Free and Open Source Software

Free and Open Source Software

Policy, Law, and Practice

Edited by

Noam Shemtov

Lecturer in Intellectual Property and Technology Law,
Queen Mary, University of London

Ian Walden

Professor of Information and Communications Law,
Queen Mary, University of London

Great Clarendon Street, Oxford, OX2 6DP,
United Kingdom

Oxford University Press is a department of the University of Oxford.
It furthers the University's objective of excellence in research, scholarship,
and education by publishing worldwide. Oxford is a registered trade mark of
Oxford University Press in the UK and in certain other countries

First edition published in 2013

Impression: 1

Published in the United States of America by Oxford University Press
198 Madison Avenue, New York, NY 10016, United States of America

British Library Cataloguing in Publication Data
Data available

Library of Congress Control Number: 2013940574

ISBN 978-0-19-968049-8

Printed in Italy by
Grafica Veneta S.p.A.

Acknowledgements

The editors wish to thank the following LLM students at the Centre for Commercial Law Studies, Queen Mary, University of London for their valuable research assistance: Stéphanie Marie Bernard, Priscilla Maria Chiara Robledo, Manuel Rey-Alvite Villar, Joanna Karina Matczuk and Martina Kuck. We are also extremely grateful for the editorial assistance of Leslie Lansman.

The editors also acknowledge the financial support received from Microsoft, during 2010–11, in the form of an academic research grant towards basic comparative research on open source licences, which has been used in the writing of Chapters 3 and 4. However, the views expressed in these chapters are those of the authors alone.

Contents

List of Abbreviations

AGPL	Affero General Public License
API	application programming interface
ASF	Apache Software Foundation
ASP	application service provider
BD	benevolent dictator
CAD	*Codice dell'Amministrazione Digitale*
CC OSS	Competence Centre Open Source Software
CDD	Compatibility Definition Document
CDPA	Copyright Designs and Patents Act 1988
CDO	cease and desist order
CII	computer implemented inventions
CPAL	Common Public Attribution License
CSIS	Center for Strategic and International Studies
CTS	Compatibility Test Suite
DG	Director-General
DMCA	Digital Millennium Copyright Act 1998
DRM	digital rights management
ECJ	European Court of Justice
EIF	European Interoperability Framework
EFF	Electronic Freedom Foundation
EPC	European Patent Convention
EPO	European Patent Office
ETSI	European Telecommunications Standards Institute
FAT	File Allocation Table
FDL	Free Documentation License
FOSS	free and open source
FRAND	fair, reasonable and non discriminatory terms
FSF	Free Software Foundation
GATT	General Agreement on Tariffs and Trade
GATS	General Agreement on Trade in Services
GEO	general exclusion order

GPA	Agreement on Government Procurement
GPL	General Public License
GUI	Graphical User Interface
HPL	Honest Public Licence
HTML	hyper-text mark-up language
http	hyper-text transfer protocol
IaaS	infrastructure as a service
IAB	Internet Architecture Board
ICT	information and communications technology
IEEE	Institute of Electrical and Electronics Engineers
IETF	Internet Engineering Task Force
IP	intellectual property
ISP	internet service provider
ISO	International Standards Organisation
IT	information technology
LEO	limited exclusion order
LGPL	Lesser General Public License
NDA	non-disclosure agreement
NIST	National Institute of Standards and Technology
NPE	non practising entity
OASIS	Organization for the Advancement of Structured Information Standards
Ofcom	Office of Communications Regulator
OFE	OpenForum Europe
OHANDA	Open Hardware and Design and Association
OIN	Open Invention Network
OKF	Open Knowledge Foundation
OSD	Open Source Definition
OSEPA	Free Open Source Software Policy for European Public Administration
OSI	Open Source Initiative
OSRM	Open Source Risk Management
OU	Open University
PaaS	platform as a service
QAA	Quality Assurance Agency
RAND	reasonable and non discriminatory terms
RF	royalty free
RPC	remote procedure call
SaaS	software as a service

SDK	software developer kit
SEP	standard essential patent
SSH	Secure Shell
SPDX	Software Package Data Exchange
SSBs	standards setting bodies
TEU	Treaty on European Union
TFEU	Treaty on the Functioning of the European Union
TPM	technological protection measures
UCITA	Uniform Computer Information Transaction Act
UEFI	Unified Extensible Firmware Interface
USPTO	US Patent office
VMs	virtual machines
WTO	World Trade Organisation
W3C	World Wide Web Consortium

List of Contributors

EDITORS

Dr Noam Shemtov is a lecturer in Intellectual Property and Technology Law at the Centre for Commercial Law Studies (CCLS) at Queen Mary, University of London. Noam is the Director of specialist intellectual property programmes at CCLS. He is a course convener for LLM courses in Computer Law and Intellectual Property in the Creative Industries as well as for the Certificate in Intellectual Property Programme in Trade Marks Law. His interest areas include IP and software protection, FOSS and international trade marks law. He has published extensively in peer-reviewed journals in these areas and managed a team in a research project on Open Source licences. Noam is a visiting professor in a number of Spanish universities. He is a qualified solicitor both in the UK and in Israel.

Ian Walden is Professor of Information and Communications Law and Head of the Institute of Computer and Communications Law in the Centre for Commercial Law Studies (CCLS) at Queen Mary, University of London. His publications include *EDI and the Law* (Blackwell, 1989), *Information Technology and the Law* (MacMillan, 1990), *EDI Audit and Control* (NCC Blackwell, 1993), *Cross-border Electronic Banking* (Lloyd's of London Press, 2nd edn, 2000), *Telecommunications Law Handbook* (Blackstone, 1997), *E-Commerce Law and Practice in Europe* (Woodhead, 2001), *Computer Crimes and Digital Investigations* (OUP, 2007), *Media Law and Practice* (OUP, 2009) and *Telecommunications Law and Regulation* (OUP, 4th edn, 2012). Ian has been involved in law reform projects for the World Bank, the European Commission, UNCTAD, ITU, UNECE and the EBRD, as well as for a number of individual states. Ian was awarded a Council of Europe Human Rights Fellowship (1987–88); was a seconded national expert to the European Commission DG-Industry (1995–96); Board Member and Trustee of the Internet Watch Foundation (2004–09); on the Executive Board of the UK Council for Child Internet Safety (2010–12) and is currently a member of the Press Complaints Commission. Ian is a solicitor and Of Counsel to Baker & McKenzie.

AUTHORS

Malcolm Bain is founding partner of *id law partners*, a boutique IP/IT law firm in Barcelona, Spain. Malcolm is an English solicitor and Spanish *abogado*, specializing among other things in free and open source law, and advises projects, IT specialists and public administrations on the creation, use, distribution and freeing of FOSS. He teaches the legal issues of FOSS at university level and has lectured on this subject at many national and international events, including before the WIPO and the EC. He is also author of various papers on this subject, and is currently co-editor of the *IFOSS L Rev*.

Amanda Brock advises diverse businesses on commercial and technology law issues from her London base. Having been General Counsel, Canonical—lead commercial sponsor of the open source operating system Ubuntu for five years, managing the worldwide legal function, she has particular expertise in open source software, cloud computing, big data and device manufacture and distribution. With over 15 years' experience of commercial and IT law, gained as an in house lawyer, including roles as European Manager at DSG International (where she was the first lawyer at the ISP, Freeserve), UK Legal Director, Aramark and General Counsel to Nicole Farhi and French Connection, her experience lends itself to her very commercial approach to legal advice. Amanda is admitted as a solicitor in England and Scotland and has a Masters in IP and IT law from Queen Mary, University of London and a Masters in Comparative Jurisprudence from NYU. Amanda is a member of the Advisory Board of the QM, University of London Open Source Centre of Excellence and has spoken internationally and written extensively on technology and commercial law. She is one of the founders of the QM Legal Incubator currently being set up to provide legal advice to the UK start up market place. Her clients range from start ups to Mozilla.

Neil Brown is a highly experienced lawyer and academic, exploring the overlaps of law, technology and society. He has particular expertise in Internet and communications regulation and policy, privacy and security, and alternative intellectual property strategies promoting the sharing of knowledge. Neil takes a grounded and yet innovative, practical approach to complex questions of law and technology, and has a sound technical and practical knowledge in a wide range of fields relating to communications and digital technology. He welcomes contact through his website: <http://neilzone.co.uk>.

Alan Cunningham completed his PhD—concerning the management of copyrights in a digital and online environment—at Queen Mary, University of London in 2007 and has taught Intellectual Property Law at Queen Mary, and La Trobe University, Melbourne. He has also undertaken research on cloud computing at Queen Mary and consults and teaches on issues relating to appropriation and art at the Node Center for Curatorial Studies, Berlin. He has published on law and technology issues in the *International Journal of Law and Information Technology* and with Oxford University Press.

Ross Gardler has over 15 years' experience in open source software development. He is currently Executive Vice President and Director of The Apache Software Foundation, one of the oldest and most influential open source foundations. Apache is responsible for over 150 high profile open source projects including the software that delivers the majority of Internet pages to your browser, 'big data' tools that drive many large-scale businesses and infrastructure components that mean it is difficult to perform any action on the Internet without using Apache software. Ross is also an advisor to open source projects and communities, such as the Outercurve Foundation. Ross has worked as an academic researcher and lecturer, software developer and open source advisor to the UK Higher and Further Education sector. At the time of contributing to this book Ross is the Programme Lead for Open Development at OpenDirective, a consultancy specializing in developing and delivering open source strategies.

W Kuan Hon is an English solicitor and New York attorney, currently non-practising. She obtained her undergraduate law degree from Trinity College, University of Cambridge; LLMs from University of Pennsylvania, USA, and (in Computer & Communications Law) from Queen Mary, University of London; and an MSc in Computing Science from Imperial College, London. Kuan is a joint law/computer science PhD candidate at Queen Mary, focusing on cloud data protection law. She is also currently consultant to the Cloud Legal Project at Queen Mary, where she worked full time in 2010–11, and is a part-time research assistant in cloud computing law at Queen Mary. Kuan participated in the UK G-Cloud programme's Commercial Workstream in summer/autumn 2011. Formerly, Kuan was a finance and insolvency lawyer in the City of London with both English and US law firms.

Andrew Katz is a partner at Moorcrofts LLP, a boutique tech-focused law firm in England's Thames Valley. He advises a wide range of businesses and other organizations on free and open source related issues. He has lectured and published widely on the subject and is a founder editor of the *IFOSS L Rev*. Andrew has also been instructed in connection with a number of international open hardware projects and is involved in the discussion and formulation of licences which can be applied effectively in the field of open hardware. He also advises on the other opens, including open standards, open content and open data.

Peter Langley is the founder and managing director of Origin Ltd, an international technology law firm, and is based in London. Peter has a degree in physics and is a solicitor, a patent attorney and a trade mark attorney. He has been voted one of the top 40 technology lawyers in the UK and one of the leading 300 IP strategists in the world. He is also Visiting Professorial Fellow in Law at the Centre for Digital Music, Queen Mary, University of London. Origin handles international patent and copyright litigation and IP-focussed M&A, strategy and transactions for technology companies, including ARM, Canonical/Ubuntu, King.com and TomTom. He has handled cases involving digital mapping, GPS, semi-conductors, computer games, holography, and operating systems.

Colm MacKernan is a director of Origin Ltd and is based in London and Washington and also Of Counsel to the Japanese law firm Nagashima & Hashimoto with offices in Tokyo. Colm has a degree in Physics and a JD from Georgetown University Law Center and is a member of the New York and Washington DC bars, a solicitor in England & Wales and the Republic of Ireland, and is admitted to practise before various US federal courts and agencies. He has published various books and articles including *A Practical Guide to Intellectual Property in Mergers and Acquisitions* (EIPR/Sweet & Maxwell, 2006) and *International Technology Law, A Practical Glossary* (Thomson/ Aspatore 2006). He was the editor of the EIPR Practice Guides series.

Luke McDonagh holds a PhD from Queen Mary, University of London (2011), an LLM from the London School of Economics (2006–07) and a BCL degree from NUI, Galway (2002–05). His current research focuses on examining how copyright works in creative spaces. He is also undertaking empirical analysis of patent litigation in the UK. His work has been published in journals including *Intellectual Property Quarterly, International Review of Intellectual Property and Competition Law* and *Civil Justice Quarterly*. Since September 2011 he has held the position of LSE Fellow in the Department of Law at the London School of Economics.

Jakub Menčl is an advocate admitted to the Czech Bar Association and works as senior associate in the Prague office of White & Case. He is also pursuing his PhD studies at the University of Economics in Prague. Jakub studied law at the Charles University in Prague and graduated in 2003. Jakub participated in the LLM in Intellectual Property programme offered jointly with the WIPO Academy and the University of Turin, where he graduated in 2009. After spending several months in the Copyright Law Division of the WIPO in Geneva, Jakub completed the LLM in Computer and Communication Law at Queen Mary, University of London.

Jakub would like to thank Dr Noam Shemtov, lecturer in intellectual property and technology law, and Michaela McDonald, PhD student, both at CCLS at Queen Mary, for their invaluable help and advice, while retaining the entire responsibility for all potential errors and omissions. Thanks go also to Jana, Jakub's wife, and Ema, their little daughter, for their support and patience.

Iain G Mitchell QC FRSA is a member of both the Scottish and English Bars. He is the UK representative on the IT Committee of the CCBE and is a member of the IT

Panel of the Bar Council of England & Wales, Chairman of the Faculty of Advocates Information Technology Group and Co-convenor of the Scottish Lawyers' European Group. He is Chairman of the Scottish Society for Computers and Law and is an honorary lecturer at the Institut für Informations-Telekommunikations-und Medienrecht at the Wilhelms-Universität, Münster, Westphalia, as well as being a Liveryman of the Worshipful Company of Information Technologists. He is also Joint Editor of *IFOSS L Rev.* His publications include contributions to *Electronic Evidence* (Butterworths, 2010) and *The Open Source Law Book* (Open Source Press, 2011), as well as frequent contributions to professional journals as well as general journalism.

Table of Cases

United Kingdom

European Union

European Commission

Court of First Instance

Court of Justice

European Court of Human Rights

European Patent Office

France

Germany

Italy

Poland

Scotland

Spain

United States of America

Harper & Row Publishers Inc v Nation Enterprises, 471 US 539 (1985) 8

i4i v Microsoft 209
Jacobsen v Katzer, 535 F.3d 1373 (Fed Cir 2008) 96–9, 300
Jacobsen v Katzer, 2007 WL 2358628 (N D Cal 2007) 96–9

LaserDynamics v Quanta, < http://www.cafc.uscourts.gov/images/stories/
opinions-orders/11-1440-1470.pdf > 206–7
Lawrence v Fox 20, N Y 268 (1959) 93

Mayo Collaborative Services v Prometheus Laboratories Inc, 566 US (2012) 147, 180
MDY Industries LLC v Blizzard Entertainment Inc and Vivendi Games Inc,
629 F.3d 928 (9th Cir 2010) 26, 33, 93, 97
Microsoft Corp v Commission of the European Communities 196
Microsoft Corp v i4i Limited Partnership 546 US_(2011) 186
Microsoft v TomTom litigation 198
Microsystems Software Inc v Scandinavia Online AB, 98 F. Supp. 2d 74 (D Mass, 2000),
aff'd 226 F.3d 35 (1st Cir 2000) 93

National Comics Publications Inc v Fawcett Publications Inc, 191 F.2d 594;
90 USPQ 274 17

Oracle America Inc v Google Inc, 798 F.Supp 2d 1111 (ND Cal 2011) 143
Oracle America Inc v Google Inc, 810 F.Supp.2d 1002 150
Oracle America Inc v Google Inc, Case 3:10-cv-03561-WHA 211
Oracle America Inc v Google Inc (2012) 872 F.Supp.2d 974 5

Planetary Motion Inc v Techplosion Inc, 261 F.3d. 1188 (11th Cir 2001) 96
ProCD v Zeidenberg, 86 F 3d 1447 (7th Cir 1996) 89, 97
Progress Software Corporation v MySQL AB, 195 F Supp 2d. 328
(D Mass 2001) 96

SG Services Inc v God's Girls Inc, 2007 WL 2315437 (CD Cal, 9 May 2007) 136
Sleep Science Partners v Lieberman and Sleeping Well LLC, 2010 US Dist LEXIS
45385, *7 (ND Cal 2010) 136
SoftMan Products Co, LLC v Adobe Systems Inc (2001) 171 F.Supp.2d 1075 26
Software Freedom Conservancy Inc v Best Buy Co Inc, 2010 WL 2985320 (SDNY) 34, 301
Specht v Netscape Communications Corp, 306 F.3d. 17 (2nd Cir 2002) 90
Stambler v Diebold, 11 USPQ 2d (NY Dist Ct 1988) 379
State Street Bank & Trust v Signature Financial Services, 149 F.3d 1368 (Fed Cir 1998),
cert denied 119 S Ct 851 (US 11 January 1999) 147–8
Symbol Techs Inc v Proxim Inc, No Civ 01-801-SLR, 2004 WL 1770290 205

Ticketmaster Corp v Tickets.com Inc, 2003 US Dist LEXIS 6483 (C D Cal 2003) 90
Two Pesos Inc v Taco Cabana Inc, 505 US 763 fn 1 (1992) 116

Table of Legislation

United Kingdom

Statutory Instruments

Belgium

England

European Union

Directives

Andalusia

Sweden

United States of America

Table of Treaties, etc

1

OPEN SOURCE AS PHILOSOPHY, METHODOLOGY, AND COMMERCE:

USING LAW WITH ATTITUDE

Ian Walden

1.1 INTRODUCTION

Software (in my opinion) is the really clever bit of computing! Software is much, if not most, of what we know as the information and communications technology ('ICT') industries. Software generally comprises two written forms: source code and object code. Source code is the language in which computer programs are generally written and which is then compiled into machine-readable object code for use by the processor, either in a form distinct from the hardware or incorporated into it, ie firmware. There are numerous programming languages structured at differing levels of abstraction; representing different generations of programming language. The conversion between source code and object code cannot be easily inverted, which acts as an effective control over the use made of object code. As a consequence, traditional commoditized proprietary software has been distributed in object code form, rather than source code, rendering modification of the software difficult.

The free and open source ('FOSS') movement is about subverting this traditional industry model, by providing access to the original source code for the user. Such access enables further development of the software, amending the existing code or writing new lines of code, for personal or public benefit. The motivations of those that pursue an 'open source' approach to software vary considerably, encompassing political, philosophical and ethical agendas as much as simple pragmatism. While acknowledging and examining this spectrum of motives, the editorial stance of the book is one of attempted neutrality, in order to understand and analyse the phenomenon of 'open source' as a legal construct.

The central fact of open source, the fact that justifies this book, is that maintaining control over source code relies on the existence and efficacy of intellectual property ('IP') laws, particularly copyright law. Copyright law is the primary statutory tool that achieves the end of openness, although implemented through private law arrangements at varying points within the software supply chain. This dependent relationship is itself a cause of concern for those philosophically in favour of 'open', with some predicting (or hoping) that the free software movement will bring about the end of copyright as a means for protecting software.[1]

This book examines various policies, and legal and commercial aspects of the FOSS phenomenon. For our purposes, FOSS is adopted as convenient shorthand for a collection of diverse users and communities, whose differences can be as great as their similarities. The common thread is their reliance on, and use of, law and legal mechanisms to govern the source code they write, use and distribute.

This chapter has three main objectives. First, to introduce the subject matter, open source software, the environment and many of the themes that are examined and analysed throughout this book. Second, the relationship between copyright law and open source is scrutinized; mapping areas of common cause and tension, as well as areas of legal uncertainty, from both a theoretical and practical perspective. Finally, the chapter is a study of how private law arrangements can be used to achieve outcomes that diverge from that intended for the applicable public law regime; using law with attitude.

1.2 THE LEGAL TREATMENT OF SOFTWARE

Before embarking on an analysis of how FOSS is used by software developers and communities, it is necessary to consider the legal treatment of software from a

[1] E Moglen, 'Anarchism Triumphant: Free Software and the Death of Copyright' in N Elkin-Koren and NW Netanel (eds), *The Commodification of Information* (Netherlands, Kluwer Law International, 2002) 107–31.

generic perspective, under intellectual property laws and within the wider legal framework.

Open source proponents utilize private law mechanisms, ie licences[2] and contracts, operating within established public law frameworks, eg copyright, patent and contract law, to achieve a particular desired outcome. For our purposes, 'public law' is used in a broader sense than the traditional concept concerning the relationship between a state and its people. Here, it encompasses legal regimes that govern relationships between people, both within and between jurisdictions.[3] These regimes not only grant legal validity and enforceability to the private law mechanisms, but also directly intervene to influence the use of these mechanisms, prohibiting certain practices, eg, and making determinations about certain conduct.

Uncertainties about how the public law will treat certain industry practices, including those of the FOSS community, are highlighted throughout the book. They include whether software should be treated as a good or a service; what constitutes a modification; whether usage is governed by contract or bare licence; whether that mechanism results in a transfer of ownership or a right to use? These questions are sometimes answered through legislative provision or judicial interpretation, but rarely without generating further areas of doubt. A private law instrument may itself be expressed in language that can deliberately or accidentally include terms that go beyond that recognized or acceptable in public law, but which remain unchallenged and unenforceable; or terms which are interpreted differently by different people or groups through inference or philosophical bent.[4] Collectively, such legal uncertainties can have a negative impact on technical and commercial innovation and development in the ICT industries. As such, one aim of the book is to try and address some of the uncertainties that surround FOSS.

In the early days of computing, software was distributed free with hardware, becoming a commodity only when it became liberated from the hardware on which it operated.[5] With the emergence of software as a discrete item, an issue arose as to the most appropriate regime within intellectual property law under which to protect it. The three leading possibilities were patent law, due to its industrial nature; copyright law, as a form of expression, or the establishment of some sui generis regime that reflected the unique features of software.[6] Copyright eventually won

[2] The legal nature of a licence can vary, as contracts or bare licences, which is examined further in ch 3. This chapter uses the term in a non-specific manner.

[3] This includes regulatory and judicial law making, as well as international and European Union law.

[4] See, eg, M Herman and J Montague, 'The elephant in the room: Patent value and open source', paper presented at the AIPLA Spring Meeting, April 2011.

[5] M Schellekens, 'Free and Open Source Software: An Answer to Commodification?' in L Guibault and B Hugenholtz, *The future of the public domain: identifying the commons in information law* (Netherlands, Kluwer Law International, 2006) 309.

[6] See, eg, the WIPO 'Model Provisions on the Protection of Computer Software', adopted in 1977.

the argument, with computer programs being accepted as a form of 'literary work':[7] although with some jurisdictions adopting a sub-set of sui generis rules to reflect some of the unique issues raised by software.[8]

What comprises 'software' or 'computer programs', however, often remains less clear.[9] As noted earlier, software is generally expressed in two forms, source code and object code, the latter being a 'translation' of the former, but both being protectable subject matter. As with other areas of law some jurisdictions attempt to define the concept in law;[10] some extend it beyond the source and object code;[11] while others are content to leave it for the courts to interpret on the basis of standard usage.[12] The European Court of Justice was recently required to examine the scope of the term in *SAS Institute Inc v World Programming Ltd*,[13] holding that a 'computer program' does not extend to the functionality of a program, the programming language or the format of data files; although the latter two may be copyrightable works in their own right (paras 29–46). In not protecting the functionality of a program, the law is constraining the scope of copyright law, which is supportive of an 'open' approach to the treatment of software as a tool. While the court distinguishes between a program and the language in which it is written, the latter often now come in the form of a program and numerous FOSS programming languages have been developed, such as Python and Ruby, licensed under open source licences.[14]

As the software industry developed and while uncertainties continued to exist, software developers tended to rely on trade secrets law and contract as the preferred mechanisms for protecting their investment. With the clarification and strengthening of the copyright regime, from the mid-1980s until recently, the software industry has relied on copyright law and licences as the primary means for governing the use of their software assets. Limitations within copyright law, however, have seen persons look to patent law as offering an alternative strategy for protecting and exploiting their software.[15] These legal mechanisms have been supplemented by technical controls that enable rights holders to further control the use of their work.

[7] WIPO Copyright Treaty, art 4. See also the Commission Green Paper, *Copyright and the Challenge of Technology*, COM(88) 172 final.

[8] eg Council Directive 91/250/EEC of 14 May 1991 'on the legal protection of computer programs' (OJ L122/42, 17.5.1991) codified in 2009, as Directive 09/24/EC (OJ L111/16, 5.5.2009), referred to here as the 'Software Directive'.

[9] In this chapter, 'software' and 'computer programs' or 'programs' are used interchangeably.

[10] eg US law, at 17 USC para 101.

[11] eg Software Directive, Article 1(1), includes 'their preparatory design material'.

[12] eg Copyright Designs and Patents Act 1988 ('CDPA').

[13] Case C-406/10, 2 May 2012. See also Case C-393/09 *Bezpečnostní softwarová asociace* [2010] ECR I-0000, paras 34–41. See the application of the ECJ decision in *SAS Institute Inc v World Programming Ltd* [2013] EWHC 69 (Ch).

[14] Note that compilers, which convert source code into object code, are also program(s) with open source versions, such as Open64.

[15] See further chs 5 and 6.

Legal uncertainties continue to exist for the software industry from the operation of the copyright regime: some are general to copyright law, such as the scope of usage exceptions; some from the application of the general rules to the specifics of software, such as its treatment as a collection, compilation or database; while others arise from the sui generis rules, such as the right to decompile. What comprises copying in a software environment has generated challenges for copyright law particularly in respect of 'non-literal' copying. Code may be written using different programming languages, enabling a person to effectively copy the internal 'structure, sequence and organisation' of another work and, or, its external 'look and feel',[16] without copying the form of expression. In some cases, such practices have been held to constitute infringement; while in others, the courts have held that a merger between idea and expression has taken place, rendering the subject matter unprotectable.[17] Current industry developments may also result in a shift away from copyright and patent law and back towards reliance on contract and trade secrets. Cloud computing and Software as a Service ('SaaS') enables applications to be accessed via networks, meaning that suppliers no longer need to give users either the source code or object code for the programs they use.[18]

The debate also continues to ebb and flow with regard to the patentability of computer programs, with the US and Europe exhibiting differing attitudes towards the issue.[19] As most FOSS licences emanate from the US, which has a liberal approach to software patenting, one consequence is that these licences have increasingly had to devote space to addressing patent rights, to ensure that the 'open' objectives continue to be maintained. Many within the FOSS community exhibit a greater dislike of patents, than of other forms of intellectual property. There are public campaigns seeking to prevent or end software patenting, for which parallels do not exist concerning copyright.[20] As such, contentious debates in some areas relating to FOSS, such as standards, often appear motivated primarily by an objection to patents rather than copyright.

Another area of controversy within copyright has been the role of technology itself as a mechanism for controlling the use and abuse of software. Technological protection measures ('TPM'), from 'dongles' to bit-encryption, together with digital rights management ('DRM') techniques, emerged with the growth of the software industry as a potentially powerful tool in the armoury of rights holders trying to stem burgeoning, industrial-scale infringement. In the 1996 WIPO Treaty, such techniques were granted legal recognition and protection under

[16] C Millard, 'Copyright in Information Technology and Data' in C Reed (ed), *Computer Law*, 7th edn (Oxford, Oxford University Press, 2011) 7.5.

[17] Millard (n 16) 7.5. See also *Oracle America, Inc v Google Inc* (2012) 872 F.Supp.2d 974.

[18] See further ch 9.

[19] See further ch 5, at 5.1.

[20] eg <http://endsoftpatents.org.nyud.net/> and <http://stopsoftwarepatents.eu/>.

international copyright law,[21] appearing in national laws often in the form of criminal prohibitions.[22] Proponents of open source, particularly within the free software movement, have been highly critical of TPM/DRM technologies and their use to further constrain end users, especially where the controls extend beyond that granted to rights holders under copyright law.[23] In Europe, such concerns were successfully raised with policy makers, who proceeded to place TPM under legal controls designed to limit their abuse.[24] While the provisions have been heavily criticized for being narrowly drawn, overly complex to apply and favourable to rights holders, they do represent some form of victory for FOSS proponents.

Distinct from the governance of software through intellectual property laws, software is developed, supplied to users, bought and sold as an asset, and comprises part of modern commercial activity. These activities are generally governed through contractual agreement between the various parties, whether business, consumers or public administrations, either distinct from, or incorporating, any IP licence terms. While such agreements are primarily established by one or other party or negotiated, certain mandatory rules of national law will shape these agreements and, indeed, generate their own uncertainties. As with the initial doubt over which intellectual property regime should apply to software, there has been an ongoing debate, in both Europe and the US, about how software supply contracts should be characterized—as a sale of goods or services or both, or some sui generis category—and the implications this determination has for the rights and remedies of the user and the obligations of the supplier.[25] European consumer protection rules, for example, impose an obligation to supply any available information about interoperability between software and 'digital content', which includes computer programs.[26] Consumer protection rules are currently being re-examined in the UK to address, in part, the lack of clarity about the sale of digital content such as software.[27]

[21] Articles 11 and 12 respectively. [22] eg in the US, 17 USC para 1204 and in the UK, CDPA, s 296ZB.

[23] eg <http://www.defectivebydesign.org/>.

[24] eg Directive 01/29/EC 'on the harmonisation of certain aspects of copyright and related rights in the information society' (OJ L167/10, 22.6.2001), referred to here as the 'Information Society Directive', Article 6(4). While the Information Society Directive, Article 1(2)(a) does not amend or affect the provisions under the Software Directive; the TPM provisions would appear to be applicable to software.

[25] For the UK, see, eg, *St Albans City & DC v International Computers Ltd* [1996] 4 All ER 481 and *The Mayor and Burgesses of the London Borough of Southwark v IBM UK Ltd* [2011] EWHC 549 (TCC). See generally, C Reed (ed), *Computer* Law, 7th edn (Oxford University Press, 2011) chs 1 and 2. For the US, see *Wofford v Apple Inc* (2011) (Case No 11-CV-0034 AJB NLS—unreported), where the judge held that software was not a tangible good or service for the purposes of California's Consumers Legal Remedies Act. See generally the American Law Institute's *Principles of the Law of Software Contracts*, 2009.

[26] Directive 11/83/EU on consumer rights (OJ L304/64, 22.11.2011), recital 19 and Articles 5(1)(h) and 6(1)(s).

[27] BIS Consultation on the supply of goods, services and digital content, July 2012.

1.3 OPEN SOURCE AS PHILOSOPHY AND POLICY

While this book examines how public and private law is used by FOSS communities and others, such as governments, it is obviously necessary to begin by understanding why the law is being used in this way; what is the end being sought by the means? Inevitably, the whys fall along a broad spectrum, some pursuing and supporting open source on the basis of deeply held philosophical beliefs about how information and knowledge should be treated in society; while others are more pragmatic, viewing open source as a means of creating better software or reducing costs for users.[28]

If 'open source' were simply a development methodology, it would not engender the types of rhetoric which have been deployed by the proprietary community[29] and vice versa.[30] Even amongst FOSS proponents, the philosophical underpinnings are viewed as starkly different; Stallman noting: 'Open source is a development methodology; free software is a social movement.'[31] It has also been described as 'a kind of recursive philanthropy,'[32] because of the manner in which participant developers devote time and energy writing code that they donate to the project community. The copyleft licences of the free software movement, with mandated contributions back to the community, can be seen as a legal limitation on a developer's ability to depart from such philanthropy, ie to change his mind.

One recent development in the open source field is the issuance of FOSS modules that are deliberately not made subject to any licence.[33] One motive behind such behaviour is a philosophical rejection of the bureaucratic governance structures required to make copyright law support open source objectives. As noted by one commentator:

> [Y]ounger devs today are about POSS—Post open source software. F*** the license and governance.[34]

However, as discussed later in respect of the public domain, copyright law cannot be ignored that easily! Whilst such views may be representative of only a small minority of the FOSS community, they may also reflect the entry of the 'born digital'

[28] See further ch 2.

[29] eg in 2001, Steve Ballmer, CEO of Microsoft, described Linux as 'a cancer that attaches itself in an intellectual property sense to everything it touches.'

[30] eg Richard Stallman, 'Writing non-free software is not an ethically legitimate activity, so if people who do this run into trouble, that's good!' <http://lists.kde.org/?l=kde-licensing&m=89249041326259&w=2>.

[31] R Stallman, 'Why Open Source misses the point of Free Software' <http://www.gnu.org/philosophy/open-source-misses-the-point.html>.

[32] G Finney, 'The evolution of GPLv3 and contributor agreements in open source software' (2009) *Journal of Technology Law and Policy*, No 14, 79–105.

[33] S Phipps, 'GitHub needs to take open source seriously,' InfoWorld, 30 November 2012 <http://www.infoworld.com/d/open-source-software/github-needs-take-open-source-seriously-208046>.

[34] Available at <http://twitter.com/monkchips/status/247584170967175169>.

generation into the software industry, many of whom have grown up in an ostensibly copyright free environment, where everything and anything is available from somewhere.

It is beyond the scope of this chapter to analyse the differing shades of belief and motivation that drive those involved in the free and open source movements. However, given the dependency on intellectual property laws, particularly copyright, the following sections consider some philosophical dimensions of copyright law of relevance to the FOSS community, including in the promotion of freedom of expression; the protection of the paternity and integrity of works, as well as its relationship with the public domain. The last sub-section shifts from the philosophical to the political, and examines how open source has become incorporated by governments into public policy initiatives, in pursuit of a range of objectives.

1.3.1 Freedom of expression

One of the most oft-quoted slogans of the free software movement is 'free' as in 'free speech,' not as in 'free beer.'[35] To achieve this free speech, copyright law is used to facilitate reuse, new expression through modification and to prevent exclusivity. The term 'copyleft' was chosen to denote that the objective of copyright was being deliberately turned on its head: 'the inverse of "right".'[36] Copyright is therefore situated as being antithetical to free speech. This perspective is shared by those that view the statutory defences to copyright, such as fair use and fair dealing, as mechanisms for reconciling free speech with copyright.[37]

Yet this has not always been, indeed is not now, the only way of viewing the relationship between copyright and free speech. As noted by the US Supreme Court, as recently as 1985:

> [I]t should not be forgotten that the Framers intended copyright itself to be the engine of free expression. By establishing a marketable right to the use of one's expression, copyright supplies the economic incentive to create and disseminate ideas.[38]

Here copyright is seen as being supportive of free speech through the granting of exclusive economic rights. Those rights obviously also exclude certain types of speech, but, so the reasoning goes, as long as the totality of copyright as an 'incentive to create' is greater that the effect of the constraint, the net outcome is beneficial and

[35] <http://www.gnu.org/philosophy/free-sw.html>.

[36] 'What is copyleft?' <http://www.gnu.org/copyleft/>.

[37] See, eg, P Masiyakurima, 'The Free Speech Benefits of Fair Dealing Defences' in P Torremans (ed), *Intellectual Property and Human Rights* (Netherlands, Kluwer Law International, 2008) 235–56.

[38] *Harper & Row Publishers, Inc v Nation Enterprises* 471 US 539, 558 (1985). While in *Eldred v Ashcroft* (01-618) 537 US 186 (2003), the Supreme Court noted that 'copyright's purpose is to promote the creation and publication of free expression' (at 219).

copyright law can rightly claim to be a tool of free speech.[39] Alternatively, it has been argued that the purpose of copyright should not be seen as a spur to creativity and a societal distributive mechanism, but rather as a means to 'affirm the inherent dignity of the author as a speaking being', where acts of infringement are viewed as compelled speech and defences as enabling the communicative acts of others.[40] Whichever perspective you adopt, this 'paradox' between copyright as both an enemy and friend of free speech has been the subject of ongoing debate.[41]

It is also widely accepted that there has been a shift over recent decades, in favour of copyright as constraint. With the emergence of information-based economies, copyright has become central to the protection of economic value in intangible information assets. As copyright's economic importance grew, so did calls for the regime to be extended and strengthened. Greater prevalence, coupled with enhanced rights and more effective and dissuasive sanctions, has resulted in numerous examples of copyright being used to chill speech, whether political, artistic or commercial.[42]

Free speech or freedom of expression is a human right expressly recognized in most legal systems. In some jurisdictions, particularly the US, free speech is accorded pre-eminent status compared with other rights, such as privacy.[43] In Europe, freedom of expression is granted equal status with other rights, including the right of property, which includes intellectual property.[44] As with copyright, freedom of expression is not absolute, it is limited in scope and is generally weighed in the balance against other protected rights and values.[45] Source code represents a protected form of expression under both free speech and copyright regimes. While aligned with literary works under copyright law, its treatment as a form of expression under a human rights analysis varies considerably depending on the specific circumstance. Equating source code with speech has resulted in judicial scrutiny when attempts have been made to constrain the distribution of source code. During the 1990s, governments sought to restrain the export of cryptographic software under export control rules; treating such code as 'dual-use', having both civil and military application.[46] Export rules have long

[39] For a positive view of this trade-off, see RA Cass and KN Hylton, *Laws of Creation* (Cambridge, MA, Harvard University Press, 2013). For a negative perspective, see M Boldrin and DK Levine, *Against Intellectual Property* (Cambridge, Cambridge University Press, 2008).

[40] A Drassinower, 'Copyright infringement as compelled speech' in A Lever (ed), *New Frontiers in the Philosophy of Intellectual Property* (Cambridge, Cambridge University Press, 2012).

[41] See NW Netanel, *Copyright's Paradox* (Oxford, Oxford University Press, 2008) and J Griffiths and U Suthersanen (eds), *Copyright and Free Speech: Comparative and International Analyses* (Oxford, Oxford University Press, 2005).

[42] Netanel (n 41) 6.

[43] US Constitution, First Amendment, 'Freedom of Religion, Press and Expression'.

[44] Convention for the Protection of Human Rights and Fundamental Freedoms (1950), Articles 10 and 1 of the First Protocol. See also the Charter of Fundamental Rights of the European Union (2007), Articles 11 and 17.

[45] See, in particular, *Ashby Donald and others v France*, App No 36769/08, ECtHR (5th Sec) 10 January 2013 and *Neij and Sunde Kolmisoppi v Sweden*, App No 40397/12, ECtHR (5th Sec) 19 February 2013.

[46] eg Wassenaar Arrangement on export controls for conventional arms and dual-use goods and technologies, 'List of dual-use goods and technologies' (December 2012) <http://www.wassenaar.org/index.html>.

existed, but in relation to physical items rather than intangible information. In trying to update these rules for a digital era, they inevitably came into conflict with free expression rights. In *Bernstein v US Department of State*,[47] the US Court of Appeals held that the source code of encryption software was expressive speech for the purposes of the First Amendment and that the existing rules, as a form of prior restraint, violated the protection granted under it. Conversely, in *Universal City Studios, Inc v Corley*,[48] an injunction prohibiting website owners from posting source code enabling the decryption of movies, or providing links to such code, was considered a permissible constraint on speech.

Where copyright and freedom of expression critically differ as legal regimes, however, is in the role of private law mechanisms in the delineation and enforcement of the respective rights and obligations of the parties. Contract and licence are tools of copyright not freedom of expression, and it is this feature that renders copyright such a powerful tool, both in the hands of proprietary rights holders and, now, for those promoting and protecting FOSS, the 'commons' and 'free culture'.[49] While private law is generally viewed as forming a lower stratum of any legal system, private law engages persons directly in a manner that the 'higher' levels, from the constitution to statutory provision, often fail to do. People are forced, metaphorically rather than literally, to 'agree' to contractual conditions and a licensee must have notice of the licence terms. Notice and consent are both public law requirements of validity and enforceability for private law arrangements, but are also methods for obtaining individual engagement with the rights and interests of others, even if it is not always supportive. Indeed, it can be said, that it is the private law tools of copyright law which enable the FOSS community to reassert copyright's historic role as an 'engine of free expression'.

1.3.2 Moral rights

To the extent that support for FOSS is driven by moral and ethical concerns, the moral rights regime within copyright law deserves consideration. As Välimäki has noted: 'One way to look at open source is to see it promoting the original ideals of authors' inalienable rights to control the integrity and paternity of their personal creations'.[50] This section considers the affinity between moral rights and an open source approach.

While copyright is primarily about economic rights, the Berne Convention also grants authors certain moral rights in respect of their works; commonly referred to as the right of paternity or attribution and the right of integrity:

[47] 176 F.3d 1132 (9th Cir 1999). [48] 273 F.3d 429 (2nd Cir 2001).

[49] See J Boyle, *The Public Domain: Enclosing the Commons of the Mind* (Yale University Press, 2008) and L Lessig, *Free Culture* (Penguin, 2004).

[50] M Välimäki, *The Rise of Open Source Licensing* (Turre Publishing, 2005).

> Independently of the author's economic rights, and even after the transfer of the said rights, the author shall have the right to claim authorship of the work and to object to any distortion, mutilation or other modification of, or other derogatory action in relation to, the said work, which would be prejudicial to his honor or reputation.[51]

Moral rights reflect a belief, originating in Continental European countries, that an author of a work has interests in the work that 'transcend the ordinary motives of commercial gain'.[52] While recognized in the Berne Convention, the treatment of moral rights varies significantly between jurisdictions.[53] Common law countries generally elaborate the least comprehensive regimes, with US copyright law adopting the narrowest statutory conception.[54] By contrast, in civil law countries moral rights are often more extensive than those provided for in Berne.[55]

Moral rights exist independently of the economic rights granted under copyright and are inalienable, generally not capable of being assigned to another,[56] although they can usually be waived.[57] This independent existence enables a divergence to appear between the interests of the creator and the owner of a copyright work. Such divergence has the potential to create problems for governance in an open source software project, were certain collaborating creators to try to assert their moral rights against the entity owning the copyright and exercising control through an open source licence.

The paternity right is bolstered in many copyright systems through the evidential presumption that the named author is the copyright holder;[58] although the right of paternity must be asserted by the author, ie brought to the attention of others, through some means.[59] Open source licences are clearly supportive of the paternity right, especially in respect of acts of redistribution, generally requiring that any copyright notices be retained, either in copies of the source code, the original package or the related documentation.

With respect to modifications, the interrelationship between moral rights and open source is more complex. Indeed, it has been argued that open source could be seen as

[51] Berne Convention for the Protection of Literary and Artistic Works (1886), art 6*bis*(a). Inserted in 1928. Transposed into UK law by Chapter IV of the CDPA 1988, ss 77–89.

[52] MT Sundara Rajan, 'Moral rights in information technology: A new kind of "personal right"?' (2004) *International Journal of Law and Information Technology*, vol 12, no 1, 2.

[53] See E Adeney, *The Moral Rights of Authors and Performers: An international and Comparative Analysis* (Oxford, Oxford University Press, 2006).

[54] 17 USC para 106A 'Rights of certain authors to attribution and integrity', inserted by the Visual Artists' Rights Act 1990.

[55] eg the French Intellectual Property Code recognizes a right of disclosure (art L 121-2, '*droit de divulgation*') and a right of display (art L 121-4, '*droit de repentir ou de retrait*').

[56] eg CDPA 1988, s 94.

[57] CDPA 1988, s 87(2) 'by instrument in writing signed', although contract or estoppel may operate in respect of informal waivers (s 87(4)). Waiver is not always permissible, eg France.

[58] CDPA 1988, s 104.

[59] CDPA 1988, s 78.

sundering the traditional link between the integrity of a work and its author, which historically justified the moral rights doctrine.[60] The integrity right is restricted in scope to modifications and other actions which are 'prejudicial' to the author's honour or reputation. Non-prejudicial modifications, such as a derivative work or an 'adaptation', do not constitute an infringement of the right to integrity, although the right of paternity continues to exist.[61] In common law systems, the evidential burden in an infringement action will generally lie with the claimant (ie the author) to demonstrate to the satisfaction of a court that prejudice results from the modification to his work.[62] In civil law systems, however, the courts are more likely to defer to the subjective view of the claimant author as to the work's derogatory treatment.[63] Derogatory treatment could relate to the content of the work itself, ie rewritten code, or the context within which the code is placed, eg incorporation within a disreputable application, such as a virus. The former would rarely give rise to a claim, since rewritten code which is poor quality, potentially damaging the reputation of the original author, is unlikely to be taken up by the community (the collaborative peer review nature of open source communities operating as the control mechanism); while actions based on contextual harm could be constrained by the non-discriminatory rights of use granted with the work. It would also raise the possibility of disproportionate interference in the right of free expression, which is a central element of the open source movement. As such, the integrity right is more akin to defamation, which is seen both as an aspect of a person's right to privacy as well as an exception to the right to freedom of expression;[64] rather than a mechanism to 'govern modifications' akin to the control paradigm of copyright.[65]

The relationship between moral rights and software varies between jurisdictions. Most make no distinction, others tailor the rights with respect to software;[66] while under English law, computer programs are specifically exempt from the moral rights regime.[67] Such an exemption is not manifest in the Berne Convention or other international copyright instruments and has not been followed in other jurisdictions.[68] One suggested reason for exempting computer programs from the moral rights regime is the dependency of 'programmers being able to build on pre-existing programs'.[69] Protecting integrity, in particular, is therefore seen as a potential obstacle to technical

[60] S Dusollier, 'Open Source and Copyleft: Authorship Reconsidered?'(2002–03) 26 Colum JL & Arts 281, 294.

[61] CDPA 1988, s 77(2).

[62] See, eg, *Confetti Records v Warner Music UK Ltd (t/a East West Records)* [2003] EWHC 1274, paras 149–57.

[63] I Eagles and L Longdin, 'Technological creativity and moral rights: A comparative perspective' (2004) *International Journal of Law and Information Technology*, vol 12, no 2, 209, 234.

[64] See H Fenwick and G Phillipson, *Media Freedom under the Human Rights Act* (Oxford, Oxford University Press, 2006) 1068–70.

[65] G Vetter, 'The Collaborative Integrity of Open-Source Software' (2004) *Utah L Rev* 565, 663.

[66] eg France, IPC, Article L 121-7.

[67] CDPA 1988, ss 79(2)(a) and 81(2).

[68] The TRIPS Agreement expressly states that the moral rights specified under the Berne Convention do not bestow rights or obligations under TRIPS (Article 9(1)).

[69] Sundara (n 52) 47. See also Vetter (n 65), who states that a right of integrity 'would be counterproductive to the sequential and successive processes used to develop software' (663).

progress and development. This argument, however, would seem equally applicable to all forms of right that enable control over the use of information. Another reason given is based on the view that moral rights are not appropriate for technological or functional works, as opposed to 'artistic creations' or expressive works.[70] Such an argument would seem to deny the individuality that can be expressed through programming or the existence of a distinct culture that recognizes and celebrates 'elegant' programming techniques and solutions.[71] A third argument has been summarized by the European Commission as follows:

> [S]erious doubts exist as to the suitability of their [ie moral rights] application to works frequently produced collectively, having a technical, industrial or commercial character and subject to successive modifications.[72]

As well as expressing reservations about technical/functional works, the key feature of concern is the collective nature of the creative process and the extent of modifications to a work that takes place; common characteristics of open source communities (although also features of closed and proprietary development systems). How could a right of attribution and integrity operate effectively within such an environment?

On collective attribution, the problem would seem no different in nature from that applicable to 'joint authorship' under copyright law and, indeed, some moral right provisions already address such issues.[73] From a governance perspective, community contributors may be obliged to waive moral rights as a condition of participation. Alternatively, while the rights themselves may not be assignable, the right to enforce can be delegated to the community or some other entity,[74] which would create greater certainty for both the community and the users of the code. In terms of the code itself, it would seem feasible to establish naming protocols for the development process, which would enable concerned persons to ensure that their name is appropriately associated with the bits of code to which they contributed.

On successive modifications, a clear threshold of what constitutes 'derogatory treatment' would likely prevent any excessive assertions of a right to integrity. Indeed, similar to the patent retaliation provisions in open source licences,[75] any person wishing to assert his right to integrity would first have to ensure that he is not exposed to any similar such claim from any source code which he modified in the course of producing his contribution, which may itself be a significant threshold issue. Alternatively, the concept of integrity could be recast, shifting the locus of protection from individual modifications

[70] Sundara (n 52) 49 and Vetter (n 65) 663.

[71] For one description of this culture, see P Himanen, *The Hacker Ethic and the Spirit of the Information Age* (Vintage 2001).

[72] Commission Communication, Green Paper 'on copyright and the challenge of technology', COM(88) 172 final, 7 June 1988.

[73] eg CDPA 1988, s 88. [74] Eagles and Longdin (n 63) 216. [75] See further ch 5.

to the collective output of the community; integrity being infringed where the 'open' nature of the code is undermined through technical or legal means.

The Open Source Initiative ('OSI') open source definition refers to source code integrity in the following terms:

> 4. Integrity of The Author's Source Code
>
> The license may restrict source-code from being distributed in modified form *only* if the license allows the distribution of 'patch files' with the source code for the purpose of modifying the program at build time. The license must explicitly permit distribution of software built from modified source code. The license may require derived works to carry a different name or version number from the original software.[76]

The rationale refers both to the right of users to transparency about whose code they are using, as well as the author's right to protect his reputation. The right of attribution is not directly referenced, although the OSI content is itself licensed under the Creative Commons Attribution licence. However, user transparency can be seen as the flip-side of the right of paternity; viewing the right as an obligation.

The Creative Commons licences refer to moral rights, noting that they are not affected by the licence.[77] By contrast, the European Union Public licence requires the licensor to waive his moral rights, but only 'in order to make effective the licence of the economic rights' provided for under the licence.[78] The Open Database licence requires the licensor to waive all moral rights 'to the fullest extent possible' or agree not to assert such rights. If neither option is permitted by law, the licence cryptically states that 'the author may retain their moral rights over certain aspects of the Database', without specifying what such aspects may be.[79] The GNU GPL makes no reference to moral rights, which reflects its US origins.

It has been argued that moral-type rights should be recast for a digital age, rather than abandoned or avoided.[80] Others have suggested that a distinction could be made between the application of moral rights to object code and source code, especially when the former generates an audio-visual work.[81] Were moral rights to be reinvigorated as a category of intellectual property, what impact would it have on the open source community? The answer, as with most legal questions, is: it depends! As Ginsburg asks, should moral rights in a digital age 'be achieved by conveying more information about the copy, or by controlling the copy itself?'[82] As noted earlier, the attribution right would seem perfectly aligned with the philosophy of the

[76] <http://opensource.org/osd-annotated>. [77] <http://creativecommons.org/licenses/by-nc-sa/3.0/>.
[78] EUPL, v.1.1 (2007), cl 2. [79] ODbL v.1.0, cl 5.
[80] See, eg, J Ginsburg, 'Have moral rights come of (digital) age in the United States' (2001) *Cardoza Arts & Entertainment Law Journal*, vol 9, no 1, 9.
[81] eg Vetter (n 65). [82] Ginsburg (n 80) 17.

open source movement, subject only to the need to facilitate collective attribution. It is with respect to modifications that our historic conception of moral rights may require recasting to reflect the phenomenon of open source.

1.3.3 The public domain

The central objective of the FOSS community is to make source code widely and freely available for use. As such, it begs the question: why not place the source code in the public domain, rather than using the tools of copyright law to achieve the same ends?

The concept of 'public domain' information has a specific meaning within intellectual property law distinct from the state of information being publicly available.[83] In some contexts, however, the term 'open source' is used in law as a synonym for publicly available data, rather than software-related.[84] A 'public domain' work is not subject to any intellectual property rights; it is an alternative state in which information may be. The literature sometimes confuses these two states. Schellekens, for example, notes that software in its pre-commodification state 'belonged to the public domain', which incorrectly equates free, as in speech or beer, with free as in without IP protection.[85] Meanwhile Boldrin and Levine describe the open source movement as having 'relinquished its intellectual monopoly',[86] which implies an abandonment of intellectual property laws rather than their subversion.

There are various reasons why something may not be subject to intellectual property laws. First, the intellectual property laws that pertain to a particular work can expire. Copyright only subsists in a literary work for between 50 and 70 years following the death of the author.[87] Differing time periods exist for different forms of intellectual property, with perpetual protection being possible.[88]

Second, certain types of information are not considered protectable subject matter; therefore a particular IP regime may not apply. Under European patent law, 'programs for computers' are not considered inventions.[89] While under US copyright law, works of the US Government are not protectable.[90] Copyright also protects forms of expression, rather than the underlying ideas and principles that generate

[83] See L Guibault and B Hugenholtz, *The future of the public domain: identifying the commons in information law* (Netherlands, Kluwer Law International, 2006).

[84] eg Council of Europe Convention on Cybercrime (2001), Article 32(a).

[85] Schellekens (n 5) 309.

[86] Boldrin and Levine (n 39) 17.

[87] The Berne Convention provides for 50 years (Article 7(1)), while UK law provides for 70 years (CDPA 1988, s 12(2)).

[88] ie confidential information, as long as it remains secret; trademarks, provided the registration is maintained and it does not lose its distinct characteristics, and database right, where a substantial change or investment is made to the contents.

[89] European Patent Convention, art 52(2)(c). See further ch 5, at 5.1.

[90] 17 USC para 105.

that expression. As such, ideas fall outside international[91] and national[92] copyright regimes and access to such ideas may require specific statutory protection, as provided for in respect of computer software under European Union law.[93]

Public domain must also be distinguished from exceptions that are carved into IP regimes. With the latter, the right subsists in the information, but the rights holder is prevented from exercising that right against a particular use made of that information. In the case of software, European law recognizes various exceptions that permit a lawful user to use the software for error correction or back-up purposes.[94] Specific provision is also made for a lawful user to obtain protected information that is 'necessary to achieve the interoperability of an independently created computer program with other programs',[95] which was designed to stimulate competition in the software market.

Use exceptions may be drafted broadly, such as the US concept of 'fair use',[96] or narrowly list specific usage scenarios or purposes, as provided for under European law.[97] Copyright exceptions are a topic of ongoing debate in many jurisdictions, revolving around what constitutes the right balance between the competing public interests and rights of control and access. These arguments are, in part, about what constitutes the proper scope of the public domain, although taking place firmly within the paradigm of copyright control.

Finally, public domain works should also be distinguished from so-called 'orphan works', where it is impossible to identify the copyright owner, but which are still subject to copyright and therefore constrained from being freely used.[98] Within the software industry there is another variation of the orphan work, so-called 'abandonware'. Here the software remains protected by copyright, but the owner is no longer interested in the code, providing no support or other related input, and not interested in policing or enforcing against violations of his copyright.[99] Reasons for abandonment vary, but can obviously include the owner going out of business.

The initial question (why not place source code in the public domain?) generates two further questions. First, does the applicable IP regime enable a rights holder to place protected subject matter in the public domain; ie can they shed the source code of its protective legal coating? Second, if source code can be placed in the public

[91] eg TRIPS Agreement, Article 9(2); Copyright Treaty, Article 2.

[92] eg 17 USC para 102(b): 'In no case does copyright protection for an original work of authorship extend to any idea, procedure, process, system, method of operation, concept, principle, or discovery, regardless of the form in which it is described, explained, illustrated, or embodied in such work.'

[93] Software Directive, Article 5(3).

[94] Software Directive, Article 5(1) and (2). See similarly 17 USC para 117.

[95] Software Directive, Article 6(1).

[96] 17 USC para 107.

[97] Information Society Directive, Article 5.

[98] See Directive 2012/28/EU 'on certain permitted uses of orphan works' (OJ L299/5, 27.10.2012).

[99] See D Khong, 'Orphan Works, Abandonware and the Missing Mark for Copyrighted Goods' (2006) 15 *International Journal of Law and Information Technology* 54.

domain, what implications does this change of status have in terms of the ceding person's ability to control subsequent users of the code?

In respect of the first issue, the problem is noted in the Creative Commons CC0 Public Domain Dedication:

> [M]any legal systems effectively prohibit any attempt by these owners to surrender rights automatically conferred by law, particularly moral rights, even when the author wishing to do so is well informed and resolute about doing so and contributing their work to the public domain.

US copyright law recognizes the concept of abandonment, which can be argued as a defence to a claim of infringement. It requires a defendant to show that the copyright owner intends to surrender his rights in the work and has overtly acted in a manner evidencing such intention.[100] Whilst this may prove a substantial hurdle in the case of orphan works, such intent could be easily manifest in an open source context through appropriate notices dedicating the work to the public. No similar doctrine of abandonment clearly exists under English law of copyright,[101] while in European civil law jurisdictions, the doctrine appears to be generally unacceptable.[102]

The difficulties in abandoning copyright is in stark contrast to the treatment of other intellectual property rights, especially the registered rights, patents and trade mark,[103] as well as moral rights discussed earlier. As well as a statutory recognition of surrender, patent rights are also vulnerable to community practices, such as defensive publication, which can undermine the secrecy required when applying for the patent.[104]

An alternative would be for the copyright owner to grant a licence to the world, without any restriction on use. Such a licence remains revocable at the copyright holder's will, except where constrained by estoppel.[105] The ability to revoke would enable a community to respond in the event that their source code was being used in an unacceptable manner, although the related complexity and legal uncertainty would represent a significant threshold to the taking of such action.

With regard to the second issue, placing source code in the public domain would enable a user to incorporate the code within another work, thereby essentially reprivatizing the code, to the extent that it could not be used except on the terms granted by the new copyright owner. As such, the public domain may be viewed as resulting in a loss of control, potentially undermining the objectives of the FOSS movement.

[100] *National Comics Publications, Inc v Fawcett Publications, Inc* 191 F.2d 594, 90 USPQ 274. See MW Turetsky, 'Applying Copyright Abandonment in the Digital Age' (2010) *Duke L & Tech Rev* 19, 22.

[101] P Johnson, '"Dedicating" Copyright to the Public Domain' (2008) 71 *Modern Law Review* 587. Also *Copinger and Skone James on Copyright* (Sweet & Maxwell, 2012) 6–88.

[102] E Hudson and R Burrell, 'Abandonment, copyright and orphaned works: What does it mean to take the proprietary nature of intellectual property rights seriously?' (2011) *Melbourne University Law Review*, vol 35, 971.

[103] Patents Act 1977, s 29 and Trade Marks Act 1994, s 45.

[104] See further ch 6, at 6.9.

[105] Johnson (n 101) 607.

1.3.4 Open source policies

A sometimes intensely political area of computing, it is inevitable that FOSS has come to the attention of politicians and policy makers. Historically, politicians in the US and Europe have been highly supportive of intellectual property laws and the need to strengthen existing rules to reflect the shift to service-based, information-led, economies in a rapidly evolving digital environment.

At the same time, however, governments have become increasingly attracted by open source software for various reasons. First, as users of ICTs, the public sector has often experienced significant disappointments with the deployment of ICTs designed to achieve more efficient and cheaper government. Some have seized upon FOSS as a means of addressing these past failures, based on assertions about its technical superiority and its cost advantages. Second, there is a general desire to stimulate innovation within national economies and FOSS is viewed as contributing to that objective. Third, the dominance of certain market players, particularly from the US, has raised concerns about the competitive position of domestic software industries, which may be bolstered by the adoption of FOSS.[106] Finally, the trend towards more open government, in terms of transparency, such as freedom of information legislation, has chimed with the concept of open source and its 'transparency of process.'[107]

International organizations have embraced FOSS. UNESCO has noted that FOSS can play a significant role in ensuring attainment of the UN's Millennium Development Goals.[108] In terms of national, regional or local government policies towards open source, the Center for Strategic and International Studies (CSIS) carried out surveys of published policies between 2002 and 2010, which it groups into four categories:[109]

- R&D-related initiatives, such as encouraging the formation of FOSS development communities;
- awareness and advisory initiatives, where FOSS is brought to the attention of communities of users, again usually the public sector;[110]
- granting preferential treatment for FOSS; or
- mandating the use of open source by public administrations.

The latter two policy categories are variants that directly increase the adoption of FOSS within the public sector. Over the period, adoption was the most

[106] See H Varian and C Shapiro, *Linux adoption in the public sector: an economic analysis*, mimeo, (University of Berkeley, California, 2003).

[107] OSI Mission Statement <http://opensource.org/about>.

[108] <http://www.unesco.org/new/en/communication-and-information/access-to-knowledge/free-and-open-source-software-foss/unescos-free-and-open-source-software-portal/>.

[109] See the March 2010 version <http://csis.org/files/publication/100416_Open_Source_Policies.pdf>. In 2010, some 364 FOSS initiatives were identified from public sources.

[110] See, eg, the European Commission's 'Joinup' initiative, available at <http://joinup.ec.europa.eu/>.

prevalent policy approach; a finding confirmed in another survey of European initiatives.[111]

In general, preferential treatment has targeted the procurement of FOSS-related ICTs ('inbound preference'); ranging from favourable treatment in procurement processes to direct financial subsidy where FOSS is adopted.[112] In some jurisdictions, FOSS has also been adopted as the preferred approach for the dissemination of public sector developed code ('outbound preference'). In 2007, eg, the European Commission approved the European Union Public licence for the purpose of distributing its own software under a private law arrangement that corresponded with the requirements of European law.[113] However, as with R&D initiatives, promoting the use of particular licence terms for 'publicly' developed or funded software may itself generate controversy, particularly when choosing the use of copyleft rather than more permissive FOSS licences.[114]

Various tools may be used by governments to facilitate FOSS, especially public procurement procedures and an 'open' standards policy.[115] The former is a demand-side competition measure, given the purchasing power of the public sector. The latter can improve supply-side competition, by facilitating interoperability between devices, software and data. While FOSS does not equate with 'free' as in no payment or charge, payment issues do arise in the area of standards and patents, where there is an ongoing debate about whether existing royalty-bearing or mandated royalty-free 'FRAND' licensing arrangements discriminate against either the proprietary or FOSS community, resulting in a market failure that justifies government intervention.[116]

It has been noted that one element in the adoption of pro-FOSS national policies has been anti-Americanism and the associated brands of large companies such as Microsoft. The CSIS suggests that trends in open source policies may also reflect market developments in the proprietary software market. So, eg, the launch of Windows Vista in 2006–07 and the resultant criticism and negative press coincided with a rise in the number of published open source policies.[117]

In terms of implementation, R&D and advisory policy initiatives generally arise through decision-making within public administrations, which is likely to reduce the political capital required for their approval. By contrast, adoption initiatives,

[111] S Comino, F Manenti and A Rossi, 'On the role of public policies supporting free/open source software' in K St Amant and B Still (eds), *Handbook of Research on Open Source Software* (IGI Global, 2007) ch XXXII.

[112] S Comino, F Manenti and A Rossi, 'On the role of public policies supporting free/open source software' in St Amant and Still (eds), *Handbook of Research on Open Source Software* (IGI Global, 2007) ch XXXII.

[113] See <http://joinup.ec.europa.eu/software/page/eupl/introduction-eupl-licence#section-2>.

[114] See L Lessig, 'Open source baselines: compare to what?' in RW Hahn (ed), *Government policy toward open source software* (Brookings Institution Press, 2002) 64 *et seq*.

[115] See further chs 9 and 10.

[116] See, eg, M Välimäki and V Oksanen, 'Patents on Compatibility Standards and Open Source—Do Patent Law Exceptions and Royalty-Free Requirements Make Sense?,' (2005) 2:3 *SCRIPTed* 397.

[117] CSIS (n 109).

particularly through mandation, will often require, or take, a more 'legal' route, through legislative or regulatory measures. Indeed, proposals for mandation are usually instigated within national or local legislatures, which increase the possibility of political and legal challenge. The CSIS survey indicates that the failure rate is considerably greatly for adoption initiatives; with mandation measures experiencing more failures than approvals.[118]

Pro-FOSS policies have inevitably generated controversy and a response from the software and wider ICT industries, generally pitching the proprietary rights holders against the FOSS community. Concerns have also been raised by academic commentators that such policies can represent 'industrial policy by stealth'.[119] To a degree, the issues are analogous to debates in other sectors, especially the utility industries, about the best means of achieving open and competitive markets: does establishing a 'level playing field' require some form of preferential or discriminatory treatment when overcoming certain entrenched market structures?

1.4 'OPEN' WHAT?

While the previous sections identified some of the philosophical and political dimensions that underpin debates about open source, they do not provide a complete description of what 'open' means in terms of its distinguishing characteristics. At an abstract level, 'open' can be defined positively in terms of the freedoms users are granted to use, modify and share something; as specified most clearly in the 'four freedoms' of the Free Software Foundation ('FSF').[120] Alternatively, 'open' can have more negative connotations, through requirements designed to prevent certain behaviours and attempts to exert control; examples of which can be found in the criteria of the OSI.[121] Open often equates to accessibility and transparency. Source code should be made accessible for examination and scrutiny by others, to enable the ideas and principles that comprise its design and functionality to be discerned and peer reviewed, without necessarily involving any further 'use' in the form of interaction. Although 'free' and 'open' are seen as denoting difference in a FOSS context, since cost is often an element in determining whether something is accessible, 'free' as in 'free beer' often comprises an aspect of what it means to be 'open'. Open can also imply freedom of choice and conduct, facilitating adoption, take-up and use, as much as rejection and the utilization of alternatives. Universality is also a connotation of 'open', which links to issues of standardization

[118] CSIS (n 109). [119] J Lerner and M Schankerman, *The Co-Mingled Code* (Cambridge, MA, MIT Press, 2010) 197.
[120] <http://www.gnu.org/philosophy/free-sw.html>. See further ch 12.
[121] eg prohibitions on discrimination against persons, groups or fields of endeavour. See <http://opensource.org/osd-annotated>.

and interoperability, critical issues for the software industry and examined elsewhere in the book.[122]

The open source movement relies upon licences, copyright and patent law to enable the *use* of source code by others, specifically its *modification* and *redistribution*. While 'use' is obviously a catch-all term, as well as a synonym for copying in a digital environment, the focus on acts of modification and redistribution are key to the control expressed in licences. A licensor is usually concerned with how a licensee uses the code in two circumstances: where the licensee redistributes the code or where it is modified and then redistributed. The licensor will want to govern the conduct of users downstream from the licensee as much as licensee himself; liberating or restraining depending on your perspective.

Each of these forms of conduct, use modification and redistribution, can raise concerns for the original creators. As in many areas of law, uncertainties and disagreements can exist about the precise meaning of terms used in statutory copyright regimes, both at a national level and from their interaction in a multi-jurisdictional environment. Language is imbued with cultural and historical meanings that find expression through law and legal interpretation. Private law mechanisms can therefore be a tool to address such uncertainties, either building on the existing framework, filling the gaps, or creating an alternative language. The free software movement, particularly through the GPL, has embraced the latter approach, using terms and defining concepts that are deliberately disassociated from those commonly found within copyright law:

> Over the years, we learned that some jurisdictions used this same word in their own copyright laws, but gave it different meanings. We invented these new terms to make our intent as clear as possible no matter where the license is interpreted. They are not used in any copyright law in the world, and we provide their definitions directly in the license.[123]

This attempt to liberate open source from national and copyright law prejudices, whilst deliberately remaining firmly within the jurisdiction of these public law regimes, obviously generates its own challenges and uncertainties for developers and users, as evidenced by the ongoing, sometimes fiercely argued, debates within the open source community.

The following sections briefly examine the concepts of modification and redistribution within copyright law and some of the implications and debates within the open source community surrounding each concept. Although substantially harmonized, national copyright laws retain enough particularities and peculiarities to

[122] See further ch 10.

[123] Why did you invent the new terms 'propagate' and 'convey' in GPLv3? In 'Frequently asked questions about the GNU licences' <http://www.gnu.org/licenses/gpl-faq.html#WhyPropagateAndConvey>.

render coverage of all jurisdictions impossible. As such, the analysis focuses on US, UK and European copyright law.

1.4.1 Modifications

Modifying source code is an exclusive right granted to a rights holder.[124] What constitutes modification however is much less obvious, varying in terminology and scope between jurisdictions. The act of modifying source code will also generally involve an act of reproduction, which begs the question whether these purportedly distinct rights are effectively inseparable. However, it is widely assumed or accepted that the distinction has important implications, not least by the FOSS community.[125] It is therefore necessary to examine the concept in an open source context.

As most open source licences originate in the US, we start with the term 'derivative work,' which is widely used and is statutorily defined as:

> a work based upon one or more preexisting works, such as a translation, musical arrangement, dramatization, fictionalization, motion picture version, sound recording, art reproduction, abridgment, condensation, or any other form in which a work may be recast, transformed, or adapted. A work consisting of editorial revisions, annotations, elaborations, or other modifications which, as a whole, represent an original work of authorship, is a 'derivative work.'[126]

This is an elaborated version of the definition used in the Berne Convention.[127] Under English law, the restricted conduct is the making of an 'adaptation,' with the term being given a specific meaning in respect of a computer program, as 'an arrangement or altered version of the program or a translation of it,'[128] which originates in EU law.[129] However, adaptation is more narrowly conceived than the US concept, which generates its own uncertainty when transplanting US-originating licences into an English law context.

A derivative work is granted a new and distinct copyright under US law, although to be derivative, the new work must substantially copy the original and must involve more than a minimal contribution to the original.[130] A derivative work should also

[124] eg 17 USC para 106(2) and Software Directive, Article 4(1)(b). Note that this right is not harmonized in the EU for other types of work (see Information Society Directive).

[125] See generally L Determann, 'Dangerous Liaisons—Software combinations as derivative works? Distribution, Installation, and Execution of Linked Programs under Copyright Law, and the GPL' *Berkeley Technology Law Journal*, (2006) vol 21, no 4, Fall, 1421.

[126] 17 USC para 101.

[127] Article 2(3): 'Translations, adaptations, arrangements of music and other alterations of a literary or artistic work shall be protected as original works without prejudice to the copyright in the original work.'

[128] CDPA 1988, s 21(3)(ab). At (4) translation 'includes a version of the program in which it is converted into or out of a computer language or code or into a different computer language or code.'

[129] Software Directive, Article 4(1)(b).

[130] *Nimmer on Copyright* (Matthew Bender, 1963, Loose Leaf) paras 3.01 and 3.03[A].

be distinguished from an original work that derives only its ideas from another work. To create a derivative work requires consent from the original owner, which is granted under an open source licence, subject to conditions such as paternity notices or contribution back. However, some licence schemes permit copyright owners to refuse by default to allow derivative works to be created.[131] If the licence conditions are breached, the consent is withdrawn and the owner of the derivative work can no longer distribute the whole work, but could (theoretically) continue to distribute his contribution. As such, a derivative can be seen as residing somewhere between a joint work, where the work is viewed as an undivided whole,[132] and a collective work, where ownership in the parts is distinct from ownership in the whole.

In a software development context, the focus is on the nature of the interaction between the component source code written by the various contributors. Is the contributed code 'based upon' an existing work? If it is, then is the contributed code sufficiently substantial and original to create a derivative work? If it is not, then is the contributed code sufficiently original to constitute an original work in its own right, which can then be assembled with other such works to form a compilation or collective work?

One central and highly charged debate within the open source community, and beyond, concerns the concept of 'linking' and the legal consequences when open source code interacts with proprietary code through usage. Linking is a normal feature of programming and usually refers to the interaction between a program and so-called 'library code'; which provides reusable functions for multiple and independent programs.[133] Broadly speaking, the nature of the interaction may either be static or dynamic, according to the decision of the program designer, the former being generally viewed as an interaction that creates a derivative work, while the latter is not.

The term 'linking' is often used in open source literature as shorthand for the multitude of different ways in which distinct pieces of code can interact, interoperate or 'couple' with other code; other methods include remote procedure calls ('RPC'), system calls and plug-ins.[134] Such interaction matters because where two or more pieces of code are licensed under different terms (free, open, proprietary or other) and the resultant work would be considered 'derivative' or similar under copyright law, then uncertainty is generated both about the licence applicable to the resultant work and whether the modification constitutes an infringement of a licence applicable to any part of the contributing code. Within the open source community, not all modifications are possible, because of licence incompatibilities, which can

[131] eg Creative Commons 'Attribution-NoDerivs 3.0 unported.'

[132] See further at 1.5.

[133] See <http://en.wikipedia.org/wiki/Library_(computing)>.

[134] See the Free Software Foundation Europe, *'Working Paper on the legal implication of certain forms of Software Interactions (a.k.a linking)'*, available at <http://www.ifosslr.org/public/LinkingDocument.odt>.

prevent two open source pieces of code being combined to create a third.[135] Where a contributing licence is 'copyleft' in nature, such as GPLv2, then the resultant work may have to be made subject to that same licence or the terms of the contributing licence will have been breached and will terminate. As such, one result of copyleft licensing is that the operation of copyright law, whether through its application or uncertainties about its application, has led to the use of software development techniques designed specifically to minimize the risk of any interaction triggering a legal consequence.[136]

Indeed, hardware controls have also been developed and deployed specifically to constrain the effective operation of copy-left licences. TiVo, the producer of digital video recorders, utilized Linux and GNU software within their device, but designed the system to use digital signatures such that modified versions of the source code would not run on the device as the digital signatures would not match. The validity of this approach generated significant controversy within the open source community, with some, particularly the FSF, viewing such 'Tivoization' as unacceptable;[137] while others, such as Linus Torvalds, viewed it as a legitimate business practice.[138]

As with much in law, the answer to these uncertainties will depend on a range of factors, specifically the technical nature of the interaction taking place; the person causing the modification to occur; the jurisdiction in which such modification takes place, and the applicable licence. First, all computer code is designed to interact at some level with something else, whether other code, hardware or otherwise. As such, 'mere' interaction or interoperation between codes is not sufficient to render the outcome either a work or a derivative work. Works may interact but remain distinct and separable, each its own copyrighted work. The works may be used together and be redistributed as a package, but remain distinct within a collective or composite work,[139] also referred to as 'mere aggregation'.[140] Second, the end user receiving the composite work may create a derivative work for his own purposes, without further redistribution. As such, the end user's conduct may differ from that of the intermediary distributor, because the conditions of the licence are only triggered by an act of modification *and* redistribution. Third, the copyright law of the jurisdiction in which the interaction takes place may interpret what constitutes a derivative work differently from its neighbouring jurisdictions, whether more narrowly or broadly. Finally, while the wording of any applicable licence may not survive judicial review under either a copyright or contractual analysis, a licensee is generally advised to

[135] See further ch 3. [136] See further n 134 and ch 7.

[137] See <http://www.gnu.org/licenses/gpl-faq.html#Tivoization> and GNU GPLv3, 6, paras 4–5.

[138] See <http://groups.google.com/forum/?fromgroups#!topic/fa.linux.kernel/L5NRD_ONkIk>.

[139] eg Berne Convention, Article 2(5).

[140] See the GPL FAQs <http://www.gnu.org/licenses/old-licenses/gpl-2.0-faq.html#MereAggregation>. See also the GPLv3, 5.

give due consideration to such wording, which may differ in important respects from the governing legal framework, particularly when adopting a broad interpretation of what constitutes modification. The GPLv2 governs not only derived works, but works that 'in whole or in part contain'[141] the licensed code, which would appear to include collective works where the distinct copyrighted works may interact only in a minimal way.

1.4.2 Distribution

Under the WIPO Copyright Treaty (1996), distribution is recognized as an exclusive right of an author:

> Authors of literary and artistic works shall enjoy the exclusive right of authorizing the making available to the public of the original and copies of their works through sale or other transfer of ownership.[142]

Under EU law, the distribution of computer programs to the public is one of the exclusive rights granted to the rights holder.[143]

While an act of distribution extends both to the original work and copies, it is generally only engaged where copying is involved. Under traditional copyright principles, where a copy of a work is redistributed, without a further copy being made, then the copyright owner is constrained from prohibiting such conduct under the doctrine of 'first sale'[144] or 'exhaustion'[145] of the distribution right. The historic rationale for this doctrine is that the copyright owner should be remunerated for the copy, but not any further economic value derived from its further sale down a chain of consumers.[146] While the doctrine refers to 'sale', it is in fact applicable to other situations where the copy is passed on to others, whether for remuneration or otherwise.[147] In the European Union, the doctrine is also used as a tool to promote the single market and prevent market partitioning,[148] which fundamentally distinguishes its application from that in the US.

In the US, the exhaustion doctrine has been held not to apply to pure 'digital works' both by the courts and the relevant authorities.[149] In addition, the courts

[141] GNU GPLv2 (1991), 2(b). [142] Article 6(1). [143] eg Software Directive, Article 4(1)(c).

[144] 17 USC para 109(a). [145] Copyright Treaty, Article 6(2).

[146] Under EU law, such remuneration should also be that which is 'appropriate', rather than the 'highest possible remuneration'; see *Football Association Premier League Ltd and others v QC Leisure and others, Murphy v Media Protection Services Ltd* [2012] 1 CMLR 29, paras 108–09.

[147] eg in the UK, the CDPA 1988, s 18(3), refers to a loan.

[148] eg Case C-200/96 *Metronome Musik* [1998] ECR I-1953, para 14. This principle is limited to distribution within the EEA and does not apply internationally (see *Laserdisken ApS v Kulturministeriet*, Case C-479/04, [2007] 1 CMLR 6, para 24).

[149] See *Capitol Records LLC v ReDigi Inc*, No 12 Civ. 95 (RJS), 30 March 2013; also United States Copyright Office, DMCA Section 104 Report (August 2001) 97 *et seq*.

have specifically held in relation to software licences that where the copyright holder clearly indicates that the user is a licensee; restricts the user's right to transfer the licence, and restricts the use made of the software, the first sale doctrine is not applicable.[150] The doctrine could apply to a software transaction, however, were the circumstances such that a licensor/licensee relationship was not successfully established, but title in the software was held to have transferred instead.[151] In the absence of evidence of an agreement or conduct indicating acceptance by the user, such so-called 'shrink-wrap', 'label' or unilateral licenses may not be considered enforceable, which equates to the question of whether FOSS licences are considered contracts or not.[152]

Under EU law, the exhaustion doctrine is expressly extended to computer programs,[153] although until recently its application was widely seen as being restricted to the distribution of tangible copies. This limitation was recently rejected by the European Court of Justice in *UsedSoft GmbH v Oracle International Corp* (2012).[154] Here, Oracle made client-server software available for downloading from a website free of charge, but subject to a usage licence. Oracle offered group licences that permitted up to 25 users, while if a licensee had more users, they would have to obtain another 25-user licence. UsedSoft obtained these group user licences from Oracle's customers and offered any unused user permissions for sale to others, which Oracle considered to be an infringing act. The Court held that where a copy of the program was transferred to a user, whether through a tangible medium such as a DVD or made available for downloading from a website, together with a licence granting a right to use the program for an unlimited period, then that constituted a 'first sale' for the purpose of the exhaustion doctrine (paragraph 49).[155] Quoting approvingly the Advocate General's opinion, it stated that to distinguish a contract as being either a licence, to which the exhaustion doctrine does not apply, or a sale, to which it does, would be to undermine the purpose of the provision itself (paragraph 49). Previously, it had been widely believed that making software available for download was an act of 'communication to the public', which is a different exclusive right granted to the rights holder and one to which the doctrine of exhaustion does not apply.[156] However, the Court held that the transfer of ownership or 'sale' that resulted from the downloading of a copy and the granting of a licence to use rendered the conduct within the scope of the distribution right (paragraph 52).

[150] *Vernor v Autodesk, Inc*, 621 F.3d 1102, C.A.9 (Wash) 2010. See also *Apple Inc v Psystar Corp*, 658 F.3d 1150, CA9 (Cal) 2011 and *MDY Industries v Blizzard Entertainment*, 629 F. 3d 928 CA 9 (Ariz) 2010.

[151] *UMG Recordings, Inc v Augusto* 628 F.3d 1175 (9th Cir 2011), which involved the distribution of digital content on physical CDs. See also *SoftMan Products Co, LLC v Adobe Systems, Inc* (2001) 171 F.Supp.2d 1075.

[152] See further ch 3. [153] Software Directive, Article 4(2). [154] 3 CMLR 44.

[155] Oracle's licence stated that it was 'non-transferable', but this was effectively ignored by the Court.

[156] See Copyright Treaty, Article 8 and Information Society Directive, Article 3.

One implication of this decision is likely to be to encourage licensors to alter their distribution model, shifting away from a 'sale' business model towards a 'rental' subscription model, which also reflects an industry trend towards SaaS and cloud computing.[157] For the FOSS community, however, cloud itself can be seen as an alternative mechanism for restricting the freedom of users to modify the software they use and depend on; controlling rather than liberating.

Under FOSS licences, redistribution is not simply about copying the actual code, but also about the conditions under which the recipient receives the code, either requiring the original rights to be matched throughout the distribution chain (copyleft) or enabling the substitution of different rights for subsequent users, which may be more restrictive. The term 'viral' has been used to describe the manner in which certain open source licences operate, also referred to as copyleft, by imposing obligations down the software distribution chain.[158] While all commercial agreements attempt, in some degree, to ensure that obligations are appropriately reflected either upstream or downstream, the viral phraseology arises from the self-executing nature of the licence, relying on copyright law, rather than contract. Other examples of 'viral' laws are some export control regimes, which apply to specific applications, such as encryption modules within devices, but which can operate such as to make the whole product subject to, or 'infected' by, the control regime.

While the right to 'distribute' is commonly used within copyright regimes, concerns about jurisdictional differences about its scope has seen the FSF deploy the term 'convey' in the GPL, defined as follows:

> [A] work means any kind of propagation that enables other parties to make or receive copies. Mere interaction with a user through a computer network, with no transfer of a copy, is not conveying.[159]

The second part of this definition is important in the context of cloud computing and is examined elsewhere.[160]

Under international, regional and national copyright rules, the concept of distribution is qualified by the phrase 'to the public', which suggests the possibility of non-public offerings of copies of a work. Understanding where the boundary exists between the two can obviously be important in the context of FOSS development. The actual numbers of persons in receipt of a work, while a factor for consideration, is likely to be less determinative than the manner in which the copies of the work were made available; 'what counts is the general *opportunity* given to the public.'[161]

[157] See further ch 9.

[158] eg A Guadamuz Gonzalez, 'Viral contracts or unenforceable documents? Contractual validity of copyleft licences' (2004) *EIPR* 26(8), 331–9.

[159] GNU GPLv3 (2007), 0.

[160] See ch 9.

[161] S Ricketson and J Ginsburg, *International Copyright and Neighbouring Rights* (Oxford, Oxford University Press, 2006) 11.91.

The Court of Justice, in *Sociedad General de Autores y Editores de Espana (SGAE) v Rafael Hotels SL*,[162] has noted in respect of the right to communicate a work to the public, that 'it is sufficient that the work is made available to the public in such a way that the persons forming that public may access it' (paragraph 42). This has potential implications for the governance of open source projects, since the more restrictive the conditions of participation are made, the stronger the argument that the distribution of code among participants does not constitute an exercise of the exclusive right in respect of the code, which could trigger certain consequences under the applicable licence. Conversely, restrictive membership runs counter to the open collaborative model that underpins open source.

The 'to the public' qualification is absent from the concept of 'conveying' used in the GPLv3, which raises the question whether certain forms of distribution, whilst not a breach of copyright law per se, may result in a breach of a licence? In a development context, code may be distributed to participants within a community or forum, which extends beyond a single organization, or demo code may be given to certain selected customers for the purpose of testing under a non-disclosure agreement ('NDA'). The restricted nature of the distribution would not appear to be 'to the public', yet it could give rise to a technical breach of the GPL because 'another' party has received a copy. The GPLv3 does provide that conveyance may be to 'others', but only where it is carried out 'exclusively on your behalf, under your direction and control',[163] which recognizes the non-public nature of the distribution. However, it also states that such conveyance is only permitted for the 'purpose of having them make modifications exclusively for you, or provide you with facilities for running those works', which would suggest an employer/employee, principal/agent or customer/supplier-like relationship between the parties, but would not necessarily cover either the community distribution or the 'testing' scenario.[164]

As distribution of the source code and any accompanying text is the central behavioural obligation placed on users, disputes have inevitably arisen about whether this obligation has been properly met, particularly in the context of retail products.[165] The code may be distributed on some associated media distributed with the product, or may be offered to the end user, often in the form of a web-based download. In either case, but often in the latter, uncertainties can arise as to whether the availability or offer of the code is made *sufficiently* transparent to the end user to meet the licence requirements. Such issues are analogous to other requirements in law concerning notice, such as the contractual incorporation of terms, and availability, such as the

[162] Case C-306/05, 7 December 2006; [2007] ECDR 2. See also Case C-607/11, *ITV Broadcasting Ltd & ors v TVCatchup Ltd*, 7 March 2013.

[163] GNU GPLv3 (2007), 2.

[164] See also ch 9, for its application in a cloud context.

[165] eg *Welte v D-Link Deutschland GmbH* (2006) <http://www.jbb.de/judgment_dc_frankfurt_gpl.pdf>.

decompilation obligation.[166] Retail products often generate particular issues where marketing, design and brand concerns are to the fore.

As with modifications, by focusing on the concept of distribution as the trigger for certain legal consequences, whether desirable or otherwise, attention inevitably converges on the meaning of the term, with, as in much of law, plenty of scope for argument and debate. The traditional venue for interpretation is the courts, although there is scant directly applicable guidance available to date. The licensor is left with the option of trying to draft appropriate and sufficiently precise provisions to address any uncertainties; a complex task in such a rapidly developing environment.

1.5 OPEN SOURCE AS DEVELOPMENT METHODOLOGY

Software development or engineering has evolved considerably since the early days of computing, as processing capacity and programming languages have enabled ever more sophisticated systems to be developed. Greater sophistication of the end product, the source code, has also required more formalized development processes, in order to adequately address the needs of users; reflect those needs in feature design, and test and verify the resultant product. Concomitant to these developments, we have seen the industry try to professionalize itself, establishing qualifications and standards which programmers can obtain and meet. Various standards and development methodologies have been promulgated to capture the various stages of the software life-cycle and, thereby, improve the quality of source code,[167] such as the 'Waterfall' model, Spiral and Agile. The latter is seen as the most widely adopted methodology with the FOSS community.[168]

Open source communities can also be seen as a development methodology in their own right, as noted by the OSI:

> Open source is a development method for software that harnesses the power of distributed peer review and transparency of process. The promise of open source is better quality, higher reliability, more flexibility, lower cost, and an end to predatory vendor lock-in.[169]

Whatever the benefits of open source as a development methodology, from a copyright law perspective such collaborative working can have important implications.

First, in the absence of agreement to the contrary, the code produced by a FOSS community project is likely to be a work of joint authorship. Joint works can arise

[166] Software Directive, Article 6(1)(b), which restricts the decompilation right where the necessary information has been made 'readily available'. Similar wording is used in the US, at 17 USC para 1201(f)(1).

[167] eg ISO/IEC 12207: 2008 *Systems and software engineering—Software life cycle processes*.

[168] See further ch 7, at 7.2.5.

[169] OSI Mission Statement <http://opensource.org/about>.

where the contribution of an individual author is either not objectively distinct from that of other authors, or is intended to form part of 'unitary whole'.[170] Where a contribution is distinct, then the author may own that contribution separately from the work as a whole; which itself may be characterized as a 'compilation', 'database', 'derivative' or 'collective work'. To add further complexity, the contribution of the individual must itself meet a minimum threshold in terms of substantiality in order to constitute joint authorship.[171] As such, identifying the 'authors' and the nature of their contribution could be a significant forensic challenge for FOSS development projects. Critically with joint works, the exclusive rights have to be exercised with the consent of all the authors, each having an 'undivided ownership in the entire work',[172] rather than independently by each. Such distributed ownership can therefore represent a barrier to the objectives of the FOSS movement. Hence the need for developer participants to agree to abide by private law agreements to address these concerns, either through a licence or assignment of rights, in respect of any in-bound contributions to the entity holding the rights in the code as a whole.[173]

Second, contributors will not generally work for a single organization, but will be operating from a variety of different positions. Some will be employed, either for the purpose of engaging in FOSS projects or otherwise engaged in software development. Others will be independent contractors or self-employed freelance developers. The legal status of the contributor also impacts directly on the issue of ownership in the code. Copyright law grants rights to employers, eg, in respect of works created by employees 'in the course of their employment' or 'made for hire'.[174] Again, private law agreements can be used to alter the statutory default position, while their absence can create legal uncertainty.

Finally, collaborative development will often involve persons from multiple jurisdictions. While copyright and patent laws are substantially harmonized at an international level, there remains plenty of divergent national rules that reflect historical or cultural specificities. As such, there is the potential for the assertion and application of multiple conflicting laws to the work product of a FOSS development community; another source of uncertainty and constraint over use.

Together these consequences of the operation of copyright law can create significant challenges for the open source movement, challenges which may supersede the public attention paid to the manner in which the resultant code is then licensed for

[170] CDPA 1988, s 10 and 17 USC para 101 respectively. While intent to create a joint work is not a requirement under English law, the parties should have intended to collaborate in some form (*Cala Homes (South) v Alfred McAlpine Homes East* [1995] FSR 818, 835).

[171] See L Bently and B Sherman, *Intellectual Property Law*, 3rd edn (Oxford, Oxford University Press, 2009) 2.3 and *Nimmer on Copyright* (n 130) para 6.07[A][1].

[172] *Nimmer on Copyright* (n 130) para 6.02.

[173] See further ch 7, at 7.3.1.

[174] CDPA 1988, s 11(2) and 17 USC para 201(b) respectively. Note that the latter US concept would extend to other types of commissioner, such as a customer of bespoke software, while under English law it is limited to employees.

use by others. Such challenges can also be fully and adequately addressed through private law ordering, but this imposes an additional dependency for the open source movement on the effective operation of law.

1.6 OPEN SOURCE AS COMMERCE

One recurrent theme has been to acknowledge the philosophical and political ideas that underpin the open source movement, whilst at the same time treating open source apolitically, ie as a reality that organizations need to be aware of, to act appropriately towards and may consider as an alternative means of doing business.

Awareness is obvious, yet organizations, as much as individuals, exhibit a tendency to turn a blind eye to those things which are not well understood or seem difficult. In the author's experience, while open source is widely known, there is a considerable lack of knowledge and uncertainty about the legal implications of using FOSS.

Acting appropriately, once aware, requires consideration of how open source may impact the organization both internally and externally, with regard to suppliers, partners and customers. Internal considerations include regulating employee contributions to projects and use of open source code; while external issues include auditing for open source code in due diligence procedures.[175] A key objective of most organizations is to manage their risk and to protect their assets.

There are a variety of ways in which FOSS can be used to generate economic value, through so-called 'hybrid strategies'.[176] The range of possible business models reflects the complexity of the ICT eco-system. Companies may distribute FOSS code produced by others, either stand-alone or as part of a collection, which is then modified to suit the specific needs of the customer. The value is in the customization process and operates similarly to the proprietary software ecosystem. The company will often also offer operational support services in relation to the FOSS, such as assistance in its deployment and integration with the customer's legacy systems. This model has been successfully adopted by RedHat, which reported revenues in excess of a billion dollars in 2012.[177]

Copyright owners have the freedom to license their code under whatever terms they choose. This includes the possibility of offering dual or multiple licences in respect of an identical piece of code. Code could be licensed under the GPL for certain users, free of charge; with other customers being charged fees under a traditional proprietary style of licence, without the conditions applicable under the GPL.

[175] See further ch 8.

[176] See 'Living apart together: Hybrid business strategies on the edge of the commons' in R van Wendel de Joode et al, *Protecting the Virtual Commons* (The Hague, Asser Press, 2003) 93–107.

[177] <http://investors.redhat.com/releasedetail.cfm?ReleaseID=660156>.

Customers get to choose the terms of use, while the licensor can generate revenues from a sub-set of its market. Such a 'dual-licensing' model does, however, require the owner to have all the legal rights in the distributed code.[178]

As discussed in Chapter 2, FOSS is usually generated within communities. These communities will emerge and may divide or peter out over time. Divisions within communities can result in 'forking,' where the code base is developed along separate and distinct lines, sometimes acrimoniously following a dispute between participant developers, or simply in pursuit of different outcomes. As such, a development line may be established specifically to meet the needs of a particular group of customers, another form of customization, who are prepared to pay for the privilege. Alternatively, for companies that invest in hardware development and do not view software as a means of differentiating their product, expending resource on FOSS community projects, whether through kind (ie employee participation) or a direct financial contribution, can be a cost-efficient approach to software development.

Interoperability between software applications and between applications and hardware, devices and peripherals is widely seen as the life blood of the industry;[179] as well as a policy objective to facilitate and maintain competition in the market, through either ex ante measures or ex post interventions.[180] Ensuring that products can operate with FOSS can be seen as a commercial imperative in certain market segments. As such, a company that supplies a new product may outsource to third party FOSS developers the writing and testing of the necessary code, encouraging its free distribution in the hope that wide availability will help build market share for its product.[181]

In generating revenues, FOSS distributors become part of a 'normal' business community. Revenues have implications for those in the FOSS community that argue against the discriminatory impact of the payment of royalties for IP-protected components, most commonly patents in standards. Revenues also tend to render organizations a target for litigants, legitimate or otherwise.

1.7 ENFORCING OPEN SOURCE

As discussed throughout this book, the open source community relies on copyright law and contract law, and to a greater or lesser extent patent and trade mark law, to govern the conduct of users of their code. As such, user non-compliance with either the terms of a licence or the underlying statutory obligations, gives rise to the

[178] M Välimäki, 'Dual licensing in open source software industry' (2003) *Systemes d'Information et Management*, vol 8, no 1, 63–75.

[179] See further ch 10.

[180] eg respectively, the Software Directive, Article 6 and Case No COMP M.5984—Intel/McAfee, 26 January 2011. See generally A van Rooijen, *The Software Interface between Copyright and Competition Law* (Netherlands, Wolters Kluwer, 2010).

[181] van Wendel de Joode et al (n 176) 99–101.

possibility of enforcement action being taken against code-users, as licensees or otherwise. Indeed, enforcement, or the realistic threat and risk of it, must be seen as an essential component of any effective legal regime, whether based in private or public law; although fear of enforcement may not be the primary reason why laws are respected.[182]

Intellectual property laws provide a range of civil and criminal remedies against infringers; although to date the enforcement of open source licences has only relied on civil remedies. Rights holders may seek protective remedies, such as an injunction; compensatory remedies, such as damages, or restitutionary remedies, such as an account of profits. By contrast, remedies for breach of contract tend to be less varied and robust, depending on the nature of the breach, and may be subject to different jurisdictional regimes.[183] As such, rights holders will tend to favour the former over the latter. However, the availability of these different remedies can depend on the characterization of the breach as either being copyright or contractual in nature,[184] which generates another layer of uncertainty for the enforcement of open source licences.[185]

Enforcement actions may also arise under other complementary legal regimes, such as consumer protection laws designed to prevent the defrauding of end users. One example is so-called 'subscription traps', where sites offer open source software for prohibitive and hidden fees, which have been the subject of criminal proceedings in Germany.[186]

As well as actions by FOSS rights holders against code-users, disputes also arise between rights holders and other rights holders, whether FOSS or proprietary. Given the risks and costs associated with enforcement actions, potential defendants will commonly adopt a range of strategic IP management measures intended to mitigate such risks, from technical 'design-a-rounds' to the defensive acquisition of IP rights.[187]

National procedures governing the enforcement of intellectual property rights vary significantly and substantially more than the substantive rights themselves, despite recent harmonization initiatives.[188] One consequence of these differences is that the incentives for enforcement and deterrence effect of potential remedies can

[182] See further C Reed, *Making Laws for Cyberspace* (Oxford, Oxford University Press, 2012).

[183] eg in the US, a contractual breach would be subject to state jurisdiction, while copyright breaches are enforced at a federal level.

[184] In the US, see *MDY Industries v Blizzard Entertainment*, 629 F.3d 928 CA9 (Ariz) 2010, where the court held that a contractual breach did not have the necessary 'nexus between the condition and the licensor's exclusive rights of copyright'.

[185] See RW Gomulkiewicz, 'Enforcement of open source licenses: The MDY Trio's inconvenient complications' (2011) 14 *Yale JL & Tech* 106.

[186] LG Hamburg, Judgment of 21 March 2012, Az 608 KL 8/11 <http://openjur.de/u/432081.html>.

[187] See further ch 6, at 6.9.

[188] See EU Directive 2004/48/EC on the enforcement of intellectual property rights (OJ L195/16, 2.6.2004) and the Anti-Counterfeiting Trade Agreement (ACTA), October 2011.

vary considerably between jurisdictions. In the US, eg, the ability to elect an award of statutory damages, rather than having to prove actual damage,[189] significantly reduces the burden on a claimant and the size of award made against the defendant. In some jurisdictions, registration of copyright with a public authority bestows procedural and evidential advantages on the registrant in the event of legal proceedings.[190] Such formalities impose another dimension of legal dependency on the open source community and impacts on the governance of open source projects.[191]

To date, compliance with licence terms and the risk of enforcement in the event of non-compliance would seem to differ in a FOSS environment from that in other areas of the software industry. The political nature of certain FOSS communities means a normal risk assessment of the likelihood of legal action may be inappropriate; as Bain notes:

> [F]rom a business point of view the community view may be of equal if not more relevance that the strict legal interpretation of a licence, for the purpose of assessing risks and benefits when taking a decision about the licensing and distribution of inter-related components of software.... There is a difference between dealing with a vociferous, if not necessarily legally correct, community... and one where there is space to discuss and reach a consensus on the matter at hand.[192]

Traditional injunctive relief prohibiting certain infringing behaviour has been sought in open source claims, especially where the infringement involves physical products, such as routers and mobile handsets.[193] Non-compliance often involves either a failure to provide certain required information (eg the licence and notification of modifications) or the removal of required notices (eg about the rights being asserted and their attribution). The defendant could be required by a court to rectify the breach, by recalling and reissuing the product, and, or, publicize the presence of the incorrect licence, with the associated reputational damage.[194] In this scenario, traditional compensatory measures for damage are unlikely to amount to much, except in relation to any reputational loss from non- or mis-attribution.[195] Where an injunction is not appropriate, claims would seem more likely to be couched in restitutionary

[189] 17 USC para 504(c). See, eg, *Software Freedom Conservancy Inc v Best Buy Co, Inc* 2010 WL 2985320 (SDNY).

[190] eg 17 USC paras 408–412. Registration is made with the US Copyright Office. In Europe, France and Spain have voluntary schemes.

[191] eg E Moglen, 'Why the FSF gets copyright assignments from contributors' <http://www.gnu.org/licenses/why-assign.html>.

[192] M Bain, 'Software Interactions and the GNU General Public Licence' (2010) *International Free and Open Source Software Law Review*, vol 2, no 2.

[193] eg in the US, see *Software Freedom Conservancy Inc v Best Buy Co, Inc* 2010 WL 2985320 (SDNY); in Germany, see *Welte v Sitecom*, District Court of Munich, Case No 21 0 6123/04. See also ch 6, at 6.3.3.

[194] eg Directive 04/48/EC 'on the enforcement of intellectual property rights'(OJ L 157/45, 30.4.2005), Article 15 'Publication of judicial decisions'.

[195] More akin to a claim for defamation, as discussed in respect of moral rights at 1.3.2.

terms, to deprive the defendant of any profits accrued from the infringement, rather than compensatory.[196]

Traditional rights holders, either as individual companies or, more often, through cooperative industry vehicles[197] engage in pro-active enforcement activities to identify infringers; from attending physical markets, to the scanning of web-based resources and the participation in P2P networks. Similarly, FOSS communities sometimes engage in pro-active enforcement activities, including assigning rights of action to third parties, so-called 'assertion entities'.[198] Despite such activities, as well as the fact that open source has existed for nearly three decades, there is scant case law available to provide an additional layer of legal certainty to code-users, whether FOSS advocates or opponents.

1.8 CONCLUDING REMARKS

This chapter has identified numerous features of FOSS-related conduct which generate legal uncertainties; uncertainties that can operate to the detriment of both proponents and users of open source software. These include the language used in most FOSS licences taken from US copyright law, which can differ in important respects when transplanted into other jurisdictions. The crafting and deployment in some licences of new terms, which while designed to better meet the objectives of the community, are unfamiliar and untested before the courts. The collaborative working structures in FOSS communities are also unfamiliar to many and are therefore often ignored or managed poorly, as well as generating complexities for the application of the law.

Certain developments may also weaken the influence of current open source licence arrangements over time, particularly those pursuing a copyleft philosophy. In terms of markets, the shift to cloud computing means that software distribution is becoming less important in a SaaS environment, except in the context of the operation of the physical access device itself. Evolving copyright law, driven as much through judicial decision-making as legislative reform, may increasingly constrain

[196] eg in *LG Bochum*, judgment of 20.01.2011, Az I-8 O 293/09, the court ordered the defendant to disclose all revenues generated from an infringing use of the claimants LGPL-licensed software (<http://www.telemedicus.info/urteile/Urheberrecht/Open-Source/1148-LG-Bochum-Az-I-8-O-29309-Ansprueche-bei-Verletzung-der-LGPL.html>). In March 2013, the parties eventually settled after the defendant agreed to pay €15k (see <http://www.h-online.com/open/news/item/German-court-case-confirms-validity-of-the-LGPL-1822882.html>).

[197] eg the Business Software Alliance (<http://www.bsa.org>).

[198] eg gpl-violations.org. See further ch 8, at 8.5.2. Under English law, the right to assign a cause of action to a third party may be unlawful where the assignee does not have 'sufficient interest' to justify the proceedings for his own benefit, which does not include the pursuance of a 'campaign', which could be pertinent to FOSS-related actions. See *Jennifer Simpson (as assignee of Alan Catchpole) v Norfolk and Norwich Hospital NHS Trust* (2011) EWCA Civ 1149, 24.

the application of copyright law to software; reducing its efficacy as a control regime while, from a technical perspective, the use of increasingly sophisticated techniques designed to limit the interaction of software components subject to divergent licensing arrangements, may reduce the viral impact of copyleft licences.

As noted at the start, this chapter has tried to avoid making normative statements about open source. Those that promote, defend and use FOSS may pursue particular philosophical, ethical or political aims, which are noted and respected. Instead, the focus has been on how public law regimes, particularly copyright law, interacts with open source software to facilitate and constrain the aims of FOSS proponents and the use of private law arrangements to achieve specified outcomes; outcomes that can be designed to subvert the public law settlement. All the evidence shows open source development and usage increasing substantially. This is likely to result in greater judicial consideration of how the language and law of open source operates; hopefully reducing some areas of uncertainty. What is more unpredictable, however, is whether governments and legislators will address the rise of FOSS; redesigning areas of public law to reflect the critical role and unique features of software in society and the economy.

2

OPEN SOURCE AND GOVERNANCE

Ross Gardler

2.1 COLLABORATION AND COMMUNITIES

Hundreds of thousands of years ago a woman stood in the snow watching a burning tree created in a recent lightning storm. She enjoyed the warmth but feared the beast itself. She'd seen the damage it would do to the tree and anyone who touched it. Yet something about it fascinated her.

A shuffling of feet caught her attention and there, holding a dead rabbit, was a young man. Together they watched the flames, their confidence growing. The woman picked up a stick and poked the fire. It caught alight and the woman watched it in awe. Fascinated the man brought the rabbit to the fire, its hair burned quickly and brightly. In fear the man dropped the rabbit and the pair withdrew to a safe distance.

As their confidence grew again the two strangers experimented more. They discovered that the rabbit had been 'cooked' and tasted good, while the woman's stick had been consumed. The man fed the beast, experimenting with different materials. The woman discovered new beasts could be created closer to her cave by carrying a small part of it on the end of a stick. A third person joined the experiments. They discovered rocks grew hot but were not consumed, and soon the first heated cave was 'built'.

Over time more people congregated around the fire which had now been tamed. Hunters and gatherers from nearby groups took up residence near the beast. Some helped feed it. Some used it to cook meat and melt snow rather than take the long walk to the river. Others experimented with the beast, creating new opportunities for the growing community. Each member of the community had their role; nearly all contributed to communal well-being in some way. Those who didn't soon found they were shunned by the community. Either they began to contribute, and were accepted, or they chose to leave, usually taking with them a mini-beast on a stick of their own.

This story of early community is used[1] by Stephen Walli, Technical Director of the Outercurve Foundation, to illustrate the fact that humans are natural collaborators. The forming of communities to make best use of available resources, both material and intellectual, is nothing new. When we consider this it might seem strange that a modern model of software production, which takes advantage of our inbuilt desire to collaborate for the benefit of all, can be such a difficult concept to understand. Nevertheless, the success of open source software remains a mystery to most.

2.1.1 Scarcity and false markets

The difficulty most of us experience in understanding the concept of open source software is a direct response to recent history. We each have a drive to collaborate as illustrated above, but we have an even greater drive for self-preservation. Hundreds of thousands of years ago our survival was dependent on the basic physiological need for food, water, and sleep. Such needs are easier to satisfy through collaboration. Some people would gather nuts and berries, others would hunt animals, and others still would find suitably well defended caves to rest in. We would each understand where our skills were best placed in the community and, over time, we would become an efficient 'machine' built to satisfy those basic needs.

[1] E Tatham, 'OSS Watch Open Source Junction, Oxford, 28–89 March 2011' (*OSS Watch team blog*, 12 April 2011) <http://osswatch.jiscinvolve.org/wp/2011/04/12/oss-watch-open-source-junction-oxford-28%E2%80%9329-march-2011> accessed 5 April 2013.

Today however, at least for those of us lucky enough to live in developed parts of the world, things are very different. We no longer need to worry about the basics of life. We are not seeking to find our place in a community that can only serve our basic needs. Instead we seek to raise our standard of living by seeking higher rewards.[2] We have turned to market forces as a means to ensure the creation of efficient models of production and supply. Such markets allow us to specialize in much narrower fields than our ancient ancestors were able to. For example, most readers of this book will be seeking to understand the legal models underpinning open source software development. This is a very narrow field and will not feed many of us directly. However, economic models that decouple the 'purchaser' of this expertise from the 'provider' of basic needs make such specialist knowledge valuable and transferable.

Most economic models are based on the principles of scarcity. That is, they recognize that the means of production (raw materials, expertise, and so forth) are scarce and thus we need to manage supply and demand carefully. The emergence of an artificially scarce exchange mechanism (money) has enabled us to assign value to each scarce resource. We no longer know the farmer, and we no longer need to have skills or goods the farmer demands. However, it is not normally in an individual's interests to share their expertise freely as that could reduce the scarcity of that expertise and devalue it in the market. The result is a competitive marketplace in which unrestricted collaboration is routinely avoided since such collaboration is seen to be an inefficient use of resources.

In the case of software products, scarcity only exists in the provision of labour and supporting resources. The cost of reproducing software, once it has been created, is negligible. Software is just a series of electronic zeros and ones that can be duplicated and shared with minimal additional impact on scarce resources. This means that the vast majority of costs in software solutions are found in the production, and in the subsequent maintenance and support of that software.

Users of software may be offered a level of support alongside the digital software product. If this is the case then an increase in the number of users will result in an increased drain on a scarce resource (predominantly staff time). That is, offering users support consumes significant scarce resources, distribution of software does not. Therefore, it can be seen that the economic costs associated with software provision are not incurred automatically by the distribution of the non-scarce software code. Instead they are incurred in the initial production phases and subsequent support phases.

We need to separate out the costs associated with software production (one-off costs), distribution (negligible costs), and support (recurring costs). If we avoid the

[2] AH Maslow, 'A Theory of Human Motivation' (*Psychclassics*, 1943) <http://psychclassics.yorku.ca/Maslow/motivation.htm> accessed 5 April 2013.

assumption that the sharing of software code automatically implies the provision of support then we no longer need to consider software distribution as part of an economic model. That is, by uncoupling the distribution of software from the provision of ongoing support, we are free to consider models of distribution that seek to reduce the cost of production whilst enabling us to continue to monetize maintenance and support activities. Open source software is a model of software production and distribution that does just this.

2.1.2 Open source software as a non-scarce resource

Open source software is a software licensing, production, and distribution model that exploits the non-scarce nature of software applications.[3] As a licensing and distribution mechanism it provides software under terms that allow users to do as they please. However, in order to ensure the software and its users place no demands on scarce resources, the supplier provides no warranties, on-demand support, or additional services alongside the software. Such resource intensive user demands form a part of the company's revenue stream. Users may choose to purchase these additional products and services via the market mechanisms we have grown accustomed to. Alternatively, users may choose to become a part of the production process itself via ancient models of collaboration, such as those illustrated in the introduction.

As a means of production the open source model minimizes the cost of production through efficient collaboration. The open source development model allows individuals to bring their specialist and valuable knowledge and share it with others. In return for their contributions they receive an improved software product. Open source software allows individuals and organizations that potentially compete in the marketplace for scarce products and services to collaborate seamlessly on software components and systems that, once created, are not scarce. The unrestricted distribution of such software results in a larger number of potential collaborators and thus facilitates a further reduction in the cost of production.

The effectiveness of this model of production can be seen in many open source projects. Consider, eg, the Apache Hadoop project.[4] This is an implementation of Google's Map Reduce algorithm. Hadoop contains significant contributions from many companies that operate in overlapping markets. Participants include large software companies such as Microsoft, Facebook, Twitter, and LinkedIn as well as SMEs, universities, and government organizations. There are even some individuals involved. All contribute on equal terms, regardless of their size, to the production and maintenance of the Hadoop software. Most contribute in order to reduce the costs and increase the quality of software that forms a core part of their unique

[3] See further ch 1.

[4] Hadoop <http://hadoop.apache.org> accessed 5 April 2013.

business models; a few contribute for more personal reasons, such as professional development.

For this model of production to work it is necessary for each participant to realize more value than they contribute. Participants must also feel that their future is protected and that their contributions cannot be abused by other collaborators now or in the future. It is the combination of a community based development model, backed by modern internet based collaboration tools and an open source licence, that ensures such collaborations are possible.

2.1.3 Licences to facilitate collaboration

The advancement of internet based communications technologies has facilitated the means of co-production found in open source software communities. Alongside this, copyright law has been leveraged to create a range of licences that protect the intellectual property contributed by each partner, whilst still allowing for the unrestricted distribution of the work. Today there are many different open source licences to choose from. Which one is chosen by a given project will have significant impact on the kind of community, and thus the kind of production model, that a project will adopt.

One group of licences, commonly known as reciprocal or 'copyleft' licences, legally enforces the sharing of contributions. These licences prevent some business models, such as the creation of proprietary derivatives, but ensure that no third party can abuse the open development model by simply consuming the projects outputs without contributing back.[5]

At the other end of the licensing spectrum are permissive licences. These allow the adoption of any business model, including the creation of proprietary derivatives.[6] These licences rely on economic and community pressure to encourage contribution back to the project. Permissively licensed projects therefore require a well-defined community governance model.

Later in this chapter we will examine the impact of licence choice and community structure on an open source project. We will see that the interplay between licensing regimes and models of development can be both subtle and impactful. First we must examine the culture of open source.

2.2 OPEN SOURCE CULTURE

When reading about open source one will often find reference to 'the open source community'. This implies a single coherent community that rallies around the open

[5] See further ch 3. [6] See ch 3.

source banner and all it represents. However, there is no such community, just as there is no 'closed source community'. Instead, there are a number of distinct communities who rally around specific software projects, modes of licensing and development models to address specific needs. These communities do not form a part of a larger coordinated and coherent 'open source community', although they may be related in one or more ways with other sub-communities. There are therefore a number of distinct clusters of communities that for a variety of reasons gather in a single place. The following few paragraphs examine some of the common reasons for such clustering.

Clustering can simplify the management of common factors across projects. For example, intellectual property ('IP') and project infrastructure facilities might be provided by a central body. There are multiple places where such gatherings occur, eg, the Outercurve Foundation[7] provides an IP shelter while GitHub[8] provides technical infrastructure. This kind of co-location does not, under normal circumstances, lead to the creation of a single unified community across projects.

Projects may also gather together in order to share community management expertise. An example of such a community can be seen in the Apache Software Foundation ('ASF') (see Case Study: The Apache Software Foundation). The ASF has a governance model in which it is not possible to buy influence, the only currency of value to the ASF is merit in recognition of productive engagement. This provides a neutral space in which people can openly collaborate. In such clusters cross-project collaboration is more likely, but it is a by-product of standardization of governance models and IP management rather than a requirement of the community structure.

Other community structures can be developed to enforce cross-project collaboration. This is useful when a number of organizations choose to collaborate on a specific set of common shared software projects. In order to enforce a certain level of commitment to these projects, partners may choose a model in which strategic influence is a reward for adhering to the rules of participation. Those rules may or may not involve an element of directly productive contributions to software code. Such an environment is designed to be less neutral than a pure community model but they still cannot be controlled by a single participant. An example of such an organization is the OpenStack Foundation[9] in which two thirds of the Board of Director seats are essentially 'paid for' while the final third are representatives of the active community regardless of their financial contributions. In these kinds of clusters collaboration levels across projects are high since there is a tight focus and clear strategy for the products being produced.

[7] OuterCurve Foundation <http://www.outercurve.org> accessed 5 April 2013.

[8] Github <http://github.com> accessed 5 April 2013.

[9] Openstack, 'Open source software for building private and public clouds' <http://www.openstack.org> accessed 5 April 2013.

In busting the myth of 'the open source community' we need to understand that the primary driver for collaboration is to benefit from the outputs of the community rather than to rally behind a generic open source banner. In these cases open source is nothing more than a means of production; however, there is one final type of community that is usually referred to as the free software community.

The free software community feels that open source and its focus on methods of production is sub-optimal. Members of this community prefer the term free software, rather than open source software, as they are concerned with the provision and protection of software that respects the users' freedom to run, copy, distribute, study, change, and improve the software. The free software community coalesces around the Free Software Foundation ('FSF').

These ethical considerations are important but are often seen as understated by more pragmatic open source participants. We will discuss this in more detail in the next section. Having established the importance of the ethical position we need to set, we will continue to use the term open source to mean software that is licensed in such a way that it is considered to be both open source software and free software. Where we wish to make a distinction between the legal protection of IP in software and the ethical considerations of the FSF, we will use the term free software.

It can be seen that while there is no single 'open source community' there are a great many sub-communities that are often referred to, incorrectly, as a single community. These communities are linked by one or more of the following characteristics:

- sharing of a legal structure for intellectual property management;
- sharing of project infrastructure (website, version control, mail lists, and so forth);
- adoption of an agreed collaborative software development model;
- requirement for a neutral space for collaboration;
- sharing of common needs that can be solved with software outputs;
- enforced collaboration on shared software components;
- an ethical belief that all software should be free (as in speech).

The one common factor across all of these communities is the adoption of an open source licence for their outputs. In theory this means that the various projects can share their outputs and contribute to one another's code across the defined communities. Unfortunately, it is not quite as simple as this. Due to the incompatibility of licences designed to prevent non-free derivatives of free software such reuse is not always possible. In summary permissively licensed code can be reused in code using a reciprocal (copyleft) licence but the reverse is not always true.[10]

[10] See further ch 3.

This situation is further complicated when we introduce the concept of 'partial copyleft.' Partial copyleft licences are ones that only demand reciprocal sharing of modifications to the free software, but do permit embedding of this code in proprietary products. In some cases partial copyleft free software can be included in permissively licensed open source software. It is beyond the scope of this chapter to go into detail about open source licence compatibility, this is covered elsewhere in this book.[11] However, we do need to acknowledge the existence of this concern since licence choice clearly influences how and when communities can share their code.

When sharing across projects is facilitated through the use of compatible licences we see immediate benefits in the code production cycle.[12] By sharing resources in the production of non-differentiating code companies are able to reduce the cost and increase quality of outputs. By 'non-differentiating software' we mean software that does not mark the participants as unique in the marketplace, whether they provide software, services, or some other output produced through software use.

However, regardless of licence choice not all open source software communities are open, collaborative communities. The licence guarantees that everyone has certain rights with respect to the use of the software code, but it says nothing about the development model adopted. In some cases the owners of the software may choose to maintain a development model in which only a very limited number of people are able to participate in the software development process. This may influence potential users' decision to use the software or not, which in turn affects the likelihood of third parties contributing to the production of the software.

A combination of the development model adopted and the licence chosen for the software will influence the kind of community one can expect to find around an open source software product. This in turn influences the kind of revenue creation or cost saving opportunities available. We will return to these points later in this chapter, but first we will dig deeper into the political and ethical considerations that influence the decisions behind community structure and licence choice.

2.3 THE POLITICS AND ETHICS OF OPEN SOURCE

So far we have examined open source software in its role as a production technique in which an IP licensing model protects participants who choose to collaborate in that process. We've indicated that this is only a part of the story, and that there are also important political and ethical considerations to be taken into account. The term

[11] See ch 3.

[12] Dirk Riehle, 'The Economic Motivation of Open Source Software: Stakeholder Perspectives' *IEEE Computer*, vol 40, no 4 (April 2007) 25–32, available at <http://dirkriehle.com/computer-science/research/2007/computer-2007-article.html> accessed 5 April 2013.

free software is used to refer to these issues. However, the term open source does not necessarily exclude the same arguments since all open source software is also free software.

The term 'free software' was adopted by the FSF and pre-dates the term open source software. For some, it is the preferable term as they do not wish to associate themselves with the term open source because it has become 'associated with a different approach, a different philosophy, different values, and even a different criterion for which licenses are acceptable.'[13]

Free software must not be confused with 'freeware', which is software that can be acquired at no cost but for which source code is not available. Freeware provides none of the benefits of code-sharing that we see in free software. That is, whilst the cost of the software is zero it is not possible to adapt the software to suit one's specific needs. In addition the lack of source code makes it impossible for users of that code to share their experience, and thus reduce the cost of further development and software maintenance.

While freeware focuses on the lack of a licence fee, free software is considered to be more of a social movement that adopts a specific IP licensing methodology, whereas open source is more of a software development movement using a broadly similar IP licensing model. For the free software movement non-free software is a social problem while for the open source movement it is a suboptimal solution. Whilst the two groups disagree on some basic principles they do agree, in the main, on the practical recommendations they make. This section describes the differences between the two movements' basic principles.

2.3.1 The free software definition

The term 'free software' refers to software that respects users' freedom and community. Everyone has the freedom to run, copy, distribute, study, change, and improve the software. These freedoms ensure that users (collectively or individually) are able, if they so desire, to control the program and what it does for them. The FSF argues that when users are unable to control the program then the program controls them. As a result such non-free software is sometimes seen as 'an instrument of unjust power.'[14] Free software is therefore a matter of liberty, not price: 'free' as in 'free speech,' not as in 'free beer.'[15]

In order to establish whether or not software is free software the FSF has defined four essential freedoms. To be free software, the terms under which it is distributed and used must provide all four freedoms. These freedoms are discussed in more detail in Case Study: Free Software Foundation, an ethical community, later in this chapter.

[13] GNU, 'Why "Free Software" is better than "Open Source"' <http://www.gnu.org/philosophy/free-software-for-freedom.html> accessed 5 April 2013.

[14] GNU, 'What is free software?' <http://www.gnu.org/philosophy/free-sw.html> accessed 5 April 2013.

[15] GNU (n 14).

It is important to note that there is nothing in these four freedoms that would indicate that free software is non-commercial. In fact, the four freedoms ensure that commercial use, development, and distribution are possible. Another important clarification is that the freedom to modify the software does not imply that third parties must accept your modifications. The value of any changes in the software is a subjective matter, and the four freedoms do not seek to provide any guidance on the acceptance or otherwise of modifications. They only seek to ensure a user's right to make and redistribute modifications.

A free software licence may require a change of name and branding for a product that has been modified, but as long as these requirements are not onerous, they are not considered to be a restriction on a user's right to modify. This provision enables third parties to build value in their version of the software, and thus generate revenue streams that will pay for further development of the software.

Case Study: Free Software Foundation, an ethical community

The FSF is a non-profit organization founded by Richard Stallman in 1985 to encourage, foster, and promote the free exchange of computer software and information related to computers. Furthermore the FSF creates, distributes and disseminates software. Finally it seeks to increase the public's access to computers. In short, the FSF advocates on behalf of the free software movement and drives development of the GNU suite of free software applications, libraries and developer tools.

An extremely important part of the FSF's advocacy is the definition of, and maintenance of, the four freedoms. These freedoms state that users have the freedom to run, copy, distribute, study, change, and improve the software. The FSF claims that 'When users don't control the program, the program controls the users. The developer controls the program, and through it controls the users. This non-free or "proprietary" program is therefore an instrument of unjust power.'[16] The precise definition of free software is software that provides users with four essential freedoms:

- The freedom to run the program, for any purpose (freedom 0).
- The freedom to study how the program works, and change it so it does your computing as you wish (freedom 1). Access to the source code is a precondition for this.
- The freedom to redistribute copies so you can help your neighbour (freedom 2).
- The freedom to distribute copies of your modified versions to others (freedom 3). By doing this you can give the whole community a chance to benefit from your changes. Access to the source code is a precondition for this.

[16] GNU (n 14).

It can be seen from this definition that 'free' in the context of free software is a matter of liberty and not a matter of price.

The foundation has a very strong preference for 'copyleft' licences, such as its own GNU General Public License. The term 'copyleft' is a play on the well-recognized word copyright. It describes the practice of using copyright law to ensure that free software remains free. This is achieved by providing a licence to the work which permits redistribution of the original, and any modified works, only under the same terms the original work was obtained. This preference for 'copyleft' licences is rooted in the FSF's ethical position that all software should be free in order to 'secure freedom for computer users'.[17]

The FSF holds copyright on a large proportion of the GNU operating system, and other free software. Contributors to these projects, both corporate and individual, assign their copyright to the foundation; the foundation in turn enforces the licence under which they distribute that software, typically the GNU General Public License.

The GNU General Public License ('GNU GPL'), a reciprocal licence, is the most commonly used free software licence in terms of absolute numbers of software projects. It was originally written in 1989 with the express purpose of promoting and preserving software freedom, and was updated to version two in 1991 and version three in 2007. The FSF publishes other licences including the GNU Lesser General Public License ('GNU LGPL'), the GNU Affero General Public License ('GNU AGPL'), and the GNU Free Document License ('GNU FDL').

The FSF also actively campaigns for free software adoption. These campaigns usually concentrate on the perceived threats non-free software products present to the individual, as well as initiatives that are seen to limit the production of free software, such as digital rights management (DRM),[18] software patents, patent encumbered standards, and Secure Boot.[19]

The majority of these activities are carried out by volunteers, although the FSF does employ a small staff of around 12 people (in 2012). Funding comes from a combination of individual donations, (non-voting) membership dues, and patrons. Membership or patronage of the FSF does not provide influence over the strategy of the FSF. Strategy is set by the Board of Directors who are elected by the voting membership which is distinct from the supporting membership.

[17] Free Software Foundation <http://www.fsf.org/about> accessed 5 April 2013.

[18] Digital rights management (DRM) are access control technologies that allow the restriction of digital content and devices after sale. They are commonly used to prevent content being shared between individuals and devices.

[19] Secure Boot provides control over what software can be run on a device. Typically only software 'approved' by the manufacturer will execute on the device.

2.3.2 The open source definition

We have seen that the four freedoms focus on a perceived social need for software to be free. We have also seen that whilst the open source movement sees non-free software as suboptimal their more pragmatic position serves to de-emphasize the need for software freedom. Finally we have seen that whilst the free software and open source software movements differ in motivation, they agree on most of the practical recommendations.

The rough equivalent of the FSF for the open source movement is the Open Source Initiative ('OSI,' see Case Study: Open Source Initiative, a pragmatic community). The OSI provides the Open Source Definition[20] (OSD) that defines the ten considerations that an open source licence must address. These are:

1. **Free redistribution**
   There can be no restrictions that prevent the software being distributed either alone or aggregated with other software. This includes no requirement for royalties or fees. However, as with free software this does not mean that open source is non-commercial.
2. **Source code**
   Software distributions must include source code in a form that is usable by a typical programmer.
3. **Derived works**
   The licence must allow derived works that can be distributed under the same terms as the original software. Note, this requirement does not extend to other software distributed alongside open source software, only to derivatives of the open source software itself.
4. **Integrity of the author's source code**
   If there is any restriction on the distribution of modified source code then it must allow distribution of 'patch' files to allow programmers to re-apply any modifications made. No restrictions on the distribution of binaries built from modified source, beyond requiring different branding, are allowed.
5. **No discrimination against persons or groups**
   The licence must be identical for all persons and groups.
6. **No discrimination against fields of endeavour**
   The licence must be identical for all types of use.
7. **Distribution of licence**
   The rights assigned in the licence must apply to everyone who receives a copy of the program.
8. **Licence must not be specific to a product**
   The licence cannot depend on the software being distributed in a specific form or as part of a specific product.

[20] Open Source Initiative, 'The Open Source Definition,' available at <http://opensource.org/docs/osd> accessed 5 April 2013.

9. **Licence must not restrict other software**
   The licence must not affect other software distributed alongside the licensed software.
10. **License must be technology neutral**
   No provision of the licence may depend upon a specific technology or style of interface.

A careful comparison of the OSD and the four freedoms will show that they are compatible. Any software that is open source is also free, and vice versa. As we discussed earlier, the main difference between the two movements is that the free software movement is driven by social need while the open source movement is driven by pragmatism. These different motivating factors lead to a possible division on the type of user that is best served by each model.

Case Study: Open Source Initiative, a pragmatic community

The Open Source Initiative ('OSI') is a non-profit corporation that was formed in 1998 to educate about, and advocate for, the benefits of open source software. It also seeks to build bridges among different constituencies in the open source community. The OSI defines open source as 'a development method for software that harnesses the power of distributed peer review and transparency of process. The promise of open source is better quality, higher reliability, more flexibility, lower cost, and an end to predatory vendor lock-in.'[21]

The OSI chose the term 'open source' rather than 'free software' as it felt that the latter term had come to be associated with a philosophically and politically focussed group. The OSI sought to focus more on pragmatism and the business case for the collaborative development of software. While the motivation for their advocacy was quite different to that of the FSF, the end result is largely the same practical behaviour: the development of free and open source software.

The OSI acts as a form of standards body, maintaining the OSD and a trademark that creates a nexus of trust around which developers, users, corporations, and governments can organize open source cooperation. In order to use the OSI trademark software must be released under one of the licences that the OSI have reviewed and approved as being in conformance with the OSD.

The OSI's mission to define the conditions under which participants can openly collaborate on free and open source software is harder than the more tightly bounded mission of the FSF to build only free software (see FSF case study

[21] Open Source Initiative, <http://opensource.org> accessed 5 April 2013.

earlier in the chapter), or the Apache Software Foundation's mission to build only permissively licensed software (see ASF case study later in the chapter). The OSI seeks to be pragmatic and business-case driven, but it is hard to imagine a situation in which all-comers will converge on a single position.

The difficulty of reaching unanimous consensus across all parties led to the strange situation in which a foundation created to promote collaboration is itself a closed organization. The OSI bylaws[22] do not allow a membership to be formed, and thus all authority is vested in the Board of Directors. The Board consists of between five and 21 individuals, each of whom is elected by the existing Board of Directors. There are currently (2012) 11 members of the Board of Directors. This arrangement allowed the OSI to complete the difficult task of defining the OSD and the associated licence approval process. However, this approach has limited the foundation's ability to have a significant impact beyond this initial work.

In 2008 an attempt was made to reform governance of the organization. The OSI Board invited 50 individuals to join a 'chartered members" group, 42 of whom agreed. However, this group conducted its business on a private mailing list, and its membership was never made public. The group seemed to make no visible progress in reforming the OSI.

In 2012 an initiative was undertaken to transition towards a membership-based governance structure. The first two phases of this have been completed at the time of writing. A free affiliate membership programme has been introduced for 'government-recognised non-profit charitable and not-for-profit industry associations and academic institutions.' Individuals can now join as 'individual members' for a small fee. A third phase is planned in which corporate members will be invited to join. At the time of writing (December 2012) none of these membership types have any formal influence over the foundation since the bylaws have not yet been updated.

It is important to note that because the foundation does not generate outputs that contribute directly to the products and services provided by most commercial free and open source software companies it has found it difficult to generate significant contributions in the form of volunteer energy. The OSI seeks to be more effective with the greater financial resources membership will make available. For example, the current Board of Directors expects the need for 'dedicated, long-term advocacy, and organizing to require the provision of resource such as permanent staff and/or fellowship positions organizing.'[23]

[22] Open Source Initiative, 'Bylaws of the Open Source Initiative' <http://opensource.org/bylaws> accessed 5 April 2013.

[23] Open Source Initiative, 'Become an OSI Individual Member' <http://opensource.org/members> accessed 5 April 2013.

2.3.3 Pragmatism versus ethics

For the open source movement the focus is on providing the maximum flexibility for producers of software. That is, producers are free to do anything they want, including produce non-free software that incorporates open source software. The free software movement, on the other hand, seeks to protect the end-users freedoms by ensuring all software is free.

Where producers choose to produce only free and open source software, users retain the four freedoms. However, where producers choose to include open source software in proprietary (non-free) software those freedoms are, at least in part, lost. The open source movement accepts that some producers of software will continue to produce proprietary software. This movement therefore seeks to ensure that all software producers can collaborate on open source software regardless of their chosen product licence strategy. Since a significant portion of the software industry is built on the capability of software producers to create false scarcity through the use of restrictive licensing models, this situation might be seen as a necessary compromise.

Despite the willingness of the open source movement to accept this compromise position it would be unreasonable to suggest that this compromise is a necessity. As free software, and the business models that exist around it, become better understood we are seeing the creation of more companies that are built exclusively around free software (eg RedHat, Suse, Acquia, and Wordpress). Nevertheless, the predominant model remains one of proprietary control. The pragmatism of the open source movement allows software producers to choose the point at which to draw the line between free software and proprietary software.

It is this ability to define one's own boundaries that enhances the flexibility for the software producer when engaging with open source software projects. However, without the legal requirement of a reciprocal licence to ensure derivative products are also free software, the driver for development collaboration is less obvious. What is to prevent software producers benefiting from the open source software without contributing to its development?

Before we attempt to answer this question we must consider the damage caused by those who use, but do not contribute, to open source software. First, the cost of distribution is not proportional to the number of users as is the case for a physical product. Furthermore, an open source licence provides no warranty and no assurances of support, and thus no significant drain on resources. Therefore, there is no significant direct cost when someone chooses to use an open source product.

Whilst there is no financial cost attached to the unrestricted distribution of open source software, there may be hidden costs to community partners. For example, a user of open source software may build a product that is in direct competition with other users of that software, and this competition could be damaging to the business of those users that choose to collaborate openly. However, in this situation the non-collaborating partner will bear the full costs of maintenance of the software within their systems, while the collaborating partners will share their costs. For successful reusers of open source code the costs associated with this maintenance will increase over time as the user continues to diverge from the publicly shared code. Consequently, over time, the economic pressures to collaborate increase.

Supporters of the more pragmatic open source movement point to these economic drivers for collaboration as evidence that, over time, more and more software will become a part of the open source projects. Supporters of the free software movement acknowledge this, but insist that the process should be accelerated by ensuring all distributed software (as opposed to modified software for personal use) must be made available under a free software licence.

Case Study: The Apache Software Foundation

The Apache Software Foundation ('ASF') is a hugely influential organization. It houses some of the most important open source software projects, and has a long history of producing successful software. It is an example of an organization that uses permissive licences to maximize the options for reuse, while a community focused development model seeks to ensure that all participants have an equal influence on the projects strategy.

In this case study we will see that this success is because the original creators worked hard to define a method of production that was as inclusive as possible. Unlike, eg, the FSF, the ASF focuses on the means of software production rather than the legal protection of software freedom. To many this is a suboptimal approach, but the model has been proven successful and repeatable in well over 100 Apache projects.

In February 1995 a small group of eight people created the Apache Group. These people had been independently maintaining the previously aborted, but public domain, NCSA web server. They had been sharing ideas and notes and decided that it was best to provide a level of legal protection, and provide a limited amount of structure around their collaboration. The result was the Apache License v 1.0, a permissive licence that allowed third parties to use the code in any way they desired. The corporate structure was informal but provided a means for coordinated decision making within the group.

In 1999 the group had grown to 21 members and a multi-national company wanted to use their software in a mainstream product. However, this company's lawyers were concerned about the lack of legal structure behind the licence. The solution was to create a US based public charity (501(c)(3)) in the parlance of the

US Internal Revenue Codes). The mission of the foundation is to 'provide support for the Apache community of open source software projects. The Apache projects are characterised by a collaborative, consensus based development process, an open and pragmatic software licence, and a desire to create high quality software that leads the way in its field.' Perhaps more important than the mission is the tagline the ASF uses: 'not simply a group of projects sharing a server, we are a community of developers and users.'[24]

This emphasis on the 'community of developers and users' is present in the bylaws of the ASF and the licence used. The ASF is operated with one simple goal: to ensure that a community of project developers can do what they do best: produce software for the benefit of all. The ASF exists only to provide the social, legal, and technical infrastructure to facilitate those developers.

The ASF places a heavy emphasis on the social aspects of collaboration. All Apache projects adopt a development model that is often called the 'Apache Way.' This is a transparent, open, and meritocratic governance model that defines a small set of rules that all Apache projects observe. These rules ensure appropriate management of intellectual property rights and community engagement. Those familiar with Apache projects will recognize that there is often more emphasis placed on community development than any other aspect of project management. This is possible because, eg, much of the legal overhead of managing an Apache project has been reduced by using a standard licence across all projects which significantly reduces the overhead in addressing legal issues in individual projects.

An important aspect of this community focus is a constant drive to ensure that all community members are seen as equal. For this reason the ASF does not pay for software development. All contributors to an Apache project are considered volunteers within the project. This means that there are no management structures within the projects, and no individual's opinion is regarded as more important than any other. This is supported by a clearly defined meritocratic and consensus based decision-making process that is surprisingly efficient in its application. This equality among volunteers is extremely important to the ASF and is fiercely protected. It is this equality that allows anyone, regardless of the resources available to them, to contribute in a meaningful way, whilst still being protected against the most serious potential abuses of their time.

The ASF uses economics to ensure contributions are made back to the foundation wherever it is strategically appropriate to do so. That is, if a user of ASF software chooses to modify Apache code without contributing back, they are introducing

[24] The Apache Software Foundation, <http://www.apache.org> accessed 5 April 2013.

a maintenance overhead that other participants do not have. This means that competitors can enter the market and benefit from lower development and maintenance costs by actively engaging with the community. In many cases this reduction in costs can make them more competitive in the marketplace.

Traditionally Apache projects have focused on infrastructure components which are more easily reused in derivative products. However, in 2011 the foundation created its first significant end-user project in the form of Apache OpenOffice. This suite of productivity tools is intended to be installed and used as a single multi-function product. The success of this end-user product at the ASF is testament to the Apache model of software development working beyond infrastructure projects.

The ASF created a structure that has successfully and repeatedly produced open source software that is used to deliver immense value to modern business. Its software is used in large internet commerce sites, social networks, space faring vehicles and control centres, government agencies, universities, schools, banks, and even children's toys. It is hard to imagine any computer that doesn't have Apache software embedded within it somewhere. All this is achieved through the provision of a genuinely neutral collaboration space, enabled by an open source licence, and a model of meritocratic, bottom up decision making that is both efficient and fair to all participants.

2.4 GOVERNANCE OF OPEN SOURCE

The OSI describes open source as 'a development method for software that harnesses the power of distributed peer review and transparency of process.' Note that this definition does not reference licences. Nobody will deny open source licences are vital. Without them we cannot guarantee the four freedoms, nor can we conform to the OSI's Open Source Definition. However, there is more to open source than a licence.

If we want to realize the full potential of open source as a development methodology we also need to consider 'governance models,' that is how a project is managed. A clear governance model ensures that all contributors understand how to engage, what is expected of them, and what protections are provided for their status as a contributor. It defines the rules of engagement and decision making.

Open source licences provide the legal framework within which parties collaborate. A governance model provides the social framework for that collaboration. A combination of open source licence and a transparent governance is what makes open source software successful. So what is a good governance model?

This is a question the Outercurve Foundation explored in a series of blog posts in 2012. This section is a reworking of those materials. The Outercurve Foundation is a not-for-profit open source software foundation created 'to enable the exchange of code and understanding among software companies and open source communities.'[25] Similar materials exploring the community aspects of open source can be found on their site.

2.4.1 People versus process

An open source governance model need not be, indeed should not be, a complex document that attempts to cover every possible circumstance. It is a guidance document covering the most common community processes. It should recognize that written rules can be both empowering and constraining. Rules make a process predictable and repeatable, but they can also make a community resistant to change, or even blind to the need for change. The goal is to create an environment in which people feel comfortable engaging with the project on a long term basis.

In reality most software developers just want to be able to get work done in an efficient way. This is especially true in a community led open source project in which people are not paid by the project itself, but by some external entity. A good governance model is therefore about enabling flexibility, empowering individuals to lead on specific activities, and preventing (occasionally resolving) conflict.

However, this in turn can present a problem. Many people find working in a self-directed, bottom-up, and collaborative environment challenging. This is where leadership comes in. In an open source, project leadership is not about directing, it is about getting results and empowering others.

A common concern about community led open source projects is that they will quickly descend into anarchy because they adopt a bottom-up, leaderless approach to coordination. Finding the right balance between bottom-up anarchy and top-down leadership is hard. This is where the governance model comes in. It provides the social scaffolding for collaboration. It empowers individuals who just want to get things done, and it provides mechanisms by which community deadlocks can be broken.

An open source licence is only a small part of this governance model. As we discussed earlier, some licences legally enforce a sharing of code modifications. Others depend upon economic and social pressures. Choosing the right licence and the right style of project governance is critical to the success of an open source project. Whilst this book focuses on the legal aspects, it is important to understand some of the choices a project must make about its social governance.

[25] OuterCurve Foundation <http://www.outercurve.org/About> accessed 5 April 2013.

The next two sections will outline two examples of common governance models. These two approaches appear to be diametrically opposed. The first is the benevolent dictator model, where a single individual has absolute authority. The second is the meritocratic model, where valuable contributions are rewarded with collective leadership authority. Once you understand both of these 'extremes' you will see that, in practice, they are not as dissimilar as they appear.

2.4.2 The benevolent dictator governance model

A benevolent dictator (BD) is an individual who has complete control over the decision-making process in an open source project. Linus Torvalds[26] is perhaps the most well-known 'benevolent dictator'. Being a benevolent dictator is not an easy job. It requires diplomacy and community building skills, in-depth technical knowledge of all aspects of the project, and exceptional levels of commitment and dedication. However, as Linus' Linux Kernel[27] project illustrates, it can be very effective.

The benevolent dictator model relies heavily on the fact that an open source licence allows anyone to take the code and spin up their own project. This means that although the leader has full control over their project, they must still work to ensure that community needs are met. Failure to do so will result in a splintering of the community as objectors set up their own projects based on the same code. A benevolent dictator who wishes to create a vibrant community project must therefore seek to ensure each decision is both understood, and supported by as many community members as possible. Consequently, diplomacy, mediation, and clarity are just three of the softer skills that a BD needs.

Although BDs are usually highly skilled from a technical perspective they are unlikely to be the best person to make every technical decision. A good BD recognizes this, and seeks to enable the community to collectively make decisions under the guidance of the most skilled members. When the community is unable to reach consensus the BD will intervene by making what they believe to be the most appropriate decision. In this way a BD seeks to prevent the project from becoming paralysed by indecision.

It is therefore the BD's job to resolve disputes within the community, and to ensure that the project is able to progress in a coordinated way. In turn, it is the community's job to guide the decisions of the BD through active engagement and contribution. Consequently the benevolent dictator model can accommodate large scale projects because, in the majority of cases, the BD is not needed to allow the community to progress.

[26] Wikipedia, 'Linu Torvalds' <http://en.wikipedia.org/wiki/Linus_Torvalds> accessed 5 April 2013.

[27] The Linux Kernel Archives <http://www.kernel.org> accessed 5 April 2013.

Typically, the benevolent dictator is self-appointed. They will usually be the originator of the project or their appointed successor. In many ways, the role of the benevolent dictator is less about dictatorship and more about diplomacy. The key is to ensure that, as the project expands, the right people (those who concur with the BDs vision) are recognized as community leaders.

2.4.3 The meritocratic governance model

In centralized models of governance the gating of contributions through a single individual becomes a bottleneck. A meritocracy recognizes this and provides a defined mechanism by which individuals can earn direct influence over the project. This process is quite different to approaches within which employment status, experience, or financial contributions might earn 'power'. In the meritocratic model, anyone contributing in any positive way earns equal authority.

This process of empowering those who contribute scales very well. Furthermore, it minimizes friction because it recognizes power and influence as scarce resources. Newcomers are seen as volunteers who want to help, rather than people who want to grab a share of the resource. A true meritocracy lacks artificial filters for contributions that are commonly found in other models. Examples of such artificial filters are the ability to buy influence with cash rather than technical contribution. This lack of artificial filters ensures the broadest possible range of contributors who are aligned to a common goal. When managed well this process creates an environment in which everyone, regardless of their relationships outside of a project, can collaborate. However, because there is no defined leader, there needs to be a clear set of rules by which the community operates. Failure to provide clear rules of engagement usually results in a model that looks more like a top-down leadership model than a bottom-up community model.

A meritocracy is typically leaderless, that is, whoever is best equipped to lead in any specific situation will be the leader for that situation only. People lead through action, not authority; they don't have any more authority than any other participant. This often causes newcomers to meritocracy to assume that a project will inevitably grind to a halt since it will be unable to make decisions. In a healthy meritocracy it is possible for those with less experience to drive a given objective forwards through action, since all work is in the open to those with more experience (but less time) who can provide feedback. Where that feedback is seen as appropriate it will be recognized as meritorious and included in the final outputs.

Fortunately, in software development the vast majority of decisions are easily reversible. As long as mistakes are identified early they can be reversed with minimal negative impact. Consequently, most decisions in a software project are made through a process called 'lazy consensus'. This is where the community lazily assumes that anyone with sufficient merit to take action is going to do so with good intentions. The community reviews all actions quickly and, if necessary raises, discusses, and acts upon any objections. In the unlikely event that consensus cannot be reached a conflict resolution process is enacted.

Potentially controversial actions may be brought to the community's attention for feedback and approval prior to work being carried out. This can reduce the number of 'roll-backs' necessary since consensus is sought before work commences. Since those with merit have already demonstrated a sensitivity to when this is necessary, there need not be hard rules in place to manage this. All that is needed is full transparency on all actions and their motivation.

2.4.4 Implications of licence choice and IP management on governance models

The benevolent dictator presents an organizationally simple model that can work extremely well, but only if the right leader can be found. The meritocratic model, on the other hand, does not depend on the availability of a single individual to act as project leader; however it brings with it a more complex social structure that requires more engaged governance processes.

A potential downside of the benevolent dictator model is that it requires the community to fully trust a single individual, both today and in an undefined future. For many people this dependence on a central figure puts the project at risk since individual circumstances change, as do employers' objectives. In a meritocratic model contributors need not put their trust in a single individual, but they must, at the very least, actively monitor the community to ensure it remains aligned to their own goals. The use of an open source licence, which allows any community member to 'fork' the project and make it their own, goes some way towards protecting the community. However, the choice of licence and the treatment of contributed intellectual property (IP) can have a significant effect on a community's confidence in this model.

As an example of this interplay between licence choice, IP management, and project governance, consider the fact that a reciprocal licence coupled with copyright assignment of all contributions centralizes legal control. The concern here is that it is not difficult to acquire full control of the open source project. This is especially true when a BD can exercise complete control over the project. With full control of both the legal and community aspects of the project it would be possible to act in ways counter to the community's interests. At its extreme this would mean the copyright holder can make all future development work closed source, while third party contributors would still be bound by the original reciprocal open source licence. Thus, there can be significant potential benefits to the 'owner' of a centralized, copyleft project.

In order to minimize the risk one could seek to manage copyright in third party contributions differently. For example, rather than centralizing ownership in an organization that can be acquired, one could use a suitable not-for-profit vehicle. This can ensure the safe-keeping of all contributions for the community because, eg, it would not be possible to purchase the assets of the not-for-profit copyright owner. Alternatively, one could avoid centralizing copyright in the first place. This is achieved by only requiring contributors to grant a licence to reuse contributions in open source software, as opposed to assigning copyright to a centralized owner. In this instance relicensing of the code would require the permission of all contributors.

It is also possible to minimize the impact of a community leader closing future developments by using a permissive licence rather than a reciprocal one. This does not prevent the creation of closed source derivatives, but it does mean that all community members have equal rights to do so. However, in this instance we have moved the problem from a legal one to a social one. As we have seen in earlier sections this tension between the pragmatic and ethical case for open source versus free software requires some careful consideration.

The matrix that follows this paragraph (Table 2.1) presents an overview of the kinds of project that are created by various combinations of licence and copyright ownership. It should be noted that there is a third licence type, known as 'partial copyleft' which is not displayed in this model. A common partial copyleft licence is the Lesser GNU Public License (LGPL). This licence requires any derivatives of the code to be released under the LGPL, that is, it is reciprocal. However, unlike a full copyleft licence such as the GPL, LGPL code can be included in unmodified form in proprietary products. We have not included discussion of this licence type here in order to simplify this chapter. We feel justified in this decision since the FSF does not recommend the use of partial copyleft licences in most circumstances[28] (despite the fact that the FSF is the author of the LGPL). Other chapters of this book will discuss this kind of licence in detail.[29]

It is outside the scope of this chapter to explore the many interactions between licence choice and project governance. Our intention here is to simply highlight the inter-relationships between the two by providing a few illustrative examples. As you continue to read this book you will come to identify many more cross-dependencies between the legal and social models of open source software development.

[28] GNU, 'Why you shouldn't use the Lesser GPL for your next library' <http://www.gnu.org/philosophy/why-not-lgpl.html> accessed 5 April 2013.

[29] See further chs 3 and 9.

Table 2.1 Copyright management's influence on community type

		Copyright Ownership Model	
		Centralized	**Distributed**
Licence type	**Reciprocal**	**Economic Community**	
		All licensees have the same rights under a reciprocal licence and thus the status of copyright owner has no special bearing. All licensees are free to share modifications or to withhold them.	
	Copyleft	**Owned community**	**Enforced community**
		Under a reciprocal licence all licensees have the same rights. All modifications affected by the licence must be made available under the same licence. However, the centralization of copyright means that the copyright holder is not bound by the same requirement and may choose to issue modifications under a different licence.	Under a reciprocal licence all licensees have the same rights. All modifications made by licensees must be made available under the same licence. Where copyright in each contribution is owned by individual contributors no single entity is entitled to withhold modifications affected by the licence.

2.5 THE BUSINESS OF OPEN SOURCE

One of the reasons that some people choose to use the term 'open source software' rather than 'free software' is that the term 'free' is commonly used to mean free of cost. Free software, however, is not necessarily free of cost. In the context of free software, free refers to freedom. This confusion can sometimes lead to misunderstandings about free software. One of those misunderstandings is that free and open source software solutions are more difficult, or even impossible, to generate revenue from.

This particular misunderstanding goes beyond the term 'free' and is rooted in the fact that an open source software licence can place no restriction on redistribution of the software. This leads people to assume that 'if you can't stop your customers sharing your software with their friends then it won't be long before there are no customers willing to pay you.' This is, of course, true. However, this thinking is narrow in that it assumes the only way to generate revenue from software products is to charge a fee for the software itself.

It is also a common assumption that open source is, in itself, a business model. That is the use of an open source licence defines a specific kind of software business.

The assumption is that any one 'open source business' adopts the same business model as any other 'open source business.' This is incorrect. Open source is a licensing and development model, it is not a business model. There are, in fact, as many open source business models as there are closed source models.

These business models include (but are not limited to):

- software licensing (including licensing of proprietary products)
- installation and maintenance
- training
- user support
- customization
- warranties

Only one of these models (software licensing) is impacted by the choice of an open source licence. Even in this case alternative models are sometimes available, such as dual licensing[30] (for reciprocal licences) or proprietary enhancements (for permissive licences). It is beyond the scope of this chapter to explore business models in detail, for now it is only important that we recognize that an open source licence does not, in any way, preclude the creation of a revenue generating business.[31]

In addition to the ability to generate revenue, a well-managed, cooperative, open source software production process can help to reduce costs and thus increase profit margins. Consider, eg, that Red Hat, a leading provider of open source solutions, reported a gross profit margin of 85.16 per cent in the quarter leading up to 31 August 2012; Microsoft, a leading provider of closed source solutions, reported gross profit margins of 73.47 per cent in the quarter ending 30 September 2012. Apple, a leading supplier of hardware supported by closed source software, reported 40.04 per cent in the same quarter, and Google, a software based service provider, reported 52.53 per cent margins.[32] All of these companies use and contribute to open source software. But only one of them can be considered a free software business in the sense that all their products are available under a free software licence: Red Hat.

The use of an open source licence on a software solution will have a significant impact on the production and business models chosen. It is therefore vital that significant thought be put into the chosen licence early in the creation of an open source project.

[30] OSS Watch, 'Dual-Licensing As A Business Model' <http://www.oss-watch.ac.uk/resources/duallicence2> accessed 5 April 2013.

[31] See further ch 1, at 1.6.

[32] All Gross Margin statistics from YCharts <http://ycharts.com> accessed 5 April 2013.

2.6 STANDARDIZATION FACILITATES INNOVATION

We have established that open source licences protect the interests of those contributing to shared outputs. We have also seen that the open development model provides a mechanism by which we can coordinate this co-production. The final piece in the open source puzzle is the opportunity to accelerate innovation through the adoption of openness in general.

Henry Chesbrough promotes the term 'open innovation,' defined as: 'a paradigm that assumes that firms can and should use external ideas as well as internal ideas, and internal and external paths to market, as the firms look to advance their technology.'[33] On the surface it would seem that the open development of open source software is a form of open innovation.

There are certainly many parallels between open software development and open innovation. For example, Chesbrough's criticism of closed, vertical organizations is similar to Eric Raymond's criticism of closed source 'cathedrals' in 'The Cathedral and the Bazaar,'[34] an essay that was an essential catalyst in the early days of the open source movement. These closed models favour internal expertise over external, and thus are potentially losing advantages that access to a wider market of ideas could bring. However, for Chesbrough open innovation depends on exchanges of technology that are protected by patents and their associated paid licensing models. This is at odds with the open source approach of facilitating exchange through the universal granting of a copyright licence, complete with either implicit or explicit patent grants.

This different approach to licensing means that the open innovation approaches discussed by Chesbrough cannot be blindly applied to the open development of software. However, it would be a mistake to think that the different licence models make the two approaches to innovation mutually exclusive. To see the similarities it is better to look past specific licensing techniques, and towards the standardization of the interfaces in both finished products, and the development processes that produce them.

If we look to history we can see many examples which demonstrate that a more open approach to interoperability has resulted in faster innovation.[35] Consider, eg, the humble nut and bolt. The first screw thread was created around the third century BC. By the first century BC wooden screws were in common use throughout the Mediterranean. In the fifteenth century metal screws became common. The first nut and bolt assembly, which allowed screw threads to be used to bind materials that

[33] H Chesbrough, *Open Innovation: The new imperative for creating and profiting from technology* (Boston, Harvard Business School Press, 2003).

[34] 'The Cathedral and the Bazaar' <http://www.catb.org/esr/writings/homesteading> accessed 5 April 2013.

[35] See further ch 10.

were harder than the screw itself, is thought to have been created in the sixteenth century.

It took three more centuries and the invention of the auto lathe in 1810 for the mass production of standardized hardware, such as standard sized nuts and bolts, to become the norm. It was these standardized components that allowed individual companies to specialize in more generally reusable components. For example, all fittings could be made to accept standard sized fasteners; therefore there was no longer a need to work directly with your customers on all aspects of component design. This in turn led to a significant spike in innovation since it enabled reuse in unexpected products, as well as more productive collaboration on innovations involving specific partners.

In this story we can see that standardization, not licensing, was the key to accelerated innovation. It can be argued that innovation should follow the Pareto principle:[36] that is they should aim to standardize 80 per cent of their product offering, and customise 20 per cent in order to offer something unique whilst benefiting from the specialisms of third parties. Chesbrough's work on open innovation focuses on the controlling of key knowledge assets, through patents, rather than on the process of standardization. That is, Chesbrough drives collaboration by encouraging the cross licensing of these assets. For Chesbrough revenue is generated from the licensing of the 20 per cent.

The open source movement, in contrast to Chesbrough, focuses on accelerating the standardization of software components through a managed co-development process rather than the licensing of key knowledge assets. The sharing of these components enables collaboration, cost reduction, and standardization on non-differentiating parts of software systems. This facilitates the creation of an ecosystem in which additional services and software can be developed and delivered. Unlike the Chesbrough model, open source development defines a model for cost reduction in the act of open collaboration, rather than a process for managing the licensing of internal knowledge.

This highlights an apparent difference between Chesbrough's open innovation and the open source movement's open development. Chesbrough defines an open innovation model as one that seeks to identify how to enhance the value of one's protected works through collaborating with a small set of partners in a closely controlled way. The open source model seeks to minimize production costs through collaboration on a much larger shared work. Participants in an open source model are rewarded through shared costs where their needs overlap with others, as well as the opportunity to sell internal knowledge where that asset differentiates them from other participants in the ecosystem. Both open innovation and open source development seek

[36] Wikipedia, 'Pareto principle' <http://en.wikipedia.org/wiki/Pareto_principle> accessed 5 April 2013.

to externalize internal knowledge assets for financial gain. It can therefore be argued that the open development process is nothing more than an open innovation process viewed from a different angle.

Chesbrough argues that this is not the case:

> Open Innovation is sometimes conflated with open source methodologies for software development. There are some concepts that are shared between the two, such as the idea of greater external sources of information to create value. However, open innovation explicitly incorporates the business model as the source of both value creation and value capture. This latter role of the business model enables the organization to sustain its position in the industry value chain over time. While open source shares the focus on value creation throughout an industry value chain, its proponents usually deny or downplay the importance of value capture.[37]

Whilst this argument can be reasonably levelled at the production model of the free software movement, it is much harder to make this argument when focusing on the development model rather than the ethical position. The free software and open source movements have different opinions on what constitutes appropriate value capture. The provision of services relating to software products is a source of revenue for any software whether it be free software or proprietary. The licensing of proprietary software, whether it is built upon permissively licensed free software or not, is an acceptable revenue model for the open source movement, but not for the free software movement. The licensing of such proprietary software facilitates 'traditional' commercial models of software licensing. In other words value capture is an important part of the open source development model, just as service provision as a means of value capture is important to the free software movement.

Once we accept that value creation, as well as cost reduction, is an important part of both the free software and open source movements, Chesbrough's differentiation of open innovation and open source starts to break down. Consequently open source software development practices can be seen as a means of open innovation through the sharing of common software components. The following three sections explore how open source software development has standardised more than just software outputs in order to facilitate open innovation in software related products and services.

2.6.1 Standardized development practices

Software is a digital asset. It costs a negligible amount to reproduce once written. Furthermore, with the rapid growth of the internet since the early 1990s the cost of

[37] H Chesbrough, W Vanhaverbeke and J West, *Open Innovation: Researching a New Paradigm* (Oxford, Oxford University Press, 2006) 1–2.

distribution has tended towards zero. Consequently we are in a position today where the free (as in cost) sharing of software assets is a reality for most of the developed world and an increasing proportion of the developing world.

The same technology that allows software to be shared at negligible cost has had a similar effect on communication across borders, both geographic and organizational. Collaboration on software has never been easier. Consequently the FSF's vision of a world in which all software is free is much more realistic today than it was when the foundation was created in 1985.

The internet, however, is not the only enabler of free and open source software. The practice of software development itself has also been maturing. The first software versioning tool was released in 1972 (Source Code Control Systems).[38] Tools such as this, along with other tools like issue trackers and automated testing suites, are an important part of modern software development, regardless of the licence and development model adopted.[39] For distributed teams working on open source software they are vital. It is these tools, coupled with the cheap and seamless communication tools of the internet age, that facilitate the open collaboration that is necessary to realize the innovation benefit of open development.

Whilst there is no single open source software development model, it is possible to find common, some might say 'standard,' practices that recur in many, or even most open source projects.[40] These practices revolve around common (or 'standard') collaboration tools that have emerged in recent years. It is this standardization that has allowed expertise to flow freely from project to project as need demands.

2.6.2 Standardized intellectual property management

In order to license software, it is necessary to track the ownership of any intellectual property embedded within it. In a closed development environment this is relatively easy to do since all contributors to the project will usually be on the payroll of the organization providing the licence. However, in an openly collaborative development such as that found in open source software, it is unlikely that all contributions will come from the same organization. For this reason it becomes necessary to track who contributes what IP and under what terms.

Other chapters will discuss the details of specific IP management processes.[41] However, it is important to recognize that the open source movement has adopted

[38] MJ Rochkind, 'The Source Code Control System' (December 1975) *IEEE Transactions on Software Engineering*, SE-1 (4), 364–70.

[39] OSS Watch, 'Essential Tools for Running A Community-Led Project' <http://www.oss-watch.ac.uk/resources/communitytools> accessed 5 April 2013.

[40] Those interested in reading further about common open source development practices should see K Fogel, *Producing Open Source* <http://producingoss.com> accessed 5 April 2013.

[41] See further chs 7 and 8.

standard models for tracking individual contributions. There are a number of different approaches to this, but all tend to revolve around the fact that modern software development tools provide a traceable record of activity by tracking who made what changes, when, and with what permissions.[42] By ensuring this record is appropriately cross-referenced and archived an efficient process of IP management can be developed.

The implementation of such processes is critical to the successful management of open source projects. The majority of contributors do not want to concern themselves with legal documentation and due diligence beyond their own contributions. Even when managing their own IP most individuals seek to minimize their direct engagement with the process. Thanks to the maturity of the open development model and the tools that support it, most contributors will find that the overhead placed on them is negligible.

Unfortunately, such practices are not currently taught in most computer science degrees. Consequently many projects, both open and closed source, fail to follow best practice. It is the strict enforcement of these policies within organizations such as the Apache Software Foundation that enables companies to safely use open source produced within these organizations. If controlled and verifiable process are not in place companies will typically insist on performing their own due diligence, often at considerable cost. When the cost of such due diligence outstrips the savings from reuse, they will often opt to reimplement, rather than reuse.

2.6.3 Standardized licences

In order to facilitate open collaboration all participants must be able to evaluate their legal rights within the community. The four freedoms and the OSD define what a free and open source licence must look like. Therefore, on the surface it would appear to be sufficient to ensure that the software licence in use appears on one of the lists of free and open source software licences maintained by the FSF and the OSI. Unfortunately, it is not as simple as this.

There are many different licences that meet all the criteria required by the FSF and/or the OSI. However, when considering any two or more open source licences there can be no guarantee that they will be legally compatible. This presents a significant barrier to collaboration; each licence must be fully understood before a composite product is created from the 'nuts and bolts' open source components.

In 2004 the OSI acknowledged that there was a proliferation of approved OSI open source licences. They also acknowledged that this was a barrier to uptake and collaboration in open source projects. Despite this the OSI continues to receive requests

[42] S Yeates, 'What is Version Control? Why Is It Important for Due Diligence?' (*OSS Watch*, 1 January 2005) <http://www.oss-watch.ac.uk/resources/versioncontrol> accessed 5 April 2013.

to approve new licences. The FSF has an even larger number of approved free software licences.

In 2006 the OSI published a report on licence proliferation which identified the extent of the problem, and made suggestions on how to tackle it. The report recategorized existing OSI approved licences based on usage. This action and the process of categorizing licences helped to bring wider awareness to the overall problem of licence proliferation; it reduced the creation and use of new licences; and it prompted a number of licences to be officially retired by their authors. The report identified just nine licences which are recommended for use in most circumstances. This category was described as 'licences that are popular and widely used or with strong communities.'[43]

At the time of writing,[44] one of those original nine licences has been superseded, at the request of the licence copyright holder, by another of the original nine. Thus the number of common licences was reduced to eight.[45] However, the total number of common licences has again risen to nine with the addition of another licence to the list.

Even within this narrow list of nine licences there are a number that are incompatible with one another, eg, the FSF maintains that the GPLv2 is incompatible with the Apache License V2.[46] Nevertheless, having a small number of recommended licences for use makes the process of auditing licences in composite software products more manageable. Legal teams need only understand which of these licences are compatible and standardize on these.

An alternative approach to minimizing the legal overhead on open source software reuse is to rely on a third party organization to do the appropriate due diligence on licence compatibility. For example, if you choose only to produce software under the GNU Public License you can turn to the FSF's list of GPL compatible licences for guidance,[47] similarly if you choose to use only the Apache Software License you can turn to the ASF for guidance.[48]

2.7 CONCLUSION

Collaboration of the type we find in open source software is not a new concept. We have been collaborating for individual and group benefit for at least as long as we

[43] Open Source Initiative, 'Report of License Proliferation Committee and draft FAQ' <http://opensource.org/proliferation-report> accessed 5 April 2013.

[44] March 2013. [45] March 2013.

[46] The Apache Software Foundation <http://www.apache.org/licenses/GPL-compatibility.html> accessed 5 April 2013.

[47] GNU, 'GPL-Compatible Free Software Licenses' <http://www.gnu.org/licenses/license-list.html#GPLCompatibleLicenses> accessed 5 April 2013.

[48] The Apache Software Foundation <http://www.apache.org/legal/resolved.html> accessed 5 April 2013.

have been defending our territory. Closed source software teams may choose to collaborate beyond their organizational borders, but here sharing is the exception rather than the rule.

Open source software teams, on the other hand, make sharing the default position. These teams rely upon the fact that the reproduction of completed software components does not consume a scarce resource. Furthermore, open source communities recognize that because large portions of their products can be standardized, and thus shared with collaborators at minimal cost, there is an opportunity to reduce the initial cost of production and ongoing costs of maintenance.

Fundamental to the success of this model of software production is the adoption of an open source licence. It is the licence that protects each participant from exploitation. The licence seeks to ensure that all contributors remain on equal terms. For this to work one needs to carefully consider both the licence chosen and the processes adopted to allow the software to be released under this licence. The rest of this book will explore, in detail, the role of open source licences.

Part I

INTELLECTUAL PROPERTY REGIMES

3

COPYRIGHT, CONTRACT, AND FOSS

Luke McDonagh

3.1 INTRODUCTION

Over the course of this chapter three crucial aspects of the law's relationship with FOSS licences are reviewed. First, a comparison of the licences themselves is outlined with particular regard to copyright provisions. In this respect, it is noted that while there is a great diversity of FOSS licences, the licences broadly fall into one of three categories: 'no copyleft', 'weak copyleft', and 'strong copyleft'. Secondly, the debate over enforcement is discussed, focusing on the question of whether these licences typically operate as 'bare licences' or whether they are in fact 'contracts'. This is an important issue because different legal consequences flow with regard to each category. Moreover, this is an issue which is difficult to resolve given the fact that FOSS typically operates online and across national boundaries, while different legal rules apply in various national jurisdictions. Thirdly, the compatibility of the most significant FOSS licences is examined.[1]

3.2 COMPARATIVE ANALYSIS OF KEY LICENCES—'NO COPYLEFT' VERSUS 'WEAK COPYLEFT' VERSUS 'STRONG COPYLEFT'

Original works of software are protected under copyright laws.[2] Several different copyrights can arise in this context. For an entirely new original work of authorship, the authors are the first owners of the copyright.[3] Furthermore, for a later work consisting of new modifications to existing code, a separate copyright will arise with respect to this new original material, which in the US is commonly referred to as a 'derivative work'.[4] There is also the possibility for a copyright in an aggregated 'compilation'.[5]

[1] C Thorne, 'Open Source Software—UK perspective' (Reynolds Porter Chamberlain LLP Presentation, 2010) <http://www.scl.org/bin_1/6.%20Clive%20Thorne.pdf>. According to Thorne, the major GPL licences together account for 65% of the total OSS license world—GPLv2 accounts for 50%, LGPLv2 accounts for 10%, while GPLv3 accounts for 5%. See also J Lovejoy, 'Understanding the Three Most Common Open Source Licenses' Open Logic; available at <http://www.openlogic.com/resources-library/webinar-understanding-the-most-common-oss-licenses> both accessed 4 April 2013. According to Lovejoy, by percentage of projects, 70% use GPL, while 7.6% use Apache and 6.7% use LGPL.

[2] 17 USC 101; CDPA 1988, s 3(1b). Directive 2009/24/EC of the European Parliament and of the Council of 23 April 2009 on the legal protection of computer programs.

[3] On the originality standard, in the US see *Feist Publication Inc v Rural Telephone Service Inc* (1991) 499 US 340, 345; for the UK see *University of London Press Ltd v University Tutorial Press Ltd* [1916] 2 Ch 601 and *Newspaper Licensing Agency v Meltwater* [2010] EWHC 3099 (Ch); for the EU see Case C-5/08 *Infopaq International A/S v Danske Dagblades Forening* [2009] ECR I-6569 (ECJ (4th Chamber)), [2009] ECDR 16 259.

[4] 17 USC ss 101 and 103. For the UK see *Ibcos Computers Ltd v Barclays Mercantile Highland Finance* [1994] FSR 275.

[5] CDPA 1988, s 3(1)(a). See also 17 USC 101.

As noted earlier, there is copyright in works of software. However, the concept of 'copyleft' must also be briefly explained. This concept has been described as 'a general method for making a program (or other work) free, and requiring all modified and extended versions of the program to be free as well.'[6] In this sense, 'free' does not mean 'free of all restrictions' or 'free of copyright.' In fact, the key concept at the heart of 'copyleft' is that the person who creates the software has the right, as the copyright-owner, to license the work as he or she sees fit. In this regard, the collaborative nature of FOSS operates so that initial authorship is 'the first link in the chain.'[7] Every new creator/collaborator produces new original modifications to the code, and then licenses these new modifications onwards. As described in detail later, what is crucial about the various FOSS licences is that some of the copyleft licences, including the 'weak copyleft' and 'strong copyleft' licences, require that this derivative material must be licensed under the same licence as the first work in the chain. The 'no copyleft' licences on the other hand typically allow modifications to be issued under any other licence.

One final thing must be outlined here, the difference between static and dynamic linking. This distinction is of key concern as different legal conditions may apply to each category. The crucial difference between the two is how and when the linking takes place. 'Static linking' typically involves combining components 'through compilation, copying them into the target application and producing a merged object file that is a stand-alone executable'; on the other hand, 'dynamic linking' typically involves the use of components 'at the time the application is loaded (load time) or during execution (run time).'[8] Of particular importance is the following question—when a piece of software is 'linked' to another piece of software should the resulting software be described as a derivative work, or, to use a non-US description, a work which requires the authorization of the copyright holder? The FSF generally takes an expansive view, arguing that even dynamic linking can create a 'derivative work.'[9] Nonetheless, the view taken in this chapter is that if the linking is static it is likely that a 'derivative work' is produced; however, if the linking is dynamic then it is likely that no 'derivative work' is produced; thus, the licensor has no copyright interest which would enable him or her to place conditions on use.[10]

[6] GNU, 'What is Copyleft?' <http://www.gnu.org/copyleft>.

[7] L Rosen, *Open Source Licensing—Software Freedom and Intellectual Property Law* (Upper Saddle River, NJ, Prentice Hall PTR, 2004) 28.

[8] See discussion of differences between static and dynamic linking at <http://joinup.ec.europa.eu/software/page/eupl/eupl-compatible-open-source-licences#section-3> accessed 4 April 2013.

[9] See FSF's discussion of dynamic linking at GNU, 'The LGPL and Java' <http://www.gnu.org/licenses/lgpl-java.html> accessed 4 April 2013.

[10] ML Stoltz, 'The Penguin Paradox: How the Scope of Derivative Works in Copyright Affects the Effectiveness of GPL' (2005) 85 *Boston University Law Review* 1439, 1451. See also discussion of 'derivative works' in this context at <http://joinup.ec.europa.eu/software/page/eupl/eupl-compatible-open-source-licences#section-3>. See also comments of J Leonard, 'A Practical Guide to Using Open Source Software': 'In the case of static linking, the various portions of

3.3 OUTLINING THE KEY TERMS OF FOSS LICENCES—'DISTRIBUTION' AND 'DERIVATIVE WORKS'

Generally all FOSS licences allow the user to make private use of the software. It is when the user seeks to redistribute the software, or distribute a 'modified' version of the software, that the differences between the various FOSS licences become clear. A number of key terms recur in many FOSS licences and understanding these terms is integral to comprehending the difference between the licences. In this regard, it is particularly necessary to discuss the much debated FOSS concept of 'distribution.' Figure 3.1 illustrates the various types of distribution that typically occur in the context of FOSS. These terms are described here as including notions of 'making available,' 'centralized' distribution, 'distribution of non-derivative works,' and 'distribution of derivative works.'

In this context, the idea of 'making available'[11] refers to the use of FOSS code in the making available of a product or facility. Google[12] and Facebook[13] are notable

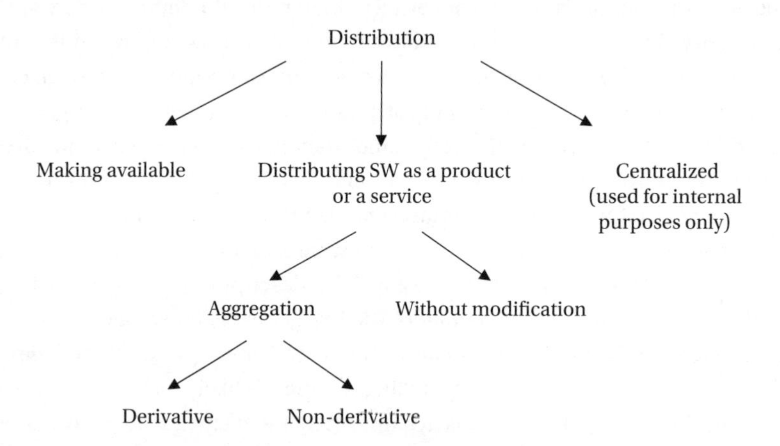

Figure 3.1 Possible FOSS Distribution channels

software are linked prior to compiling. If static linking used is with open source and proprietary software, then, arguably, the open source has been modified and all of the source code that was linked to the open source software would need to be disclosed upon distribution. By contrast, however, in the case of dynamic linking, it might be argued that since modified software is really only created at the time the program is actually run and dynamically linked to others software. Thus, there may be no distribution since the modified software may only be created on an end-user's machine.' <http://c.ymcdn.com/sites/www.coloradotechnology.org/resource/collection/335E7C59-E3F5-428F-9FAB-F318428051F4/A_Guide_to_Using_Open_Source_Software-FW_J._Leonard.pdf> both accessed 4 April 2013.

[11] This category is self-standing for the purpose of this chapter and it bears no resemblance to any other known category of 'making available' as sometimes defined under copyright law.

[12] J Corbet, 'How Google Uses Linux' (*LWN*, 21 October 2009) <http://lwn.net/Articles/357658> accessed 4 April 2013.

[13] S Campbell, 'How Does Facebook Work? The Nuts and Bolts [Technology Explained]' (*Makeuseof*, 27 February 2010) <http://www.makeuseof.com/tag/facebook-work-nuts-bolts-technology-explained> accessed 4 April 2013.

examples of this. For instance, although FOSS code is used to facilitate the Google search engine, the FOSS code itself is not distributed. Within this type of use FOSS code may be interacting with proprietary code (which may be held as a trade secret and which is not released). For this reason, many FOSS licences do not seek to bind the licensee by placing restrictions on this type of use.[14]

The notion of 'centralized' distribution, on the other hand, covers internal distribution within a company or use on an intranet. In general, this type of use or distribution is not specifically addressed by a FOSS licence's provisions. Moreover, it is strongly arguable that since there is no distribution to another natural or legal person, this type of use is within the scope of a FOSS licence, unless it is specifically forbidden.[15]

The idea of 'distribution of non-derivative works' includes distribution of original works and aggregations,[16] such as via dynamic linking, which do not create derivative works. The idea of 'distribution of derivative works' includes distribution of modified works and aggregations, such as via static linking, which do result in derivative works. In this regard, as outlined earlier, understanding the difference between static and dynamic linking is crucial.

The interpretation of the definition of 'derivative work' in court will be of great significance, as will the interpretation of other common terms found in many FOSS licences such as 'modified work' and 'contribution'. For instance, from the copyright perspective it is important to note that the term 'derivative work' does not have a universal meaning. Typically it is has a meaning under US law but it is a contestable notion in other jurisdictions such as those in Europe.[17] Some licensors attempt to clarify what they mean by the use of the term 'derivative work' in the text of the licence. For example, Linus Torvalds puts forward the notion that user-space programs, such as non-kernel applications running on the Linux kernel, do not create 'derivative works'.[18] Nevertheless, the ultimate authority for deciding this question remains the court.

[14] One exception is the Affero GPLv3 licence, which was specifically designed in order to capture this kind of activity: GNU, 'GNU Affero General Public License' <http://www.gnu.org/licenses/agpl-3.0.html> accessed 4 April 2013.

[15] It is notable that the Affero GPLv3 licence, which was designed to capture some forms of network/web use, eg, 'making available', specifically allows this 'centralized' use. See AGPL Frequently Asked Questions <http://www.affero.org/oagf.html>. See also comments at Free Software Foundation Question and Answer section: <http://www.gnu.org/licenses/gpl-faq.html#WhyPropagateAndConvey>; <http://www.gnu.org/licenses/gpl-faq.html#ConveyVsDistribute>; and <http://www.gnu.org/licenses/gpl-faq.html#NoDistributionRequirements> all accessed 4 April 2013.

[16] The FSF uses a slightly narrower use of the term 'aggregation' than the one in this chapter. The FSF clarifies that in its view 'mere aggregation' means distributing discrete non-derivative works on the same storage medium, eg, on the same compact disc; the FSF states that this will not trigger the copyleft requirement—see <http://www.gnu.org/licenses/gpl-faq.html#MereAggregation> accessed 4 April 2013. This chapter makes use of the term 'aggregation' where relevant to cover distribution of both derivative and non-derivative works. Therefore, it can be said that this chapter refers to 'aggregation' in a general sense instead of the FSF's term 'mere aggregation'.

[17] T Jaeger, 'Enforcement of the GNU GPL in Germany and Europe' (2010) 1 *JIPITEC* 34.

[18] Kernel.org, 'GNU General public license' (June 1991) <http://www.kernel.org/pub/linux/kernel/COPYING> accessed 4 April 2013, noting the disclaimer at the top of GPL.

As will be described, there are three main categories of licence: 'no copyleft', 'weak copyleft', and 'strong copyleft', all of which outline different permissions and restrictions with regard to distribution, and in particular distribution of derivative works. As already noted, the contestability of some of the terms commonly found in FOSS licences adds uncertainty to the meaning of licence terms. As a result, a certain amount of reasoned speculation is inevitable. The licence comparison analysis given here must be read with this in mind.

3.4 LICENCES FEATURING NO COPYLEFT PROVISIONS—APACHE 2.0, BSD, AND MIT

'No copyleft' licences are licences with limited or virtually non-existent copyleft provisions. Typically software released under 'no copyleft' licences can be used in nearly all distribution models, including proprietary and closed software models. These licences tend to impose minimal or no restrictions on use and distribution, eg, affixation of notices, requiring specific trademark permissions, and so forth.

The most prominent and popular 'no copyleft' licence is *Apache 2.0*. It is written by the Apache Software Foundation ('ASF').[19] With respect to licensing FOSS works under Apache, copying and linking are permitted under the licence.[20] Regarding the key issue of distribution, distribution of the original version of the work is expressly allowed with minimal restrictions.[21] Similarly distribution of the 'work' with modifications is allowed under the same terms.[22] The minimal restrictions include requiring a permission notice (licence text) to appear in all copies of the source code, necessitating the provision of a copy of the licence (s 4.1), requiring the retention of all notices (s 4.3–4), and requiring the giving of a notice of modifications (s 4.2).[23]

Apache 2.0 also provides a definition of 'derivative work'. It explicitly excludes 'works that remain separable from, or merely link (or bind by name) to the interfaces of, the Work and Derivative Works thereof'. Under this definition, linked works are excluded from the notion of derivative work; any work being linked to such a derivative work would most

[19] Open Source Initiative, 'Apache License, Version 2.0' <http://opensource.org/licenses/Apache-2.0> accessed 4 April 2013.

[20] The licence states that 'each Contributor hereby grants to You a perpetual, worldwide, non-exclusive, no-charge, royalty-free, irrevocable copyright license to reproduce, prepare Derivative Works of, publicly display, publicly perform, sublicense, and distribute the Work and such Derivative Works in Source or Object form'.

[21] The licence states 'You may reproduce and distribute copies of the Work or Derivative Works thereof, in any medium, with or without modifications, and in Source or Object form…'.

[22] 'You may reproduce and distribute copies of the Work or Derivative Works thereof, in any medium, with or without modifications, and in Source or Object form'. Cu, PN, AM, CL-Apache License only has limited effect. The 'key' to these abbreviations is found in Annex I of this chapter.

[23] Different rules apply in s 5 to works submitted as a contribution to the ASF; Copyleft clause applies 'unless you explicitly state otherwise' and only to 'any Contribution intentionally submitted for inclusion in the Work by you to the Licensor…'.

probably not be deemed by a court to be part of such derivative work. The reason for this is that both works would remain separable even if they are linked statically.

The licence also gives a definition of 'contribution' and 'contributor'.[24] There are three additional requirements within the terms of Apache 2.0, two of which have caused some controversy with regard to compatibility with other licences, as discussed in section 3 of this chapter. The first and least controversial requirement is a trade mark permission clause (s 6).[25] There is also a patent retaliation (termination) clause (s 3), as well as an indemnity clause which operates in the case additional support is offered by a licensee (s 9).

Given the permissive nature of Apache 2.0 it can be said to be generally suitable for all types of distribution discussed in this section: making available, centralized distribution, distribution of non-derivative works, and distribution of derivative works.[26] Provided that the minimal requirements of the licence are met, any person is able to modify the source code and release, commercially or non-commercially, a free/open or proprietary/closed version of Apache-licensed software.

The *BSD* licences are a series of permissive, 'no copyleft' licences authored by UC Berkeley.[27] The most common BSD licences are the three-clause 'modified' BSD licence and the two-clause 'simplified' BSD licence. The primary difference between the two main BSD licences is that the 'simplified' two-clause version omits the non-endorsement clause found in the 'modified' three-clause version. Copying and linking are permitted under the licences; dynamic linking to the work is possible with no restrictions while static linking to the work falls within the scope of the permission to copy; redistribution and use, both in source and binary forms, and with or without modification, are broadly permitted.[28] Distribution of the work is generally allowed with or without modifications.[29]

[24] Under the licence it is defined as 'any work of authorship, including the original version of the Work and any modifications or additions to that Work or Derivative Works thereof, that is intentionally submitted to Licensor for inclusion in the Work by the copyright owner or by an individual or Legal Entity authorized to submit on behalf of the copyright owner. For the purposes of this definition, "submitted" means any form of electronic, verbal, or written communication sent to the Licensor or its representatives, including but not limited to communication on electronic mailing lists, source code control systems, and issue tracking systems that are managed by, or on behalf of, the Licensor for the purpose of discussing and improving the Work, but excluding communication that is conspicuously marked or otherwise designated in writing by the copyright owner as "Not a Contribution." ' The license states ' "Contributor" shall mean Licensor and any individual or Legal Entity on behalf of whom a Contribution has been received by Licensor and subsequently incorporated within the Work'.

[25] See further ch 4.

[26] However, given the patent retaliation provision, the use of Apache 2.0 may not suit a distributor or business that seeks to enforce software patents in the manner described in the retaliation provision.

[27] Two-clause (simplified) BSD licence: <http://opensource.org/licenses/BSD-2-Clause>; and three-clause (modified) BSD licence: <http://opensource.org/licenses/BSD-3-Clause> both accessed 4 April 2013.

[28] For the purposes of clarity and space, abbreviations are used here to give detail regarding the terms of the licences. The key for these abbreviations is included as Annex I at the end of this chapter. For this licence the relevant abbreviations are C+ and PN+.

[29] 'Redistribution and use in source and binary forms, with or without modification, are permitted...' modified BSD licence (C+, NA, PN+) and simplified BSD licence (C+, PN+).

BSD licences are very short at merely two or three clauses. This potentially leaves a lot open to interpretation. For example, no definition of derivative work is given. However, the permissive nature of the licences is undeniable. The minimal requirements of the licences consist of requiring the affixation of both a copyright notice, and a related liability disclaimer (which applies to source code and binary code). Moreover, it is stated in the three-clause licence that the name of the copyright holder and/or of the organization that created the licence may not be used in advertising without prior permission. Like Apache 2.0, the three-clause BSD licence is generally suitable for all types of distribution discussed here: making available, centralized distribution, distribution of non-derivative works, and distribution of derivative works. As noted earlier, provided that the minimal requirements of the licence are met, any person is able to modify the source code and release, commercially or non-commercially, a free/open or proprietary/closed version of BSD-licensed software.

The *MIT* licence is a permissive, 'no copyleft' licence developed by the Massachusetts Institute of Technology.[30] Copying and linking are permitted under the licence.[31] Dynamic linking to the work is possible with no restrictions. Static linking to the work falls within the scope of the permission to copy. The minimalist requirements of this licence consist of the affixation of a copyright notice, and the use of a contract and tort disclaimer. Distribution of the 'work' with or without modifications is allowed.[32] Like the BSD licences, the MIT licence is very short. Nonetheless, its permissive nature is clear. As a 'no copyleft' licence it is generally suitable for all types of distribution discussed here: making available, centralized distribution, distribution of non-derivative works, and distribution of derivative works. As before, provided that the minimal requirements of the licence are met, any person is able to modify the source code and release, commercially or non-commercially, a free/open or proprietary/closed version of MIT-licensed software.

In conclusion, it must be noted that the 'no copyleft' licences examined in this section are sometimes described by commentators as 'permissive' or 'copyfree'.[33] Regarding the notion of a 'permissive' or 'copyfree' licence, for the purpose of this chapter the key concept at the heart of these licences is 'no copyleft', referring to the lack of copyleft provisions restricting how the software can be redistributed. It is this that makes the licences 'permissive' or 'free'. For this reason, and for the purpose

[30] Open Source Initative, 'The MIT License': <http://opensource.org/licenses/MIT> accessed 4 April 2013.

[31] 'Permission is hereby granted... to deal in the Software without restrictions, including without limitations the rights to use, copy, modify, merge, publish, distribute, sublicense, and/or sell copies of the Software, and to permit persons to whom the Software is furnished to do so...'—C++, PN++.

[32] 'Permission is hereby granted... to deal in the Software without restrictions, including without limitations the rights to use, copy, modify, merge, publish, distribute, sublicense, and/or sell copies of the Software, and to permit persons to whom the Software is furnished to do so...'—C++, PN++.

[33] Copyfree, 'The Copyfree Standard Definition' <http://copyfree.org/standard> accessed 4 April 2013.

of clarity, the term 'copyleft' is used. It is also important to reiterate that software released under a 'no copyleft' licence can be used 'permissively' or 'freely' not only by the general computer programmer/user; companies can also make use of the code and incorporate it under stricter 'weak copyleft' or 'strong copyleft' licences, as described in 3.5 and 3.6.

3.5 LICENCES FEATURING WEAK COPYLEFT PROVISIONS—MPL AND LGPL

Licences with 'weak copyleft' provisions can be easily utilized in some distribution models, but not in others. For example, the provisions in these licences usually require that derivative works must be issued under the particular licence in question. However, non-derivative and/or 'linked' works may be distributed under another licence, something which envisages commercial use in 'proprietary' software models. Therefore, the source code for linked software can remain closed even if this software is linked with open source code (which must itself remain open). Typically, there are other requirements with respect to trade marks, the use and availability of source code provisions, and so on. Examples of these types of licences are the Mozilla Public License 1.1 and the GNU Library or 'Lesser' General Public License v 2.1.

The *Mozilla Public License 1.1 (MPL)* is a weak copyleft licence written by the Mozilla Foundation.[34] Copying, display, performance, and use are explicitly permitted.[35] As discussed later with regard to compatibility, sub-licensing is also permitted.[36] The definition of the 'Covered Code' includes both the 'Original Code' and its 'Modifications'. Regarding distribution, there are different conditions that apply to distribution in object code[37] and in source code.[38] Each contributor must inform recipients about any third party IP rights applicable to the software by including such information in a text file named 'LEGAL.'[39] It is noted in MPL s 4 that if the recipient of the licence cannot comply with all of its terms due to statute, regulation, or judicial order, he or she can still use the work provided he or she complies with the terms to

[34] Open Source Initiative, 'Open Source Initiative OSI—Mozilla Public License 1.1' <http://opensource.org/licenses/MPL-1.1> accessed 4 April 2013.

[35] C, PND.

[36] The licence notes in MPL s 2.1: 'The Initial Developer hereby grants You a world-wide, royalty-free, non-exclusive license...to use, reproduce,..., display, perform, sublicense...the Original Code (or portions thereof) with or without Modifications'. MPL s 2.2 ensures each contributor makes the same grant.

[37] ASC+ (source code must be made available for redistribution under conditions described hereafter).

[38] C, PN, CL—MPL.

[39] MPL s 3.4 states: 'If Contributor has knowledge that a license under a third party's intellectual property rights is required to exercise the rights granted by such Contributor under Sections 2.1 or 2.2, Contributor must include a text file with the Source Code distribution titled "LEGAL" which describes the claim and the party making the claim in sufficient detail that a recipient will know whom to contact'.

the maximum extent possible, and provides the reasons why compliance is not possible in the LEGAL file.

Overall, it can be said that distribution of the 'work' with modifications is allowed, but with restrictions. As stated earlier, there are different conditions that apply to distribution in object code[40] and source code,[41] and each contributor must inform recipients about any third party IP rights.[42] With regard to 'modifications' (the point which potentially relates to derivative works), the licence permits the recipient to create 'Larger Works.' The notion of a larger work is defined as 'a work which combines Covered Code or portions thereof with code not governed by the terms.' This explicitly provides that in such case it is only the 'Covered Code' or portions thereof that must be subject to MPL, not the other parts of such larger work. This permission encompasses both the situation where another program links to the 'Covered Code' (either statically or dynamically) as well as the circumstances where modified 'Covered Code' links to another program. In both cases the restrictions prescribed by the licence apply only to the 'Covered Code' and not to other parts of the larger work, which may be licensed under different terms. This gives the MPL its 'weak copyleft' character. The meanings of 'Contributor' and 'Contributor Version' are defined in s 1.1 and s 1.2. 'Contributor' is said to mean 'each entity that creates or contributes to the creation of "Modifications",' while 'Contributor Version' means 'the combination of the Original Code, prior Modifications used by a Contributor, and the Modifications made by that particular Contributor.'

Other requirements of the MPL include the fact that source code must be published for a period of twelve months (or six months in the case of a modification) from the time the executable version was made available. Furthermore, there must be affixation of a copyright notice. The licence therefore requires the inclusion of the source code for any software licensed under MPL for a limited time. As will be noted in 3.8 with respect to compatibility, MPL envisages the use of other licences, such as GPL. Overall it can be said that with respect to distribution, MPL is suitable for making available and centralized distribution (though no specific provisions are given on these issues). The distribution of non-derivative works is allowable with the condition that the MPL-licensed code must be left open and accessible for a specified time (there are different requirements for object and source). The major limitation comes in the context of 'modifications.' MPL can also be used for distribution of derivative works, but the MPL requires that the derivative content must be licensed under MPL (though not the entire larger work).[43] As noted earlier, what typifies the

[40] AM, ASC+ (source code must be licensed under conditions described hereafter).

[41] C, PN, AM, CL—Mozilla PL.

[42] MPL s 3.4, fn 40

[43] In this regard the MPL code must be left open and accessible, with acknowledgement of the different requirements for object and source.

'weak copyleft' category of licence is the fact that derivative content must be licensed under MPL, but in the case of any other type of interaction between the MPL-code and other code, such as interaction via static or dynamic linking, another licence may be utilized.

The *GNU Library or 'Lesser' General Public License v 2.1 (LGPL)* is a 'weak copyleft' licence authored by the Free Software Foundation ('FSF').[44] Copying is explicitly permitted.[45] Distribution of the unmodified work is allowed, but there are different conditions that apply to distribution in object code[46] and in source code.[47] Distribution of the work featuring modifications is also allowed, with different conditions that apply to distribution in object[48] and in source code.[49] Permission to modify the 'Library' and to copy and distribute its 'modified' versions is subject to two additional conditions. First, the 'modified' work itself must be a software library. Secondly, it is noted that 'if a facility in the modified Library refers to a function or a table of data to be supplied by an application program that uses the facility... then you must make a good faith effort to ensure that, in the event an application does not supply such function or table, the facility still operates, and performs whatever part of its purpose remains meaningful.'[50] These requirements apply to the modified work as a whole, including separable parts that are not derived from the 'Library.' However, it is crucial to note that mere aggregation of another work with the 'Library' on a volume of a storage or distribution medium does not bring the other work under the scope of LGPL. Therefore, works based on the 'Library' can be placed in a single library with other library facilities not covered by LGPL, and be distributed within such a combined library, provided that access to the works based on the 'Library' is granted under LGPL. Works that do not contain the 'Library,' or any portion thereof, but which are designed to work with the 'Library' by being compiled or linked with it are called 'works that use the Library.' These works have a specific regime described under the 'Linking' section of the LGPL.

Works which merely engage in dynamic linking with the 'Library' most probably fall outside of the scope of the LGPL (despite the contrary intentions of its drafters).[51] As noted earlier, dynamically linked works are unlikely to create a copyright interest

[44] Open Source Initiative, 'The GNU Lesser General Public License, version 2.1' <http://opensource.org/licenses/lgpl-2.1.php> accessed 4 April 2013.

[45] C, Pnus.

[46] ASC+ (complete source code must be made available for redistribution under conditions described hereafter).

[47] 'You may copy and distribute verbatim copies of the Library's source code as you receive it, in any medium...'—C, PNus, PN?, or CL-GPLv2 or any later version of GPL.

[48] ASC+ (complete source code must be made available for redistribution under conditions described hereafter).

[49] 'You may modify your copy or copies of the Library or any portion of it, thus forming a work based on the Library, and copy and distribute such modifications or work...'—C, PNus, PN?, AM, CL-LGPL, or GPLv2 or any later version of GPL.

[50] LGPL, s 2(d).

[51] GNU, 'GNU Lesser General Public License (section 5 LGPL appears designed to apply to all linking)' <http://www.gnu.org/licenses/lgpl-2.1.html> accessed 4 April 2013.

as a 'derivative work' which would enable the licensor to place conditions on the use of these works.

Works statically linking to the 'Library' fall out of the scope of the LGPL until they are compiled with the 'Library'. 'Executables' created by linking a work that uses the 'Library' with the 'Library' are treated under the LGPL as derivatives of the 'Library'. These 'derivative works' can be said to fall under the LGPL; thus, they have a special regime different from modifications of the 'Library' itself.[52] The combining or linking of a work that uses the 'Library' with the 'Library' itself (in order to produce a work containing parts of the 'Library') is permitted, as is distribution of the resulting work under any terms, provided that the terms permit modification of the work for the customer´s own use and allow reverse engineering for debugging such modifications.[53]

In light of the above, it is clear that LGPL is a 'weak copyleft' licence. Overall, it can be said that the LGPL is suitable for making available and centralized distribution (including use as part of a 'Library' since works can be used for personal internal purposes subject to conditions).[54] The licence is also suitable for the distribution of non-derivative works, including software that merely links to the LGPL library, and which is not considered to be a derivative work. However, all LGPL code must be left open and accessible. The LGPL is suitable for the distribution of derivative works, but crucially the LGPL requires that derivative content must be licensed under LGPL/GPLv2 (see following section).

3.6 LICENCES FEATURING STRONG COPYLEFT PROVISIONS—GPLv2 AND GPLv3

Licences with 'strong copyleft' provisions can only be used restrictively. These licences typically maintain that derivative works cannot be distributed under any other licence and that full source code must be provided. Moreover, these licences typically try to catch as much software 'material' within the remit of the licence as possible by taking a wide a definition of derivative work. For example, a 'strong copyleft' licence will typically seek to prevent all linked works, whether linking statically or dynamically, from being issued under another licence.[55]

[52] This is the case except in relation to object files that use only numerical parameters, data structure layouts, small macros and small inline functions (up to ten lines in length). Such object files are unrestricted by the LGPL.

[53] The following conditions relate only to the Library itself: C?, Ca, PN?, ASC+CL-LGPL, GPLv2 or any later version of GPL, or using suitable shared library mechanism.

[54] Conditions include affixation of copyright notice and disclaimer, the modified work must be a software library and be licensed to third parties with no charge, source code to be attached to any distributed works.

[55] GNU Affero allows distribution (subject to conditions) on a web but not full distribution as a product or service; GNU, 'GNU Affero General Public License' <http://www.gnu.org/licenses/agpl-3.0.html> accessed 4 April 2013.

The *GNU General Public License (GPL) v 2* is a strong copyleft licence written by the FSF in 1991.[56] Copying is explicitly permitted.[57] The licence grants the licensee the right to copy, distribute, and modify the software on the crucial condition the software is again distributed under the conditions of GPLv2. The requirements of the licence include making reference to GPLv2 (together with the GPL licence text), providing the source code, and making reference to the disclaimer of warranty. There is a clear provision stating that failure to follow the licence terms will result in the revocation of the licence, although third parties are deemed to be unaffected.

Distribution of the unmodified 'work' is allowed, though there are different conditions that apply to distribution in object code[58] and in source code.[59] The obligation to grant access to the source code in case of distribution of executable copies covers 'complete source code'; this is defined as 'all the source code for all modules it contains, plus any associated interface definition files, plus the scripts used to control compilation and installation of the executable.'[60]

Distribution of the 'work' with modifications is allowed, with different conditions that apply to distribution in object code[61] and in source code, but these derivative works must also be licensed under GPLv2.[62] The obligation to grant access to the source code in the context of distribution of executable copies covers 'complete source code.'[63]

It is not exactly clear what is deemed to be part of the modified or derivative work and what is not. A work based on the 'Program' is defined as 'any derivative work under copyright law: that is to say, a work containing the Program or a portion of it.' Regarding aggregation, it is explicitly stated in GPLv2 that 'mere aggregation of another work not based on the Program with the Program... on a volume of a storage or distribution medium does not bring the other work under the scope of this License.' GPLv2 further states that when sections of the new work that can be reasonably considered independent and separate works in themselves are distributed as part of a whole, which is a work based on the Program, the distribution of the

[56] Open Source Initiative, 'GNU General Public License, version 2' <http://opensource.org/licenses/GPL-2.0> accessed 4 April 2013.

[57] C, Pnus.

[58] ASC+ (complete source code must be made available for redistribution under conditions described hereafter).

[59] 'You may copy and distribute verbatim copies of the Program´s source code as you receive it, in any medium...'—C, PNus, PN?

[60] It is explicitly stated that 'the source code distributed need not include anything that is normally distributed... with the major components (compiler, kernel, and so on) of the operating system on which the executable normally runs, unless this component itself accompanies the executable.'

[61] ASC+ (complete source code must be made available for redistribution under conditions described hereafter).

[62] 'You may modify your copy or copies of the Program´s source code or any portion of it, thus forming a work based on the Program, and copy and distribute such modifications or work...'—C, Ca, PNus, PN?, AM, CL-GPL.

[63] 'Complete source code' is defined as 'all the source code for all modules it contains, plus any associated interface definition files, plus the scripts used to control compilation and installation of the executable of the modified work as a whole.'

whole must be on the terms of GPLv2. With respect to the drafters' intention, GPLv2 explicitly mentions that the intent of the licence 'is to exercise the right to control the distribution of derivative or collective works based on the Program'; further to this, the second part of the definition of 'a work based on the Program' also suggests that collective works that include the 'Program' or a portion thereof are deemed to be 'works based on the Program.'[64]

Despite the drafters' intentions, under copyright law where the new work, including the modification of the 'Program,' could not be defined as a whole to be a derivative of the 'Program,' it would instead be seen as a 'collective work.'[65] Regarding this collective work, it would typically be composed of 'a work based on the Program' and other separate works. These other separate works would not have to be licensed under GPLv2, despite the intention of the drafters.[66]

With respect to linking, it was noted earlier that due to the fact that GPLv2's restrictions apply to 'derivative works,' anything that is outside the definition of a derivative work will not be affected by the licence's restrictions. According to the licence, if a modified work links to another program (statically or dynamically) such program is deemed to form part of the modified work and it must be treated accordingly. Static linking to the work falls within the scope of the permission to copy.[67] However, if the resulting work is distributed the licence states it must be treated as a modified work (a work based on the Program). The drafters of the GPL licence also firmly state that dynamic linking to the work makes the program linking to the work 'a work based on the Program' as well. However, this is probably not true. It is strongly arguable that the mere act of dynamic linking does not constitute use of the work in this respect. Furthermore, if the new program linking to such work is not distributed together with the work it arguably cannot be caught under the GPL. Statically linked code on the other hand is more likely to be found to be 'derivative' - in this respect, the GPL-derived code would have to be left open and accessible (acknowledging the different requirements for object and source code).

Ultimately, it can be said that GPLv2 is a 'strong copyleft' licence. It is generally suitable for making available and centralized distribution (though no specific provisions on these issues). It is also suitable for distribution of non-derivative works, but any GPLv2 code must be open and accessible (and there are different

[64] GNU, 'GNU General Public License, version 2, s 0' <http://www.gnu.org/licenses/gpl-2.0.html> accessed 4 April 2013

[65] See discussion of 'derivative work' in ch 1 and n 10.

[66] GNU, 'GNU General Public License, version 2, s 0' <http://www.gnu.org/licenses/gpl-2.0.html> accessed 4 April 2013. It is also notable that even under the FSF's expansive view, not all collective works including the Program would be deemed to be 'works based on the Program'; only those that form one functional application would be, eg, according to the FSF if one internal module of MS Word was a program licensed under GPLv2, the whole of MS Word would have to be licensed under GPLv2, but not the complete MS Office package.

[67] C, Pnus.

requirements for object and source). The licence is suitable for distribution of derivative works, but GPLv2 requires that derivative content must be licensed under the same terms. As noted earlier, the confusion in the licence concerning the definition of a derivative work leaves the court with some room for interpretation, particularly regarding dynamically linked works. It is argued here that the attempt of the drafters to catch all varieties of linking within the GPL licence is probably not successful.

The *GNU General Public License (GPL) v 3* is a strong copyleft licence authored by the FSF.[68] Under the licence it is explicitly permitted to run the unmodified 'Program' and to make, run, and propagate works that are not conveyed without restrictions. Under GPLv3 Works can be distributed subject to a number of conditions: there must be affixation of a copyright notice and disclaimer, modifications must be licensed back to the public under the same terms, source code must be attached to any distributed works, and respect for the anti-tivoization clause must be given.[69]

Distribution of the unmodified work is allowed.[70] In this respect, if the work is distributed in object code the 'Corresponding Source' must be provided together with the work as described in the licence.[71] If the work in object code is distributed in, with, or specifically for use in a 'User Product', and the right of possession of the product is transferred to the recipient, and anybody retains the ability to install modified object code on the 'User Product', the 'Corresponding Source' must be accompanied by the Installation Information.[72] As Asay has stated, this essentially means that for any such user or consumer products 'any encryption keys or other information necessary to operate modified GPLv3'ed software on such products (such as the Installation Information) must be provided as part of the Corresponding Source'.[73]

Distribution of the work with modifications is permitted subject to the licence restrictions.[74] Dates of alterations must also be provided. If the work is distributed in object code the corresponding source must be provided together with the work by

[68] Open Source Initiative, 'GNU General Public License, version 3' <http://opensource.org/licenses/GPL-3.0> accessed 4 April 2013.

[69] It also allows use with Affero GNUv3 licensed-works.

[70] 'You may convey verbatim copies of the Program's source code as you receive it, in any medium... You may convey a covered work in object code...'—C?, PN?, ASC.

[71] 'Corresponding Source' means 'all the source code needed to generate, install, and (for an executable work) run the object code and to modify the work, including scripts to control those activities. However it does not include the work's System Libraries or general purpose tools or generally available free programs which are used unmodified in performing those activities but which are not part of the work'.

[72] The requirements concern all information, authorization keys and methods required to install and execute modified versions of the work in such a 'User Product'; this also known as the 'anti-tivoization' clause.

[73] CD Asay, 'The General Public License version 3.0: Making or Breaking the FOSS Movement' (2008) 14 *Mich Telecomm Tech L Rev* 265, 275.

[74] 'You may convey a work based on the Program, or the modifications to produce it from the Program, in the form of source code... You may convey a covered work in object code...'—C?, Ca, PN?, AM, ASC, CL-GPLv3.

one of the ways described in the licence.[75] There is also a requirement that seeks to bypass the requirements of the Digital Millennium Copyright Act 1998 ('DMCA');[76] if anybody conveys a covered work, it is stated that he or she waives 'any legal power to forbid circumvention of TPMs to the extent such circumvention is effected by exercising rights under this License'.[77] Regarding the DMCA provision, GPLv3 provides that no covered work shall be deemed part of an effective technological measure under any applicable law. However, the effectiveness of this provision is to some extent uncertain. For instance, it is very difficult to foresee in advance how a court or jurisdiction may interpret the notion of 'applicable law'. It is also possible that the program licensed under GPLv3 may be used as part of TPMs protecting access to works, eg, via online access, without being distributed together with such works, and therefore, without the necessity to license that program to recipients of such works.

Regarding derivative content, sub-licensing is not allowed at all under GPLv3. Nonetheless, with regard to aggregations, the licence explicitly states that inclusion of a covered work into an aggregate[78] does not cause GPLv3 to apply to the other parts of the aggregate. With respect to the issue of linking, although it is clear that the GPLv3 drafters intended to catch linking within the meaning of 'modification' as defined in the licence,[79] it is doubtful whether this is really the case. It is strongly arguable that if a covered work dynamically or statically links to another program, the source code of such program must be provided as part of the 'Corresponding Source', unless it is a 'System Library' (and unless it is a 'Major Component', eg, a kernel or window system of the specific operating system). It is more unclear whether the program linked to by a modified work forms part of such modified work and must, therefore, be licensed under GPLv3. The drafters of the licence believe the answer is yes.[80] However, given the fact that some kind of derivative work must have been created in order for the licence to be binding, the answer is most probably no in relation to dynamically linked programs, and it may also be no even in relation to statically linked programs, depending on the nature of the modified work, as noted later.

[75] Corresponding source refers to 'all the source code needed to generate, install, and (for an executable work) run the object code and to modify the work, including scripts to control those activities. However it does not include the work's System Libraries or general purpose tools or generally available free programs which are used unmodified in performing those activities but which are not part of the work'.

[76] Digital Millennium Copyright Act 1998 (DMCA) Pub L No 105-304, 112 Stat 2860 (28 Oct 1998).

[77] 'TPM' means a technological protection measure.

[78] Defined as 'a compilation of a covered work with other separate and independent works, which are not by their nature extensions of the covered work, and which are not combined with it such as to form a larger program, in or on a volume of a storage or distribution medium', but only 'if the compilation and its resulting copyright are not used to limit the access or legal rights of the compilation's users beyond what the individual works permit'. If the work in object code is distributed in, with or specifically for use in a user product, and the right of possession of the product is transferred to the recipient, and anybody retains the ability to install modified object code on the 'User Product', the 'Corresponding Source' must be accompanied by the 'Installation Information'.

[79] See GNU 'FAQ' <http://www.gnu.org/licenses/gpl-faq.html> accessed 4 April 2013.

[80] See GNU 'FAQ' (n 79).

The drafters believe that if another program links to a covered work such program must be licensed under GPLv3 'because the program as it is actually run includes the library.'[81] Nonetheless, this reasoning seems to be flawed. The licence does not impose any restrictions on running the covered work, only on conveying modified works; furthermore, the program dynamically linking to a covered work does not convey nor modify the work in any way. Granted static linking to a covered program would arguably result in a modified work that would have to be conveyed under GPLv3, but it would depend on the nature of the resulting program, such as whether this program could be defined as an aggregate, as defined above. Surprisingly, the licence does not mention specifically the situations in which covered works are deemed to be 'linked to' by other programs.

Overall, GPLv3 is generally suitable for making available (though no specific provisions are provided on this issue).[82] With regard to centralized distribution it appears that the GPLv3 does attempt to tackle this issue by introducing two new terms: 'propagation' and 'conveying.'[83] Under this view, mere 'propagation' that does not amount to 'conveying' of software licensed under GPLv3 will not trigger the copyleft requirement. This appears to allow centralized distribution.

GPLv3 is also suitable for distribution of non-derivative works, though any GPLv3 code must be open and accessible (there are different requirements for object and source). It is also possible to use the licence for distribution of derivative works but according to the licence terms, distribution of statically or dynamically linked works must be under the terms of the GPL (noting that GPL code and any linked code must remain open and accessible). However, despite the contrary intention of the drafters of GPLv3, it is likely that only derivative content is bound under GPL. In other words, dynamically-linked programs are probably not affected by this provision since they are unlikely to be considered to be modified or 'derivative' works.

3.7 FOSS LICENCES—'CONTRACTS' OR 'BARE LICENCES'?

There has been a tremendous amount of academic debate concerning whether FOSS 'licences' are 'bare licences' in the legal sense, or whether they are in fact 'contracts.' In this respect, there is some overlap between the different categories. Generally, it is the case that a licence can be a contract, but it does not necessarily have to be one. A licence is said to be analogous to giving permission—a licensor gives a licensee

[81] See GNU 'FAQ' (n 79).

[82] As noted at nn 14 and 15, there is a separate licence, Affero GPLv3, which does specifically attempt to capture the 'making available' of FOSS.

[83] GNU, 'GNU General Public License, definitions' section of GPLv3' <http://www.gnu.org/licenses/gpl.html> accessed 4 April 2013.

permission to do something which otherwise the licensee would not be able to do.[84] Over the course of this sub-section, an assessment is made of the requirements for 'contracts' and 'bare licences'; this is coupled with an analysis of the consequences of a finding that a FOSS licence falls into either category.

3.7.1 Assessing the requirements of a contract in the FOSS context

The question of whether FOSS licences are valid contracts has been much debated. For instance, on one hand Gomulkiewicz has argued that GPL licences fulfil the legal requirements of a contract under the US model code Uniform Computer Information Transaction Act (UCITA).[85] However, the UCITA has been accused by Richard Stallman of being more suitable for use in the context of 'proprietary' software than FOSS; this is one reason the FSF has not accepted the idea that the GPL is a contract.[86]

On this point Moglen has argued:

> A contract...is an exchange of obligations, either of promises for promises or of promises of future performance for present performance or payment. The idea that 'licenses' to use patents or copyrights must be contracts is an artefact of twentieth-century practice, in which licensors offered an exchange of promises with users: 'We will give you a copy of our copyrighted work,' in essence, 'if you pay us and promise to enter into certain obligations concerning the work.' With respect to software, those obligations by users include promises not to decompile or reverse-engineer the software, and not to transfer the software.[87]

In order to evaluate whether a FOSS licence can properly be considered to be a contract, it is necessary to discuss the requirements for the formation of a valid contract under the Anglo-American common law legal system, whereby formation typically occurs via 'offer,' 'acceptance,' and 'consideration.'[88] Generally, contractual terms must also be sufficiently drawn to the attention of the contracting party[89] and be within the 'reasonable expectations of the parties.'[90]

[84] CDPA 1988, s 16; 17 USC s 106.

[85] RW Gomulkiewicz, 'How Copyleft Uses License Rights to Succeed in the Open Source Software Revolution and the Implications for Article 2B' (1999) 36 *Houston Law Review* 179. UCITA, s 102(a)(41) refers to a licence as 'a contract that authorises access to, or use, distribution, performance, modification, or reproduction of, informational rights, but expressly limits the access or uses authorized or expressly grants fewer than all rights in the information, whether or not the transferee has title to a licensed copy.'

[86] R Stallman, 'Why We Must Fight UCITA' (*Linux Today*, 6 February 2000) <http://www.gnu.org/philosophy/ucita.html> accessed 4 April 2013.

[87] Moglen quote reported by P Jones, 'The GPL Is a License, not a Contract' (2003) <http://lwn.net/Articles/61292> accessed 4 April 2013.

[88] J Beatson, *Anson's Law of Contract*, 28th edn (Oxford, Oxford University Press, 2002) 1–37, 88–9.

[89] *Thornton v Shoe Lane Parking* [1971] 2 QB 163.

[90] *Equitable Life v Hyman* [2000] UKHL 39, [2002] 1 AC 408.

In this respect, finding the offer in the FOSS context is relatively straightforward. Zhu has defined an offer in the FOSS context as 'a licensor's manifested willingness to give users permission to access, use, modify or redistribute a piece of FOSS', and he stated that these permissions are usually accompanied by 'some restrictions pursuant to Free Software Definition and Open Source Definition.'[91] Meanwhile Rosen has remarked that posting the offer to an accessible FOSS repository/website demonstrates a willingness to offer.[92]

With respect to acceptance, the situation is more complex. It is generally the case that it must correspond exactly with the terms of the offer. In this vein, it must be 'absolute' and it must leave no doubt 'as to the fact of acceptance, or as to the coincidence of terms of the acceptance with those of the offer.'[93] In the software area, there is some case law regarding acceptance via 'shrinkwrap', 'clickwrap', and 'browsewrap'. The idea of 'shrinkwrap' concerns the consumer tearing off the shrinkable clear plastic on the software box. Once this has been done, the consumer is said to have assented to the terms of the licence. In the US, this type of acceptance was found to be valid in *ProCD v Zeidenberg*.[94] Nonetheless, this type of acceptance is controversial; Lemley has stated that the conduct supposedly showing evidence of a shrinkwrap contract 'is hardly unambiguous evidence of assent.'[95] In any event, most FOSS licences are not accepted via 'shrinkwrap' because FOSS software often does not come in a box package, but is instead downloaded online. The categories of 'clickwrap' and 'browsewrap' are more relevant to FOSS.

Zhu has remarked that 'clickwrap' licences 'require affirmative actions from licensees to manifest their acceptance.'[96] Typically, in the context of this kind of licence the user clicks a button to say 'Yes, I accept the license terms'. Kim has stated that since the user has notice of the terms and the ability to engage with them prior to acceptance, these types of licences are generally less controversial than 'shrinkwrap' licences.[97] Under a 'browsewrap' licence it is assumed that because a user has

[91] C Zhu, 'Authoring collaborative projects: a study of intellectual property and free and open source software (FOSS) licensing schemes from a relational contract perspective' (*LSE Theses Online*, PhD thesis, 2011) 148 <http://etheses.lse.ac.uk/294>. See also American Law Institute, s 24, Restatement (Second) of Contracts, which defines an offer as the 'manifestation of willingness to enter into a bargain so made as to justify another person in understanding that his assent to that bargain is invited and will conclude it', available at <http://www.lexinter.net/LOTWVers4/restatement_(second)_of_contracts.htm> both accessed 4 April 2013.

[92] In this sense 'all prospective licensees will be able to retrieve the software under the terms of the license'. Rosen (n 7) 60.

[93] Beatson (n 88) 37.

[94] *ProCD v Zeidenberg* 86 F 3d 1447 (7th Cir 1996). See also F Easterbrook, 'Copyright and Contract' (2005) 42(4) *Houston Law Review* 953.

[95] M Lemley, 'Terms of Use' (2006) 91 *Minnesota Law Review* 459, 468.

[96] Zhu (n 91) 153.

[97] NS Kim, 'Clicking and Cringing' (2007) 86 *Oregon Law Review* 797, 842–3. Zhu has also noted that some FOSS software licenses also attempt to manifest acceptance via mere use of the software, as is the case with the Google Chrome Browser—see n 92.

installed the software the user is effectively a 'licensee'; in other words, the user has agreed to the terms of the licence, which can usually be viewed or 'browsed' on a webpage. The key element appears to be that there must be prominent notice of the licence terms.[98] In this respect, GPLv3 section 5 requires that 'prominent notices' must be given by licensors/downstream distributor, something which potentially means that GPL code does not require the 'clickwrap' licence. The OSI also stipulates that 'non-clickwrap' licences are acceptable.[99] Nevertheless, from the point of view of 'acceptance' the 'browsewrap' licences are more difficult to comprehend, and courts may be less willing to enforce them.[100]

Consideration is the final major requirement for the formation of a valid contract. In *Currie v Misa*, Lush J stated that 'a valuable consideration, in the sense of the law, may consist in some right, interest, profit, or benefit accruing to the one party, or some forbearance, detriment, loss, or responsibility given, suffered, or undertaken by the other.'[101] Treitel has noted that 'an act, forbearance or promise' amounts to consideration only if the court recognises that it has some economic value, even if that value cannot be precisely quantified.[102] Chen-Wishart has remarked that consideration must of the 'right kind' under the law; in this context, 'non-monetary performance' which is of 'doubtful economic value' is difficult to assess.[103] Indeed, with regard to FOSS 'volunteer licensees' Zhu has remarked that their contributions are mostly non-monetary performances, eg, reporting bugs, testing submitted patches, and so forth; therefore, it is not clear whether these performances can have the right 'economic values' to qualify as consideration.[104] It also must be noted that the UK and US positions on consideration are not identical, something which adds another layer of complexity to these issues.[105]

Nonetheless, Wacha has taken the view that in the context of FOSS licences, including GPL, there is valid consideration in the form of 'reciprocal promises' undertaken between the licensor and licensee(s) which require the licensees to do a number of things, eg, to post requisite notices, to distribute the code under the

[98] See *Ticketmaster Corp v Tickets.com, Inc* 2003 US Dist LEXIS 6483 (C D Cal 2003) and *Specht v Netscape Communications Corp* 306 F.3d. 17 (2nd Cir 2002).

[99] OSI, 'Open Source Definition Criterion 10, Rationale' <http://opensource.org/osd-annotated> accessed 4 April 2013.

[100] It has been noted that browsewrap licenses are more frequently enforced against businesses, rather than individuals—Lemley (n 95) 459, 476.

[101] *Currie v Misa* (1975) L R 10 Ex 153, 162.

[102] G Treitel, *The Law of Contract*, 11th edn (London, Sweet and Maxwell, 2003) 83.

[103] M Chen-Wishart, *Contract Law*, 2nd edn (Oxford, Oxford University Press, 2008) 134.

[104] Zhu (n 91) 158.

[105] For an examination of the English notion of 'consideration' see Treitel (n 102) 67 and 83. For an examination of the US notion of 'consideration,' which consists of a performance or promise which is bargained for and given in exchange for promise, see American Law Institute, *Restatement (Second) of the Law of Contracts* (1981) s 71, available at <http://www.lexinter.net/LOTWVers4/restatement_(second)_of_contracts.htm> accessed 4 April 2013.

same terms, and so on, in return for making use of the FOSS software.[106] On the other hand, Kumar has argued that the adherence to the requirements of the FOSS licence cannot be consideration because this adherence does not 'directly benefit the licensor'.[107] Within this dichotomy, Zhu has pointed out that there are generally two types of FOSS licensee: one type of licensee is a mere consumer of the software, but the second type of licensee makes efforts to improve the FOSS software and often passes these changes on to the FOSS community.[108] In this view, the assessment of consideration may depend on the court's view of the licensee's use of the software.

3.7.2 Assessing the requirements of a bare licence in the FOSS context

A licence does not have to be a contract; it may be unilateral and thus, it will not require mutual assent. Such a licence is known as a 'bare licence'. As a legal concept it has its roots in land law in common law systems.[109] Moglen has remarked:

> The word 'license' has, and has had for hundreds of years, a specific technical meaning in the law of property. A license is a unilateral permission to use someone else's property. The traditional example given in the first year law school Property course is an invitation to come to dinner at my house. If, when you cross my threshold, I sue you for trespass, you plead my 'license,' that is, my unilateral permission to enter on and use my property.[110]

This is a more straightforward concept than a contract, as the requirements of offer, acceptance, and consideration are not present. As noted earlier, a bare licence is a unilateral permission to use the work in a manner that would otherwise infringe.[111]

The FSF claims that GPL is a unilateral bare licence, arguing that the GPL licensees are not required to 'accept' the licence:[112]

> The GPL, however, is a true copyright license: a unilateral permission, in which no obligations are reciprocally required by the licensor.[113]

[106] JB Wacha, 'Taking the Case: Is the GPL Enforceable' (2005) 21 *Santa Clara Computer and High Technology Law Journal* 451, 474.

[107] S Kumar, 'Enforcing the GNU GPL' (2006) *University of Illinois Journal of Law, Technology and Policy* 1, 19–21.

[108] Zhu (n 91) 159.

[109] IJ Dawson and RA Pearce, *Licenses Relating to the Occupation or Use of Land* (London, Butterworths, 1979) 1. See also *Thomas v Sorrell* (1673) Vaugh 330, 351.

[110] Moglen quote reported by P Jones, 'The GPL Is a License, not a Contract' (2003) <http://lwn.net/Articles/61292> accessed 4 April 2013.

[111] Rosen (n 7) 65–6.

[112] E Moglen and R Stallman, 'Transcript of Opening session of first international GPLv3 conference, January 16th 2006' (2006) <http://www.ifso.ie/documents/gplv3-launch-2006-01-16.html> accessed 4 April 2013.

[113] E Moglen, 'Free Software Matters: Enforcing the GPL' (2001) <http://emoglen.law.columbia.edu/publications/lu-12.pdf> accessed 4 April 2013. See also A Guadamuz, 'Viral contracts or unenforceable documents? Contractual validity of copyleft licences' (2004) 26 (8) *European Intellectual Property Review* 331.

Regarding the question of whether FOSS licences are bare licences, the following passage from GPLv2 is of note:

> [You] are not required to accept this License, since you have not signed it. However, nothing else grants you permission to modify or distribute the Program or its derivative works. These actions are prohibited by law if you do not accept this License. Therefore, by modifying or distributing the Program... you indicate your acceptance of this License to do so, and all its terms and conditions for copying, distributing or modifying the Program or works based on it.[114]

This passage is intended to lay down the concept that since exclusive rights cannot be exercised without the permission of the copyright owner, a licensee must either follow the terms of the licence, or not exercise the rights, as any other action amounts to copyright infringement. A similar provision can be found in GPLv3, section 9, which explicitly states that acceptance is not required for the licence to operate.[115] No acceptance of a bare licence is therefore required. As noted in 3.7.3, if a FOSS licence is found to be a bare licence rather than a contract this will have a number of legal consequences.

3.7.3 What are the consequences of a FOSS licence being held to be either a contract or a bare licence?

A number of consequences would arise from a finding that a FOSS licence is either a contract or a bare licence.[116] Regarding enforceability, if FOSS licences are held to be contracts the doctrine of privity of contract (which would not apply in the case of a bare licence) has significant implications. The traditional understanding of this doctrine refers to the 'contractual relationship' which exists between the parties to a contract.[117] This relationship allows them to take legal action against each other in the case that one party is dissatisfied with the enforcement of the contract. However, the nature of the contractual relationship is that it binds only the parties to it; as a general rule, a contract cannot confer rights or impose obligations arising under it on any person except the parties to it. For instance, in the FOSS context a third party who made use of the FOSS might not be bound by the contract. Nonetheless, it must be noted that for some time now the courts have taken a relaxed approach to this doctrine both

[114] GPLv2 s 5.

[115] GPLv3 s 9 states 'You are not required to accept this License in order to receive or run a copy of the Program' and '...nothing other than this License grants you permission to propagate or modify any covered work. These actions infringe copyright if you do not accept this License. Therefore, by modifying or propagating a covered work, you indicate your acceptance of this License to do so.'

[116] M Henley, '*Jacobsen v Katzer and Kamind Associates*—an English legal perspective' (2009) 1(1) *IFOSS L Rev* 41.

[117] The UK Law Commission, 'Privity of Contract: Contracts for the Benefit of Third Parties' (31 July 1996) <http://lawcommission.justice.gov.uk/docs/lc242_privity_of_contract_for_the_benefit_of_third_parties.pdf> accessed 4 April 2013.

in the US[118] and in the UK, which alleviates this concern to some extent.[119] If, on the other hand, the FOSS licence is held to be a bare licence then it would not be enforceable against the licensor, with the exception of estoppel, as discussed further later.

Henley has further argued that in the case of a contract courts tend to be willing to look beyond mere terminology; in fact, they often try to give effect to the intentions of the parties. The interpretation of terms is of great importance in this respect. In the absence of contract law, bare licences would be merely regulated by intellectual property law, which typically says very little on interpretation of licence terms. There is, therefore, some uncertainty about terms that are not consistent with consumer protection laws, eg, warranty disclaimers as limitations of liability. One major reason for the FSF's claim that a FOSS licence is a bare licence is that the FSF seeks to avoid the diversity of contract law in preference for the more uniform application of copyright law under Berne. In particular, it is notable that in the US copyright is largely a matter within the jurisdiction of the federal courts, whereas contract is much more within the various individual states' jurisdictions.[120] However, the interpretation of copyright law in various national jurisdictions is not as unitary as the FSF claims, particularly with regard to the concept of 'derivative work.' Furthermore, the different interpretations of contract law concepts in various national jurisdictions are not as divergent as the FSF claims. Moreover, the question of whether a FOSS licence is a contract or a bare licence is also significant because there is the possibility that national legislation will include specific provisions regulating contracts which will not automatically apply to bare licences.[121]

In addition, Henley has stated that unlike a contract a bare licence can be interpreted solely at the licensor's will—it is revocable.[122] In this respect, GPLv2 states:

> [A]ll rights granted under this License are granted for the term of copyright on the Program, and are irrevocable provided the stated conditions are met...

However, unless this term is part of a contract, this statement is merely a promise. As such, it may be revoked by the licensor at will. In this regard, Zhu has argued that the

[118] See *Lawrence v Fox* 20 N Y 268 (1959) and *Burr v Beers* 24 N Y 178 (1861), which refer to an 'Intent to Benefit Test' which suggests that a third party ought to be able to enforce a contract if the parties intended to benefit such a party.

[119] For the UK, see Contracts (Rights of Third Parties) Act 1999. See also New Zealand legislation—the Contracts (Privity) Act 1982.

[120] See, eg, the recent case of *MDY Industries, LLC v Blizzard Entertainment, Inc and Vivendi Games, Inc*, 629 F 3d 928 (9th Cir 2010) and the discussion on point by RW Gomulkiewicz, 'Enforcement of Open Source Software Licenses: The MDY Trio's Inconvenient Complications' (2011) 14 *Yale J L & Tech* 106.

[121] See examples in the UK—Sale of Goods Act 1979, applying to contracts of sale of goods; Supply of Goods and Services Act 1982, applying to contracts; and the Unfair Contract Terms Act 1977, which also governs contracts.

[122] *Microsystems Software, Inc v Scandinavia Online* AB, 98 F. Supp. 2d 74 (D Mass, 2000), aff'd, 226 F.3d 35 (1st Cir 2000). See also D McGowan, 'Legal Implications of Open-source Software' (2001) 1 *University of Illinois Law Review* 241, 302, fn 283 at 302.

equitable doctrine of estoppel could empower a licensee to stop the full revocation of the licence from taking place.[123] Promissory estoppel would work in this context where there is 'detrimental reliance' on the part of the licensee.[124]

It is also notable that the applicable governing law may differ in each case. For instance, under UK law 'the governing law for a contract dispute is determined by the Rome Convention on the Law Applicable to Contractual Obligations.'[125] In the case of non-contractual obligations it will be decided 'by the Rome II Regulation or another statute of Private International Law.'[126] In fact, it is logical to conclude that different laws apply to contractual disputes and disputes over bare licences. In addition as stated earlier, the FSF seeks to avoid the diversity of contract law in preference for what it sees as the more uniform application of copyright under federal law in the US, whereas contract is generally said to come within the various individual states' jurisdictions.[127] However, as noted earlier, the extent to which copyright is interpreted in a uniform fashion tends to be overstated by the FSF.

As will be assessed, there are also different remedies which are applicable in each case. In the context of breach of contract, the unique doctrines of part performance and specific performance are potentially available.[128] Generally, in the common law arena of contract damages are the usual remedy, but are limited to those within the 'contemplation of the parties.'[129] Similarly damages are the usual remedy for breach of contract in many European civil law jurisdictions. In France, the amount of damages is allocated depending on the importance of the breach and its consequences.[130] In Germany, in a case of a breach of contract, or a breach of any obligation set forth under the contract, the main remedies/methods of compensation are damages or termination of the contract, or a mixture of both.[131]

[123] Denning MR in *Moorgate Mercantile Co Ltd v Twitchings* [1976] 1 QB 225, CA, 241. See also *Central London Property Trust Ltd v High Trees House Ltd* [1947] KB 130.

[124] E Cooke, *The Modern Law of Estoppel* (Oxford, Oxford University Press, 2000) 105. See C Patterson, 'Copyright Misuse and Modified Copyleft: New Solutions to the Challenges of Internet Standardization,' (2000) 98 *Michigan Law Review* 1351.

[125] Henley (n 116) 41–4. [126] Henley (n 116) 41–4. [127] Zhu (n 91) 161–3.

[128] Where a claimant partly performs their contractual obligations under the expectation the defendant will perform its obligations, a court may order specific performance. An order for specific performance is an equitable remedy to compel actual performance of contractual obligations.

[129] *Hadley v Baxendale* [1854] EWHC J70.

[130] Article 1142 of Civil Code (*Code Civil)*: Any obligation to do or not to do resolves itself into damages, in case of non-performance on the part of the debtor, available at <http://www.legifrance.gouv.fr/affichCodeArticle.do?cidTexte=LEGITEXT000006070721&idArticle=LEGIARTI000006436337&dateTexte=20130222> accessed 4 April 2013. See also Articles 1142 and 1589 of Civil Code (*Code Civil)*.

[131] Section 280 *et seq* of Civil Law Code (*Bürgerliches Gesetzbuch*), available at <http://www.gesetze-im-internet.de/englisch_bgb/englisch_bgb.html#p0828> accessed 4 April 2013. The termination of a contract depends on the sort of contract and how the contract was breached, s 346 *et seq* of Civil Law Code (*Bürgerliches Gesetzbuch*).

Finding a mechanism for calculating appropriate damages in the case of FOSS is not straightforward.[132] Regarding attorney fees and legal costs, in the US these are usually only recoverable if expressly provided for within the contract. In the UK and most European systems, such as the German one, there is a loser pays costs system, whereby the loser pays not only his own costs but the costs, or the majority of the costs, of the winner as well.[133]

Furthermore, if FOSS licences are bare licences a licensor cannot restrict activities that do not amount to copyright infringement such as dynamic linking.[134] This is important because in the context of copyright, injunctions can only be granted to prevent infringing distribution. In common law jurisdictions, injunctions are generally available as a remedy in copyright law, but it is usually difficult, though not impossible, to get an injunction for breach of contract.[135] In European jurisdictions there may also be a difference in remedies available with respect to contract and copyright. To take the example of Spain, in a case of copyright infringement the available remedies are cessation, damages, and the granting of an injunction.[136] In a case of breach of contract, the norm is to either enforce performance, or claim termination of the relevant obligation, and to claim damages.[137]

With respect to damages, in the UK both tortious damages, in the form of reasonable compensation, and statutory damages are potentially available in the copyright context.[138] Other potential remedies include an account of profits and 'delivery up.'[139] Additionally, criminal remedies often exist for commercial scale copyright infringement, while these generally do not exist with respect to breach of contract.

With regard to remedies, one other thing is of significance: in the field of copyright only copyright owners have the ability to enforce these rights in court. This could prove to be problematic in the FOSS context. As noted earlier, FOSS software typically involves numerous contributors, who are not sole copyright owners of every right

[132] Typically, there are two ways to calculate expectation loss—a 'cost of cure' analysis and—a 'difference in value' analysis, neither of which seem to suit the FOSS context.

[133] M Gryphon, 'Assessing the Effects of A "Loser Pays" Rule on the American Legal System: An Economic Analysis and Proposal for Reform' (2011) 8 *Rutgers Journal of Law & Public Policy* 567.

[134] eg, 'strong copyleft' licences, such as GPLv2 and GPLv3, include clauses restricting dynamic linking and derivative works.

[135] See for instance *Warner Brothers v Nelson* [1937] 1 KB 209 and *Page One Records v Britton* [1968] 1 WLR 157.

[136] WIPO, 'Consolidated text of the Law on Intellectual Property, regularizing, clarifying and harmonizing the Applicable Statutory Provisions (approved by Royal Legislative Decree No. 1/1996 of April 12, 1996, and last amended by Royal Decree No. 20/2011 of December 30, 2011)' Articles 138–141 <http://www.wipo.int/wipolex/en/details.jsp?id=11050> accessed 4 April 2013.

[137] Article 1124 of the Civil Code (*Código Civil*) <http://www.wipo.int/wipolex/en/text.jsp?file_id=221319> accessed 4 April 2013.

[138] CDPA 1988, s 97(2).

[139] Directive 2004/48/EC of the European Parliament and of the Council of 29 April 2004 on the enforcement of intellectual property rights, available at <http://eur-lex.europa.eu/LexUriServ/LexUriServ.do?uri=CELEX:32004L0048R(01):EN:HTML> accessed 4 April 2013.

which exists in the work, but instead own only a part of the copyright. It may prove to be difficult both to identify and to distinguish between the owner and the distributor without imposing large costs on potential users and developers.

3.7.4 Legal enforceability of FOSS licences—enforcement in the US and Europe

It is likely that the enforceability of FOSS licences, including the question of whether a FOSS licence is a bare licence or a contract, will be jurisdiction-dependent. Regarding the US jurisdiction, the case of *Jacobsen v Katzer* is of significance to the enforcement of FOSS licences.[140]

The *Jacobsen* case hinged upon the meaning of a term of the *Artistic License* (AL).[141] Jacobsen devised software for controlling model trains and he released the software under the AL. A key obligation of the licence is that when distributing the work, the user must include attribution notices, and identify any modifications. Katzer, the defendant, had failed to provide attribution or give identification of modifications. This key term fell to be considered by the courts.

Henley has remarked that the issue turned on whether the provision breached was 'a condition of the licence, or a mere covenant.'[142] In other words, the case hinged upon whether the crucial term of the AL would be interpreted by the court as amounting to either a condition of the contract or as a mere covenant. In the District Court the court stated that the licence included both contractual covenants and copyright conditions:

> [T]he condition that the user insert[s] a prominent notice of attribution does not limit the scope of the license.

Thus, according to the District Court, violation of the AL's terms constituted a breach of contract, rather than copyright infringement. This decision affected the type of relief available to Jacobsen. Typically, injunctive relief, which is available in the context of copyright infringement, is unlikely to be available for breach of contract.

Nevertheless, the Court of Appeals for the Ninth Circuit overruled the District Court's ruling.[143] The court found that Katzer's obligations did amount to conditions

[140] *Jacobsen v Katzer*, 2007 WL 2358628 (N D Cal 2007); Pre-Jacobsen US cases include—*Progress Software Corporation v MySQL* AB, 195 F Supp 2d. 328, 239 (D Mass 2001); Complaint, *Drew Technologies, Inc v Society of Auto Engineers, Inc*, No 2:03-CV-74535 (DT), 2003 WL 238562505; *Planetary Motion, Inc v Techplosion, Inc* 261 F.3d. 1188 (11th Cir 2001); *Computer Associates International v Quest Software, Inc*, 333 F Supp 2d 688, 697–8 (ND III, 2004). See also the various cases taken by the Software Freedom Law Center assessed in detail by H Meeker, 'Open Source and the Age of Enforcement' (2012) 4(2) *Hastings Science and Technology Journal* 267, 271–4.

[141] Open Source Initiative, 'Artistic Licenses' <http://opensource.org/licenses/artistic-license> accessed 4 April 2013.

[142] Henley (n 116) 41–4.

[143] *Jacobsen v Katzer*, 535 F.3d 1373 (Fed Cir 2008).

limiting the scope of the licence; these were not independent contractual covenants. With respect to the key contract question of consideration, the court stated:

> The choice to exact consideration in the form of compliance with the open source requirements of disclosure and explanation of changes, rather than as a dollar-denominated fee, is entitled to no less legal recognition.

Thus, the court found that the licence was of a 'hybrid' nature, which did include enforceable copyright conditions. Katzer's actions had gone beyond the scope of the licence by failing to comply with these conditions. Therefore, an action for copyright infringement could legitimately be brought by the licensor and the appropriate remedies could be sought.[144]

The *Jacobsen* case was undoubtedly an important one for the enforceability of FOSS licences.[145] By finding that the term was a contractually enforceable condition of the contract, the court confirmed that such licences can be legally binding and enforceable in the US jurisdiction. A significant post-*Jacobsen* case, although it does not directly concern FOSS licences, is *MDY v Blizzard*.[146] In this case, the Ninth Circuit stated that a term prohibiting the use of 'bots' was a covenant, not a condition. Crucially, in making this decision it cited relevant state law, whereas in the *Jacobsen* decision the court did not defer to state law.[147] Gomulkiewicz has remarked that the effect of this case may lead to 'inconvenient complications' arising in the future with regard to FOSS licences.[148] In particular, he has argued that the method of delineating between contractual covenants and licence conditions laid down in *MDY* may make it more difficult for open source licensors to obtain injunctive relief. Nonetheless, the overall picture for FOSS enforceability in the US jurisdiction is a positive one.

Indeed, in light of this analysis of *Jacobsen* it is worth considering whether the major licences explored over the course of this chapter, Apache 2.0, BSD, MIT, MPL, LGPL, GPLv2, and GPLv3, are likely to be interpreted as contracts or bare licences under *Jacobsen*. Menon has argued that the terms of GPLv2 are likely to be interpreted as conditions because they use the appropriate language, including conditional phrases

[144] The case eventually reached a court settlement on 19 February 2010. Katzer agreed to pay Jacobsen $100,000. Katzer also accepted a permanent injunction against his copying or modifying the relevant software; settlement reported at <http://yro.slashdot.org/story/10/02/19/1614216/jacobsen-v-katzer-settled-victory-for-foss> accessed 4 April 2013.

[145] C Zhu, '"Copyleft" Reconsidered: Why Software Licensing Jurisprudence Needs Insights from Relational Contract Theory' (forthcoming, 2013) *Social & Legal Studies* (draft copy on file with author) has nonetheless argued that the *Jacobsen* ruling does not radically deviate from the still dominant neo-classical software licensing jurisprudence since the *ProCD* ruling.

[146] *MDY Industries, LLC v Blizzard Entertainment, Inc and Vivendi Games, Inc*, 629 F.3d 928 (9th Cir 2010).

[147] H Meeker, 'Open Source and the Age of Enforcement' (2012) 4(2) *Hastings Science and Technology Journal* 267, 286.

[148] RW Gomulkiewicz, 'Enforcement of Open Source Software Licenses: The MDY Trio's Inconvenient Complications' (2011) 14 *Yale J L & Tech* 106.

such as 'provided that'.[149] This would expose the user to copyright liability. The same can be said with respect to other GNU licences such as LGPL and GPLv3, which also use conditional terminology.[150] Apache 2.0 uses traditional contractual language, subjecting use to terms and conditions. As such, its provisions can largely be considered to be conditions, and the same can be said for the BSD and MIT licences.[151] Moreover, MPL uses terms more traditionally associated with covenants rather than conditions, such as 'must do' and 'curing the breach', and features a termination clause which is undoubtedly conditional.[152]

Nevertheless, Goss has remarked that since FOSS licences depend on contract law for enforcement, this may present challenges for courts, particularly since contractual issues may vary from jurisdiction to jurisdiction. In other words, even though a FOSS licence could be enforceable in the US jurisdiction, in another jurisdiction the interpretation of the law may well be different.

As yet, there is no UK case concerning the validity of FOSS licences. Despite this, it has been argued that if a case similar to *Jacobsen v Katzer* were to come before the courts in the UK jurisdiction, a different conclusion would be reached on whether a contract exists between the licensor and licensee.[153] For instance, Shemtov has argued that in line with *Currie v Misa*[154] UK courts may not find a binding contract to have been formed due to the lack of consideration.[155] On this point Henley has remarked that the courts of England and Wales would likely consider the AL to be a bare licence rather than a contract.[156] Moreover, with respect to the condition/covenant distinction, which was of crucial importance under US law in *Jacobsen v Katzer*, it must be stated that many European jurisdictions including France, Germany, and Italy do not feature this same condition/covenant distinction.[157] Nevertheless, a number of courts in civil law jurisdictions such as Germany and France have accepted that such licences are legally valid.[158] For instance,

[149] Y Menon, 'Jacobsen Revisited: Conditions, Covenants and the Future of Open-Source Software Licenses' (2011) 6(4) *Washington Journal of Law, Technology and the Arts* 311, 336–8.

[150] Menon (n 149) 338–40. However, Menon has further noted that GPLv3 also includes other terms, such as the DRM clause, which may not be considered to be conditions by a court.

[151] Menon (n 149) 343–7. [152] Menon (n 149) 347–9. [153] Henley (n 116) 41–4.

[154] (1975) L R 10 Ex 153.

[155] N Shemtov, 'FOSS License: Bare License or Contract', presentation available at <http://web.ua.es/es/contratos-id/documentos/itipupdate2011/shemtov.pdf> accessed 4 April 2013.

[156] Henley (n 116) 41–4.

[157] Regarding the relevant French legal terms 'obligation', 'conditions precedent', and 'conditions subsequent', see Articles 1168, 1181 and 1182 of the French Civil Code. In Germany, parties to an agreement may draft a contract based on s 311 and s 241 Civil Law Code, while 'conditions' are regulated by virtue of s 158 *et seq* German Civil Law Code. Under Italian contract law the relevant definitions of 'conditions' are set forth in s 1353 of Italian Civil Code.

[158] German cases include *Welte v Sitecom Deutschland GmbH* District Court of Munich, 19 May 2004, case 21 O 6123/04; *Welte v Skype Technologies S A* District Court of Munich, 12 July 2007, case 7 O 5245/07. The major French case is *EDU 4 v AFPA*, Cour d'Appel de Paris, Pole 5, Chambre 10, no: 294. Many European cases have been taken by Harald Welte, founder of http://www.gpl-violations.org. Welte has a case pending against Iliad, a French telecom company, over the failure to disclose source code with regard to 'Freebox' a DSL technology which extensively uses GPL-licensed software; details available at <http://gpl-violations.org/links.html> both accessed 4 April 2013.

the German case of *Welte v Sitecom Deutschland GmbH* is of significance due to the fact that the Munich District Court held that failing to comply with GPL licence terms could constitute both a breach of contract and copyright infringement.[159] This is in line with *Jacobsen v Katzer*. In France, the case of *EDU v AFPA*, also known as the 'Paris GPL case', is of significance because the court seemed to accept that a violation of GPL terms could bring copyright infringement considerations into play.[160]

To some extent the fact that civil law jurisdictions have so far found FOSS licences to be valid and enforceable ought to come as no surprise. Civil law jurisdictions typically consider licence agreements, including FOSS licences, to be enforceable contracts because consideration is generally not a formal requirement of contract formation.[161] Moreover, it seems less likely that a FOSS licence could be considered as akin to a bare licence, since, as noted earlier, this is a concept which has its roots in land law in common law jurisdictions.

Ultimately, Shemtov has remarked that FOSS licences in civil law jurisdictions appear to have a 'dual nature'; indeed, where relevant either, or both, contract law and copyright law may provide remedies.[162] In light of the above analysis, it seems that the terms of FOSS licences are valid and enforceable conditions. Nonetheless, case law in all jurisdictions is still in its infancy, which means the above assessment of the enforceability of FOSS licences must be greeted with a degree of caution.

3.8 EXAMINING LICENCE COMPATIBILITY

It has been argued that open source licences are now overly diverse, and that this diversity could lead to legal complications.[163] For instance, the proliferation of different licences that are potentially available to programmers may make it difficult for later users/contributors/distributors to comprehend which uses are acceptable and legal.[164] For this reason, the Open Source Initiative has tried to curb the enactment of new licences, and some obsolete and poorly designed licences have effectively been 'retired' from use. Nevertheless, it has been argued that these efforts have

[159] Jaeger (n 17). It was also noted in this case that GPL licensors can rely on Directive 2004/48/EC of the European Parliament and of the Council of 29 April 2004 on the enforcement of intellectual property rights, available at <http://eur-lex.europa.eu/LexUriServ/LexUriServ.do?uri=OJ:L:2004:195:0016:0025:en:PDF> accessed 4 April 2013.

[160] M von Willebrand, 'Case law report: A look at EDU 4 v AFPA, also known as the "Paris GPL case"' (2009) 1(2) *IFOSSLR* 123.

[161] A Guadamuz-Gonzalez, 'The License/Contract Dichotomy in Open Licenses: A Comparative Analysis' (2009) 30(2) *University of La Verne Law Review* 296, 302–4. See also H MacQueen and JM Thomson, *Contract Law in Scotland*, 2nd edn (Edinburgh, Tottel Publishing, 2007) 54–6.

[162] Shemtov (n 156).

[163] L Guibault and O van Daalen, *Unravelling the Myth around Open Source Licenses: An Analysis from a Dutch and European Law Perspective* (The Netherlands, TMC Asser Press, 2006) 4.

[164] RW Gomulkiewicz, 'Open Source License Proliferation: Helpful Diversity or Hopeless Confusion?' (2009) 30 *Washington University Journal of Law and Policy* 261, 261–3.

largely failed to prevent the negative aspects of proliferation from taking place.[165] On the issue of proliferation, it has been argued that represents both 'helpful diversity' and 'hopeless confusion'.[166] In other words, it is unfortunate that confusion often results from licence proliferation, but there may be no other way to satisfy the diverse licensing needs of the software programmers. On other hand, the majority of software programs are released via one of the popular licences examined over the course of this chapter, which to some extent mitigates the proliferation problem.

The assessment undertaken in this section discusses compatibility in terms of 'one way compatibility' and 'two way compatibility'. In considering two licences, one way compatibility refers to the situation that exists when material which works under licence A can be taken, modified, and licensed under licence B, but material under licence B cannot be taken, modified, and incorporated under licence A. In other words, the licences are compatible in one direction only. Typically, licence A is a 'no copyleft' licence and licence B is a 'weak copyleft' or a 'strong copyleft' licence. Two way compatibility implies some degree of reflexive/reciprocal compatibility, such as via licensing or via linked works.

There is also an important jurisdictional concern which arises here. As noted earlier, the term 'derivative work' has a meaning under US law,[167] but it is a contestable concept in other jurisdictions such as those in Europe.[168] The jurisdictional interpretation of the boundaries of a derivative work, or a work featuring modifications, will be of great significance. Indeed, the question of whether dynamic and/or static linking creates a derivative work could be answered differently in the various jurisdictions of the US and Europe. Furthermore, as already described, the notion of 'distribution' may not have a uniform meaning. The notions of distribution discussed here are in line with those discussed in section 1 of this chapter: making available, centralized distribution, distribution of non-derivative works, and distribution of derivative works.

3.8.1 Compatibility between the 'no copyleft' licences—Apache 2.0, BSD, and MIT

Few complications arise with respect to compatibility between the 'no copyleft' licences; indeed, it is the permissive nature of the licences which allows broad compatibility. Copying and linking are broadly permitted by all three licences examined here, with only minimal requirements. As noted earlier, the most popular 'no copyleft' licence is Apache 2.0. It is broadly two way compatible with BSD. In other words, Apache and BSD material can be incorporated under either licence. With respect to two way compatibility between Apache 2.0 and MIT, Apache, and MIT materials can

[165] Gomulkiewicz (n 164) 291.
[166] Gomulkiewicz (n 164) 291.
[167] See further ch 1, at 1.4.3.
[168] Jaeger (n 17).

be incorporated under either licence. Similarly, BSD is two way compatible with MIT; in other words, BSD and MIT materials can be incorporated under either licence.

3.8.2 Compatibility between the 'weak copyleft' licences—MPL and LGPL

With respect to compatibility, the weak copyleft licences tend to have limited two way compatibility. A weak copyleft licence typically stipulates that derivative content must be licensed under that same licence. However, these restrictions tend to not be applied in the context of 'linked' works. Therefore, these licences generally allow and encourage linking.

In line with this, MPL has two way limited compatibility with LGPL. In this respect, there is no compatibility regarding derivative works: these must be licensed under either MPL or LGPL. However, linking is permitted by both LGPL and MPL which means that in the context of 'non-derivative works' the licences are compatible. Furthermore, clause 13 of MPL concerns choices made by the 'initial developer', whereby the latter can designate portions of the covered code as 'multi-licensed'. It appears to be the case that if you follow 'Exhibit A' in the MPL (as referred to by clause 13), you may enable third parties to utilize parts of the code that you released under MPL under other licences of your choice. Therefore, clause 13 allows alternative use of LGPL/GPL in limited circumstances.

3.8.3 Compatibility between the 'strong copyleft' Licences—GPLv2 and GPLv3

There are compatibility problems between the strong copyleft licences.[169] Under the strict terms of these licences, there is little that can be done with the material that apparently causes the copyleft clauses to come into effect. In this respect, GPLv2 is generally thought to be incompatible with GPLv3.[170] Nonetheless, v2 envisages use via the terms of later versions of the GPL. Therefore, there is a possibility that v2 code may be used under GPLv3 in those circumstances.

3.8.4 Compatibility between the 'no copyleft' licences and the 'weak copyleft' licences

With regard to compatibility between the 'no copyleft' licences and the 'weak copyleft' licences there is one way compatibility between the licences. In this sense, derivative 'no copyleft' material can be incorporated under the 'weak copyleft' licence, but not vice

[169] GNU, 'GPL-Compatible Free Software Licenses' <http://www.gnu.org/licenses/license-list.html#GPLCompatibleLicenses> accessed 4 April 2013.

[170] GNU 'FAQ' (n 79).

versa; nevertheless, it must be noted that there are typically some exceptions allowing limited two way compatibility between the licences for 'linked' works, as will be discussed.

Apache 2.0 is one way compatible with MPL; MPL requires that derivative content be licensed under MPL. In other words, Apache-derived material can be incorporated under MPL, but not vice versa. However, under MPL clause 13 if the programmer follows 'Exhibit A' in the MPL (as referred to by clause 13) he or she may enable third parties to utilise parts of the code that were released under MPL under other licences of choice. Therefore, MPL clause 13 allows alternative use of Apache 2.0 in limited circumstances, and thus, there is some two way compatibility between the licences. As with MPL, Apache 2.0 is generally one way compatible with LGPL in that LGPL requires derivative content to be licensed under MPL.[171] Therefore, Apache-derived works can be incorporated under LGPL, but not vice versa. As with MPL, there is also the possibility of two way compatibility via linking, software that links to LGPL library is not considered a derivative work (clause 5).

BSD is one way compatible with MPL; MPL requires that derived content be licensed under MPL. BSD material can be incorporated under MPL but not vice versa (unless specifically indicated under MPL clause 13). Similarly, BSD is one way compatible with LGPL; BSD material can be incorporated under a LGPL but not vice versa since LGPL requires that content be licensed under GPL or LGPL (clause 2).

MIT is one way compatible with MPL; MIT-derived works can be incorporated under MPL, not vice versa, unless specifically indicated under MPL clause 13. Derivative works must be licensed under MPL. MIT is one way compatible with LGPL. In other words, MIT-derived works can be incorporated under LGPL, not vice versa.

3.8.5 Compatibility between the 'no copyleft' licences and the 'strong copyleft' licences

There is clear one way compatibility between the 'no copyleft' licences and the 'strong copyleft' licences. The terms of the strict 'strong copyleft' licences mean that 'no copyleft' content can be integrated under a 'strong copyleft' licence, but this does not work the other way around because the 'strong copyleft' licence requirements do not allow this. Moreover, as outlined earlier, the 'strong copyleft' licences typically try to catch any 'linked' material within the terms of the licence.

Regarding GPLv2, Apache 2.0 has one way compatibility with the licence. In other words, Apache material can be incorporated under GPLv2 but not vice versa. Linking is broadly permitted by Apache (clause 2) but GPLv2 requires that derivative works must be licensed under GPL. However, since GPLv2 refers to 'derivative works' it is likely that anything which is outside the definition of a 'derivative work' will not be affected. In addition, with respect to the contract/bare licence debate

[171] Derivative content must be licensed under GNU GPL or GNU LGPL, clause 2.

already discussed, in a jurisdiction where a FOSS licence is considered to be a bare licence rather than a contract, it may not be possible legally to impose these types of obligations on downstream users.

The FSF claims that GPLv2 is not compatible with Apache because the patent retaliation clause and the indemnity clause could be seen as 'further restrictions'.[172] Nonetheless, Lovejoy has noted that this interpretation is not accepted by the ASF, which argues that the terms are in line with GPLv2.[173] Furthermore, given the 'no copyleft' nature of Apache 2.0 it is possible that a court would take this permissive nature into account when determining compatibility; indeed, it seems unlikely that the court would take a restrictive view of the Apache 2.0 requirements.

BSD licences have one way compatibility with GPLv2. As before, BSD material can be incorporated under GPLv2 but not vice versa. Copying and linking are broadly permitted by BSD, but GPL requires that derivative works be licensed under GPL. However, since GPLv2 refers to 'derivative works' anything which is outside the law's definition of a 'derivative work' will likely not be affected. As noted earlier, in a jurisdiction where such a licence is considered to be a bare licence rather than a contract, it is not possible legally to impose these types of obligations on downstream users. Further to this, MIT also has one way compatibility with GPLv2; MIT-derived works can be incorporated under GPL, but not vice versa. As detailed earlier, any derivative GPLv2 content must be GNU GPL licensed (clause 2).

Regarding GPLv3, Apache 2.0 has one way compatibility with the licence; Apache material can be incorporated under GPLv3 but not vice versa. Copying and linking are broadly permitted by Apache (clause 2) but GPLv3 requires that 'derivative' content must be licensed under GPLv3 (clause 5). Similarly, BSD is one way compatible with GPLv3; BSD material can be incorporated under GPLv3 but not vice versa. Linking is permitted by BSD, but GPLv3 requires that content must be licensed under GPLv3 (clause 5).

Finally, MIT has one way compatibility with GPLv3; MIT material can be incorporated under GPLv3, but not vice versa. Copying and linking are broadly permitted by MIT, but GPLv3 requires that content must be licensed under GPLv3 (clause 5).

3.8.6 Compatibility between the 'weak copyleft' licences and the 'strong copyleft' licences

Generally 'weak copyleft' licences have one way limited compatibility with 'strong copyleft' licences with respect to non-derivative 'linked' content, rather than 'derivative' content.

[172] GNU, 'GPL-Incompatible Free Software Licenses' <http://www.gnu.org/licenses/license-list.html#GPLIncompatibleLicenses> accessed 4 April 2013.

[173] J Lovejoy, 'Understanding the Three Most Common Open Source Licenses' (*Open Logic*) <http://www.openlogic.com/resources-library/webinar-understanding-the-most-common-oss-licenses> accessed 4 April 2013.

In this vein, MPL has one way limited compatibility with GPLv2. Under clause 13 of MPL, a GPL can be used alongside MPL code if specifically indicated under MPL clause 13, as will be described. However, GPL does not have a similar provision. Copying and linking are permitted by both licences but both licences have restrictive clauses with respect to modified or 'derivative' works: such works must be licensed under MPL or GPL. Moreover, since GPLv2 refers to 'derivative works' it is likely that anything which is outside the definition of a 'derivative work' will not be affected. Regarding clause 13 MPL, it is notable that it is first and foremost about choices made by the 'initial developer', where the latter can designate portions of the covered code as 'multi-licensed'. It seems that if a person follows 'Exhibit A' in the MPL (as referred to by clause 13) that person may enable third parties to utilise parts of the code that were released under MPL under other licences. Thus, clause 13 allows alternative use of GPL in limited circumstances. Similarly, LGPLv2 has one-way compatibility with GPLv2; LGPL-derived material can be licensed under GPL. It is notable, however, that software that links to LGPL library is not considered to be a derivative work (clause 5). Therefore, there is also some two way limited compatibility with regard to GPL works linking to the LGPL library.

MPL has one way limited compatibility with GPLv3. Copying and linking are permitted by both licences but derivative works must be licensed under either MPL or GPL as is relevant. As before, since GPLv3 refers to 'derivative works', anything which is outside the definition of a 'derivative' work will not be affected. As noted earlier, under MPL clause 13 GPL can be utilized in certain limited circumstances; clause 13 MPL is primarily concerned with choices made by the 'initial developer', whereby the latter can designate portions of the covered code as 'multi-licensed'. According to the licence, if you follow 'Exhibit A' as described in MPL clause 13 you may enable third parties to utilize parts of the code that you released under MPL under other licences of your choice. Therefore, MPL clause 13 allows alternative use of GPLv3 in limited circumstances. Nonetheless, as stated earlier, there is no compatibility for derivative works. LGPL has two way compatibility via linking with GPLv3. Copying and linking are allowed by both LGPL and GPLv3. Moreover, LGPL clause 5 states that software that links to the library is not considered a derivative work, so this must be borne in mind. Derivative content must be licensed under GNU LGPL/GPLv3 (clause 2).

3.9 CONCLUSION

This chapter has outlined and compared the terms of the various types of FOSS licences: 'no copyleft', 'weak copyleft', and 'strong copyleft'. The possible effects of the contract/bare licence debate have also been explored, along with the relevant compatibility issues. Ultimately, it is clear that while there are challenges to the legality of FOSS licences, these challenges are not insurmountable. The diversity of licences does create legal complexities with respect to compatibility, but given the diverse nature of FOSS programmers, a certain amount of proliferation of different FOSS licences seems inevitable.

On this point, one element in particular warrants further reflection; so far there is a relative paucity of FOSS case law concerning the issues discussed in this chapter. Given the widespread adoption of FOSS it is surprising that there are no cases on enforcement in the UK, and few in other jurisdictions such as the US, France, or Germany. This in itself implies that open source programmers and users, even commercial ones, are not getting tied up in costly and time-consuming legal actions. Furthermore, there may be a number of reasons for the lack of cases. For example, it may be that disputes do arise, but they are largely of a minor nature and can be easily rectified before a court hearing is required. It may also be the case that many licences are actually breached in practice, but these breaches simply go unnoticed by FOSS licensors. The underlying DIY ethos of FOSS may also have a role to play. Nonetheless, it stands to reason that given the diversity and complexity outlined here, 'hard cases' will inevitably come up in the future, and these in turn may alter the FOSS legal landscape. In particular, given the fact that FOSS thrives online in a global environment, if jurisdictional legal differences kick in over the next few years, this may have a detrimental effect on the continued 'viral' spread of FOSS globally.

Overall, there is much work yet to be done to bring clarity to the crucial enforceability and compatibility issues outlined in this chapter. All the parties involved, the FOSS developers, individual FOSS users, and businesses which make use of FOSS, need guidance as to the legal ramifications of their actions. The recent EU 'Joinup' initiative, which maps licence compatibility issues, is one such helpful guide; this chapter provides another.[174]

ANNEX I—KEY OF LICENCE ABBREVIATIONS USED IN FOOTNOTES

A acknowledgment must be included in any redistribution.

Ca if the program is interactive and such announcements are customary for similar kind of programs, copyright notice must be displayed or printed at each time the program commences operation or at the request of the user, depending on custom practice related to the kind of programs in question.

[174] <http://joinup.ec.europa.eu/software/page/licence_compatibility_and_interoperability%20>.

C? copyright notice must be included (but no explicit obligation to include permission notice in the source code, object code, or documentation).

Cu copyright notice must remain unchanged as included in the original package (but no explicit obligation to include copyright notices in the source code, object code, or documentation).

Cus copyright notice must retained in the source code as included in the original source code.

Cs copyright notice must appear in all copies of the source code (but not necessarily in the documentation).

C copyright notice must appear in all copies of the source code and in the documentation (but no obligation to provide any supporting documentation with the binary code).

C+ copyright notice must appear in all copies of the source code and in the documentation that must be provided with the binary code (but not necessarily in the binary code).

Cc+ copyright notice must appear in all copies of the code, but no obligation to include it in the documentation.

C++ copyright notice must appear in all copies and in supporting documentation.

PN? permission notice (licence text) must be included (but no explicit obligation to include permission notice in the source code, object code or documentation).

Pnu permission notice (licence text) must remain unchanged as included in the original package (but no explicit obligation to include copyright notices in the source code, object code, or documentation).

PNus permission notice must retained in the source code as included in the original source code.

PN permission notice (licence text) must appear in all copies of the source code.

PND permission notice (licence text) must appear in supporting documentation.

PN+ permission notice (licence text) must appear in all copies of the source code and in the documentation (but not necessarily in the binary code).

PNc+ permission notice (licence text) must appear in all copies of the code, but no obligation to include it in the documentation.

PN++ permission notice (licence text) must appear in all copies and in supporting documentation.

NA name of the copyright holder and/or of the organization which created the license may not be used in advertising without prior permission.

NC name of the original program cannot be changed.

NP name of the original program cannot be used in connection with any derived programs.

AM altered versions must be plainly marked as such.

ASC access to the source code must be provided to each recipient of the Work.

AWP access to the modified work must be provided to the public.

CL copyleft clause, conditions are described. If CL appears with the name(s) of specific licences it means that modifications must be licensed exclusively under this licence or those licences. Mere obligation to include original permission notice or licence text is *not* considered as copyleft clause for purpose of this definition.

F cannot be sold, must be distributed for free.

4

TRADE MARKS AND FOSS

Noam Shemtov

4.1 INTRODUCTION

It is safe to state that in the pecking order of intellectual property rights in the context of the FOSS legal ecosystem, it is trade marks that have traditionally attracted less attention and discussion in comparison to copyrights and patents. This position, however, is changing. As this chapter will illustrate, trade mark rights present a distinct set of challenges to the FOSS model, and must be taken into consideration by actors in the FOSS community, whether as licensees or licensors.

Although trade mark law may come into play in the FOSS context in a manner that is no different than other industries, there are a number of particular areas of friction that this chapter will seek to highlight and explore. These can be traced to the unique sharing culture in FOSS communities, which might view trade mark enforcement policies by some of its members unfavourably.

This chapter is divided into four substantive parts. It first seeks to set the scene for the ensuing examination of the mentioned friction areas. In order to understand the potential clash between trade mark law and FOSS models, it is first necessary to examine the functions that trade marks perform, and the scope of the legal monopoly that is granted to a trade mark proprietor as a result. Although this chapter is mainly concerned with the position under EU trade mark law jurisprudence, as well as the relevant domestic trade mark law in some of largest EU member states, references to the legal position under US law will also be made for the purpose of illustration. Next, the chapter will discuss the FOSS development model and, in particular, the characteristics that render certain patterns of behaviour under this model susceptible to challenge under trade mark law. The third section of the chapter examines and maps the various trade mark policies that are taken under some of the most commercially popular FOSS licences. At this stage the discussion will turn to the impact that EU trade mark law might have on the FOSS development model and policies adopted. Based on the preceding examination of trade mark law and FOSS model friction zones, this chapter will conclude with a set of recommendations to participants in the FOSS community.

4.2 THE FUNCTIONS OF TRADE MARKS

It is useful to consider the recognized and protected functions that trade marks perform in our system of trade before examining the effect that trade mark law might have on the FOSS model. Identifying the recognized functions that trade marks perform assists us in analysing the scope of the legal monopoly granted to a trade mark proprietor, and thus whether and when certain patterns of behaviour practised by participants in the FOSS model are incompatible with the said functions and may impinge on such monopoly.

4.2.1 The main function of trade marks

In the US, at least initially, it appeared that trade mark law's objective was two-fold. Explaining the basis for trade mark protection under the 1946 Lanham Act, the Senate proclaimed:

> The purpose underlying any trade mark statute is twofold. One is to protect the public so it may be confident that, in purchasing a product bearing a particular trade mark which it favorably knows, it will get the product which it asks for and wants to get. Secondly, where the owner of a trade mark has spent energy, time, and money in presenting to the public the product, he is protected in his investment from its misappropriation by pirates and cheats. This is the well-established rule of law protecting both the public and the trade mark owner.[1]

For a number of reasons, the discussion of which goes beyond the scope of this chapter, subsequent US cases tended to focus on the consumer protection aspect of trade mark law rather than investment protection. This aspect is guaranteed by maintaining a trade mark regime where trade marks function as indicators of origin.

The position in the EU is somewhat different, but it too emphasizes the consumer protection aspect, as guaranteed through the origin-indicating function of trade marks. Thus, eg, in *Arsenal v Reed*[2] the European Court of Justice (ECJ) explained that although trade marks may have a number of recognized and protected functions, the main or essential function of a trade mark is to guarantee the identity of origin of the marked goods or services to the consumer or the end user by enabling him, without any possibility of confusion, to distinguish these goods or services from those offered by other undertakings.

The core function of the trade mark is thus to enable commercial entities to establish an exclusive link between them and a distinctive sign. Such a sign serves as a source identifier in the mind of the relevant consumers. Protecting usage of a sign as an exclusive source identifier allows fair competition, restricts the possibility for consumer confusion, and furthers a mercantile economy where consumers are able to express their preferences for particular goods or services.

In order to maintain this function trade mark law protects against the use of a protected mark, or a mark similar to it, in a manner that gives rise to likelihood of probable confusion.

In the US, section 32 of the Lanham Act[3] provides that using a registered mark in a manner that is likely to cause confusion, to cause mistake, or to deceive, may amount

[1] S Rep No 1333, 79th Cong, 2d Sess, 3 (1946).

[2] Case C-206/01 *Arsenal Football Club v Matthew Reed*.

[3] US Code, Title 15.

to infringement of such a mark. The greater the similarity to the proprietor's mark, the more likely it is that the requisite level of confusion will be established in the defendant's mark and infringement will be found.[4]

Similarly, the legal position in the EU also emphasizes the relationship between the marks in terms of their identity or similarity as a crucial factor in assessing confusion. Thus, Article 5(1) of the Trade Marks Directive[5] provides that a party would be liable for trade mark infringement where he uses in the course of trade an identical mark with respect to identical goods.[6] Where a party uses a mark similar, rather than identical, to the claimant's mark, Article 5(2) provides that such use might trigger a finding of infringement, where it gives rise to likelihood of confusion. Thus, where the similarity between the marks, and the relationship between the relevant goods or services (that is they are either identical or sufficiently similar) is such so as to give rise to likelihood of confusion, a finding of prima facie infringement would follow.

It is noteworthy that confusion in this context does not necessarily mean confusing one product with another. It is sufficient that consumers are mistaken to believe that the products in question originate from the same company or affiliated companies. Moreover, actionable confusion can also arise where the relevant public is likely to believe that the second product is authorized, sponsored, or approved by the original company.

4.2.2 Other protectable functions of trade marks

As mentioned, in the case of the US it is the consumer protection aspect of trade mark law that courts tended to focus on. Thus, it is mainly activities that interfere with the origin-indicating function of a trade mark that courts find necessary to regulate, as it is this function that safeguards and maintains the consumer protection aspect of trade mark law. As is the case in the EU, in order to be considered as jeopardizing this function of a trade mark, the contested activity must give rise to likelihood of confusion.

It should be noted that, irrespective of the core function of trade marks, both US and EU systems recognize other protectable functions of trade marks.

[4] See, eg, the first factor in the DuPont test concerning actionable trade marks confusion on whether the two marks are confusingly similar, according to which the courts should assess the similarity or dissimilarity of the marks in their entirety (*re E I DuPont de Nemours & Co*, 476 F.2d 1357, 177 USPQ 563 (CCPA 1973)).

[5] First Council Directive 89/104/EEC.

[6] Unlike the position in the US, under the EU trade marks regime there is no need to establish confusion where such 'double identity' is present. This is so since in such a case confusion will almost be certain to occur. In the exceptional circumstances where this is not the case, the defendant can invoke one of the available defences, some of which are likely to be applicable to scenarios that involve a double identity use but without confusion (eg in the case of comparative advertising under Article 6(1)(b)).

In the US this is done via the Lanham Act dilution provision,[7] introduced as a consequence of the implementation of Trade mark Dilution Revision Act 2006. In the EU, it is Article 5(2) of the Trade Marks Directive that provides protection against dilution.[8]

Unlike the indication of origin function, dilution as a concept in trade mark law is not as consumer-centred. Dilution concerns the withering away of the capacity of a famous mark to distinguish goods or services, whether or not confusion is present in the mind of the relevant public, and irrespective of whether the claimant and defendant are in competition. The distinctive character of the mark is diluted as a result of either blurring or tarnishment of the famous mark. Dilution protects against the use of a sufficiently similar mark regardless of the goods associated with the potentially diluting mark. It provides protection over and above the prevention of confusion, and is usually justified on the grounds that the diluted mark is a famous mark or a mark with reputation and thus deserves a greater scope of protection. It is the investment of the trade mark proprietor in elevating the mark to its present status as a famous mark that stands at the heart of this doctrine.[9]

In addition, the EU trade mark regime provides protection against what might be described as the taking of an unfair advantage or 'free riding' on a mark with reputation in contexts that do not involve either confusion or dilution.[10] It was in *L'Oreal v Bellure*[11] that the ECJ stipulated that the taking of unfair advantage in this context takes place when a party seeks by the contested use to ride on the coat-tails of a mark with a reputation in order to benefit from the power of attraction, the reputation, and the prestige of that mark and to exploit, without paying any financial compensation, the marketing effort expended by the proprietor of the mark in order to create and maintain the mark's image.[12]

On the basis of the abovementioned provisions, the ECJ recognized a number of protected trade mark functions, other than the long-established origin function. Of importance to the context of this chapter, the ECJ recognized the quality guarantee and advertising functions,[13] as well as the investment function.[14]

[7] Section 43(c), US Code Title 15. [8] See n 5.

[9] For a detailed discussion of dilution theory, see Mark D Janis and Peter K Yu, 'International Comparative Aspects of Trade mark Dilution' (2008) Faculty Publications Paper 362, available at <http://www.repository.law.indiana.edu/facpub/362> accessed 10 April 2013.

[10] As promulgated under Article 5(2) of the Trade Marks Directive. [11] C-487/07.

[12] C-487/07, para 50.

[13] Case C-236/08 *Google France and Google* (the advertising function, sometimes called the communication function, concerns the trade mark's ability to communicate to the public an advertising message through the use of the trade mark; it is thus connected to the trade mark's goodwill function).

[14] Case C-323/09 *Interflora Inc and Interflora British Unit v Marks & Spencer plc and Flowers Direct Online Limited* (according to which infringing activity 'may adversely affects the trade mark's investment function if it substantially interferes with the proprietor's use of its trade mark to acquire or preserve a reputation capable of attracting consumers and retaining their loyalty').

All of the aforementioned protected trade mark functions are of clear relevance to actors in the FOSS scene. As we shall see, certain patterns of behaviour by participants in FOSS communities, stemming from community norms and licensing models, may prove incompatible with the scope of protection offered under trade mark law.[15] The next three sections of the chapter highlight the main friction zones of trade mark law with the FOSS model.

4.3 THE FOSS MODEL AND TRADE MARK LAW

The FOSS model essentially permits use, reproduction, modification, and redistribution of the licensed code. These freedoms are subject to various conditions, depending on the licence in question, but are nevertheless on offer whereupon the licensee complies with the said conditions.

One condition, which is common to most licences, is that a licensee that does any of the abovementioned permissible activities, and then releases the product of these activities back into the market, has to make the 'source code', namely the human understandable language in which the program was written, available to interested parties who may wish to study it, improve upon it, and modify it. There are other conditions that may be common to different families of licences, each of which may embody the philosophy and development model that is shared by members and participants in a particular sub-community on the FOSS landscape.

4.3.1 Creating FOSS code

Like all software, FOSS code is written in source code format. Thus, it is created using human readable computer languages, such as Java, C++, PHP, or Python. Computers, however, cannot read instructions written in such languages. Such languages need to be 'translated' to a language that the computer can read; namely, to 'executable code'.[16] This 'translation' or compilation is done by a compiler, which is a computer program, or a set of programs, that converts a program that was written in source code format to executable code format.[17]

It is noteworthy that compiling the same source code will not necessarily result in the same outcome time and time again; factors, such as the compiler's version, and the hardware on which the code is intended to operate, will have an impact on the final form of the executable code. Furthermore, upon creating an executable file

[15] See further ch 2. [16] Often referred to as 'object code' or low level language.

[17] This is a very simplified explanation regarding the manner in which programs are written and executed by computers. For a comprehensive explanation, see, eg, E Felton, 'Freedom to Tinker, Source Code and Object Code' (4 September 2002) <http://freedom-to-tinker.com/blog/felten/source-code> accessed 10 April 2013.

from source code, a party might decide to make a number of changes, eg, in order to improve upon the original version and add new functions or fix bugs.[18]

Organizations or projects that provide code in executable form, often accompany it with a digital signature, essentially certifying the authenticity of the source of the executable code as coming from those organisations or originating from the said projects. It is in this context that the peculiar nature of FOSS software should be examined: unlike the case of proprietary software, FOSS software exists in an open environment in which it is available to changes and modifications. Executable code originating from a FOSS project might have been tinkered with by someone who could have modified it, and, eg, introduced some malicious code. Thus, assurances as to the source of the relevant code are of particular importance within the FOSS context.[19] This assurance is often given by reference to an organization's or project's trade name. The crucial role of a trade mark right in protecting the integrity of such trade name, as indicating a single source, might explain the vigilant trade mark policies that some actors in the FOSS community adopt.

4.3.2 Contributing to FOSS projects: a sense of ownership

As Chestek explains, being a product of a collaborative endeavour and taking part in the development process of FOSS often leads contributors and participants to develop a sense of ownership regarding the resulting code, which may spill over to a sense of entitlement to use a trade mark associated with the project.[20] As discussed in the following sections, such attitudes may prove incompatible with both trade mark law and various FOSS licence trade mark policies.

4.3.3 FOSS and trade-dress protection

'Trade-dress refers to the image and overall appearance of a product. It embodies that arrangement of identifying characteristics or decorations connected with a product, whether by packaging or otherwise, [that] make[s] the source of the product distinguishable from another and... promote[s] its sale.'[21] Trade-dress 'may include features such as size, shape, color or color combinations, texture, graphics, or even

[18] See P Chestek's excellent discussion on this point in, 'The Uneasy Role of Trade marks in Free and Open Source Software: You Can Share My Code, But You Can't Share My Brand' (July–August 2012) 102(4) *The Trade Mark Reporter* 1031.

[19] Chestek (n 18) 1032.

[20] Chestek (n 18) fn 23. Chestek refers to an example of such sense of entitlement for using a project's trade mark by a contributor to such project, who commented 'Do you know that feeling when you feel treated unjust? When someone has done wrong to you and you simply cannot do anything against it? This is exactly what I am feeling again and again these days ever since I heard about the trade mark registrations of handhelds.org especially done by George France.'

[21] *Esercizio v Roberts* 944 F.2d 1235, 1238–9 (6th Cir 1992).

particular sales techniques.'[22] Protection of trade-dress applies to 'a combination of any elements in which the product is presented to the buyer' including the shape and design of the product.[23] In the context of computer programs, trade-dress protection might be relevant in relation to user experience and the overall look and feel of the program. This might apply, eg, to elements such as the following and their combination thereof: design, layout, colours, fonts, shapes, interface, style, impression, feel, Graphical User Interface (GUI), and more.

4.4 TRADE MARK POLICY UNDER FOSS LICENCES

Licensing plays a pivotal role within the FOSS ecosystem; it is the tool with which rights are conveyed and conditions for redistribution are imposed. As discussed elsewhere in this book, such licences are mainly concerned with copyright and patent rights with respect to the actual code of the FOSS program at issue and its functionality. Thus, they grant conditioned permissions to use, modify, and redistribute the said code with respect to copyrights and patents, held or enjoyed by the licensor, which may cover the said code. The licences' approach towards trade marks is different. First, it might be useful to recall that trade marks do not concern the same subject matter as copyright and patents. Thus, although all of the said intellectual property rights might protect a given FOSS program, it is different aspects of such programs that they will usually be concerned with. While copyrights[24] and patents concern the underlying code and its functionality, trade marks do not; trade marks concern brand names, logos, or other distinguishing features of the program. It is noteworthy that none of the FOSS licences convey trade mark rights in a manner similar to the grants made with respect to copyright and patents. As will be discussed, there is a good reason for this different approach which stems from the nature and characteristics of trade marks as an intellectual property right.[25]

There are around 69 licences approved by the Open Source Initiative ('OSI').[26] Of these, around 20 are completely silent about trade marks, a similar number prohibit the use of trade marks for the purposes of advertising and endorsements, around 26 outright exclude a trade mark grant, and a few more prohibit particular uses of names or marks. Moreover, and in addition to grants conveyed or excluded by the actual licences, FOSS publishers often take additional practical steps in order to ensure and

[22] *Two Pesos, Inc v Taco Cabana, Inc* 505 US 763, 764 fn 1 (1992).

[23] *Art Attacks Ink, LLC v MGA Entm't Inc* 581 F.3d 1138, 1145 (9th Cir 2009).

[24] It noteworthy that copyright might protect the 'look and feel' aspects of a computer program, or at least parts of it. However, as discussed later, such copyright is almost never the subject matter of a grant under a FOSS licence.

[25] As discussed later, unlike copyrights and patents, such trade mark grants may lead to the proprietor's loss of the mark.

[26] OSI website <http://opensource.org/licenses/alphabetical> accessed 10 April 2013.

make clear that the permissions granted under the licence do not apply to trade mark rights; eg, they may incorporate logos and trade mark files in different directories with different headers.[27]

The trade mark policies of some of the most commercially popular FOSS licences will be discussed,[28] and the differences in attitudes between copyright and patent grants on the one hand, and trade marks on the other hand, will be highlighted.

4.4.1 GPL versions 2 and 3

The main GPL licences are considered to be 'strong copyleft' type of licences, where they restrict the ability to integrate code released under another licence that had restrictions of a type not already present under the GPL into a GPLed project. Such licences are considered incompatible with the GPL.[29] However, the FSF, the publisher of GPL licences, makes it clear that its attitude towards further restriction does not apply to prohibitions against the use of trade marks, logos, and trade names. Thus, referring to such prohibitions, the FSF explains:

> That's not really an additional restriction: if that clause wasn't there, you still wouldn't have permission to use the trade mark.[30] We always said those licenses were compatible with GPLv2....[31]

As regards GPLv3, it explicitly provides:

> Notwithstanding any other provision of this License, for material you add to a covered work, you may (if authorized by the copyright holders of that material) supplement the terms of this License with terms:
>
> ...
>
> Declining to grant rights under trade mark law for use of some trade names, trade marks, or service marks.'[32]

Thus, GPLv3 specifically allows licensors to refuse to grant rights for using their trade names, trade marks, and service marks.[33]

[27] T Dare and H Anderson, 'Passport Without A Visa: Open Source Software Licensing and Trade marks' (2009) 1(2) *IFOSSLR* 99–110.

[28] As representative case studies, the trade mark approaches of a strong copyright type of licence: the GPL, weak copyleft licence, MPL and permissive licence, and Apache will be examined.

[29] See further ch 3.

[30] It is noteworthy that this assertion overlooks prohibitions that restrict trade mark uses allowed under trade mark law.

[31] The GNU Project, available at <http://www.gnu.org/licenses/quick-guide-gplv3.pdf> (3) accessed 10 April 2013.

[32] The GNU Project, 'The GNU General Public License v3', s 7(e) <http://www.gnu.org/licenses/gpl.html> accessed 10 April 2013.

[33] A trade name is the name that a business uses to identify itself, whether or not registered as a trade mark. A service mark is used to identify and distinguish the source of a service rather than goods. The term 'trade mark' is often used to refer to both trade marks and service marks.

4.4.2 MPL versions 1.1 and 2.0

MPL 2.0 was the result of a two-year process that revised MPL 1.1. It sought to clarify and simplify Mozilla Foundation's position regarding trade marks grants.

MPL 1.1's stance regarding use of trade marks and logos merely provides that the grants given under the licence, to use, reproduce, distribute, and so forth do not cover patents and trade marks.[34]

In its Frequently Asked Questions section regarding MPL 1.1, it seeks to clarify that unless the scenario at issue involves the distribution of complete and unchanged binary packages provided by Mozilla, all other scenarios involving distribution where the licensee wishes to use Mozilla's trade marks (eg Firefox) must obtain a separate Mozilla Foundation trade mark license.[35] Such scenarios comprise distribution of MPL-covered code that the licensee has compiled himself but not changed, or a modified version thereof.

In contrast MPL 2.0 takes a more direct approach to the issue of use of trade marks by licensees, where it clearly states:

> This License does not grant any rights in the trade marks, service marks, or logos of any Contributor (except as may be necessary to comply with the notice requirements in Section 3.4).[36]

Thus, it is clear that the wording of the licence is aligned with the position of the Mozilla Foundation regarding use of its trade marks: any use that is not sanctioned under trade mark law, eg, purely descriptive use in the case of distribution of complete and unchanged binary packages provided by Mozilla, requires a separate permission or licence from Mozilla, as it is explicitly not covered by the licence.

4.4.3 Apache 1.0, 1.1, and 2.0

The Apache Software Foundation ('ASF') has a long-standing stance regarding the use of its trade marks by third parties. In its earlier versions, the Apache licence approached the issue by attempting to prohibit the use of its trade names without permission, independent of the grants given under the licence. Thus, both versions 1.0[37] and 1.1[38] stipulate:

[34] See s 2(1)(a) and (2)(a) as to grants by the Initial Developer and Contributor respectively, available at <http://www.mozilla.org/MPL/1.1> accessed 10 April 2013.

[35] <http://www.mozilla.org/MPL/1.1/FAQ.html> accessed 10 April 2013.

[36] MPL 2.0, s 2(3), available at <http://www.mozilla.org/MPL/2.0> accessed 10 April 2013. Section 3.4 concerns compliance with notice requirements and provides that 'you may not remove or alter the substance of any license notices (including copyright notices, patent notices, disclaimers of warranty, or limitations of liability) contained within the Source Code Form of the Covered Software, except that You may alter any license notices to the extent required to remedy known factual inaccuracies.'

[37] <http://www.apache.org/licenses/LICENSE-1.0> accessed 10 April 2013.

[38] <http://www.apache.org/licenses/LICENSE-1.1> accessed 10 April 2013.

> The names 'Apache' and 'Apache Software Foundation' must not be used to endorse or promote products derived from this software without prior written permission. For written permission, please contact apache@apache.org.[39]
>
> Products derived from this software may not be called 'Apache', nor may 'Apache' appear in their name, without prior written permission of the Apache Software Foundation.[40]

As in the case of the MPL, growing awareness of questions surrounding use of a trade mark by licensees who compiled the 'work' themselves or modified it resulted in the most recent version of Apache directly addressing the issues surrounding use of its trade marks. Thus, version 2.0[41] provides:

> This License does not grant permission to use the trade names, trade marks, service marks, or product names of the Licensor, except as required for reasonable and customary use in describing the origin of the Work and reproducing the content of the NOTICE file.[42]

In its Frequently Asked Question section,[43] the ASF explains that a licensee may not use the Apache marks in the primary or secondary branding of any third party product or service names. Recognizing the needs of actors in the Apache ecosystem, where, eg, such actors might build products or services that are supersets of the functionality of an Apache product, the ASF trade mark policy allows the use of the'Powered by...' form of the Apache brand name of the related product under certain circumstances.[44]

4.4.4 Compatibility warning

It is submitted that a trade mark provision should not seek to define the scope of permissible or non-permissible trade mark use. Defined in this manner, it runs the risk of contravening the no further restriction conditions as in GPLv2[45] and GPLv3.[46] This is so since a licence that seeks to prohibit certain explicitly defined uses may turn out to restrict uses that are allowed under trade mark law in a given jurisdiction.[47] The FSF explanation of the compatibility of GPL licences with a trade mark clause is that it is not really a restriction since it is prohibited by trade mark law in any event.[48] This reasoning would not be valid where the licence at issue seeks to restrict that which trade mark laws allow. It is arguable that under such circumstances the said clause

39 <http://www.apache.org/licenses/LICENSE-1.1> fnn 38, 39, s 4 accessed 10 April 2013.

40 <http://www.apache.org/licenses/LICENSE-1.1> fnn 38, 39, s 5 accessed 10 April 2013.

41 <http://www.apache.org/licenses/LICENSE-2.0.html> accessed 10 April 2013.

42 <http://www.apache.org/licenses/LICENSE-2.0.html> s 6 accessed 10 April 2013.

43 <http://www.apache.org/foundation/marks/faq> accessed 10 April 2013.

44 <http://www.apache.org/foundation/marks/faq> accessed 10 April 2013.

45 See s 6 of this licence.

46 See s 10 of this licence.

47 See 4.2.

48 See 4.2.2 and 4.2.3, n 31.

will amount to a further restriction. It is thus preferable to define the scope of permitted trade mark related uses by reference to the lack of any trade mark grant given under the licence, rather then use language as found in the earlier Apache versions which stipulated 'Products derived from this software may not be called "Apache", nor may "Apache" appear in their name'. As we shall see, it is sometimes permissible to make unauthorized use of a trade mark with respect to a product derived from the trade marked product.

4.4.5 Other trade mark licensing—related issues

Not granting trade mark permissions under the licence, whether impliedly or explicitly, is not the only manner to address the question of trade mark use by licensees. The Common Public Attribution License ('CPAL'), an OSI-approved licence based on the MPL 1.0, takes things even further. Not only does it not grant licensees the right to use the relevant trade marks, it explicitly requires them to acknowledge the trade mark proprietor's exclusive right with respect to such trade marks:

> You acknowledge that all trade marks, service marks and/or trade names contained within the Attribution Information distributed with the Covered Code are the exclusive property of their owners and may only be used with the permission of their owners, or under circumstances otherwise permitted by law or as expressly set out in this License.[49]

As mentioned, around 20 licences do not address trade mark issues at all. An example of such a licence is the MIT licence, which is silent about trade marks.[50] What is the legal position regarding such licences? Being an exclusive intellectual property right, trade mark enforcement is not dependent on an 'opt-in' system, where a proprietor must state that it intends to safeguard and enforce its trade mark rights. This being so, it is only by 'opting-out' that a trade mark proprietor might render its trade mark right unenforceable. Such opt-out might be either explicit, as in granting trade mark permissions under a licence, or implicit, where the circumstances of the case might give rise to it. It is submitted that within the context of a FOSS licence, merely keeping silent about the issue of trade mark grant, while giving various grants regarding copyright and patents in the underling code, is not likely to constitute a sufficient basis for such an implied licence.[51]

[49] <http://opensource.org/licenses/CPAL-1.0>, s 14(d), accessed 10 April 2013.

[50] It is a fairly popular licence that has 11.28% of the FOSS licences 'market' (see licence proliferation table at <http://www.blackducksoftware.com/oss/licenses> accessed 10 April 2013).

[51] The same conclusion applies to licences that merely prohibit using a mark in a manner that might give the impression of endorsement or advertising, although in this case it might be argued, as a matter of legal interpretation, that opting to prohibit only these specific types of behaviour may suggest that the licensor consents to all other uses of its trade names and logos which do not correspond to the ones specifically prohibited.

This position is supported by a decision of the Higher Regional Court ('OLG') Dusseldorf.[52] In this case the court was required to determine whether the use of a protected trade mark could be derived from a GPLv2 licence. The court rejected this option and held that a GPL licence only grants the user rights with regard to copyright. Even an implied permission to make use of the trade mark could not be derived.

One of the issues in dispute concerned a notice of the defendant in a forum to make an 'xt: Commerce SP2.1 Update', hence offering the update available online. The claimant regarded this announcement as a trade mark infringement, since it did not agree to the use of its trade mark to market modified versions of the program. Furthermore, a permission to market software updates under the trade marked original name could not be derived from the GPL. The Court of Appeal agreed with this assessment. The court explained:

> The GPL governs only the copyright aspects of the use of a computer program, provisions regarding the use of trade marks are not contained within this set of rules. An (implied) right to use the trade mark does also not arise from the nature of things. The permission to use the copyright does not run empty without permitting the use of the trade mark: the beneficiary is able to market the legally reproduced program under a different (own) name.[53]

To avoid any doubt, it is nevertheless preferable, where possible, for a party who is concerned about unregulated use of its trade marks by licensees to opt for a licence that makes it absolutely clear that the licence in question does not cover rights to use its trade marks and that such permission should be separately sought.[54]

4.5 TRADE MARK LAW'S ZONES OF INFLUENCE ON FOSS TRADE MARK POLICIES

This book examines the various grants that FOSS licences give with respect to copyrights and patents. We have seen that whether implicitly or explicitly such grants do not cover trade mark rights. Irrespective of the collaborative ethos of the FOSS community and the sharing culture that surrounds it, permissions to use one's trade mark are kept at arm's length, and require agreements independent of any permissions given under the said licences.

There are valid reasons for this approach, which are based on a number of unique characteristics of trade mark law, as well as on the shared norms of the FOSS community. Starting with the latter, the FOSS movement is essentially about collaborative

[52] See (Az I-20 U 41/09); I am grateful to Marc Mimler for the translation of this decision.

[53] Az I-20 U 41/09.

[54] This could be accompanied by a clear trade mark policy, as in the Apache Foundation policy in its FAQ section, which addresses the issues surrounding use of the Foundation's trade marks (see 4.4.3).

creative effort, access, and freedom to reproduce, modify, and redistribute the program's code.[55] Whether one examines the FSF manifesto or the OSI one, it is clear that the emphasis is on intellectual property grants that deal with the freedoms and rights relating to the code of the program at issue in its functional sense.[56] It should be noted that this is not a question of differentiating between what is or is not covered by the licence grants by reference to the intellectual property rights involved. Rather, it is about which aspects of the software product are viewed as part of the FOSS model. Indeed, even in the case of copyright, which is the focal point of all FOSS licences, it is clear that the licence covers copyright grants as long as those relate to the program's code. To this author's best knowledge, there is no licence that grants copyright in relation to the overall 'look and feel' of the program, to the extent that such look and feel aspects are protected under copyright law in the first place.[57]

Thus, rather than being a question of which intellectual property right is at issue and, on this basis, determining whether or not it is covered by the grants made under the licence, it is ultimately a question of which aspects of the software product at issue are intended to be subject to FOSS freedoms and rights. It is submitted that branding badges and indications of origin are not intended to be part of, and do not naturally fit within, FOSS licences' sphere of influence.

Notwithstanding the aforementioned, could a licensor decide that it wishes to provide grants over and above that which is usually provided for under FOSS licences, and include a right to use its trade mark to downstream licensees? As discussed later, such a decision entails serious risks in terms of the well-being of the trade mark and should be handled with care.

4.5.1 Bare licensing and the risk of trade mark loss

Unlike other intellectual property rights, trade marks' ongoing maintenance and survival sometime depends on the licensor exercising quality control over the licensee's use of the mark. Such condition is compatible with the main function of the trade mark, as discussed earlier, which is source indication where such trade mark is being licensed. As long as the licensor keeps control over the quality of the good or services offered by the licensee under the licensor's mark, such goods or services could be considered as originating from a single source.

A trade mark proprietor is not under an obligation to provide goods or services of a certain level of quality in order for the use of the trade mark in question to be

[55] See further ch 2.

[56] Of course, outside the scope of such IP grants these manifestos also address non-functional aspects, for example author integrity and non-discriminatory use (both of which are addressed in ch 1).

[57] Ultimately this is a jurisdiction-specific matter; nevertheless, in the case of user interfaces, certain features will prove eligible to copyright protection in most jurisdictions.

compatible with the source identifying function of the trade mark. Rather, it must provide goods or services under the mark of a quality that is consistent and thus predictable.

> The chief function of a trade mark is a kind of 'warranty' to purchasers that they will receive, when they purchase goods bearing the mark, goods of the same character and source, anonymous as it may be, as other goods previously purchased bearing the mark that have already given the purchaser satisfaction.[58]

Thus, according to the quality control principle, as long as the licensee maintains a level of quality controlled by the licensor, the mark is deemed to identify the single source of origin, and thus distinguish the goods or services offered under the mark from those offered by others under different marks. The reverse side of this principle might have a crucial impact on the validity of the trade mark in question: if unregulated use of a trade mark is made by a licensee, where no quality control by the licensor takes place, the mark might not be able to function anymore as a source identifier, and thus may become susceptible to cancellation. Therefore, a trade mark proprietor that is an actor in the FOSS community, who is prepared to permit licensees of his FOSS program to use its trade marks with respect to derivative works they create, may run the risk of having its mark revoked due to the absence of quality control.[59] A trade mark licence of this type, which does not involve a sufficient level of quality control, is often referred to as a 'naked' or 'bare' licence.

The focal point of this book is FOSS in Europe. It is nevertheless the case that most of the organizations that write FOSS licences,[60] as well as most of the persons who call the shots on FOSS trade mark policies, are situated in the US. A review of the position in the US is provided for the purposes of illustration, and a reference point for comparison. Nevertheless, the main bulk of the ensuing discussion will focus on the legal position in the EU.

4.5.2 United States

When it comes to trade mark licensing, sections 5 and 45 of the Lanham Act[61] set forth the requirements for the validity of such licensing and both, arguably,[62] serve as

[58] J Thomas McCarthy, *McCarthy on Trade marks and Unfair Competition*, 4th edn (USA, West, 2011).

[59] Effectively, such permission amounts to a trade mark licence.

[60] Thus, the majority of these licences are written by legally trained US lawyers, with US law in mind.

[61] 15 USC Ch 22, Title 15.

[62] On the question on whether it is primarily s 5 or s 45 which embodies the underlying policy of the 'Naked Licensing' doctrine, see, eg, the inter-blog debate between Tim Bukher, 'Trade mark: 7th Circuit confirms "naked licensing" depends on control not abandonment' <http://www.lawtechie.com/2011/05/trademark-7th-circuit-confirms-naked-licensing-depends-on-control-not-abandonment>; and Pamela Chestek, 'Ninth Circuit Ignores the Law Again' <http://propertyintangible.com/2010/11/ninth-circuit-ignores-law-again.html?utm_source=feedburner&utm_medium=feed&utm_campaign=Feed%3A+PropertyIntangible+%28Property%2C+intangible%29> both accessed 10 April 2013.

the basis for the US 'Naked Licensing' doctrine.[63] Although section 5 of the Lanham Act recognizes that the origin indication function of a trade mark could still be served where the mark is used by 'related companies', such use must take place in manner that does not involve deception of the relevant public.

> [w]here a registered mark or a mark sought to be registered is or may be used legitimately by related companies, such use shall inure to the benefit of the registrant or applicant for registration, and such use shall not affect the validity of such mark or of its registration, provided such mark is not used in such manner as to deceive the public.[64]

Section 45 clarifies the scope of such use by defining the term 'related company' as:

> any person whose use of a mark is controlled by the owner of the mark with respect to the nature and quality of the goods or services on or in connection with which the mark is used.

Thus, in order to have an effective trade mark licence that will not jeopardize the validity and survival of the trade mark itself, these provisions of the Lanham Act in effect require that (a) control is exercised by the proprietor over the nature and quality of the goods or services offered under the mark by the licensee and, (b) such control must be of an adequate level so as not to result in public deception.

A discussion over the necessary level of quality control in order to keep a trade mark out of harm's way within the context of trade mark licensing goes beyond the scope of this chapter.[65] It is clear that in the FOSS context, there are no restrictions imposed within the framework of a FOSS licence regarding the quality of the code that licensees may produce.[66] In fact, imposing such restrictions is likely to contravene the norms underlying some of the most popular and widely used licences.[67]

However, it is clear that in the absence of any quality control arrangements or mechanisms, the proprietor of a trade mark is likely to have its mark invalidated. This is so since without quality control a trade mark proprietor cannot guarantee that the level of quality is consistent.[68]

[63] The naked licensing doctrine essentially means that a trade mark licence that does not contain an adequate quality control scheme is a 'naked' licence and, therefore, may lead to the loss of the trade mark itself. For a detailed discussion on the doctrine see, eg, R J Kuss, 'The Naked Licensing Doctrine Exposed: How Courts Interpret the Lanham Act to Require Licensors to Police Their Licensees & Why This Requirement Conflicts With Modern Licensing Realities & The Goals of Trade mark Law' (2005) 9 *Marq Intell Prop L Rev* 361.

[64] Lanham Act, s 5. [65] For such discussion see, eg Kuss (n 63).

[66] In fact it is questionable whether mere contractual control, rather than actual control, is sufficient to keep a trade mark valid in the US in this context; see, eg, NJ Wilkof and D Burkitt, *Trade Mark Licensing* (London, Sweet & Maxwell, 2005) 6-23.

[67] See, eg, GPLv2, s 6, which provides: 'You may not impose any further restrictions on the recipients' exercise of the rights granted herein', available at <http://www.gnu.org/licenses/gpl-2.0.html> accessed 10 April 2013 (quality control related restrictions are likely to be considered as 'further restrictions' in this context).

[68] Thus, where the proprietor fails to exercise adequate control over the quality of goods or services offered under the mark by the licensee, the trade mark licence at issue is likely to be deemed by US courts as 'naked', the

Applying the above to the FOSS context, it appears that where a licensee redistributes a complete and unchanged binary package initially provided by the trade mark proprietor, and uses the proprietor's mark while doing do, the proprietor has little to fear by authorizing such use. This is so since there is no risk that the public will be deceived as a result of being exposed to products that, although they bear the same mark, are not consistent in their quality. Things become more complicated where the case involves a licensee who wishes to distribute executable code, created by it from the proprietor's project source code. As mentioned, although the base source code is identical, compiling it will not necessarily result in an identical executable code; factors, such as the compiler's version and the hardware on which the code is intended to operate will have an impact on the final form of the executable code. Furthermore, upon creating an executable file from source code, a party might decide to make a number of changes, eg, in order to improve the original version, add new functions or fix bugs. Thus, under such circumstances it may be argued that there is no guarantee that executable code offered under the same mark by licensor and licensee will manifest a consistent and predictable level of quality. A trade mark proprietor that consents to such use with respect to its mark[69] runs the risk of having its mark declared abandoned. Obviously, the same applies to distribution of executable code based on a modified version of the proprietor's source code.

It is noteworthy that some types of use by third parties in the US do not require authorization by the rights holder. When no authorization is given, it is more difficult to establish that a trade mark licence was granted.[70] Under such circumstances, the licence at issue is not considered 'naked' and the trade mark is not likely to be lost. Nevertheless, even where no authorization can be established, there are instances where a licensee may use a licensor's trade mark with impunity. A FOSS licensee that uses the licensor's mark without authorization, may rely on the doctrine of nominative fair use. The doctrine have been describe by Justice Renbdell in *Century 21* as follows:

> Nominative fair use is said to occur when the alleged infringer uses the trade mark holder's product, even if the alleged infringer's ultimate goal is to describe his own product. Nominative fair use also occurs if the only practical way to refer to something is to use the trade marked term....
>
> [W]e adopt a two-step approach in nominative fair use cases. The plaintiff must first prove that confusion is likely due to the defendant's use of plaintiff's mark....Once plaintiff has met its burden of proving that confusion is likely, the burden then shifts

mark is considered abandoned, and the owner loses the trade mark. See, eg, *Barcamerica Int'l USA Trust v Tyfield Importers, Inc* 289 F.3d 589 (9th Cir 2002); *FreecycleSunnyvale v The Freecycle Network*, No 08-16382 (9th Cir, 24 Nov 2010); *Eva's Bridal Ltd v Halanick Enter, Inc* No 10-2863 (7th Cir 10 May 2011).

[69] Thus, effectively granting a trade mark licence.

[70] Unless one goes down the route of implied licence.

> to defendant to show that its nominative use of plaintiff's mark is nonetheless fair. To demonstrate fairness, the defendant must satisfy a three-pronged nominative fair use test... (1) that the use of plaintiff's mark is necessary to describe both the plaintiff's product or service and the defendant's product or service; (2) that the defendant uses only so much of the plaintiff's mark as is necessary to describe plaintiff's product; and (3) that the defendant's conduct or language reflect the true and accurate relationship between plaintiff and defendant's products or services.[71]

As is evident from the nature of the test and the factors that are to be taken into consideration, the outcome of its application is fact-specific and should be assessed on a case by case basis. In the FOSS context, after the proprietor establishes that the contested use is likely to give rise to confusion, the burden would shift to the licensee to show that the use is nevertheless fair on the basis of the abovementioned three-pronged test. This, of course, depends, on the nature of the licensee's product, and the type of use to which the proprietor's mark has been subjected. For example, statements such as 'based on,' or 'derived from' might not result in confusion in the first place. But even where likelihood of confusion might be established, the contested use might still be considered as 'fair' due to the nature of market, the proprietor's product, the licensee's product, and the use the licensee makes of the proprietor's mark.[72]

4.5.3 United Kingdom

The legal position in the UK regarding 'naked' or 'bare' licensing should be viewed in relation to two time periods: pre- and post-Trade Marks Act 1994.

The Trade Mark Act 1938 provided that as a condition for registering a 'registered user,' the parties should state 'the degree of control by the proprietor'[73] over the licensee.[74] There was no definition, however, of what was meant by 'degree' and 'control.' Case law decided under the 1938 Act appeared to recognize two types of control: contractual control over the quality of licensee's goods or service, and financial control by the proprietor over the licensee's relevant activities. In exceptional circumstances[75] UK courts were prepared to find that irrespective of the quality control level stated on the register, the de facto quality control as exercised by the licensor was inadequate, which resulted in the loss of the trade mark at issue.[76]

[71] *Century 21 Real Estate Corp v Lendingtree, Inc* 425 F.3d 211 (2005).

[72] It is likely that for the defence to apply, the use of the proprietor's mark must be done so as to refer to the proprietor's product, rather than as the trade name for the licensee's product.

[73] Section 28(4)(a).

[74] Under the 1938 Act, for the first time a trade mark licence could be registered with the trade mark registry; once registered, quality control was presumed (it is noted that registration as a 'registered user' was regarded as optional rather than mandatory by the courts).

[75] See, eg, *McGregor T M* [1979] RPC 36; *Job Trade Mark Case* [1993] FSR 118.

[76] For a detailed discussion on the legal position regarding the quality control requirement and 'bare' licensing under the 1938 Act, see Wilkof and Burkitt (n 66) 6.04–6.18.

The above UK approach changed markedly following the implementation of the Trade Marks Directive[77] and, as a result, the enactment of the 1994 Trade Marks Act.

Following the enactment of the 1994 Act, UK trade marks jurisprudence changed. The provisions regarding 'registered user' were dispensed with, and although new provisions concerning the registration of trade mark licences were introduced,[78] these were mainly concerned with transparency regarding various details of the licence at issue. Importantly, there was no mention of quality control in the new Act.

Thus, in the face of the lack of any EU jurisprudence on the matter, UK courts could have chosen to follow one of the following three approaches: (a) they could have discarded any requirement for quality control all together; (b) they could have maintained such a requirement as a matter of fact, even in the absence of statutory provision to this effect; (c) they could have developed fresh jurisprudence on the matter.[79] As we shall see, it appears that UK courts opted for the last option.

It was in *Scadecor*[80] that the House of Lords was required to determine, for the first time, on the post-1994 Act position regarding quality control, or the lack of it, in a licensor/licensee relationship. The facts of the case are highly complex. For the purpose of the current discussion, they may be reduced to the question on the legal position regarding a 'bare' or 'naked' exclusive trade mark licence, which contained no quality control provisions or mechanisms. It should be noted that the licence at issue, although being 'bare', was exclusive.

In *Scandecor*, the House of Lords appeared inclined to accept that a bare licence, where no quality control mechanisms exist, no longer leads automatically to loss of the trade mark on the grounds of the mark ceasing to be distinctive and becoming deceptive.[81] The court found that even where no quality control is exercised the mark does not necessarily stop functioning as an indication or origin. This was so since, according to the court, consumer perception regarding the origin of goods or services offered under a mark in a licensing context has changed over the years. According to the court, the important question was which person, the licensor or the (bare) licensee did the public perceive as the source of the goods in question? The court explained that under the former law there could have been only one source to goods or services offered under the mark: the trade mark proprietor. As long as the latter continued to exercise quality control over the activities of the licensee, the law regarded goods or services offered by the licensee as ultimately emanating form the proprietor or licensor. This, explained the court, was no longer the case. Due to the

[77] Wilkof and Burkitt (n 66) 6.04–6.18 fn 4. [78] See ss 28-31.

[79] For a detailed discussion on the options available to UK courts prior to the *Scandecor* decision, see J de Werra, *Research Handbook On Intellectual Property Licensing* (Cheltenham, Edward Elgar, 2013) 205.

[80] *Scandecor Developments AB v Scandecor Marketing AB* [2001] UKHL 21.

[81] Under s 46(1)(d) of the 1994 Act a trade mark could be revoked on the grounds of it becoming deceptive in eyes of the relevant public (this mirrors Article 12(2)(b) of the Trade Marks Directive).

changes made to the 1994 Act, and the fact that trade mark licensing became commonplace and thus consumers viewed it accordingly, the 'source' of the goods could now be legitimately viewed either as the proprietor or the exclusive licensee. Giving the lead judgment and referring to public perception during the exclusive licence period, Lord Nicholls stated:

> The mere fact that, during this period, some customers may associate the trade mark with the exclusive licensee does not mean that it has become deceptive or that it lacks distinctiveness. During the licence period the goods come from only one source, namely the licensee, and the mark is distinctive of that source.[82]

Thus, it appears that, according to the House of Lords, in the case of a bare licence the crucial question is not whether the proprietor exercises quality control, but rather who does the relevant public identify as the source of the goods. If, as a matter of fact, it is the exclusive licensee that is so identified rather than the proprietor, then the trade mark continues to perform its source indicating function in a satisfactory manner.

Notwithstanding the views expressed by the House of Lords in the judgment, their Lordships were also of the view that the legal position regarding a number of questions was not clear, and thus guidance should be sought from the ECJ on these issues. Amongst the questions referred to the ECJ was the following one:

> Is a trade mark to be regarded as liable to mislead the public within the meaning of Article 12(2)(b) of the EC Harmonisation Directive (from which Section 46(1)(d) of the 1994 Act is derived) if the origin of the goods denoted by the mark is a bare licensee?[83]

In an unfortunate twist for trade mark aficionados, the parties in *Scandecor* settled before the ECJ gave its decision. Since then, the ECJ has not been called upon to decide on the matter. This leaves us with the *Scendacor* decision, at least as far as the legal position in the UK is concerned. It is submitted that it provides limited comfort to actors in the FOSS scene. First, on a general note, although the House of Lords expressed its inclination to discard the previously held position where a bare licence was considered deceptive, it clearly thought it could not reach such conclusion without first seeking guidance from the ECJ. Thus, any fresh dispute in the UK that will hinge on this legal question is likely to find its way to the ECJ on terms similar to the ones in the referral made by the House of Lords in *Scandecor*. Furthermore, even if one is prepared to consider the view expressed by the House of Lords in *Scandecor* as binding, it may be of limited application to the FOSS context. As mentioned, the dispute in *Scandecor* concerned an exclusive licence in the UK territory. Thus, no other party used the trade mark at issue in the UK during the term of the licence. It was

[82] *Scandecor* (n 80) para 42. [83] *Scandecor* (n 80) para 50.

against this backdrop that the House of Lords found that the public might view the licensee as the sole source of the goods. However, the FOSS model does not involve exclusive licensing. It concerns non-exclusive licensing that enables a potentially unlimited number of licensees to use, modify, and redistribute the licensor's code. It is yet to be seen whether the reasoning and rationale of the court in *Scandecor* would equally apply to such a scenario.

4.5.4 The legal position in other EU Member States

As mentioned, the *Scandecor* case was settled before the ECJ had the opportunity to give its decision. Thus, at the time of writing, there is no EU harmonized position regarding the grant of 'bare' licence, without exercising quality control by the licensor, and a potential loss of the trade mark at issue as a result.

Examining the legal position of domestic jurisprudence in the five largest EU jurisdictions[84] suggests that there is no unified position on this question. With the excepiton of Italy, none of these jurisdictions (namely Germany, France, Spain, and Poland) directly address the question of a 'bare' licence and its impact on the licensor's trade mark's validity. While it is true that, under certain circumstances, failing to exercise quality control may lead to the mark becoming misleading and hence revoked, this conclusion does not follow automatically from a lack of quality control arrangement. Such circumstances will be discussed in detail in 4.6.1.

Italian law appears to be unique in its position on quality control within a licensing framework. There are two provisions under the Italian Intellectual Property Code[85] that should be taken into consideration within the current context.

> Article 23.2 provides that a trade mark can be licensed, even on a non-exclusive basis, for the whole or for part of the products or service it has been registered for and for the whole or part of the national territory; but only if, in case of non-exclusive license, the licensee expressly undertakes to use the trade mark only for the same products or services that are put into the market with the same trade mark by the proprietor or by other licensees in the national territory.
>
> Article 23.4 provides that in any event, the transfer and the license of the trade mark must not generate deception as regards the characteristics of the product or services which are fundamental in the public's judgment.[86]

It should be noted that these provisions are not based on the Trade Marks Directive and appear to be 'home-grown' provisions. They appear to stem from a dominant 'consumer protection' stance that has been intertwined with Italian trade mark law

[84] In addition to the UK, the legal position of which was discussed in 4.5.3.

[85] Italian Industrial Property Code (Legislative Decree no 30/2005).

[86] I am grateful to my LLM student, Priscilla Robledo, for providing me with the translation and her views on these provisions.

prior to the implementation of the Directive. Thus, prior to implementation of the Directive, it was not possible to transfer or license a trade mark in Italy without also transferring at the same time the business or branch thereof; this was in order to ensure that the quality of the products offered under the mark would be stable and predictable. This was in order to ensure that the quality of the branded product would never change over time. Known as 'one trade mark one business', this principle was grounded in consumer protection considerations.

As a result, it appears that through the operation of these provisions, any trade mark licence imposes on the licensee a type of 'obligation of conformity' with goods or services bearing the same trade mark and already circulating in the market. This obligation is imposed by the operation of law, rather than due to a quality control licensing provision. One may query what would be the case where, notwithstanding the said obligation, the licensor pays little attention to the quality and nature of the goods or services offered under the mark by the licensee, and fails to enforce the said obligation where the quality and nature of the goods or services offered by licensee are markedly different from those it offers? In that case the licensor runs the risk that the mark may be revoked on the grounds of becoming misleading according to Article 14.2 of the Code, which implements Article 12(2)(b) of the Trade Marks Directive.

Applying this principle to a FOSS environment, it appears that a licence that also grants permission to use the trade mark of the licensor may carry with it, by implication of law, an obligation to use the mark only with respect to the products or services equivalent to the ones offered by the licensor under that mark. However, it is still up to the licensor to enforce that obligation. Thus, failure to guarantee that this obligation is observed by the licensee may lead to the loss of the mark due to it becoming misleading in the eyes of the relevant public. Hence, eg, where a FOSS licence appears to permit the use of a FOSS project mark, and a subsequent licensee/distributor uses the project mark for its own executable file built from project source code, not to mention for its own derivative work based on the project source code, it is for the licensor to enforce the above mentioned obligation of conformity. Failure to do so renders the mark susceptible to revocation under Article 14.2 of the Italian Intellectual Property Code.

4.5.5 Misleading marks: revocation

Article 12(2)(b) of the Trade Marks Directive states:

> A trade mark shall also be liable to revocation if, after the date on which it was registered... in consequence of the use made of it by the proprietor of the trade mark or with his consent in respect of the goods or services for which it is registered, it is liable to mislead the public, particularly as to the nature, quality or geographical origin of those goods or services.

This provision stipulates one of the grounds for revocation under the EU harmonized trade marks regime. It is noteworthy that the provision refers to use made by the proprietor or *with his consent*. The latter clearly covers a scenario where a licence to use the trade mark has been granted. Therefore, the question is whether granting such a licence, without exercising quality control, will render the mark at issue liable to mislead the public. It should also be noted in this context that the list of characteristics with respect to which the public might be misled is a non-exhaustive one and might also cover origin per se.

Elizabeth Emanuel[87] is one of the only ECJ decisions where the applicability of Article 12(2)(b) of the Directive was examined. The facts of the case may be summarized as follows. Elizabeth Emanuel, a famous dressmaker, sold her business, which she had conducted under her personal name, to the defendant. The sale included the transfer of a UK registered trade mark: ELIZABETH EMANUEL. Subsequently, Ms Emanuel's relationship with the defendant broke down and she sought to challenge the registration on the grounds that the name ELIZABETH EMANUEL would mislead the public into believing that she was still involved in the design or manufacturing of the products sold under the mark.

The ECJ did not find Ms Emanuel's arguments convincing. It essentially held that even if consumers were confused about the trade origin of the goods, they still correctly assumed that the goods came from a *single* source. It was the latter that was crucial for the purposes of revocation in this context. Thus, for a trade mark to remain valid, it must indicate *one* source of origin, whatever such origin may be. As we have seen, a similar line of reasoning could be identified in the House of Lords' *Scandecor* decision.

But the FOSS scenario does not involve an assignment, nor does it involve an exclusive licence; rather it is a 'bare' or 'naked' non-exclusive licence, which is at issue. Obviously, by definition there could not be a de facto single source for goods or services in the case of a non-exclusive licence, as there could be multiple licensees, and a requirement that the consumer must perceive all the goods or services offered under the mark as coming from a single source is incompatible with this licensing model. It is submitted that it is here that a quality control mechanism may prove crucial: rather than concentrating on a de facto single source, it focuses attention on whether the licensees are subject to quality control by the licensor. However, we have seen that this is not a feasible option for a FOSS licensor since placing further restrictions associated with quality control requirements might prove incompatible with FOSS norms. Of course, it is open to a licensor to impose such obligations separately from, and independent of, the FOSS licence; eg, in a separate trade mark licence which does not form a part of the FOSS licence.

[87] Case C-259/04 *Elizabeth Florence Emanuel v Continental Shelf 128 Ltd.*

It may therefore be concluded that since a FOSS licensor cannot incorporate a quality control scheme into a FOSS licence, he should not grant any permissions regarding his trade marks under this licence. If he does, he runs the risk of having his mark revoked.

4.6 THE CONSEQUENCES OF USING A FOSS TRADE MARK WITHOUT AUTHORIZATION

We have seen that a trade mark proprietor, who is also a FOSS licensor, will be well advised to keep his trade marks at arm's length from the permissions he may grant under a FOSS licence, or else the trade mark might be lost altogether. Absent such authorization, a FOSS licensee may nevertheless decide to use a licensor's mark. This section is concerned with two main aspects of such unauthorized use: (a) where the proprietor fails to enforce its trade marks rights: revocation on the grounds of the mark becoming generic and, (b) the defences available to the licensee where the proprietor does attempt to enforce its rights.

4.6.1 Failure to enforce trade mark rights: the risk of the mark becoming generic

Article 12(2)(a) of the Trade Marks Directive states:

> A trade mark shall also be liable to revocation if, after the date on which it was registered... in consequence of acts or inactivity of the proprietor, it has become the common name in the trade for a product or service in respect of which it is registered;

The rationale behind this provision is that marks that become a generic name for the goods or services for which they were registered lose their distinctive character and, thus, lose their capacity to distinguish the goods or services of one person from those of another. Namely, they can no longer fulfill their source indicating function. For example, if the term 'googling' becomes customary for carrying out a search in an internet search engine, rather than for carrying out a search in Google's search engine, the registered trade mark 'Google' may be held to have become generic and therefore revoked. The type of harm that may occur if a generic mark is allowed to stay on the Register is two fold:

(a) To consumers: when asked by consumers to provide a type of product, which consumers refer to by using the generic term, a seller is likely to provide the trade marked version of that product.[88] Under these circumstances consumers are likely to be offered only the proprietor's version of the product.

[88] This is so since the generic term and the trade mark on the trade mark's proprietor version would be identical. Thus, rather than being offered the choices available to a given product in the market place, consumers are likely to end up with being offered only one version of it: the one that uses the generic term as a trade mark.

(b) To competitors: a registered trade mark which is also a generic term will have the effect of barring competitors from legitimately using a term that consumers use to refer to the mark. In the FOSS context it is easy to imagine the anti-competitive effect of having a term that refers to a class or type of goods or service being subject to the proprietor's legal monopoly to the exclusion of all competitors in the market place.

The main question is how does a mark become generic as a matter of law, and what should a proprietor do in order to ensure that it does not? The most important factor in such an assessment is who is the relevant class of persons in the eyes of whom the mark may have become generic. The *Procordia Food*[89] decision suggests:

> [I]n cases where intermediaries participate in the distribution to the consumer or the end user of a product which is the subject of a registered trade mark, the relevant classes of persons whose views fall to be taken into account in determining whether that trade mark has become the common name in the trade for the product in question comprise all consumers and end users and, depending on the features of the market concerned, all those in the trade who deal with that product commercially.[90]

However, it is the perception of consumers or end users that will play a decisive role.

What type of evidence may be brought in order to support a claim that end users, consumers and, where appropriate, intermediaries view the mark at issue as customary?[91] UKIPO refers to the decision of the Appointed Person in *STASH TM* [BL 0-281-04][92] as indicative to the type of evidence that should be taken into account when making this assessment. In particular, the following factors, which could be relevant to a FOSS scenario, will be taken into consideration by the court:

a) Use of the sign in widely read publications offering the goods/services to the relevant public may carry more weight than limited uses on obscure web sites;
b) Journalistic use, whilst not irrelevant (because it leads to use by the public), is less relevant than use in the course of trade;
c) Private use (in 'chat rooms' and the like) is of little relevance;
d) The size and nature of the market for the goods/services is a relevant factor: the amount of use required to show that a sign has become 'customary' or 'established' in a specialized market is liable to be less than that which is required to

[89] Case C-371/02 *Bjornekulla Fruktindustrier AB v Procordia Food AB* [2005] 3 CMLR 16.

[90] Case C-371/02 *Bjornekulla Fruktindustrier AB v Procordia Food AB* [2005] 3 CMLR 16, para 26.

[91] The term 'customary' should be considered synonymous with 'generic'.

[92] See the Trade Marks Manual, 12, para 6, available at <http://www.ipo.gov.uk/tmmanual-chap3-exam.pdf> accessed 10 April 2013.

show the same things in relation to a much bigger market for general products or services.

Bearing these factors in mind should give a FOSS trade mark proprietor an indication as to the type of uses that are most likely to render his trade mark generic, assist him in carefully crafting a trade mark strategy, and police the use of his mark in the market place.

4.6.2 Descriptive use or use intended to indicate the intended purpose

Article 6 of the Trade Marks Directive provides that:

> The trade mark shall not entitle the proprietor to prohibit a third party from using, in the course of trade,
>
> ...
>
> (b) indications concerning the kind, quality, quantity, intended purpose, value, geographical origin, the time of production of goods or of rendering of the service, or other characteristics of goods or services;
>
> (c) the trade mark where it is necessary to indicate the intended purpose of a product or service...;
>
> provided he uses them in accordance with honest practices in industrial or commercial matters.

4.6.2.1 Descriptive use

Article 6(b) is concerned with descriptive use. Thus, eg, where a FOSS licensee uses a FOSS project trade mark without authorization, in order to indicate a characteristic of his product, he may be excused as long as that use is considered to be in accordance with honest practices.

Such situation may arise in numerous instances within the FOSS context. A fairly recent preliminary injunction decision of the Higher Regional Court of Dusseldorf[93] may provide an interesting example for factors taken into account by a court conducting such an assessment. The case will thus be discussed in detail.

The facts of this case were essentially as follows.[94] The claimant owned the rights to the community trade mark 'Enigma', which was registered with respect to 'operating systems, drivers, set top boxes, satellite receivers and digital TV units'. The claimant had granted its affiliate an exclusive licence to use the trade mark name. The affiliate had marketed and distributed set top boxes based on the Linux open-source operating system under the name 'Dreambox' for more than 10 years. To that end,

[93] I-20 U 176/11.

[94] Translation of the case taken from JBB Blog German IT Law, available at <http://germanitlaw.com/wp-content/uploads/2012/05/Higher-Regional-Court-Duesseldorf-final.pdf> accessed 10 April 2013.

the affiliate developed a user interface under the name 'Enigma' and subsequently licensed it under GPLv2. Since 2006, the affiliate has been marketing and distributing an 'Enigma 2' user interface, also licensed under GPLv2. Various competitors also used the user interface in their own set top boxes. It is noteworthy that the said user interface necessitated certain compatibility-related modifications if it was to be used on different set top boxes.

The defendant distributed a set top box which featured the Linux operating system and the 'Enigma 2' user interface developed by the affiliate, although with modifications added to it so it would be compatible with the defendant's own device. The defendant promoted the device in a Flyer, which read:

> VU+DUO Your Smart Linux TV Player. The VU+ DUO is a fully equipped HDTV twin tuner PVR with the Linux Enigma 2 operating system...

In addition, the device was being described as follows:

> 400 Mhz CPU + Linux OS Enigma 2 + Internal HDD (2.5/3.5) + Twin DVB-S2 Tuner + E-SATA/3 x USB + PVR (2.5"/3.5" HDD) + WiFi USB (Option) + low power consumption (Standby: 0.5 W).

Further, the 'Enigma' name was displayed when choosing the menu item 'About', showing the software data in detail.

The claimant argued that this use infringed its community trade mark.

Of particular importance to the present discussion, the court found that the manner in which the defendant used the term 'Enigma 2' was permitted by Article 12(b) of the Community Trade Marks Regulation:[95] 'Enigma 2' was used by the defendant in order to inform (potential) customers about the characteristics of its product. Interestingly, the court was of the view that this conclusion applied irrespective of the fact that the defendant was distributing a modified version of the claimant's program. This was so since the court was prepared to take into consideration that the program might not be used on different types of hardware without being adequately modified. Moreover, the court was even prepared to accept that offering under the trade mark a modified version of the program, with some new functions, may also be permissible under Article 12(b) as long as the essential features of the original trade marked program remained unchanged.

The decision interprets the defence under Article 6(b) broadly. If this line of rationale was to be widely adopted, EU law would appear to allow FOSS licensees to use the licensor's trade mark with respect to a modified version of its program as long as the essential features of the program remain unchanged and third party plug-ins

[95] It is equivalent to Article 6(b) of the Trade Marks Directive.

continue to work with that version.[96] Of course, such permissible use must be in accordance with honest practices.[97]

4.6.2.2 Use intended to indicate the intended purpose

Article 6(c) is sometimes referred to as the 'spare parts' provision, although the provision is not limited to spare parts and accessories.[98] In the FOSS context this defence might be useful, eg, where a party wished to inform the public that he offers maintenance or enhancement services to the FOSS trade marked proprietor's product, or that his product is compatible with the trade marked proprietor's product. Doing so may necessitate a reference to the proprietor's trade marked product, using the actual trade mark as an identifier. Namely, the licensee does not use the trade mark as a trade name for its own product, but rather uses it to identify the trade mark proprietor's product. As with Article 6(b), such use must be in accordance with honest practice.

4.7 A BRIEF NOTE ON TRADE-DRESS PROTECTION

As mentioned earlier,[99] trade-dress protection for 'look and feel' aspects of a computer program might be available under laws concerning unregistered trade marks, passing off, or unfair competition. A program's 'look and feel' will usually not be eligible to protection as a registered trade mark, since, as a subject matter, its description lacks clarity and precision normally required for registration.

Section 43(a) of the Lanham Act protects against infringement of unregistered trade-dress. A trade-dress infringement claim requires a plaintiff to show that: (a) the trade-dress is not functional; (b) the trade-dress has acquired secondary meaning; and (c) there is a substantial likelihood of confusion.[100] It is submitted that elements (a) and (b) are not easy to establish in the case of computer programs. There are numerous decisions dealing with trade-dress protection of internet websites,[101] but to the best of this author's knowledge, there are none to date that deal with computer programs in a more general sense.

[96] This might be the case if the licence at issue is GPLv2 as in the instance just noted. It might be different where the licence explicitly prohibits such use. However, in such a case it might be argued that placing a restriction that goes further than that which is restricted under trade mark law contravenes FOSS norms.

[97] For the factors taken into account while assessing 'honest practices' see Case C-228/03 *Gillette Group Finland Oy v LA-Laboratories Ltd Oy*.

[98] Case C-228/03 *Gillette Group Finland Oy v LA-Laboratories Ltd Oy*.

[99] See 4.3.3.

[100] *Art Attacks Ink, LLC v MGA Entertainment Inc* 581 F.3d 1138, 1145 (9th Cir 2009).

[101] See, eg, *Sleep Science Partners v Lieberman and Sleeping Well, LLC*, 2010 US Dist LEXIS 45385, *7 (ND Cal 2010); *Conference Archives v Sound Images*, 2010 WL 1626072 (WD Pa 31 Mar 2010); *Biosafe-One, Inc v Hawks*, 524 F.Supp. 2d 452 (SDNY 2007); *SG Services Inc v God's Girls Inc* 2007 WL 2315437 (CD Cal 9 May 2007); *Blue Nile, Inc v Ice.com, Inc* 478 F.Supp.2d 1240 (WD Washington 2007).

In the EU, protection against appropriation of unregistered aspects of a business or a product is not harmonized within a trade mark law context.[102] Thus, different EU member states might provide protection against such appropriation on a domestic level, but such regimes are not harmonized on a community level.

In general, EU common law countries, namely the UK and Ireland, might offer protection against such appropriation under the law of 'passing off', while the majority of countries that follow the civil law tradition, namely the remaining 25 member states, might offer protection under a broader unfair competition regime.[103]

In order to bring a successful action in passing off in relation to trade-dress, the claimant must show:

(a) that the trade-dress under which his products were offered has become associated in the minds of substantial numbers of the purchasing public specifically and exclusively with him or the said products;
(b) that the trade-dress under which the defendant proposed to market his product amount to a representation by the defendant that his products are the claimant's or associated with the claimant, which might lead to a substantial number of members of the public being misled into purchasing the defendant's products;
(c) as a consequence of the above misrepresentation, the claimant's goodwill suffers, or likely to suffer, damage.[104]

Similar to the position under the Lanham Act, the law of passing off requires the showing of confusion. Thus, the defendant must have appropriated sufficient amount of the 'look and feel' aspects of the claimant's program that the public will be misled into believing that the two are connected (or are the same). Except for the question of public deception, it is establishing that the look and feel elements of the program at issue acquired goodwill which is likely to be difficult to prove, as the claimant will need to show that there is a mental association in the mind of the relevant public between his program's 'look and feel' and a single source of that program. Namely, that the way in which the program looks and behaves, and the experience it conveys, is distinctive to a single source. It is noteworthy that unlike the US, UK passing off jurisprudence does not have a functionality doctrine per se, where functional elements are excluded from protection.[105] Thus, while in the US it is clear that functional

[102] There is a level of harmonization outside trade mark law where the aspect of the business or product in question is copyrightable, and thus does not require registration. Also, elements such as on-screen icons might be protected under EU registered and unregistered design rights. A discussion of the protectability of 'look and feel' aspects of computer programs under copyright and design rights is beyond the scope of this chapter.

[103] eg, see later discussion regarding France, Belgium, and Germany.

[104] *IRC v Muller & Co Margarine Limited* [1901] AC 217.

[105] It is likely, though, that the courts would be less inclined to acknowledge goodwill in functional aspects. They would be more likely to hold that the public will view such features for what they are, ie, aspects designed to serve a functional objective, rather than as a source identifier.

trade-dress elements are excluded from protection on the basis of their functional nature,[106] UK passing off law does not contain such an exclusion.

In contrast to the position under the Lanham Act, or the law of passing off, some domestic laws of unfair competition do not necessarily require a showing of confusion. Thus, eg, the 'parasitism' branch of French unfair competition law focuses more on diversion of investment and creative effort, than on consumer confusion,[107] while the Belgian Trade Practices and Consumer Protection Act[108] might apply in certain cases[109] even where no confusion can be established. German law on unfair competition is generally applicable with respect to subject matter that is not protected by any intellectual property right and is usually enforced against imitators; thus, trade-dress as a whole is eligible for such protection.[110] To bring an action under unfair competition law, a claimant in Germany needs to show:[111]

(a) that its product's trade-dress manifests 'competitive distinctiveness'—namely, that the trade-dress at issue, or certain distinctive elements thereof might serve as an indication of origin;
(b) that its product is distributed in Germany and enjoys good reputation;
(c) the defendant's products generate confusion as to their origin, or are taking unfair advantage of or inflict damage on the reputation of claimant's product.

Protection of trade-dress or 'look and feel' elements of programs could be of significance to actors in the FOSS community. This is especially the case where a party modifies a FOSS product so as to create a derivative work, but keeps the overall look and feel of the original reputable program. While creating a derivative work might be permissible under the relevant FOSS licence in respect of the actual code, and as long as this is done in compliance with the terms of the licence, consideration must be given to the 'look and feel' elements of the program in question since permissions under the licence rarely apply to them.

[106] See, eg, the decision in *Art Attacks* (n 100).

[107] See INTA, 'European & Central Asia Legislation And Regulatory Sub-Committee, Unfair Competition Report' (2007) 27, available at <http://www.inta.org/Advocacy/Documents/INTAUnfairCompetitionEurope2007.pdf> accessed 10 April 2013.

[108] Trade Practices and Consumer Protection Act of 14 July 1991 (which entered into force on 29 February 1992).

[109] eg where a particularly distinctive mark (or trade-dress) is being used by a party in manner that takes unfair advantage of or is detrimental to it.

[110] It is noteworthy that copyright protection might be available to some aspects of a program's 'look and feel,' such as elements of its Graphical User Interface. Where this is the case, unfair competition protection is not available for such elements. For an overview of design and trade-dress protection in Germany, see K Jonas and HK Budde, 'Design and Trade Dress in Germany' (July-August 2008) *World Trade Mark Review* 76.

[111] The German Act against Unfair Competition (*Gesetz gegen den unlauteren Wettbewerb*, UWG), 3 July 2004 (BGBl. I 2004 32/1414).

4.8 SUMMATION

At first glance trade mark law does not immediately come to mind in the FOSS context. After all, the community ethos and the freedoms and rights granted under FOSS licences have to do with improving the functionality of the base code, and not with the manner in which a licensee may brand and represent its own program. FOSS actors who might not be as familiar with trade mark law as they are with copyright or even patents, might wrongly assume that the sharing norms embodied in the FOSS model apply to trade marks. As was illustrated in this chapter, this is not the case, and there are good reasons for it being so. FOSS participants should nevertheless be aware that, irrespective of whether or not the licence at issue purports to grant trade mark rights, there are circumstances that may entitle them to use a FOSS project or organization trade mark; however, such unauthorized use is highly fact-sensitive and should be handled with care.

5

PATENTS AND FOSS

Malcolm Bain[1]

5.1 INTRODUCTION

Free and open source software ('FOSS') is basically a copyright licensing regime, and not, at least expressly in the beginnings, a means for dealing with patent rights.

[1] With thanks to Peter Langley for comments in general, and contributions to the final section on OIN and Linux Defenders.

The BSD licence,[2] one of the first open source licences to be used (probably *c* 1988), states:

> Redistribution and use in source and binary forms are permitted provided that the above copyright notice and this paragraph are duplicated in all such forms and that any documentation, advertising materials, and other materials related to such distribution and use acknowledge that the software was developed by the <organization>.

No express mention is made of patents. However if we look at the latest two significant FOSS licences to be approved by the Open Source Initiative ('OSI'), the GNU General Public License v 3 (GPLv3 2007) and the Mozilla Public License v 2 (MPL v 2 2012), we see that they deal quite extensively with patents. For example, relevant portions of the MPL v 2[3] read:

> 2.1. Grants
>
> Each Contributor hereby grants You a world-wide, royalty-free, non-exclusive license: . . . under Patent Claims of such Contributor to make, use, sell, offer for sale, have made, import, and otherwise transfer either its Contributions or its Contributor Version.
>
> . . .
>
> 5.2. If You initiate litigation against any entity by asserting a patent infringement claim (excluding declaratory judgment actions, counter-claims, and cross-claims) alleging that a Contributor Version directly or indirectly infringes any patent, then the rights granted to You by any and all Contributors for the Covered Software under Section 2.1 of this License shall terminate.

In fact, even since the original draft of the GNU General Public License (versions 1 and 2, in 1989), software patents have been considered a risk for free software, a risk often voiced by the Free Software Foundation ('FSF'). The GPLv2 warned of patent threats in its preamble: 'Finally, any free program is threatened constantly by software patents. We wish to avoid the danger that redistributors of a free program will individually obtain patent licenses, in effect making the program proprietary . . .', and did in fact include provisions dealing with patents, the rather dramatically called 'Liberty or Death clause', 'the clause that says if somebody uses a patent or something else to effectively make a program non-free then it cannot be distributed at all.'[4]

[2] The text of the different versions of the BSD license can be found at Wikipedia, 'BSD licenses' <http://en.wikipedia.org/wiki/BSD_licenses> accessed 9 April 2013.

[3] Open Source Initiative, 'Mozilla Public License' <http://opensource.org/licenses/MPL-2.0>. Released 3 January 2012. Mozilla.org, 'Announcing Version 2.0 of the Mozilla Public License' <https://mpl.mozilla.org/announcements/> both accessed 9 April 2013.

[4] FSFE, 'Transcript of Richard Stalman at the 2nd international GPLv3 conference; 21st April 2006' <fsfe.org/campaigns/gplv3/fisl-rms-transcript.en.html> accessed 9 April 2013.

> [P]atents not only do not assist in the production of innovative software, they can potentially destroy the free software production system, which is the world's most important source of software innovation.
>
> Eben Moglen[5]

While over the years FOSS licences themselves have become more sophisticated with regard to patents, more recently several initiatives involving the FOSS community have been set up to fend off the threat of the use of patents to limit the creation and use of free software, which will be discussed in more detail in this chapter and the next. To name some, Open Invention Network,[6] a patent pool for defending the GNU/Linux operating system, the Public Patent Foundation,[7] working to improve the patent system (by opposing or requesting the re-examination of non-inventive patents, among other things), and Linux Defenders,[8] who promote defensive publication of new ideas to avoid their being patented by third parties.

And, as will be commented on in more detail in the next chapter, recent litigation in the open source space—more specifically *Oracle America, Inc v Google Inc*[9]—was specifically related to patent infringement claims in relation to Java, a programming language and framework developed originally by Sun Microsystems Inc. and subsequently licensed under the GPLv2 free software licence.

A lot has happened in this area in the last 25 years or so.

What seems paradoxical is that patents and free software appear to share the same objective: to promote development and innovation through transparency and disclosure. It is on the basis of disclosing and sharing knowledge, in patent applications or through access to source code, that new inventions or innovations may be made over existing technology, whether in an incremental manner or by 'intuitive' leaps. Even the legal technique established for promoting inventions via the patent system, ie granting monopolistic rights that may be exercised by the inventor to control the exploitation of the invention and eventually obtain royalties, should not have been a problem: a similar legal framework in the area of copyright has been used by the free software community from the start as the very basis for granting and ensuring software freedoms.[10]

However, there are significant friction areas between the two models or approaches to innovation; particularly the fact that patents provide for the monopolization of all and any implementations of an idea, and not just one expression of that idea, which

[5] E Moglen, 'Free Software Matters: Patently controversial' (*Moglen Law*, 2001) <http://moglen.law.columbia.edu/publications/lu-16.html> accessed 8 April 2013.

[6] Open invention Network <www.openinventionnetwork.com> accessed 8 April 2013.

[7] Public Patent Foundation <http://www.pubpat.org> accessed 8 April 2013.

[8] Linux Defenders: <http://linuxdefenders.org> accessed 8 April 2013.

[9] *Oracle America, Inc v Google Inc* 798 F.Supp2d 1111 (ND Cal 2011).

[10] RM Stallman, 'The Free Software Definition' in *Free Software, Free Society: The Selected Essays of Richard M. Stallman*, 2nd edn (Boston, GNU Press, Free Software Foundation, 2002–10), available at <http://www.gnu.org/philosophy/fsfs/rms-essays.pdf> accessed 8 April 2013.

gives rise to problems and eventually legal risks for free software. The purpose of this chapter is to explore these issues, to understand how the FOSS community tries to deal with patents with the aim of ensuring software freedoms, and we will conclude by commenting on proposals that have been made to remedy the situation and mitigate the risks.

Therefore, in this chapter we first look at why patents are relevant to FOSS, briefly, the question of *software patentability* and the differences with copyright, and then, taking into account the free software development and licensing models, we consider in 5.3 what the impacts are for FOSS: the interrelations and frictions areas between free software licensing models and patents. Section 5.4 focuses on the particular issue of patents over standards and the licensing of such patents under 'RAND' terms, and how this may impact free software implementations of those standards and interoperability. In section 5.5 we then look at how patents are dealt with by the community from a structural point of view—particularly patent-related licensing provisions in free software licences. Finally, section 5.6 considers how the risk posed by patents—or the way patents are wielded—to the FOSS community may be mitigated, if not removed entirely.

5.2 PATENTS 101: WHY ARE PATENTS RELEVANT TO FREE SOFTWARE?

Patents are exclusionary rights[11] granted to inventors over an invention, rights to exclude anyone else from commercially exploiting the invention in the specific territory, for a limited period, in return for the full disclosure of the invention to the public. They are granted on application to territorial patent offices (eg the UK Intellectual Property Office), after examination for patentability under the applicable rules.

5.2.1 In Europe

Within Europe, patents are regulated on a regional basis by the European Patent Convention ('EPC'), which creates a European patent with potential effects in the territories of the signatories to the Convention, and on national bases by the corresponding national patent laws, eg, the UK Patents Act 1977, or the Spanish *Ley 11/1986 de Patentes*. In this chapter we will mainly comment on the EPC provisions with respect to software, though it is important to note that it is the national courts applying the law of the member states who ultimately decide on patent validity or infringement, though they tend to follow the European Patent Office ('EPO') practice and Board of Appeal decisions.

[11] Patents are not 'exclusive' rights, ie, a positive and exclusive right to do something, but rather a negative right to exclude others from implementing the claims established in the patent document.

The state of patenting in the software industry is controversial, and there are many arguments as to whether software does or should constitute patentable subject matter to begin with. Patents are granted for inventions in all fields of technology that are new, involve an inventive step, and are capable of industrial application.[12] The EPC does not define what an 'invention' is. It does, however, provide a negative limitation, giving examples of what are not to be regarded as inventions. Relevant for our purposes is the specific exclusion, under Article 52.2 EPC, of 'programs for computers'.

A 52(2).The following, in particular, shall not be regarded as inventions:

a) discoveries, scientific theories, mathematical methods;

b) aesthetic creations;

c) schemes, rules and methods for performing mental acts, playing games or doing business, and programs for computers;

d) presentations of information.

However this exclusion is then limited by Article 52.3 which provides that these items are excluded 'only to the extent to which a European patent application relates to such subject matter or activities as such'. It is these last two words, 'as such', that have caused an ongoing and acrimonious debate about software patentability under the EPC, and also under the European national legislations, many of which provide a translation or approximation of this double exclusion/limitation with regard to software,[13] and which ultimately are the benchmark against which the validity of the European patent is measured.[14]

It is not the purpose of this chapter to review the situation of software patentability within Europe, as we aim to focus on the interaction between software patents—however well or justifiably granted—and free and open source software.[15] Suffice to say that the EPO is currently granting patents over what have been named 'computer implemented inventions' ('CII'), on the basis that they are granting patents over inventions that have technical character, and a technical effect that goes beyond the normal interaction of the software with the computer, although ironically 'technical' is not defined in the EPC.[16] And European national courts

[12] EPC, Article 52. [13] eg Spanish Patent Act 11/1986, Article 4.

[14] This may be changed with the proposed Unified Patent Court, under the Agreement on a Unified Patent Court and associated Regulations, recently approved by the European Council of Ministers and European Parliament.

[15] There are a significant number of thoughtful papers written on this subject. Recently, see N Shemtov, 'Software Patents and Open Source Models in Europe: Does the FOSS community need to worry about current attitudes at the EPO?' (2010) *IFOSS L Rev* 2(2), 51–164; A Freeman, 'Patentable Subject Matter: the View From Europe' (2011) *IFOSS L Rev* 3(1) 59–80; CV Chien, 'From Arms Race to Marketplace: The Complex Patent Ecosystem and Its Implications for the Patent System' (2010) *Hastings Law Journal*, vol 62, 297; MA Lemley, 'Software Patents and the Return of Functional Claiming' (25 July 2012) Stanford Public Law Working Paper No 2117302. Available at <http://ssrn.com/abstract=2117302 or http://dx.doi.org/10.2139/ssrn.2117302>.

[16] EPO Board of Appeal Decisions: Computer program I/IBM (T1173/97) and Computer program II/IBM (T 0935/97). See: EPO, Guidelines for Examination in the European Patent Office, C-IV 1.2 (2009), available at <http://www.epo.org/law-practice/legal-texts/guidelines.html> accessed 9 April 2013.

(with some reticence, it was thought, in England and Wales, but more recently not so) are upholding those grants.[17] What is more, in the light of the debate about software patentability, the Enlarged Board of the EPO rejected the EPO President's request to undertake a full review of the situation, at the instigation of the English High Court, considering that the 'case law' created by the EPO Boards of Appeal is sufficiently clear.[18]

> Indeed if the Boards continue to follow the precepts of T 1173/97 *IBM* it follows that a claim to a computer implemented method or a computer program on a computer-readable storage medium will never fall within the exclusion of claimed subject-matter under Articles 52(2) and (3) EPC, just as a claim to a picture on a cup will also never fall under this exclusion. However, this does not mean that the list of subject-matters in Article 52(2) EPC (including in particular 'programs for computers') has no effect on such claims. An elaborate system for taking that effect into account in the assessment of whether there is an inventive step has been developed, as laid out in T 154/04, *Duns*. While it is not the task of the Enlarged Board in this Opinion to judge whether this system is correct, since none of the questions put relate directly to its use, it is evident from its frequent use in decisions of the Boards of Appeal that the list of 'non-inventions' in Article 52(2) EPC can play a very important role in determining whether claimed subject-matter is inventive... It would appear that the case law, as summarised in T 154/04, has created a practicable system for delimiting the innovations for which a patent may be granted.

In practice, as stated on various occasions by examiners of the EPO,[19] while they consider software based inventions with technical effect as patentable subject matter, many if not most software patent applications are being rejected on the basis of lack of novelty (the second hurdle, considering 'patentable subject matter' as the first) or lack of inventive step (the third hurdle).[20] In particular, mere computer- or software-based automation of constraints imposed by non technical aspects,

[17] eg, *Aerotel Ltd v Telco Holdings Ltd* [2007] RPC 7; and *Macrossan's Application* 2006 [EWCA], followed by *Symbian Ltd v Comptroller General of Patents* [2008] EWCA Civ 1066; and more recently *Halliburton Energy Inc's Patent* [2011] EWHC 2508 (Pat).

[18] Enlarged Board of Appeal Opinion G3/08. For commentary, see Freeman (n 15).

[19] See EPO presentations by N Ciarelli, Patentability of Computer-Implemented Inventions at the EPO (Brussels, EPO Conference on CII, 2007); D Hanon, 'What makes an Invention—How patent applications are examined at the European Patent Office' (Barcelona, 6-10 October 2008); E Archontopoulos, 'Spot the Differences, A computer-implemented Invention or a Software Patent?' (6th Annual Conference of the EPIP Association, Brussels, 2011); D Closa, 'What is this?' (Barcelona, 2012).

[20] In particular, features making no contribution to the technical character cannot support the presence of inventive step (*Comvik* (T0641/00) and *Duns Licensing* (T0154/04)). See EPO presentations on the subject, eg, 'Patentability of Computer Implemented Inventions at the European Patent Office' in the EPO online course, available at <https://e-courses.epo.org/course/view.php?id=30>; and <https://e-courses.epo.org/course/view.php?id=64> both accessed 9 April 2013, by J Beatty, I Bozas, S Krishner. Also D Hanon 'What makes an Invention—How patent applications are examined at the European Patent Office' and E Archontopoulos (n 19).

specifically those that are excluded by the EPC, notably mental acts, games, business methods, or methods for presenting information, are allegedly not being granted patent protection.[21]

5.2.2 In the USA

In the US, for many years the leading decisions in the debate on software patentability were *Diamond v Diehr*[22] and subsequently *State Street Bank & Trust v Signature Financial Services*[23] where the Court of Appeals for the Federal Circuit held that a computerized algorithm for managing an investment fund structure constituted patentable subject matter which should be evaluated under the usual tests of usefulness, novelty, and non-obviousness.[24] More recently, however, in *In re Bilski*, the Federal Circuit seemed to have started a more strict approach towards software patentability:[25] it found that a patent on a method of hedging financial risk in commodity trading claimed 'neither a new machine nor a transformation of matter', and thus was too abstract and non-patentable subject matter. However the Supreme Court then mitigated this to a certain extent, holding that the 'machine-or-transformation test' is not the only test for determining the patent eligibility of a process (but rather 'a useful and important clue, ... an investigative tool, for determining whether some claimed inventions are processes under §101').[26] And in *Mayo Collaborative Services v Prometheus Laboratories, Inc*,[27] the US Supreme Court reaffirmed the judicially created exception that makes 'laws of nature, natural phenomena, and abstract ideas' ineligible for patenting, opening the judicial 'door' to making the oft-stated argument that software code is merely a series of mathematical algorithms, and as such, a description of abstract laws of nature. The usefulness of this decision regarding medical testing methods in the software space has been reinforced by the Supreme Court's holding in *WildTangent, Inc v ULTRAMERCIAL*,[28] rejecting a decision by the Federal Circuit regarding the patentability of an online method for distributing copyrighted works, and ordering the appellate court to review its decision in the light of *Mayo*. It remains yet to be seen

[21] *Ricoh Decision* T 03/0172; *Hitachi Decision* T 03/0258.

[22] 450 US 175 (1981).

[23] 149 F.3d 1368 (Fed Cir 1998) cert denied; 119 S Ct 851 (US 11 January 1999).

[24] See, eg, P Toren, 'Software and Business Methods are Patentable in the U.S. (Get over it)', *Patent World*, September 2000 at 7. See also: CL Ogden, 'Patentability of Algorithms After State Street Bank: The Death of the Physicality Requirement' (2000) No 10 Vol 82 *Journal of Patent and Trademark Office Society* 721, 724ff.

[25] *In re Bilski* 545 F.3d 943 (Fed Cir 2008) (en banc). For comment, see, eg, D Crouch and J Rantanen, 'In re Bilski: Patentable Process Must Either (1) be Tied to a particular machine or (2) Transform a Particular Article' (*Patentlyo*, 30 October 2008) <http://www.patentlyo.com/patent/2008/10/in-re-bilski.html> accessed 9 April 2013.

[26] *Bilski v Kappos*, No 08-964, 561 US (2010). Comment by Crouch and Rantanen (n 25).

[27] *Mayo Collaborative Services v Prometheus Laboratories, Inc* 566 US (2012). Decision available at <http://www.supremecourt.gov/opinions/11pdf/10-1150.pdf> accessed 9 April 2013.

[28] *WildTangent v Ultramercial* (Supreme Court 2012) Docket No 11-962.

how this question will pan out in the US, as there are more cases in the pipeline, like *CLS Bank v Alice Corporation*.[29]

In the meantime, since *State Street Bank* in particular, a significant number of 'software patents' have been granted, and applications have been made to such an extent that the USPTO is bogged down, only being able to dedicate an average of 18 hours to study each case.[30] This has also led to the issue of a significant number of weak, if not totally trivial, patents being issued, on both sides of the Atlantic, and the creation of patent 'thickets' of overlapping and poor quality patents, which close down innovation and make it difficult to operate in this sector.[31]

So all in all, current industry practice, the pressure from large software industry companies and other non-industry players such as non practising entities, combined with the lack of resources and time for reviewing patents at the patent offices and the lack of access to relevant prior art in the field,[32] together mean that software patents have been and are still being granted over software implemented processes and methods, on both sides of the Atlantic and also in Japan, another key jurisdiction. Specific examples include security algorithms for encryption, audiovisual data codification and decodification (codecs), online data back-up, graphical user interface features, 'one-click' online shopping systems, frames for displaying information on computer interfaces, and the list goes on.[33]

5.2.3 Differences with copyright

When a patent is granted over a software-based invention or CII, it doesn't just grant exclusionary rights over the exploitation of a specific implementation of that invention, but *any* implementation of the invention: it protects the functional features of the 'invention,' the underlying methodologies, in any manner or form of expression.

[29] *CLS Bank v Alice Corporation* (Fed Cir 2013). Commented online at Groklaw, 'CLS Bank v Alice—Some Amicus Briefs' <http://www.groklaw.net/articlebasic.php?story=20121230021614863>; D Crouch, 'CLS Bank v. Alice Corp: Oral Arguments Lead to More Questions' (*Patentlyo*, 9 February 2013) <http://www.patentlyo.com/patent/2013/02/cls-bank-v-alice-corp-oral-arguments-lead-to-more-questions.html> both accessed 9 April 2013.

[30] J Nightingale, 'Patent Reform Fails to Halt Fee Diversion' (*Inventors Digest*) <http://www.inventorsdigest.com/archives/7664>. For commentary see, eg, P Samuelson, 'Benson Revisited: The Case Against Patent Protection for Algorithms and Other Computer Program-Related Inventions' (1990) 39 *Emory LJ* 1025; and P Menell and M Meurer, 'Nonpatentability of Business Methods: Legal and Economic Analysis' (*SSRN*, 2 October 2009) <http://papers.ssrn.com/sol3/papers.cfm?abstract_id=1482022> both accessed 9 April 2013.

[31] RM Ballardini, 'The Software Patent Thicket: A Matter Of Disclosure' (2009) 6:2 *SCRIPTed* <http://www.law.ed.ac.uk/ahrc/script-ed/vol6-2/ballardini.asp> (accessed 8 April 2013), DOI: 10.2966/scrip.060209.207.

[32] Software patenting basically started in 1989, 40 years after modern computing was invented, and thus no 'prior art' was previously published in a meaningful manner, particularly in patent office databases, for disclosure against subsequent patenting.

[33] An interesting series of software patents can be found at End Soft Patents wiki, 'Example software patents' <http://en.swpat.org/wiki/Example_software_patents>; and at FFII.org, 'European Software Patents: Assorted Examples' <http://eupat.ffii.org/patents/samples/index.en.html> both accessed 9 April 2013.

This is in contrast with copyright protection that only protects source and binary code expression embodied in the software, and preparatory materials.

This means that while copyright protection may seem weaker than patent protection, it is more specific, referring only to the concrete expression of the code developed by the programmer. This has the advantages of providing legal certainty with regard to what exactly is prohibited or restricted by copyright, particularly verbatim copying,[34] and what is permitted: alternative or clean room development of similar functions, incremental development of additional functionalities, or complementary development of other programs using software interfaces and interoperability characteristics. Being more specific and restricted to expression (code), copyright enables alternative implementations and improvements of a same idea or function, through different algorithms, coding languages, or architectures.

> There is a crucial distinction between the way patent and copyright concepts respond to the challenge free software poses. Copyright law, as the US Supreme Court has said, is primarily intended to cover expressions, not ideas. So if in a particular instance software copyright inhibits progress in making better, more reliable, or more effective software, the inhibition can be overcome: It is always possible for programmers to sit down and rewrite from scratch whatever program needs to be available in a freely-modifiable version. This may be time-consuming, but it cannot be forbidden. But patent law prohibits anyone from 'practicing the teaching' of the patent—or using the technological ideas the patent describes—without license. It does not matter how you came by the idea the patent discloses, even if you invented it for yourself in complete ignorance of the patent and the prior art it references: Without a license you cannot embody your idea in any way covered by the patent's often very general claims.[35]

Patents, on the other hand, are broader and provide protection against all forms of implementation of the process that is patented, even if they are independently developed. This enables patent holders to restrict competition by other developers in the market wishing to implement similar functionalities in their own programs. Patents are also vaguer or less definite, particularly in the way software patents are currently drafted and, as we mention later, it is often difficult to determine exactly if a patented software process is being used, and thus if any development, distribution, or use of the code would be infringing the patent. This creates significant legal uncertainty.

In addition, the law has recognized that the ideas and principles underlying a software program, and in particular its interfaces, should be exempted from copyright

[34] To a major extent, although there are always questions about non-verbatim copying and derivative works which the courts deal with on a fairly regular basis.

[35] E Moglen, 'Free Software Matters: The Patent Problem' (9 October 2000) <http://moglen.law.columbia.edu/publications/lu-05.html> accessed 9 April 2013.

protection.[36] Software interfaces basically consist of information and eventually code that define how a particular program may interact with or be used by other programs. As software becomes more and more modular ('component based'), and software architectures have more layers (operating systems, databases, application servers, and so on) and operate over or across networks, the interfaces between programs become more important. This specific aspect of software copyright law (in particular the lack of protection for ideas and principles underlying a software program's interfaces, and the ability to access and use information necessary to achieve interoperability) thus permits independent interoperable software programs to be created, an important aspect in an ever more connected world, and providing a level playing field for innovation.[37]

The law on software patents on the other hand has developed separately, and there is no exemption for interfaces. As an interface is a set of definitions or specification of a method or process (for using the program or data), it is particularly prone to being 'patentable'. So not only are we finding patents over specific computer-based processes and data formats, but also there are patents over software interfaces that provide information on how to connect with and use these software processes and data formats.[38]

Another significant difference between copyright and patents (relevant for FOSS) is the characteristics and structure of creation and ownership of rights: copyright in a software program belongs originally to its creator (or the company where the creator works), who has invested time and effort in developing the code, and the rights may be licensed or assigned, usually to someone who wishes to use or further develop the program. Thus, copyright rights are generally held by parties interested in exploiting the software. A patent is first owned by its inventor, who may or may not be a software developer. As there is not necessarily any 'software development' involved in inventing a process that may be embodied by software, the patent rights may be held by any party, who may or may not be interested in implementing the patented process or method.

This situation is illustrated by what have been now called 'non practising entities' ('NPEs') or 'patent trolls'.[39] These are persons or companies that do not have any

[36] The general concept set out in Article 1.2 of the EC Software Directive, providing that 'Ideas and principles which underlie any element of a computer program, including those which underlie its interfaces, are not protected by copyright under this Directive', is reinforced by Article 6 'Decompilation' which enables third parties, under certain conditions, to reproduce and translate software code (decompile it) if this is 'indispensable to obtain the information necessary to achieve the interoperability of an independently created computer program with other programs'. In the US, the recent decision in *Oracle America, Inc v Google Inc* (810 F.Supp.2d 1002) has confirmed this point on the other side of the Atlantic.

[37] This has been recognized, eg, by the efforts to create 'interoperability frameworks' for public administration systems, such as the EU interoperability framework (EIF), now in its version 2, commented on later.

[38] More below in section 4 (patents on software standards).

[39] Wikipedia, 'Patent troll' <http://en.wikipedia.org/wiki/Patent_troll> accessed 9 April 2013.

particular interest themselves in exploiting the software that implements the patented processes, but only in exploiting the patent rights against participants of the software industry interested in the invention. While this is a legitimate function of patent rights under the current regime, this creates a significant imbalance in the software sector and can constitute a major block on innovation.[40] This is not to say that there are not 'copyright trolls', monetizing copyrights through litigation.[41] We will comment further on this later, when looking at the interactions and frictions between FOSS and patents.

5.2.4 Remedies

Finally, it is essential to understand the remedies available to patent holders in the case of infringement. National courts are competent to hear infringement cases and determine remedies of both European patents and patents issued by their national offices. However, the national court's decision will only apply in its territory, and if the infringement occurs in several states, then proceedings would have to be brought independently in each country.[42] This should change with the recently formed Unified Patent Court,[43] a specialized patent court with exclusive jurisdiction for litigation relating to European patents and European patents with unitary effect (unitary patents). In practice, at the moment Germany seems to be one of the favourite states to start infringement proceedings, as they are relatively cheaper and faster there (many decisions are made under the fast injunction procedure), something that has been seen in the case of the *Apple v Samsung* proceedings relating to Galaxy Tab 10.1.[44]

Remedies have been broadly harmonized across the EU through Directive 2004/48/EC of the European Parliament and of the Council of 29 April 2004 on the enforcement of intellectual property rights.[45] Remedies include both precautionary

[40] For recent commentary, see JE Bessen, MJ Meurer and JL Ford, 'The Private and Social Costs of Patent Trolls' (19 September 2011) Boston University School of Law, Law and Economics Research Paper No 11-45 <http://ssrn.com/abstract=1930272> or <http://dx.doi.org/10.2139/ssrn.1930272>.

[41] While this is more common with regard to photographs or news, SCO has been accused of being a 'copyright troll' in the FOSS space when it claimed copyright royalties from many companies, and sued IBM (on behalf, maybe, of other industry players) for alleged breach of its copyrights through distribution of GNU/Linux based operating system.

[42] Unique procedures may be brought against the defendant in its jurisdiction of residence, if there are multiple territorial patents, and the local courts may in this case handle infringements across the relevant EU territories.

[43] The Agreement on the UPC was endorsed by EU ministers in the Competitiveness Council on 10 December 2012 and by the European Parliament on 11 December 2012.

[44] See C Foresman, 'Apple stops Samsung, wins EU-wide injunction against Galaxy Tab 10.1' (*ArsTecnica*, 9 August 2011) <http://arstechnica.com/apple/2011/08/samsung-facing-eu-wide-injunction-against-galaxy-tab-101>. Germany is a preferred venue, see comment by K O'Brien, 'German Courts at Epicenter of Global Patent Battles Among Tech Rivals', *New York Times* (8 April 2012) available at <http://www.nytimes.com/2012/04/09/technology/09iht-patent09.html?_r=3&pagewanted=all&> both accessed 9 April 2013.

[45] *Official Journal of the European Union* L157 of 30 April 2004.

measures, such as preliminary injunctions and seizure, as well as permanent orders and monetary damages.

As the patent holder's main goal is to stop the infringing party's actions, it will mainly aim for preliminary and then permanent injunctions to cease the manufacture, distribution, commercialization, and use of the infringing product. In addition, at the preliminary stage the patentee may request an order to seize or produce for audit products, tools (including computer equipment), production plants, books of account, invoices, and advertising materials, the latter in order to collect documentary evidence of the infringement and its extent; and a blocking order to stop imports at the national borders. In the extreme, a patentee may also request freezing the allegedly infringing party's bank accounts. Thereafter, when infringement is finally determined, the rights holder can request a declaration of the validity of the patent and the destruction of the infringing items.

If infringement is found, damages may be applied for to compensate for the infringing activities, either as accounts for profits made, monetary compensation for lost profit of the patent holder, or the fees the patentee would have charged for granting a licence (probably the preferred method, as proving lost profits or trying to work out the infringer's illegitimate profit made on the basis of the patented item, is extremely difficult).

We will see in the following section how difficult it is to apply these concepts in the open source software context. Not only are the 'original infringers' of a computer implemented invention potentially unknown or difficult to identify or locate (assuming that the FOSS project is the 'person' infringing a third party's patent), but also it can be extraordinarily difficult to prevent distribution of intangible goods (that may infringe on patent rights) on the internet.[46]

This is not the case when the software is embedded in hardware devices, such as smart phones, set-top boxes, or routers, whereby the patent holder may pursue any member of the supply chain (in particular the retailer and the importer) to obtain the injunctive relief and subsequent claim for damages. This is probably one of the reasons patent litigation has been so popular in the mobile device industry recently, as there are specific goods or devices to identify for remedial action.

Thus there is a series of reasons why patents are relevant to software, in particular their very existence with respect to software implemented inventions, their nature and scope, and their differences with copyright, many of which, as we will see next, enter into conflict with the principles and reality of FOSS.

[46] See, eg, how OpenSuse community deals with audiovisual codecs encumbered by patents: oSC, 'Restricted formats' <http://opensuse-community.org/Restricted_Formats> accessed 9 April 2013.

5.3 PATENT AND FOSS INTERACTIONS

To understand the interactions between free and open source software and patents, we must briefly review the nature and characteristics of FOSS and its development process. As we will then see in this section, these are anathema if not antithetical to the patent system (as legislated and practised), leading to a variety of areas and types of friction. In the next section of this chapter, we will look at how the FOSS community tries to deal with these frictions, both in the licensing regimes and in practice.

5.3.1 Development and innovation in free software

Free software is software that is distributed under a free software licence. This is a broad, royalty-free licence that allows all persons to use, copy, modify, and distribute the original code and its derivative works.[47] Thus FOSS is characterized by the granting to others of the ability to exploit the software, with access to its source code as a requirement to be able to enjoy those rights.

The FOSS licence is in fact a practical expression of the ideals and objectives of the software creators, using copyright rights to allow and enforce openness and freedom with respect to the software code and the knowledge contained therein. FOSS licensing increases public accessibility to this knowledge. Under copyleft licences,[48] a sub-group of FOSS licences, this knowledge and these freedoms to exploit and innovate are guaranteed for all third parties through obligations to maintain the free software licensing terms in downstream distributions of the product and its derivative works.[49]

In practice, this usually leads to a decentralized software development model, the 'bazaar', as Eric Raymond has called it,[50] whereby developers from all parts of the world may participate in and contribute to a FOSS project. These participants form what has generically been called the 'community' of the project, and these communities together form the 'FOSS community' or movement as a whole. These communities are extremely heterogeneous, including individual programmers and users, institutions, companies, and public bodies, and can be formed by one or two persons, or a significant number of participants such as the Open Document or GNU/Linux communities.[51] The community participants, acting

[47] Stallman (n 10). See also 'Open Source Definition' available at <http://www.opensource.org> accessed 9 April 2013.

[48] Stallman (n 10) 127.

[49] And eventually collective or composed works containing the original code.

[50] ES Raymond, 'The Cathedral and the Bazaar' (2000) <http://www.catb.org/~esr/writings/cathedral-bazaar/cathedral-bazaar> accessed 9 April 2013.

[51] See, eg, Linux Foundation Annual Report 2012, estimating 7800 contributors since 2005. Linux Foundation, 'The Linux Foundation Releases Annual Linux Development Report' (3 April 2012) <http://www.linuxfoundation.org/news-media/announcements/2012/04/linux-foundation-releases-annual-linux-development-report> accessed 9 April 2013.

usually remotely over the web, maintain, develop, and correct the project software according to a roadmap that may or may not be an agreed 'master' document. In some communities, such as the Mozilla, Ubuntu, or Alfresco projects, the project may be led or structured by a foundation or corporate entity, which guides development and may exploit the software (or services based on the software) commercially.

Innovation in these communities is varied, either incremental—developers building on previous contributions made by themselves or other participants, or complementary—developing new functionalities and modules through standard and open interfaces. However, in all circumstances, innovation is based on the principles of freedom and openness: taking advantage of broad rights to copy, share and improve the code, along with open access to the source and interoperability information of the project code.[52]

The certainty provided by the standardized copyright licensing terms established by the project FOSS licence provides reliability and trust among the participants, increasing network effects and providing a strong basis for further innovation.[53] In transaction cost analysis terms, this 'lowers the informational and transactional cost of licensing, as the terms are standard and transparent to all parties, so there is no information asymmetry and no need to negotiate terms.'[54]

5.3.2 Frictions with the patent regime: differences in concept

This form of innovation through sharing, however, runs counter to the justification for patent protection, which is based on the historical and theoretical foundation of intellectual property rights regimes, that of providing economic incentives to creativity and innovation through the artificial creation of exclusivity.[55] Yochai Benkler, among others, has clearly argued that in the information society, as exemplified by free software production models, this justification is not necessarily correct, as there are (many) other incentives to innovation, including curiosity, need, benefits to

[52] C diBona, 'Introduction' in C DiBona, S Ockman and M Stone (eds), *Open Sources: Voices from the Open Source Revolution* (O'Reilly Media, 1999).

[53] Notwithstanding the difficulties of interpreting certain licences in certain conditions, eg, the copyleft scope of the GPL. However, the most vibrant FOSS community, the Linux Community, uses the GPLv2 as its legal foundation, showing that this is not an impediment to innovation and sharing.

[54] J Schultz and JM Urban, 'Protecting Open Innovation: The Defensive Patent License as a New Approach to Patent Threats, Transaction Costs, and Tactical Disarmament' (2012) 26 *Harvard Journal of Law and Technology* 15.

[55] See, eg, PA David 'Intellectual Property Institutions and the Panda's Thumb: Patents, Copyright, and Trade Secrets in Economic Theory and History' in MB Wallerstein, ME Mogee and RA Schoen (eds), *Global Dimensions of Intellectual Property Rights in Science and Technology* (National Academies Press, 1993) 19–62; or GK Hadfield, 'The economics of copyright' (1992 38 *Copyright L Symp* 1); reviewed in C Handke, 'The Economics of Copyright and Digitisation: A Report on the Literature and the Need for Further Research' (2010) *SABIP*. For counter arguments, see M Boldrin and D Levine, *Against Intellectual Monopoly* (Cambridge, Cambridge University Press, 2008) esp ch 7, 'Defenses of Intellectual Monopoly'.

reputation, the simple desire to share knowledge, or stimulating demand for a related product or service.[56]

Patents also offer the risk of over protection: going back to the historical debate of how to protect and incentivize the creation of software, there were arguments against the broad protection granted by patent rights over 'any' implementation of a particular process, its functionalities, its interoperability, and the impossibility of carrying out reverse engineering, as being too wide and hindering competition and innovation in this sector.[57] Recognizing this, the copyright legal regime for software provides express exclusions for interoperability and reverse engineering to study the principles and ideas behind a software program, eg, to be able to reproduce in a new manner its functionalities.[58]

This is particularly important for FOSS, one of whose main areas of development is the reverse engineering of proprietary software formats and functionalities, to create and distribute under FOSS licence terms both programs with similar features and software that is interoperable with proprietary formats (eg OpenOffice.org/ LibreOffice or SAMBA[59]).

In *SAS Institute v Worldwide Programming*,[60] the European Court of Justice reviewed the question of the protection by copyright of software functionalities, in the context of innovation and technical progress, concluding that:

> On the basis of those considerations, it must be stated that, with regard to the elements of a computer program which are the subject of Questions 1 to 5, neither the functionality of a computer program nor the programming language and the format of data files used in a computer program in order to exploit certain of its functions constitute a form of expression of that program for the purposes of Article 1(2) of Directive 91/250.
>
> As the Advocate General states in point 57 of his Opinion, to accept that the functionality of a computer program can be protected by copyright would amount to making it possible to monopolise ideas, to the detriment of technological progress and industrial development.[61]

However, what is granted by the copyright regime (reverse engineering and interoperability), can be taken away by the patent regime. And although the law clearly states

[56] Y Benkler, *The Wealth of Networks: How Social Production Transforms Markets and Freedom* (New Haven, Yale Press, 2006) 63. Collaborative development models are also described in various articles in DiBona et al (eds) (n 52); and, eg, Chris DiBona's ch 2, 'Open Source and Proprietary Software Development' in C DiBona, D Cooper, and M Stone (eds), *Open Sources 2.0: the continuing evolution* (O'Reilly and Associates, 2006).

[57] See debates of WIPO, Advisory Group of Governmental Experts on the Protection of Computer Programs, *Copyright* (WIPO's monthly bulletin) March 1971, 5–40; and WIPO Group of Experts on the Legal Protection of Computer Software, *Draft Treaty for the Protection of Computer Software* (Geneva, 13–17 June 1983).

[58] See WIPO Model Provisions for the Protection of Software 1983 and, eg, EC Software Directive, Articles 5 and 6.

[59] Libre Office: <http://www.libreoffice.org> and Samba: <http://www.samba.org> accessed 9 April 2013.

[60] *SAS Institute Inc v World Programming Ltd*, C-406/10.

[61] ECJ decision C-406/10, paras 39, 40.

that copyright and patent regimes are complementary and non-exclusionary, this seems illogical taking into account that the objectives of the two regimes, to incentivize and reward creativity and innovation, are basically the same.

5.3.3 Frictions in practice

Not just on a theoretical basis, but also in practice, there is a significant number of friction areas between the legal regime for patents and FOSS and its production and distribution models.

First, as regards obtaining patents—if the FOSS community did ever want to patent inventive processes of a project—in environments where innovation is incremental and distributed throughout a community, it may be difficult if not impossible to determine who the author of an invention is. And who should be the beneficiary and rights holder of the patent rights? There is often no such figure or entity to hold them.

Second, from a risk analysis point of view, the risk of infringing copyright in software is far lower than the risk of infringing a patent. Copyright infringement can be avoided by implementing good development practices and (if need be) creating new and independent versions of copyrighted software. With regard to FOSS licensed code, it is in fact quite difficult to infringe copyright, as most exclusive copyright rights in the original code that you may be working on or with, are granted. Conversely, a patent over a software process can stop anyone from making, using, or selling the patented invention, even if there is no copying of the inventor's original software (if any). This means that it may be impossible to avoid infringing a patent regardless of how much care is taken, particularly essential patents on standards. Studies released in 2004, eg, indicate that the GNU/Linux operating system may infringe some 280 software patents.[62] What's more, the source code availability of FOSS allows a patent based plaintiff to evaluate infringement easily, while a reverse evaluation of binary code would be more difficult.

> Software patents are dangerous to software developers because they impose monopolies on software ideas. It is not feasible or safe to develop nontrivial software if you must thread a maze of patents.[63]

Moreover, it is argued that this situation is worse for FOSS than for proprietary projects.[64] As we have commented, FOSS is often developed by many

[62] See D Lyons, 'Linux Scare Tactics' (*Forbes Magazine*, 8 February 2004) <http://www.forbes.com/2004/08/02/cz_dl_0802linux.html> accessed 9 April 2013; and *Open Source Risk Management Position Paper—Mitigating Patent Risks* (2 August 2004).

[63] R Stallman, 'Europe's "Unitary Patent" Could Mean Unlimited Software Patents' <http://www.gnu.org/philosophy/europes-unitary-patent.html> accessed 9 April 2013.

[64] J V Morgan, 'Chaining Open Source Software: The Case Against Software Patents' (1999) <http://progfree.org/Patents/chaining-oss.html> accessed 9 April 2013.

persons—volunteers—in 'open' communities. These communities rarely have any company or institution providing (legal or financial) support, and thus the individual developers are more vulnerable to litigation. They certainly don't have the financial resources to cover the cost of dealing with patent issues, which can cost thousands if not millions of euros. However, a counter argument is that these individuals are not worth pursuing by patent holders, which may be one of the reasons that to date there are few if any patent-based cases against non-commercial FOSS projects.

However, any corporate end users are vulnerable to attack. While copyright focuses on the potentially infringing copying, transformation, and distribution of software (thus acts carried out by persons in the software industry), any person that also *uses* software that infringes a patent is liable and can have monetary damages and an injunction awarded against them, regardless of whether they were aware of the patent or had any intent to infringe it, and regardless of whether they have any technical or other expertise in dealing with patents. This has a significant impact across industry, raising development expenses, and increasing legal risks and insurance premiums. This also hinders the uptake of the FOSS projects' output through fear of prosecution, or making it more expensive by encouraging participants to take a royalty bearing patent licence (Novell's agreement with Microsoft is an example of this, as are the companies taking Microsoft or Apple patent licences for the distribution of Android devices).

For a non-commercial FOSS project (and most commercial ones too), taking a patent licence is also nearly impossible. Patent licences and associated royalties are usually based on usage, and a FOSS project rarely if ever knows how its software is used, improved, or redistributed. In addition, in the event of using any FOSS under copyleft licences, in particular the GPL, the patent licence would have to contemplate redistribution of the code unencumbered by any downstream patent restrictions so to enable the code to remain free; the patent holder would have to be willing to grant wide downstream user rights, something they are unlikely to be willing to do, absent any numerical data on usage.[65]

> We cannot just buy a patent license, because though free software isn't always free like free beer, it cannot exist at all unless it is free like free speech: everyone has to be allowed to take free code from one place and use it in another, or build on it, so long as she is willing to share and share alike.[66]

Rarely can this be done in a manner to achieve compatibility with copyleft licensing, even on RAND (reasonable and non-discriminatory terms),[67] although Red Hat has

[65] See Clause 7 of the GPLv2 available at <http://www.gnu.org/licenses/old-licenses/gpl-2.0.html> accessed 9 April 2013, noted later.

[66] Moglen (n 5).

[67] Discussed at length in IG Mitchell and S Mason, 'Compatibility Of The Licensing Of Embedded Patents With Open Source Licensing Terms' (2010) *IFOSS LRev* 3(1), 25–58.

achieved it through its widely publicized agreement with Firestar. But Red Hat is in the unique position of having both the financial means and legal resources to negotiate such a licence.[68]

Often in cases of (corporate) patent litigation, the parties involved can and often do come to settlement through cross-licensing and patent peace agreements. These agreements are non-aggression agreements providing each party royalty-free access to a determined part of the other party's patent portfolio. This is prevalent in areas such as hardware manufacturing or biotech, and royalty-free cross-licences are quite common in the computer hardware and software industry among proprietary companies. However, the nature of FOSS makes cross-licensing non-viable; first, very few (if any) FOSS projects have any patents with which to 'trade' with a potential plaintiff. Second, there is usually no particular institution or entity with which to negotiate such an agreement (with the exception of corporate sponsored developments, such as Red Hat, which as we have mentioned, can and have negotiated patent licences). Third, any potential legal entanglement due to software patents creates uncertainty and significant fear within the project community. As Georg Greve, founder and former president of the FSF Europe stated before the European Commission, few FOSS projects are going to go near any patented technology or process—if they ever get to know about it—merely due to the risk of patent litigation and the transaction costs for dealing with the patent situation.[69]

It has been argued, in the context of patents over standards, that from an economic perspective patent licences and royalties may be compatible with FOSS development models: it is just a question of implementing an appropriate technological or business process for licensing and collecting the dues.[70] Indeed, there are FOSS projects such as Fluendo[71] whose very existence and business model lies in dealing with patents rights over audiovisual codecs, and interested third parties can purchase licences to these patent rights so as to implement and distribute proprietary patented codecs in FOSS multimedia environments. However, above and beyond the legal incompatibility when using copyleft licences, most non-commercial (and many commercial) FOSS projects are particularly incompatible with royalty-bearing technologies, since an essential characteristic of the project is to share the code easily among community participants (including users), and they have no visibility or control of downstream

[68] See Red Hat press release Legal Team, 'Red Hat Puts Patent Issues to Rest' *(Red Hat,* 11 June 2008) <http://www.redhat.com/about/news/archive/2008/6/red-hat-puts-patent-issue-to-rest>; commented on online at Grocklaw, 'The Red Hat-FireStar Settlement Agreement is Published' (15 July 2008) <http://www.groklaw.net/articlebasic.php?story=20080715054748526> both accessed 9 April 2013.

[69] European Commission Workshop on IPR and Standardisation, 22 November 2012: 'Implementing FRAND standards in Open Source: Business as usual or mission impossible?' papers available at <http://ec.europa.eu/enterprise/sectors/ict/standards/extended/event_open_source_en.htm> accessed 9 April 2013.

[70] JP Kesan, 'The Fallacy of OSS Discrimination by FRAND Licensing: An Empirical Analysis' (22 February 2011) *Illinois Public Law Research Paper* No 10-14.

[71] Available at Fluendo <http://www.fluendo.com> accessed 9 April 2013.

users. Requiring even minimal royalties would greatly hinder the freedom of developers to share and distribute the code they write.

This is reinforced by the sheer number of software related patents that are applied for and issued annually (particularly in the US), as well as the legal uncertainty about many of those that are issued (for lack of novelty, inventiveness, or patentable subject matter, as discussed earlier).[72] It would be impossible—if not counterproductive, as they could then be claimed to be knowingly infringing a patent, if subsequently litigated—for software developers to read through all the software patents relevant in their area of expertise (let alone 'all' software patents generally), and subsequently take an informed view on the validity or not of those patents.

Another significant area of concern for the FOSS community is the accumulation of patents in proprietary software companies and their associated companies. Usually, large companies like IBM, HP, or Novell use patents defensively. As they know that other companies in the industry will apply for patents, and then may sue for patent infringement in order to gain a competitive advantage, a company that wants to defend itself files for its own patents to use against its competitors. This either creates a massive patent war, such as that occurring in the mobile device space,[73] or creates a *détente* or hold-off between the company and its competitors, each could sue the other in a similar way, so neither one does (and eventually they enter into cross-licensing agreements such as those mentioned earlier). However, members of the FOSS community are becoming increasingly concerned by ongoing moves from large proprietary corporations, directly or through entities such as Intellectual Ventures,[74] to acquire a range of software patents that they can potentially use in the future to attack and try to restrict the development and distribution of free software.

Finally, and this is linked to the previous point, we must mention patent trolls, or 'non-practising entities'.[75] As we have mentioned, these are entities that accumulate patent portfolios for the mere purpose of demanding patent royalties from third parties, and do not themselves 'practise' or implement their patents. They do not make, use, import, sell, or offer for sale anything that could be infringing, inoculating them against countersuits. There are a significant number of these entities, such as Acacia Media, Trend Micro, IP Innovation, or Intellectual Ventures, holding large portfolios of patents of often dubious validity (Intellectual Ventures is alleged to hold over 30,000 existing patents).[76] While one would think they would target their activities against commercial entities, in particular proprietary software publishers with funds

[72] Ballardini (n 31) 207.

[73] Involving Samsung, HTC, Motorola, and Apple, among others. See ch 6.

[74] D Crouch and J Rantanen, 'Intellectual Ventures: Revealing Investors' (*Patentlyo*, 18 May 20122) <http://www.patentlyo.com/patent/2011/05/intellectual-ventures-revealing-investors.html> accessed 9 April 2013.

[75] See BT Yeh, 'An Overview of the "Patent Trolls" Debate' (2012) Congressional Research Service, for a good overview of this problem.

[76] T Bishop, 'Intellectual Ventures sues HP, Dell and others over patents' (*Geekwire*, 12 July 2011) <http://www.geekwire.com/2011/intellectual-ventures-sues-hp-dell-patents> accessed 9 April 2013.

to pay for royalties, more recently they have been targeting the FOSS community, in particular FOSS based commercial entities such as Red Hat, who had to deal, eg, with Firestar.[77] As opposed to litigation against industrial entities, where (negatively) the threat of patent retaliation or (positively) the offer of a cross-licence may be made, it is nearly impossible to use such a strategy against patent trolls, leaving only the expensive (prohibitively so, for FOSS communities) options of paying a royalty or challenging the validity of the alleged patents; or, abandoning the allegedly infringing software altogether.

Thus in the end the patenting regime for software benefits nearly exclusively large (proprietary) software companies with economic resources to apply for, defend, and litigate software patents, to the detriment of the open source communities who are behind many of the current innovations in ICTs.

In summary, software patents are expensive to acquire and enforce, and outside most FOSS projects economic capabilities. They are a philosophical, cultural, and political anathema to many FOSS communities and their members, as a restriction on innovation. Many of them are of dubious validity, due to lack of novelty or inventiveness; and even when they appear to be acquired for 'defensive' or other altruistic purposes, there has been no guarantee against someone later 'weaponizing' them for use in an offensive attack.[78]

This has led the FOSS community as a whole to reject the current legal regime whose uncertainty enables obtaining patent protection (in any form, even the allegedly 'highly filtered' protection granted by the EPO) for software, arguing on the one hand that the whole system is too expensive for FOSS projects and small software publishers to benefit from (if they wanted to) and, on basis of their own experience and that of the software industry as a whole, that copyright provides sufficiently strong protection for software and incentive to innovate and create more.

In a now often quoted memo, Bill Gates said in 1991 'If people had understood how patents would be granted when most of today's ideas were invented, and had taken out patents, the industry would be at a complete standstill today.'[79] On this issue Richard Stallman stated in 2004: 'Software patents are the software project equivalent of land mines: each design decision carries a risk of stepping on a patent, which can destroy your project. Because every such patent covers some idea and the use of that idea, which by giving monopoly on patents inhibits the development of software.'[80]

[77] Reported online. F Marinescu, 'Red Hat Sued Over Hibernate 3 ORM Patent Infringement Claim' (*Infoq*, 30 June 2006) <http://www.infoq.com/news/RedHat-Sued-Due-to-Hibernate-3-O> accessed 9 April 2013, settled in 2008.

[78] Schultz and Urban (n 54).

[79] B Gates, 'Challenges and Strategy Memo' (16 May 1991) <http://en.swpat.org/wiki/Bill_Gates_on_software_patents> accessed 9 April 2013.

[80] R Stallman, 'Fighting Software Patents—Singly and Together' (2004) <http://www.gnu.org/philosophy/fighting-software-patents.html> accessed 9 April 2013.

5.4 PATENTS, STANDARDS, AND FOSS

One area where FOSS and patents interact significantly is in the context of standards, particularly standards for file formats, interfaces, and interoperability protocols. While the policy issues of open source, standards, and innovation are discussed in Chapter 10 of this work, I think it is relevant to consider here the specific relationship between patents and software standards (and interoperability standards in particular), and the potential conflicts for free and open source software implementations of patent encumbered standards.

5.4.1 Software interoperability

Most programs are not designed to work by themselves, but to interact with other programs either via data exchange (with defined data formats) or through common application interfaces (with defined interface information and protocols). So for a program to interoperate with another, it has to 'support' a protocol, an interface, or a data format that the other program uses. In other words, both programs have to use a common standard to interoperate.

One way to achieve this type of interoperability is to provide open access to the interface information and source code of the applications, so that any other developer can learn and use this information to create new interoperable software programs. But not all programs are open source; accordingly even if a program is 'closed source', it is important to publish the interoperability information if interoperability with other programs is desired.[81]

A means for achieving coherent software architectures and systems, and also competition among software publishers to provide programs for these systems, is to ensure that data formats and interface specifications for software programs are open and standard. Hence the involvement of standards setting bodies ('SSBs'), such as ETSI, IEEE, IETF, OASIS (with regard to XML-based technologies), W3C (for web related standards), or the Object Management Group, each of which provide a forum for industry participants to suggest and define the specification of standards relevant for the body, and among which the standards for information systems interoperability are some of the most important.

Access to and use of interoperability information is all the more important for integrated information system 'frameworks' such as that aimed at by the European Interoperability Framework ('EIF'), a set of guidelines and recommendations for ensuring interoperable public administration information technology

[81] In fact, if you do not publish this information, European copyright law for software allows third parties to reverse engineer your code so as to obtain this information (EU Software Directive, Article 6.1).

systems.[82] The current version of the EIF requires the use of 'open' specifications, being those in which all can participate in their elaboration; that the specification document is available; and with respect to IP rights in the standards, they 'are licensed on Free Reasonable and Non-Discriminatory terms or on a royalty-free basis in a way that allows implementation in both proprietary and open source software'.

A software standard can be seen as a definition or specification setting out how the format of data or the process of a software program or system for data exchange should be. This specification can be protected by law, either as a trade secret (if the information is proprietary and protected against unauthorized disclosure to third parties) or, more relevantly for the current purposes, by patent claims over the standard's methods and/or processes. Thus a standard is particularly susceptible to being patented, whereas the software reference implementation would be protected by copyright. Hence, the law can be used to restrict access to and use of standards, by invoking trade secret or patent protection.

> While the patent system and the standards system share certain common objectives, inherent tensions exist between patents and standards. These become particularly apparent when the implementation of a standard calls for the use of technology covered by one or more patents. Indeed, on the one hand, the objective of standardization, which in many cases involves companies interested in the development of the technology in question, is to establish standardized technology that can be used as widely as possible in the market. On the other hand, patent owners in the relevant area who have invested resources in developing the patented technology may have an interest in the adoption, in the standard, of their own patented technology which may bring them, at a later stage when the standard is being implemented and applied, royalty income.[83]

The potential to hold a patent over a standard is an incentive for existing or prospective patent holders—in particular large industry players who are members of SSBs—to orient standardization efforts towards adopting standards involving formats, methods, or processes covered by their patents. Consequently, if a method is 'essential' for the standard, that is it cannot be avoided, any person interested in implementing the standard would have to obtain the patent rights holder's authorization to do so.

[82] European Commission, IDABC, 'Linking up Europe: the Importance of Interoperability for eGovernment Services, Commission Staff Working Paper' 7 (*EC,* 2003) <http://europa.eu.int/idabc/servlets/Doc?id=1675> accessed 9 April 2013. EIF version 2 is in COM (2010) 744 final Communication, Towards interoperability for European public services, European Interoperability Framework for European Public Services v2, para 5.2.1.

[83] WIPO, Standing Committee on the Law of Patents, Thirteenth Session, Geneva, 23–27 March 2009, SCP/13/2, 18 February 2009.

5.4.2 RAND licensing terms and copyleft

To control or prevent legally enforced restrictions being imposed with respect to interoperability standards established and subsequently published by SSBs, these organizations have 'IP policies' that require their participants (members) to declare ex ante any patents they may hold over formats, processes or methods submitted for standardization, and enter into patent licensing agreements with all third parties if the process or information is subsequently accepted as part of the recognized standard.

The problem that arises is with respect to the terms of the licences over patents that are material or essential to the standards. The IP policies of some standards setting bodies, such as the W3C or the OMG, require that such patents be freely available to all, on non-discriminatory and royalty free terms.[84] These policies are compatible with implementation of the standards by software licensed under FOSS terms, as there are no downstream restrictions on redistribution and redevelopment using the patented technology or process. However, many other important standards bodies in the software sector, such as ETSI, IEEE, or IETF, only require essential patent licences to be granted on what has become to be known as 'fair, reasonable and non-discriminatory terms' (FRAND, or just RAND).[85] 'Non-discriminatory' signifies that the licensor must not refuse to license different parties who are similarly situated on materially similar terms. However there is no definition of RAND, especially with regard to any economic impact, and little if no guidance provided by the standards setting bodies that establish this as their IP policy.[86] In fact, many SSBs do not guarantee that their standards may be used in FOSS programs, since they allow restrictions to be imposed that are incompatible with the software freedoms we have already mentioned.

In addition to this, there may well be patents granted over the specification held by patentees who are not participants in the standardization process, and who are therefore not bound by the disclosure and the RAND/RF licensing obligations.

[84] eg, see DJ Weitzner, 'Current Patent Practice' (*W3C*, January 2002) fn 24 <http://www.w3.org/TR/patent-practice> accessed 9 April 2013.

[85] See ch 10 of this work, which discusses the different positions of the SSBs towards patent licensing. Also, see ETSI example in P Treacy and S Lawrance, 'FRANDly fire: are industry standards doing more harm than good?' (2008) *Journal of Intellectual Property Law & Practice*, vol 3, no 1, 22–9. Also, a summary in M Välimäki and V Oksanen, 'Patents on Compatibility Standards and Open Source—Do Patent Law Exceptions and Royalty-Free Requirements Make Sense?' (2007) 2 *SCRIPTed* 397, 398.

[86] For a more detailed study, see M Välimäki, 'A Practical Approach to the Problem of Open Source and Software Patents' (December 2004) 26(12) *EIPR* 523–7. Note however that there may be competition issues with providing strict guidelines or rules as to RAND patent licensing (price fixing), and SSBs are wary of doing so (or so they argue). See MA Lemley, 'Intellectual Property Rights and Standard-Setting Organizations' (2002) 90 *Cal L Rev* 1889 available at <http://scholarship.law.berkeley.edu/californialawreview/vol90/iss6/3> accessed 9 April 2013. See also, R Shapiro, 'Navigating the Patent Thicket: Cross Licenses, Patent Pools and Standard Setting' in AB Jaffe, J Lerner, and S Stern (eds), *Innovation Policy And The Economy* (NBER Book Series Innovation Policy and the Economy, Boston, MIT Press, 2001) 119–50.

Above and beyond the issue of whether submitting a technology for standardization and then demanding patent royalties is fair and reasonable in any circumstances, and despite the economic question of what exactly are RAND terms in a variety of circumstances (both for closed and open source software projects), the requirement to pay royalties for use of a patented standard, and the imposition of other restrictions often found in patent licences, such as cross licensing obligations,[87] are legally incompatible with many FOSS licences, in particular copyleft licences such as the GPL or other members of the GPL family (LGPL, AferroGPL).[88] This is because these copyleft licences require that original software and any derivative works be redistributed under the same (royalty free) terms as the original licence, *with no further restrictions*. As we have noted earlier, the GPL therefore does not permit patent-style 'additional' restrictions being imposed on recipients of the code (including the payment of even RAND royalties). If they were, and this would be the case if downstream recipients of the code had to pay royalty fees to a third party, then the licensor is not permitted to redistribute the code at all unless it obtains a patent licence for all users.[89] This means that, absent a specifically negotiated licence with the patent holder to cover downstream licensing and licensees, software under copylefted licence terms cannot be used to implement these standards.[90]

In addition, regardless of the purely legal position, there are market-based strategic considerations in play in this context, derived from differing business models between proprietary and FOSS licensing, which are discussed in more detail in Chapter 10. In particular, using patents as a means to increase transaction costs for competing products implementing the standard (including therefore, and in particular, FOSS projects, one of whose competitive arguments is that the code is economically free (gratis), currently a strong business incentive, particularly for government procurement); and holding up competing implementations in order to get first mover advantage or maintain a significant market position.

Beyond the conflicts between patents and free software licensing and development methods previously discussed, and evidence that the concept of software patents may not only be flawed but also does not provide any incentive for innovation,[91] their actual implementation and use as strategic tools can and have

[87] See Microsoft standards patent licences: Microsoft Work Group Server Protocol Program License Agreement or Microsoft Business Process Execution Language for Web Services License.

[88] While they may seem to be only a fraction of recognized FOSS licenses, a statistical analysis of available FOSS repository information (source forge, github, and so on) indicates that copyleft licence terms are used by more than 85% of free software projects, and the GPL family covers around 60%.

[89] GPL2 cl 7 and GPLv3 cl 12. See s 5.5.

[90] For a detailed analysis, see Mitchell and Mason (n 67). Also G Greve, 'Analysis on Balance: Standardisation and Patents' (*FSFE*, 2 December 2008) <http://fsfe.org/projects/os/ps.en.pdf> accessed 9 April 2013. For arguments en contra, see Kesan (n 70).

[91] M Boldrin and DK Levine, 'The Case against Patents' (2013) *Journal of Economic Perspective* 27(1): 3–22. Also online at <http://research.stlouisfed.org/wp/2012/2012-035.pdf> accessed 9 April 2013.

constituted serious risks in restricting the operation of standards and interoperability.[92] A recent study on standards for Open Standards for IT in Government in the UK[93] concludes by asking whether there is any economic justification to encourage patent protection of interfaces and data formats, and whether there is a failure of the market which has not been corrected by the adoption of SSBs of FRAND policies, to which the UK Cabinet Office has answered in the negative for the first question, and promoted a 'royalty free' standards policy.[94] This is analysed from a policy perspective in Chapter 10.

5.5 HOW FOSS DEALS WITH PATENTS

We now turn to see how the community has reacted to and deals with the several interactions and friction areas between patents and FOSS, and the perceived patent threat.

The FOSS community's actions in this respect can be divided into two types of action: preventive measures, to minimize the impact of software patents on software freedoms, and reactive measures, taking action to invalidate and neutralize the current patent threats to free software development.

5.5.1 Patent clauses in FOSS licences

The first and most 'structural' preventive measure to deal with software patents is the incorporation of patent related terms in FOSS licences. As we noted in the introduction, a FOSS project's community norms and guidelines are reflected in the chosen licence terms: they set out the rules for participation, in particular for contributing to and using the project software. So the community has leveraged the licences to set out rules regarding patent grants and non-assertion among participants.

5.5.2 First generation FOSS licences

The first generation of FOSS licences, particularly the no copyleft licences such as the BSD, Apache 1.0 and 1.1 or the X11/MIT licences, did not expressly deal with patents,

[92] The case of *European Commission v Microsoft* is evidence of use of patents (and secrecy) for strategic purposes to restrict interoperability and competition by the SAMBA free software project. A Orlowski, 'Samba shakes hands with Microsoft' (*The Register*, 21 December 2007) <http://www.theregister.co.uk/2007/12/21/samba_microsoft_agreement> accessed 9 April 2013.

[93] S Weston and M Kretschmer, 'Open standards in government it: a review of the evidence' (*Centre for Intellectual Property Policy & Management (CIPPM)*, Bournemouth University, 2011) <http://www.cippm.org.uk/publications/open-standards-in-government-it-study.html> accessed 9 April 2013.

[94] HM Government, 'Welcome to the Open Standards Consultation' <http://consultation.cabinetoffice.gov.uk/openstandards> accessed 8 April 2013, esp ch 1, 'Criteria for Open Standards'.

though on the wording of the licences, there are arguments that an implicit licence is granted (a licence to 'use' the software). Unfortunately, while these licences do grant rights to 'use' the software (use being one of the acts restricted by patent rights, as opposed to copyright) many legal writers believe that implicit patent licences are uncertain and not binding (in particular when there is no consideration), giving rise to questions regarding their scope or duration, the impact of combing potentially patented software distributed under these licences with other programs or hardware, and the creation of derivative works.[95] This is not a happy situation with regard to legal certainty for the FOSS community, and while these licences are still popular, contributors with significant patent portfolios, in particular universities or large corporations such as IBM, eschew these licences in favour of more recent versions with explicit patent provisions.[96]

Where a company did recently want to use one of these more permissive licences (Google Inc, in this instance, with regard to WebM VP8 video codec technologies), it added a patent licence grant and peace terms in an additional clause, tying the patent grant to its implementation of the patent claims.[97] The impact of this is twofold: the code that Google has distributed is effectively granted under the MIT licence, a recognized and standard FOSS licence permitting easy use and adoption, while users of Google's version of the code are given comfort and protection as regards claims with respect to patents that Google and other contributors may hold in the codec.[98]

The GPLv2, published in 1991, did in fact have some wording dealing with patents, with the principal aim of making GPL'd software redistribution incompatible with software patents rights assertion. GPLv2 does not have a patent grant or non-assertion covenant. While a licence by the original creator cannot take away patent assertion rights of a third party patent holder (rights to restrict distribution and use of a software that embodies the patent for example against payment of a royalty), what it can do is prevent the redistribution of the original software at all if such distribution under the terms of the GPL2 is prevented by patents encumbering the software; hence the name of Clause 7 of GPLv2, 'liberty or death.'

> 7. If, as a consequence of a court judgment or allegation of patent infringement or for any other reason (not limited to patent issues), conditions are imposed on you

[95] H Meeker, *The Open Source Alternative* (New Jersey, John Wiley and Sons, 2008).

[96] IBM is the primary drafter of the Common Public License (now the Eclipse Public License). Universities in the US have promoted the Education Community License, a derivate of the Apache Software License 2.0 with specific patent related clauses (see comment by Wheeler et al, 'Open Source Collaboration in Higher Education: Guidelines and Report of the Licensing and Policy Framework Summit for Software Sharing in Higher Education' (*Scholar Works*, March 2007) <https://scholarworks.iu.edu/dspace/handle/2022/3076> accessed 9 April 2013).

[97] Google's WebM, 'Additional IP Rights Grant (Patents)' <http://www.webmproject.org/license/additional> accessed 9 April 2013.

[98] This of course does not guarantee that 'all' potential patent rights in the codec are licensed, as Google may not hold all those rights.

> (whether by court order, agreement or otherwise) that contradict the conditions of this License, they do not excuse you from the conditions of this License. If you cannot distribute so as to satisfy simultaneously your obligations under this License and any other pertinent obligations, then as a consequence you may not distribute the Program at all. For example, if a patent license would not permit royalty-free redistribution of the Program by all those who receive copies directly or indirectly through you, then the only way you could satisfy both it and this License would be to refrain entirely from distribution of the Program.

The GPL2 also forbids imposing any additional restrictions (such as patent encumbrances) on the rights granted by the licence to the recipients of the software. If a distributor does so, eg, by asserting patent rights, his or her licence under the GPL is cancelled. This effectively means that a patent holder who distributes a software program based on GPLv2 code, embodying one or more of its patents, may no longer assert those patent rights against downstream licensees who redistribute that program onwards, or who incorporate the program in their own product. What's more, this has the effect that if a GPL licensee does get a third party patent licence to exploit the software, then to be able to redistribute it they must effectively ensure that all downstream licensees are covered. This was made explicit in GPLv3, published in 2007,[99] and Red Hat achieved this in its agreement with Firestar (with respect to one of its FOSS programs, called Hibernate).

5.5.3 Second generation FOSS licences

This situation was not a happy one from a legal point of view, due to the uncertainty of the terms, and not acceptable for a corporation such as Netscape that was considering freeing its 'Navigator' web browser in 1998. So the drafters of Netscape Public License (migrated into the Mozilla Public License 1.1) included express patent provisions in this licence, and since then most recent FOSS licences do so too.

These 'patent provisions' generally do two things: first, they grant a patent licence over patent rights that the initial developer or any contributor to the project may have in his or her contribution. Secondly, they provide for patent peace and retaliation, through licence termination in the event of initiating aggressive patent litigation with respect to the software. However, there are several interesting variations among the main FOSS licences.

For example, as regards patent grants, the Apache Software Foundation 2.0 licence[100] provides a licence from each contributor to 'make, have made, use, offer to sell, sell, import, and otherwise transfer the Work'. This grant covers the contributor's

[99] GNU, 'GNU General Public License' <http://www.gnu.org/licenses/gpl.html> accessed 9 April 2013.

[100] The Apache Software Foundation, 'Apache License, Version 2.0' <http://www.apache.org/licenses/LICENSE-2.0.html> accessed 9 April 2013.

contribution by itself, or when combined with the software to which it is contributed. The MPL1.1 (1998)[101] patent grant, by the initial developer and contributors, is under 'Patents Claims infringed by the making, using or selling of [Original Code or *Modifications], to make, have made, use, practice, sell, and offer for sale, and/or otherwise dispose of the [Original code or Modification]*,' and excludes deletions from, or modifications made to, the code or combinations of the code with other software or devices. It is interesting to note that 'patent claims' cover both current patents (existing at the time of distribution) and future patents that the developer/contributor may subsequently acquire. The MPL 2.0 (2012)[102] patent grant is similar, covering the present and future patents rights regarding the 'making, using, selling, offering for sale, having made, import, or transfer of either [the Contributor's] Contributions or its Contributor Version.'

GPLv3 (2007) also has a patent grant: clause 11 provides:

> Each contributor grants you [the user] a non-exclusive, worldwide, royalty-free patent license under the contributor's essential patent claims, to make, use, sell, offer for sale, import and otherwise run, modify and propagate the contents of its contributor version.

Essential patent claims are defined as

> all patent claims owned or controlled by the contributor, whether already acquired or hereafter acquired, that would be infringed by some manner, permitted by this License, of making, using, or selling its contributor version, but do not include claims that would be infringed only as a consequence of further modification of the contributor version. For purposes of this definition, 'control' includes the right to grant patent sublicenses in a manner consistent with the requirements of this License.

The last point regarding 'control' is interesting, as in practice it permitted the flexibility for Red Hat to acquire downstream patent sublicensing rights from Firestar, so as to ensure valid onward GPL-based licensing of the (allegedly) patented code.[103]

[101] Mozilla, 'Public License Version 1.1' <http://www.mozilla.org/MPL/1.1> accessed 9 April 2013.

[102] Mozilla, 'Public License Version 2.0' <http://www.mozilla.org/MPL/2.0> accessed 9 April 2013.

[103] This is reinforced by paras in cl 11 of the GPLv3 that provide for this very situation: 'If you convey a covered work, knowingly relying on a patent license, and the Corresponding Source of the work is not available for anyone to copy, free of charge and under the terms of this License, through a publicly available network server or other readily accessible means, then you must either (1) cause the Corresponding Source to be so available, or (2) arrange to deprive yourself of the benefit of the patent license for this particular work, or (3) arrange, in a manner consistent with the requirements of this License, to extend the patent license to downstream recipients.

If, pursuant to or in connection with a single transaction or arrangement, you convey, or propagate by procuring conveyance of, a covered work, and grant a patent license to some of the parties receiving the covered work authorizing them to use, propagate, modify or convey a specific copy of the covered work, then the patent license you grant is automatically extended to all recipients of the covered work and works based on it.'

The overall aim of this is to ensure a level playing field, and guarantee freedoms for the whole chain of licensees taking a copy of the code under the GPL.

These clauses ensure that users of software under these licences get all the specified patent rights from the upstream contributors to the work. This does not mean that use of the software is free of patent risks, as third parties may have patent rights over the work and may not have granted the user any licence. But, at least the user is protected from patent claims by the contributors, who—if the contribution is of original code—are usually the persons most likely to have any patent rights.

5.5.4 Patent peace clauses

As regards patent peace or retaliation clauses, there are several 'flavours', depending on the scope and conditions for triggering the clause. Patent peace provisions are structured as legally binding undertakings given by licensees, either as a general covenant not to sue, or as a specific licence grant to use a particular technology (part of the code). They can be weaker (covenants by licensees not to sue the initial or subsequent contributors with respect to patent rights over a specific code contribution), or stronger (protecting any third party, against any suits based on patent rights over any software, not just the licensed software). The provision may also revoke patent rights or all rights granted under the FOSS licence. In Table 5.1 that follows, we will look at four licences, chronologically the MPL1.1, ASL2, CPL/EPL, and GPLv3.

Table 5.1 Comparison of Patent Peace Clauses

MPL1.1: Clause 8.2	
If You initiate litigation by asserting a patent infringement claim (excluding declaratory judgment actions) against *Initial Developer or a Contributor* ('Participant')... alleging that • such *Participant's Contributor Version* directly or indirectly infringes any patent, then any and *all rights* granted by such Participant to You... shall, upon 60 days notice from Participant terminate prospectively, unless [a royalty arrangement is worked out or the litigation is withdrawn.] • *any software, hardware, or device*, other than such Participant's Contributor Version, directly or indirectly infringes any patent, then *any [patent] rights* granted to You by such Participant... are revoked effective as of the date You first made, used, sold, distributed, or had made, Modifications made by that Participant [my emphasis in italics].	This clause is a mix: on the one hand, it only covers claims against original authors and contributors to the code (ie upstream), on the other, that protection is triggered not just by claims relating to the code itself, but also to any software, hardware or device. The main interest here is in protecting the developers and project members, and making their 'patent weapons' available to them in the event of patent litigation from a licensee. The MPL1.1 drafting is the basis for many subsequent licences.

continued

Table 5.1 (continued)

ASL 2: Clause 3	
If You institute patent litigation against *any entity* (including a cross-claim or counterclaim in a lawsuit) alleging that the *Work or a Contribution* incorporated within the Work constitutes direct or contributory patent infringement, then any *patent licenses* granted to You under this License for that Work shall terminate as of the date such litigation is filed. [my emphasis in italics]	The ASL (released in 2004) has slightly different clause. Thus, on the one hand it seems wider (it covers claims against any entity), but on the other, it is limited to claims with regard to the covered code, and only revokes potential patent right grants; it does not purport to terminate any copyright licence. This clause protects the wider Apache community, including end-users, and not just the code contributors.
CPL 1.0: Clause 7	
• If Recipient institutes patent litigation *against a Contributor* with respect to a patent applicable to *software* (including a cross-claim or counterclaim in a lawsuit), then *any patent licenses* granted by that Contributor to such Recipient under this Agreement shall terminate as of the date such litigation is filed. • In addition, if Recipient institutes patent litigation against *any entity* (including a cross-claim or counterclaim in a lawsuit) alleging that the *Program itself* (excluding combinations of the Program with other software or hardware) infringes such Recipient's patent(s), then such Recipient's *rights granted under Section 2(b)* [patent rights] shall terminate as of the date such litigation is filed. [my emphasis in italics]	In the CPL (drafted by IBM) the MPL1.1's patent wording is mapped, but not quite in the same terms. Clause 7 seems to be a mix of the Mozilla and Apache terms: it has provisions for claims against both (a) the contributors with respect to any software, whereupon all rights are revoked, and (b) any entities, with regard to the software in question, in which case only patent rights are revoked. The first provision provides wider protection for the specific project members and contributors, while the second gives narrower protection related to the specific software, but for the wider FOSS community of users of the software. The CPL was retired and substituted by the Eclipse Public License, which only includes the second provision.
GPLv3: Clause 10	
You may not impose any further restrictions on the exercise of the rights granted or affirmed under this License. For example, you may not impose a license fee, royalty, or other charge for exercise of rights granted under this License, and you may not initiate litigation (including a cross-claim or counterclaim in a lawsuit) alleging that any patent claim is infringed by making, using, selling, offering for sale, or importing the Program or any portion of it.	The GPLv3, released 2007, maintains similar 'liberty or death' provisions as its version 2, commented on in the introduction (now called 'No Surrender of Others' Freedom' clause), and includes this patent peace clause.Breach of this undertaking (not to initiate patent-based litigation with respect to the software in question) would mean breach of the licence, and revocation of all licence rights subject to the reinstatement provisions (eg, if the litigation is withdrawn).The GPL does not limit this litigation against 'developers' but would cover litigation against 'any entity,' similar to the Apache and Eclipse licences commented above.

The GPLv3 provisions were heavily negotiated among stakeholders during the community drafting process of the GPLv3, in order to achieve a specific balance between the interests of the (non-patent holding) volunteer community, who wanted as wide a patent protection as possible, and the more commercially oriented (patent holding) corporate participants, who did not want their whole software patent portfolio to lose value or 'assertability' because the corporation had licensed some code under the GPL. This issue was also commented on again more recently during the drafting of MPL v 2. The Eclipse Public License is also symptomatic, drafted by IBM, a corporation holding possibly the world's largest (software) patent portfolio: the patent grants are as limited as possible, while the patent protections (with regard to third party patents) are much wider.

What do these provisions achieve? On the one hand, as we have noted, FOSS participants using software under these licences have a certain degree of safety from patent related threats from contributors (upstream) and other licensees (downstream users); this provides 'patent peace' among community participants. The more participants involved in the community, the greater the peace, and all the more so if the licence is copyleft, and thus maintains the same licensing terms downstream and throughout the community of users. The stronger the retaliation clause, the wider this peace may be extended, even outside the community of users ('any entity'), or beyond the functionalities of the software in question ('any software, hardware, or device'). This contributes to the ideals of the FOSS community, of providing (safe) access to knowledge of FOSS technologies (and derivative works thereof) and freedom to innovate.

> Licensees and their sublicensees should not be able to benefit from free and open source software while at the same time forcing the licensor to pay royalties for patents embodied in that very software.[104]

However, the scope of this protection does vary, and it is important (especially for patent holding users or contributors to FOSS projects) to understand the scope of the patent peace clauses and how they interact with their patent portfolios, in particular in the case of stronger retaliation clauses. These clauses may discourage patent holders from participating in communities with strong patent peace clauses, for fear of contagion and loss of value of their patents unrelated to the FOSS code, without significant benefits. An example of this is where a company drafted a modification to the MPL1.1 in order to protect this portfolio, rather than use the standard version of the licence.[105]

In addition, there may be questions of validity of parts of these clauses. First, with regard to 'future' acquired patents and patent rights, and second, with regard

[104] L Rosen, 'Dealing with Patents in Software Licences' (2001) *Linux Journal* 1 January 2002 <http://www.linuxjournal.com/article/5575> accessed 9 April 2013.

[105] MXM Public license submission, OSI Review, 'For approval: MXM Public license' (*Crynwr*, 8 April 2009) <http://www.crynwr.com/cgi-bin/ezmlm-cgi?17:mss:717:200904:chenjkbbnllffijebmno>, commented on by G Moody 'Should an Open Source Licence Ever Be Patent-Agnostic?' (*Linux Journal*, 9 April 2009) <http://www.linuxjournal.com/content/should-open-source-licence-ever-be-patent-agnostic> both accessed 9 April 2013.

to extending the benefits of the clauses to non-licensees, or extending the obligations either to future users (holding other patents) of the FOSS technologies, or future holders of relevant patents (eg through acquisition), who may be able to argue they are not party to the original bargain. This may be a question of privity of contract, if licences are deemed to be contracts in this respect; though for licences that are considered to be unilateral authorizations (and not contracts), the provisions would only be effective against licensees (ie users) of the code, as a condition of the licence grant.

The issue of how binding and effective this type of undertaking is in practice, has been raised in particular in the context of standards setting organizations, whose members commit to royalty-free or FRAND licensing terms over patents incorporated in a standard, but whose commitments may not necessarily bind future holders of those patents if they are sold off to a third party.

5.5.5 Open source software as prior art, peer to patent, and defensive publication

Another way of the dealing with the negative impacts of software patents in a preventive manner is to help avoid them being granted ab initio. We have noted in the first section the fight to get software processes—computer implemented inventions—totally excluded (in theory and in practice) from patentability, and the current jurisprudence in this area. In the meantime, while this battle is still being fought in parliament and the courts, there are other projects working to ensure that, during the patent examination process, poor quality applications are rejected for lack of conformity with the main requirements for patentability: novelty and inventive step.

One of the main criticisms aimed at the current patent granting process, in terms of quality, is that patent examiners normally only search patent databases, and occasionally scientific publications, to discover prior art. This means that a significant amount, if not all, of previously published software and software related documentation—both proprietary and FOSS—is not being taken into account during the prior art search stage of the examination process.

Open Source as Prior Art, a project launched in 2005, is an initiative to enable open source software repositories to be considered during this prior art search stage, 'improving accessibility by patent examiners and others to electronically published source code and its related documentation as a source of prior art.'[106] Unfortunately, software in online repositories is not published in a manner that can easily be mapped against the way patent applications describe the claimed methods

[106] The Linux Foundation, 'Open Source as Prior Art (OSAPA)' <http://www.linuxfoundation.org/programs/legal/osapa> accessed 9 April 2013.

or processes. To ensure such software is taken into consideration, it needs to be time stamped, documented, and ideally categorised or described in a manner that can be searched. While this aim is laudable, in practice is has been found to be particularly difficult and time consuming, so it seems the project is currently somewhat 'on hold'. Some interesting know-how has been developed, mainly forward looking for future releases of software, rather than for analysing and tagging existing repositories.

In another attempt at improving patent quality, 'Peer to Patent' is a project launched by the US Patent Office ('USPTO') together with New York Law School, aimed at taking advantage of the software community to supply the USPTO with information and discussion relevant to assessing the claims of patent applications during the examination process, opening this process to public participation, and 'community reviewing'.[107] Within this project, third parties can identify, submit, and rank prior art that is relevant to a patent application. There are also online fora for discussing the validity and strength of the submissions, and this can also lead to the identification of experts in the field who can assist in determining if a claimed process is inventive or not. The results of this project, reviewing 226 applications in a first pilot in the software area, and then 308 applications in a second, were encouraging; several patent applications were rejected or narrowed as a consequence of peer reviewing.[108]

While there have been several criticisms,[109] this project has been seen as one of the factors leading to the creation of certain new processes for improving the quality of patents under the US federal America Invents Act of September 2011,[110] notably the possibility for third parties to file pre-issuance submissions, something similar to the observations phase of European Patent applications.[111] In addition, this project has highlighted the need to take into account all prior art, not just in theory but also in practice, that is relevant to the patent applications they are reviewing: websites, journals, textbooks, software development, user manuals, and other non-patent databases. Community involvement and online discussion also helps find this information. This has a positive economic effect, as avoiding ab initio the issue of poor quality and/or invalid patents is significantly cheaper than a re-examination

[107] Peer to Patent, available at <http://peertopatent.org>. There was also an Australian pilot, available at <http://www.peertopatent.org.au>; and a UK pilot, described in K Hall, 'IPO's Peer to Patent site gets 100 reviewers to assess computing patent applications' (*Computer Weekly*, 13 June 2011) <http://www.computerweekly.com/news/2240104743/IPOs-Peer-to-Patent-site-gets-100-reviewers-to-assess-computing-patent-applications> all accessed 9 April 2013.

[108] See results commented on by A Casillas, 'Peer to Patent Pilot 2 Results' <http://www.slideshare.net/acasillas11/peer-to-patent-pilot-2> accessed 9 April 2013.

[109] Summarized at Wikipedia, 'Peer-to-Patent Criticisms' <http://en.wikipedia.org/wiki/Peer-to-Patent#Criticisms> accessed 9 April 2013.

[110] HR 1246 (112th).

[111] WIPO has also taken up this idea for PCT applications, WIPO, 'Patent Cooperation Treaty (PCT) Working Group' (14-18 June 2010) <http://193.5.93.80/edocs/mdocs/pct/en/pct_wg_3/pct_wg_3_6.pdf> accessed 9 April 2013.

or post-grant review process, or invalidity procedures before the courts. And it will gradually reduce the ability and scope for patent trolls with large portfolios of poor quality patents to threaten FOSS projects.

As a third leg in the strategy for avoiding 'bad patents,' that is those that are of poor quality or invalid for lack of novelty or inventiveness, *defensive publication* is coming to be seen as one of the most efficient and effective measures. Linux Defenders,[112] a program for defending the Linux operating system and the FOSS community as a whole against patent concerns and threats, and which also supports the Peer to Patent project, is leading the Defensive Publications initiative.

Linux Defenders state[113] that:

> Defensive publications are documents that provide descriptions and artwork of a product, device or method so that it enters the public domain and becomes prior art upon publication. This powerful preemptive disclosure prevents other parties from obtaining a patent on a product, device or method that is known though not previously patented. It enables the original inventor to ensure access to the invention across the community by preventing others from later making patent claims on it.
>
> We are attempting to mobilize the creativity and innovative capacities of the Linux and broader open source community to codify the universe of preexisting inventions in defensive publications that upon publication in the IP.COM database will immediately serve as effective prior art that prevents anyone from having a patent issued that claims inventions that have already been document in a defensive publication. In addition to creating a vehicle to utilize this highly effective form of IP rights management for known inventions, it is hoped that the community will use defensive publications as a means of codifying future inventions should the inventors prefer not to make their invention the subject of a patent disclosure and application.

The Defensive Publications site provides guidance for developers and creators on drafting a publication in a form that is easy for patent examiners to review and use as prior art, as well as enables the publication to be posted to the IP.com prior art database, which the patent offices worldwide include in their patent searches.

5.6 PATENT BUSTING AND PATENT POOLS

Peer-to-Patent and Defensive Publication are aimed at preventing the issue of poor quality patents in the software sector. Another question for the FOSS community has been: what can be done about existing 'bad' patents that can be used to threaten the FOSS—and indeed proprietary software—community and potentially demand

[112] Linux Defenders: <http://linuxdefenders.org> accessed 9 April 2013.

[113] Defensive Publications, 'What is a defensive publication?' <http://www.defensivepublications.org> accessed 9 April 2013.

exorbitant patent royalties? This a question of 'problem containment' and the strongest proposals so far focus on post-grant patent review and re-examination, and creating defensive patent pools to protect specific areas of technology. Notably, these proposals are centred in the US, where the software and business method patent problem is most acute.

As regards patent review, there are several community initiatives: one is the Linux Defenders project called 'Post-Issue Peer to Patent'[114] which solicits prior art contribution from Linux and the broader open source community to permit the invalidation of previously issued patents that were issued in error because of the patent office's lack of awareness of relevant prior art. Another is the 'Patent Busters' project, launched in 2004 by Electronic Freedom Foundation ('EFF'),[115] which organizes collaborative community efforts to challenge existing patents that it has pinpointed as being particularly harmful to innovation. It then files for re-examination of the patent, which it has done with certain success. The Public Patent Foundation at the Benjamin N Cardozo School of Law ('PUBPAT')[116] runs a similar project, with the aim of challenging through re-examination US patents that the project members believe are invalid. This project works in all areas of technology, not just software.[117]

These actions have been supported in the US by the introduction of the (allegedly cheaper) post-grant review process under the America Invents Act. This enables third parties to submit evidence of invalidity of a recently granted patent (within nine months of issuance). Grounds for invalidity include both the existence of prior art and non-obviousness based on evidence of public use, on-sale activity, or other public disclosures, as well as non-compliance with description, enablement, or patent eligibility rules. Unfortunately, just as for many post-grant actions such as declaratory judgments, invalidity proceedings, or re-examination, the cost of this still surpasses the available funds of standard FOSS community projects.

To overcome this individual weakness, the solution—as often in the FOSS space—is a collaborative effort. Open Invention Network is one of these.

Open Invention Network ('OIN'),[118] controls a patent pool and has the mandate to defend Linux and Android (as well as some other FOSS packages) from patent attacks. It was launched in 2005, and has received investment from IBM, NEC, Novell, Philips, Red Hat, and Sony. OIN has so far acquired a large (400+) portfolio of patents, 'all available royalty-free to any company, institution or individual that agrees not to

[114] Post Issue, 'Post-Issue Peer to Patent—Improving Patent Quality' <http://www.post-issue.org> accessed 9 April 2013.

[115] EFF, 'Patent Busting Project' <https://www.eff.org/patent-busting> accessed 9 April 2013.

[116] Public Patent Foundation, 'Undeserved Patents and Unsound Patent Policy Harm the Public' <http://www.pubpat.org> accessed 9 April 2013.

[117] Successes are listed at Public Patent Foundation, 'Protecting the public domain' <http://www.pubpat.org/Protecting.htm> accessed 9 April 2013.

[118] OIN <http://www.openinventionnetwork.com> accessed 9 April 2013.

assert its patents against the Linux System'. OIN will therefore buy patents (a) to stop them falling into the hands of non-practising entities, who might otherwise assert them against Linux-based companies;[119] and (b) to provide a portfolio of patents that can be asserted against companies that attack Linux.[120] Over 400 companies are currently members.

Because all of the patents of all of the members are in effect licensed royalty-free to all the other members in relation to Linux and Android, that equates to a collective patent portfolio of over an estimated 350,000 patents and applications.

OIN has acted successfully in at least one action that has been made public, when TomTom was sued by Microsoft over FAT filesystem patents.[121] While there is little statistical data yet regarding patent threats and assertions, it is believed that the mere existence of OIN is a useful factor among industry players for reducing patent threats, at least in the Linux space. Obviously, it has little effect against non-practising entities or trolls who are not frightened of any patent-based counter-claim.

OIN is not itself an assertion entity, that is, it does not itself commence litigation against companies attacking FOSS, although some commentators have suggested—wildly, in my view—that an assertion entity acting on behalf of the FOSS community to recoup sums paid in patent licensing might have attractions.[122]

More recently, in March 2013, Google published an initiative to establish and standardize defensive patent pools, with the objective of reducing the patent litigation concerns, particularly by patent trolls/non-practising entities.[123] Google has outlined 'four multi-party, self-help, patent licensing approaches' to increase companies' freedom to operate while reducing patent assertions, that is to operate in a patent-free or patent assertion-free environment.[124] The main objective or mechanism is to reduce patent

[119] See, eg, OIN's purchase of 22 Silicon Graphics patents that Microsoft placed with Allied Security Trust to sell: P Rooney, 'OIN outmanuevers Microsoft, buys Linux patents' (*ZDnet*, 9 September 2009) <http://www.zdnet.com/blog/open-source/oin-outmanuevers-microsoft-buys-linux-patents/4800> accessed 9 April 2013.

[120] See, eg, OIN's transfer of four patents to Salesforce.com after Salesforce.com was sued for patent infringement by Microsoft: F Mueller, 'The OIN gave Salesforce.com four patents to assert against Microsoft' (*Fosspatents*, 31 May 2011) <http://www.fosspatents.com/2011/05/oin-gave-salesforcecom-four-patents-to.html> accessed 9 April 2013.

[121] See comment by Software Freedom Law Center, 'Settled, But Not Over Yet' (30 March 2009) <http://www.softwarefreedom.org/news/2009/mar/30/settled-not-over-yet> accessed 9 April 2013.

[122] F Mueller, 'The DPL and the "Fair Troll" business model: make money fighting patents with patents' (*FOSS Patents*, 18 May 2010) <http://www.fosspatents.com/2010/05/dpl-and-fair-troll-business-model-make.html> accessed 9 April 2013.

[123] E Schulman, 'Working together to reduce patent litigation' (*Google Public Policy Blog*, 12 March 2013) <http://googlepublicpolicy.blogspot.co.uk/2013/03/working-together-to-reduce-patent.html> accessed 9 April 2013.

[124] Google Royalty-Free Patent Licensing, 'Patent Licensing to Encourage Innovation' <http://www.google.com/patents/licensing> accessed 9 April 2013. The four proposals are a *License On Transfer Agreement* (when a patent in the pool is transferred to a third party, the transferred patent automatically becomes licensed to other participating companies); a *Non-Sticky Defensive Patent License* (patent non assertion which survives transfers out of the pool); a *Sticky Defensive Patent License*, (as the former, but irrevocable, even if the patent holder leaves the pool); and a *Field-of-Use Agreement* (patent pool limited to certain field of technology, similar to the OIN patent pool in the Linux operating system field). Google and Oracle are both members of OIN, and the limited field of use restriction did not prevent Oracle suing Google in relation to Java technologies in Android.

litigation through non-assertion (or patent grant). Not all companies are parties to FOSS licences and their patent peace/non-assertion provisions noted earlier, and even if they are, those non-assertion clauses often only refer to the technologies covered by the licence. Google is suggesting therefore that, just as patent holders in a particular area (audiovisual codecs, eg), band together to license their patents on unitary basis, companies could band together and agree not to assert the patents against each other, either generically (portfolio wide), or with respect to specific areas of technology. An interesting aspect of Google's proposal is the evolutionary aspect: ie dealing with what happens when companies evolve through merger or splitting up, or when patents get transferred to third parties. Google's proposal is still very much an outline, and we have yet to see its impact on the market.

Finally, during the 2000s, various companies made patent pledges in favour of individuals and groups working on open source software; unilateral promises not to assert patents against developers, provided that certain conditions are met. They operate as an enforceable covenant not to sue, and equitable estoppel precludes the patent holder from bringing suit against those within the safe harbour defined by the pledge.

Notable patent pledges include: Red Hat,[125] Nokia,[126] Computer Associates,[127] and IBM.[128] Even Microsoft has made a patent pledge[129] for openSUSE.org.

One major unresolved issue is whether a pledge binds a new owner of a patent, an issue of great practical significance given the powerful and accelerating trend for major patent holders to divest some parts of their patent stock to patent assertion entities. This issue is also being considered in the context of whether FRAND obligations bind successors in title, as we have commented above when discussing patents and standards.

5.7 CONCLUSIONS

The free and open source community attitude to patents has gone from raising the issue—rejecting software patents on principle—to implementing sophisticated

[125] Promise at Red Hat, 'Statement of Position and Our Promise on Software Patents' <http://www.redhat.com/legal/patent_policy.html> accessed 9 April 2013.

[126] Nokia, 'Nokia announces patent support to the Linux Kernel' (25 May 2005 <http://press.nokia.com/2005/05/25/nokia-announces-patent-support-to-the-linux-kernel> accessed 9 April 2013. But it is unclear if that would constrain anyone Nokia transferred its patents to; further, the pledge covers only patents with a priority date on or before 31 December 2005.

[127] CA, 'CA Supports IBM's Open Source Patent Pledge as Companies Announce Long-Term Licensing Agreement' <http://investor.ca.com/releasedetail.cfm?releaseid=315793> accessed 9 April 2013.

[128] IBM, 'IBM Pledges 500 US Patents to Open Source in Support of Innovation and Open Standards' (11 January 2005) <http://www-03.ibm.com/press/us/en/pressrelease/7473.wss> accessed 9 April 2013.

[129] Microsoft, 'Community Commitments—Microsoft & Novell Interoperability Collaboration' (2 November 2006) <http://www.microsoft.com/about/legal/en/us/IntellectualProperty/IPLicensing/customercovenant/msnovellcollab/community.aspx> accessed 9 April 2013.

mechanisms for dealing with them, both on a structural basis (in FOSS licences) and in public and private initiatives. Looking back at our initial objective of exploring the relationship between patents and FOSS, we have seen that there are several areas of friction, creating risk and uncertainty. However, the different mechanisms we have mentioned that aim to reduce these issues are far from completing the task. So what more can be done?

5.7.1 If you can't beat them, ... should you join them?

One view to take is that as the software patent system seems to be here to stay (in one form or another), the FOSS community should become a participant in the system if it wishes to protect itself from the threats of patent thickets, ITC proceedings, patent encumbered standards, and ridiculously high awards in the event of infringement findings.[130] This means not only applying for patents and using them as defensive or aggressive weapons (something the Open Invention Network is partially involved in), creating patent pools for open source environments, but also providing open source technologies and ideas as searchable prior art[131] and eventually taking a patent licence over FOSS technologies in terms that benefit the whole community, and even comply with copyleft licensing terms.[132]

However this seems unreal in economic terms, considering the financial status of the great majority of FOSS projects (commercial or not), and only available in exceptional circumstances, such as the Open Invention Network, who has the financial backing of significant market players such as Philips, NEC, Sony, IBM, Red Hat, and Novell.

5.7.2 Patent reform

More recently, there have been a number of proposals for patent reform in this area, the idea being that in the context of these conflicts, rather than forcing FOSS development to change and adapt its ways and methods (having been proven to provide significant innovation contribution and to the 'Progress of Science and useful Arts')[133] to an archaic legal framework that is outdated and unaligned with reality, it is the legal system itself that should be improved. Indeed, there seems to be growing evidence that the patent

[130] See, eg, the arguments of Schultz and Urban (n 54).

[131] While the 'Open Source as Prior Art' Project (available at <http://www.linuxfoundation.org/programs/legal/osapa>) seems to be at a standstill, Defensive Publications are growing (principal site available at <http://www.defensivepublications.org> both accessed 9 April 2013).

[132] Such as the Red Hat/Firestar licence agreement.

[133] US Const, Art I, s 8, cl 8, known as the copyright clause.

system in general has not led to greater innovation, especially in the field of software, as much as constituting a block on innovation and progress.[134]

Some writers have suggested significantly modifying the patent system, reducing the strength of patent protection, if not getting rid of patents altogether (at least for software), a view taken not only by the FSF[135] and the Foundation for a Free Information Infrastructure,[136] but also some leading academics in the field.[137] Proposals include expressly eliminating or limiting software as patentable subject matter, tailoring the length of patent protection to software (not 20 years!), or awarding patents only when strictly needed on economic grounds (when providing proof of this, something that may not be realistic, or on the contrary, too easily achieved).

Along similar lines, other more moderate changes have been proposed, to limit the effect of patents in the context of software. At a recent conference on Patent Reform at Santa Clara Law School,[138] Professor Mark Lemley, one of the leading advocates of patent reform in the US, suggested that the interpretation of US patent law should be tightened up, to prevent software patents from being drafted in general functional terms (thus prohibiting any implementation of the functional idea, creating an overbroad patent), and limit enforceable claims to the actual algorithms disclosed by the patentees and their equivalents. This rule is something that the courts in the US should be doing under the Patent Act of 1952,[139] increasing disclosure obligations for software related patents and details of computer implemented functional claims, obliging applicants, eg, to use diagrams, flowcharts, or pseudocodes along with a clear description of the invention in natural language, and reducing the abstract nature of claims. This idea is also of some interest to the European Patent Convention

[134] J Bessen and MJ Meurer, *Patent Failure* (Princeton, Princeton University Press, 2008), have found evidence that patents can actually harm innovation. E von Hippel concluded that 'empirical data seem to suggest that the patent grant has little value to innovators in most fields' in E von Hippel, *Sources of Innovation* (Oxford, Oxford University Press, 1988) available online at <http://web.mit.edu/evhippel/www/sources.htm> accessed 9 April 2013. In *The Wealth of Networks* (New Haven, Yale University Press, 2006), Y Benkler suggests that patents may result in a drop in productivity. In J Lerner, 'Patent Protection and Innovation over 150 Years' (Nat'l Bureau of Economic Research, Working Paper No 8977, 2002), the author noted that strengthening available patent protection tended to yield less patenting of new innovations by domestic inventors, which may correlate with reduced rates of technological innovation.

[135] RM Stallman, 'Software patents—Obstacles to software development' in *Free Software, Free Society: The Selected Essays of Richard M. Stallman* (Boston, GNU Press, 2002).

[136] FFII <http://www.ffii.org>; and Stop Software Patents, 'Petition to stop software patents in Europe' <http://stopsoftwarepatents.eu/211000297544> both accessed 9 April 2013.

[137] Boldrin and Levine (n 91) conclude that 'a system that at one time served to limit the power of royalty to reward favored individuals with monopolies has become with the passage of time a system that serves primarily to encourage failing monopolists to inhibit competition by blocking innovation' (at 20). See also J Bessen and MJ Meurer, in 'The private costs of patent litigation' (Boston University School of Law Working Paper Series, Law and Economics, Working Paper No 07-08, online at <http://dx.doi.org/10.2139/ssrn.983736> accessed 9 April 2013), the authors conclude that 'In the worst case, the net effect of patents today may be to reduce the profits of public firms and to possibly impose disincentives on innovative activity as well.'

[138] Santa Clara Law, 'Solutions to the Software Patent Problem' (16 November 2012) <http://law.scu.edu/hightech/2012-solutions-to-the-software-patent-problem.cfm> accessed 9 April 2013.

[139] US Patent Act—35 USC, Article 112. See M Lemley and J Cohen, 'Patent Scope and Innovation in the Software Industry' (2001) 89 *California Law Review* 1. See also Ballardini (n 31).

regime, which generally allows functional claims but only to the extent that any more precise definition would reduce the scope of the invention (which is in fact the very purpose of ruling out functional claims).[140] The EPO Guidelines develop this, prohibiting attempts to define an invention purely in terms of the result to be achieved (thus claiming the underlying technical problem), particularly if a claim is formulated in such a way as to embrace other means, or all means, of performing the function.[141]

Another suggested idea is not to attack the upstream source of the problem, the patentability of software, which is proving to be fairly immutable,[142] but to limit the effect or enforceability of software patents on the market, reducing the liability risk for FOSS projects and users. One proposal is to legislate a 'safe harbour' from patent claims for software that runs on 'general purpose machines' (PCs and servers, terminal and mobile devices such as smart phones, routers, and set-up boxes, and so forth).[143] This may seem rather conservative, eg, it would not apply to specifically programmed hardware devices, and doesn't really deal with existing patents (unless the effect would be retroactive with regard to issued patents). Another suggested approach is to focus on interoperability and standards, and only allow software patents to be enforced against implementations of standards where the patents had been previously declared during the standard setting process. 'All other software contexts should become off-limits for patent enforcement.'[144]

As regards standards setting bodies, in the absence of moving to RF (royalty free) IP policies, suggested reforms include ensuring that the SSBs actually enforce their policies regarding RAND terms and compatibility with open source implementations, and—if no patents are disclosed up front by standards setting participants and members—improved research into existing patents over the proposed standards, through better searches of the patent databases.

In the absence of any reform, FOSS projects must resort to classic defence strategies to deal with patent risks: obtaining a licence, proving non-infringement, proving invalidity due to lack of novelty or inventiveness (or requesting re-examination, on the same bases), getting legal opinion support for invalidity or non-infringement (to reduce claims of wilful infringement), looking for other grounds for non-enforceability such as expiry, and eventually, of course, the technical solution of designing around the patent.[145]

[140] Article 83 EPC. See *Synergestic herbicides/CIBA GEIGY* T68/85, and subsequent cases.

[141] EPO Guidelines, C-III, 4.10 and 6.5.

[142] But not without some progress, in the US, considering *In re Bilski* and *Mayo v Promotheus*, and further limitations likely to come out of *CLS Bank International v Alice Corporation Pty Ltd*, No 2011-1301 (Fed Cir, 9 July 2012).

[143] R Stallman, 'Let's Limit the Effect of Software Patents, Since We Can't Eliminate Them' (*Wired*, 1 November 2012) <http://www.wired.com/opinion/2012/11/richard-stallman-software-patents> accessed 9 April 2013.

[144] S Phipps, 'Stop patent mischief by curbing patent enforcement' (*Infoworld*, 9 November 2012) <http://www.infoworld.com/d/open-source-software/stop-patent-mischief-curbing-patent-enforcement-206658> accessed 9 April 2013.

[145] See R Fontana et al, 'A Legal Issues Primer for Open Source and Free Software Projects' (*Software Freedom Law Center*, 2008) <http://www.softwarefreedom.org/resources/2008/foss-primer.html> accessed 9 April 2013.

6

PATENT LITIGATION AND PATENT WARS

Peter Langley and Colm MacKernan

6.1 POLICY ISSUES

6.1.1 Introduction

Clausewitz, that most romantic of military theorists, might have observed that 'Litigation is the continuation of *Politik* by other means'. But precisely what issues of policy or politics are involved in the area of law that will be the focus of this chapter, *patent litigation*? How are the private policies of corporations impacted as they collide against the larger issues of government or state policy? In the current 'Smartphone Wars'[1], largely targeting Android, we see patent litigation used in a global jockeying for advantage in the smartphone market, where Android now, in early 2013, enjoys a 75 per cent market share[2] in a global smartphone market of over 200 million unit sales per quarter.[3] And despite this litigious environment, we see other Linux-based mobile platforms waiting in the wings (Firefox OS, Sailfish, Tizen, Ubuntu).

The Smartphone Wars expose the grinding cogs and gears of the complex and obscure machine of multi-country patent litigation at work, a machine that asks us to think about the nature of markets, about capitalism, about creative destruction, about national rights in our borderless world, about the role of government (and regulators) to operate the machinery of incentivising innovation. How can we best understand this cryptic mechanism, to set contemporary patent litigation in a firm context of relevance to practitioners working in the FOSS context? As with everything FOSS, there is a body of theory, ideology even. In this chapter, we task ourselves with outlining some of the key developing issues in patent litigation, but also with providing practical and crisp lessons for practitioners (including IP litigators starting to engage with FOSS, and FOSS law specialists starting to engage with IP litigation; we doubt we have anything to teach IP litigators already expert in FOSS). For example, we will not merely ask whether patent litigation poses an existential risk to FOSS, but what, in the harsh and the ordinary (or fresh and invigorating, depending on your temperament) business realities have FOSS adherents done to re-risk; and what have proprietary software companies done to impose costs and uncertainty on FOSS?

It is clear enough that patent litigation remains a sport of kings, available only to the wealthiest corporations, with cases costing typically $3 million to over $100 million;[4]

[1] Patent litigation commenced in 2009 by Nokia against Apple, and subsequently extending out to multiple suits in multiple jurisdictions involving Apple Inc, Google, Samsung, Microsoft, Nokia, Motorola, HTC amongst others.

[2] S Webster, 'IDC: Android hits 75% market share on fourth anniversary of platform' (*IDC*, 2 November 2012) <http://www.androidguys.com/2012/11/02/idc-android-hits-75-market-share-on-fourth-anniversary-of-platform> accessed 10 April 2013.

[3] Gartner, 'Gartner Says Worldwide Mobile Phone Sales Declined 1.7 percent in 2012' (13 February 2012) <http://www.gartner.com/newsroom/id/2335616> accessed 10 April 2013.

[4] J Golson, 'Apple's Legal Fees Rumored to top $100M on HTC Patent Dispute Alone' (*Macrumors*, 23 January 2012) <http://www.macrumors.com/2012/01/23/apples-legal-fees-rumored-to-top-100m-on-htc-patent-dispute-alone>;

no doubt the Smartphone Wars will ultimately end up with complex cross-licensing settlements between the major players, with substantial net balancing payments flowing between corporations. But whether the Smartphone Wars will ever deliver against their instigators' original intent is doubtful, but then again, do wars ever?

Quite likely, some of the patents cross-licensed will be patents that (arguably) impact core functionality in Android and perhaps Linux, and possibly also on the web's open standards. Over time, as Linux itself becomes superceded, there will no doubt be other patents that cover any successors to Linux.

Open source software is, as a practical matter, at a substantial disadvantage in the patent wars. The open availability of source code facilitates patent infringement investigation of FOSS, while the diverse and often voluntary nature of contributions to the code base means that many 'inventors' in the FOSS world do not patent their inventions (and may be ideologically opposed to software patents), and even if they do the patents are held by a plethora of smaller entities. By contrast, proprietary software is less amenable to infringement investigation because the source code is confidential, so that even if FOSS users had suitable patents, they would find it difficult to reach the level of good faith belief that there is infringement necessary to file a US patent infringement suit. It is thus highly likely that creators of proprietary software, while loudly denouncing FOSS free riders on their inventions, are in fact substantial free riders on FOSS themselves.

And here lies the greatest danger to FOSS (and an opportunity for proprietary software companies): once the dust settles on the Smartphone Wars, we may well find ourselves in a world where the legal precedents have been set for imposing substantial patent royalty-based financial costs on software functions that are both global and ubiquitous, controlling a vast number of devices (and with the Internet of Things, the size of the potential market to tax with patents will dwarf even the smartphone market).[5] Moreover, much of the patent royalties will accrue, possibly quite unfairly, to the closed/proprietary software vendors who will freely use inventions that originated in FOSS.

Furthermore, patent licensing fees that are 'FRAND' (fair, reasonable, and non-discriminatory) can impose costs that are simply unsustainable for many companies working with FOSS, let alone individual contributors, and those companies that can absorb those costs will inevitably have less to invest in R&D, marketing, and so forth. And because FOSS code by definition can be readily inspected, patent

WR Towns, 'US Contingency Fees: A Level Playing Field?' (*WIPO Magazine*, February 2010) <http://www.wipo.int/wipo_magazine/en/2010/01/article_0002.html> both accessed 10 April 2013.

[5] Every light bulb, thermostat, perhaps any device for which some kind of communication over the internet could possibly be useful will need an operating system of sorts (probably Linux based for reasons of quality, cost, customisability, scalability, and reliability) and web connectivity, so the Smartphone Wars may set the stage for a yet bigger patent battle in the internet of things. Precedents (royalty rates) established now could be vastly valuable and entrench the ability of a small group of patent holders to tax a massive global industry.

owners will face few practical difficulties in testing FOSS code to see whether or not it infringes.

So patent litigation poses the most acute of dangers to FOSS, just as it offers tremendous opportunities to proprietary companies to tax FOSS and impose control over it, eg, to chill its further development. And in patent litigation, we see most strikingly the clash of convictions: for the adherents of the current patent system, the absolute conviction that patents are essential for there to be R&D; for the adherents of FOSS, the absolute conviction that patents are entirely irrelevant to R&D. We have two sharply conflicting and mutually exclusive systems of social organization and innovation;[6] on the one hand, large corporations acting to maximize profit and on the other, FOSS. To illustrate the latter, Professor Eben Moglen sees creativity as being hard-wired in humans: 'It's an emergent property of connected human minds that they create things for one another's pleasure and to conquer their uneasy sense of being too alone.'[7] Or, as his Metaphorical Corollary to Faraday's Law puts it: 'Wrap the Internet around every brain on the planet and spin the planet. Software flows in the wires. It's an emergent property of human minds to create.' But the end-game of the Smartphone Wars (and perhaps other, as-yet-unplanned patent litigation, targeting software) may be to reinforce the dominance of orthodox legal models of social organization and innovation, and hence to turn the FOSS global motor of software creativity into an engine of patent royalty cash, flowing to the major patent holders, entrenching their oligopolies, and gradually depleting the ability for other players, including those adopting FOSS, to effectively compete.

Or just possibly, and more benignly, the end-game of the current round of smartphone patent litigation could be the re-establishment of low-cost[8] (or at least sustainable, for all impacted) cross-licensing as the way industry resolves patent issues.

US patent law is currently evolving in a manner quite favourable to FOSS. We may be seeing the start of a major fork in the patent system, with one fork for pharma and other sectors where innovation is slow and costly and a single product is protected by a small family of related patents (and that fork will retain much of the characteristics of the established patent enforcement regime), and a second, new fork, where injunctions are in practice hard to obtain, and damages are low, for tech areas where innovation is fast, cheap, and incremental, and a product is covered by thousands of unconnected families of patents: FOSS operates almost exclusively in this second fork.

This kind of solution also promotes and supports innovation sharing, paradoxically aligning closely with FOSS' aim of open, cooperative sharing of innovation. It's

[6] For a political economist's view on open source, see S Weber, *The Success of Open Source* (Cambridge, Harvard University Press, 2004).

[7] E Moglen, 'Anarchism Triumphant: Free Software and the Death of Copyright' (2 August 1999) *First Monday*, vol 4, no 8.

[8] It is worth reminding ourselves that the pioneering work done by Bell Labs on Unix and much else besides was in effect given to the world entirely royalty-free, albeit because of concerns for anti-trust scrutiny.

arguable that the objectives of FOSS and a forked patent system may then converge upon a similar end-point, and the current wave of industry-led litigation (we'll put to one side here non-practising entity litigation) is just the tectonic plates shifting momentarily as they release some stresses and then settle back to their old and long established equilibrium. FOSS may find that it can co-exist within a forked patent system, or otherwise co-opt the patent system to its specific needs.

In later sections we will put aside speculation and look instead at how the Smartphone Wars impact FOSS, and what in practice FOSS adherents are doing to defend against the perceived dangers of patents and patent litigation.

6.1.2 An historical perspective

Many of the experts in this space have a largely US perspective; in this chapter, we'll look not only through a US lens, but also with an English law perspective. For the non-US practitioner, an understanding of applicable US law and practice is essential; for the US practitioner, an understanding of non-US approaches is becoming increasingly important (and interesting) because of the tactical advantages in bringing patent litigation not just in the US, but also in other countries too, notably Germany and the United Kingdom.

One might start this particular enquiry at one beginning: we take as our point of inception the contrasting origins of those most superficially related of legal traditions, the patent laws in England and the United States. The divergence of attitude reflected in these differing origins affects outcomes even today.

For England, we begin with the Statute of Monopolies of 1624, which codified patents as:

> Grants of privilege for the term of fourteen years or under, hereafter to be made, of the sole working or making of any manner of new manufactures within this realm (c) to the true and first inventor (d) and inventors of such manufactures, which others at the time of making such letters patents and grants shall not use (e), so as also they be not contrary to the law nor mischievous to the state by raising prices of commodities at home, or hurt of trade, or generally inconvenient....

The notion that one must guard against patent monopolies becoming 'mischievous to the state by raising prices of commodities at home, or hurt of trade, or generally inconvenient' is a lesson with contemporary resonance[9] in the FOSS context. One might characterize the English attitude as follows: those who exercise monopolies,

[9] A muffled echo of this language can be heard in the EU 'Enforcement Directive' (Directive 2004/48/EC of the European Parliament and of the Council of 29 April 2004 on the enforcement of intellectual property rights), where measures, procedures and remedies for infringement shall be 'fair and equitable' and 'shall also be effective, proportionate and dissuasive and shall be applied in such a manner as to avoid the creation of barriers to legitimate trade and to provide for safeguards against their abuse', Article 3(2).

be they seventeenth century English kings, or twenty-first century tech companies, have an innate and inevitable tendency to extract ever-increasing benefits from their monopolies in a manner that fits perfectly well with their commercial self-interest, but nevertheless may cause harm to consumers and to competitors. The courts, the antitrust, or the competition authorities must be continuously astute to provide the essential checks and balances necessary to bring the system back into equilibrium.

But this compulsion to be always alive to the mischief that monopolies may bring is a somewhat English perspective; one can contrast the English Statute of Monopolies of 1624 with Article I, section 8 of the United States Constitution, empowering the United States Congress:

> To promote the Progress of Science and useful Arts, by securing for limited Times to Authors and Inventors the exclusive Right to their respective Writings and Discoveries.

Article I, section 8 is silent on the potential for monopolies to raise prices, to damage trade, or to be generally inconvenient. The consequences of this difference in legal traditions can be seen most starkly in the context of patent litigation where the validity of a patent is in play: English courts, with a certain weary cynicism, invalidate patents with a regularity and resourcefulness that is not often seen in the US. In the US, patents enjoy a presumption of validity, and proving invalidity requires clear and convincing evidence, whereas in the English system, there is no such presumption, and the balance of probabilities standard to proving invalidity applies.[10] One suspects a deeper cultural affection for patents in the US system, although, as we will see, much of the impetus for contemporary reform of the patent system flows from the US.

The entrenched importance of patents in the US system can be seen in an antecedent to the current Smartphone Patent Wars; the early twentieth century patent conflict between the Wright Brothers and Glenn Curtiss, involving US patent 821,393 covering basic methods of controlling the flight of an airplane. This conflict is widely regarded as having impeded the development of the aircraft industry in the United States from shortly after the first flight at Kitty Hawk, ceding technological leadership in the industry to Europe, where it largely remained until the Second World War. Earlier litigation brought by George Selden who had secured a broad patent covering automobiles in 1895 was finally overturned in a suit by Henry Ford in 1911.[11] Again, the uncertainty that the intellectual property situation created is argued to have impeded the development in the US of the auto industry. Conversely, in Europe, there was intense debate about the need for there to be a patent system at all; eg, the Netherlands abolished their patent systems in 1869, although subsequently re-established it in 1912.

[10] See US Supreme Court in *Microsoft Corp v i4i Limited Partnership* 546 US (2011) available at <http://www.supremecourt.gov/opinions/10pdf/10-290.pdf> accessed 10 April 2013.

[11] US Patent 549,160.

6.1.3 Contrasting patent rights with free and open innovation: Filippo Brunelleschi

We are faced with many alien and novel issues when looking at how patent litigation impacts FOSS. But there are some old precedents contrasting ideas that were promoted and protected by monopoly rights, and those shared freely, openly, and collaboratively. To illustrate, it is interesting and instructive to go back even further in time than the English 1624 Statute of Monopolies, to one of the earliest patents on record.

In 1421, the great Renaissance architect Filippo Brunelleschi had been commissioned to design and build the great dome of the Santa Maria del Fiore, the Duomo, and would stand to make a not inconsiderable profit if he were able to efficiently transport the quantities of marble needed for the dome up from the quarries of Carrara to Florence, along the hostile and unpredictable River Arno. Brunelleschi designed an apparently ingenious barge for carrying the marble, christened 'Il Badalone'. Fearing it would be copied, he persuaded the ruling council of Florence to grant him a three-year monopoly to the design of Il Badalone (and in fact to *any* new design of ship whatsoever, the notion of the scope of the monopoly being limited to the innovations actually made by the inventor was not present, but of course critics of the contemporary patent system might argue that nothing much has changed). It is interesting to read the declaration in full, as it is pregnant with so much of the future of patent law:

> The Magnificent and Powerful Lords, Lords Magistrate and Standard Bearer of Justice,
>
> Considering that the admirable Filippo Brunelleschi, a man of the most perspicacious intellect, industry and invention, a citizen of Florence, has invented some machine or kind of ship, by means of which he thinks he can easily, at any time, bring in any merchandise and load on the river Arno and on any other river or water, for less money than usual, and with several other benefits to merchants and others, and that he refuses to make such machine available to the public, in order that the fruit of his genius and skill may not be reaped by another without his will and consent; and that, if he enjoyed some prerogative concerning this, he would open up what he is hiding and would disclose it to all;
>
> And desiring that this matter, so withheld and hidden without fruit, shall be brought to light to be of profit to both said Filippo and our whole country and others, and that some privilege be created for said Filippo as hereinafter described, so that he may be animated more fervently to even higher pursuits and stimulated to more subtle investigations, they deliberated on 19 June 1421;
>
> That no person alive, wherever born and of whatever status, dignity, quality and grade, shall dare or presume, within three years next following from the day when the present provision has been approved in the Council of Florence, to commit any of the following acts on the river Arno, any other river, stagnant water, swamp, or water

> running or existing in the territory of Florence: to have, hold or use in any manner, be it newly invented or made in new form, a machine or ship or other instrument designed to import or ship or transport on water any merchandise or any things or goods, except such ship or machine or instrument as they may have used until now for similar operations, or to ship or transport, or to have shipped or transported, any merchandise or goods on ships, machines or instruments for water transport other than such as were familiar and usual until now, and further that any such new or newly shaped machine etc. shall be burned;
>
> Provided however that the foregoing shall not be held to cover, and shall not apply to, any newly invented or newly shaped machine etc., designed to ship, transport or travel on water, which may be made by Filippo Brunelleschi or with his will and consent; also, that any merchandise, things or goods which may be shipped with such newly invented ships, within three years next following, shall be free from the imposition, requirement or levy of any new tax not previously imposed.[12]

The barge sank on its inaugural voyage, dumping its cargo of marble to the bed of the River Arno, and according to those in the FOSS camp, it has been wholly downhill for patents ever since. Brunelleschi was compelled to clad the cupola of the Duomo with marble taken from old tombstones, which might also serve as a *momento mori* to those attracted by the idea of a morality lesson for those seeking a spot of patent adventurism.

But, far more successfully, Brunelleschi earlier in the fifteenth century invented single point linear perspective; according to Vasari, he demonstrated that openly in the doorway of the Duomo and it was rapidly (and widely) copied.

Single-point linear perspective was widely shared in and beyond Brunelleschi's circle; it was developed and enhanced by many others and became one of the foundations of Renaissance Western art. One can only wonder if Brunelleschi had been prompted to seek a monopoly for his great barge because of the widespread adoption of single-point linear perspective, from which he failed to profit in direct financial terms. Or whether he might, after the financial disaster of his patented barge, have after all preferred the free and open use of his ideas.

FOSS adherents might claim this as an important lesson for those regulators and law-makers interested in where ideas come from, and how creativity can be cultured. And those firmly on the side of proprietary, patented software might take a moment to acknowledge this most creative and exceptional of men, and the sizeable part of his personal fortune he lost when his great barge Il Badalone sank, protected by patent against copyists, but not against the capricious and chaotic currents of the River Arno.

[12] Taken from FD Prager and G Scaglia, *Brunelleschi: studies of his Technology and Inventions* (New York, MIT Press, 1970).

6.2 PORTER FORCES—A PRACTICAL STRATEGIC CONTEXT FOR UNDERSTANDING PATENT LITIGATION

Patent litigation, particularly the Smartphone Wars, presents a picture of chaos,[13] much like the black and turbulent waters of the Arno as it swamped Il Badalone.

To give some tools to permit that clearer, strategic understanding of patents and patent litigation that will be essential to practitioners advising in relation to how patent litigation impacts FOSS, we look in this section at the five strategic forces (referred to as Porter Forces)[14] which determine industry attractiveness, structure, and profitability. The forces are:

- Barriers to entry
- Rivalry
- Supplier bargaining power
- Customer leverage and
- Threat of substitutes.

The Smartphone Wars, and any future wars directly impacting FOSS, can helpfully be seen through the lens of this kind of strategic understanding. We can summarize this in Table 6.1, as follows:

Table 6.1 Mapping how patents impact FOSS using Porter Forces

Porter Forces	Patents
Barriers to entry	Patents can lead to injunctions and import exclusion orders against products including FOSS and services provided using FOSS, denying entry entirely to new FOSS-based market entrants.Patents can lead to substantial royalties having to be paid on products including FOSS and services provided using FOSS, dis-incentivising FOSS-based market entrants.Patents can force FOSS-based companies to look for invent-arounds, which may take time and lead to incompatibilities with existing de facto standards.Patents can create economic uncertainty, inhibiting investment in the development of new FOSS based technologies and businesses.

continued

[13] Federal Judge Richard Posner, questioning Apple Inc's bid for an injunction against Google Inc's Motorola Mobility unit, at an oral hearing on 20 June 2012, called the US patent system 'chaos' and said an order barring the sale of Motorola phones could have 'catastrophic effects'. *Apple, Inc and Next Software Inc v Motorola, Inc and Motorola Mobility, Inc* 11-cv-8540.

[14] ME Porter, 'How Competitive Forces Shape Strategy' (March/April 1979) *Harvard Business Review*.

Table 6.1 (continued)

Porter Forces	Patents
Rivalry	Patents can reduce or eliminate FOSS-based rivals, eg by imposing unsustainable costs on those FOSS-based rivals (eg by forcing them to spend time and money defending costly patent litigation, entering into patent settlements and costly licences). Patents can reduce the numbers of FOSS-based new entrants by making them unattractive to investors.
Supplier bargaining power	Patents can give bargaining power to suppliers over FOSS-based, potentially infringing alternatives. A proprietary software company could, eg, grant broad patent infringement indemnities to customers, which a FOSS entity might be unable to match; the ability to indemnify can provide suppliers with significant bargaining power.
Customer leverage	Patents decrease customer leverage since customers are less able to divert their custom to FOSS-based but potentially infringing alternatives.
Threat of substitutes	Patents reduce the threat of FOSS-based potentially infringing alternatives.

For these reasons, patents are often an exceptionally powerful way for large, proprietary software companies to preserve and extend their oligopolies over FOSS-based rivals.

6.3 HOW GREAT A THREAT ARE PATENTS, AMPLIFIED THROUGH PATENT LITIGATION, TO FOSS?

6.3.1 Some views from the protagonists

> Grand theft. . . . I will spend my last dying breath if I need to, and I will spend every penny of Apple's $40 billion in the bank, to right this wrong. I'm going to destroy Android, because it's a stolen product. I'm willing to go thermonuclear war on this.
>
> Steve Jobs[15]

But contrast with an interview between Google's CEO Larry Page:[16]

[15] W Isaacson, *Steve Jobs: The Exclusive Biography* (London, Simon & Schuster, 2011) 512.

[16] S Levy, 'Google's Larry Page on Why Moon Shots Matter' (*Wired*, 17 January 2013) <http://www.wired.com/business/2013/01/ff-qa-larry-page/all> accessed 10 April 2013.

Page: . . . But show me a company that failed because of litigation. I just don't see it. Companies fail because they do the wrong things or they aren't ambitious, not because of litigation or competition.
Wired: Steve Jobs felt competitive enough to claim that he was willing to 'go to thermonuclear war' on Android.
Page: How well is that working?

FOSS is of course much larger than Android (and we leave it to others to debate to what extent Android is even FOSS), but the consequences for FOSS generally, arising from the Smartphone Wars, may well be considerable. In this section, we look in more detail at some of the specific kinds of threats (or remedies, depending on your viewpoint) relevant to FOSS.

6.3.2 Settlements and licences

WSJ: You're still charging a license fee for the software.
Mr Ballmer: Sure.
WSJ: Is that difficult in an environment where Android is free?
Mr Ballmer: Android has a patent fee. It's not like Android's free. You do have to license patents. HTC's signed a licence with us and you're going to see licence fees clearly for Android as well as for Windows.
WSJ: It doesn't seem like the licence fee alone is a big financial opportunity for Microsoft.
Mr Ballmer: It's one of the opportunities. One.
WSJ: It's one of them.
Mr Ballmer: Look, anything that can sell in the tens to hundreds of millions is a big opportunity, and we see big opportunity. Even in the world today, there's a bunch of different models in place.

See *Wall Street Journal*, 3 October 2010 'Ballmer Aims to Overcome Mobile Missteps.'

Settlements (in the Smartphone Wars and elsewhere) establish trends that place intense pressure on FOSS entities to follow, so Android settlements (eg HTC, Samsung and others with Microsoft; HTC with Apple; see later) will heavily influence how patents impact FOSS in the future. Critically, these kinds of settlements tend to impose significant financial costs on FOSS, but the actual amounts paid are generally confidential and the important detail concealed. The Smartphone Wars shed some public light on the level of patent royalties being sought and are worth understanding.

Table 6.2 Patent royalties sought in the Smartphone Wars

Patent holder	Royalty sought	Circumstances
Motorola/Google	2.25% total sales—but specifically for standard essential patents, not a total portfolio licence including non-SEP patents.Approx 1% of sales for a single patent.	See, eg, Google's letter to IEEE dated 8 February 2012,[17] committing to a maximum per-unit royalty of 2.25% of the net-selling price of a handset to license MMI's standard essential patents, subject to any offsets for the value of any cross-licences and so forth. Net-selling price is the selling price of a handset, tablet, and so on before any subsidies or discounts.
Apple	1%–2.5% ASP (or $5–$15 per device).	Unconfirmed industry rumours[18,19] relating to settlement proposals made by Apple to Samsung and Motorola. Hence, likely to be for a portfolio licence, but with a no-clone provision to protect Apple's product differentiation (see 6.3.4 for details on the no-clone provision imposed by Apple on HTC).
Samsung	2.4% ASP but specifically for standard essential patents, not a total portfolio licence.	See, eg, letter from Apple to Samsung[20] dated 30 April 2012 regarding licensing of UMTS patents, confirming that Samsung is asking for 2.4%. In the letter Apple states that Samsung's demand would imply a 44% aggregate royalty burden on UMTS products, and refers to a case where Samsung argued for a 5–7% aggregate royalty as appropriate. Apple further argues that the royalty base needs to be the baseband chip (which typically costs $10) and not the entire iPhone (which might retail at $500). Following the same lines, Apple offers to license its own UMTS patents for $0.33 per unit if Samsung agrees to use the same royalty base (that is the baseband chip) in their calculation.
Microsoft	1.4%, but for a portfolio licence.	Unconfirmed industry rumours based on the HTC settlement.[21] Would likely include some kind of no-clone provision to ensure product differentiation based on say 'live tiles' in Windows Phone.

[17] <http://www.scribd.com/doc/80976133/12-02-08-Google-to-IEEE-on-MMI-Patents> accessed 10 April 2013.

[18] R Liu, 'Apple considering royalties to settle Android patent lawsuits' (*Slash Gear*, 6 March 2012) <http://www.slashgear.com/apple-considering-royalties-to-settle-android-patent-lawsuits-06217068> accessed 10 April 2013.

[19] <http://appleinsider.com/articles/12/03/06/apple_seeks_up_to_15_per_android_device_in_settlements_offered_to_motorola_samsung> accessed 18 June 2013.

[20] 'Apple Samsung Teksler-Kim Letter Re FRAND' <http://www.scribd.com/doc/108832665/12-04-30-Apple-Samsung-Teksler-Kim-Letter-Re-FRAND> accessed 10 April 2013.

[21] J Yarow, 'HTC Pays Microsoft $5 Per Android Phone, Says Citi' (*Business Insider*, 27 May 2011) <http://www.businessinsider.com/htc-pays-microsoft-5-per-android-phone-2011-5> accessed 10 April 2013.

These figures largely align with other public pronouncements for royalties for LTE[22] under FRAND royalty commitments, as per Table 6.3:

Table 6.3 Royalties sought for LTE patents

Patent holder	Royalty sought
Qualcomm	3.5% ASP
Nokia	1.5% ASP
Ericsson	1.5% ASP
Alcatel-Lucent	Under 2% ASP
Huawei	Under 1.5% ASP
ZTE	Under 1% ASP

Apple has also argued[23] that Samsung is entitled to a maximum of $0.0049 per infringing Apple device for each infringed standard essential patent ('SEP'); contrast that with the per-device infringing value it ascribes to its own non-SEP UX patents and designs:

- $2.02 for the 'over-scroll bounce' (or 'rubber-banding') patent;
- $3.10 for the 'scrolling API' patent;
- $2.02 for the 'tap to zoom and navigate' patent;
- $24 for use of any of Apple's design patents or trade dress rights.

These product differentiation patents are seen (by Apple at least) as far more valuable than standard essential patents. Whether the courts will sanction that is an ongoing saga; one thing we can say about the Smartphone Wars is that they are giving the courts (and regulators) rich opportunities to clarify the value of patents. 2013 will see a number of trials in key jurisdictions, which will directly address the appropriate rate for a standard essential patent under FRAND commitments; the outcomes are likely to influence very significantly the landscape for settling patent disputes through licensing. But since, at the time of writing, those judgments are unwritten, we will look in the following sections at some of the historical precedents already set.

6.3.3 Microsoft settlements and licences

We start with a relatively recent settlement: on 27 April 2010 HTC signed[24] an agreement with Microsoft to pay royalties on Android-based devices, rumoured

[22] LTE: Long-Term Evolution. A standard for wireless communication of high-speed data for mobile phones and data terminals.

[23] <http://www.fosspatents.com/2012/07/apple-seeks-25-billion-in-damages-from.html>.

[24] 'Microsoft Announce Patent Agreement with HTC' (27 April 2010) <http://www.microsoft.com/en-us/news/press/2010/apr10/04-27MSHTCPR.aspx> accessed 10 April 2013.

to be $5 per handset (equivalent to a royalty rate of approximately 1.4 per cent of the average retail selling price of $350, perhaps 3 per cent of the ex-factory price), but not verified in any public documents. That $5 might not be accurate or even be a net amount (eg, Microsoft could be receiving $5 per Android device from HTC, but be paying back a significant sum to HTC to license HTC's substantial patent portfolio, or to incentivise HTC to adopt Windows Phone). But the details remain confidential.

In any event, publicly announced Microsoft Android or Linux patent licences (or other kind of patent 'cover', we will explain the term 'cover' in relation to the Microsoft Novell patent settlement below) include:

Amazon[25] (22 February 2010)
HTC[26] (27 April 2010)
General Dynamc Itronix[27] (27 June 2011)
Velocity Micro[28] (29 June 2011)
Onkyo[29] (30 June 2011)
Wistron[30] (5 July 2011)
Acer[31] (8 September 2011)
ViewSonic[32] (8 September 2011)
Samsung[33] (28 September 2011)
Quanta[34] (13 October 2011)
Compal[35] (23 October 2011)

[25] 'Microsoft and Amazon.com Sigh Patent Agreement' (22 February 2010) <http://www.microsoft.com/en-us/news/press/2010/feb10/02-22msamazonpr.aspx> accessed 10 April 2013.

[26] 'Microsoft Announce Patent Agreement with HTC' (27 April 2010) <http://www.microsoft.com/en-us/news/press/2010/apr10/04-27MSHTCPR.aspx> accessed 10 April 2013.

[27] 'Microsoft and General Dynamics Itronix Sign Patent Agreement' (27 June 2011) <http://www.microsoft.com/en-us/news/press/2011/jun11/06-27ItronixPR.aspx> accessed 10 April 2013.

[28] 'Microsoft and Velocity Micro, Inc, Sign Patent Agreement Covering Android-Based Devices' <http://www.microsoft.com/en-us/news/press/2011/jun11/06-29VelocityMicroPR.aspx> accessed 10 April 2013.

[29] 'Microsoft and Onkyo Corp Sign Patent Agreement Covering Android-Based Tablets' (30 June 2011) <http://www.microsoft.com/en-us/news/press/2011/jun11/06-30OnkyoPR.aspx> accessed 10 April 2013.

[30] 'Microsoft and Wistron Sign Patent Agreement' (5 July 2011) <http://www.microsoft.com/en-us/news/press/2011/jul11/07-05WistronPR.aspx> accessed 10 April 2013.

[31] 'Microsoft and Acer Sign Patent License Agreement' (8 September 2011) <https://www.microsoft.com/en-us/news/press/2011/sep11/09-08AcerPR.aspx> accessed 10 April 2013.

[32] 'Microsoft and ViewSonic Sign Patent Agreement' (8 September 2011) <http://www.microsoft.com/en-us/news/press/2011/sep11/09-08ViewSonicPR.aspx> accessed 10 April 2013.

[33] 'Microsoft and Samsung Broaden Smartphone Partnership' (28 September 2011) <http://www.microsoft.com/en-us/news/press/2011/sep11/09-28SamsungPR.aspx> accessed 10 April 2013.

[34] 'Microsoft and Quanta Computer Sign Patent Agreement Covering Android and Chrome-Based Devices' (13 October 2011) <http://www.prnewswire.com/news-releases/microsoft-and-quanta-computer-sign-patent-agreement-covering-android-and-chrome-based-devices-131793888.html> accessed 10 April 2013.

[35] 'Microsoft and Compal Electronics Sign Patent Agreement Covering Android and Chrome Based Devices' (23 October 2011) <http://www.microsoft.com/en-us/news/press/2011/oct11/10-23CompalPR.aspx> accessed 10 April 2013.

LG Electronics[36] (12 January 2012)
Pegatron[37] (25 April 2012)
Barnes & Noble[38] (30 April 2012)
Honeywell[39] (2 August 2012)
EINS[40] (11 December 2012)
Hoeft & Wessel AG[41] (11 December 2012)
Coby Electronics[41a] (9 July 2012)
Aluratek[42] (9 July 2012)

Microsoft claimed in January 2012 that: 'more than 70 percent of all Android smartphones sold in the US are now receiving coverage under Microsoft's patent portfolio.'[43]

The licensing deals with Wistron, Compal, and Quanta are particularly interesting because these are Original Design Manufacturers ('ODMs'), who build Android devices for sale under others' brands. So the practical consequence is that if you have an Android or Chrome design (or whatever else is covered by the Microsoft agreements, all of which are confidential), then these ODMs will make it for you, but they will presumably be subject to a Microsoft patent royalty at source. Given the vast amount of manufacturing done by ODMs, Microsoft's strategy in going direct to the ODM manufacturers makes complete sense. In October 2011, Microsoft claimed that 'Together with the license agreements signed in the past few months with Wistron and Quanta Computer, today's agreement with Compal means more than half of the world's ODM industry for Android and Chrome devices is now under license to Microsoft's patent portfolio.'[44]

[36] 'Microsoft and LG Sign Patent Agreement Covering Android and Chrome OS Based Devices' (12 January 2012) <http://www.microsoft.com/en-us/news/press/2012/jan12/01-12LGPR.aspx> accessed 10 April 2013.

[37] 'Microsoft and Pegatron Corp Sign Patent Agreement Covering Android- and Chrome-Based Devices' (25 April 2012) <http://www.microsoft.com/en-us/news/Press/2012/Apr12/04-25PegatronPR.aspx> accessed 10 April 2013.

[38] 'Barnes & Noble, Microsoft Form Strategic Partnership to Advance World-Class Digital Reading Experiences for Consumers' (30 April 2012) <http://www.microsoft.com/en-us/news/Press/2012/Apr12/04-30CorpNews.aspx> accessed 10 April 2013.

[39] 'Honeywell Introduces First Android-Based Enterprise Digital Assistant' (2 August 2012) <http://honeywell.com/News/Pages/Honeywell-Introduces-First-Android-Based-Enterprise-Digital-Assistant.aspx> accessed 10 April 2013.

[40] 'Microsoft and EINS Sign Android Patent Agreement' (11 December 2012) <http://www.microsoft.com/en-us/news/Press/2012/Dec12/12-11EINSPR.aspx> accessed 10 April 2013.

[41] 'Microsoft and Hoeft & Wessel AG Sign Patent Agreement' (11 December 2012) <http://www.prnewswire.com/news-releases/microsoft-and-hoeft--wessel-ag-sign-patent-agreement-182973461.html> accessed 10 April 2013.

[41a] 'Microsoft and Coby Electronics Sign Patent Agreement Covering Android and Chrome Based Devices' (9 July 2012) <http://www.microsoft.com/en-us/news/Press/2012/Jul12/07-09CobyPR.aspx> accessed 10 April 2013.

[42] 'Microsoft and Aluratek Inc Sign Patent Agreement Covering Android and Chrome Based Devices' (9 July 2012) <http://www.microsoft.com/en-us/news/Press/2012/Jul12/07-09AluratekPR.aspx> accessed 10 April 2013.

[43] 'Microsoft and LG Sign Patent Agreement Covering Android and Chrome OS Based Devices' (12 January 2012) <http://www.microsoft.com/en-us/news/press/2012/jan12/01-12LGPR.aspx> accessed 10 April 2013.

[44] 'Microsoft and Compaq Electronics Sign Patent Agreement Covering Android and Chrome Based Devices' (23 October 2011) <http://www.microsoft.com/en-us/news/press/2011/oct11/10-23CompalPR.aspx> accessed 10 April 2013.

For device manufacturers using Android and Chrome, it looks like a Microsoft patent royalty (perhaps of the order of $5, perhaps more for some device categories, perhaps less in others; the details of Microsoft's licensing terms have not been exposed in any litigation to date) may well be an item that needs to be factored in to the 'Bill of Royalties' cost that sits alongside the more familiar Bill of Materials cost, unless that manufacturer has patents or other assets of commercial value to Microsoft, or is willing to provide value to Microsoft in other ways: eg, Samsung's stated willingness to embrace Windows Phone as part of its settlement with Microsoft:

> We are pleased to build upon our long history of working together to open a new chapter of collaboration beginning with our Windows Phone 'Mango' launch this fall.[45]

To date, we have not seen companies being put out of business through Microsoft's patent licensing costs. Microsoft might need to be cautious about setting their patent royalty rates at such a level that margins are so squeezed to render a business not viable for antitrust reasons, but FOSS adherents could, with some justification, point out that antitrust liability has not in the past deterred Microsoft from pursuing a course of action that it deemed in its over-riding commercial interests.[46]

Although we have focussed so far on the more recent Microsoft patent settlements affecting Android, we shouldn't omit where it all started: Microsoft's 2 November 2006 patent settlement with Novell.[47] GPLv2 precludes a FOSS target of patent litigation from settling and taking a licence under the asserted patents. There are two complementary reasons; first, the FOSS entity has to be able to distribute source code unencumbered by obligations to pay patent fees. So, if the patent holder granted a patent licence to the FOSS entity, structured to enable the FOSS entity to distribute unencumbered, then the patent holder would be able to secure only the one patent licence, since anyone else would be able to get the code from the FOSS entity and use it royalty-free since the patent holder's rights would be exhausted. So that fails from the patent holder's perspective. Second, the patent holder could grant a patent licence limited to just the FOSS entity, with no rights flowing through the FOSS entity to anyone the FOSS entity distributes to, but then the FOSS entity is in a bind because

[45] 'Microsoft and Samsung Broaden Smartphone Partnership' (28 September 2011) <http://www.microsoft.com/en-us/news/press/2011/sep11/09-28SamsungPR.aspx> accessed 10 April 2013.

[46] See *United States of America v Microsoft Corporation* at <http://www.justice.gov/atr/cases/f3800/msjudgex.htm and also *Microsoft Corp v Commission of the European Communities* at http://eur-lex.europa.eu/LexUriServ/LexUriServ.do?uri=CELEX:32007D0053:EN:NOT> accessed 10 April 2013.

[47] 'Patent Cooperation Agreement—Microsoft & Novell Interoperability Collaboration' (2 November 2006) <http://www.microsoft.com/about/legal/en/us/IntellectualProperty/IPLicensing/customercovenant/msnovellcollab/patent_agreement.aspx> accessed 10 April 2013.

GPLv2 permits distribution only if the FOSS entity can pass on to others the same rights it enjoys.[48] Each side is stymied. The ingenious solution, (or rank betrayal, depending on your perspective) arising out of a complex set of business needs on the part of both Microsoft and Novell[49] was for Microsoft not to grant a licence to the FOSS entity (in this case, Novell), but instead to grant a covenant not to sue the FOSS entity's customers.[50] Condemnation of the Novell settlement from the FOSS community was swift and at times brutal.[51] And so started Microsoft's FOSS patent licensing programme, which continues to date.

One important element of the Microsoft FOSS strategy is its FAT patent licensing programme. The FAT or File Allocation Table was a solution to a problem that had arisen with Microsoft's naming conventions for its operating system. Originally the operating system supported only short 8.3 file names, that is eight characters separated by a dot and then three characters. Later, this proved to be inadequate for more powerful computers and larger data storage devices, and a new long-name system called vFAT was developed. However, Microsoft chose to keep both long and short file names so as to maintain backwards compatibility, and came up with technical solutions to make this possible, patenting those solutions. Problematically for the rest of the technology industry, to connect with Microsoft Windows based computers required compatibility with FAT and possibly use of what Microsoft had patented. Since 98 per cent of the world's computers ran on Windows, FAT became unavoidable, even if derided by some software engineers as a 'kludge'.

In May 2007, Roger Parloff, *Fortune* senior editor, reported[52] that Microsoft had determined that Linux infringed on 235 Microsoft patents: the Linux kernel (42 patents); the Linux graphical user interfaces (65 patents); the Open Office suite of programs (45 patents); E-mail programs (15 patents); and assorted FOSS programs (68 patents). Microsoft declined to identify these (retaliatory action to invalidate them might well have followed, as well as work to invent beyond them). It was not until Microsoft sued TomTom,[53] the GPS device vendor whose personal navigation

[48] See preamble to GPLv2: '. . . we have made it clear that any patent must be licensed for everyone's free use or not licensed at all'—the so-called: 'liberty-or-death' provision. And see also GPLv2 cl 7.

[49] For the commercial background, see R Parloff, 'Microsoft takes on the free world (cont)' (*CNN Money,* 14 May 2007) <http://money.cnn.com/magazines/fortune/fortune_archive/2007/05/28/100033867/index2.htm> accessed 10 April 2013.

[50] <http://www.microsoft.com/about/legal/en/us/IntellectualProperty/IPLicensing/customercovenant/msnovellcollab/patent_agreement.aspx> accessed 10 April 2013.

[51] See W Togami, founder of Fedora Project, Red Hat, Inc: 'But the price of liberty is not free, nor is it comfortable. And unfortunately, some "leaders" of our community are willing to compromise liberty for short-term convenience. I am disgusted by people like this, and by Novell's betrayal of the community today', Wtogami, 'Fedora Will Never Compromise' (11 March 2006) <http://wtogami.livejournal.com/11305.html> accessed 10 April 2013.

[52] R Parloff, 'Microsoft takes on the free world' (*CNN Money*, 14 May 2007) <http://money.cnn.com/magazines/fortune/fortune_archive/2007/05/28/100033867/index.htm> accessed 10 April 2013.

[53] By way of disclosure, the authors acted for TomTom in this litigation and the settlement negotiations.

devices are all Linux-based, in the ITC and US Federal Court, that it specifically identified a small set of these.

The patents asserted by Microsoft against TomTom included the FAT patents.[54] Microsoft has a licensing program specifically directed to these patents,[55] which have now been licensed to a number of companies (including RIM[56] Sharp,[57] Canon, Tuxera, Panasonic,[58] Aspen Avionics).[59] The FAT patents illustrate the inconsistent scrutiny afforded to patents in different jurisdictions: their validity has been upheld in Germany by the Federal Court of Justice of Germany[60] (*Bundesgerichtshof*, BGH), the highest appellate court (apart from the Federal Constitutional Court of Germany, which hears only matters of constitutional significance). Back in 2006, the Public Patent Foundation failed in its attempt to get the USPTO to reject the equivalent two US patents; the ITC later expressed scepticism on their validity, based in part on evidence from Linus Torvalds.[61]

The *Microsoft v TomTom* litigation illustrates a fairly typical litigation-settlement chronology: Microsoft sues for patent infringement (ITC, and in Federal District Court in Washington); a few weeks later, TomTom counter-sues Microsoft for infringing its own patents (Delaware); TomTom starts working with the FOSS community and a few weeks after that, the parties settle. The terms remain confidential, but the settlement was not reported as material in TomTom's public accounts. As Jim Zemlin[62] put it:

> There is another silver lining here. We read the outcome of this case as a testament to the power of a concerted and well-coordinated effort by the Linux industry and organizations such as the Open Invention Network, the SFLC and

[54] TomTom's issue was that, while its devices ran on Linux, users needed to connect them to Microsoft PCs from time to time to download data updates, and TomTom had therefore needed to make its software capable of interacting with the Windows file system and allegedly with FAT.

[55] 'exFAT file system' <http://www.microsoft.com/About/legal/en/us/intellectualproperty/iplicensing/programs/exfatfilesystem.aspx> accessed 10 April 2013.

[56] 'Microsoft Signs Licensing Agreement with Research in Motion' (18 September 2012) <http://www.microsoft.com/en-us/news/Press/2012/Sep12/09-18RIMPR.aspx> accessed 10 April 2013.

[57] 'Microsoft Signs Licensing Agreements for exFAT With Sharp, Sigma, NextoDi, Black Magic and Atomos Global' (7 November 2012) <http://www.microsoft.com/en-us/news/Press/2012/Nov12/11-07FiveDealsPR.aspx> accessed 10 April 2013.

[58] 'Microsoft Enters Intellectual Property Licensing Agreement with Panasonic' (25 February 2010) <http://www.microsoft.com/en-us/news/press/2010/feb10/02-25MSPanasonicPR.aspx> accessed 10 April 2013.

[59] 'Microsoft Signs Patent Licensing Agreement with Aspen Avionics' (3 May 2012) <http://www.microsoft.com/en-us/news/Press/2012/May12/05-03AspenPR.aspx> accessed 10 April 2013.

[60] <http://www.jurablogs.com/de/microsofts-controversal-fat-patent-upheld-german-federal-court-justice>; <http://www.visaepatentes.com/2010/04/microsofts-controversal-fat-patent.html> both accessed 10 April 2013; BGH Sentence, 20 April 2010, X ZR 27/07.

[61] <https://groups.google.com/forum/?fromgroups=#!topic/comp.os.minix/0rgZpprg_Eo> accessed 10 April 2013.

[62] 'TomTom Settlement Aftermath: Get the FAT Out' (*Groklaw*, 1 April 2009) <http://groklaw.net/article.php?story=20090401152339514> accessed 10 April 2013.

> the Linux Foundation. This was not merely a typical David vs. Goliath story. This time David aligned itself with the multiple slingshots of the Linux community. Microsoft relented as soon as TomTom showed they were aligned with that community and ready to fight. The system is working. There is one other fact clear from this case. Microsoft does not appear to be a leopard capable of changing its spots. Maybe it's time developers go on a diet from Microsoft and get the FAT out of their products.

Significant hold-outs from licensing Microsoft as of early 2013 include Google/Motorola and Red Hat.

6.3.4 Apple settlements and licences

Apple and HTC settled[63] their numerous lawsuits (52 suits, in the ITC and courts in the US, Germany, UK) on 11 November 2012. A heavily redacted version[64] of the Patent License and Settlement Agreement indicates that Apple imposed an anti-cloning requirement in which HTC is in effect precluded from releasing 'Cloned Products', namely products which include a human interface with a distinctive visual appearance which it has created (that is it's not a clone if the UX feature is in Android) and which (a) infringes an Apple patent and (b) Apple products also implement that Apple patent and (c) shares the same visual appearance as the Apple implementation and (d) is not a result of requirements from Google, or the Open Handset Alliance ('OHA'), or any carrier or any standard-setting body Apple belongs to and (e) there is an alternative available to HTC that realizes the functional, cost, and performance advantages of the Apple patented feature. An arbitration mechanism applies to any dispute as to whether or not HTC has produced a 'Cloned Product'. One example that attracted much attention in this litigation was Apple's patent to the 'swipe-to-unlock' idea of dragging an object from a start location to an 'unlock region' (see US Patent 8,046,721 and US Patent 8,286,103). Exhibit A of the settlement states that other bubble slider animations, or an animation at the side of the screen (as opposed to the bottom of the screen) would not be a 'Cloned Feature'. It has also been reported that Apple licensed patents to Microsoft, again with a 'No-clone' provision.[65] It's becoming tolerably clear that the 'No-clone' provision is at the heart of Apple's product differentiation strategy, supported by its extensive patent litigation.

[63] 'HTC and Apple Settle Patent Dispute' <http://www.apple.com/pr/library/2012/11/11HTC-and-Apple-Settle-Patent-Dispute.html> accessed 10 April 2013.

[64] <http://www.scribd.com/doc/115715526/2182-5> accessed 10 April 2013.

[65] D Levine and E Chan, 'Apple expert shines light on Samsung sales in US' (*Reuters*, 13 August 2012) <http://www.reuters.com/article/2012/08/13/us-apple-samsung-idUSBRE87C0SC20120813> accessed 10 April 2013.

One aspect of the Apple and HTC patent settlement is perhaps worth mentioning: we saw earlier that for Microsoft to craft a settlement that enabled its licensees to remain GPLv2 compliant (at least in the eyes of Microsoft's counsel), it had to forego granting a direct licence on any patents that might cover GPLv2 code (eg, the Linux kernel), and instead grant a covenant not to sue the licensee's customers. That kind of mechanism is absent from the Apple and HTC settlement;[66] the reasons for that absence are opaque and not discussed by either party. Whilst Android itself would not be licensed to HTC under GPLv2, but instead the more permissive Apache Version 2.0, which permits users of Android to enter into patent licences (that is it includes no equivalent to the GPLv2 clause 7 language), the kernel and patches would be licensed under GPLv2. To date, no GPLv2 enforcement action against HTC has been reported.

One could go into tremendous detail for each of the many different cases in the Smartphone Wars,[67] but that is not the purpose of this chapter (and it would also render it out-of-date immediately on publication). Instead, we will focus on using the Smartphone Wars to illustrate principles and practices, which are likely to apply to any litigation brought against FOSS. Most litigation ends up with a settlement of sorts; a great deal of money is spent; most patents are held invalid or not-infringed; money is often paid (even where both sides have large patent arsenals) and it can be a significant amount, but those amounts are concealed from public scrutiny. It's not an especially welcoming vista to FOSS adherents.

6.4 INJUNCTIONS

Particularly unappealing is the threat of an injunction preventing the sale entirely of infringing products. Injunctions against Motorola in Germany have forced it to withdraw all Android products from that market. Microsoft moved its European distribution centre from Germany to the Netherlands, citing the unacceptable risk of injunctions from Motorola in Germany as the reason.[68]

We can summarize the current legal position, as of end 2012, for injunctions against Android product in Table 6.4 as follows:

[66] See, eg, Groklaw's analysis at <http://www.groklaw.net/articlebasic.php?story=20121206022939920> accessed 10 April 2013.

[67] For a detailed exegesis and insightful commentary, see <http://www.groklaw.net> and also F Mueller's <http://www.fosspatents.com> both accessed 10 April 2013.

[68] 'Microsoft shuts German distribution center in patent dispute' (2 April 2012) <http://www.reuters.com/article/2012/04/02/us-microsoft-germany-idUSBRE8310IN20120402> accessed 10 April 2013.

Table 6.4 SmartPhone Wars—Patent injunctions obtained against Android products

Patent No	Short description	Date	Plaintiff	Defendant	Region
EP2059868	Photo gallery page-flipping	24/11/2011	Apple	Samsung	Europe
		01/03/2012	Apple	MMI	Germany
EP1964022	Slide-to-unlock	16/02/2012	Apple	MMI	Germany
US6,370,566	Generating meeting requests and group scheduling	18/05/2012	MS	MMI	US
EP1304891	Communicating multi-part messages	24/05/2012	MS	MMI (Google)	Germany
EP0618540	Common name space for long and short filenames	27/07/2012	MS	MMI (Google)	Germany
EP2126678	Overscroll-bounce	13/09/2012	Apple	MMI (Google)	Germany
EP1040406	Soft input panel system and method	20/09/2012	MS	MMI (Google)	Germany

Google's primary strategy for Android against Microsoft has been to assert Motorola's standards essential patents (eg H.264 video coding patents against Microsoft's Xbox gaming console), seeking injunctions in numerous jurisdictions that, if granted, would give it the leverage over Microsoft needed to secure a broad settlement that would force Microsoft to cease hostilities against Android. But standard essential patents are subject to FRAND obligations (where the patent holder commits to a standards body such as the International Telecommunication Union or the European Telecommunication Standards Institute that it will license any of its patents that are essential to the standard controlled by that standards body, on fair, reasonable, and non-discriminatory terms).[69]

The precise circumstances in which an injunction can be secured for so called SEPs has been a matter of fast-evolving case law over the course of the SmartPhone Wars, with increasing involvement from the antitrust regulators (see European Commission's 21 December 2012 Statement of Objections[70]—'The European Commission has informed Samsung of its preliminary view that Samsung's seeking of injunctions against Apple in various Member States on the basis of its mobile phone standard-essential patents

[69] See further ch 9.

[70] European Commission, 'Antitrust: Commission sends Statement of Objections to Samsung on potential misuse of mobile phone standard-essential patents' (21 December 2012) <http://europa.eu/rapid/press-release_IP-12-1448_en.htm> accessed 10 April 2013.

("SEPs") amounts to an abuse of a dominant position prohibited by EU antitrust rules.' Samsung had dropped all of its injunction requests against Apple in Germany, UK, France, Italy, and the Netherlands on 18 December 2012.

Google entered into a consent decree[71] with the FTC, announced 3 January 2013, in which it undertook not to seek injunctions for infringement of its standard essential patents (other than in highly constrained circumstances). Although the consent decree is silent on the current litigation, it seems probable that MMI will withdraw all pending injunction requests.

The current position, as of January 2013, is that no injunctions based on standard essential patents have been obtained, and the prospects of any company ever being granted one in normal circumstances in most countries are both remote and ever-receding; further US courts may grant global anti-suit injunctions, precluding a SEP holder subject to FRAND obligation seeking injunctive relief anywhere in the world.[72]

Motorola has secured one injunction against Apple in respect of a non-standards essential patent, shown in Table 6.5.

Table 6.5 Patent injunctions obtained against companies accusing Android products

Patent No	Short description	Date	Plaintiff	Defendant	Region	Type
EP847654	Multiple pager status synchronization	03/02/2012	MMI	Apple	Germany	Permanent

Germany is without doubt the most injunction-friendly major jurisdiction, and for that reason alone it will no doubt continue to attract patent owners.

We summarize briefly the law relating to injunctions in the US, UK, and Germany in Table 6.6.

Table 6.6 Summary of US, UK and German law on injunctions

Country	Rules for injunctions
USA	For preliminary/provisional injunctions,[73] before a trial on the merits: • A likelihood of success on the merits. • A showing of likely irreparable harm without an injunction. • The balance of equities must tip in the plaintiff's favour. • To be in the public interest.

continued

[71] FTC, 'Google Agrees to Change Its Business Practices to Resolve FTC Competition Concerns In the Markets for Devices Like Smart Phones, Games and Tablets, and in Online Search' (3 January 2013) <http://ftc.gov/opa/2013/01/google.shtm> accessed 10 April 2013.

[72] Groklaw, 'Surprise Surprise... NOT. Seattle Judge Grants MS Motion, Bans Injunctions for Motorola's RAND Patents' (30 November 2012) <http://www.groklaw.net/articlebasic.php?story=20121130235041754> accessed 10 April 2013.

[73] *Winter v Natural Resources Defense Council, Inc* 129 S Ct 365, 376–7 (2008).

Table 6.6 (continued)

Country	Rules for injunctions
	For permanent injunctions, after a trial on the merits, the criteria[74] to weigh are essentially the same: • Irreparable harm (but rejecting notion that a patent holder is entitled to a presumption of irreparable harm if his patent is held valid and infringed; imposing a requirement to prove a sufficiently strong *causal nexus* relating the alleged harm to the alleged infringement, which requires showing that consumers buy the infringing product '*because it is equipped with the apparatus claimed in the patent and not merely because it includes a feature of the type covered by the patent*').[75] For many cases involving FOSS, this *causal nexus* may well prove to be exceptionally difficult to establish. That Apple was denied an injunction[76] against Samsung, despite the 21 August 2012 jury returning a verdict of infringement, shows how difficult in practice meeting this standard can be when the trial court applies the 'causal nexus' standard strictly. The Federal Circuit will hear Apple's appeal from this judgment in mid-2013; it will be one of the defining moments of the Smartphone Wars. If the Federal Circuit supports the rigorous application of the 'causal nexus' test, then they will in effect have forked the US patent system, with one fork covering say pharma, where causal nexus can generally be established and so injunctions will be available, and a fork covering electronics/software, where causal nexus will be exceptionally hard to prove and so injunctions will in practice not be available, a highly attractive outcome for FOSS. • Inadequacy of legal remedies, that is money damages for the past, a running royalty for the future. • Balance of hardships. • The public interest. Here again, case law may favour FOSS interests because in most cases, a patent covering a function implemented by FOSS will be just one function out of many tens of thousands (see:[77] 'the public interest does not support removing phones from the market when the infringing components constitute such limited parts of complex, multi-faceted products'). The only available relief at the ITC under section 337 is an injunction; complainants need therefore to prove (i) an unfair act (eg patent infringement); (ii) importation into the US of infringing goods and (iii) that the complainant meets the domestic industry standard.[78] Exclusion orders can be limited (a

continued

[74] *eBay Inc v Merc Exchange, LLC* 547 US 388 (2006).

[75] The Federal Circuit's *Apple II* opinion: *Apple, Inc v Samsung Electronics Co., Ltd* 695 F.3d 1370 1374 1376 (Fed Cir 2012).

[76] See order Denying Motion for Permanent Injunction, *Apple, Inc v Samsung Electronics Co, Ltd* Case No 11-CV-01846-LHK, on appeal to the Federal Circuit as of early 2013.

[77] See Order Denying Motion for Permanent Injunction, *Apple, Inc v Samsung Electronics Co., Ltd* Case No 11-CV-01846-LHK, on appeal to the Federal Circuit as of early 2013.

[78] The s 337 domestic industry requirement involves an economic prong (the complainant must have, in the US, with respect to its (or its licensees') products covered by the asserted patent, a significant investment in plant and machinery, significant employment of labour or capital, substantial investment in R&D, or licensing relevant to the patent; the complainant's products (or its licensees') products must itself practice the asserted patent).

Table 6.6 (continued)

Country	Rules for injunctions
	'LEO') to the named respondent, or general (a 'GEO'), barring importation of all infringing goods, irrespective of the importer. A cease and desist order (a 'CDO'), preventing further distribution of good already in the US, may also be granted. Injunctions and exclusion orders will likely[79,80,81] not be available for infringement of standard essential patents, voluntarily subject to FRAND obligations in most cases (but injunctions may perhaps be given where the accused is unable or refuses to license on FRAND terms, refuses to negotiate, is outside of the jurisdiction of a court that could award damages in lieu of an injunction). The ITC must take into account as an *overriding consideration,*[82] the public interest, including the assurance of competitive conditions in the US economy, when determining its remedies. It is possible that the ITC may be reluctant to grant an exclusion order against say a tablet running a FOSS operating system, when faced with a complaint or suit brought by a major patent holder purely based on an infringement associated with, eg, a minor function implemented by a few lines of code in the millions of lines of code Linux, running on chip that can be bought for a few dollars. See Justice Kennedy's concurring opinion in *eBay*: 'when the patented invention is but a small component of the product the companies seek to produce and the threat of an injunction is employed simply for undue leverage in negotiations, legal damages may well be sufficient to compensate for infringement and an injunction may not serve the public interest'.
UK	For preliminary/provisional injunctions before a trial on the merits, the court has a broad discretion, applying the following criteria:[83] • Is there a serious question to be tried? • If 'yes', would damages be an adequate remedy by a party injured by the court's grant, or failure to grant an injunction? • If not, where does the balance of convenience lie?For final injunctions, the court again has an unfettered discretion, but generally awards an injunction: it may however award damages in lieu of an injunction where[84] the infringement is small, the claimant can be compensated by a small monetary payment and the

continued

[79] See 'Third Party United States Federal Trade Commission's Statement on the Public Interest' filed on 6 June 2012 in *In re Certain Wireless Communication Devices, Portable Music & Data Processing Devices, Computers & Components Thereof*, Inv No 337-TA-745 at <http://www.ftc.gov/os/2012/06/1206ftcwirelesscom.pdf> accessed 10 April 2013.

[80] See, eg, United States Department of Justice and United States Patent & Trademark Office; Policy Statement on Remedies for Standards-Essential Patents Subject to Voluntary F/RAND Commitments dated 8 January 2013 at <http://www.justice.gov/atr/public/guidelines/290994.pdf> accessed 10 April 2013.

[81] See Opinion and Order of 22 June 2012, *Apple, Inc and next Software Inc v Motorola, Inc, and Motorola Mobility, Inc*, Case No 1:11-cv-08540.

[82] Certain Inclined Field Acceleration Tubes & Components Thereof, Inv No 337-TA-67, USITC Pub 1119, Comm'n Op, at 22 (December 1980).

[83] *American Cyanamid v Ethicon* [1975] FSR 101.

[84] *Shelfer v City of London Electric Lighting Co* [1895] 2 Ch 388.

Table 6.6 (continued)

Country	Rules for injunctions
	grant of an injunction would be oppressive (that is grossly disproportionate to the right protected). These factors may well apply to FOSS patent infringement associated with relatively minor but patented functions. Where the motive for an injunction is merely to improve a negotiating position, an injunction may be refused.[85] Again, that may well apply in those practical circumstances where there is litigation against FOSS. Broader public interest issues may provide further and important areas of legal development.
Germany	For preliminary/provisional injunctions before a trial on the merits, the court needs to conclude that infringement is likely, and that the interests of the patent holder prevail over those of the alleged infringer in a balance of convenience test (urgency, irreparable harm, patent likely to be valid).For final injunctions, if infringement is found and the case is not stayed (eg pending a nullity action, a common occurrence because in the German split system, the infringement action can be heard a year or more in advance of the nullity action), then the grant is automatic, unless there are exceptional grounds justifying the use (eg a prior user defence).Where a permanent injunction is granted by the first instance court ('Landgericht') then, pending an appeal, a defendant can seek a stay, subject to payment of security and a showing of irreparable harm, and that the defendant's interests in securing a stay outweigh the plaintiff's interests in enforcing the injunction.The German system is seen as significantly more favourable to plaintiffs than, eg, the UK. Recent experience in the Smartphone Wars appears to bear that out, with Germany being the only major European court granting injunctions to any of the players. If there is European anti-FOSS patent litigation, then Germany is likely to prove the venue of choice for patent holders.

6.5 WHAT ARE PATENTS WORTH? ENTIRE MARKET VALUE, RATE STACKING, THE GEORGIA PACIFIC FACTORS, HOLD-UP VALUE

6.5.1 Typical royalty rates in software

As a rough rule of thumb, reasonable royalty rates to compensate for infringement of a single software patent, as determined at trial in the US, have historically tended to hover around 1 per cent of sales. There is no hard and fast rule as to how this number should scale with increasing numbers of patents, but in practice reasonable royalty rates tend not to go much higher than 2 per cent of sales, even with significantly more patents. There are of course exceptions; eg, Symbol was awarded[86] a 6 per cent royalty

[85] *Banks v EMI Songs (formerly CBS Songs Ltd) (No 2)* [1996] EMLR 452.

[86] See *Symbol Techs, Inc v Proxim Inc*, No Civ 01-801-SLR, 2004 WL 1770290.

rate for infringement of its patent relating to the 802.11 standard. The practical issues of providing admissible evidence as to the value of a patent should not however be underestimated: eg, Judge Posner, dismissing with prejudice[87] patent suits brought by Apple and Microsoft, characterized Motorola's failure as:

> We say it's 2.25 per cent, *but I'm not going to be able to prove to you that that's the right number today* (emphasis added). And now it's too late.

We expect to see significant developments in this key area in the coming years, and we will focus on these in this section. Because US law is disproportionately more influential than the laws of other countries when it comes to assessing the value of patents, and US approaches tend to dominate the everyday practice of negotiating patent licences and settlements, we focus here on US law issues.

6.5.2 Entire Market Value Rule

A key issue in all patent licensing negotiations, and indeed any other context involving royalty rate disputes, is invariably the identity of the royalty base; is the royalty rate to be applied to the entire market value of say a smartphone, or should it be applied to a component, such as a chip in the device. Invariably, patent holders seeking royalties will base their demands on the entire market value of the end product, since it is the most valuable element in the chain of commerce, even though their patents might cover features which are relevant to just a single component in the device (perhaps the processor), and there are dozens of other components in the final product. The first crack in the entire market value rule came in *Uniloc USA, Inc and Uniloc Singapore Private Limited v Microsoft Corporation*,[88] in which Microsoft successfully fought back an effort to use as a royalty basis 'Microsoft's approximate total revenue for Office and Windows of $19.28 billion' during the relevant calculation period.

The *Uniloc* decision was further clarified in a more recent case from the Federal Circuit, *LaserDynamics v Quanta*, holding:[89]

> We reaffirm that in any case involving multi-component products, patentees may not calculate damages based on sales of the entire product, as opposed to the smallest salable patent practising unit, without showing that the demand for the entire product is attributable to the patented feature.

LaserDynamics had patented a disc discrimination method but

> [f]ailed to present evidence showing that the patented disc discrimination method drove demand for the laptop computers. It is not enough to merely show that the disc

[87] See Opinion and Order of 22 June 2012, *Apple, Inc and next Software Inc, v Motorola, Inc, and Motorola Mobility, Inc*, Case No 1:11-cv-08540.

[88] 632 F.3d 1292 (Fed Cir 2011).

[89] <http://www.cafc.uscourts.gov/images/stories/opinions-orders/11-1440-1470.pdf> accessed 10 April 2013.

> discrimination method is viewed as valuable, important or even essential to the use of the laptop computer. Nor is it enough to show that a laptop computer without an ODD practising the disc discrimination method would be commercially unviable. Were this sufficient, a plethora of features of a laptop computer could be deemed to drive demand for the entire product. To name a few, a high resolution screen, responsive keyboard, fast wireless network receiver and extended-life battery are all in a sense important or essential features to a laptop computer; take away one of these features and consumers are unlikely to select such a laptop computer in the marketplace. But proof that consumers would not want a laptop computer without such features is not tantamount to proof that any one of those features alone drives the market for laptop computers.[90]

The upshot was a vast reduction in Quanta's liability, down from the $52 million awarded at trial. In practical terms, proving that a specific patented feature drives demand can be exceptionally difficult, as we saw earlier in relation to Apple's failure to secure an injunction against Samsung, where the same test of proving that a patented feature drives demand applies to the grant of an injunction. For many FOSS functions, patent holders asserting against FOSS will face substantial challenges meeting this evidentiary burden. Further, even if they can establish sufficient proof that their patented feature drives demand, in many cases, the 'smallest saleable unit' for software patents will be the chip or chip+ROM module in the accused products, or code itself, and that will be priced at a small fraction of the finished consumer item. So we can discern a possible trend that could be highly favourable to FOSS.

6.5.3 Royalty rate stacking

We have seen earlier, in relation to the declared royalty rates for LTE wireless essential patents, that where there are multiple patent holders, each claiming royalties against the same product, the overall royalty burden is not only difficult to predict with any accuracy but can, if patent holders get what they say they deserve, quickly become commercially unsupportable, at least for licensees with nothing to cross-license. If there are 100 companies, all looking for 1 per cent of sales, then the stacking of these royalties to 100 per cent of sales is clearly wrong.

It may also be that the Federal Circuit's requirement to use as a royalty base the smallest salable, patent practising unit (except in those very rare cases when the plaintiff can prove that their patented feature drives demand), will go some way towards softening the royalty rate stacking problem. But we also expect, during 2013, to see a number of trials in the US and in the UK that directly address royalty rate stacking, in the context of FRAND rates; at the time of writing, we can only wait in

[90] <http://www.cafc.uscourts.gov/images/stories/opinions-orders/11-1440-1470.pdf> accessed 10 April 2013.

expectation. It is possible, perhaps likely, that we will see in the US some significant developments to the way that royalties are calculated, developing the Georgia Pacific factors, which are currently controlling. It is worth reciting these in full:

1. The royalties received by the patentee for the licensing of the patent in suit, proving or tending to prove an established royalty.
2. The rates paid by the licensee for the use of other patents comparable to the patent in suit.
3. The nature and scope of the licence, as exclusive or non exclusive; or as restricted or non restricted in terms of territory or with respect to whom the manufactured product may be sold.
4. The licensor's established policy and marketing program to maintain his patent monopoly by not licensing others to use the invention or by granting licences under special conditions designed to preserve that monopoly.
5. The commercial relationship between the licensor and licensee, such as, whether they are competitors in the same territory, in the same line of business, or whether they are inventor and promoter.
6. The effect of selling the patented specialty in promoting sales of other products of the licensee; the existing value of the invention to the licensor as a generator of sales of his non-patented items; and the extent of such derivative or convoyed sales.
7. The duration of the patent and the term of the licence.
8. The established profitability of the product made under the patent; its commercial success; and its current popularity.
9. The utility and advantages of the patent property over the old modes or devices, if any that had been used for working out similar results.
10. The nature of the patented invention; the character of the commercial embodiment of it as owned and produced by the licensor; and the benefits to those who have used the invention.
11. The extent to which the infringer has made use of the invention; and any evidence probative of the value of that use.
12. The portion of the profit or of the selling price that may be customary in the particular business, or in comparable businesses to allow for the use of the invention or analogous inventions.
13. The portion of the realizable profit that should be credited to the invention as distinguished from non-patented elements, the manufacturing process, business risks, or significant features or improvements added by the infringer.
14. The opinion testimony of qualified experts.
15. The amount that a licensor (such as the patentee) and a licensee (such as the infringer) would have agreed upon (at the time the infringement began) if both

> had been reasonably and voluntarily trying to reach an agreement; that is, the amount which a prudent licensee—who desired, as a business proposition, to obtain a licence to manufacture and sell a particular article embodying the patented invention—would have been willing to pay as a royalty, and yet be able to make a reasonable profit; and which amount would have been acceptable by a prudent patentee who was willing to grant a licence.

As we have noted earlier, if there are 100 companies, all looking for 1 per cent of sales, then the stacking of these royalties to 100 per cent of sales is clearly wrong. Yet, the current system is in practice entirely consistent with that absurdity, even though factor 15 in the *Georgia Pacific* factors envisages that the reasonable royalty should still enable the licensee to make a 'reasonable profit'. We may see case law explore the contours of this 'reasonable profit' concept more fully.

Damages to compensate for past infringements and running royalties for future acts are notoriously difficult to generalize about; patent trials are always highly fact specific, and the bearing on damages/running royalties can be colossal. Take, at one extreme, the facts of *i4i v Microsoft*, where a $290 million damages claim was affirmed at the Federal Circuit and Supreme Court. In that case, damages (which are meant in US patent cases to compensate the injured party for the infringement) were set high for a number of factors that would typically not apply in most FOSS contexts. Specifically, i4i's main focus was a product that allowed Microsoft Word to be used as an editor for XML (the subject of their patent). The evidence was that Microsoft, at the time that i4i released its product, had no idea how to achieve that goal, and that they relied heavily on i4i and its product in securing the approval of various US defence and security agencies, praising both i4i and its product in its presentations to those agencies. Yet Microsoft, without telling i4i, was incorporating the i4i technique into Word 2003 to provide its custom XML capability; and stated publicly that custom XML was 90 per cent of the value of XML, and that XML was fundamental to Word 2003 and 2007. Word 2003 and Word 2007 proceeded to enjoy huge market success, but that in turn had the effect of dramatically limiting i4i's business. i4i sought 2 per cent of Microsoft's profits from its sales of Word, amounting to $200 million. Microsoft countered with a damages assessment at $13,000. The jury sided with i4i; US juries have historically tended to disapprove strongly of what they perceive as underhand treatment by a big corporation in capturing much of the value in a market pioneered by a small innovator. Complex stories are often simplified (perhaps to the point of falsification, if you don't come out on top).

So it would be wrong for FOSS adherents to point to the huge sum that Microsoft ultimately paid to i4i as indicative that the value of software patents is astronomically disproportionate. Patents rarely have any intrinsic value, but take their value from the circumstances around them. In the circumstances of the i4i litigation, the compensation due to i4i amounted to a great deal of money because of the exceptional market success of Word 2003 and 2007.

At the other end of the spectrum, we could imagine a patent infringement case brought by a major software company against a much smaller FOSS entity. Let's suppose that the patented software function is something that (like most patented software functions) can be invented around. Let's suppose that the major software company suffers minimal losses as a result of the smaller FOSS entity's commercial activities. What then is the appropriate compensation? One argument, suggested by Judge Posner in his highly influential Opinion and Order dismissing with prejudice patent suits brought by Apple and Microsoft,[91] is to say that compensation for the major software company is 'royalties capped at the minimum design-around costs' since that equates to what a prudent infringer would have paid to secure a licence. Where the design-around costs for the FOSS entity are small (and possibly close to zero), as they often will be when the community collaborates to design or invent-around a software patent, the damages due would then be minimal. This possible strand of legal thinking could prove highly favourable to FOSS.

6.5.4 Hold-up value

In royalty or patent licensing negotiations that occur under the threat of an injunction or exclusion order, the patent holder typically seeks to realize royalty rates or settlement amounts that do not reflect the inherent value of the patent relative to alternatives, but a greatly enhanced value (associated with the costs and effects of switching), referred to as the hold-up value.[92] The problem is especially acute for standard essential patents, because once the standard is adopted, then a patent that covers the standard, even though it might be entirely trivial, must be practised. There is no option but to take a licence; the value of the patent has increased because it has been declared (albeit voluntarily by the patent holder, without external scrutiny) as standard essential.

Hold-up value is a major focus for antitrust regulators looking at potential abuses of the standard-setting process (and standard-setting bodies exist solely on the sufferance of the antitrust regulators). But arguably hold-ups can occur whenever a company with disproportionate bargaining power seeks patent royalties from an entity with no effective means of negotiating a licence at rates that genuinely reflect the value of the patents being licensed, as opposed to the artificially enhanced value they have by virtue of that disproportionate bargaining power in the hands of the

[91] See Opinion and Order of 22 June 2012, *Apple, Inc. and next Software Inc v Motorola, Inc, and Motorola Mobility, Inc*, Case No 1:11-cv-08540.

[92] For a comprehensive and influential analysis, see M Lemley and C Shapiro, 'Patent Holdup and Royalty Stacking' <http://faculty.haas.berkeley.edu/shapiro/stacking.pdf> accessed 10 April 2013.

patent holder. This is often the case with SME FOSS targets: eg the patent holder has far greater financial resources, access to skilled legal advisors, and relative immunity from counter-assertions than the target; the target has neither the financial nor personnel resources to litigate or bring antitrust complaints.

So we may, perhaps, see a broadening of antitrust focus from licensing of standard essential patents, to licensing wherever the patent holder has disproportionate bargaining power. And as the US case law evolves to make injunctions and exclusion orders exceptionally difficult for standards essential patents (see Table 6.6), the debate will likely shift back onto attempting to craft ways of more fairly determining the true value of patents. These twin trends may prove to be significantly favourable to FOSS.

6.6 SMARTPHONE WARS—ORACLE V GOOGLE

We have already discussed the ongoing Smartphone Wars and extracted some lessons for FOSS. The weapons in the wars we have been discussing are principally patents (including design patents in the case of Apple v Samsung). Copyright has not featured, but it remains the sole focus of Oracle's litigation against Google,[93] alleging that Google's Android infringes various patents, together with copyrights in Java, in Oracle's hands after Oracle acquired Sun in April 2009; $6 billion in damages were sought by Oracle.

May 2012 saw the first jury trial in the Smartphone Wars. A verdict of non-infringement of all the asserted patents was returned, a significant win for FOSS, and an illustration of the important lessons that, for most patents that might arguably cover FOSS, there are likely to be some ways of inventing-around (also known as 'design-arounds'). Invent-arounds may well become a key aspect of FOSS creativity.

Judge Alsop also decided the issue of the inherent copyrightability of the JAVA APIs; he held[94] that:

> So long as the specific code used to implement a method is different, anyone is free under the Copyright Act to write his or her own code to carry out exactly the same function or specification of any methods used in the Java API.

He further held that the method header line is not protectable because Java requires that a method's header line be identical to declare the same functionality, even when the method's implementation is different. Protectability is denied under the merger doctrine (when there is only one way to express a function, no-one can monopolise that expression). Finally, he held that the command structure of the Java API packages was not protectable because it was a method of operation (excluded from

[93] *Oracle America, Inc v Google Inc*, Case3:10-cv-03561-WHA.

[94] <http://www.groklaw.net/pdf3/OraGoogle-1202.pdf> accessed 10 April 2013.

copyright under statute) and duplication of this command structure is necessary for interoperability.

The case is on appeal, with a hearing due mid 2013. Importantly for the FOSS community, Oracle dropped all of its patent infringement assertions for that appeal, focussing exclusively on copyrightability of APIs, despite the case commencing principally as a patent case. As Judge Alsop noted:

> A close follower of this case will know that Oracle did not place great importance on its copyright claims until after its asserted patents started disappearing upon PTO reexamination (indeed, Oracle's first damages report barely mentioned copyright claims). Oracle did not bring its API copyright claim for the benefit of addressing 'a landmark issue of national importance,' but instead fell back on an overreaching (albeit somewhat novel) theory of copyright infringement for its own financial interests late in litigation.

For FOSS, the copyright issues in the case remain of central importance, and are analysed elsewhere.

6.7 HOW DO ANTI-FOSS PATENTS PRACTICALLY IMPACT SME VENDORS WITH FOSS PRODUCTS?

In this section, we summarize the practical impact that anti-FOSS patents might have on SME vendors with FOSS products, given the current state of the patent system.

- SMEs with successful FOSS products may be compelled to pay patent royalties because they are in a weak bargaining position when faced with a patent holder with a large anti-FOSS patent arsenal; the SME cannot fund acquisition or creation of their own counter-balancing patent portfolio; cannot afford defensive litigation (at between $3million and $10 million per case) or take even a small risk of an adverse ruling; cannot fund antitrust litigation; and may have no ability to invent-around in advance of a suit (or have the FOSS community do so) because the patent holder may refuse to publicly define their anti-FOSS patent arsenals.
- SMEs typically lack access to patent royalty data since there is no open and transparent process discovery mechanism for licensing anti-FOSS patents (other than litigation). This puts them at a disadvantage in negotiations and also in attracting investment.
- SMEs will also typically be faced with a patent holder threatening to fragment their patent holdings, selling some to non practising entities ('NPEs') so multiplying the source of threats, to leverage a settlement. This again puts the SME at a disadvantage in negotiations. (In May 2012, Google filed a complaint with the European Commission alleging anticompetitive consequences to Microsoft and Nokia's

recent disposal of 1,200 patents to an independent enforcement entity, MOSAID; patent fragmentation of this sort can proliferate the sources of threats to FOSS entities and insulate the patent seller from the adverse consequences of directly attacking the FOSS community).

- There are rarely any FRAND commitments around anti-FOSS patents because the patent holders do not participate in any of the standard-setting for FOSS.
- There is no transparency as to what anti-FOSS patents actually exist, and who owns what. Many software patents can, if known about, be invented-around, but secrecy about what patents are allegedly infringed precludes pre-emptive inventing-around. This again puts the SME at a disadvantage in negotiations.
- Royalty rate stacking is an especially glaring issue for FOSS since there could be hundreds, perhaps thousands of relevant patents impacting FOSS code in a single product.
- The application of the Smallest Saleable Unit as the proper base for royalties is uncertain when applied to FOSS patents; what is the Smallest Saleable Unit for purposes of say a patent that covers a kernel technique, and the patent claims the final end-user product? Is it the price of the chip that the operating system runs on?
- What should patent damages and royalty rates be when only minimal investment is needed to devise a software function that is subsequently patented, and FOSS community developers independently devise the same idea rapidly with no investment requirements at all? What would damages sufficient to compensate the patent holder look like? What would a reasonable royalty look like if inventing-around is trivial? And, on a practical note, does the SME have the resources to extract maximum leverage from these kinds of arguments in negotiations?

6.8 FOSS COMMUNITY'S RESPONSE TO PATENT THREATS

In this section, we will survey briefly how the FOSS community has chosen to respond to the perceived patent threat.

6.8.1 Open source licence terms

Open source licences may include a patent licence under all of the patents owned by each contributor, plus a 'yank clause' that automatically terminates those patent licences in the event that the licensee initiates patent litigation. This induces a stable, patent-litigation free equilibrium throughout the ecosystem of licensees and contributors. See, eg, the Apache License v2.0.[95]

[95] <http://www.apache.org/licenses/LICENSE-2.0> accessed 10 April 2013.

> 3. **Grant of Patent License**. Subject to the terms and conditions of this License, each Contributor hereby grants to You a perpetual, worldwide, non-exclusive, no-charge, royalty-free, irrevocable (except as stated in this section) patent license to make, have made, use, offer to sell, sell, import, and otherwise transfer the Work, where such license applies only to those patent claims licensable by such Contributor that are necessarily infringed by their Contribution(s) alone or by combination of their Contribution(s) with the Work to which such Contribution(s) was submitted. If You institute patent litigation against any entity (including a cross-claim or counterclaim in a lawsuit) alleging that the Work or a Contribution incorporated within the Work constitutes direct or contributory patent infringement, then any patent licenses granted to You under this License for that Work shall terminate as of the date such litigation is filed.

And the Apache Individual Contributor License Agreement v2.0:

> 3. **Grant of Patent License**. Subject to the terms and conditions of this Agreement, You hereby grant to the Foundation and to recipients of software distributed by the Foundation a perpetual, worldwide, non-exclusive, no-charge, royalty-free, irrevocable (except as stated in this section) patent license to make, have made, use, offer to sell, sell, import, and otherwise transfer the Work, where such license applies only to those patent claims licensable by You that are necessarily infringed by Your Contribution(s) alone or by combination of Your Contribution(s) with the Work to which such Contribution(s) was submitted. If any entity institutes patent litigation against You or any other entity (including a cross-claim or counterclaim in a lawsuit) alleging that your Contribution, or the Work to which you have contributed, constitutes direct or contributory patent infringement, then any patent licenses granted to that entity under this Agreement for that Contribution or Work shall terminate as of the date such litigation is filed.

In addition, Google is currently surveying the community to build consensus around different Royalty-Free Patent Licensing models.[96] Four different licensing models are under review:

- **Licence on Transfer Agreement (LOT):** Companies entering into this kind of agreement pledge to give a licence to all members to any patent that they might transfer to a third party.
- **Non-sticky Defensive Patent Licence:** A portfolio-wide, royalty-free licence available to anyone agreeing to do the same with their portfolio. Inbound and outbound licences are terminated upon withdrawal.
- **Sticky Defensive Patent Licence:** Same as the Non-sticky alternative, except that issued licences are not terminated upon withdrawal.

[96] <http://www.google.com/patents/licensing> accessed 10 April 2013.

- **Field-of-Use Agreement:** A royalty-free, field-of-use licence similar to the OIN patent pool. This kind of licence is limited in scope, as opposed to the Defensive Patent Licences which are portfolio-wide.

Each of these proposed alternatives are potentially positive from a FOSS perspective, as they all aim to reduce the risk of being on the receiving end of patent assertions.

6.8.2 Community action

The FOSS community has set up several initiatives to deal with patents, as has been commented in the preceding chapter. These are coming together to create a more cohesive response to perceived patent threats, including:

- **Practical guidance** to community members has been offered on how to treat patents and patent threats. The Debian Position on Software Patents[97] is a well-known example.
- **Defensive patent pools**: eg Open Invention Network,[98] which controls a patent pool and has the mandate to defend Linux and Android (as well as some other FOSS packages) from patent attacks.
- **Defensive publication:** Linux Defenders is organizing and disseminating defensive publications, as a means to create prior art. There are interesting historical precedents[99] to information sharing networks of this sort; in the 1880s, the US railroads were subject to an intense degree of patent litigation from suppliers and what we would today call non practising entities; costs and damages were potentially life threatening. The railroads countered by forming two associations, the Eastern and the Western Railroad Association, each tasked with jointly defending its members from suit, and pooling information relating to patents that might affect members and advising on invent-arounds. The strategy was remarkably successful in dampening down litigation, and Congress twice rejected petitions that the associations violated antitrust laws.
- **Patent Promises and Pledges (Red Hat, Nokia, IBM, Google).** As the preceding chapter notes, various companies have made patent pledges, unilateral promises not to assert patents against developers, provided that certain conditions are met; they operate as an enforceable covenant not to sue, equitable estoppel precludes the patent holder from bringing suit against those within the safe harbour defined by the pledge.

[97] See <http://www.debian.org/legal/patent> accessed 10 April 2013.

[98] <http://www.openinventionnetwork.com> accessed 10 April 2013.

[99] SW Usselman, *Regulating Railroad Innovation* (Cambridge, Cambridge University Press, 2002).

6.8.3 Defensive patent portfolio development and acquisition

In addition to community action, 'corporate' FOSS stakeholders seem to be building portfolios, a priori for defensive purposes. Google's acquisition of the Motorola patent portfolio in its $12.5 billion acquisition of Motorola Mobility may be the high-water mark for patent acquisitions, but filing patents as a prudent, defensive measure within FOSS is not unknown. For example, Red Hat, Inc has over 400 granted US patents:[100]

> Red Hat has consistently taken the position that software patents generally impede innovation in software development and that software patents are inconsistent with open source/free software...
>
> At the same time, we are forced to live in the world as it is, and that world currently permits software patents. A relatively small number of very large companies have amassed large numbers of software patents. We believe such massive software patent portfolios are ripe for misuse because of the questionable nature of many software patents generally and because of the high cost of patent litigation.
>
> One defense against such misuse is to develop a corresponding portfolio of software patents for defensive purposes. Many software companies, both open source and proprietary, pursue this strategy. In the interests of our company and in an attempt to protect and promote the open source community, Red Hat has elected to adopt this same stance. We do so reluctantly because of the perceived inconsistency with our stance against software patents; however, prudence dictates this position.

6.8.4 Re-examinations and reviews

We have seen earlier, in relation to Google's defence against Oracle's patent and copyright suit (where the copyright suit focussed on various Javi APIs), that re-examinations filed by Google at the USPTO played a significant role in diffusing the patent threat. In re-examinations, inter-partes, and post-grant reviews, the US Patent Office will re-assess the patentability of an invention in the light of new prior art. As noted in the preceding chapter, it can be difficult, for practical reasons, for Patent Office examiners to access the most pertinent prior art, which may be obscure and known only to members of the FOSS community. And in these circumstances, re-examinations may well be desirable. But the cost can easily run from $100,000 to $200,000, so is generally out of reach for all but the wealthiest potential defendants.

6.8.5 Challenging software patentability

The FOSS community has in the past been extremely vocal about software even being patentable; however, in practical terms, substantive reform in the US to deny

[100] See Statement of Position and our Promise on Software Patents, Red Hat Inc available at <http://www.redhat.com/legal/patent_policy.html> (last modified 2004) accessed 10 April 2013.

patentability to software (and in Europe, to deny patentability where the software makes a technical contribution to a field that is not excluded from patentability by statute) remains a distant prospect. In Germany, we have seen the decision to uphold the validity of the Microsoft FAT patents by the Federal Court of Justice of Germany (*Bundesgerichtshof*, BGH);[101] but against that, we see an increasing trend to invalidate software-related patents where the innovation is seen as not technical because it lay in the user interface or user interaction. The forthcoming (mid-2013) nullity action in respect of Apple's slide-to-unlock patent in Germany may well clarify this area. As a practical matter, it probably does not serve the commercial interests of any of the major players in the Smartphone Wars (or indeed major pro-FOSS companies like IBM) to try and roll-back patentability to exclude software; all of the major actors have invested hundreds of millions of dollars, and in Google's case a lot more.

6.9 SOME FINAL THOUGHTS: PATENT REFORM

There are notable legal scholars and jurists advocating reform. (Beneficiaries of the current system unsurprisingly believe it to be working well; vested interests run deep and broad in this area of law and policy.) To take one example, Judge Posner, currently a judge on the United States Court of Appeal for the Seventh Circuit and influential legal theorist, notes that 'the need for patent protection in order to provide incentives for innovation varies greatly across industries,'[102] adding:

> In an industry in which teams of engineers are employed on a salaried basis to conduct research on and development of product improvements, the cost of a specific improvement may be small, and when that is true it is difficult to make a case for granting a patent. The improvement will be made anyway, without patent protection, as part of the normal competitive process in markets where patents are unimportant. It is true that the easier it is to get a patent, the sooner inventions will be made. But 'patent races' (races, induced by hope of obtaining a patent, to be the first with a product improvement) can result in excessive resources being devoted to inventive activity. A patent race is winner take all. The firm that makes an invention and files for a patent one day before his competitors reaps the entire profit from the invention, though the benefit to consumers of obtaining the product a day earlier may be far less than the cost of the accelerated invention process.

Judge Posner's comments apply with great force to software. In the same article, he continues:

[101] 'Microsoft's controversial FAT patent upheld by German Federal Court of Justice' <http://www.jurablogs.com/de/microsofts-controversal-fat-patent-upheld-german-federal-court-justice>; <http://www.visaepatentes.com/2010/04/microsofts-controversal-fat-patent.html>; BGH Sentence, 20 April 2010, X ZR 27/07.

[102] RA Posner, 'Why there are too many patents in America' (*The Atlantic*, 12 July 2012) <http://www.theatlantic.com/business/archive/2012/07/why-there-are-too-many-patents-in-america/259725>.

> There are a variety of measures that could be taken to alleviate the problems I've described. They include: reducing the patent term for inventors in industries that do not have the peculiar characteristics of pharmaceuticals that I described; instituting a system of compulsory licensing of patented inventions; eliminating court trials including jury trials in patent cases by expanding the authority and procedures of the Patent and Trademark Office to make it the trier of patent cases, subject to limited appellate review in the courts; forbidding patent trolling by requiring the patentee to produce the patented invention within a specified period, or lose the patent; and (what is beginning) provide special training for federal judges who volunteer to preside over patent litigation.

Legal innovation of this sort, especially when ranged against highly influential corporations with vested interests against such change, may be slow and uncertain. But the Smartphone Wars provide intense incentives for reform and some of these reforms are potentially very significant:

- Royalty base to be the smallest salable unit and not the entire market value of a product absent proof that the patented feature drives demand for the entire product (and that kind of proof may well be illusive for patents allegedly covering FOSS implemented features);
- Injunctions unavailable where the patent holder cannot prove a causal nexus between the patented feature and the demand (as will generally be the case with software patents);
- Reasonable royalty limited to the costs associated with inventing-around (which may well be close to zero for FOSS);
- Antitrust concerns on hold-up value extended from FRAND to whenever the patent holder wields disproportionate bargaining power (as will generally be the case where software patents are asserted against SME FOSS entities).

Each of these reforms could prove to be highly favourable to FOSS entities. In combination they could be transformative and in effect constitute forking the patent system in a way that preserves its strengths for sectors such as pharma, but curtails overcharges and overreaching in sectors such as software, perhaps realizing that earlier objective of curtailing monopolies that are 'mischievous to the state by raising prices of commodities at home, or hurt of trade, or generally inconvenient.' But innovative legal reform is generally slow and unpredictable. In the meantime, there is always the Latin adage, 'If you want peace, prepare for war.'[103]

[103] *'Si vis pacem, para bellum'* Publius Flavius Vegetius Renatu (*De Re Militari*).

Part II

BUSINESS MODELS AND USAGE

7

COMMERCIAL AGREEMENTS

Amanda Brock

7.1 INTRODUCTION

FOSS involves some of the world's best coders in the software industry, working on their dream projects. This means that they push the bounds of technology and development. Their work is often in new areas, with technical issues that need to be understood to undertake a legal analysis. This chapter examines the commercial aspects of FOSS-related agreements and is aligned with Chapter 8, examining the business implications of FOSS.

In many ways the fact that an agreement relates to an open source product, makes no difference to the content of the agreement for that product. If a business or project is looking to distribute FOSS software as a business, then it needs to consider a significant number of the standard clauses that we would expect to find in any contract or agreement. I will deal with this at a couple of points in this discussion.

Within the context of this chapter, as agreement and contract mean the same thing, that is they are simply terms for the legally binding document under which the transaction will happen, from this point on I will refer throughout the chapter to 'agreement'.

Ideally once the agreement is signed it will never be looked at again. But, it might be, so let's try and get it right. Why are lawyers perceived as being so annoying and accused of slowing down deals? Generally it's caused by an honest attempt on the lawyer's part to 'get it right'. And by 'it', in this case, I don't just mean the terms of the agreement, I mean the deal. The main purpose of the agreement is of course to set out in legally binding language, at an appropriate level of detail, what the deal is all about.

It is often the case that when you try to sit down to write out the details of a deal, questions come up. Key commercial elements may not have been thoroughly hammered out and outstanding issues may float to the surface. It is often only at the point of negotiating the agreement, that many of the deal's commercial terms are finessed and agreed. So, it is important for lawyers not only to understand what the legal terms mean but also what the deal is all about, and what if any risk is created by it. The nuances of a deal which involves FOSS require an understanding of some key aspects of the software and in turn open source and how it is developed.

A wise man once said to me, 'keep it simple'. On that basis the first three things to remember when writing down a deal (open source or otherwise) are:

- What is being bought, sold, or transferred?;
- How much is it going to cost, if anything, or what is the consideration?;[1] and
- How do the parties get out of the agreement if either should want to do so?

Of course a negotiation may go into detail on the impact of licence terms applicable to the software, issues around combining software, and who should bear the risk of a deal? However, in any negotiation or drafting any agreement, don't lose that holistic view. Try to keep in mind what the deal is for. There is no point in spending months worrying about the detail if you don't get the deal done or don't get the basics right. A deal that isn't closed is worth nothing to anyone and even worse may leave both parties in a position where the commercial reality takes over and the deal is contractually unfinished, but the commercial and technical people are ready to deliver, or

[1] See further ch 3.

even worse, have delivered, without an agreement. This is not a way to make yourself popular with your colleagues or clients, and may potentially leave lots of exposure on both sides.

7.2 WHAT NEEDS TO BE CONSIDERED?

In any agreement, the terms to be included depend on the nature of the deal being done.

Many open source based businesses work from business models that mean that they do not in fact distribute open source software as part of their agreements, but have utilized instead, open source software to enable a low cost of entry for their products, and in fact use open source software which sits server side and they have based a commercial business on this software. However, as no code is distributed in these models, they have few distinct open source issues. Open source challenges are relevant in these business models in the commissioning and development of the software on which the businesses are built, and the agreements around these will be considered.

In an agreement for open source software some of the key considerations are whether the software is to be used internally by the recipient, or whether it is for inclusion in their product and will be subject to onward distribution? Further, it is important to consider whether the software being provided is on a standard product basis, or whether it is going to be tailor-made or bespoke for the customer?

These and other factors need to be considered in terms of what the appropriate agreement terms will be, and I will now consider how these are relevant or may make a difference to an open source agreement.

7.2.1 What is being purchased or transferred?

Is software being delivered with services or support?

It may seem unlikely, but during my time negotiating open source agreements there has often been confusion as to whether the agreement entered into with an open source company is actually for software, support services, or both. The answer to this depends to some extent on whether the agreement is purely for services for software already freely available under its own licence(s), or whether the agreement is in fact a software distribution and service agreement. This is not, of course, the same scenario as a business utilizing open source server side but is, in fact, relevant to businesses working on a support or subscription model. Clearly this clarification is essential up front, as the terms to be included in an agreement are different depending on whether the agreement includes software delivery. Many organizations which distribute open source software, 'free as in beer,' will have a support based revenue model, which offers an opportunity for the commercialization of that open source software, and revenue/profit to be generated allowing the ongoing existence of the free open source distribution.

Depending on the commercial model utilized by the FOSS company, it is more than possible that there is no software covered by the agreement at all. This can be a very confusing situation for lawyers used only to dealing with agreements of a closed or proprietary nature. Without a written licence somewhere in the agreement, they understandably believe that their organization has no ability or right to utilize the software for which the services are purchased.

In the case of companies like Canonical, the support agreement utilized by the organization to support Ubuntu does not include the delivery of software. The Ubuntu software is freely available and can be downloaded by anyone. Unlike some other distributions, Canonical does not use a true subscription model (more of this later) and so there is no charge for updates. The agreement to sell support for Ubuntu is therefore a pure services agreement, and does not include software delivery.

However, if a customer wished to purchase its own tailored version of Ubuntu and was adding its own flavour to the vanilla software distributed freely, then the agreement might change. In that situation there would be a deliverable which was a version of Ubuntu and clearly software, so the agreement would include provisions regarding the software. Any rights granted in the commercial agreement that included the software, would be subject to open source licences. Where open source software is provided, the software is provided on its own approved open source licence terms, and these should be the terms of a package's distribution. If modifications are made to the software, these modifications would generally be distributed on the terms of the FOSS licence applicable to the base software that has been modified. It is possible that for some permissive licences the licence terms of a future distribution could be different, but it is important to remember in such an instance that there may be requirements around notices and attributions.

There is generally no need to draft a full licence with standard terms such as the duration of the licence, the global or territorial reach of the licence, or any royalties for the software itself, as the applicable FOSS licence covers these elements already. If you plan to charge for the code, then you can of course specify that and there is nothing in principle to stop you (with the terms of a few exceptional FOSS licences). However, the fact that the software is delivered subject to these licences for individual components ought to be stated in the agreement and might, as a matter of good practice, be referenced to in any general licence granted under the agreement, ie by including a statement such as 'All FOSS is provided on its underlying FOSS licence'.

Chapter 3 sets out an analysis of the various types of free and open source licences, some of their terms, their approval, and their compatibility with each other. It also goes into detail as to whether FOSS licences are bare licences or contracts, and whether or not, and how, they would be enforceable. In negotiating commercial agreements for FOSS, this knowledge and understanding of licences should almost be a given, so if you are not aware of this, I advise becoming familiar with Chapter 3.

For what it is worth, I tend to agree with Jason Wacha of MontaVista's view:

> There is valid consideration in the form of 'reciprocal promises' undertaken between the licensor and licensee(s), which require the licensees to do a number of things e.g. to post requisite notices, to distribute the code under the same terms etc., in return for making use of the FOSS software.[2]

The purpose of my chapter is not to analyse FOSS licences, but to work out how commercialization can work successfully from a contractual standpoint. I am going to take it as a given that FOSS licences are binding and enforceable. Whether they are in fact a bare licence or an agreement is not entirely relevant to the commercial agreement, so long as their binding nature and their enforceability is in some form accepted. My recommendations for commercial agreements therefore work on the basis that the applicable FOSS licences are binding.

In considering service agreements, I am going to take a short diversion into the world of FOSS operating systems. Their business models are best known to me, but also are replicated in other areas of FOSS distribution and commercialization.

A model used by many distributions like RHEL,[3] is the subscription model, where software may be provided free as a standard release under open source licences, but the updates to that software are charged for along with a number of services, so whilst they are still on open or 'free as in speech' licences they are not 'free as in beer'. However, as with any open source distribution, third parties may take the freely licensed code from the distribution and redistribute it with any 'owned IP' removed. The Centos OS[4] 'is an Enterprise-class Linux Distribution derived from sources freely provided to the public by a prominent North American Enterprise Linux vendor.'[5] The RHEL trade marks are removed and some packages changed. The Centos distribution has binary compatibility with RHEL. There may in fact be a new compilation of the code. Red Hat is one of the world's most successful open source companies, and its ability to co-exist alongside a free, if slightly modified version, is no mean feat.

I mentioned that Canonical's Ubuntu distribution is distributed free and that updates are also distributed without charge. Canoncial sells support services. It is a free distribution model where support services, rather than a more traditional software subscription, are sold by Canonical. Canonical does not distribute both a community and a commercial version of its operating system but a single version of Ubuntu. Red Hat and Novell, its two big competitors each distribute both a free

[2] MIT licence is a good example of this.

[3] Red Hat Enterprise Linux, the commercial operating system distributed by Red Hat the first open source company with an annual turnover of more than $1 billion, which it hit in 2012.

[4] Centos <http://www.centos.org> accessed 6 April 2013.

[5] Wikipedia states: 'CentOS (*Community Enterprise Operating System*) is a Linux distribution which attempts to provide a free enterprise class computing platform which has 100% binary compatibility with its upstream source, Red Hat Enterprise Linux (RHEL)' <http://en.wikipedia.org/wiki/CentOS>.

community version and a charged for enterprise version. In the case of Red Hat, they successfully distribute Fedora as a community distribution, then commercialize this with Red Hat Enterprise Linux. RHEL is the commercial product distributed with a charged subscription model Fedora is free.

Bearing in mind the differences in these models, support agreements for Ubuntu will inevitably be different than for RHEL. As the Ubuntu Wiki states: 'There will never be a difference between the "commercial" product and the "free" product, as there is with Red Hat (RHEL and Fedora).'[6] Agreements for Ubuntu support services are not for software updates, just for support, whereas agreements for support of RHEL, being on a subscription model are for software updates as well as support and other services. With RHEL you will not receive updates unless you have purchased that subscription. Code is clearly being purchased from Red Hat along with support, and the agreement should reflect that by including provisions for software.

If software is delivered then the agreement should make clear, to the extent possible (ie if the software already exists), what the software is and what licence it is distributed under. If the agreement is for updates, then it should make clear what the software to be updated is or may be, and what licence will apply to the update (if known). If this covers many different pieces of software, then a general statement would be included to the effect that the updates would be under the base licence unless otherwise agreed, eg, if an update was made on a bespoke basis for a client and was not going to be distributed by the client, it might not be contributed back to the open source project if it was for internal usage only.[7]

If the agreement is not going to include software, as the software is standard and freely available under a FOSS licence, and updates will also be freely available, there is little or no point wasting time negotiating either a list of software or the terms applicable to delivery of software into an agreement, that agreement being purely for services.

Having the software terms included despite no software being delivered may seem like a belts and braces approach to negotiating the agreement. Unfortunately, I have seen several agreements fail to complete; deals that could happily have moved forward, where the blocker has been a lawyer's insistence on including software licences, warranties, indemnities, and liabilities where no software is to be provided. Easy to argue that if none is being delivered there is no risk in giving these, but to my mind there is a risk.

Agreements between two entities sit in a bigger commercial context where there may be multiple services and agreements between those parties, over time. If there are not already multiple agreements in existence at the time of negotiation, then there may well be in the future. A provider may offer terms that they otherwise would not accept purely on the basis that they do not matter; being irrelevant to the deal in question may set a precedent between the two parties that is incorrect or unwise.

[6] Wikipedia, 'Ubuntu' <https://wiki.ubuntu.com> accessed 6 April 2013.

[7] See further ch 1, at 1.4.1.

For example, in a later negotiation, trying to say that a software indemnity was provided for open source software solely because no such software was going to be delivered under the support services agreement may not be a helpful negotiating position for the provider in the future, and may undermine the provider's reasonable position at a later stage where they do not wish to give that indemnity for open source software when such is actually delivered. This lack of indemnity is standard in most open source software distribution. The software is freely available without warranty or indemnity.

In this situation a purchaser may feel let down when the second deal comes around and software is it to be delivered. The purchaser may be unhappy that the supplier could not give the same contractual commitment previously given when there was no code delivery or risk. The customer could consider that the parties had created a course of dealing between them. The supplier might well feel cheated, as in the first instance they had been clear that giving the wide commitment was only possible as it was not relevant to that deal. It felt reasonable to concede the risk only because there was no risk of it crystallizing as the deal had not included delivery of any software. There could well be problems in the second deal being closed due to the supplier's earlier approach of taking the easy option, and conceding to something they would not agree if it was a reality in a deal.

A further risk, depending on the structure and efficiency of the contract management system being used, is that if the reason for the concession of an otherwise inappropriate term is not clearly flagged on that contract management system, at a later date the agreement might be amended to include further services. If these later services include the delivery of software, then the liabilities that the supplier unwisely accepted in the first deal but would not normally agree to, might apply to that later deal and become a real risk. Effectively the provider could accept unwise provisions they would not generally agree upon by the back door or unintentionally. Best just to be clear that no software or open source software is delivered and no liability taken; that is to get it right and make sure that both parties understand what is being purchased.

A more technical consequence of the delivery of software can be the applicable statutes that apply to a transaction unless they are, and to the extent they can be, successfully disclaimed. The Sale of Goods Act 1979 will not apply to software under English law as it is not a sale of goods. In *Southwark London Borough Council v IBM*,[8] it was held that the provision of a licence for software was not a sale of goods, the software itself is not a good, and protection applies to consumers only to the extent of the physical medium on which it is provided if any. In a world of downloads, there is little or no protection here for consumers.[9]

[8] [2011] EWHC 549 (TCC). [9] See ch 1, at 1.2.

7.2.2 If software is being delivered is it open source?

Where software is going to be delivered as part of the agreement, then it is essential to understand what it is that is being delivered and what licence it will be delivered under. If the software is FOSS then it will be delivered, within the agreement's definition of open source software, under an approved licence.

Of course, with very limited case law, there are open discussions on the interpretation of the licence terms and their meanings, and these are not entirely agreed upon. It is important to know what those licences are, and therefore to understand their terms as much as reasonably possible.

If your organization has a FOSS strategy/policy it is possible that you have preferences on licensing, or do not accept software under certain licences as you perceive practical problems in their usage. This will be your opportunity to review the licence list and decide that the software is appropriate for your needs.[10] Better still, have your procurement team understand the policy and make any prohibited licences or concerns known to the supplier long before negotiating the agreement.

If the software to be delivered is going to be a mixture of open source and proprietary software how will this work? The open source software will be provided under the standard FOSS licences. There will be a need for a proprietary licence in the commercial agreement on the same terms as any other proprietary licence, setting out what is covered by the licence grant, how long the grant is for, what territories are covered by the grant, whether the licence can be revoked, and what fee is to apply, if any? If there is a sub-licence requirement in the usage of the software to be delivered, then that should also be included, and if any sub-licence granted is to terminate with the head licence then that should be noted.[11] As always, the software and applicable licences need to be specified and, in the case of proprietary packages, the list should simply cross reference the proprietary licence, whether that is a general licence in the agreement or, in the case of a redistributed third party package, the specific licence terms, which should be attached to the agreement.

Many advocates of open source will be galled by the very idea of proprietary code being distributed by a company that primarily provides open source code, but the commercial reality remains that many open source suppliers also make proprietary software available to their customers, and so this chapter and commercial agreements must take that on board.

The legalities of distributing a mixture of open source and proprietary software from the perspective of licensing are discussed in Chapter 3, but in short there is a

[10] See further ch 8.

[11] Note that as a result of *VLM Holdings Limited v Ravensworth Digital Services Limited* [2013] EWHC 228 (Ch), it is possible depending on the circumstances for a sub-licence to survive termination of the head licence.

general fear of the viral effect of copyleft[12] licences, particularly those regarded as stronger copyleft licences such as GPL. Copyleft is a concept intended to guard the ongoing free nature of the original code by requiring all distributed modifications and versions to be distributed under the original licence as a share alike type model embedded in their licences. If a copyleft licensed piece of code is combined with a permissively licensed piece of code or code under a proprietary licence, then should this be deemed to have created a derivative work. The copyleft licence may cause 'infection' of the other code and the software that was previously licensed either permissively or under a proprietary licence may become subject to the copyleft licence, that is combined code may be combined in such a way that they are deemed one, or a derivative work,[13] the whole of which will be under a single licence and, due to the nature of copyleft, this would be the copyleft licence. The owner of the proprietary code may rightly fear the loss of their valuable code if it accidentally becomes open source and the world can share their secret sauce.

For companies that hold large stocks of proprietary code, or even small stocks of very valuable proprietary software, or where their business is dependant on revenue generated from licensing proprietary software, a grave concern of this potential consequence makes absolute sense. For those companies, their secret sauce is all. This concern means that this type of company is likely to have IP policies in place, and that these will include a stance on FOSS software and copyleft licences in particular. If they don't they should!

Technical experts have put a lot of time and effort into creating structures and methods of combining code that they understand will allow for the combination of open or copyleft code and closed code, without the creation of a derivative work.

In Europe, whether code combinations amount to the creation of a derivative work is not generally defined purely by technical matters but is also a question of law. The technology and architecture has a strong impact as to how the interface between code is structured and is crucial to this, but you also have to look beyond that to define and understand what is or becomes one work on code combination, and where despite combination, the code remains as two independent works. However, this fear may generally be more 'FUD'[14] than real concern. Like many legal concerns in open source, the concern is generally appropriately resolved by appropriate up

[12] Copyleft, is a pun or play on copyright. It means in short that where any new work is derived from a work under a copyleft licence, then the new work must be distributed and contributed back under the original licence. The best example of copyleft is the GNU GPL. The concept works to ensure that Richard Stallman's Free Software Definition, published by the FSF is enforced by the licence, that is there is a requirement to share all changes and modifications under the original licence.

[13] For a discussion of 'derivative works', see chs 1 and 9.

[14] Wikipedia, 'FUD—Fear, uncertainty and doubt' <http://en.wikipedia.org/wiki/Fear,_uncertainty_and_doubt> accessed 7 April 2013; MSFT are credited with this due to their past partial patent assertions, by many open source developers.

front thinking and with use of state of the art technological practices. If a business takes sensible technical steps this risk should be alleviated and not be a real concern.

Technical routes, such as forms of dynamic linking or RPC,[15] in the combination or running of proprietary and open source software, follow state of the art technology to combine the code in a way that is not believed to create a permanent combination or derivative work, and so are assumed to avoid the risk of infection. Other routes that are generally considered not to create derivatives are IPC (inter-process communication), pipes and sockets, and Application Binary Interface (system calls).

Linus Torvalis, the creator of the Linux operating system, has himself issued a note on the complex topic of derivative works. In this he says:

> I'm just pointing out that you should not assume that 'derivative' is something simple. If an author claims your work is derivative, you should step very very lightly.[16]

There is no case law on point at this time (at least of which I am aware) but the consequences of managing code to speak to code in a way that does not create static links, is certainly industry accepted as not creating a derivative work. If there is a concern that this could be a possibility, this should be dealt with at an early stage in the negotiations.

If something goes wrong the immediate effect is also not necessarily that of a viral infection by the copyleft licence. It may well be possible under the applicable open source licences to 'stop ship' and rectify any problem in that way. Perhaps this is not the ideal solution, but generally, it is not as bad as the perceived risk of code infection.

7.2.3 Internal usage versus distribution

I often think of this as the Google question. In the case where open source software is utilized by business which modifies that code provided under an open source licence, but does not then distribute the modified code, it may keep those amendments to itself, and is not required to contribute these back under the open source licence. The requirements of sharing in copyleft licences do not take effect until the point of distribution of the code, so if there is no distribution, there is no requirement to share alike. This is perhaps not in the true spirit of open source, but should the recipient of the code who has modified it decide to share their modified version of the code, then the copyleft share alike provisions will apply, that is, the sharing will be the equivalent of distribution of the code, and there will be a requirement to share the code.

[15] Wikipedia, 'RPC, remote procedure call' <http://en.wikipedia.org/wiki/Remote_procedure_call> accessed 7 April 2013.

[16] LKML.org, <https://lkml.org/lkml/2003/12/10/123> accessed 7 April 2013.

> **Goobuntu** is a Linux distribution, based on the 'long term support' versions of Ubuntu, that is internally used by almost half of the 20,000 employees of Google. It adds a number of packages for in-house use, including security features and disables the installation of some applications, but does not have any other stark differences. Thomas Bushnell, the Google manager for the company's Linux desktops, displayed Goobuntu at LinuxCon 2012. Bushnell explained that 'Goobuntu is simply a light skin over standard Ubuntu.'[17]

So, Google are able to use the freely available open source distribution Ubuntu, modify it, use it internally, and not share their modifications (unless they choose to, which in some instances they do share as contributions to the Ubuntu project) despite the existence of copyleft licences in many Ubuntu packages. They are able to do this as the provisions requiring contribution back of modifications, that is the copyleft piece in such licences, are generally viewed not to kick in until the point of distribution.

What is the point at which distribution of code will occur? This may be very important with respect to the open source code and the associated licence obligations. Would sharing code with a supplier amount to distribution, what about sharing it with contractors in your own business?

This ability not to share modifications or contributions, and the point in time that the requirement to share kicks in and makes that requirement, may be important to agreements. If you are commissioning a specific development for internal usage, you may want to add requirements into the agreement that the code will not be shared. If you are drafting an agreement to demo new code, perhaps under NDA, then the demo agreement may also have to deal with sharing and distribution.

In a world of servers and virtualization[18] where services may be purchased by end users, whether for personal or business usage, without code being distributed, conveyed, or propagated, many are able to utilize open source code in a commercial or for profit context. If the code they are utilizing is not distributed they are able to do so without sharing their changes. In terms of commercial agreements, the code will not be distributed, and will not generally need to form part of a customer facing agreement. The agreement will generally be purely for services. To the extent that code is mentioned, it is likely to be in a commercial agreement, and purely in the sense that the provider of the services may be asked (depending on bargaining power and use of standard terms) to confirm that their use of software in providing services is not an infringement of third party rights.

If the code utilized is open source, then it is more than likely that the service provider will want to call out that this is the case, and add a statement that whilst known

[17] Wikipedia, 'Goodbuntu' <http://en.wikipedia.org/wiki/Goobuntu> accessed 7 April 2013.

[18] See further ch 9.

open source licences are complied with, it cannot warrant or indemnify against the open source code.

It occurred to me whilst watching the Facebook movie, 'Social Network' and hearing another Apache server being ordered in the movie, that open source really has a place in our world of social media and server driven services. Many of the best known end user services such as Facebook and Gmail are run on open source software stacks. In these environments, services are provided to end users, but code is not. The legal issues around distribution of open source code will not be faced by the service providers. The agreements for open source relevant to these organisations will be in commissioning code for their services as opposed to distribution.

Organizations developing open source code may develop that code in different ways, demonstrating differing levels of openness. Ubuntu, eg, has been developed publicly with a pure open source methodology, and a mixture of Canonical employee and community contribution to that development. There is transparency in the development and its possible to follow what is being done as the project, its goals, time frames, and in-development code are in the public domain. Canonical's founder Mark Shuttleworth has recently blogged about his intention to involve community participation in the company's secret development projects as well as in the open Ubuntu project. So, as time passes, some code may be developed behind closed doors and not be publicly available during its development phase, but only once it is released, at which time, the point of distribution, it will become available to the world under open source licences, and both the binary and source code will be publicly available.

This would follow the Google Android development model to some extent. In this model, the code for distribution is not developed publicly, and only becomes publicly available at the point of time of release, that is complete code internally developed and tested is released under open source licences. Some purists would argue that this is not really open source, and it is certainly not the traditional model for open source development.

Distribution points are certainly worth thinking about in any agreement where the purchaser makes a significant payment for code to be developed, and may not want to have others taking that code until such time as its ready to be shipped/deployed for commercial usage, or where there is a desire to remove knowledge of bugs between alpha and beta releases from the public domain. This model allows the purchaser a short first mover advantage in return for its investment. If an agreement is intended to cover this situation then the development practices applicable to the project and method of release should be specified in the agreement. Without this there would be a risk of public sharing prior to the agreed time.

Historically it has been common practice in some organizations for open source packages to be distributed alongside proprietary code, such as drivers for open source consumer operating systems (where suitable open source equivalents were not available), but for those not to be run until the point in time at which the code was booted. You will often see a reference to the code forming the drivers as the binary blob, that is a closed source code where no source code is provided, simply the binary element. This has been particularly common for operating systems on devices distributed for consumer use.

On that basis, the proprietary code would arguably not be combined with open source code until the point of end user boot when the programs would run and statically link, potentially creating a derivative work. The practice was based on the view the proprietary code was not being distributed in combination with the open source code, and so no derivative work was distributed.

Assuming that the recipient then used the combined code without further distribution, this should mean that the combined code would not be subject to distribution or the impact of copyleft licences in the open source code on the combined open source and driver code. A derivative work may well be created by the combination on boot, but without distribution this would not affect the proprietary code provided. The practice is becoming less common as the driver providers are increasingly open sourcing their drivers and suitable open alternatives are becoming available, so fewer proprietary drivers are being shipped with open source operating systems.

7.2.4 Standard versus bespoke open source products

Where the software being delivered under an agreement is part of a release of standard code it should be set out in the list of software and associated licences. However, it is important to understand whether the agreement includes any particular development work, where the provider is being paid to develop code, and to list out the code that is being developed, and any special provisions with regard to it.

If code is created for you, on what basis is this being provided?

One of the basic concerns a business faces in purchasing open source software, is what is in the deliverable? The obvious reason for this concern is that a business needs to know what code it is receiving and using. It needs to understand what licences attach to that code, and the obligations associated with it that it is required to comply with. To meet this, there first needs to be a clear list of code, and secondly a list of associated licences. This should be a requirement of any deliverable in a software distribution.

With FOSS, as opposed to proprietary software, the licences will generally be standard licences. They will be licences that fall within the open source initiative ('OSI') definition of open source,[19] and therefore the licences will be on terms that

[19] OSI 'Open Source Definition' <http://opensource.org/osd-annotated> accessed 7 April 2013. The OSI also approves open source licences.

are approved by the OSI. In many respects this is a simplifying factor in favour of open source. The licences will be known by name and contain standard terms. They may be permissive or copyleft.[20] Whichever they are, they should not be new or unusual, as they are standardized through the approval process. This standardization contributes to making the use of open source a relatively straightforward process. There are various articles by both the creators of the standard licences and those who use them, with appropriate FAQs and clarifications. What was intended by any ambiguity can be discovered; whether this would be upheld by a court remains to be seen.

The list of software and associated licences is as long as the list of packages to be included in the deliverable. It will reference named licences as opposed to their terms, eg:

X code GPLv3
Y code Apache

The full terms of the actual licences will not be set out in this list, simply referenced. Their content, due to the OSI approval and effective standardization of the licence terms, will be a given. You can find the actual licence wording online.[21] The software itself will also contain this information. Along with any IP notices (copyright ownership, a list of the individuals who have developed the code, trade mark assertions) the applicable licence will be stated and generally linked to in the code's header. In some licences, such as the MIT licence, there may be a requirement to add a contract and tort notice or the like which will also be found in that header. There is a form of wording to use for this purpose in the licence and this exercise should be nothing more than a pass through of notices.

SPDX is a project to standardize lists of code and is considered in more detail later. Any provisions warranting this list should be in the body of the agreement itself, and not in an exhibit or attachment, that is not in the list itself. It is normal for such a list to be without any warranty or promise due to the nature of FOSS.

When considering bespoke code, as in code that will be open sourced but which is specifically developed for a project, as opposed to standard packages, many lawyers will ask for the same warranties and indemnities as they would ask for with respect to proprietary code. It is generally accepted that these should not be provided for FOSS whether it is bespoke or standard. It makes sense that lawyers who are less familiar with the nature of open source development would want to treat this bespoke code more like proprietary or closed source code even although it is being created as open source or to be released as open source.

The types of warranties requested may relate to the originality of the IP, as the IP is apparently being created by the software house on a bespoke basis and they should

[20] See further ch 3. [21] OSI licence terms.

know what is in that code. It is not immediately obvious why that would be any different from proprietary code and in some instances, if the developers can be 100 per cent sure that all of the code being delivered has been created by them and does not link to or incorporate any third party code, then this might be possible. However, it is rare for any code that will become open source code, to be really developed 100 per cent from scratch. It is far more likely that the so called bespoke code is a modification or customization of existing code, or will read on open source software libraries, and is in fact not 100 per cent bespoke but contains a bespoke element. On that basis bespoke code should generally be treated in the same way as any other open source software, with the exception that the point of distribution may be restricted, that is if the code is not distributed there may not be a need to share it.

This may take a bit of discussion and negotiation. The purchaser is paying for something to be developed and open sourced, and may find it a little odd that this payment does not create any additional rights or security around the code created and delivered under the project. If it is really important to a deal that code is being created from scratch and that traditional proprietary warranties or indemnities should apply to that code, then it is important to have the discussion around this at the earliest stage, and to clarify both what is being purchased or delivered, and what protection should apply to this. The argument that the code is being provided for free so should not come with warranties does not really stand the test in this situation.

7.2.5 Specifications and agile

Where services are being provided these are obviously, as with any other tech agreement, captured in the technical specification that is attached to the agreement. As with all good lawyers, I am sure that your goal will be to detail as fully as possible what the software to be created is, how it is to be used, what the outcomes or deliverables are, and what services are to be provided. You will want to document this to create certainty. This protects the parties from a legal perspective by helping to create a legally binding agreement, and commercially as each party has clarity as to what to expect.

Although it is not exclusive to open source, agile development methodologies are prevalent in open source, its proponents having a tendency to be early adopters, and the collaborative style of agile development sits well with the ideology and collaborative methodologies of open source. Agile development is probably best defined as a structure for software development that is based on particular methodologies allowing for iterative development and collaboration between parties that in the case of any commercial agreement requires agreement between the provider and customer.

The issue with this is, of course, that where the specification is not buttoned down and the final goals are fluid, there are likely to be multiple or ongoing changes over time. A traditional technical specification will therefore not do the job. It is increasingly common that the contracting parties will sit down to put an agreement in place and know what the end output should roughly look like or be, but not be able to agree on the detail of that output, or even the services to be provided, in a way that would traditionally be acceptable to a lawyer.

When setting up an agile project based on collaboration and development, whilst there are goals to work towards, there may not be any absolute requirements of the provider that can be defined in great detail. The parties may well be at the stage of knowing very generally that they want something, and so are able to set out only a process and general objectives in the agreement. Where there are requirements to be included in a commercial agreement, eg, perhaps the use of or compatibility of some software being developed with particular drivers or hardware components, then these will be very loosely stated in the agreement to avoid the need for a change notice being issued under the change control process every time that there is a development in what the end goal or the known requirements are. The project, being about development and collaboration, means the agreement must allow fluidity. This is something that is surprisingly difficult for lawyers to draft.

A frequently used approach is to include phased development, with phase one (and potentially later phases) being the exploratory work needed to get to the stage of a specification for the development required. Phased development may well be accompanied by milestones and payment triggers. Milestones are not something that can be committed to by projects with community involvement due to the lack of control over those providing the deliverables. However, in the case of a community developed project, or one that involves their contributions, the project will probably be willing to share and demonstrate publicly available project timelines and a reference to these (although not an absolute obligation to meet them) may be included in the agreement.

Bespoke code development and commercial services may also be affected by community contributions in two ways. First, the achievement of certain milestones or paid for goals may have community dependencies listed in its dependencies section. Secondly, and somewhat perversely, whilst the project may not be able to commit timescales in a legally binding or contractual way, it may require a commercial customer to commit to timescales. If a customer wishes something to be a fixed deliverable in a project that includes community development, then the customer may be required to commit to provide certain code or other required deliverables such as demo devices for the software to be tested on, within specified time frames. Generally and intentionally, community projects run like a train. They have a schedule and it will be stuck to. Despite payment, there cannot be exceptions that if the customer does not deliver in time the publicly shared community timescales will be stopped.

The risk of an agreement which does not have an adequately described deliverable is that one party will believe the work has been done completely or to an appropriate standard, and the other party will not. To my mind the loser in this situation is always the supplier. They are likely to try to meet the customer's expectations. They are likely to do more work than they envisaged if the customer expects it. If they don't go the extra mile they are a bad supplier, and are not likely to stay in business. To others with different experience, they may believe that the customer is always the loser as they have paid (and will not be entitled to a refund), whether it is on a time and materials or fixed fee basis for work to be done, but have not achieved a usable deliverable.

The development teams from each party, if both are participating in the development of the code, need to be put together in a collaborative way. In such an agreement, the teams will be required to work closely together towards common goals to be successful. The process and governance around how it will operate may well need to be more detailed than you might expect in a standard software services agreement to achieve harmonious working between the parties. Developers used to FOSS projects will also be familiar with this kind of governance, and be used to contributing to projects that utilize codes of conduct for their contributions.[22] There is unlikely to be much developer resistance to the existence of process or structure, so long as there is appropriate consultation and input as to the practicality of it. Building this into the agreement will be a little unusual for the lawyers drafting it who should take care to ensure that it is not too restrictive or bureaucratic, and guard against its suffocating the project.

If only the supplier is actually creating code, the customer may well still want to see a detailed governance structure in place. This may have less detail in the agreement and be done by reference in the agreement to specific existing documents/web sites.

If the customer is more participative in the development agreement, than in a standard agreement, this may lead to conversations around IP ownership. Although the code is licensed under an open source agreement, there will of course be an ownership of the IP in it. Models that are open to this may include shared ownership or each party owning the IP their teams create. Joint ownership may leave parties in a difficult position; it may be all but impossible to establish which team has created the IP. If the work is being contributed to an existing open source project that may in fact make this issue simpler.

7.2.6 SPDX—Software Package Data Exchange

The list of software identifying what is being delivered being attached to any agreement probably sounds like a simple piece of the FOSS puzzle. My experience is that it is not quite so straightforward. If the code has been developed purely by one person or business then fine, they should be able to list out what is included with some

[22] See further ch 2.

certainty. But, the reality is very different. A key benefit of FOSS is the ability to modify and share code. On that basis, it is more than likely, probably a certainty, that the code delivered by any business or person will link to or include third party code, even if only in its utilisation of libraries.

On the basis that FOSS is provided by the creator of the code, or owner of the work, under licences that state that the software comes without warranty as to its origin and IP, the fact that almost all code contains or links to third party code or IP means that there is a potential issue with the list being complete and correct. Any developer is able to list the code that he is aware of that has been incorporated into a project, but what if a third party who has contributed, or whose code interfaces, has failed to list something? For any package there is likely to be thousands of files, and many of these will be built from multiple authors or pieces of code. If something was not listed from this vast number of components, that would mean that not only was the omitted code missing in the third party's list of software, but that an omission would have a waterfall effect, caused by the initial omission, and which will seep through the levels of distribution.

Due to the sharing nature of FOSS and this risk of third party error, the list of code should never be guaranteed. No sensible business is able to warrant that the list is complete or accurate, or to provide an indemnity against this. There is a legal risk here. There is a risk that the software delivered includes third party code that has not been listed or licensed, and that a third party will assert its rights, claiming infringement.[23]

The software is generally not paid for and it is generally accepted that it is a reasonable stance that the risk is passed through the waterfall without any indemnity provision. That is not to say that a list should not be provided.

Companies taking in open source code with an associated commercial agreement, often have a preferred format for this list. I have seen it called a variety of names, including a certificate of originality (a derivation of the Linux kernel's name for this).

It is important to a supplier providing code listed on a customer format to be attached to an agreement, that the format itself is set out in the agreement and cannot be overridden accidentally by technical or business people at a later stage. If you are providing code and listing it in such a document, then make sure that any warranties and indemnities that may end up in such a document, even if not included in the body of the agreement, have been removed in the format being attached. It may also be wise to add a disclaimer to the list itself to ensure that this works.

The wide variety of formats of these lists utilized by industry sits at odds with an industry built on standards and apparent self-regulation. It is not a surprise that an initiative to standardize the list format was created. Esteban Rockett and John Ellis (formerly of Motorola) got together with Kate Stewart (formerly of Freescale) at

[23] A similar risk arises in a corporate acquisition, see further ch 8, at 8.7.

LinuxCon 2009, and started merging the ideas from their separate efforts to create the concept of SPDX. Momentum gathered in 2010 as notable participants such as Black Duck, HP, Windriver, OpenLogic, and several others started contributing to this effort as well and it came to be sponsored by the Linux Foundation.

SPDX is an ongoing industry initiative to standardize the format of code lists. As stated on the organization's website: the SPDX specification 'is a standard format for communicating the components, licenses and copyrights associated with a software package'.[24] This allows for standardization of the licence and IP information across the supply chain, through a standard for data exchange formats. The Linux foundation is the home of the SPDX working group.[25]

Utilization of SPDX will not only assist lawyers in drafting commercial agreements with some certainty and standardization, but will allow businesses in turn to have better internal open source compliance and housekeeping. However, as with any disruptive project in the legal sphere, a number of challenges have been faced by the working party putting their efforts into this. One issue has been the question of whether any implied or explicit warranty is provided by a company that adds data to the certificate. If a major conglomerate was to add a list of packages, would they in fact be warranting the content as complete and accurate for the rest of the world's use? Obviously this would not be right and would deter companies of any size from participating.

Should SPDX come to a successful conclusion as a project, the addition of a barcode to any embedded device would allow a manufacturer to scan the product and find the required list of the software known to be contained and listed in an SPDX list for that device. This project may be responsible for major changes in certainty and consistency in the world of FOSS.

7.3 OWNED OR THIRD PARTY CODE

7.3.1 Where has the code come from and contribution agreements

Is the copyright in the code owned or created by the distributor, or are they are a redistributor of third party code?

If the code has been developed by a community project, as opposed to a business, then there is little or no point in looking for any financial liability from the provider. A promise or commitment from the developers that the code is to the best of their knowledge not stolen or in breach of their employment contracts may well be the

[24] SPDX <http://www.spdx.org> SPDX is a work in progress, but the site currently provides a list of licences: SPDX, 'Standard Licenses' <http://www.spdx.org/licenses> both accessed 7 April 2013.

[25] The Linux Foundation, 'Software Package Data Exchange (SPDX) Workgroup' <http://www.linuxfoundation.org/collaborate/workgroups/spdx> accessed 7 April 2013.

best that can be expected. In projects that utilize contribution agreements, this type of statement is likely to be included in the contribution agreement but may have little or no teeth. Project Harmony was established in 2010 to standardize these contribution agreements.[26] The whole area of contribution agreements raises mixed emotions in the open source community.

The purpose of a contribution agreement in an open source project is to create some pedigree as to the code contributed to a project and ultimately the project's output. Contribution agreements are one way of doing this, and have the benefit of greater legal certainty. This can never be a full certainty as the nature of FOSS projects means contributors are located globally, and the laws of many jurisdictions could apply but not be accommodated by the project. Some projects work happily and well without contribution agreements, probably the well administered Linux kernel, with its gate keeping and technical advisory board, being one of the best known and managed of these.

One of the key benefits of Project Harmony was to create a suite of documents that had received input, if not final blessing of the legal community around FOSS. This allowed for many issues to be hammered through and thought out. Prior to this forum a problem facing those using contribution agreements was that they might not do what they said on the tin.

I first became aware of contribution agreements when I was asked to review developer contributions on behalf of a company that had asked them to participate in a project. The Free Software Foundation Europe ('FSFE'), with the best of intentions, utilize a document that is called a licence to undertake an assignment. For an honourable organization this is not a problem, however other organizations whose intentions may not be so honourable have followed similar practices. This leaves developers understandably confused, and means that lawyers really do need to read the documents for contributions if they are to know what is actually happening. For example, an open source business policy which says no need for legal to review a licence to a project which your business employees contribute to may not work if the licence turns out to be an assignment, and you accidentally contribute the copyright through an assignment rather than licence it as you expected.

Harmony offers a variety of different forms of contribution agreements including those with licences to the project and assignments of code.

It is reasonable for any lawyer who works in open source to expect to review contribution agreements for individuals and companies' contributions to open source projects. Of course the starting point is to work out where the code being contributed is really coming from. Is the individual contributing to a project under the auspices

[26] Harmony, 'What is harmony' <http://www.harmonyagreements.org/about.html>; Wikipedia, 'Project Harmony (FOSS group)' <http://en.wikipedia.org/wiki/Project_Harmony_%28FOSS_group%29> both accessed 7 April 2013.

of employment, during working hours, or as reasonably requested by his employer? If he is then it is probably going to be the company that owns the code, whether the individual is a fully fledged employee or contractor. So, the company or business is likely to be the contributor. If, however, as is frequently the case, the code is contributed under the individual's own steam then the individual will sign. It is important in the first instance to get this right, and to work out who should be signing. The next thing to determine is whether the contribution agreement is an assignment or a licence of the code created to the project.

Some contribution agreements have different terms for companies and individuals; a company can unwittingly end up taking on liability for open source contributions to a project that are unreasonable.

Some trusted industry bodies, such as the Free Software Foundation ('FSF'), offer assignment agreements to the development community on terms that would seem unacceptable if the code was going to a commercial body. This raises two issues, first that the development community is willing to accept these terms due to the party to whom the assignment is being made. This may not seem reasonable to a lawyer, but may be something your organization is willing to live with. Second, as a trusted body, the organization's terms may well be replicated by third parties believing that they are doing the right thing. Whilst objectionable terms may be agreed with an industry body of such standing, the same terms may not be acceptable with a commercial or other organization.

Contribution agreements which expect developers to take on financial liability are in my opinion unreasonable and contrary to the spirit of open source. However, it is fine to expect that the developer make some effort to ensure that he is doing the right thing in providing code, and that he does not to breach his terms of employment with a third party employer in providing code to a project, nor knowingly take someone else's code or breach their copyright.

From the point of view of the recipient of the code, the question is whether this belongs to the third party, or whether it is merely being redistributed to you? In each case it is likely that the code will simply be distributed without warranty, as per the open source licences attaching to the code itself. It is not reasonable to expect any additional warranty, indemnity, or liability from any individual or organization redistributing code. It is industry standard that no liability will be taken by a party passing code through to another party. If the code is owned then it may be possible to negotiate some form of further assurance, but this may well be limited to what is in the contribution agreement or project governance, and again this will depend on the code not interfacing with other open source code where no assurances are possible.

If an organization has a major concern or need to hold the types of warranties, indemnities, or assurances that you would expect for proprietary code from open source code, the best advice to them is probably either don't use open source code, or possibly to buy insurance against IP infringement. The alternative is to accept that the code may have some exposure, to perform appropriate inbound checks on the code, and to participate in OIN.

7.4 DUAL LICENSING AND OPEN CORE

If code is being commissioned or created, then it is of course reasonable for the purchaser to ask that it be supplied under a specific licence and this should be stated in the agreement, assuming that no pre-existing code is being included (which would already have its own licence). What licence is most appropriate will depend on a number of considerations, including the purchaser's open source policy, the use of the software, and also the use that the software provider will put it to later.

If you are in the position of owning the copyright in the code (it is fairly rare for anyone in open source to be in that position) then you may also distribute the code under more than one licence. Only the copyright holder may change the licence of code or distribute it under a different licence. There are exceptions to this right. In an open source project, it is possible that despite having a contribution agreement with an assignment, which would in theory transfer the rights, that the assignment may contain conditions that restrict the licences on which the code may be distributed.

The FSFE utilize the fiduciary licence as an assignment document.[27] This assignment form adds a commitment that the code will only be redistributed under a free licence, within the FSF definition of 'free'.

If the provider of code is the owner of the copyright in the code and the purchaser has an issue with the particular open source licence used, then it is possible that the provider may also be able to provide the code under a different licence. They will have the option to distribute as the copyright holder under a second open source licence, or even under a proprietary licence.

It is also possible if you are not the owner of the copyright, but have received code under a permissive licence such as BSD that you may be able to change the licence of code and follow this model.

There is a degree of scepticism around dual licensing in the open source development community and as a consequence many developers are against assigning their copyright to organizations. If multiple individuals hold copyright then they all have to consent to the code being distributed under an alternative licence.[28] They also all have to consent to a change of licence over time, which has proven problematic.

[27] FSFE, 'Fiduciary Licence Agreement' <http://fsfe.org/activities/ftf/fla.en.html> accessed 7 April 2013.
[28] See further ch 1, at 1.5.

Contributors know the licence utilized by the project they contribute to. They have consented to this by contributing. If they assign their code, and the project can change licence or dual license, then some would argue that the project could do something with the code that the contributor would not have agreed to such as dual licence the code on a proprietary licence.

Social and political issues aside, I have seen agreements where due to a company's policy on particular licences, there has been a requirement to dual license. If the distributor does not hold the entire copyright this is not possible. If there is to be any dual licensing, the alternative licence and confirmation of the distributor's right to release the code must be stated in the agreement. Note, however, that dual licensing does not give the project or distributor the right to withdraw code previously released under another licence.

So, if a project has released code under GPLv2, then is asked to also release the same code under an Apache licence, if it holds the entire copyright and the right to licence the code, it may do so. However, it cannot remove the right of anyone to take the previous release code which was released and utilised under GPLv2. So the code would be available under both licences. However, the project could release a later version 2.0 solely under the Apache licence. This would effectively fork the GPLv2 code so that 1.0 was available under GPLv2 or Apache, but the forked version 2.0 was available only under Apache.

Where, different versions of the code become available with variations as a result of this, it is known as forking. 'A project fork happens when developers take a copy of source code from one software package and start independent development on it, creating a distinct piece of software.' This is more common in open source software as, 'open source software may be legally forked without the approval of those currently managing a software project or distributing the software.'[29] In the case of copyleft code the fork will be restricted to the original licence. Forking is a likely consequence of dual licensing. Where dual licensing creates a risk of forking or additional work to maintain two streams, then it may come at a price.

Since 2010, the name Open Core has been applied to this model where the additions are not open source, and in this situation a feature rich and a standard model of the code will exist. The feature rich version will gain its richness from proprietary add-ons. The version that is not feature rich is sometimes referred to as a crippled version, and this naming goes some way to demonstrate the antagonism which exists in the community around this.

However, from a contractual perspective it may be commercially useful to a purchaser with prohibitive internal open source policies. Yet, there may be licensing

[29] Wikipedia, 'Fork (software development)' <http://en.wikipedia.org/wiki/Fork_%28software_development%29# Forking_free_and_open_source_software> accessed 7 April 2013.

issues in adding proprietary software to the basic vanilla open source. The assurances in the proprietary code itself would of course be standard proprietary IP warranties and indemnities, then the combination would be subject to both industry good practices, and a warranty and indemnity confirming the right of whichever party is providing that code to do so for the purpose and in the manner utilised under the agreement.

7.5 PROJECTS AND THEIR GOVERNANCE[30]

Projects taking in code contributions and distributing these under open source licences, will generally be well governed and administered. Agreements that deal with community provided code should include a requirement from the project as an assurance of this type of governance in the project, whether a contribution agreement is used by that project or not. Accept that it is unlikely that a project will confirm that it has all the IP in the code it distributes, but that it is possible to require that the project has a code of conduct, contribution policy or agreement, and that all code provided has been provided under the rules of that, and that these have been accepted by the community contributors and administered in a way that is legally effective.

The roles played by community advocates such as Ubuntu's Jono Bacon and Perl's Allison Randall should be recognized, and in your due diligence it is worth considering how well managed a project is/whether they have a strong team managing the contributions.

It is not uncommon for projects to incorporate issues like who owns the code (IP in code can, of course, only be held by a legal person whether that's a foundation, a body corporate, or an individual) in these policies. This also flags the issue that to contract with an open source project the project must in fact be a legal entity or person. This is generally not an issue, but is something that has to be checked.

The types of agreements a lawyer may see with open source foundations may go well beyond code distribution. Many foundations are made up of well-recognized companies who contribute to the foundations at various levels, eg, Platinum, Gold, and Silver.[31] Structures of this nature will require membership agreements and the benefits of the membership may well include board participation and attending committees such as lawyers joining the IP policy committee. A good example of this is the Open Stack Foundation.[32] The policies should consider where the code is being accepted from, ownership of the code, and the licences under which the code is distributed.

[30] See also ch 2. [31] eg, <http://www.openstack.org/foundation/companies/>.
[32] <http://www.openstack.org/foundation/>.

Outercurve[33] is an organization advising on setting up foundations, and may be a good source of advice if you find yourself part of this type of discussion. It is also worth pointing out that the foundations involve industry competitors who fund open source projects for the greater good. Commendable as this is, there are likely to be anti-trust or competition issues caused by these innovative competitive collaborations. As a consequence of this, all parties will generally be required to sign identical agreements, and there will be little if any room for a single member to negotiate the membership agreements; this seems perfectly understandable. It does mean that if you wish to be part of a foundation, it's worth being at the table early on when any suggestions you have for the agreement's content or the IP policy can be heard. Once set in stone these are difficult to change.

7.6 OPEN SOURCE POLICIES AND STRATEGIES

Chapter 8 explains how to put in place an open source policy for a business. As a business with such a policy, that policy will be taken into consideration by a purchaser of open source software. However, whether it is reasonable to impose or require the policy to be complied with will be dependent on what is being brought into your business, what the purpose of this is, and from whom it is obtained.

If the product is a standard off the shelf product, whether additional services are being purchased or not, it is a reasonable expectation that the licences applicable to software distributed will be the standard licence for that project. If the product is bespoke to the procurer, then the purchaser may well want to specify the licences that the deliverable will be provided under. Again, whether this will be possible will very much depend on who the owner of the deliverable is. If it is repackaged third party code, then it is unlikely that the provider will have the ability to change the licence.

Issues like potential interoperability and availability of support should be considered in this process.

7.7 APP STORES

As open source guru, Simon Phipps, points out in his blog: 'When mobile phones started to gain the ability to run apps, many companies realized that installing them was going to be an issue. The solution was package management, but presented to the end-user as a shopping experience. Generally, these app stores were a failure, lacking the critical mass to attract developers because they were too fragmented

[33] Outercurve Foundation, <http://www.outercurve.org> accessed 7 April 2013.

across handset brands and carriers, and because the apps involved were not sufficiently compelling—until Apple embraced the concept. It is worth identifying app store agreements as a distinct area as they are such a large source of distribution, and may raise concerns for open source apps.'

Apple's App Store for mobile devices took the idea of shopping-themed package management and made it succeed by creating a compelling need for apps, and by aggregating the markets of all their resellers. Neither alone would probably have been sufficient, but together, they were able to create the necessary critical mass. Other vendors have tried to follow suit; Google and Amazon have both been able to repeat the same trick successfully, using Android as a base.[34]

And the rise of the app store, as a means of distributing software to end users, has meant that for those who wish to distribute software to consumers, the app store is probably the genre through which a huge percentage of their volume currently flows.

Apps may be native, that is modified through an app store's API[35] to run in the environment of that app store, platform, or device. Most app stores wish to keep the apps in their store and native, providing developers with an API which will allow the developer to build a new app or modify an existing app to run in their store and potentially on their devices, eg, Apple's App Store for Apple Devices and Google Play for Android. In effect the app store has a captive audience associated to its devices.

A native app will be locally installed on the device, generally a smartphone, and may work (depending on its functionality) without internet connectivity, as opposed to a web app which will run inside the browser. Whether developing open or closed source apps, an issued faced by developers who build native apps is the risk of fragmentation of their apps through the multiple technologies used by various app stores.

Native and web apps do not form black and white alternatives. Mozilla's mobile phone OS, 'Firefox OS' utilizes web apps with a native wrapper, allowing a mix of the two technologies, and a light touch approach to customization for the Firefox app distribution.

Web app technology has not been able to provide the same user functionality as native apps, but that distinction is now blurring, and the gap between the two is decreasing. HTML5 is the term used to cover the protocols that define the content, layout, and navigation of web pages through browsers and in which web apps are developed.[36] HTML5 is generally recognized as allowing the development of feature rich apps. The technology will of course continue to develop.

This will leave app development in an interesting space, as developers wishing to reduce the work involved in developing and distributing apps are likely to push

[34] S Phipps, 'How to make app stores open source-friendly' (*Infoworld*, 25 January 2013) <http://www.infoworld.com/d/open-source-software/how-make-app-stores-open-source-friendly-211511> accessed 7 April 2013.

[35] Application programming interface.

[36] See further <http://www.w3.org/html/wg/drafts/html/master> accessed 8 April 2013.

towards web based apps, whilst app stores demand native apps to support the current lucrative business models.

Developers who wish to create native apps are required to sign up to developer terms with the app store and will then generally be provided with both an API licence to allow them to develop the native app and a set of principles or contribution policies defining what they may and may not contribute to the store. Generally these are fairly inoffensive, although the developer agreement can be problematic in terms of open source software. The code is then distributed by the store and there may be further issues in the distribution agreements.

The theory perhaps ought to be that, like any other means of on-line sales transaction, there ought to be nothing more than website user terms or terms of sale if a charge is applicable and the licence under which the software is distributed in an app store. Assuming that the terms of use of the site and any applicable terms of sale do not contradict the software's licence terms, there should be no legal issue in the software being distributed under its licence. However, the various terms of app stores have in fact contradicted some open source licence terms.

The FSF's VLC enforcement action against Apple in 2011[37] demonstrated that if app stores include contract provisions in their terms of use or the terms applicable to developers' contributions to the app store, and those terms either contradict or are not compliant with licence under which the software is distributed, then problems may arise.

In this instance, developer Rémi Denis-Courmont flagged a contradiction between the VLC's GPLv2 licence and the terms of the Apple App store. He was one of a number of contributors to the VLC project and assigned his copyright to the FSF who were therefore able to act to enforce the GPLv2 against Apple. The action was based on the fact that the DRM[38] restrictions in the Apple App store terms contradicted GPLv2's no further restriction provision.

In respect of software distributed under a copyleft open source licence (such as the GPL) including provisions such as DRM, or restrictions on the number of copies that can be made in the app store's terms can be problematic. This is because distribution on this basis may breach the copyleft licence.

If the code has been created by a single individual and that individual owns all copyright in the work, then the copyright owner can not only put the copyleft licensed software onto the app store, but may choose not to enforce that software's licence, if the app store's terms cause a breach of the licence. Bradley Khune said at FOSDEM 2013,[39] 'an unenforced copyleft licence is the same is a permissive licence'. However,

[37] B Smith, 'VLC developer takes a stand against DRM enforcement in Apple's App Store' (*FSF*, 29 October 2010) <http://www.fsf.org/blogs/licensing/vlc-enforcement> accessed 7 April 2013.

[38] Wikipedia, 'Digital rights management' <http://en.wikipedia.org/wiki/Digital_rights_management> accessed 7 April 2013.

[39] Fosdem <https://fosdem.org/2013> accessed 7 April 2013.

the fact remains that the owner of the copyright licensed under GPL, or any copyleft, or any other licence has the right not to enforce the licence.

As was the case with the VLC media player, there will generally be multiple copyright holders. Each holder may enforce the copyright in such jointly held copyright. Should one copyright holder chose to put the software on an app store with potentially infringing terms, and decide to do so even if the app store's terms cause a breach, this would not bind the other holders. Despite consent from one of the software's creators, the other holder(s) of the copyright might chose to enforce against the app store for the infringement the store's terms caused.

In the case of the VLC enforcement, the action may well be considered to have backfired. Rather than change the App Store terms to make them GPL (copyleft) compliant, Apple simply removed the VLC software.

This removal was done under the standard 'take down' policy utilized by the Apple App store. App stores, so long as they do not monitor content and therefore do not have knowledge of what is going onto their app store, may benefit from the safe harbour provisions of the Digital Millennium Copyright Act ('DMCA')[40] and E-Commerce Directive provisions,[41] and they are heavily reliant on these to remove their risk and potential liability. The provisions of these laws may allow the app store to avoid liability for the content provided, but require them to react to complaints.

From the perspective of the app store owners, great reliance has been placed on the safe harbour type provisions of DMCA in the US and the E-Commerce Directive in Europe.

Under the EU's E-Commerce Directive internet service providers ('ISPs') and website hosts are generally not liable for illegal content communicated by others, but are required to act to remove the material under certain circumstances, using 'notice and take-down' procedures. The DMCA is clearer as to the process required, whilst the current E-Commerce Directive's current status leaves variation and a lack of consistency in how ISPs operate this.[42] The public consultation ended in September 2012, but as of yet, no firm guidelines have been provided.

If an app store wishes to benefit from safe harbour, and it is likely that it will, it cannot go through the processes of checking that many software repositories. This really depends on what the store undertakes in its checking process. The ECJ concluded[43] that the safe harbour for hosting providers only applies to third party data processing that is merely technical and automated, as well as passive and neutral.

[40] 17 USC para 512 (inserted by the Digital Millennium Copyright Act 1998).

[41] Directive 00/31/EC on certain legal aspects of information society services, in particular electronic commerce, in the Internal Market (17 September 2000) OJ L178/1, Article 14.

[42] See, eg, *Payam Tamiz v Google Inc* [2012] EWHC 449 (QB).

[43] *L'Oréal and Others v eBay International AG and others* [2012] EMLR 6.

So, a technical or automated check would not remove the benefit of safe harbour, following this logic.

Moving away from take down notices and back to the alleged VLC software GPL infringement, in January 2013 there was a recent and interesting development on the app store front in Microsoft's app store terms. These seem to have dealt with the issue of licences being contradicted in app store terms in rather a neat way:

> 4) d: ...Your license terms must not conflict with the Standard Application License Terms in any way, except that if your Application or In-App Product includes FOSS, your license terms may conflict with the limitations set forth in Section 3 of the Standard Application License Terms, but only to the extent required by the FOSS that you use.
>
> 5) e: If your Application includes FOSS, (i) you must comply with all applicable FOSS license terms, including any source code availability requirements, and (ii) the Application must not cause any non-FOSS Microsoft software to become subject to the terms of any FOSS license.

These appear to allow the app store to include the potentially contradictory terms it wishes to have for the no copyleft code, but to the extent that they would contradict and breach a copyleft licence, the terms will be overridden by the copyleft licence. This seems to be an ideal solution to that issue. In short, whilst not removing the conflicting terms from their app store terms and conditions, Microsoft have manoeuvred around the open source adverse consequences of these by adding a carve out where there is any contradiction.

There are a few further open source issues that need to be considered in the app store arena. The app store, to be licence compliant, must make an offer for the source code where the code distributed through the app store is in binary form, as it often will be. There are a number of simple ways that this can be done.

Modifications to the code should be possible. Also the individual who modifies code distributed under a copyleft licence is required to contribute that back on the same licence terms. App stores may not want such changes to the code on the app store. One solution to that would be to contribute the modified app as a further app on the store.

If the app store has standard terms which require any modifications or contributions to be licensed back under the app store's terms, as opposed to being provided under the code's prevailing licence, this will also potentially infringe copyleft licences.

Further issues may be faced in app store developer terms and/or the user terms, where warranties are required. FOSS software is generally distributed free and without warranty. Any warranties implied by law will generally be disclaimed to the fullest extent permitted at law. So, if the terms require that the content be warranted, whether this is a warranty that the software does not violate any law or that the software does not infringe any IP, the developer providing that warranty may end up in a risk position.

This risk could be two fold. First, the provider's code is being warranted and the liability that is being taken on may be unlimited. Secondly, if that code is a modification of or includes third party code, there may be warranties that are wide enough to cover that third party code from the developer to the app store, but no back to back warranty from the third party. So, the risk taken on by the developer to the app store may not be backed off.

7.8 CLAUSES, SOME SPECIFICS

This final section works through a mixture of clauses for agreements, some real law and some open source issues that don't really fit anywhere else, but which are generally good to know.

- Definition of Open Source Software:
  A good starting point for this is software that falls under a licence within the OSI's definition. In order to tie liabilities or carve out open source software from liabilities it is essential to include such a definition.
- Grant of Licence:
  Any open source software should be included in the list of Software and Licences under which it is distributed. There may be a need for a licence for any non software deliverables and in the trade mark. Trade marks are not covered by the open source licence in the code, and their usage will be very much dependent on the distributor of the code's Trade Mark Policy. Generally these will allow non-commercial usage at no charge, but may impose a cost where the usage is commercial or for profit.[44]
  Any licence which encompasses the open source software should both make clear that it is subject to the licences in the individual packages, and that it neither changes these nor adds any further conditions or terms.
- Interoperability
  As well as a significant cost saving in the upfront acquisition costs of software, one of the key benefits of open source software, particularly the utilization of standard packages, is the fact that software may be interoperable, meaning packages from multiple vendors will work together. If updates are provided for free this will be particularly true. For a business, the benefit of the disruption of transition will be

[44] See further ch 4.

the long term security offered by this but also there is the fact that packages will work together around open source standards.
With open source, the fact that the software source code, the human readable component, is available to utilize allows businesses to build their own add-ons and to lift compatible open source software.
This is not something that is generally specified in agreements for open source, but if the purchaser is looking to have code developed and wishes it to work with particular standards or to interoperate with specific code, then this should be stated as a term of the agreement, or at least in any development specification.

- Combining Code:
  As discussed in Chapter 3 and at various points in this chapter, if code is being combined at your request, you will want to add a warranty that this will not result in viral infection of any proprietary code, or at least that the combination will be done using state of the art methods with a goal to achieve this. A general statement that all code forming part of the deliverable will be combined on appropriate licences is also appropriate. If there are proprietary components to be combined the provider of these should take on the burden of confirming that the licences allow the actions proposed to be taken.
- Versioning:
  One of the benefits of open source is the pace of development. However, where an organization does not have the internal infrastructure in place to manage that pace of change, they may want to stick to updating their internal code only where there is a long term release. If this is to be the case, the duration of support to be provided by the supplier should be investigated and stated in the agreement, to ensure that whilst only adopting certain versions of the free code, this does not leave an organisation without appropriate support.

7.8.1 Risk—we warrant, represent, and undertake

This section may be of particular interest to lawyers looking to do business under English law in the open source sector. Under English law, there is a history of case law around warranties and representations that impact both the meaning of the particular words used and the consequences of these.[45]

A warranty is a contractual assurance or promise as to a set of facts or state of affairs. They have become a standardized checklist in technology licensing agreements. As a breach of a warranty would go to the root of the agreement, any warranty, being a fundamental term of the agreement, means the innocent party may claim damages. The measure of damages would be that required to put the innocent party

[45] See generally *Chitty on Contract*.

into the position it would have been in if there had been no breach of the warranty. Unlike a contractual condition, a warranty does not allow for the innocent party to terminate an agreement.

A representation is a statement (which may be in the agreement or not) which has the intention of persuading or inducing someone to take an action in reliance on that particular statement, and in this case has induced them into entering into the agreement.

Representations can be made accidentally by sales people and such, which can go beyond what is written in the agreement.[46] It is worth making sure your sales team are trained to know what the agreements are and not make a false representation by accident. If there is a breach of a representation, a claim may be made for damages based on tort (not contractual damages). The measure of these damages is intended to put the innocent party in the same position as if the misrepresentation had not been made. These may in fact be significantly higher damages than if the same provision had been a warranty where the damages would be based on contractual losses.

The consequences of a breach of representation may go beyond damages and may give rise to a right to rescind the agreement, which is to have the agreement set aside for all purposes. This combined with the tortious measure of damages will put the parties back in the position that they would have been in had the agreement not been made. Rescission of the agreement means that the agreement would be set-aside for all purposes, and that the parties will be restored to their pre-agreement position, which is in fact quite different from termination.

If you remove the word representation, is there a danger that any warranty you give would be considered also to be a representation? It was held in 2012 that this was not the case, and that a warranty would not be deemed to be a contractual representation.[47]

It is also possible to qualify warranties, to put the other party on notice of a particular situation, and so to avoid any claim. Whether it suits you to have a representation in an agreement depends on whether you are the provider or the recipient of the representation.

With respect to caps on liability it has been held that it is not possible to exclude liability for a fraudulent misrepresentation under English law.[48] So, to avoid a cap on liability clause being unenforceable it is necessary to carve out misrepresentation from the cap on liability.

In English agreements there is a third term that may be associated with the promises section, undertakings where the party 'undertakes' to do something. This will

[46] See, eg, *BSkyB v EDS* [2010] EWHC 86 (TCC).

[47] *Sycamore Bidco v Breslin & Anor* [2012] EWHC 3443 (Ch).

[48] See n 47.

be a contractual condition and breach of such a condition would allow the innocent party to terminate the agreement. Again, whether you wish to have that in an agreement depends on whether you are the recipient or provider.

So, knowing what these terms mean under English law, what is appropriate for an open source agreement? If the agreement is for services then it should contain the same warranties as any other service agreement which may include warranties around the quality of the workers, their workmanship, and their commitment to doing the work. However, the goalposts are a little different when it comes to the delivery of software. When proprietary software is created, it is appropriate for the creator, who is the originator of the work and being paid for the code's development, to take responsibility for the code, and to give a warranty that they own the IP in the code. This has been a standard agreement provision for some time and would generally have covered all IP.

Over the last few years, savvy lawyers in sophisticated companies now carve their liability for patents out of such warranties. This is an interesting development as it is a direct consequence of the rise of the software patent and companies and non practising entities/trolls enforcing software patents. Agreements also generally remove all reference to patents in their warranty and indemnity provisions. This is a marked change, and one that applies to both proprietary and open source software transfers and distributions. The area has been a long-standing source of nervousness around open source, but now this nervousness has spread to proprietary agreements.

For open source developers the landscape is different still. It is rare for a developer of open source code to write something truly from scratch. Even sitting down and doing some old-fashioned clean screen drafting, they are likely to want to interface their code or to run the code with libraries.

If code is owned, then the origin of the code may be something that can be certified, and it may be reasonable to ask for a copyright (if not a general IP) warranty and indemnity in these days of software patent wars.[49]

7.8.2 Indemnities

An indemnity is really quite different from a contractual warranty, representation, or undertakings. As opposed to being a contractual promise or reassurance, an indemnity is a commitment to protect the innocent party from a particular loss and to reimburse them. An indemnity does not require the beneficiary of that indemnity to show that the loss was caused by a breach, but simply that the loss has occurred and that it was recoverable under the provision of the indemnity as drafted and included in the

[49] See further ch 6.

agreement. It is intended generally to cover both damages and a reimbursement or protection against actual costs.

There is no magic meaning of the words indemnity or indemnify, and what an indemnity clause means depends on the words used in the clause. Whether an indemnity is covered by the cap on liability is unclear, but this is something that can be easily resolved by simply drafting the indemnity clause as being subject to the cap on liability, or by stating in the cap on liability clause that the cap will not apply to that indemnity. This should be given full and careful consideration in the agreement.

You may also want to specify, if you are the supplier, that should there be a breach of any warranty, the requirements on you to fix will be one of a number of things. These are generally to repair, replace, or remove.

7.8.3 Non-disclosure agreements

Non-disclosure or confidentiality agreements ought not to be allowed to contain provisions beyond confidentiality. Whilst software will be referenced as confidential information, whether open source should be carved out, depends on the development methodology being used. As it is possible for code to be developed in private and then open sourced it may be appropriate for NDAs to include code that will later be released under an open source licence. It is advisable to keep any licence terms or provisions on IP out of the NDA as they go beyond the purpose of an NDA. If code is actually being developed publicly then it may not make sense for it to be included, although a NDA may be required for ongoing collaborative work, or ideas.

7.8.4 Software developer kit

Software developer kit ('SDK') will generally be provided to developers for APIs in app stores or development work on a commercial basis. Generally this will be a combination of a restricted usage software licence and a confidentiality agreement. If open source code is being shared for development, there may be issues as to sharing it if it is under copyleft licences, bearing in mind the question as to what the point of distribution is.[50]

7.8.5 Secure boot

If you are working with distribution of any operating system, then the issue of secure boot needs to be considered. The Unified Extensible Firmware Interface ('UEFI')

[50] See further ch 1, at 1.4.2.

Forum was set up by a number of organizations in the PC industry with a goal of modernizing the boot process to UEFI. It is made up of chipset, hardware, system, firmware, and operating system vendor. UEFI sets a new model for the interface between PC operating systems and platform firmware. The UEFI Secure boot specification defines the secure boot firmware validation process that implements public key cryptography to verify each successive layer in the operating system boot process. Many computers now boot in this way, through UEFI, as opposed to booting through the BIOS.

Microsoft released its Windows 8 marketing guidelines in late 2011 and these required that Windows 8 PCs came to market locked to Microsoft's UEFI secure boot specification with a goal of preventing malicious software applications and unauthorized operating systems from loading during the system start-up process. So, all computers shipped with Microsoft Windows 8 have been shipped with Secure boot enabled, and will only boot operating systems that have been digitally signed with the key. An obvious knock on effect of this is that if the OS is locked on boot, end users would find it difficult to install any other operating system onto a pre-locked computer, and that Linux operating systems could not be easily used by end users as an alternative to the Microsoft operating system.

There are a number of legal issues around this including competition law, end user security/consumer rights, and of course GPLv3. This has created a heated debate around whether the installation information requirements of GPLv3 are triggered? Reviewing these in detail is not relevant here, but it is important to understand that any distribution agreement for consumer devices may need to include a provision requiring a solution to this interoperability question. In early 2013 the Linux Foundation, through one of its key developers James Bottomley, announced the Linux Foundation work around to allow Linux operating systems to work with this, but at this time the work around is only suitable for use by someone technically skilled and does not fix the end user issues. It is expected that an end user solution will be available by mid 2013.

From the point of view of a commercial agreement which includes operating system distribution, if there is a dual boot requirement, with a linux operating system being one of the potential operating systems, the Secure boot switch must not be switched off, and this and the work around to allow the switch over should be stated in the agreement.

The key to making the commercials work in open source like any other area is understanding. Taking the time to know what it is that is being done and how is critical. The lawyers who are immersed in this area are generally very experienced and sharing, so take advantage of the knowledge that they offer.

Annex: Risk Grid

Issue	Commentary	Who is best placed to bear risk?	Best mechanism to tackle risk	Sample wording	Supplier's arguments	Customer's arguments	Comments
Supplier-created code infringes copyright.	The risk of detection of infringement is easier for [F/OSS] (as the code is more readily available for comparison purposes, especially if the code is GPL and redistributed, but the ability of the customer to mitigate its loss is greater, as it automatically has access to the source code, to enable it to re-engineer infringing code itself if the Supplier will not or cannot do so.	Supplier	Indemnity/ warranty from Supplier. Supplier has right to rewrite infringing code. Version control system (VCS) shared repository and allowing audit rights.	The Supplier warrants that it has title to all Supplier-Created Code and that its delivery [assignment/ licence] to the Customer and use in accordance with this Agreement does not infringe the [copyright] of any third party.	No good ones!	Supplier is in control of code creation, and should therefore be liable for third party infringements. Supplier should use a common source code repository, to which Customer may be given access.	Note that supplier-created code may in practice amount to amendments to existing publicly available code (and create a derivative work of that code). In that case, the row below (publicly available code infringes copyright) would be more appropriate)

Issue	Commentary	Who is best placed to bear risk?	Best mechanism to tackle risk	Sample wording	Supplier's arguments	Customer's arguments	Comments
Publicly-available code (ie code acquired from third parties under a [F/OSS] licence, and incorporated into the software) infringes third party copyright.	One risk is that the publicly available code selected is inherently infringing (ie there is a provenance issue), or alternatively, the component is available under a [F/OSS] licence, but not the one attached to it. Note that 'publicly available code' will include publicly available code that has been amended by the Supplier to create a derivative work.	Varies from project to project. If the Customer specifies use of a specific component, then it should be liable for claims in relation to that component. If the Supplier selects the components, there is a stronger argument that the Supplier should bear some of the risk, or at least take care in the selection process.	Warranty or indemnity from the Supplier, to encourage Supplier to take care in source selection. A list of agreed sources of code may give the Customer comfort (even if this is by no means conclusive), and may encourage the Supplier to take fewer risks in terms of provenance. Further, if code is obtained from recognized locations, it is more likely to be heavily reused, and therefore there is arguably	The Supplier warrants that each component of Publicly Available Code incorporated in the Software has been acquired solely from the locations listed in Appendix [1] and that the source of each such acquisition shall be accurately documented [as set out in Appendix [2]]. [The Supplier further confirms that it has compiled, [with reasonable skill and care], documentation required by the licence[s]	Each Customer has a different appetite for risk. Requiring the Customer to document how it regards the risk of accessing code from different locations, gives the Supplier more information on which to base an accurate price for the job. Alternatively, Supplier may want to give the Customer the option of a cheaper price by doing 'quick and dirty' development by scraping code from anywhere, without provenance checking, providing that the	Supplier is contracting to supply IPR, and should bear all the risk. How Supplier intends to source IPR should not be Customer's issue. In any event, where the Supplier is actively choosing the code to use, provenance checking should be a selection criterion.	Infringement can occur either because the infringing code is not available under any [F/OSS] licence (eg it is derived from proprietary code), or because it is not available under the licence supposedly attached to it (eg it is available under the GPL, but appears to be available under the BSD). It may also occur

Issue	Commentary	Who is best placed to bear risk?	Best mechanism to tackle risk	Sample wording	Supplier's arguments	Customer's arguments	Comments
			safety in numbers (ie it's been used lots of times before and there hasn't been a claim yet), and also the likelihood that if it is found to be infringing, the community will generate a non-infringing alternative.	applicable to the Publicly Available Code and will provide it to the Customer in order to enable the Customer to comply with [the notice and disclaimer] conditions applicable to such licence[s]].	Customer takes the risk. In any case, this clause as drafted could prove unduly restrictive for the Supplier. There are vast amounts of quality code available from 'grey' sites. Also, is 'reasonable skill and care' capable of consistent interpretation given the state of the art? Koders.com contains plenty of roll-your own licences, eg. Also, just because something is on sourceforge.net does not mean that it is necessarily of any better provenance than elsewhere.		because the code has not been released by complying with the appropriate notices in the licences (eg copyright notices, disclaimers). These are reasonably easy to correct.

Issue	Commentary	Who is best placed to bear risk?	Best mechanism to tackle risk	Sample wording	Supplier's arguments	Customer's arguments	Comments
	Another risk is that the Customer (as opposed to the Supplier) may specify the use of specific [F/OSS] components, and in using these components faces a similar issue as above, though with a different context for allocating potential liability.	If the Supplier selects the components, there is a stronger argument that the Supplier should bear some of the risk, or at least take care in the selection process. If the Customer performs this selection, the opposite is true.	Customer takes all risks relating to the nominated code.	The Customer acknowledges, notwithstanding any other provision of this Agreement, that the Supplier shall not be responsible for any claim, cost or expense howsoever arising from the Supplier's incorporation, use of, modification of, linking to the Customer's Specified Components [and the Customer shall indemnify the Supplier for any cost, claim or expense arising therefrom].	The Supplier's choice of component is restricted, and therefore it should not be held liable for such use.		

Issue	Commentary	Who is best placed to bear risk?	Best mechanism to tackle risk	Sample wording	Supplier's arguments	Customer's arguments	Comments
	It is possible to explicitly address the risk of publicly available code not being available under the licence apparently attached to it, and instead actually falling under a different licence and potentially incompatible licence.	This is similar to the provenance issue, in that the Customer's use/ modification/ distribution of the Software may infringe third party rights, but in this case, infringement may depend on the Customer's intended out-licence or intended use of the Software. This wording contains an option which limits the Supplier's obligations to checking that the components' attached licences are on an approved list, but not	Warranty relating to the licences attached to publicly-available code components. Optional exclusion of liability for licence incompatibility (Customer takes risk of incompatibility).	[The Supplier warrants that[, so far as it is aware,] each component of Publicly Available Code incorporated in the Software is available under one of the licences specified in Appendix [3] and has documented the provenance of each such component [as set out in Appendix [1]] [The Supplier does not warrant that use, modification or distribution by the Customer of the Software will not infringe	The Supplier does not want to be responsible for ensuring licence compatibility, as the Customer will be much better placed to determine what its intended use is. Therefore, it's more practical for the Customer to specify a list of compatible licences, than having the Supplier do compatibility checks.	The Customer selects code	

Issue	Commentary	Who is best placed to bear risk?	Best mechanism to tackle risk	Sample wording	Supplier's arguments	Customer's arguments	Comments
		that they are compatible with any intended use.		the rights of any third party, and no provision of this Agreement or implied term shall be construed as such a warranty].			
	Sweeper up warranty designed to ensure that code-selection for copyrights is within the ambit of the Supplier's services.	Supplier	Warranty that skill and care has been taken in component selection, so far as third party copyrights are concerned	[The Supplier warrants that it has taken reasonable skill and care in selecting publicly available components having regard to the non-infringement of third party copyrights [the Customer's Specified Use and the Customer's Specified Out-Licence], and has documented the provenance	This warranty is too vague, at least without qualification as to whether the licences which are attached to the components are compatible with the Customer's Specified Use or (preferably) the Customer's Specified Out-Licence.	The Supplier needs to be put under a practical obligation to make copyright compatibility/ awareness part of its selection criteria.	

Issue	Commentary	Who is best placed to bear risk?	Best mechanism to tackle risk	Sample wording	Supplier's arguments	Customer's arguments	Comments
				and licences applicable to such components [as set out in Appendix [1] and [2] [with reference to Appendix [3] where applicable]].]			
	Publicly available code is incompatible with the Customer's Specified Use or Specified Out-Licence. By requiring the Customer to specify in this way, expectations are managed, and minds are focused.	Supplier		The Supplier warrants that [so far as it is aware, but without having made any specific enquiry] the development of the Software, its delivery to the Customer and the Customer's modification, distribution and use of the Software within the Specified Use [or relicensing to third parties within	This warranty places the onus on the Supplier (at least without the awareness qualification) to ensure compatibility, which can include a legal analysis of different licences, which may be outside the scope of the ability of the Supplier, or the scope of the services intended to be provided.	The Customer has taken time to specify either the licences to be used, or the Specified Use, and it is up to the Supplier to ensure that the Software complies with this requirement.	

Issue	Commentary	Who is best placed to bear risk?	Best mechanism to tackle risk	Sample wording	Supplier's arguments	Customer's arguments	Comments
				the Specified Out-Licence] shall not infringe the licences set out in Appendix [3].			
Infringement by misuse of third party code by the Customer.		Customer		[The Customer is responsible for ensuring that its own subsequent use, modification and redistribution of the software [outside the Specified Use] is in accordance with [the licences set out in Appendix [3]].	The Supplier is developing for the Customer. Therefore the Supplier is not to be concerned about out-licensing, outside the scope of the specified use. This is the Customer's issue. Any future or different uses would be subject to a future or different agreement.	The Customer may want to distribute in the future, and may want to out-license to customers etc. Also, passing around the group, or to the acquirer of the business may be 'distribution' and therefore should be covered.	
Bought-in proprietary code infringes	A third party proprietary library may have a provenance	Supplier (through contractual relationship with provider of the	Indemnity/ warranty from Supplier - but can Supplier obtain	The Supplier [confirms that the licences under which the third	Supplier to use reasonable skill and care in selecting code,	Supplier is contracting to supply IPR, and should	The third party code may infringe because it

Issue	Commentary	Who is best placed to bear risk?	Best mechanism to tackle risk	Sample wording	Supplier's arguments	Customer's arguments	Comments
third party copyright.	issue – ie it obtains code which the supplier is not entitled to licence. This code may itself be proprietary, or it may be [F/OSS].	proprietary code) (unless use of that component is nominated by the Customer – see above).	a back to back indemnity from the provider of that code? This chain may need to extend all the way up to the ultimate provider.	party components of the Software are available [are contained within the list set out in Appendix [3] as amended from time to time by agreement between the parties]][will not be breached by the Customer's Specified Use] [permit the Customer to out-license the Software under the Specified Out-License] and that so far as it is aware [but not having made specific enquiry] the development of the Software and its delivery to the Customer do	but should not be liable for third party infringement. Similar to the supply of third party hardware. May offer to pass on any third party warranties available. May also be subject to the Customer complying with terms passed through by the Supplier.	bear all the risk. How Supplier intends to source IPR should not be Customer's issue.	contains copyleft code, but the source is not made available. This may cause the customer to be the subject of, for example, a GPL violations claim, even if the customer wishes all the code to be available under the GPL, because it does not have access to the source. The customer's remedy may therefore be to compel the supplier

Issue	Commentary	Who is best placed to bear risk?	Best mechanism to tackle risk	Sample wording	Supplier's arguments	Customer's arguments	Comments
				not infringe such licences. [The Customer is responsible for ensuring that its own subsequent use, modification and redistribution of the software [outside the Specified Use] is in accordance with such licences.][The Supplier agrees to provide reasonable assistance to the Customer in passing the benefit of any warranties associated with such third party [proprietary] components to the Customer subject to the Customer's continued compliance with the licences applicable to such code.			to release the source (which may have to pass this requirement up the supply chain). This also suggests a circumstance where the customer insists on the source code being placed in escrow, and released if there is a third party GPL violations claim.

Issue	Commentary	Who is best placed to bear risk?	Best mechanism to tackle risk	Sample wording	Supplier's arguments	Customer's arguments	Comments
Infringement of patent in Supplier Created Code.		Where Supplier has choice of implementation: Supplier. Where implementation is dictated by Customer's requirements: Customer.	Right to change implementation, if implementation is determined by Supplier. Otherwise, risk is on Customer. May be possible to negotiate risk sharing. May be possible to get insurance? Audit rights?	The Supplier warrants that [so far as the Supplier is aware [not having made any enquiry]] the use by the Customer of the Software for its Specified Use [within [jurisdictions]] will not infringe any right which any third party may hold under any valid patent.	It is not economically feasible to undertake a patent clearance prior to implementation. If the implementation is dictated by the Customer's requirements, this should not affect liability.	Supplier is contracting to supply IPR, and should bear all the risk. How Supplier intends to source IPR should not be Customer's issue.	
Infringement of patent in publicly available code.		Where Supplier has choice of implementation: Supplier. Where implementation is dictated by Customer's requirements: Customer.	Where implementation is dictated by Customer: Customer to bear risk. Otherwise, negotiated on a case by case basis.	<none>	It is not economically feasible to undertake a patent clearance prior to implementation. If the implementation is dictated by the Customer's requirements, this	Supplier is contracting to supply IPR, and should bear all the risk. How Supplier intends to source IPR should not be Customer's issue.	

Issue	Commentary	Who is best placed to bear risk?	Best mechanism to tackle risk	Sample wording	Supplier's arguments	Customer's arguments	Comments
					should not affect liability. If supplier has to accept some liability for patent infringement, again there is the potential to insure against this in the UK at a high price and the additional costs of this would be passed through to the Customer.		
Infringement of patent in bought-in proprietary code.		Where Supplier has choice of implementation: Supplier. Where implementation is dictated by Customer's requirements: Customer.	Where implementation is dictated by Customer: Customer to bear risk. Otherwise, negotiated on a case by case basis. Can Supplier obtain a back to back indemnity from the proprietary Supplier?	<none>	Supplier to use reasonable skill and care in selecting code, but should not be liable for third party infringement. Similar to the supply of third party hardware. May offer to pass on any third party warranties available, or to	Supplier is contracting to supply IPR, and should bear all the risk. How Supplier intends to source IPR should not be Customer's issue.	

Issue	Commentary	Who is best placed to bear risk?	Best mechanism to tackle risk	Sample wording	Supplier's arguments	Customer's arguments	Comments
					assist and again this may be subject to a pass through of third party restrictions.		
Trade secrets		Supplier		The Supplier warrants that, to the best of the Supplier's knowledge [but not having made any specific enquiry], its delivery [assignment/licence] to the Customer and use in accordance with this Agreement does not breach any obligations of confidentiality to a third party.			
Trademarks		Customer		For the avoidance of doubt nothing in this Agreement [except for clause []] is intended to	The Customer may wish to use the Supplier's trade mark if the code is distributed (or		

Issue	Commentary	Who is best placed to bear risk?	Best mechanism to tackle risk	Sample wording	Supplier's arguments	Customer's arguments	Comments
				grant any licence over any trade mark of the Supplier or its licensors. The Customer shall comply with the terms of the licences governing all third-party components comprised in the Software, which may include terms relating to trade marks.	accessed remotely). The parties may rely on trade mark law to tackle this, or incorporate an explicit licence permitting the use of the trade mark in relation to the Supplier's code only if it is not modified in any way.		
General Indemnity Wording				The Supplier will indemnify and hold the Customer harmless on demand against any claim or loss arising as a consequence of a breach of any of the [above warranties—warranties set out in this clause].			

Issue	Commentary	Who is best placed to bear risk?	Best mechanism to tackle risk	Sample wording	Supplier's arguments	Customer's arguments	Comments
Implied terms, pre-contractual representations				Except as expressly set out in this Agreement, the Supplier makes no representations or warranties in respect of or in connection with the Software or its use. All other representations, warranties, conditions or other terms which might have effect between the parties or be implied or incorporated into this Agreement or any collateral contract, whether by virtue of statute, common law or otherwise, are hereby excluded to the maximum extent permitted			

Issue	Commentary	Who is best placed to bear risk?	Best mechanism to tackle risk	Sample wording	Supplier's arguments	Customer's arguments	Comments
				by law, including, without limitation, implied conditions, warranties or other terms as to satisfactory quality, merchantability, fitness for purpose or the use of reasonable skill and care.			
Conduct of Claim				The Customer shall notify the Supplier promptly ('a Claim Notice') should it receive any claim that any portion of the code delivered under this Agreement infringes the rights of any third party, or where it otherwise has reason to believe that it does so. The Supplier's			

Issue	Commentary	Who is best placed to bear risk?	Best mechanism to tackle risk	Sample wording	Supplier's arguments	Customer's arguments	Comments
				obligation to indemnify the Customer under [clause [ ]] in connection with a claim against the Customer by a third party is subject to: (a) the Customer promptly serving a Claim Notice; (b) the Customer not making any admission as to liability or compromising or agreeing to any settlement of any such claim without the prior written consent of the Supplier[, which consent shall not be unreasonably withheld or delayed]; (c) at the Supplier's written			

Issue	Commentary	Who is best placed to bear risk?	Best mechanism to tackle risk	Sample wording	Supplier's arguments	Customer's arguments	Comments
				request and at its own expense, the Supplier having the conduct of and the right to settle all negotiations and litigation arising from such claim; and (d) at the Supplier's request and expense, the Customer giving the Supplier all reasonable assistance in connection with such negotiations and litigation. [The Customer shall take all reasonable steps to mitigate its loss arising from any default of the Supplier].			

Issue	Commentary	Who is best placed to bear risk?	Best mechanism to tackle risk	Sample wording	Supplier's arguments	Customer's arguments	Comments
Access to VCS repository				The Supplier undertakes that it will [during the Term] allow the Customer [read-only] access to the [VCS Repository].			
Replace or rewrite				The Supplier may at any time replace any part of the code ('the Original Portion') delivered under this Agreement where it reasonably believes that such code infringes the rights of any third party or where a claim of such infringement has been made, provided that such replacement code materially complies with the Specification. The			

Issue	Commentary	Who is best placed to bear risk?	Best mechanism to tackle risk	Sample wording	Supplier's arguments	Customer's arguments	Comments
				Supplier shall cease to be liable to the Customer for any claim relating to the Original Portion to the extent that it arises after delivery of the Replacement Code, except where such claims apply to items already created or manufactured and currently being deployed to market.			
Licence of Collective Work	The Software is likely to consist of a number of components, and the list of components itself will amount to a collective work. Although in many jurisdictions,			The Supplier acknowledges that the combination of the components within the Software constitutes a collective work. The Supplier hereby grants a non-exclusive licence to such collective work			

Issue	Commentary	Who is best placed to bear risk?	Best mechanism to tackle risk	Sample wording	Supplier's arguments	Customer's arguments	Comments
	the collective work will be implied, in some jurisdictions, eg Spain, it may need to be explicitly granted. Note also that the GPL may not be an appropriate licence for a collective work – FDL, or creative commons may be more appropriate as they do not introduce source code complications.			to the Licensee [consistent with the rest of this Agreement] [consistent with the Specified Use].			
Limitations and exclusions of liability				The Supplier's liability under or in connection with this Agreement (whether in contract, tort	On a risk and reward basis the Supplier will wish to limit to the fees for the specific project.		

Issue	Commentary	Who is best placed to bear risk?	Best mechanism to tackle risk	Sample wording	Supplier's arguments	Customer's arguments	Comments
				(including negligence) or otherwise) is limited as follows: (a) the Supplier will have no liability for any loss of profits, loss of business, loss of goodwill, loss of anticipated savings, loss of or corruption to data or for any indirect or consequential loss or damage; and (b) the maximum aggregate amount of any such liability which is not excluded by (a) shall be [ ]. Nothing in this Agreement shall limit the Supplier's liability for death or personal injury or arising as a result of fraud.			

Issue	Commentary	Who is best placed to bear risk?	Best mechanism to tackle risk	Sample wording	Supplier's arguments	Customer's arguments	Comments
Status of Supplier	This needs to be considered carefully in the context of each licence. Generally, the Supplier will want to be providing services to the Customer, rather than deliverables. This has issues for distribution, acquired rights directive, liability.			The Supplier is [an independent contractor][acts as Agent for the Customer in developing the Software].			
Failure of software to meet specification: Supplier created	Note that the source is automatically available. No need for escrow. More natural to have documentation available.	Supplier	Warranty from Supplier + ability to rewrite non-performing code.	To the extent that any Supplier-Created Code fails to meet the Specification, the Supplier shall during the Warranty Period [replace such Supplier Created Code with code that is compliant][insert SLA].	Offer SLA? Maintenance agreement. Warranty period. Source is automatically available.	Warranty that Software will perform to spec.	

Issue	Commentary	Who is best placed to bear risk?	Best mechanism to tackle risk	Sample wording	Supplier's arguments	Customer's arguments	Comments
Failure of software to meet specification: publicly available		Supplier, generally	Warranty (negotiated) from Supplier + ability to rewrite non-performing code.	To the extent that any Publicly-Available Code fails to meet the Specification, the Supplier shall during the Warranty Period [replace such Publicly Available Code with code that is compliant][insert SLA].	The Supplier should not be responsible for the performance of third party code.	The Customer should not be concerned about how the Supplier opts to select code. Further, for Publicly-Available Code, the Supplier has access to the source, and can therefore treat that code as simply a more-rapidly-developed version of its own code. There is therefore no reason why it cannot give a warranty.	

Issue	Commentary	Who is best placed to bear risk?	Best mechanism to tackle risk	Sample wording	Supplier's arguments	Customer's arguments	Comments
Failure of software to meet specification: proprietary.		Original supplier—can supplier pass on warranties etc?	Back to back warranty from supplier, or mechanism to enable customer to benefit from original suppliers' warranties (agency, third party beneficiary, collateral warranty).	The Supplier shall take reasonable steps to assist the Customer with the enforcement of any warranties applicable to proprietary code, but shall [except to the extent that no reasonable supplier could have specified the use of such code] not otherwise be liable for any failure of any third party code to reach Specification.	Industry standard to use third party code. Depends on type of code (OS/database engine/DLL/Embedded component).	Software should perform to spec.	

8

BUSINESS IMPLICATIONS OF FOSS

Neil Brown

8.1 INTRODUCTION

Put bluntly, FOSS is no longer an issue which businesses can ignore. Many will be using FOSS without realizing it, whilst other, more savvy, businesses, will be using FOSS in a strategic manner to accelerate the development of their products and services, and to enable spending to be focussed on differentiation.

This chapter starts by examining the desirability of a clear FOSS strategy and policy as an underpinning for a business's use of FOSS. By using FOSS to support a business's objectives, decisions are no longer ad hoc or project centric, but rather strategic, enabling the business to extract the most value from FOSS. Although employment law is perhaps not traditionally linked closely with FOSS, it plays an important role in implementing a FOSS policy in a manner that enables a business to update it in the event of strategic changes, whilst also permitting disciplinary action in the event of a breach.

Moving from policy to practice, there are a number of key challenges facing a business using FOSS including detecting use of FOSS, licence incompatibility, and complying with licensing terms. Each of these issues is examined, and practical guidance is offered.

Of course, sometimes things do not go according to plan, and a business may find itself in violation of a FOSS licence. By understanding the motivation of the main

FOSS licence enforcement projects, and the steps which a business can take in the event of a violation report, a business may avoid serious harm to its reputation and bottom line. This section also examines the possibility of litigation in the event of a breach, looking at approaches taken by courts in the US and Europe.

The chapter concludes by examining two more specific areas of FOSS in business: the impact of competition law on FOSS usage, and considerations for businesses looking to acquire companies using FOSS.

8.2 DEVELOPING A FOSS STRATEGY AND POLICY

8.2.1 Introduction

A company may use FOSS for many different reasons, or without a reason. At one end of the spectrum there are companies using FOSS without knowing it; perhaps they have been supplied with products which contain FOSS components, or perhaps their developers have built a product or platform using their favourite FOSS code and never thought to mention it. At the other end are companies for which the use of FOSS is a measured business decision; perhaps they use FOSS to reduce their time to market, or to avoid reinventing the wheel, thereby allowing them to spend money on differentiating elements of their product or service.

The difference between using FOSS without realizing it, and using FOSS in a way which furthers the company's business objectives, is the existence of a FOSS strategy.

8.2.2 Determining the FOSS strategy and policy

Understanding a company's FOSS strategy is the starting point for developing a FOSS policy. Without a clear statement of how the company intends to use FOSS, any policy document exists in a vacuum, and is likely to have little value.

A FOSS strategy is a simple explanation of what a company intends to achieve through the use of FOSS. In developing its strategy, a company is looking to complete the statement 'We use FOSS to . . . ' The aim of this is to get a considered understanding of the company's rationale for using FOSS; eg, 'We use FOSS to keep our costs down,' or, better, 'We use FOSS to allow us to focus spending on differentiating elements of our product.'

Importantly, the company is not looking to complete 'We use FOSS because . . . .' In trying to answer this question, the company is likely to produce a list of generic statements: we use FOSS because it is cheaper; we use FOSS because it is more stable, and so on. Whilst these may or may not be true, they do not help understand the goal the company is trying to reach in the use of FOSS.

Who is involved in completing this statement will depend on each company's structure. Generally speaking, it will need to be a combination of those who understand how the company's products and services work, those who understand the company's strategic direction and how it makes money, and those who can advise on the impact of FOSS usage in different situations. The objective is not to get a statement which is to be imposed on other parts of the business, developed in isolation by the legal team or the technical team, but to develop something which recognizes the company's business reality and which, when fleshed out in the form of a policy, is something which is understood and accepted by the key parts of the business.

A FOSS strategy gives a clear direction on use of FOSS within the company. However, without operational guidance on delivering this strategy, the business will need to make ad hoc decisions on use of FOSS, which is likely to lead to inconsistent or ill-considered use of FOSS, as different business units attempt to understand what the strategy means to their operations. The FOSS strategy should thus be seen as the underpinning of a FOSS policy, which sets outs to the business the how, what, and where of FOSS usage.

By developing a FOSS policy that sets out this operational guidance, a company can encourage consistent and beneficial use of FOSS, cutting down on wasted time, and reducing the risk of inappropriate or ill-reasoned decisions.

8.2.3 The content of a FOSS policy

A good FOSS policy is an agreed approach to achieving the strategic use of FOSS, framed in an easily understood document, and accompanied with appropriate training and guidance. There is no agreed standard as to what should be included in a FOSS policy[1] as different companies will require different approaches. At a minimum, a company should consider:

- Use of third party FOSS in products and services;
- Use of third party FOSS other than in products and services;
- FOSS in the inbound supply chain;
- Releasing code as FOSS/contributing to FOSS projects;
- Handling exceptions.

The remainder of this section explores these elements in detail.

[1] See, eg, OpenLogic's 'Best Practices for Creating an Open Source Policy' <http://www.openlogic.com/wazi/bid/187982/Best-Practices-for-Creating-an-Open-Source-Policy> and Black Duck's 'How to Create an Open Source Policy' <http://opensourcedelivers.com/2012/02/27/how-to-create-an-open-source-policy> both accessed 3 April 2013.

8.2.4 Use of third party FOSS in products and services

The most critical part of a FOSS policy is a clear statement as to which licences are permitted for use in the business. This may be an absolute statement, or else the choice of licence might be dictated by the use to which the FOSS code is to be put, such as a restriction on the use of code licensed under the Affero GPL or LPGL in hosted service components. Whilst a simple approach may be attractive from a clarity and compliance perspective, a more purposive approach may attain better results for the business.

The main consideration for a purposive approach is whether the code in question is to be used in a differentiating or non-differentiating manner.[2] Generally speaking, a wider range of licences may be considered suitable for non-differentiating elements than for those which provide competitive advantage. As an example of such a situation, consider a company that is developing a product which needs to incorporate a web server utility, such as a router with a web interface. In this situation, whilst the design of the web interface might be differentiating, with a clear and simple design more favourable to consumers than a complex and convoluted interface, the actual code forming the web server itself is unlikely to improve a business's sales. In this situation, it would seem unwise to spend time and money developing a custom web server when an existing FOSS web server could be reused. The money saved on developing the web server could be better invested in the differentiating aspects of the product.

This requires a clear determination as to whether a particular element is differentiating or not; it may not always be clear to the business team in question whether this is the case, particularly where a company might be considering changing its strategy and looking to rely on competitive advantage from traditionally non-differentiating parts of its business. In this situation, it may be advisable to publish a list of aspects of products or services considered to be differentiating, which can be easily referenced.

In selecting which FOSS licences are appropriate for the company's business model, it is worth bearing in mind that all FOSS licences have conditions and obligations of some form or other, even if many are not onerous; even permissive licences contain some form of obligation, such as source code attribution or preservation of licence text in source code.[3] Whilst these obligations are unlikely to be problematic from a business perspective, the individual conditions do need to be considered, as failure to comply may result in action for copyright infringement.

[2] Considering the use to which code is to be put is not unique to licensing FOSS, as a company may seek to focus its resources on obtaining bespoke software for differentiating activities whilst relying on common, off-the-shelf, software for more general tasks.

[3] See further ch 3.

The obligations most commonly considered problematic by businesses are those contained in copyleft licences. A term of art rather than law, 'copyleft' licences contain obligations to release at least part of a program's source code if certain trigger events occur, and prohibit the charging of a royalty or licence fee, although charging for access to the code, and for value-added services, usually remains possible. The most common of these are the GNU General Public Licenses, and their Affero and Lesser siblings, but copyleft obligations are also contained in other licences, including the Mozilla Public License and the Common Development and Distribution License.[4]

The key point for a business is that, where the business is looking to incorporate the copyleft codebase into its own product, the licence may require that the business releases some or all of its source code. In some cases, particularly where the business intends to sell the resulting software through a royalty model, obligations to make source code available as a result of the inclusion of copyleft code are unlikely to be desirable. However, whilst the presence of copyleft code may be problematic in some circumstances, this is not necessarily the case, for two reasons.

First, the copyleft code may be used in such a way that the trigger events are never met, so no source code release is required. Determining this requires both a technical understanding of the code's functionality and means of interoperation, and a legal understanding of the licensing implications. Whilst most copyleft licences trigger source code release obligations on distribution of the code to third parties, some—such as the Affero GPL and the Apple Public Source License—require source code distribution where third parties interact with the code remotely, or where it is used to provide a service (eg, where the software is an external-facing web server or application).[5] Generally speaking, where the code in question is only used internally, it is unlikely to trigger source code release obligations.

Secondly, even if source code release obligations were triggered, the program in question may not be a differentiating aspect of the product or service. As discussed above, if there is no competitive disadvantage in complying with copyleft licensing obligations in respect of a given body of code (eg, where release of the source code is not detrimental to the company's business model) the benefit from using the FOSS may outweigh the costs of compliance. Similarly, a sophisticated business would also consider the extent to which source code release may have a positive impact, such as the beginnings of a vibrant development community leading to an improved product, or increased adoption.

Since the scope of copyleft obligations is not always clear (what, eg, is a 'work based on the Program' for the purposes of GNU GPL 3.0?) a business may wish to appoint a FOSS review team, comprising a technical expert and a legal expert, to assess use of copyleft code, and to determine the extent of copyleft licensing implications.

[4] See ch 3. [5] See further ch 9.

In addition to considerations around copyleft licences, a FOSS policy will need to take a position around patent licensing, in particular whether it requires licences to contain an express patent licence.[6] The rationale behind such a requirement is likely to be that, in the absence of an express grant, a licensor might seek to claim against the licensee for patent infringement on the basis that the licence covered copyright alone. As many licences do not contain an express grant of patent licence, imposing such a requirement will constrain considerably the number of FOSS licences which the business is able to use.

It is not possible to state conclusively that a FOSS licensor would be prohibited from bringing a claim of patent infringement against a business using code licensed under terms without an express grant of patent licence. There are, however, good reasons why such action may be prevented, thereby reducing the risk to businesses using licences without express patent grants.

First, a business may claim that the very nature of a FOSS licence creates an implied licence for patent claims infringed by use of the code, relying on the argument that the intention of the drafters of FOSS licences is to enable reuse of the code in question, subject only to any limitations set out in the licence.

For example, the three clause BSD licence does not grant an express patent licence but does declare that '[r]edistribution and use in source and binary forms, with or without modification, are permitted'. As a user could not enjoy this wide-ranging permission if a patent prevented her from doing so, an implied licence to any relevant patent owned by the licensor is necessary to give effect to the permission.

Secondly, an alternative analysis of the same provision would be to argue that a licensor 'having given a thing with one hand is not to take away the means of enjoying it with the other'[7] and is thus prevented from enforcing patent rights against a licensee on the basis of the maxim of non-derogation from grant.[8] To permit such enforcement would be to go against the principle of fair dealing.[9]

Thirdly, some licences contain obligations preventing the imposition of further restrictions on recipients. Whilst GNU GPL 2.0 does not include an express grant of patent licence (although it does contain wording trying to limit the impact of patents)[10] it requires that a distributor of the covered work must 'not impose any further restrictions on the recipients' exercise of the rights granted herein'.[11] The distribution of the work would be an infringement of copyright if the distributor asserted patent rights over that work against a recipient.[12]

[6] See further ch 5. [7] Birmingham Dudley & District Banking Co v Ross (1888) 38 Ch D 295 per Bowen LJ.

[8] British Leyland Motor Corp v Armstrong Patents Co [1986] UKHL 7.

[9] Johnston & Sons v Holland [1988] 1 EGLR 264, 268. [10] GNU GPL 2.0, s 7. [11] GNU GPL 2.0, s 6.

[12] This approach has an inherent limitation, as a party releasing code under a licence is not bound by the terms of that licence, and is thus not a protective measure where the code being distributed is owned entirely by the distributor.

8.2.5 Use of third party FOSS other than in products and services

Use of FOSS within a company's IT infrastructure may be acceptable under more relaxed conditions than those applying to FOSS in products and services to be delivered to customers, as, generally speaking, FOSS licences do not place obligations on merely running FOSS-licensed programs.

For example, a FOSS policy may not prohibit use of a FOSS solution for running a company's intranet, or as a browser on employees' computers.

8.2.6 FOSS in the inbound supply chain

A sensible FOSS policy, particularly one which imposes restrictions on the licences which a company's development team can use, will ensure that a company's control over FOSS usage will extend to code brought into the company through its supply chain function. The objective of the policy requirement is to ensure that the business understands what it is buying, such that it is able to make a risk-aware decision as to whether the product in question is fit for the company's purpose. If, eg, the company was buying a network router from a third party which contained FOSS code, the company will need to understand the extent of any licence compliance activities it might need to undertake, and the cost of performing those activities, as part of the cost/benefit analysis of the purchase. More importantly still, where the business is buying access to code which it intends to incorporate in its own software, it will be critical to understand the licensing requirements and implications of using that code.

An aside...

Product almost at launch stage

Someone suggests 'didn't someone mention something about Lunix?'

One page guide to use of FOSS in products circulated after training session found filed in email account

Oops—there's a process which should have been followed, starting months ago when the product was first being developed

Panicked exchange of email to work out if product contains 'Lunix'

Panicked exchange of email extends to product supplier

Panicked exchange of email extends to product supplier's supplier

Answer comes back that product probably contains 'Lunix,' but that the person who knows has quit/is on holiday/has taken a vow of silence and lives in a convent not far from Lourdes

Frantic reference to supply chain to see whether it came up in supplier due diligence

Due what?

Products ripped apart, trying to get access to code on the device; firmware run through the Binary Analysis Tool

Multiple references to FOSS code discovered

Supply chain asked to provide copy of procurement agreement, to check terms around compliance with FOSS licensing conditions and source code provision

Contract looks remarkably similar to an unmodified precedent, complete with [square brackets] where details should have been inserted or clauses modified
Numerous phone calls to supplier
Component list and source confirmed as held by supplier
In their Ugandan office
It's a national holiday in Uganda, but should be available tomorrow
Tomorrow arrives, along with tarball of source code and licensing information
Seems to match BAT output
Need to ensure copy of licence accompanies the product, along with other text and, if source is not being shipped with product, some form of written offer
Emergency briefing to external design agency about how to meet compliance obligations
Boxes already in warehouse, ready for distribution
Could we open all the boxes and put in a paper statement?
Feasible, but would not meet brand guidelines on packaging
Further frantic calls
Careful consideration given to placing an order for 'baseball bat, aluminium' on Amazon and expensing it as 'compliance training'
Brand manager placated
Paperwork printed and placed in boxes, and source code hosted on website
Sighs of relief all round
Whinge that it's all so difficult
Sharp email that it's only difficult it you don't do it properly and fail to plan it from the beginning
Commitments to do it properly next time
Training offered, accepted and delivered
One page guide circulated
Guide filed in email account
and so it begins again...

The cleanest way to do this is to require all suppliers to provide a list of FOSS components used within a product before a procurement contract is signed. It is not unreasonable to sign a confidentiality agreement in respect of this information, as it may not be something that a company wishes to have disclosed to its competitors, but, from a purchaser's point of view, it will be essential to understand what is being bought. Where the business has strict rules around which FOSS licences it will accept, providing this to the supplier during the process of identifying suitable vendors or solutions may help avoid wasting time considering products which will not suit the business's strategy. To facilitate comparison of multiple solutions, a business may ask a supplier to provide this FOSS usage information in SPDX format,[13] but, as adoption of this approach is still in its infancy, this might be impractical.

In addition to information gathering requirements, a business may wish to adjust its purchasing agreements to include warranties that all FOSS usage is declared in an annex to the agreement, and that the supplier will provide reasonable support to the business to ensure that the business's distribution of the product is compliant with all

[13] 'The Software Package Data Exchange® (SPDX®) specification is a standard format for communicating the components, licenses and copyrights associated with a software package.' <http://spdx.org> accessed 3 April 2013.

licensing requirements, and to assist in the event of a reported violation. Companies that do not have existing policies on use of FOSS in the supply chain may wish to consult the Free Software Foundation Europe's Risk Grid,[14] which provides a reasoned analysis on risk apportionment on FOSS issues in contracts.

Where the risk associated with FOSS is considered high—eg, the supplied product is part of a particularly important product, for which obligations such as source code distribution could affect adversely the business's competitive position—the business may consider imposing a requirement that all source code coming into the company must be scanned, and the output of the scan assessed in the light of the list of FOSS reported by the supplier. Code scanning is considered in more detail at 8.4.

8.2.7 Releasing code as FOSS/contributing to FOSS projects

As has been discussed earlier, certain licences impose obligations to distribute source code if a trigger condition is met. Where this is a requirement, compliance with the obligation is part of the cost of using code under that particular licence. A business's FOSS policy will want to include the conditions (if any) under which someone within the business can choose to release source code where it is not required for the purposes of licence compliance. This issue comes up mainly in the context of bug fixes and non-differentiating functionality enhancements.

Whilst the initial reaction of a more traditional company might be to decline to release any code back into FOSS projects unless legally required to do so, this approach may not be in the company's best interests. For example, where a business fixes a bug in a piece of code licensed under a permissive FOSS licence (such as the three clause BSD licence), it may choose to provide the bug fix back to the project to avoid the necessity of maintaining the patch for each new release of the project's code. As well as assisting other users of the code in question, the business reduces the time and effort in maintaining the bug fix, which it can invest instead in differentiation. It may be appropriate for all such contributions to be passed through an internal review team, to confirm that the contribution is a bug fix rather than a differentiating feature enhancement.

8.2.8 Handling exceptions

Although the aim of a policy is to set the standard for the business, the reality is that occasions will arise in which someone within the business wishes to introduce code which does not comply with the policy. Having a clear responsibility in the policy for dealing with exceptions will enable a risk/benefit analysis to be carried out in respect

[14] <http://www.ifosslr.org/ifosslr/rt/suppFiles/10/0> accessed 11 June 2013.

of the exceptional activity, to avoid missing a good business opportunity through an overly rigid policy application, whilst simultaneously preserving the business from unnecessary risk.

8.2.9 Rolling out the FOSS policy

An agreed and written FOSS policy, which implements the company's FOSS strategy is an excellent starting point for managing FOSS within a company. However, as a document alone, it is unlikely to have much impact, unless it is properly implemented.

To comply with the policy, and achieve the business's FOSS strategy, some areas of the business may need to make changes to the way in which they operate. For example, the supply chain management team may need to draft new contract clauses to deal with FOSS, to ensure that it is identified, or only provided under a specific set of licences, with agreed provision of assistance in the event of receipt of a violation report. Similarly, the R&D team may need to keep better track of the code it is using, and the licences under which that code is used.

Since the policy is likely to affect different parts of the business differently, compliance is likely to be improved by conducting specific, relevant training for each affected part of the business. The emphasis here is relevance; eg, the R&D team may not need to know the particular warranties to be included in supply agreements. Although if, as suggested earlier, the strategy and policy are developed in conjunction with key areas of the business rather than as a standalone activity, the FOSS policy should not come as a surprise, the process of training the teams may bring out new suggestions and thoughts which had not been considered in the drafting stage. The training represents a good opportunity to test the policy in a safe environment, and to develop and finesse it based on operational feedback.

A few months after the policy has been launched, it would be sensible to check back with the relevant teams as to how it is working in practice. For example, whether the policy is leading to odd decisions being made, and whether employees are unable to comply with policy requirements. Only with an opportunity to see how it has actually worked for the business in question can it be tailored most effectively to the business's objectives.

8.3 EMPLOYMENT LAW AND FOSS

8.3.1 Introduction

Although perhaps not seen as having a major bearing on FOSS, there are two particular employment law issues which arise in discussions around use of FOSS in a business. The first relates to the status of the FOSS policy, and the manner in which it is created and implemented. This is especially relevant where a business wishes to retain the right to pursue breach of the FOSS policy as a disciplinary matter, whilst also being able to modify the policy as the business's situation changes.

Secondly, employment law, and its impact on copyright and patent law, has a major bearing on the ownership of code and ideas created in the course of employment. From the point of view of both the company and its employees, ensuring that there is a clear understanding of who owns what is essential.

8.3.2 Status of FOSS policy

The preceding section discussed the role of a FOSS strategy and policy, and the value of having such a policy in gaining the maximum benefit from FOSS within the context of the business's objectives.

In a small company of objective-focussed employees, there may be little need for formality around the policy; it provides a useful guide to the use of FOSS which helps employees in their jobs, and is thus followed willingly because it is helpful. In other situations, where it has not proven possible to get agreement on the policy from all employees potentially affected by it, a stick to encourage compliance may be desirable.[15]

As with employment policies generally, it is better from an English law perspective that the FOSS policy does not form part of the employment contract, to avoid the need to obtain each employee's consent in the event any modifications are needed.[16] In particular, in the period immediately after the introduction of the policy, changes may be needed to reflect issues which arise in practice and which were unforeseen in the drafting process. Similarly, if the FOSS strategy were to change, as a result of a shift in the business's direction, key sections of the FOSS policy may need to be revisited.

A well-drafted contract of employment is likely to include language around compliance with corporate policies, and the FOSS policy should slot into this framework. However, merely documenting the policy and putting in on the intranet is unlikely to lead to successful adoption. To change behaviours, the policy should be rolled out properly through training and awareness raising exercises. If failure to follow the FOSS policy is to be a disciplinary offence, this is all the more important, to avoid any allegation that the expectations were not sufficiently communicated. As part of the training and rollout, employees should be told when the policy will come into effect, and be given a means to ask questions, seek clarifications, and express concerns about the policy. If the use of FOSS is prevalent within the organization,

[15] In some countries, it may be necessary to obtain approval from the company's works council before implementing a FOSS policy, eg, Germany.

[16] Wandsworth London Borough Council v DeSilva [1998] IRLR 193, para 31.

and the policy is a significant adjustment from previous working practice, drop-in sessions or online discussions may be in order, else a named and accessible point of contact.

If breach of the FOSS policy is to be a disciplinary offence, this should be communicated, with a clear explanation of what will happen. Action taken in the event of a breach should be in accordance with the company's disciplinary policy, although, at least in the early stages, using examples of non-compliance as a mechanism for questioning the effectiveness of the policy's implementation and roll-out might produce more desirable results in the long term.

8.3.3 Ownership of code and inventions

In addition to the specific FOSS policy, the key employment policy to consider in a FOSS context is a company's intellectual property[17] policy. Generally, a company will have an IP rights policy to determine who owns what, and to ensure that the benefit of the employee's or contractor's work attracts to the company, rather than to the employee, a position which may not be the case at law.

For example, whilst, under English law, the first owner of copyright in a literary work comprising computer software would be the work's author, where that code is written by an employee in the course of his employment, the employer would be treated as the owner absent an agreement to the contrary.[18] As it may not always be clear whether a work is created 'in the course of employment' or not[19]—eg, where an employee creates software for a FOSS project during work hours but her employment duties do not include programming, and her contract of employment would not have permitted her employer to require her to program[20]—having a clearly-defined policy is likely to be in the company's interest if it wishes to avoid potentially costly litigation. Similarly, a company engaging a contractor for a development activity is likely to want to deviate from the basic legal position, and will take steps to make it clear that any copyright created by the contractor is to vest in the company.[21]

A company is likely to have an IPR policy irrespective of its use of FOSS, as the issues that such a policy attempts to solve are not exclusive to FOSS. However, a company which is keen to make use of FOSS as a way of furthering its business will want to consider its IPR policy, to minimize harm associated with overreaching. In particular,

[17] The term 'intellectual property' is frowned upon by some in the FOSS sphere, since it considers as one discrete notions of copyright, trade mark, patents, design rights, and so on, and equates these rights with the ownership of physical objects: RM Stallman, 'Did You Say "Intellectual Property"? It's a Seductive Mirage' (GNU) <http://www.gnu.org/philosophy/not-ipr.html> accessed 3 April 2013.

[18] Copyright, Designs and Patents Act ('CDPA') 1988, s 11(2).

[19] Missing Link Software v Magee [1989] 1 FSR 361.

[20] See, eg, Stevenson Jordan & Harrison v McDonnell & Evans [1952] 1 TLR 101.

[21] Griggs v Evans [2005] EWCA Civ 11.

to what extent is it reasonable for a company's IPR policy to extend to activities that take place outside the company?[22]

It is understandable that a company would want to ensure that the outputs of work performed at its cost belong to the company, irrespective of where or when these outputs are created. It is also understandable that a company would not wish for an employee to be working on something for the company in the course of his employment, and to be creating a competing product in his own time, irrespective of whether the employee is actually copying the code in the copyright sense. Whilst a director doing this might be in breach of a fiduciary duty owed to his company,[23] it is unlikely that an employee doing this would be breaching a fiduciary duty to his employer other than in specific circumstances, such as reliance on the company's confidential information.[24]

From the point of view of an employee, it is not unreasonable for an employee to engage in creative activities outside the course of employment, for his own benefit rather than his employer's. A company recognizing this is not acting entirely selflessly, as skills developed in an employee's own time may be useful to the company, particularly in terms of familiarity with relevant FOSS packages or communities. A failure to recognize this, and an attempt to impose onerous restrictions on an employee's out of work activities, may have more serious consequences, including being unable to attract the best people for the role. It would seem odd for a company which is keen to make the most of FOSS to have a policy which prevented employees from engaging on their own projects in their own time.

These requirements and expectations need not be in conflict. A future assignment, with recognition payments where appropriate, of inventions and other outputs arising (a) in the course of employment, and (b) outside the course of employment but which relate to the employer's current or anticipated business, may protect each party's rights adequately, at least as a starting point.

Outside the IPR policy, a restrictive covenant that the employee must not compete with his employer during the course of employment, or for an appropriate period of time after employment, may be an appropriate additional protection.[25]

Where a company is engaged in a range of activities, and an employee is only responsible for working on a small subset of that range, it may be appropriate to limit the reach of an assignment for activities conducted outside the course of employment to only those which compete with the work which the employee performs for the company. For example, if the employee works on the network stack for a mobile

[22] M Mattoli, 'The Impact of Open Source on Pre-Invention Assignment Contracts' (1990) 9(1) *U Pa Journal of Labor and Employment Law* 228.

[23] Companies Act 2006, s 175(1) provides that a director must 'avoid a situation in which he has, or can have, a direct or indirect interest that conflicts . . . with the interest of the company.'

[24] University of Nottingham v Fishel [2000] ICR 1462.

[25] Thomas v Farr [2007] EWCA Civ 118.

device, but enjoys contributing to a FOSS spreadsheet application on his own time, should the fact that others in the company are writing a spreadsheet application for the company's mobile device preclude the employee from his pastime?

As a note of caution to this, if the company distributes or conveys third party code licensed under GNU GPL 2.0 and 3.0, or other similar licences, any attempt to restrict use of that code is likely to be considered a 'further restriction', which is prohibited by the licence; under GNU GPL 3.0, the presence of this restriction may be sufficient to terminate the company's licence to use the code in question, or trigger copyright infringement.[26] As both a restrictive covenant not to compete with the company and a requirement to assign any copyright created in a competing work to the company are likely to be considered 'further restrictions', a business should exclude use by an employee of GNU GPL'd code distributed or propagated by the company from any such covenants or requirements.

8.4 FOSS IN PRODUCT AND SERVICE DEVELOPMENT

8.4.1 Introduction

A good FOSS policy, implementing a company's FOSS strategy, will enable a business to enhance its products and services through the use of FOSS in a considered, risk-aware manner. Many of the key considerations for use of FOSS in product development, such as licence selection, have already been considered in the context of the FOSS policy; indeed, one of the key reasons for having a FOSS policy is to avoid the need to decide whether a particular licence is appropriate on a case by case basis.

However, in addition to the considerations outlined in the FOSS policy section 8.2, there are three areas which require particular attention in the area of product development: identifying FOSS use, licence incompatibilities, and complying with licence obligations.

8.4.2 Identifying FOSS use: code scanning

A business's FOSS policy is likely to require that, when obtaining a product containing software from a third party supplier, the supplier is asked to detail use of FOSS, to ensure that the product is suitable for the company's business model. Similarly, in a corporate acquisition, understanding the use of FOSS by the target may be an essential part of understanding what is being bought. In each case, whilst the first step is to ask the supplier/target to identify FOSS usage, the procuring or acquiring business

[26] GNU GPL 3.0, s 8 provides that 'You may not propagate or modify a covered work except as expressly provided under this License. Any attempt otherwise to propagate or modify it is void, and will automatically terminate your rights under this License . . .'.

may want a greater degree of comfort that the supplier's declaration is accurate;[27] perhaps the supplier was unable to provide a list in a timely manner, or else the business suspects that a certain FOSS component was used but is not declared (whether unintentionally or otherwise). If resolving any apparent disjunct is important for the business, an independent verification of FOSS utilisation may be appropriate. Generally, this will entail code scanning.

The objective of code scanning is straightforward: to obtain a list of FOSS in a particular piece of software. Ideally, this will include the name of the package in question, its version, and the licence under which it is released. With this information, a business can make more informed enquiries as to how the FOSS is used in the product, which facilitates, amongst other things, exploring questions of how the FOSS interacts with other components, to understand potential licence incompatibilities and copyleft implications, and to take remedial action where necessary. Where the output of a scan is different to a supplier's declared use of FOSS, there is a clear driver for further investigation, although a difference is not necessarily a sign of error or omission by the supplier, due to the possibility of false positive or false negative code scanning results.

Code scanning takes two forms: source code scanning and binary scanning. As the name suggests, source code scanning analyses the human-readable form of a computer program, whilst a binary scan analyses the executable form of a program. Using a variety of techniques, often comparing data found within the code with a database of known patterns or details of FOSS applications and their licensing information, scans attempt to identify what the code being scanned contains.

Which is appropriate for the task at hand will depend on the level of access the business has to the software. If a supplier or target is cooperative, a business may prefer to perform a source code scan, since this is more likely to produce accurate results than a binary scan; by having access to the source code, a layer of abstraction is removed. However, businesses often receive software from suppliers in binary-only form, and it may not be possible to work with the supplier on a source code scan.[28] In an ideal world, a business would conduct both a source code and binary scan, to maximize the chances of detecting any problems whilst ensuring that the code being offered as the relevant source code matches with the code forming the binary.

There are a number of tools available for code scanning, each offering different functionality and levels of support. Options include the Binary Analysis Tool,[29]

[27] M Von Willebrand and M-P Partanen, 'Package Review as a Part of Free and Open Source Software Compliance' (2010) 2(1) *IFOSS L Rev* 39.

[28] A Hemel et al, 'Finding Software License Violations Through Binary Code Clone Detection' (2011) MSR '11 Proceedings of the 8th Working Conference on Mining Software Repositories' 63.

[29] <http://binaryanalysis.org> accessed 3 April 2013; (of particular interest to businesses concerned about FOSS licence compliance, the Binary Analysis Tool is authored by Armijn Hemel, who was formerly a core member of the gpl-violations.org project, and thus has a highly relevant insight into FOSS compliance and licence enforcement).

Fossology,[30] the Ninka licence identification tool,[31] Open Logic's OSS Discovery,[32] as well as tools from Palamida,[33] and Black Duck.[34]

As many of these tools are easy to install and operate, or else are offered as an online service, the real effort involved in code scanning is the analysis of the output data. For example, whilst a scan output may identify constituent parts of a piece of software, determining whether the interaction of two components is problematic from a licence compatibility perspective will require a joint legal and technical analysis.[35] For example, a developer may have released code under a number of licences, such that post-scan analysis will need to identify under which licence the code has been used. Depending on the tools used, a scan may also highlight the unexpected inclusion of third party non-FOSS code. It is also worth noting that scans may produce false positive and false negative outcomes. Whilst undeniably useful as tools in assessing FOSS usage, it would be unwise to regard their outputs as necessarily accurate or complete, but rather as an additional source of information requiring critical evaluation, the outcome of which can be used as part of the overall risk assessment.

With this in mind, a number of companies offer support and advice on software governance and licence compliance activities.[36] Unless a business has sufficiently skilled individuals in-house, outsourcing the activity of code scanning and licence compliance assurance may be the most practical solution.

8.4.3 Licence incompatibilities

A team developing a product will need to be aware of licensing incompatibilities, to ensure that it does not produce a product that cannot be distributed in compliance with all applicable licences, or a service that cannot be provided. At a very high level, the greatest risk of incompatibility arises from the combination of a code licensed under terms which prohibit the imposition of further restrictions with code licensed under other terms.

The GNU project maintains a list of licences which it considers compatible or incompatible with different versions of the GNU GPL.[37] Of particular note, GNU GPL 2.0 is not, in itself, compatible with GNU GPL 3.0.[38] Where code is made available under 'GNU GPL 2.0 or any later version', the licensee is able to take the code under

[30] <http://www.fossology.org/projects/fossology> accessed 3 April 2013.

[31] 'Ninka, a license identification tool for Source Code' <http://ninka.turingmachine.org> accessed 3 April 2013.

[32] <http://www.openlogic.com/products/scanners>.

[33] <http://www.palamida.com/products> accessed 3 April 2013.

[34] <https://www.blackducksoftware.com> accessed 3 April 2013.

[35] M Bain, 'Software Interactions and the GNU General Public License' (2010) *IFOSS L Rev*, vol 2, no 2, 165.

[36] See, eg, <http://www.tjaldur.nl> accessed 3 April 2013.

[37] <http://www.gnu.org/licenses/license-list.html> accessed 3 April 2013.

[38] <http://www.gnu.org/licenses/license-list.html#GNUGPL> accessed 3 April 2013.

GNU GPL 3.0 instead, removing any incompatibility, but, where code is not licensed on an 'or any later version' basis, this is not possible.

8.4.4 Complying with licence obligations

A business will need to ensure compliance with any licensing obligations. To assist with this, use of FOSS within a product should be carefully documented. The cleanest way of doing this is generally in the form of a dedicated source control system, into which all product-related code is committed, along with accurate and concise information about provenance and licence terms.[39] By working in such a way, it is possible to trace how any given code was committed to a project and by whom, and to obtain easily a list of all the FOSS included in a project, which is vital for a pre-launch compliance review.

Where a mechanism is in place to obtain licensing information quickly, a pre-launch review is a relatively straightforward task. Conversely, where there is no good history of the code in the project, it may be necessary to work through each code file and identify known FOSS code. Once compliance obligations have been established, the business will need to ensure that it has a means of meeting those obligations.

For example, where a business uses code under GNU GPL 2.0, and intends to release the software in binary form (such as installed in a product), it will need to ensure that it complies with obligations around distributing the licence text and the complete relevant source code. Where a licence imposes obligations for a defined period of time, such as making source code available for a period of years after distribution of the product has ceased,[40] this will need to be tracked by the company, to ensure that it continues to meet its obligations. By having a centralized mechanism for doing this, a business avoids the risk of having essential knowledge held only by one or two individuals.

8.5 HANDLING FOSS VIOLATIONS

8.5.1 Introduction

With a sensible FOSS policy, a pragmatic governance regime for use of code in internal development activity and controlled procurement activities, the risk of

[39] Although not specific to FOSS, if the company does not have a suitable mechanism for managing their source code—eg, committing code to a versioning system, for reuse and to help understand code provenance—the company may wish to consider this alongside the adoption of a FOSS policy.

[40] eg, the 'written offer' mechanism for conveying non-source forms of the covered code under s6(b), GNU GPL 3.0 requires that the written offer is valid for at least three years from the point of conveyance and for as long as the distributor offers spare parts or customer support.

an allegation of a FOSS licence infringement should (hopefully) be low. But what should a business do if it does receive notification of a purported violation? This section explores some of the myths and realities of FOSS licence enforcement.

8.5.2 Ensuring compliance

With a wide range of people authoring FOSS, for all manner of different purposes, it would be unwise to conclude that all copyright holders would seek to resolve FOSS licence violations in the same way. Looking at comments made by those involved in the more regular and high profile violation enforcement activities, however, there is a commonality: as the Software Freedom Conservancy ('SFC'), which includes FOSS licence enforcement amongst its many other FOSS activities, puts it, '[t]he primary goal of every GPL enforcement action is to gain compliance.'[41]

gpl-violations.org,[42] which has been responsible for raising the profile of FOSS licence violations within Europe, adopts a similar mantra:

> The goal of gpl-violations is to resolve violations. We recognize that companies make mistakes. We seek amicable solutions whenever possible, but only if that solution resolves the violation.[43]

As such, whilst it would not be sensible to consider that everyone seeking to enforce the terms of a FOSS licence would only be interested in compliance, it is perhaps the most likely desired outcome.

Compliance, however, is a non-specific term; different people may take it to mean different things. As a starting point, a business would be expected to resolve the violation which was notified to it. If, eg, the licence in question required the business to make available the source code for a program, but the source code made available by the business did not match the binary being shipped, the company would be expected to ensure that the complete source code corresponding to the relevant binary was made available.

If enforcement action is taken by the SFC, merely fixing the notified violation alone is unlikely to be enough, as the SFC has stated[44] that it would commonly ask for:

- compliance with all FOSS licences in the product in question;
- the appointment of a compliance officer; and
- payment of SFC's costs.

[41] BM Kuhn, 'Some Thoughts on Conservancy's GPL Enforcement' (SFConservancy, 1 February 2012) <http://sfconservancy.org/blog/2012/feb/01/gpl-enforcement> accessed 3 April 2013.

[42] gpl-violations.org is a German project, founded by Harald Welte in 2004, which has the objective of raising awareness about past and present violations of the GNU GPL. For further information about the background of gpl-violations.org, see <http://gpl-violations.org/about.html> accessed 19th January 2012.

[43] <http://gpl-violations.org/faq/violation-faq.html> accessed 9 December 2012.

[44] <http://sfconservancy.org/blog/2012/feb/01/gpl-enforcement> accessed 3 April 2013.

8.5.3 Compliance with all FOSS licences in the product in question

Whilst the SFC may only have standing from a copyright point of view to take action in respect of a small part of the company's overall codebase,[45] the SFC would be looking for all issues of FOSS licence non-compliance to be rectified.

8.5.4 The appointment of a compliance officer

To reduce the risk of needing to bring enforcement action in respect of each product, even each software update, released by a company, the SFC has said that it will require a company to provide a single point of contact, knowledgeable about FOSS licensing issues, so that, in the event of a problem in the future, there is an easy route to the relevant part of the company.[46] In an ideal world, the compliance offer would not just wait for reports of violations from the SFC or other rights holders, but would work with the business to prevent future violations.

8.5.5 Payment of SFC's costs

A self-explanatory point, the investigation of a potential violation and the enforcement activity itself has a financial cost, and the SFC would seek to recover this.

Where a violation was particularly egregious,[47] or else it was not possible to effect compliance on a voluntary basis, both SFC and gpl-violations.org have sought to address the issue of non-compliance through litigation.

8.5.6 Litigation for FOSS licence violation

A claim often heard is that 'open source has not been tested in court.' This is a surprising argument, for two reasons.

First, from a theoretical point of view, if, in the relevant jurisdiction, failure to comply with the licence requirements means that no licence is in place, such that the action in question amounts to an infringement of copyright,[48] infringement of copyright is well

[45] A party intending to take action for infringement of copyright must have the right to do so. eg, under English law, infringement of copyright is actionable by the copyright owner (CDPA 1988, s 96), by an exclusive licensee (s 101) or by certain non-exclusive licensees (s 101A). gpl-violations.org has commented that 'some... Linux kernel developers have transferred their rights in a fiduciary license agreement to enable the successful gpl-violations.org project to enforce the GPL in cases where no code originally written by Harald Welte was used/infringed upon' (<http://gpl-violations.org/about.html#history>, accessed 19 January 2013), whilst the SFC offers to provide compliance services to its 'Member Projects' (<http://sfconservancy.org/members/services> accessed 3 April 2013).

[46] <http://sfconservancy.org/blog/2012/feb/01/gpl-enforcement> accessed 3 April 2013.

[47] Return of Organisation Exempt from Income Tax Form 990 for Software Freedom Conservancy, Inc. dated 13 January 2012, at s 4(c): <http://sfconservancy.org/docs/conservancy_Form-990_fy-2010.pdf> accessed 3 April 2013.

[48] See, eg, Jacobsen v Katzer 535 F.3d 1373 (Fed Cir 2008), in which failure to comply with the requirements of the Academic Free Licence was treated as a matter of copyright infringement.

understood by courts. Whilst a particular licence may not have been the subject of litigation, the same can be said of most proprietary software licences.

Secondly, on a more practical level, there is a growing volume of case law relating to FOSS and similar licences such as the Creative Commons licences.[49]

For example, within Europe, in Welte v Sitecom Deutschland GmbH,[50] it was held that failing to comply with the conditions of GNU GPL 2.0 meant that the defendant infringed the claimant's copyright.[51] A similar conclusion was reached in the case of Welte v Skype Technologies SA,[52] following an abortive appeal attempt by Skype.

In the US, the SFC successfully obtained an injunction against Westinghouse Digital Electronics,[53] which 'marks the first time a court in the USA has granted an injunction ordering a GPL violator to permanently cease distribution of out-of-compliance GPL'd software.'[54] In this case, the court ordered damages of $30,000, trebled to $90,000 for the wilful nature of the infringement, along with a requirement to forfeit infringing articles in its possession by giving all the defendant's stock of HDTVs containing BusyBox to the SFC.[55]

The key point for businesses is not that litigation is inevitable in the event of a violation, as it would still seem to be a matter of last resort, but that, if a violation is not rectified in a manner suitable to the claimant,[56] litigation may well be available to the claimant as a backstop.

8.5.7 Dealing with a reported violation

As well as a policy for the use of FOSS, a well-prepared business will have a plan for dealing with reports of FOSS violations.

Reports of violations, and discussions about whether a particular situation amounts to a violation, are often posted to the gpl-violations.org legal mailing list.[57] As a public list, anyone can join the list and receive messages posted to it, or else view the messages online, and representatives of businesses which distribute FOSS to customers or supply to downstream companies which distribute to customers may find that keeping an eye on the mailing list gives them advance notice of impending violation reports, as well as a chance to engage pro-actively with potential complaints.

[49] <http://wiki.creativecommons.org/Case_Law> accessed 3 April 2013.

[50] District Court of Munich, 19 May 2004, case 21 O 6123/04.

[51] T Jaeger, 'Enforcement of the GNU GPL in Germany and Europe' (2010) 1 *JIPITEC* 34, para 20.

[52] District Court of Munich, 12 July 2007, case 7 O 5245/07.

[53] Software Freedom Conservancy, Inc and Anderson v Best Buy Co Inc et al, 09 Civ 10155 (SAA), filed July 2010.

[54] <http://sfconservancy.org/news/2010/aug/03/busybox-gpl> accessed 3 April 2013.

[55] Software Freedom Conservancy, Inc and Anderson v Best Buy Co Inc and ors, 09 Civ 10155 (SAA) 14.

[56] An appropriate outcome to a FOSS claimant may be different to that of a more traditional litigant, per SFC's stated outcomes <http://sfconservancy.org/blog/2012/feb/01/gpl-enforcement/>.

[57] <http://gpl-violations.org/mailinglists.html> accessed 9 December 2012.

Unlike more traditional copyright infringement claims which are likely to come from rights holders through lawyers, FOSS violations raised to companies are often done so informally, through a customer service channel or online support forum.[58] As part of the roll out of a FOSS policy, a business will want to train its customer services teams to recognize a reported FOSS violation, and to pass it on promptly to the relevant contact within the organization.

As discussed earlier, many FOSS licensing complainants will be looking for compliance, which is likely to dictate a more FOSS-centric response, as opposed to the more legalistic response associated with more traditional copyright infringement handling. As this is a rule of thumb, exceptions will arise, and so the complaint should be checked by someone with adequate training to understand the nature of the claim being made; it may be more appropriate to immediately refer the claim to a business's legal advisors.

If the complaint is one that the business intends to resolve on a FOSS-centric basis, a standard process of communication and investigation should begin. Generally speaking, resolving a complaint is likely to entail the following steps:[59]

- Engage with the complainant;
- Understand the complaint;
- Investigate the complaint;
- Fix any valid issues;
- Communicate the outcome;
- Learn from the experience.

8.5.8 Engage with the complainant

Respond to the person who has sent in the violation report, stating that the company is looking into the issue. Reassuring the complainant that the business is taking the issue seriously may help to limit immediate reputational damage, as long as this position is believable. A business with a poor track record of compliance is less likely to be taken seriously than one which actively resolves violations. If the complaint has been made in a public forum, it would be advisable to agree with the complainant that, whilst under investigation, communications from the company will be just with the complainant. The aim of doing so is to build a trusted

[58] Posts to the gpl-violations.org mailing list often indicate failed attempts to correspond with companies in this way. eg, 'I wrote an inquiry to their customer support and they responded: "Unfortunately, we don't provide the source code of our firmware to customers".' (<http://lists.gpl-violations.org/pipermail/legal/2012-February/003220.html> accessed 19 January 2013) and 'I've asked [company name] help desk for the sources and GPL notifications, and got the predictable idiotic answer....' (<http://lists.gpl-violations.org/pipermail/legal/2012-December/003418.html> accessed 19 January 2013).

[59] A Hemel, 'Reporting and Fixing License Violations' (Fsfe, 12 August 2008) <http://fsfe.org/activities/ftf/reporting-fixing-violations.en.html> accessed 3 April 2013.

relationship with the complainant, to move towards the common goal of resolving the violation.

8.5.9 Understand the complaint

If the complaint is insufficiently precise (eg, if it is not clear from the complaint which product is apparently problematic, or the nature of the perceived problem) it will not be possible to start an investigation. Asking the complainant for more detailed information not only shows that a business is taking the complaint seriously, but may cut down on wasted investigation time; in particular, where the complainant has performed a detailed compliance analysis exercise, and the complainant may be willing to share this. As with the initial engagement, the approach here is collaborative, rather than confrontational. The business is not aiming to mock or belittle the complaint, which may have been raised without a good understanding of the licence or product, but to gain support in resolving the perceived problem. An overly legalistic approach is unlikely to be well received.

8.5.10 Investigate the complaint

Armed with sufficient information, the business can now investigate the issue. Other than in the case of the more obvious or simple violations, this is likely to involve both legal and technical representatives from the business. If the business only has the binaries, and is unable to contact the supplier to be able to vet the relevant product's source code,[60] a binary analysis scan may be the only way to approach violation resolution; as with code scanning more generally, specialist technical advice may be advisable at this point. Where the complaint relates to an upstream violation, the business's supply chain management team may need to be engaged, to make contact with the upstream supply to secure its help in resolving the issue.[61] This process is likely to take time, and the business should provide regular updates to the complainant.

8.5.11 Fix any valid issues

If the outcome of the investigation is that the report is valid, work out how to fix the issue. Some problems will be more difficult than others, particularly where the business does not have the necessary information or capability to fix the problem, eg, where the problematic element has been supplied by a third party. In this situation, the

[60] It is recommended that the procurement agreement between the company and the supplier should place obligations on the supplier to assist in such an event.

[61] A Mandelbaum, 'What to do if you get "the letter" about a GPL violation' (Open Logic, 12 July 2012) <http://www.openlogic.com/wazi/bid/187994/What-to-do-if-you-get-the-letter-about-a-GPL-violation> accessed 3 April 2013.

complainant may be willing to work with the business to approach the upstream supplier, to attempt to bring them into compliance, and, through this, securing the business's compliance.

If resolving a violation for already-shipped code is not possible, the business would need to discuss options with the complainant. Where the complainant is not the copyright holder, or does not have the right to take action on behalf of the copyright holder, and the relevant rights holder(s) are not known for taking enforcement action, the business may take a more aggressive position than in the case where the complainant would be able to bring a claim of copyright infringement. In this latter case, the business might consider withdrawing the product line in question and re-engineering the code[62] but, in the first instance, good communication will be essential.

8.5.12 Communicate the outcome

Irrespective of whether the outcome of the investigation concludes that the violation report is well-founded or not, the business will need to communicate the outcome to the complainant. If the business's conclusion is that the violation report is incorrect, the complainant is likely to expect a well-reasoned and evidenced answer, explaining the outcome; as a complainant may not be fully conversant with the licence in question or the code, it may be a genuine error, and informing the complainant of the business's reasoning may help avoid future incorrect complaints, reducing unnecessary investigations by the business. If the conclusion is that the violation report was correct, the business would communicate the remedy.

If the original report was on a public list or on the company's online forum, the business might consider responding to that place, so that there is a public record of the outcome.

8.5.13 Learn from the experience

Whilst one unintentional violation may be excused, repeated violations are unlikely to be treated favourably, particularly by those active in FOSS licence enforcement. Learning from the experience is an important part of violation handling. A business might wish, eg, to strengthen contractual rights as against suppliers, and ensure that source code is managed appropriately throughout the project, or improve documentation (whether paper-based or electronic) supplied with the product. Avoiding violations is generally a straightforward activity, and the learning from

[62] Depending on the quantity of infringing code, and the complexity of the function which it performs, this may be a relatively simple activity, dropping in alternative existing FOSS code (or proprietary code if this would not lead to licence incompatibility), or else require a more complicated 'clean room' reverse engineering of functionality and rewriting of the code.

the experience of working through a violation report should help avoid violations in the future.

8.6 COMPETITION LAW AND FOSS

8.6.1 Introduction

This section examines the competition law issues affecting a business's use of FOSS.

It will become clear quickly that, whilst competition law cannot be discounted entirely, the likelihood of competition law concerns for a business using FOSS is low. To the extent that competition law concerns are apparent, their scope is likely limited to the use of copyleft licences, rather than all FOSS licences. Competition law already plays a particularly prominent role in the standards arena, and, whilst outside the scope of this chapter,[63] copyleft FOSS licences are likely to require specific attention.

On the other side of the coin, a business developing a FOSS implementation of a dominant proprietary product may be on the receiving end of anti-competitive behaviour. This section examines the case of Microsoft v Commission, commenting on the challenges faced by the Samba project in its attempt to implement a FOSS competitor to Microsoft's Active Directory.

8.6.2 A brief overview of European competition law[64]

There are two main rules on competition applying to business within Europe: anti-competitive concerted practices between businesses, and the abuse by a business of a dominant market position.

Article 101 of the Treaty on the Functioning of the European Union (TFEU) prohibits agreements between undertakings and other forms of concerted practice which may affect trade between Member States, and which, either in practice or by design, restrict or distort competition. Any such agreements are automatically void, although exceptions to this prohibition are provided for arrangements that have an overall beneficial effect for consumers, per Article 101(3).

Article 102 TFEU prohibits the abuse of a dominant position by an undertaking where it may affect trade between Member States. Such abuse includes the imposition of unfair selling prices, or other unfair trading conditions, and applying dissimilar conditions to equivalent transactions.

[63] See further ch 10.

[64] For further information on competition law see, eg, R Whish, Competition Law, 7th edn (Oxford, Oxford University Press, 2012).

8.6.3 FOSS and competition law before the courts

Arguments that use of FOSS is anticompetitive have been advanced in at least two cases, one in the US and one in Germany.

In the US, a claimant, Wallace, alleged that IBM's use of the GNU GPL was anticompetitive, on the basis that competing with Linux was 'impossible as long as Linux and its derivatives are available for free.'[65] His argument was that IBM and others were using the GPL to eliminate competition in the operating system market, on the basis that free software is a deterrent to competition; the GPL, he alleged, was a conspiracy to restrict competition, and that the GPL's insistence of a royalty-free licence amounted to predatory pricing.

The court gave short shrift to Wallace's position, for a number of reasons: that Wallace did not contend that software available under the GPL would lead to monopoly prices, that people willingly pay for software irrespective of the existence of free alternatives, and that the GPL did not pose a threat to consumer welfare in the long term. Indeed, the court took a robust position in closing its judgment: 'the GPL and open-source software,' it said, 'have nothing to fear from the antitrust laws.'

The second case took place within Europe, following enforcement action taken by gpl-violations.org against Skype,[66] alleging non-compliance with the GNU GPL in respect of Skype's distribution of an internet telephony device. One of the arguments advanced by Skype on appeal was, according to a report by the claimant, Harald Welte, 'that the GPL is violating German antitrust legislation...'.[67] As Skype subsequently withdrew its defence and accepted the judgment of the lower court, the court was not required to rule on the issue. This is clearly disappointing from an academic point of view, although Welte's report of the case suggests that the court was not inclined towards Skype's reasoning.

8.6.4 Article 101: prohibited agreements between undertakings

In *Wallace*, the claimant attempted to argue that FOSS users were engaged in a concerted practice, aiming at restricting competition. Could a similar case be brought successfully under European principles? Whilst not impossible to rule out, the short answer is that it is unlikely.

8.6.5 Is FOSS licensing a concerted practice?

The fundamental requirement of an Article 101 claim is that there is an agreement between undertakings, or some other form of concerted practice. Unlike the Article

[65] Wallace v International Business Machines Corp et al, 467 F.3d 1104 (7th Cir 2006).

[66] Welte v Skype Technologies SA (District Court of Munich, 12 July 2007, case 7 O 5245/07).

[67] Harald Welte's blog, <http://laforge.gnumonks.org/weblog/2008/05/08> accessed 3 April 2013.

102 prohibition on dominance, Article 101 aims to tackle unfair partnerships and cooperation.

For a business using third party FOSS, this is made out very easily, as the licence permitting the performance of acts otherwise restricted by copyright establishes a relationship between the licensor and the licensee.

In *Wallace*, the claimant advanced the notion that '[t]he GPL is the conspiracy'. The extension of this is that anyone involved in working with GPL'd code, whether writing it, writing about it, or otherwise supporting it, is part of a concerted practice. Although, on first view, this argument would appear weak, as the very nature of Article 101 is that it prohibits the conjoined actions of two or more companies, not one company acting in isolation, it may not be entirely without merit.

For some, the use of Free software (as opposed to the all-encompassing 'FOSS' at this point) is a considered, even ethical, decision; a business may be making a choice to be part of the social movement comprising the Free software community.[68] This would appear to be exactly what Wallace feared, a group of undertakings joined by the notion that non-Free software is undesirable. It is likely that, from an antitrust perspective, merely aligned interests and commonality of beliefs would be insufficient to be considered a concerted practice, requiring evidence of actual co-ordinated activity, but the perceived existence of a 'FOSS community' may, in itself, go some way towards supporting Wallace's viewpoint. Where the 'FOSS community' was more than a mere description of a range of individuals with common interests and objectives, and was actually a group of actors working together, such as a group or foundation working on a particular FOSS application, an allegation of concerted practice may arise if the group is insufficiently open in terms of membership and participation.[69]

8.6.6 Can a FOSS licence affect trade?

If the existence of a concerted practice, such as the existence of a copyright licence, is established, could it affect trade between Member States?

In most FOSS licensing scenarios, it is highly unlikely that this would be the case. In its guidelines on the 'effect on trade' concept, the Commission notes that an agreement is not, in principle, capable of appreciably affecting trade between Member States if:

(a) The aggregate market share of the parties on any relevant market within the Community affected by the agreement does not exceed 5 per cent, and

[68] R Stallman, 'Why Open Source misses the point of Free Software' (GNU) <http://www.gnu.org/philosophy/open-source-misses-the-point.html> accessed 3 April 2013.

[69] See further Chapter 2.

(b) In the case of horizontal agreements, the aggregate annual Community turnover of the undertakings concerned in the products covered by the agreement does not exceed 40 million euro... In the case of vertical agreements, the aggregate annual Community turnover of the supplier in the products covered by the agreement does not exceed 40 million euro. In the case of licence agreements the relevant turnover shall be the aggregate turnover of the licensees in the products incorporating the licensed technology and the licensor's own turnover in such products.[70]

The conditions are likely to be met in the vast majority of uses of FOSS. Where the conditions are not met, the businesses involved would need to consider carefully whether an impact on trade was foreseeable, taking into account the economic and legal context of the agreement.

8.6.7 Can a FOSS licence restrict or distort competition?

At the heart of the Article 101 prohibition is the requirement that the practice in question must have, either by virtue of its object or its effect, the prevention, restriction, or distortion of competition within the internal market.

Generally speaking, it would be difficult to sustain an argument that a FOSS licence was anticompetitive by object;[71] it is more likely that the claim would be that the effect of the FOSS licensing was anticompetitive.[72]

An argument often heard within the FOSS community is that, if the would-be licensee does not like the terms of the licence, they need not use the software in question. In the case of Skype, the court made a similar observation:

> If a publisher wants to publish a book of an author that wants his book only to be published in a green envelope, then that might seem odd to you, but still you will have to do it as long as you want to publish the book and have no other agreement in place.[73]

From a copyright licensing point of view, this approach would be correct. Whilst licence conditions might be odd or unappealing, without them, there is no licence to perform acts restricted by copyright, such that a licensee intending to proceed with the act has a choice either to comply with the licence conditions, or else infringe copyright. From an antitrust point of view, if the would-be licensee would be unable to compete without a licence to the software in question, and would be unable to compete by virtue of the conditions of the licence, the licence terms may well be considered to have a distortive effect on competition.

[70] 'Commission Notice: Guidelines on the effect on trade concept' (2004) 2004/C 101/07, para 52.

[71] 'Guidelines on the applicability of Article 101 of the Treaty on the Functioning of the European Union to horizontal co-operation agreements' (2011), European Commission (2011/C 11/01).

[72] S Sheppard, 'Balancing Free with IP' (2009) *IFOSS L Rev*, vol 1, Iss 2, 73.

[73] H Welte's blog (n 67).

In practice, such a claim could only be brought in respect of a subset of FOSS licences. The more permissive FOSS licences, eg, contain important but, from a competition law perspective, relatively inconsequential requirements around retention of copyright notice and disclaimer of warranty, and obligations not to infer endorsement by the original developers. A more likely target would be licences which restrict the ability for redistribution to be monetised on a for-royalty basis, although even though the likelihood of success against such a licence would still seem to be low.

In terms of royalty-free redistribution of the licensed code, an injured party would need to claim that any solution they developed which competed with the FOSS product would not succeed in the market because they could not compete with a royalty payment by a licensee of zero. As with similar issues here, the question is one of fact, and a court would need to consider whether the claimant was, in the situation at hand, effectively prevented from entering the market. This is not an issue particular to FOSS, as a group of companies looking to develop free, but not Free, software to perform a particular function would likely be in a similar position.

For a claim to be made out, the impact of the FOSS in question would need to be particularly strong in the relevant product market, such that competing with it was impossible. This may be challenging, both because the prohibition on charging a royalty does not prevent other charging methodologies for Free software—such as charging for access to a download of the software—and because, even if made available without any charge whatsoever, many users still pay for non-Free alternatives to Free software.[74]

8.6.8 Is there an exemption?

Even if all of the above could be made out, such that the use of a FOSS licence looked anticompetitive, would the provisions of Article 101(3), which provide for certain categories of agreement to be recognized as not being anticompetitive, apply to FOSS licensing?

As an issue of licensing, the starting point would be the Technology Transfer Block Exemption Regulation.[75] It is not possible to give a general statement as to whether FOSS licensing would be exempted, as the key issue in determining the applicability of an exemption under this regulation is the need for a case by case analysis, assessing each situation on its own facts.[76]

In particular, the competitive position of parties to a FOSS licensing arrangement would need to be examined, to determine whether the basic market share analysis

[74] A Gonzalez, 'Viral Contracts or Unenforceable Documents' [2004] EIPR 331.

[75] Regulation 772/2004.

[76] 'Guidelines on the application of Article 81 of the EC Treaty to technology transfer agreements' (2004) 2004/C 101/02.

is satisfied.[77] Perhaps, unlike two similar commercial products, it would need to be determined whether two pieces of FOSS, which perform substantially similar functions, were competing or complementary. The structure of licences such as the GNU GPL plays an important role here, in that, upon distribution of GPL'd code from one party to another, the recipient receives a licence from the original licensor of the work, rather than a sub-licence from the distributor.[78] In this situation, the original licensor may not know to whom they have granted licences, and is thus not in a position to undertake an analysis as to whether or not they compete with the recipient.

In terms of hardcore restrictions, which prevent the block exemption from applying,[79] the royalty-free requirements of some licences would need to be considered in the light of prohibitions on restrictions on a party's ability to determine its prices. As before, a price may be charged otherwise than by way of royalty (eg, a distribution fee), and so it may be argued that a FOSS licence sets neither a maximum nor a minimum price for the sale of products, but the reality of this argument would need to be assessed in the situation at hand.[80] Even if it were found to be setting a price, in the case of agreements between non-competing undertakings, the setting of a maximum price is likely to be in the consumers' interest.

8.6.9 Article 101 and other FOSS collaborations?

Outside the simple FOSS licensing scenario, might companies which become members of initiatives such as the Open Innovation Network ('OIN') have more to fear from a claim of unfair concerted practice?

The OIN describes itself as 'an intellectual property company that was formed to promote the Linux system by using patents to create a collaborative environment.'[81] The basic model of the OIN is that it

> acquires patents and makes them available royalty-free to any company, institution or individual that agrees not to assert its patents against the Linux System.[82]

The protection offered by OIN is potentially two-fold. First, member companies get the benefit of patent licences from other members, as well as OIN's own patents, and so can develop Linux functionality without fear of litigation from these parties. Secondly, OIN may be able to use the threat of instigating cross-claims of infringements against third parties seeking to bring claims of patent infringement against its members, based on OIN's own patent portfolio.

[77] Regulation 772/2004, Article 3.
[78] GNU GPL 2.0, s 6 and GNU GPL 3.0, s 10.
[79] Regulation 772/2004, Article 4(1).
[80] M Valimaki, 'Copyleft Licensing and EC Competition Law' (2006) *ECLR*, vol 27, no 3, 130.
[81] <http://www.openinventionnetwork.com/about.php> accessed 3 April 2013.
[82] <http://www.openinventionnetwork.com/patents.php> accessed 3 April 2013.

From the point of view of those using Linux, the OIN's activities are likely to be seen as contributing to improving the technical and economic progress of the kernel and related functionality; rather than eliminating competition, it attempts to enable anyone to make use of the Linux kernel, and thus to bring new products to market, without fear of patent litigation.

Companies which own patents which read onto the Linux kernel, and which consider the grant of a patent, and its subsequent enforcement, as a necessity to innovation and competition, may feel differently about the OIN, and a complaint under Article 101 may be a way to voice such a feeling.

8.6.10 Article 102: abuse of dominance

For most companies, the risk to business of a claim of abuse of dominance with regard to FOSS is incredibly low. Whilst it may not be appropriate to rule out the possibility of a challenge altogether, the likelihood of the existence of the necessary factual situation is remote.

For a claim of abuse of dominance to be upheld, a complainant would first need to identify the relevant product market (a standard competition law procedure, which is heavily dependent on the situation at hand), and then demonstrate that the undertaking in question was dominant in that market. Having done so, the claimant would then need to establish that the defendant's actions affected trade between Member States. If these questions of fact can be determined, the remaining question would be to assess for the purposes of this analysis whether the use of a FOSS licence amounts to abusive behaviour.

As discussed earlier, it is unlikely that the use of most permissive FOSS licences would amount to abuse, as their requirements contain little which could be considered objectionable or hard to satisfy. Again, licences which require redistribution of the covered code to be on a royalty-free basis are more likely candidates, along with licences requiring the distribution of some or all of a party's code under the same licensing terms: copyleft licences.

If a business was unable to enter the market without agreeing to license some or all of its copyright, or to forbear from litigating on infringements of its patents, that business has no real choice but to accept the terms if it wishes to compete. Access to the market in such a situation is predicated on adherence to terms that the company may find inappropriate if it wishes to proceed with a proprietary licensing model, which may bring with it the possibility of an additional claim of abuse by virtue of dissimilar treatment.

Determining whether the dominant company is responsible for the perceived abusive behaviour may pose an unusual challenge where the abuse in question supposedly relates to FOSS licensing. In a proprietary software environment, the company that is dominant is likely to be also responsible for setting the problematic licensing practice. There is a similar linear relationship in the FOSS world in terms of a company which owns its entire codebase, and chooses to release it under a FOSS licence.

However, many successful FOSS projects have more than one contributor. In particular, projects which are based on the aggregation of multiple works are likely to have numerous authors. Whilst the company exploiting FOSS commercially may have made contributions to the code, they may not have been responsible for the decision to adopt a particular licence. This may amount to another hurdle for a would-be claimant to overcome, if it is to demonstrate successfully that a dominant company's behaviour is abusive by virtue of its choice of licence.

Unlike Article 101, Article 102 has no provision exempting from its scope behaviours that are considered beneficial. However, if the company could point to an objective justification for its behaviour, or else that its behaviour produces substantial efficiencies, it may escape a violation of Article 102.[83] A business accused of anticompetitive conduct because of its use of FOSS may seek to make arguments around technical improvements as a result of the FOSS-based model, an argument commonly used in support of an 'open source' approach to FOSS, as well a to wider societal benefits of Free software, although each argument would require an evidential basis.

8.6.11 Competing with proprietary alternatives

The focus of this section has been on the potential, if unlikely, competition law implications of the use of FOSS by businesses. On the other side of the coin are the potential anticompetitive stances a supplier of proprietary software might take towards a company seeking to use a FOSS-based business model, particularly when the supplier has a dominant position in the relevant market. Unfortunately, if Microsoft v Commission[84] is representative of such actions, it is unlikely to be a route open to most businesses, even if desirable in its eventual outcome.

The case suggests that antitrust action against a company in a dominant position that refuses to make available suitable interoperability information with the effect of stifling competition might be successful. This is clearly a positive outcome for FOSS. However, the 'own initiative' investigation by the European Commission was started in February 2000[85] and the ruling on the last remaining issue of the case (excepting an unpredictable appeal)[86] was handed down by the General Court on 27 June 2012.[87]

[83] 'Guidance on the Commission's Enforcement Priorities in Applying Article 82 EC Treaty to Abusive Exclusionary Conduct by Dominant Undertakings' (2009/C 45/02), para 27.

[84] See T-201/04 and T-167/08.

[85] 'Commission Decision of 24.03.2004 relating to a proceeding under Article 82 of the EC Treaty (Case COMP/C-3/37.792 Microsoft)' (C(2004)900 final) para 5.

[86] <http://piana.eu/msft_ends> accessed 3 April 2013.

[87] Judgment in the case of Microsoft Corp v European Commission T-167/08, dated June 2012.

For a company reliant on obtaining interoperability information from a dominant competitor to be able to launch a competitive product, the protracted nature of the case is unlikely to offer much hope.

8.6.12 Conclusion on FOSS and competition law

Overall, it is unlikely that the majority of businesses will face competition law issues relating to use of FOSS. However, it is equally unlikely that FOSS usage would automatically qualify for an exemption from antitrust law, as any exemption would be based closely on the facts of a particular case.

Businesses involved in standards setting are more likely than most to encounter competition law issues around FOSS.[88] Whilst outside the scope of this section, it may be safer for a business in this situation to propose an open standards methodology, rather than open source. As an open standard can be implemented in any way in which a company sees fit, a business choosing to implement a standard through a proprietary closed source model could do so, thereby minimizing, if not eliminating, the arguments stated here around the exclusionary nature of (certain) FOSS licences.[89]

8.7 CORPORATE ACQUISITIONS AND FOSS

8.7.1 Introduction

From the point of view of an acquirer, the critical issue in most, if not all, corporate acquisitions is an understanding of what it is that is being sold. Without a clear grasp of what is for sale, it is not possible to formulate a sensible valuation of the target, nor appreciate the risks which acquisition could bring, and which might require particular handling in deal documentation.

This section approaches the issues of corporate acquisitions and FOSS predominantly from the point of view of an acquirer. It looks first at why an acquirer might want to identify FOSS usage, and then considers mechanisms for doing this. It moves on to consider contractual terms relating to FOSS in corporate acquisitions, focussing on appropriate warranties. Lastly, it looks briefly at insurance.

A section at the end deals with the situation from the point of view of a target, or a company which hopes to be a target.

[88] For an excellent introduction to the subject, see S Sheppard's 'Balancing Free with IP' (2009) IFOSS L Rev, vol 1, iss 2, 73. See also ch 10 on standardization.

[89] See, eg, K Blind et al, 'Study on the Interplay between Standards and Intellectual Property Rights (IPRs)' available at <http://ec.europa.eu/enterprise/policies/european-standards/standardisation-policy/policy-activities/intellectual-property-rights/index_en.htm> accessed 7 April 2013.

8.7.2 Knowing what you are buying, and how much it is worth

At its heart, a corporate acquisition is much like any other transaction: one party wants what another party has. Just as one might test fruit for its ripeness, the due diligence phase of a corporate acquisition is fundamental to a would-be acquirer. Without it, an acquirer cannot determine whether the outcome of the deal would give the acquirer what it wants, nor can it make an informed decision about the target's value. An understanding of a target's use of FOSS is likely to be a small part of the due diligence phase of most transactions, but, where software plays a key part in the target's value, ensuring that an acquirer has a sound understanding of the target's use of FOSS, if any, and how this would impact its plans for the target, is critical.

As 'FOSS' is a term that encompasses a considerable number of software licences,[90] some very permissive, others less so, the mere presence of FOSS is unlikely to disrupt a deal. Instead, the impact of FOSS is likely to be more nuanced, heavily dependent on the functionality of the code, its licensing, and the intended use of the code in question.

Where the acquirer plans to incorporate the target's code base into its own products and services, the acquisition would be subject to the same considerations as any other use of FOSS, and should be handled in accordance with the acquirer's FOSS strategy and policy; considerations applicable to supply chain acquisition are similarly relevant. If certain FOSS licences would cause problems, detecting whether (a) code under these licences is present in the target's code base, and (b) whether there would be an interaction of components sufficient to require source code distribution will be essential.

Where the acquirer plans to keep the target separate, it is the target's FOSS policy that is more relevant. An acquirer would be advised to ask for a copy of this, along with a list of any FOSS used by the target. In this situation, assuming that the target is complying with all relevant FOSS obligations and is operating successfully as a business, obligations which would be of concern if they were to attract to the acquirer's code base, may be of much less concern if the target is to continue to operate independently.

Irrespective of the acquirer's proposed use of the target, an acquirer is likely to have two questions: first, whether the target's use of FOSS is compliant; and secondly, whether the FOSS licences in question could impact the acquirer's patent portfolio.

In terms of licence compliance, a failure to comply with licensing requirements may be expensive to fix. In the worst case scenario, an acquirer may not be able

[90] The Open Source Initiative currently lists 69 licences as complying with its Open Source Definition: <http://opensource.org/licenses> accessed 3 April 2013.

to use the code it has purchased without substantial reengineering,[91] potentially also requiring stock to be withdrawn. Given the potential for cost, assessing compliance will be a key part of any FOSS due diligence. The mechanics of doing this are discussed above, in the context of product development. If a violation is detected, the acquirer may wish to make the deal conditional on the target fixing the violation (a contractual modification, although this approach may be challenging in a fast-moving acquisition environment), or else reducing the purchase price to reflect the potential financial implications for the acquirer in fixing the violation (a price modification).

8.7.3 Patent considerations

In terms of patents, some FOSS licences include clauses which terminate a licensee's licence to the work in question if the licensee institutes patent infringement litigation; these are generally known are 'patent retaliation' clauses.[92] The critical question is whether, by virtue of acquiring the target, the acquirer is prevented from taking action for patent infringement.

The risk for an acquirer is that, if the target is reliant on a particular FOSS component governed by a licence with a patent retaliation clause, the acquirer may either need to refrain from initiating patent litigation against others, or else have an alternative component in place for the target to use, to ensure business continuity once litigation is filed.

The Common Development and Distribution License version 1, eg, provides that:

> If You assert a patent infringement claim (excluding declaratory judgment actions) against Initial Developer or a Contributor (the Initial Developer or Contributor against whom You assert such claim is referred to as Participant) alleging that the Participant Software (meaning the Contributor Version where the Participant is a Contributor or the Original Software where the Participant is the Initial Developer) directly or indirectly infringes any patent, then any and all rights granted directly or indirectly to You by such Participant, the Initial Developer (if the Initial Developer is not the Participant) and all Contributors under Sections 2.1 and/or 2.2 of this License shall, upon 60 days notice from Participant terminate prospectively and automatically at the expiration of such 60 day notice period, unless if within such 60 day period You withdraw Your claim with respect to the Participant Software against such Participant either unilaterally or pursuant to a written agreement with Participant.[93]

Likewise, the Mozilla Public License version 2:

> If You initiate litigation against any entity by asserting a patent infringement claim (excluding declaratory judgment actions, counter-claims, and cross-claims) alleging

[91] See 8.5.11. [92] See further Chapters 5 and 6. [93] At s 6.2.

> that a Contributor Version directly or indirectly infringes any patent, then the rights granted to You by any and all Contributors for the Covered Software under Section 2.1 of this License shall terminate.[94]

The Apache License, version 2.0 contains language similar to that of the MPL version 2, with an important difference in terms of counter- and cross-claims; according to the terms of the Apache License 2.0, using patents in these manners triggers licence termination,[95] and so may be considered as having a stronger retaliation provision than the MPL version 2.

Under the preceding licences, instituting patent infringement action against a third party for an infringement in the relevant licensed code terminates, either immediately or after a period of grace to withdraw the claim, the claimant's licence to use the code in question. If an acquirer intends to continue to use the licensed code, the cost of doing so may be effectively curtailing its right to sue certain infringing parties.

The Apple Public Source License, version 2.0, includes an even stronger form of patent retaliation clause. The APSL's scope is both broader and narrower: a litigating party's licence automatically terminates:

> if You, at any time during the term of this License, commence an action for patent infringement against Apple; provided that Apple did not first commence an action for patent infringement against You in that instance.[96]

The clause is narrower, as it only prevents patent litigation against Apple, and yet broader, as it does not relate only to infringements in the licensed code, than those stated. An acquirer who might have a right of action against Apple, might think it desirable to avoid adopting code under the APSL if it wishes to pursue infringement action.

Although proposed for GNU GPL 3.0, patent retaliation language does not appear in the final version; Stallman has commented that some of the proposed language 'didn't seem like it would be terribly effective', whilst another part related to activities which 'nobody's actually doing'.[97] Similarly, there is no retaliation language in GNU GPL 2.0. The FSF notes, however, that the absence of patent-specific language should not be taken as indicating that patent infringement action is considered acceptable:

> [A]nyone considering enforcing their patents aggressively is an enemy of the community, and we will defend ourselves against such an attack.[98]

[94] At s 5.2. [95] Apache Public License, version 2.0, cl 3.

[96] Apple Public Source License, version 2.0, cl 12.1(c).

[97] From the transcript of Richard Stallman's talk on GNU GPLv3 in Brussels, 1 April 2007: <http://fsfe.org/campaigns/gplv3/brussels-rms-transcript.en.html#retaliation> accessed 3 April 2013.

[98] Excerpt from the FSF's FAQs on the GPL: <http://www.gnu.org/licenses/gpl-faq.html#v2OrLaterPatentLicense> accessed 3 April 2013.

On first sight, it may be tempting to hold patents in one company and license FOSS into another company in the group, to avoid the reach of patent retaliation clauses. By separating the two, the company which licenses the FOSS is not the one which institutes litigation. To combat this, the licences include language attempting to bring within their scope any entity that controls, is controlled by, or is under common control with the licensee. If use of the FOSS in question forms an important part of the reason for the acquirer's interest (eg, it forms a core part of the software used by the target for making money), the acquirer may need to decide whether the benefit from ongoing use of the FOSS outweighs the harm of refraining from instituting patent infringement litigation.

In making that decision, the acquirer should consider the wider impact of taking infringement action against other users of FOSS. In particular, it may be difficult for a company to enforce patents against core Linux functionality without a counterclaim of infringement from a defensive patent pool such as the Open Innovation Network, discussed earlier.

If the reality is that the business is unlikely to litigate in respect of an infringement in a FOSS component which it needs to use, the risk associated with a patent retaliation clause is likely to be low, although a clause as wide as that in the Apple Public Source License may remain troubling.

8.7.4 Contractual protections

Assuming that due diligence is completed successfully, and the acquirer feels able to value the target and make an offer, the deal will proceed to a documentary phase. The precise nature of wording relating to FOSS will depend on what is important to the acquirer, and the state of FOSS usage by the target.

Whilst some standard form agreements will continue to include wording that the target does not use FOSS code, this is unlikely to be appropriate in the situations described here, where the target clearly does use FOSS. However, although a warranty that there is no FOSS in the target would be inappropriate, an acquirer will still want to manage its risk by ensuring that there is no undeclared use of FOSS in a target.

One approach to achieving this is to list all FOSS usage by the target in a schedule, setting out the name of the component and its version, the relevant licence and a short description on how it is used. The target warrants that, other than as declared in this schedule, there is no use of FOSS.

The parties may agree to limit this warranty to use of FOSS in customer-facing products or services, rather than in internal systems. It is unlikely to be of material risk whether the target uses Mozilla's Thunderbird as an email client, eg, and the time and resource cost of listing FOSS use across all a target's systems may be too great for the deal to bear.

Where a target is unable to list all FOSS usage, it may be appropriate to consider a warranty that the target does not use FOSS covered by certain licences considered problematic by the acquirer. For example, if the acquirer intends to use the target's technology as a web service, obligations to make available source code of that web service may not suit the acquirer's business model, and so code licensed under the Affero GPL or other similar licences would need to be avoided. However, if a company is unable to list its use of FOSS it may not be in a good position to state the licences covering its code base, and, if not already performed, a code scan may be considered as a way of mitigating this risk.

In addition to a warranty of 'no undeclared use of FOSS,' an acquirer is likely to seek a warranty that all use of FOSS complies with licence requirements. This may form part of a wider, more-encompassing warranty of non-infringement of copyright but, if there is a possibility that FOSS licences might be interpreted as contracts in the relevant jurisdiction,[99] a more specific warranty would be advisable. As with non-infringement or non-breach warranties generally, there is likely to be debate around whether the scope of a 'no FOSS violation' warranty should be limited to knowing violations.

It may be possible for an acquirer to obtain an insurance policy to deal with some of the risks associated with purchasing a company which uses FOSS, although the number of brokers offering this insurance is limited. Open Source Risk Management ('OSRM') offers a policy with coverage of up to $10 million for certain loss of profits and valuation impairment 'resulting from the requirement to distribute certain code or products, in compliance with an Open Source software license.'[100] Obtaining the policy is dependent on passing a 'risk audit,' for which the company seeking the policy must pay OSRM a non-refundable fee in advance. As with the purchase of any insurance policy, a company considering such a policy would want to consider the likelihood of any of the risks covered by the policy materializing, the cost of remediating any harm suffered, and contrast this with the cost in acquiring the policy, the coverage of the policy, and the nature of any exclusions and limitations.

8.7.5 From the viewpoint of a company using FOSS

The main focus of this section has been the impact of FOSS on the acquirer in a corporate acquisition situation. Although more limited in scope, there are a number of considerations for potential targets too.

A company that hopes to be acquired would be advised to maintain a clear, documented position on how it uses FOSS in its products and services. By implementing

[99] See further ch 3.

[100] 'Open Source Compliance Representation and Warranty Insurance data sheet' (OSRM) <http://www.osriskmanagement.com/downloads/OSRM_PROTECT_Jan07.pdf> accessed 3 April 2013.

a FOSS strategy and policy, and by putting in place compliance mechanisms such as a code management system, the additional administrative burden of doing this is minimal, and would lead to a target being able to present in a straightforward documented manner exactly what FOSS it uses where, against which an acquirer could compare the output of a code scan.

Ensuring compliance with FOSS licensing terms, and avoiding violations, is good practice for any company using FOSS but, for a potential target, it is particularly important, as distributing a product which infringes copyright is likely to be a significant detracting factor for a would-be acquirer. If a violation is detected, a documented path to fix is better than no fix (although, clearly, not as good as an actual fix) as it means that an acquirer can more easily estimate the amount of work needed to bring about compliance, and to assess the risk of non-compliance.

In considering the appropriateness of warranties relating to FOSS, a target will want to ensure it is not taking responsibility for things that are outside its control. In particular, a company using FOSS is unlikely to be in a position to warrant that there are no underlying infringements in third party FOSS code which is used, either from the point of view of being within the scope of a third party patent claim, or else that the code does not infringe third party copyright. Whilst this may be an acceptable risk in respect of proprietary software licensed on terms which back the risk off with the supplier, most FOSS licences will exclude all liability for such matters, and so a business is unlikely to have an upstream remedy. It is more reasonable, however, for a company to warrant that it is compliant with all stated licence terms, and that its overall solution (as opposed to any of the underlying third party components) does not infringe third party patent claims, as a company can take steps to check this more readily.

In terms of code created by the company, disclaiming liability for copyright infringement would be difficult to justify; but indicating that no patent clearance searching has been done such that it is not possible to warrant no infringement of third party patent claims is more reasonable.

8.8 CONCLUDING THOUGHTS

One of the problems of any detailed examination of a subject is the risk of losing sight of the bigger picture. This chapter concludes by bringing together strands from the preceding discussion into two key points.

First, by starting with a clear understanding of what a business intends to achieve, constructing a set of rules around use of FOSS becomes a relatively simple task.

Answering the simple question 'We use FOSS to...' provides a focal point for implementing measures designed to make strategic use of FOSS, rather than relying on ad hoc decision making, which, in turn, reduces risk and complexity.

Secondly, FOSS need not be a confusing or concerning area for lawyers advising businesses.

It is the author's experience that many lawyers, even those well versed in copyright or commercial law, express concerns about advising on FOSS matters. Whilst understanding the legal impact of FOSS in business may seem a daunting task, perhaps due to the often technical nature of the subject matter and its patois, the second conclusion to draw is that FOSS may not be such a special case after all:

- In a corporate acquisition, the key issue is understanding what is being sold, to be able to value it; in a procurement situation, it is understanding what is being bought.
- Where a company is developing a product or service, it will want to understand and comply with its suppliers' licensing requirements, to avoid infringement.
- Businesses with dominant market positions, or working with other companies in ways which may impede competition, will need to consider competition law implications of their behaviours.

These considerations will be business as usual for most lawyers; the involvement of FOSS may add nuances to these, which this chapter explores, but does not demand a fundamentally new approach.

Part III

PUBLIC POLICY ISSUES

9

COPYLEFT IN THE CLOUD

Jakub Menčl and W Kuan Hon

Open Source and Free Software has been significant in cloud computing's development. Its importance is unlikely to diminish as cloud use evolves further. Section 9.1 outlines cloud computing and key areas where open source software is employed in the cloud. The remaining sections analyse the main issues with running open source applications in the cloud.

9.1 CLOUD COMPUTING: INTRODUCTION

Cloud computing is increasing in profile and adoption. Analyst Gartner considers cloud to be an innovative, disruptive force which, with other forces like mobile, is revolutionizing business and technology.[1]

[1] <http://www.gartner.com/it/page.jsp?id=2209615> accessed 10 April 2013.

9.1.1 Cloud computing—definitions and model

In brief, cloud computing involves use of computing resources over a network, typically the internet, scalable up or down with user need. This means the relevant resource may be used, typically through a simple web browser, from any location where a suitable network connection is available, including via smartphones, tablets and other mobile devices as well as desktop or laptop computers. The end user device need not be powerful, it may be a 'thin client', because the substantive computing work is performed on remote servers and the outcome transmitted over the network to the device. Generally, this kind of flexible use is made possible by the shared use of pooled resources accessed over the internet.

The detailed definition of cloud computing most popularly cited is from the US National Institute of Standards and Technology ('NIST')[2] but we shall use the definition by the Cloud Legal Project at Queen Mary, University of London,[3] which defines cloud computing in a way which seeks to be neutral regarding different aspects of the cloud computing model:[4]

- Cloud computing provides flexible, location-independent access to computing resources that are quickly and seamlessly allocated or released in response to demand.
- Services (especially infrastructure) are abstracted and typically virtualised, generally being allocated from a pool shared as a fungible resource with other customers.
- Charging, where present,[5] is commonly[6] on an access basis, often in proportion to the resources used.

This definition aims to highlight aspects of cloud computing that are central to the concept, whilst distinguishing (via qualifiers such as 'typically' or 'generally') those which are common, but neither essential nor ubiquitous.

NIST has also defined cloud deployment models. With private cloud, the infrastructure is for the exclusive use of one organization; with community cloud, a group of organizations from a community with common interests (eg financial services); while public cloud is for open use by the general public. Different entities may own, manage and operate the infrastructure, which may exist on or off the user's premises (except that public cloud would be off-premise). Hybrid cloud involves distinct cloud

[2] P Mell and T Grance, *The NIST Definition of Cloud Computing, Special Publication 800-145* (US National Institute of Standards and Technology, 2011).

[3] <http://www.cloudlegal.ccls.qmul.ac.uk/> accessed 10 April 2013.

[4] See eg S Bradshaw, C Millard and I Walden, 'Contracts for clouds: comparison and analysis of the terms and conditions of cloud computing services' (2011) 19(3) *Int J Law Info Tech* 187.

[5] Many consumer services are free, advertising-funded services.

[6] Some services are charged per month per user, etc. WK Hon, C Millard and I Walden, 'Negotiating Cloud Contracts—Looking at Clouds from Both Sides Now' (2012) 16 *Stan Tech L Rev* 9.

infrastructures working together, eg private cloud 'bursting' to public cloud when extra capacity is needed.

NIST's models for cloud services are also commonly cited. In brief, with Software as a Service ('SaaS'), the resource used over a network comprises application software, installed and run on remote servers instead of on the user's device. Examples include webmail eg Yahoo! Mail, storage services like Dropbox, social networking services like Facebook, customer relationship management eg Salesforce, and office applications such as Google Apps and Microsoft Office 365.

With Infrastructure as a Service ('IaaS'), the computing resources used over a network effectively comprise a quota of 'raw' hardware—servers, storage devices, networking equipment, etc—which users are generally free to manage and use as they wish. Amazon Web Services IaaS, including EC2 for processing and S3 for storage, was the first, and probably still best known, IaaS service. Others include Rackspace. IaaS customers must manage the provided resources themselves, and therefore need some technical expertise.

With Platform as a Service ('PaaS'), the resources comprise an integrated platform for developing and hosting software applications, deployed from user-provided programming code. The application may be run over a network, typically the internet. PaaS services may incorporate databases and web servers. Examples are Google App Engine and Microsoft Windows Azure. PaaS is higher level than IaaS: users may concentrate on programming code, and need not manage virtual servers and other resources, unlike with IaaS. However, customers are restricted to the programming languages and frameworks, eg Java, supported by the particular PaaS service; some support more languages than others.

IaaS and PaaS may be used to host any application the user chooses, whether for internal use or to offer SaaS services to external customers. Some users employ IaaS or PaaS simply to host websites.[7]

9.1.2 Cloud technologies

IaaS may use 'virtual machines' ('VMs'). Virtualization technology enables a physical server to 'host', within its memory, multiple VMs. Different users may create ('instantiate') and use their own VMs in the same physical server, 'bringing down' their VMs when no longer needed. Each VM operates independently, emulating a physical computer with its own operating system and application or other software. VMs need not run the same operating system or software, even when sharing the same physical equipment. Separation between tenants (and their data) from other tenants is

[7] eg Google App Engine hosted the 2011 UK Royal Wedding website <http://www.officialroyalwedding2011.org/> while, perhaps more famously, Wikileaks was hosted on Amazon Web Services for a time before Amazon chose to take the site down <http://aws.amazon.com/message/65348/>.

enforced by virtualization software rather than through different tenants using different hardware, ie separation is logical rather than physical. Therefore, multiple 'tenants' may use the same physical infrastructure simultaneously (multi-tenancy). This promotes efficient resource utilization and enables economies of scale.

Virtualization software may be closed source, such as Microsoft Hyper-V and VMWare ESX; or open source, such as KVM, Xen and VirtualBox. Amazon Web Services' IaaS cloud computing service is based on Amazon's own modification of Xen. Google's Compute Engine IaaS, launched in mid-2012, uses KVM. Formats for VM files or machine images, used to create and boot VMs, may again be closed or based on open standards, eg OVF.[8] The operating system installed within a VM may itself also be closed or open source, eg Windows or Linux; the relevant operating system's licence may or may not permit or limit its installation on VMs (instead of directly on physical servers). Similarly, users are free to choose which applications or other software to install and run within their VMs, again subject to their licences allowing their use within VMs. Such software may be closed or open source, and may include database systems as well as end user applications.

To manage scalable use of a shared, distributed pool of resources, including instantiating and terminating VMs in physical servers that have spare capacity, and managing shared distributed storage and networking resources, software 'cloud platforms'[9] or 'cloud operating systems' have developed. These 'cloud platforms' may be closed source, eg Amazon's, or open source, eg Eucalyptus,[10] OpenStack,[11] OpenNebula[12] and CloudStack.[13] Different platforms support different virtualization technologies eg VMWare, Xen. Indeed, open source Eucalyptus supports Amazon APIs and machine images, and Amazon agreed in early 2012 to support Eucalyptus's compatibility with Amazon so that applications run on Eucalyptus can be moved to Amazon Web Services and vice versa.[14]

PaaS cloud platforms, ie software that may be installed and used to provide PaaS, are also available, such as Windows Azure and VMWare's open source Cloud Foundry.[15] Some IaaS and PaaS platforms are only usable as hosted services, such as Google App Engine, whereas others may be installed on customers' own infrastructure, eg Azure

[8] <http://dmtf.org/standards/ovf> accessed 10 April 2013.

[9] 'Platform' is used here in a broad sense, and not in the same sense as in 'Platform as a Service'.

[10] Licensed under GNU GPLv3 <http://www.eucalyptus.com/licenses/eucalyptus-software-license-agreement>—although Euca2ools tools are licensed under BSD—<http://www.eucalyptus.com/licenses/euca2ools-software-license-agreement> accessed 10 April 2013.

[11] Licensed under Apache 2.0 <http://www.openstack.org/projects/openstack-faq/> accessed 10 April 2013.

[12] <http://opennebula.org/> using Apache 2.0 <http://opennebula.org/about:faq#how_is_the_software_licensed> accessed 10 April 2013.

[13] Acquired by Citrix in mid-2011, now an incubating Apache project <http://incubator.apache.org/cloudstack/> accessed 10 April 2013.

[14] <http://www.eucalyptus.com/news/amazon-web-services-and-eucalyptus-partner> also supports Amazon APIs. However, OpenStack will not: <http://gigaom.com/cloud/the-amazon-api-battle-for-the-cloud-rages-on/> accessed 10 April 2013.

[15] Licensed under Apache 2.0 <https://github.com/cloudfoundry/vcap/blob/master/LICENSE> accessed 10 April 2013.

and Cloud Foundry. Hardware manufacturers may even sell servers with cloud platform software pre-installed.[16] While most SaaS applications are hosted services, some may be licensed for internal use or to offer as a service to the licensee's customers, eg Microsoft Office 365.

Some forms of cloud computing do not use VMs, but instead involve the conceptual reverse: instead of multiple VMs running in a single physical server, multiple physical computers are combined to work in parallel as a single supercomputer. Processing operations are 'mapped' or divided up amongst different physical servers for processing, and the results of sub-operations are 'reduced' (brought back together). This facilitates efficient processing of huge volumes of data. Such a system is also designed to be resilient, tolerant to the failure of individual hardware components, with the same sub-operation being performed on multiple servers so that the operation will complete even if a server fails. Therefore relatively low-cost, easily-replaceable commodity machines can be used, eg Linux servers. Based on Google's published details of such a framework, previously developed for its own use (MapReduce), a similar open source platform for distributed computing was developed, called Hadoop.[17] Hadoop, now an Apache Software Foundation ('ASF') project, is licensed under Apache v 2.[18] Written in Java, Hadoop uses 'clusters' of 'nodes' or servers, fragmenting data across nodes automatically and also replicating data automatically, trying to use different racks for fault-tolerance.

Many internet firms use Hadoop both internally and to provide cloud services to customers, such as eBay, Facebook and Yahoo!. While Hadoop does not require VMs, it can run on VMs instead of directly on physical machines; eg, Amazon offers 'Hadoop as a service', supporting its own version of Hadoop hosted in VMs on its IaaS service. Hadoop has spawned an ecosystem of related software. Facebook developed and open sourced Hive,[19] a higher level data warehouse infrastructure/analytics system that translates SQL, the language used to query traditional relational databases, to Hadoop MapReduce. Eschewing Hive, Yahoo! created and open sourced its own Hadoop programming query language called Pig, for analysing big data.[20] Apache

[16] eg Dell offers Canonical's cloud platform (Ubuntu Enterprise Cloud with the open source Eucalyptus platform) on Dell-manufactured servers.

[17] For a history of Hadoop see <http://www.wired.com/wiredenterprise/2011/10/how-yahoo-spawned-hadoop/>. Also see <http://www.theregister.co.uk/2010/04/27/google_licenses_mapreduce_patent_to_hadoop/> accessed 10 April 2013.

[18] <http://projects.apache.org/projects/hadoop.html> accessed 10 April 2013.

[19] <http://hive.apache.org/> licensed under Apache 2.0 <http://projects.apache.org/projects/hive.html>. See also <https://www.facebook.com/note.php?note_id=89508453919> and A Thusoo, JS Sarma, N Jain, Zheng Shao, P Chakka, Ning Zhang; S Antony, Hao Liu, R Murthy, 'Hive—a petabyte scale data warehouse using Hadoop', 2010 IEEE 26th International Conference on Data Engineering (ICDE), 996–1005, 1–6 March 2010, Long Beach USA<http://ieeexplore.ieee.org/stamp/stamp.jsp?tp=&arnumber=5447738&isnumber=5447611> accessed 10 April 2013.

[20] <http://pig.apache.org/> licensed under Apache 2.0—<http://projects.apache.org/projects/pig.html>. C Olston, B Reed, U Srivastava, R Kumar and Andrew Tomkins (2008), 'Pig latin: a not-so-foreign language for data processing.' In Proceedings of the 2008 ACM SIGMOD International Conference on Management of Data (SIGMOD '08). ACM, New York, USA, 1099–110. DOI=10.1145/1376616.1376726 <http://doi.acm.org/10.1145/1376616.1376726> accessed 10 April 2013.

Cassandra,[21] another Java application, is an increasingly popular open source distributed database management system which supports Hadoop, handling 'big data' analytics with high availability and failure tolerance using commodity hardware. Cassandra was developed and open-sourced by Facebook,[22] who has since moved to HBase, also open source.[23] Cassandra may also be hosted on Amazon EC2.[24] Some other distributed databases used in cloud are open source, such as MongoDB,[25] used by Twitter and, running on Amazon EC2, by location-based social media service FourSquare.[26]

9.1.3 Cloud supply chains

A key point about cloud computing is that it 'abstracts' IT resources away from users, who, in order to use those resources, need not be concerned, at least at a technological level,[27] with details of what underlying physical resources are used, how or where they are located. However, this also means that users may not be aware of such details. In cloud computing, users primarily procure services, not software licences, although the service may include rights to run software owned by the provider (or licensed by it from the rights owner for users to run).

The cloud computing supply chain can be complex—many hardware and software components may be used for a single cloud service, with different suppliers and owners, and chains or layers of services, including multiple cloud services, are possible. For example, an SaaS service may use hardware and software infrastructure controlled by the SaaS provider, or it may be built on top of another provider's IaaS or PaaS service, with the SaaS provider installing its own application software or third party application software on the IaaS or PaaS infrastructure. Indeed, PaaS platforms have been created using IaaS infrastructure,[28] and SaaS may be layered on such PaaS too. Application software installed by a provider may again be open

[21] <http://cassandra.apache.org> licensed under Apache 2.0 <http://projects.apache.org/projects/cassandra.html> accessed 10 April 2013.

[22] <http://nosql.mypopescu.com/post/407159447/cassandra-twitter-an-interview-with-ryan-king> accessed 10 April 2013.

[23] <http://www.facebook.com/notes/facebook-engineering/the-underlying-technology-of-messages/454991608919>. HBase <http://hbase.apache.org/> is also licensed under Apache 2.0 <http://projects.apache.org/projects/hbase.html> accessed 10 April 2013.

[24] eg <http://techblog.netflix.com/2011/11/benchmarking-cassandra-scalability-on.html> accessed 10 April 2013.

[25] <http://www.mongodb.org/>—database licensed under the Free Software Foundation's GNU AGPL v 3.0, and drivers under Apache 2.0—<http://www.mongodb.org/display/DOCS/Licensing> accessed 10 April 2013.

[26] <http://engineering.foursquare.com/2011/12/21/show-and-tell-mongodb-at-foursquare/> and <http://www.10gen.com/customers/foursquare> accessed 10 April 2013.

[27] There may, however, be issues from a legal or regulatory perspective, eg physical location of personal data is still a compliance concern. WK Hon and C Millard, 'Data Export in Cloud Computing—How can Personal Data be Transferred Outside the EEA? The Cloud of Unknowing, Part 4' (2012) 9:1 *SCRIPTed* 25 <http://script-ed.org/?p=324> accessed 10 April 2013.

[28] Such as Engine Yard <http://www.engineyard.com/> for Ruby on Rails and PHP developers accessed 10 April 2013.

or closed source. Therefore, in considering the position regarding software used for or running in the cloud, it is important to be clear as to the specific role, structure and usage concerned. For example, SaaS service Dropbox employs Amazon Web Services IaaS behind the scenes to provide SaaS storage services to Dropbox's customers. From Dropbox's perspective, it is a business user of Amazon's IaaS service. From the viewpoint of Dropbox's storage customers, they are users of Dropbox's SaaS service.

9.1.4 Summary

Much software used to provide and manage cloud computing platforms is open source, and many cloud computing services include or use open source components.

Software installed and run on cloud computing services, eg code deployed on PaaS, or applications installed in VMs with IaaS, may also be open source.

In many ways, it may be said that open source software has helped to fuel the development and use of cloud computing, from Linux servers running Hadoop, Xen VMs used for IaaS, and fully-fledged cloud platforms like OpenStack, to application software that may be installed in the cloud, such as open source database applications used to process 'big data'.

9.2 COPYLEFT

As the preceding sections have shown, many cloud computing components are, or are based on, open source software, from virtualization software, and operating systems installed or even pre-installed by providers within VMs, to application software that is installed and run on cloud infrastructure/platforms.

Copyleft is the term coined by the authors of the GNU General Public License ('GPL')[29] to describe its most characteristic feature—an obligation imposed on anyone who redistributes software licensed under the GPL, with or without changes to the software's code, to pass along the freedom to further copy and change it.[30] This copyleft obligation is sometimes called the 'reciprocity obligation'.[31] The most prominent and best known[32] copyleft licence is the GNU General Public Licence, known as GPL, which was created and promoted by the Free Software Foundation

[29] LE Rosen, *Open Source Licensing: Software Freedom and Intellectual Property Law*, 2nd edn (New Jersey, Prentice Hall Professional Technical Reference, 2005) 105.

[30] FSF, '*What Is Copyleft?*' <http://www.gnu.org/copyleft/copyleft.en.html> accessed 31 December 2012.

[31] The term 'reciprocity obligation' is sometimes used as equivalent to 'copyleft obligation', see Rosen (n 29) 106.

[32] Other examples of copyleft licences are Common Public Attribution Licence, European Union Public Licence and Mozilla Public Licence.

('FSF') and Richard Stallman, founder of FSF. Although the FSF published GPL version 3 on 29 June 2007,[33] GPL version 2 ('GPLv2') is still used for far more projects than the newer version 3,[34] and there are reasons to believe GPLv2 will remain the most popular Free Software licence at least in the near future.[35] Accordingly, this chapter will use GPL versions 2 and 3 as example of copyleft licences for the purpose of analysis.

9.2.1 GNU General Public License version 2

Section 2(b) condition is what makes GPLv2 a copyleft licence, and it is one of the most important provisions of GPLv2.[36] It provides for a bargain which is at the core of all copyleft licences: a licensee may modify the licensed software on condition that any works derived from the original software must be distributed under the same licence.[37] However, using the term 'derivative work' when discussing the copyleft obligation in section 2 of GPLv2 is problematic, for two main reasons.

The first important reason, applicable not only to GPLv2 but to many other Free Software or Open Source licences, is that the licence does not explicitly provide for its governing law. Although it seems probable that when GPLv2's drafters referred to 'any derivative work under copyright law' they envisaged the US copyright law definition,[38] this may be irrelevant in situations where the licensor-licensee relationship is governed, due to operation of applicable conflict of laws provisions, by a national law which uses the term with a different meaning.[39]

The second and main reason is that the GPLv2 section 2(b) copyleft provision does not use the term 'derivative work', or even 'work based on the Program'.[40] Instead, it refers to 'work... that in whole or in part contains or is derived from the Program or any part thereof'. This wording, which is similar but not identical to the wording used in the definition of 'work based on the Program', suggests that the scope of section 2(b) includes not only 'derivative works' of the original program, but also any works that 'contain' the original program or any part thereof, even when such works cannot be considered 'derivative works' of the original program in the strict copyright law sense. GPLv2 section 2 confirms that obligations under that section were intended to apply to a broader group of works than merely derivative works of the original program, by explicitly stating that 'the intent is to exercise the right

[33] FSF, *GNU GPL*, v3 <http://www.gnu.org/licenses/gpl.html> accessed 25 November 2012.

[34] On 31 December 2012, the Sourceforge.net database of Open Source and Free Software projects listed 14,670 GPLv3-licensed projects versus 115,995 GPLv2-licensed projects. Dice Holdings Inc., <http://sourceforge.net/directory/> accessed 31 December 2012.

[35] A Katz 'GPL—the Linking Debate' (2007) *Computers and Law*, vol 18, issue 3, 13.

[36] AM St Laurent, *Understanding Open Source and Free Software Licensing* (Sebastopol, O'Reilly Media, Inc, 2004) 39. See n 33.

[37] Rosen (n 29) 103; St Laurent (n 36) 39.

[38] 17 USC para 101.

[39] See ch 3.

[40] See ch 3.

to control the distribution of derivative *or collective* works based on the Program' (emphasis added).[41]

However, in copyright law there are fundamental differences between derivative works and collective works.[42] US copyright law defines a collective work as

> a work, such as a periodical issue, anthology, or encyclopaedia, in which a number of contributions, constituting separate and independent works in themselves, are assembled into a collective whole.[43]

A derivative work is defined as

> a work based upon one or more preexisting works, such as a translation... abridgment, condensation, or any other form in which a work may be recast, transformed, or adapted. A work consisting of editorial revisions, annotations, elaborations, or other modifications, which, as a whole, represent an original work of authorship, is a 'derivative work'.[44]

Both derivative works and collective works, ie works formed by collecting and assembling pre-existing materials or data that are selected, coordinated, or arranged in such a way that the resulting work as a whole constitutes an original work of authorship,[45] are subject to copyright in their own right, separate from and independent of any copyright in the pre-existing material.[46]

The copyright law of England and Wales differentiates between those two types of works also. A collective work is defined as a work of joint authorship or a work in which there are distinct contributions by different authors or in which works or parts of works of different authors are incorporated.[47] The Copyright, Designs and Patent Act 1988 uses the term 'adaptation' instead of 'derivative work'. Adaptation is defined, in relation to computer programs, to mean an arrangement or altered version of the program or a translation of it.[48]

There are two main differences between derivative works and collective works. The first difference is factual, not legal, and lies in the fact that a computer program

[41] FSF, *GNU GPL*. [42] Rosen (n 29) 114. [43] 17 USC para 101. [44] 17 USC para 101.

[45] 17 USC para 101: A 'compilation' is a work formed by the collection and assembling of preexisting materials or of data that are selected, coordinated, or arranged in such a way that the resulting work as a whole constitutes an original work of authorship. The term 'compilation' includes collective works.

[46] 17 USC para 103:

(a) The subject matter of copyright as specified by section 102 includes compilations and derivative works, but protection for a work employing preexisting material in which copyright subsists does not extend to any part of the work in which such material has been used unlawfully.

(b) The copyright in a compilation or derivative work extends only to the material contributed by the author of such work, as distinguished from the preexisting material employed in the work, and does not imply any exclusive right in the preexisting material. The copyright in such work is independent of, and does not affect or enlarge the scope, duration, ownership, or subsistence of, any copyright protection in the preexisting material.

[47] Copyright, Designs and Patent Act ('CDPA') 1988, s 178. [48] CDPA 1988, s 21(3)(ab).

(eg module) can be incorporated into a collective work, eg an interconnected set of modules, without being modified. The second difference is that, under legal regimes relating to derivative and collective works, while creating a derivative work without permission of the holder of copyright in the original work would infringe copyright in the original work both under US and English copyright law,[49] merely *incorporating* an original work into a collective work does not require any permission beyond permission to copy the work, and, given such permission, would not infringe copyright in the original work.

These differences between derivative and collective works play a very important role in determining the scope of section 2 of GPLv2. We consider that the correct interpretation is that, while the copyleft obligation applies to any distribution of a modified program which is governed by section 2 of the licence, it does not apply in the situation covered by section 1, which permits licensees to copy and distribute verbatim copies of the original program, and, in our view, permits licensees to incorporate the original program unmodified into a collective work. Therefore, whenever a GPLv2-licensed program is incorporated into a larger program *without* being modified, so that it forms part of a collective work rather than constituting a derivative work, section 1 permits such incorporation, but the section 2(b) copyleft obligation does *not* apply, meaning that all other parts of the collective work can be distributed under any terms and conditions, whatever the degree of interdependence of the programs forming such collective work or the importance of the GPL'd program to the collective whole.[50] This conclusion applies particularly where a program links to a GPLv2-licensed library licensed, whether statically or dynamically,[51] despite the firm stance of the FSF, Richard Stallman and others that any program linking to a GPLv2-licensed library must itself be released under GPLv2.[52][53]

Section 2's first line refers to 'thus forming a work based on a Program' (whose definition includes 'a work containing a Program'), and section 2(b) refers to work that 'contains' the Program. Could it therefore be said that a collective work incorporating the unmodified Program 'contains' the Program, and so is caught by the section 2(b) copyleft obligation? We argue not; again, only section 1 is relevant there (giving permission to copy the Program, which we consider includes incorporating an unmodified copy into a larger collective work). Because such verbatim incorporation does not 'modify' the Program, and section 2 only applies upon a modification of the Program, in our view section 2 as drafted (including the section 2(b) condition) does not apply at all to verbatim incorporation into a larger work, despite the drafters' likely intentions.[54]

[49] ie 17 USC para 106 and CDPA 1988, s 16(1)(e). [50] Rosen (n 29) 120.
[51] For a clear and concise explanation of static and dynamic linking see eg Katz (n 35) 13.
[52] See FSF, *Frequently Asked Questions about the GNU Licenses* <http://www.gnu.org/licenses/gpl-faq.en.html#IfLibraryIsGPL> accessed 1 December 2012.
[53] Katz (n 35) 14. [54] Rosen (n 29) 120.

Conversely, if a GPLv2-licensed program is modified, regardless of the importance or scope of such modification, it is clear that the copyleft obligation applies. From GPLv2's wording, the obligation to distribute any modified work exclusively under GPLv2 encompasses not only modifications of the original program, but also any collective work containing any such modified works or parts thereof,[55] and even all independent works forming part of such collective work.[56] While this seems exactly what the authors of the GPLv2 licence wanted to achieve, many other commentators argue that the GPLv2 copyleft obligation, correctly interpreted, applies only to derivative works of the original program, not to collective works that include the original program (even if modified), and still less to other independent works included in such collective works.[57] The debate continues and is unlikely to be settled unless and until a court rules definitively on the position. However, we consider the debate should be limited to scenarios where the original GPLv2-licensed program has been modified. This is because if the original program has not been modified, licensees may distribute the program under section 1 of the licence, alone or accompanied by any other programs or even integrated within a larger collective work, without being concerned about the reciprocity obligation, which applies only where the original program is modified. Otherwise, the extensive interpretation of section 2 asserted by the FSF with respect to modified works could lead to perverse results. A new original program merely linking to an unmodified GPL'd library may be distributed under any licence, even if the GPL'd library was included on the same medium. If, however, the new program's author modified the library the program links to, on the FSF's interpretation the new program must be released under GPLv2, at least if it were to be distributed on the same medium as the library. Yet if someone other than the new program's author modified the library, while the modified library would have to be released under GPLv2, the new program could link to it without triggering the copyleft obligation.[58]

9.2.2 GNU General Public License version 3[59]

9.2.2.1 Licence provisions

Basic permissions granted under GNU GPL version 3 ('GPLv3') are described in its section 2: 'you are allowed to make, run and propagate covered works that you do

[55] FSF, *GNU GPL*, v2: 'You must cause any work that you distribute or publish, that in whole or in part contains or is derived from the Program or any part thereof, to be licensed as...'; also, see C Blake and J Probst, 'Loaded Question: Examining Loadable Kernel Modules Under the General Public License v2' (2011–2012) 7 *Wash J L Tech & Arts* 290.

[56] FSF, *GNU GPL*, v2: '...distribution of the whole must be on the terms of this License, whose permissions for other licensees extend to the entire whole, and thus to each and every part regardless of who wrote it.'

[57] eg Katz (n 35) or Rosen (n 29) 120; for a contrary opinion see, eg, St Laurent (n 36) 40.

[58] Katz (n 35) 14.

[59] See ch 3, at 3.4.

not convey, without conditions so long as your license otherwise remains in force'. New terms 'propagation' and 'conveying' were chosen instead of the terms 'copying' and 'distribution' used in GPLv2, to ensure that different meanings in different jurisdictions of the traditional copyright terms 'copying' and, especially, 'distribution', would not result in different interpretations of GPLv3 from country to country.[60] To 'propagate' a work means to do anything with it that, without permission, would make you directly or secondarily liable for infringement under applicable copyright law, except executing it on a computer or modifying a private copy. Propagation includes copying, distribution (with or without modification), making available to the public, and in some countries other activities as well.[61] To 'convey' a work means any kind of propagation that enables other parties to make or receive copies. Mere interaction with a user through a computer network, with no transfer of a copy, is not conveying.[62] A 'covered work' means either the unmodified Program or a work based on the Program. To 'modify' a work means to copy from or adapt all or part of the work in a fashion requiring copyright permission, other than the making of an exact copy. The resulting work is called a 'modified version' of the earlier work or a work 'based on' the earlier work,[63] ie under GPLv3 the definition of a work 'based on' a Program is different from that in GPLv2.

Section 4 of the GPLv3 grants permission to:

> convey verbatim copies of the Program's source code as you receive it, in any medium, provided that you conspicuously and appropriately publish on each copy an appropriate copyright notice; keep intact all notices stating that this License and any non-permissive terms added in accord with section 7 apply to the code; keep intact all notices of the absence of any warranty; and give all recipients a copy of this License along with the Program.[64]

GPLv3 section 5 grants permission to distribute a modified program as follows:

> You may convey a work based on the Program, or the modifications to produce it from the Program, in the form of source code under the terms of section 4, provided that you also meet all of these conditions:
>
> a) The work must carry prominent notices stating that you modified it, and giving a relevant date.
>
> b) The work must carry prominent notices stating that it is released under this License and any conditions added under section 7. This requirement modifies the requirement in section 4 to 'keep intact all notices'.

[60] FSF, *A Quick Guide to GPLv3* <http://www.gnu.org/licenses/quick-guide-GPL v 3.html> accessed 2 December 2012.

[61] FSF, *GNU GPL*, v3 (n 60).

[62] FSF, *GNU GPL*, v3 (n 60).

[63] FSF, *GNU GPL*, v3 (n 60).

[64] FSF, *GNU GPL*, v3 (n 60).

c) You must license the entire work, as a whole, under this License to anyone who comes into possession of a copy. This License will therefore apply, along with any applicable section 7 additional terms, to the whole of the work, and all its parts, regardless of how they are packaged. This License gives no permission to license the work in any other way, but it does not invalidate such permission if you have separately received it.

d) If the work has interactive user interfaces, each must display Appropriate Legal Notices; however, if the Program has interactive interfaces that do not display Appropriate Legal Notices, your work need not make them do so.

A compilation of a covered work with other separate and independent works, which are not by their nature extensions of the covered work, and which are not combined with it such as to form a larger program, in or on a volume of a storage or distribution medium, is called an 'aggregate' if the compilation and its resulting copyright are not used to limit the access or legal rights of the compilation's users beyond what the individual works permit. Inclusion of a covered work in an aggregate does not cause this License to apply to the other parts of the aggregate.[65]

Section 6 addresses distribution of a program in object code form: 'You may convey a covered work in object code form under the terms of sections 4 and 5, provided that you also convey the machine-readable Corresponding Source[66] under the terms of this licence....'

9.2.2.2 Conveying unmodified works

Although GPLv3 introduced an explicit definition of a 'modified version' of a program, this definition does not seem to cover situations where an unmodified work is incorporated into a collective work, ie into a larger program, in cases where the code of the incorporated work is unchanged. Even if mere inclusion of an exact copy of a work in a collective work required the copyright holder's permission beyond the general permission to copy granted by GPLv3, such inclusion would not constitute 'modification'[67] but at most 'propagation'.[68] It can therefore be argued that, as with GPLv2, if the original program is not modified but is made part of a larger program,

[65] FSF, *GNU GPL*, v3 (n 60).

[66] FSF, *GNU GPL*, v3 (n 60): the 'Corresponding Source' for a work in object code form means 'all the source code needed to generate, install, and (for an executable work) run the object code and to modify the work, including scripts to control those activities. However, it does not include the work's System Libraries, or general-purpose tools or generally available free programs which are used unmodified in performing those activities but which are not part of the work. For example, Corresponding Source includes interface definition files associated with source files for the work, and the source code for shared libraries and dynamically linked subprograms that the work is specifically designed to require, such as by intimate data communication or control flow between those subprograms and other parts of the work.'

[67] See the definition of 'modify' in 9.2.2.1. In our view (as discussed in 9.2.1), incorporating an unmodified work into a collective work does not constitute 'copying from' or 'adapting' all or part of the work, but making an exact copy of it. Making an exact copy is specifically excluded from the definition of 'modify'.

[68] See the definition of 'propagation' in 9.2.2.1.

ie a collective work, the copyleft obligation is not triggered. This argument is even stronger if the unmodified original program is merely linked to by another, separately developed, program. On the other hand, if the words 'making of an exact copy' in the GPLv3 definition of 'modify' were interpreted strictly, it could be argued that copying even the unmodified program to include it in a collective work is not 'making an exact copy', and that therefore the collective work resulting from such inclusion falls within the definition of a 'modified work' or 'work based on the program'.[69] The FSF, unsurprisingly, adheres to the latter interpretation. However, there is one important difference between GPLv2 and GPLv3. While the scope of the GPLv2 copyleft obligation is the same with respect to programs whether in source or object code form, under GPLv3 the foregoing discussion applies to conveying the work in source form only; the GPLv3 reciprocity obligation is much wider when the modified work is conveyed in non-source form, as explained later.

According to the FSF, every program that merely dynamically links to a GPLv3-licensed library must itself be released under GPLv3.[70] At least with respect to dynamic linking, the FSF's interpretation seems to extend the scope of protection far beyond that granted by copyright law. Dynamic linking to a library involves neither adaptation of nor copying from that library, and accordingly does not require copyright permission from the library's author.[71] If a GPLv3-licensed library is 'conveyed' together with the program which links to it, that certainly requires permission and it is arguable, at least theoretically, that the library and the program together constitute a collective work, and that such work must, under the interpretation advocated by the FSF, be deemed to be a modified work, so that it can be conveyed only under the terms and conditions applicable to modified works. It is however much more difficult to argue that the library and a program linking to it form part of a collective work if the library is not conveyed with the program, as will often be the case.

9.2.2.3 Conveying modified works

Despite its new terminology, GPLv3 seems to have failed to remove the uncertainty regarding the scope of the copyleft provision in relation to modified programs. It is true that GPLv3 explicitly provides that 'this license will therefore apply... to the whole of the work (based on the program), and all its parts, regardless how they are packaged', but despite the deletion of all references to 'derivative works',[72] confusion remains as to what constitutes a work 'based on' a program.

As mentioned earlier, it is unclear whether inclusion of an unmodified program in a larger collective work constitutes 'modification' of the original work

[69] JA Chern, 'Testing Open Source Waters: Derivative Works Under GPLv3' (2009–10) 13 *Chap L Rev* 154.

[70] FSF, *Why you shouldn't use the Lesser GPL for your next library* <http://www.gnu.org/licenses/why-not-lgpl.html> accessed 4 December 2012.

[71] Similarly Katz (n 35) 14.

[72] G Finney, 'The Evolution of GPLv3' (2009) 14 *J Tech L & Pol'y* 94.

under GPLv3.[73] GPLv3 section 5's last paragraph seemingly attempts to clarify the extent to which the copyleft obligation applies to collective works by defining 'aggregate', and explicitly excluding from the scope of the copyleft obligation other independent works forming part of an 'aggregate'. However, this provision seems to do nothing more than confirm that a covered work can be conveyed in a package together with completely separate and unrelated programs. It fails to clarify the position sufficiently, because it uses undefined terms such as 'compilation', 'combine', 'extensions of a covered work' or 'to form a larger program'. 'Compilation' does not seem to be used here in the same sense as 'compiler' is used elsewhere in GPLv3, so what does it mean? Are 'extensions' of a covered work 'derivative works', or something broader? What does 'form a larger program' mean, and where does such 'larger program' end? For example, if a GPLv3-licensed module for calculating square roots was included in Microsoft Excel, must Excel or even the whole Microsoft Office suite be licensed under GPLv3? Unfortunately the scope of the copyleft obligation under GPLv3 is no clearer than under GPLv2.[74]

9.2.2.4 Corresponding source

The scope of the GPLv3 copyleft obligation is further blurred by the definition of 'Corresponding Source', which must also be conveyed when conveying any work in non-source form. It seems 'Corresponding Source' encompasses more than the 'covered work' itself, as it includes 'all the source code needed to generate, install, and (for an executable work) run the object code and to modify the work, including scripts to control those activities', and more specifically any 'shared libraries and dynamically linked subprograms that the work is specifically designed to require'. Yet some parts of what might be considered constituents of a 'covered work' are excluded from 'Corresponding Source': 'the work's System Libraries,[75] or general purpose tools or generally available free programs which are used unmodified in performing those activities but which are not part of the work'.

It must be stressed that the obligation to convey 'Corresponding Source' under GPLv3 applies to both unmodified and modified works where such works are conveyed in any non-source form. To understand the scope of the copyleft obligation it is necessary to determine not only what constitutes the 'covered work', which may be

[73] Chern (n 69). [74] Finney (n 72).

[75] FSF, *GNU GPL*, v3 (n 60): The 'System Libraries' of an executable work include anything, other than the work as a whole, that (a) is included in the normal form of packaging a Major Component, but which is not part of that Major Component, and (b) serves only to enable use of the work with that Major Component, or to implement a Standard Interface for which an implementation is available to the public in source code form. A 'Major Component', in this context, means a major essential component (kernel, window system, and so on) of the specific operating system (if any) on which the executable work runs, or a compiler used to produce the work, or an object code interpreter used to run it. A 'Standard Interface' means an interface that either is an official standard defined by a recognized standards body, or, in the case of interfaces specified for a particular programming language, one that is widely used among developers working in that language.

difficult, as has been shown, but also what constitutes the 'Corresponding Source' for such covered work.

While the definition of 'Corresponding Source' may initially appear to extend the copyleft obligation explicitly to shared libraries and dynamically linked subprograms,[76] on closer analysis it is clear that the provision does not do so, at least certainly not to the extent advocated by the FSF. 'Corresponding Source' relates to a 'covered work'; the definition can therefore include only libraries and subprograms that are dynamically *linked to by* a covered work, but not independent programs *linking to* a covered work. Instead of clarifying the position regarding dynamic linking under GPLv3, the 'Corresponding Source' provisions actually increase confusion regarding the licence's scope,[77] raising new questions. What is decisive in determining whether a program has been 'specifically designed to require' a shared library? Does it mean that where the program dynamically links to a specific library the source code of such library must be provided, whereas where the program links to any library with certain interfaces, but not to a specific library, there is no need to do so? What kind of data communication or control flow is 'intimate' enough to include the library into the code covered by the copyleft obligation? Moreover, can the definition of Corresponding Source be interpreted widely enough to cover the operating system under which the program is supposed to run, or at least the part of such operating system needed to generate, install, and run the object code, where the operating system is not a 'generally available free program'?

It seems that GPLv3, in attempting to clarify the scope of its copyleft obligation, exacerbated the situation for free software developers by extending the application of the copyleft obligation to code other than the code of the original program, including certain dynamically linked libraries and subprograms, without clarifying where the copyleft obligation ends. However, GPLv3 has not changed the position of developers of proprietary software dynamically linking to GPL'd libraries—such software will probably remain unaffected by GPLv3.

9.3 COPYLEFT AND CLOUD

9.3.1 ASP loophole

Despite the high level of legal uncertainty regarding the scope of the reciprocity provisions in both GPLv2 and GPLv3, some legal issues related thereto seem to be much less controversial and are interpreted in the same way by most commentators. One example of such consistent understanding is that it is generally agreed

[76] J Tsai, 'For Better or Worse: Introducing the GNU General Public Licence Version 3' (2008) 23 *Berkeley Tech LJ* 566.

[77] Tsai (n 76).

that the copyleft obligation under both GPLv2 and GPLv3 is triggered only when a modified program is distributed, not when it is modified or run by the licensee who modified it.[78]

GPLv2 section 0 explicitly provides that 'the act of running the Program is not restricted.' This is interpreted, consistently with definitions of Open Source[79] and Free Software,[80] as a grant of unconditional permission to run the program without any limitations and for any purposes.[81] GPLv2 section 3 permits modification subject to conditions described in paragraphs (a) and (c) therein, but the copyleft provision under paragraph (b) applies only when the modified work is distributed or published.

GPLv3's section 2 contains more precise and better drafted permissions, allowing licensees to 'make, run and propagate covered works that you do not convey, without conditions.' GPLv3 goes further than GPLv2, explicitly permitting not only modifying the licensed program but also having others modify it, provided certain conditions are met.[82]

As explained earlier, GPL'd programs may be freely modified without releasing the modified version's source code, where such modified programs are not further distributed by the entity that made such modifications (or, in case of GPLv3, had them made by others). This remains true even where a GNU GPL-licensed program is modified by the licensee to provide services where third parties run the program online, whether such services are considered 'ASP,' IaaS, PaaS or SaaS[83,84] or any combination thereof.[85] That situation was perceived by certain free software developers and commentators as unfair because it allowed anybody to use modified software

[78] B Richard, 'The GPL Has No (Networked) Future' <http://www.linux-mag.com/id/3017/> accessed 4 December 2012; T Gue, 'Triggering Infection: Distribution and Derivative Works under the GNU General Public License" (2012) *U Ill JL Tech & Pol'y* 112.

[79] OSI, 'The Open Source Definition' <http://opensource.org/osd> accessed 8 December 2012: Criterion 6—'The license must not restrict anyone from making use of the program in a specific field of endeavour. . . .'

[80] FSF, 'What Is Free Software? The Free Software Definition' <http://www.gnu.org/philosophy/free-sw.en.html> accessed 8 December 2012: 'A program is free software if the program's users have the four essential freedoms: The freedom to run the program, for any purpose (freedom 0).'

[81] RW Gomulkiewicz, 'De-Bugging Open Source Software Licensing' (2002–03) 64 *U Pitt L Rev* 85.

[82] FSF, *GNU GPL*, v3 (n 60): 'You may convey covered works to others for the sole purpose of having them make modifications exclusively for you, or provide you with facilities for running those works, provided that you comply with the terms of this License in conveying all material for which you do not control copyright. Those thus making or running the covered works for you must do so exclusively on your behalf, under your direction and control, on terms that prohibit them from making any copies of your copyrighted material outside their relationship with you.'

[83] SC Crandall, 'A Practical Guide to the GPL' <http://www.jw.com/publications/article/1013> accessed 29 December 2012.

[84] As mentioned by user 'RandyGee' in a discussion in Richard (n 78), if the frontend of a web application in the form of a webpage was itself licensed under GNU GPL, it could be argued that such webpage is being distributed to the user and the source code of any modifications to the webpage must therefore be licensed under GPLv3. This would certainly be the case under GPLv3 which explicitly includes the act of 'making the work (ie the webpage) available to the public' as one of the forms of 'conveying.'

[85] As an example of an opposite view, see F Capobianco, 'The Honest Public License' <http://www.fabcapo.com/2006/08/honest-public-license.html> accessed 4 December 2012.

licensed under GNU GPL or another copyleft licence to provide web services where third party users ran the modified software online, without giving the open source community access to any modifications.[86] The fact that GPLv2 permitted such behaviour was perceived as a loophole in the licence, often referred to as the 'ASP (application service provider) loophole',[87] or 'SaaS loophole'.[88]

As early as the late 1990s, some commentators noted the increasing importance of applications provided as a service through the web, identifying this as an incipient shift in the software usage paradigm.[89] The increasing number and popularity of applications offered as a service brought the ASP loophole to the attention of the FOSS community. Many viewed business models providing software as a service as a fundamental challenge to the FOSS movement[90] and the community began considering how the loophole could be closed.

9.3.2 First attempts to close the ASP loophole

9.3.2.1 Affero General Public License v 1

The first licence attempting to close the ASP loophole, the Affero General Public License ('AGPL v 1'), was the result of cooperation between Henry Poole of Affero, Inc and Bradley M Kuhn and Eben Moglen of the FSF, and was published in March 2002.[91] This licence is based on and is almost identical to GPLv2, with the sole addition of a new section 2(d):

> If the Program as you received it is intended to interact with users through a computer network and if, in the version you received, any user interacting with the Program was given the opportunity to request transmission to that user of the Program's complete source code, you must not remove that facility from your modified version of the Program or work based on the Program, and must offer an equivalent opportunity for all users interacting with your Program through a computer network to request immediate transmission by HTTP of the complete source code of your modified version or other derivative work.

[86] Capobianco (n 85).

[87] Capobianco (n 85). ASP-hosted software refers to software applications that were offered for running online, pre-cloud; see M Tiemann, 'GNU Affero GPL version 3 and the "ASP loophole"' <http://opensource.org/node/152> accessed 8 December 2012.

[88] Richard (n 78).

[89] T O'Reilly, 'The New Age of Infoware: Open Source and the Web', speech given in 1999 in Berlin, available at <http://oreilly.com/tim/archives/mikro_age_of_infoware.pdf> accessed 8 December 2012; R McGillan, 'Tim O'Reilly: Software licenses don't work' <http://www.infoworld.com/d/developer-world/tim-oreilly-software-licenses-dont-work-261?page=0,1> accessed 8 December 2012.

[90] PH Arne, 'GNU Affero General Public License: Risks and Opportunities' <http://www.mmmtechlaw.com/2010/12/14/gnu-affero-general-public-license-risks-and-opportunities/> accessed 8 December 2012.

[91] Affero General Public License, in *Wikipedia, The Free Encyclopedia* <http://en.wikipedia.org/w/index.php?title=Affero_General_Public_License&oldid=526005594> accessed 8 December 2012.

New section 2(d) introduces copyleft obligations triggered, not by distribution of a modified version of the computer program, but by offering users the opportunity to interact with the modified program through a computer network. However, the copyleft obligation applies only if the original program allowed its users 'to request transmission of the program's complete source code' and if the original program was 'intended to interact with users through a computer network', which makes its scope very limited.

It seems that, for the reciprocity obligation to apply, the opportunity to request transmission of the source code must be an integral part of the program that is to be modified, as was the case with Affero's own software, which enabled any user to download its complete source code on any screen in the user interface.[92] Such interpretation is supported by the wording of the licence referring to the opportunity being given 'in the version you received.' Adopting a more extensive interpretation of 'being given the opportunity to request transmission' which would include, eg, giving users the opportunity to request access to the source code by a public promise made on a webpage or in documentation distributed together with the program, could cause difficulties. This is because it is hard to imagine what kind of a search would have to be performed by the licensee to find out whether such an opportunity had been given so that the licensee could understand the extent of its obligations under the licence.

The second factor limiting the applicability of AGPL v 1 is that the copyleft obligation does not apply to all programs which interact with users through a computer network, but only to those which are *intended* to do so. In our view this means that, eg, if the OpenOffice program suite,[93] which was not originally intended to be run online, had been distributed under AGPL v 1, anybody who modified it and offered it as SaaS would have no obligation to grant users access to the source code of such modifications (although if the person who modified it then licensed their own modified version under AGPL v 1, anyone who further modified *that* modified version would be so obliged).

9.3.2.2 Honest Public Licence

In 2006, Fabrizio Capobianco of Funambol wrote another licence attempting to close the ASP loophole, the Honest Public Licence ('HPL').[94] Like AGPL v 1, HPL was based on GPLv2. Capobianco made amendments in two main areas.

The first notable change was adding 'communication of the program to the public' to the rights explicitly permitted by the licence. It is unclear whether this was to avoid potential restrictive interpretations of the term 'distribution' in jurisdictions where this term relates only to distribution of tangible copies and does not include making

[92] FSF, 'Free Software Foundation Announces Support of the Affero General Public License, the First Copyleft License for Web Services' <http://www.gnu.org/press/2002-03-19-Affero.html> accessed 8 December 2012.

[93] <http://www.openoffice.org/>.

[94] Capobianco (n 85).

the program available for downloading, which is treated as one of the forms of communicating the work to the public under EU copyright law, or whether Capobianco thought that allowing users to use a program through a computer network constitutes communication of such program to the public. Although the idea that the right of public performance may be more suitable to address the ASP loophole than the distribution right was raised also in academic debate,[95] it was never seriously developed. The main problem with this idea is that copyright protects mainly the source code of computer programs, but where a program can be accessed by users over a network as SaaS, the program is not 'made available' to users in the copyright sense—the *code* is not publicly performed or communicated at all; the only part of the program which may be considered to be 'communicated to the public' is the graphical user interface ('GUI').

The main difference between HPL and GPLv2 is that HPL has a new section 2(d), which reads as follows:

> For the purposes of determining the right to obtain copies of the source code (as well as the right to modify and distribute such source code and object code), the term distribution shall include the communication of the Program or work based on the Program which is intended to interact with third party users (meaning anyone other than you or if you are an entity such as a corporation and not an individual, that corporation), through a computer network and the user shall have the right to obtain the source code of the Program or work based on the Program. This provision is an express condition for the grants of license hereunder and any such communication shall be considered a distribution under Section 1, 2 and 3.

The reference to 'communication of the Program' is unfortunate as it suggests that section 2(d) applies only when making the program available for download, although it is clear that Capobianco's intention was to capture all scenarios where a program can be used as SaaS.[96] It is unclear whether the obligation to provide users with the source code is triggered also by offering the program as SaaS without any modifications. The wording of section 2(d) suggests that such triggering was Capobianco's intention ('...user shall have the right to obtain the source code *of the Program* or work based on the Program...' (my emphasis)). However it seems that offering an unmodified program as SaaS would not trigger the reciprocity obligation due to the fact that, instead of adding a specific new obligation, section 2(d) merely extends the scope of section 2(b), which applies only to distribution of modified programs.

HPL is only one example of a licence created by a member of the Free Software community to address the ASP loophole in GPLv2. HPL was never submitted for approval

[95] RW Gomulkiewicz, 'General Public License 3—Hacking the Free Software Movement's Constitution' (2005-06) 42 *Hous L Rev* 1030, fn. 85.

[96] Capobianco (n 85).

by the Open Source Initiative because it was created as a temporary solution to the ASP loophole until an OSI approved licence emerges to address that issue. After the OSI approved the Affero General Public License version 3, Funambol immediately switched to it.[97] There are also other licences addressing the ASP loophole. For example, the Common Public Attribution Licence imposes the copyleft obligation not only on licensees distributing the program but also on those who 'externally deploy'[98] it. The Reciprocal Public Licence goes further, imposing the copyleft obligation on any licensee who modifies the code, even if the modified program is used only by such licensee for its internal purposes, except where such use is for non-commercial or research purposes.[99]

9.3.3 GPLv3 drafting process

Many members of the free software community believed that GPLv3 would close the ASP loophole,[100] and this was one of the main reasons for initiating the process of updating GPLv2.[101]

On 16 January 2006, the FSF published the first draft of GPLv3.[102] The draft did not include any mandatory provision extending the copyleft obligation to acts of enabling users to interact with the program through a computer network, but section 7(d) of the draft allowed software developers releasing their own work based on a program licensed under this draft to add a term requiring that the work contain functioning facilities allowing users immediately to obtain copies of the source code. Section 7(d) of the first draft did not specifically refer to programs intended for use over a computer network; the additional requirement described therein would, theoretically, have been applicable to programs whether used locally or over a network.

In the second draft of the GPLv3,[103] published on 27 July 2006, section 7 had been substantially redrafted. Section 7(b)(4) of the second draft contained the permitted

[97] S Yegulalp, 'Honest Public Licensing: Q&A With Fabrizio Capobianco' <http://www.informationweek.com/software/honest-public-licensing-qa-with-fabrizio/229211923> accessed 27 December 2012.

[98] OSI, 'Common Public Attribution License Version 1.0 (CPAL-1.0)' <http://opensource.org/licenses/cpal_1.0> accessed 27 December 2012: Section 15: 'The term "External Deployment" means the use, distribution, or communication of the Original Code or Modifications in any way such that the Original Code or Modifications may be used by anyone other than You, whether those works are distributed or communicated to those persons or made available as an application intended for use over a network...'.

[99] OSI, 'Reciprocal Public Licence 1.5 (RPL-1.5)' <http://opensource.org/licenses/RPL-1.5> accessed 27 December 2012.

[100] eg Capobianco (n 85).

[101] BM Kuhn, 'stet and AGPL v 3' <http://web.archive.org/web/20080315231323/http://www.softwarefreedom.org/technology/blog/2007/nov/21/stet-and-agplv3/> accessed 27 December 2012.

[102] FSF, 'GNU General Public License—Discussion Draft 1 of Version 3' <http://GPL v 3.fsf.org/comments/gplv3-draft-1.html> accessed 27 December 2012.

[103] FSF, 'GNU General Public License—Discussion Draft 2 of Version 3' <http://GPL v 3.fsf.org/comments/gplv3-draft-2.html> accessed 27 December 2012.

additional requirement which replaced the one included in section 7(d) of the first draft. Section 7(b)(4) of the second draft allowed software developers to add terms requiring that any modified work intended to interact with users through a computer network must allow users to obtain copies of the source code of the work through the same session. Such requirement was similar to the obligation imposed by AGPL v 1 as it necessitated creation of a specific facility within the program allowing users to download the source code. However GPLv3 draft section 7(b)(4) went further than AGPL v 1. AGPL v 1 only obliged licensees to keep the facility already included in the original program intact in any modified version, while the proposed additional requirement under GPLv3 would have permitted imposing the obligation to create a new facility where there was none in the original work.

Section 7(d) of the first draft, and especially section 7(b)(4) of the second draft, were amongst those provisions of the drafts which attracted the most comments from the community. Some comments criticized the optional nature of the extension of the copyleft obligation to SaaS. Others argued that any licensee should be allowed to use the modified program without any restrictions or additional requirements for any purposes, including offering the program for users to run as SaaS. After considering the community's comments, the FSF ultimately decided not to include in GPLv3 even the possibility to add the option to extend the copyleft obligation to SaaS,[104] and no provision similar to section 7(b)(4) of the second draft appeared in any subsequent draft or in the final version of the licence. Instead of dealing with the ASP loophole in GPLv3, it was decided to create a separate licence[105] based on GPLv3, inspired by the AGPL v 1.[106]

9.3.4 Affero General Public License version 3

Following this decision, the FSF worked with Affero to create a version of the Affero licence based on GPLv3 rather than GPLv2.[107] The new Affero licence based on GPLv3 was published on 19 November 2007[108] and named GNU Affero General Public License version 3 ('AGPL v 3'), even though there was no version 2, to highlight the fact that it was based on GPLv3. Version 2 of the AGPL[109] was also published in November 2007 and is just a transitional licence allowing users of programs licensed

[104] FSF, *Frequently Asked Questions about the GNU Licenses* <http://www.gnu.org/licenses/gpl-faq.en.html#SeparateAffero> accessed 27 December 2012.

[105] Kuhn (n 101).

[106] R Wilson, 'GPLv3—What's New?' <http://www.oss-watch.ac.uk/resources/gpl3final> accessed 27 December 2012.

[107] Wilson (n 106).

[108] FSF, 'GNU Affero General Public License Version 3' <http://www.gnu.org/licenses/agpl.html> accessed 28 December 2012.

[109] Affero Inc., 'Affero General Public Licence Version 2' <http://www.affero.org/agpl2.html> accessed 28 December 2012.

under AGPL v 1 to distribute such programs or their modifications under AGPL v 3 as well.[110]

Apart from the preamble, AGPL v 3 is almost identical to GPLv3. The only substantive difference lies in one provision. Section 13 of AGPL v 3, entitled 'Remote Network Interaction; Use with the GNU General Public License', reads as follows:

> Notwithstanding any other provision of this License, if you modify the Program, your modified version must prominently offer all users interacting with it remotely through a computer network (if your version supports such interaction) an opportunity to receive the Corresponding Source of your version by providing access to the Corresponding Source from a network server at no charge, through some standard or customary means of facilitating copying of software. This Corresponding Source shall include the Corresponding Source for any work covered by version 3 of the GNU General Public License that is incorporated pursuant to the following paragraph.
>
> Notwithstanding any other provision of this License, you have permission to link or combine any covered work with a work licensed under version 3 of the GNU General Public License into a single combined work, and to convey the resulting work. The terms of this License will continue to apply to the part which is the covered work, but the work with which it is combined will remain governed by version 3 of the GNU General Public License.

Section 13 of AGPL v 3 suffers from similar shortcomings as discussed above with respect to copyleft provisions of GPLv2 and GPLv3: use of undefined terms leads to uncertainty as to the scope of the copyleft obligation. In order to determine exactly when the copyleft obligation is triggered, it is necessary to interpret at least three unclear terms: 'user', 'interacting remotely through a computer network', and 'supporting such interaction'.

9.3.3.1 Users—what are they actually using?

We shall use social networking service Facebook as an example in order to illustrate the problematic nature of those terms. Let us start with 'user'. There may be little doubt that those with Facebook accounts are users of Facebook's frontend, ie the part of the application which they access and can interact with through the frontend web GUI. However, are they also 'users' of the software used by Facebook Inc. to determine eg what content uploaded by Facebook users will be shown to which of their friends? While Facebook users uploading content cannot directly command such software as there is no option to interact with it directly through a GUI, arguably, they are 'using' such software, because operations performed by such software are necessary

[110] Affero General Public License (n 91).

to provide Facebook users with the output they wanted to achieve by uploading the content in combination with setting their preferences regarding who should be able to see such content.

What about the software that manages how uploaded content is stored across different Facebook servers? What about such servers' operating systems? Is everybody who uses Facebook a 'user' of such management software and operating systems software also, or is only Facebook Inc. a 'user' of such software?[111]

9.3.3.2 Remote interaction—which interaction counts?

Interpreting the term 'remote interaction through a computer network' is closely related to interpreting 'user', and raises similar questions. Does 'interaction' mean only direct interaction by users influencing the application's behaviour through their own commands submitted through a GUI? Or does it include any situation where a program performs a function as a consequence of certain user action, although such performance is only ancillary to such action, and users may even not know their action triggered the function?

9.3.3.3 Impact of unclear definitions in cloud

The importance of these questions becomes apparent when analysing the various cloud service models, ie IaaS, PaaS and SaaS. It seems clear that the copyleft obligation is triggered upon offering an AGPL v 3-licensed program as SaaS, eg office productivity, webmail, etc. The same is true when an AGPL v 3-licensed tool is offered for direct use by IaaS or PaaS users. In both cases, users can use the program as such, and allowing users to use the program is the only purpose, with SaaS, or part of a larger service, with IaaS or PaaS. Where the service is not direct application usage functionality for IaaS or PaaS users, but computing power, networking or storage space or deployment of users' applications, it is much less clear whether using an AGPL v 3-licensed program to provide IaaS or to support the infrastructure or code development/deployment part of a PaaS offering triggers the copyleft obligation. In our opinion, under AGPL v 3's section 13, the copyleft obligation is triggered only if users are enabled to use an AGPL v 3-licensed program's functionality directly, not by providers using the program to provide IaaS or other cloud services, or even to support provision of SaaS, provided the program is not *itself* offered as SaaS. This would mean AGPL v 3 has not closed the ASP loophole as regards organizations such as Google or Amazon which may use open source programs to offer services not involving direct use of program functionality as SaaS; many consider that such organizations'

[111] Comment of user 'frx' on the AGPL v 3 draft in the discussion on the FSF webpage dated 3 September 2007 <http://gplv3.fsf.org/comments/rt/readsay.html?filename=debug-intense&Query=%20%27CF.NoteStartNodeId%27%20LIKE%20%gplv3.remotenetworkandgnu.p0.s1%27%20AND%20%27CF.NoteUrl%27%20LIKE%20%27agplv3-draft-2%27> accessed 29 December 2012.

use of open source programs without any copyleft obligations is the loophole's main negative consequence.[112]

9.3.3.4 Does internal use trigger copyleft?

Another relevant question in this context is the following: is the copyleft obligation triggered by modifying an AGPL v 3-licensed program, if the program is modified and deployed exclusively for internal use within the organization making or commissioning the modifications, eg installing the modified program exclusively in a private cloud, or in a public cloud where remote access to the program is granted only to that organization's employees? It is tempting to argue that no copyleft obligation exists here, as the program is neither distributed nor offered for use to any entity other than the organization making the modifications. AGPL v 1's drafters made it clear that a commercial enterprise which runs an AGPL-licensed program internally need not release the modified source code.[113] However, the FSF website's FAQ section does not provide similar guidance regarding AGPL v 3, nor does AGPL v 3's wording support this interpretation. The copyleft obligation is not triggered by making the modified program available for third party use, but by making the modification, provided the modified version supports remote interaction with the program through a computer network. It is therefore irrelevant whether the modified program is made available for use and whether users are third parties or employees of the organization modifying the program—once the program is modified, the copyleft obligation is triggered and the modified program itself must provide its users the opportunity to receive the Corresponding Source.

9.3.3.5 To support or not to support remote interaction

Another undefined term which requires interpretation is 'to support [remote] interaction [via computer network]' between the user and the program. The most logical and consistent interpretation is that the copyleft obligation only applies to programs created for use either exclusively over a computer network (eg Facebook apps) or offline but with specific features allowing their use over a network. Programs originally intended for offline use, but made usable remotely via additional tools such as Secure Shell ('SSH') or VNC, should not be classified as supporting remote interaction for this purpose, so the section 13 copyleft obligation should not apply to them, provided the combination of original program and additional tool is not considered a modified version of the original program.[114]

[112] eg M Asay, 'Google's festering problem with the AGPL' <http://news.cnet.com/8301-13505_3-9917947-16.html> accessed 29 December 2012; M Asay, 'We can't open up because we're too monolithic (Yahoo! and Google)' <http://asay.blogspot.cz/2006/07/we-cant-open-up-because-were-too.html> accessed 29 December 2012; and Capobianco (n 85).

[113] Affero Inc, 'AGPL Frequently Asked Questions' <http://www.affero.org/oagf.html> accessed 31 December 2012.

[114] Comment of user 'larzhu' on AGPL v 3 draft in the discussion on the FSF webpage dated 21 August 2007 <http://gplv3.fsf.org/comments/rt/readsay.html?filename=debug-intense&Query=%20%27CF.NoteStartNodeId%27%20LIKE%20%27agplv3.remotenetworkandgnu.p0.s1%27%20AND%20%27CF.NoteUrl%27%20LIKE%20%27agplv3-draft-2%27> accessed 29 December 2012.

9.3.3.6 'Modification' in the cloud

Certain limitations on the copyleft obligation's scope appear, at least initially, to be clear and unambiguous. The most important such limitation is that licensees who merely offer the unmodified program as SaaS have no reciprocity obligation: the obligation is triggered by modifying the program, not by offering the unmodified program as SaaS. However, this returns us to the question of what constitutes 'modification' under AGPL v 3. As discussed in section 9.2.2 it is unclear whether 'modification' covers incorporating an exact copy of the original program into a larger whole, regardless of whether or not such larger program constitutes a collective work. The FSF considers, unsurprisingly, that any inclusion of a covered work in a larger program constitutes 'modification', but even the FSF cannot draw a clear line between combining a covered work with separate programs, which does not constitute 'modification' of such covered work, and combining a covered work with other programs so 'intimately' that the combination constitutes a new single program.[115]

When analysing what constitutes a modified version of a program in the cloud, there is one particular aspect that does not arise in non-cloud scenarios. As pointed out earlier, the cloud supply chain can be complex—different software components across different service 'layers' (IaaS, PaaS and SaaS), which could be supplied by different providers, may be used to provide a single cloud service. For example, an SaaS service may be built upon a PaaS platform which in turn uses IaaS infrastructure. Under AGPL v 3, should software used in different 'layers' of a cloud service, such as a a PaaS/IaaS provider's software infrastructure or platform on which a cloud user's modified AGPL v 3-licensed application is built, be considered part of a new program, being a work based on the original AGPL v 3-licensed program? We consider such an interpretation would be excessive and inappropriate given the nature of cloud computing. Where a cloud user deploys an AGPL v 3-licensed application in the cloud, 'layered' atop other software offered as part of a provider's cloud services, we believe that the copyleft obligation should not encompass such other software, especially where those services are in a different cloud 'layer'. In other words, we believe any licensee of AGPL v 3-licensed applications wishing to modify and deploy such an application in the cloud is obliged to release source code for the modified application and all source code needed to install, modify and run the application *in the same cloud environment*, but nothing more. Imposing a broader copyleft obligation requiring release of source code of software provided by third parties as part of their cloud service offerings would, we believe, based on our understanding

[115] FSF, *Frequently Asked Questions about the GNU Licenses* <http://www.gnu.org/licenses/gpl-faq.en.html#MereAggregation> accessed 29 December 2012.

of relevant market policy considerations, dramatically limit AGPL v 3's practical usability and popularity.

9.3.3.7 Corresponding source in cloud

It is not only the unclear scope of the term 'modification' which could extend the scope of the copyleft obligation to other cloud layers, but also the 'Corresponding Source' definition.[116] As the GPLv3 section noted, this definition covers not only the source code of the work itself, but all source code needed to generate, install and run the object code and to modify the work. The definition certainly extends to certain shared libraries and dynamically linked subprograms, and might even extend to the operating system on which the work is to run, although the courts are unlikely to adopt such an extensive interpretation. PaaS offerings often include libraries, databases and other software tools customers can use in building their own applications. Where a SaaS application written by a PaaS customer is a modification of an AGPL v 3-licensed program meeting the section 13 criteria, and the application is 'specifically designed to require' a library or database, etc offered by the PaaS provider, the library's source code must be provided as part of the 'Corresponding Source'. Realistically, this would prohibit modifying any AGPL v 3-licensed works to deploy SaaS applications that require any library offered by the PaaS provider, unless the library has been made available under an open source licence compatible with AGPL v 3. Similarly, this would also prohibit modification of any AGPL v 3-licensed works to deploy SaaS applications that require any library offered by any IaaS services that offer libraries, databases etc for use with user applications, unless that library or database had been made available under an AGPL v 3-compatible open source licence. Conversely, a SaaS application's Corresponding Source[117] would not include the source code of software used only to provide the infrastructure on which the application or platform supporting the application runs.

9.3.3.8 Is AGPL v 3 really a copyleft licence?

Interestingly, section 13 only obliges licensees to 'provide access to the Corresponding Source from a network server at no charge', but does not explicitly impose any obligation to license the modified code under AGPL v 3 or another open source licence. This is potentially a significant further loophole. Its drafters probably believed that once a licensee makes their modified work available under section 13, section 5 necessarily requires the licensee to license the modified code under AGPL v 3. However, in our opinion, section 5 is not automatically applicable. Section 5 determines what the licensee can do without infringing copyright.

[116] See n 66. [117] See 9.2.2.

It cannot be a copyright infringement to do, with respect to a work, something the copyright holder's licence requires, eg providing access to Corresponding Source. Licensees could therefore argue that, when they provide such access to users of the modified program pursuant to section 13, section 5 does not apply to require them to release their modified code under AGPL v 3. If a court upheld this interpretation, AGPL v 3 would lose any practical effect as a separate licence; it would become identical to GPLv3.

Certain differences between AGPL v 3 section 13 on the one hand and sections 4, 5 and 6 (permission to convey the work) on the other, are worth noting. While the critical obligations under sections 4, 5 and 6, including the section 5(c) copyleft obligation, are clearly formulated as conditions of the licence grant (eg section 5(c): 'you may convey... provided that you also meet all of these conditions...'), section 13 is not formulated in the same manner. It is therefore unclear whether section 13's provisions constitute licence conditions or mere contractual covenants. If the obligation to offer users an opportunity to receive the program's source code were considered a mere covenant, this would have significant implications—upon any breach of the obligation by a licensee, the licensor, at least in jurisdictions such as the US, would be unable to seek injunctive relief or other remedies for copyright infringement, but could only seek damages for breach of contract.[118] This would make enforcement of such obligation more complicated and less effective.

9.4 CONCLUSION

Despite several attempts, including AGPL v 3, the ASP loophole remains open. As shown in this chapter, none of the licences attempting to close the loophole have achieved this goal completely. More importantly, licences explicitly addressing this issue are much less popular amongst software developers than other copyleft licences, namely GPLv2 and GPLv3.[119]

Some FOSS community members, including those who had previously campaigned for closing this loophole,[120] expressed the opinion that closing the loophole may adversely impact on adoption of FOSS, especially by enterprises.[121] As FOSS

[118] Gue (n 78) 103.

[119] On 31 December 2012, a database of Open Source and Free Software projects available on Sourceforge.net listed 115,995 projects licensed under GPLv2 and 14,670 projects under GPLv3, versus only 1,127 projects under AGPL v 3. Dice Holdings Inc, <http://sourceforge.net/directory/> accessed 31 December 2012.

[120] M Asay, 'Would closing the ASP loophole create more problems than it solves?' <http://news.cnet.com/8301-13505_3-9941510-16.html> accessed 31 December 2012.

[121] G Haff, 'Do we need to protect open source from the cloud?' <http://news.cnet.com/8301-13556_3-9939131-61.html> accessed 31 December 2012.

underlies many cloud implementations,[122] arguably it was the very existence of this loophole that contributed to the success of FOSS in the cloud.

The cloud poses other important challenges to users' freedom, such as portability of data[123] to competing cloud services or for use in-house. Also, open standards, which would allow developers to create software and services compatible and interoperable with existing offerings, are lacking or not widely adopted.[124] Perhaps the attention of the FOSS community will switch from attempting to close the ASP loophole to addressing these other challenges, and in some areas the process has been ongoing for some time.[125]

[122] As described in 9.1; also see JG Vikram, 'Building the Cloud with Open Source and Open Standards' <http://www.linuxforu.com/2011/04/building-cloud-open-source-open-standards/> accessed 31 December 2012.

[123] Asay (n 120).

[124] Vikram (n 122); also see discussion in ch 10.

[125] eg OSI, 'Open Standards Requirement' < http://opensource.org/osr-intro> accessed 31 December 2012.

10

OPEN SOURCE, STANDARDIZATION, AND INNOVATION

Alan Cunningham

10.1 STANDARDIZATION

Standards—those 'agreed ways of doing things',[1] whether social, economic, political, or, indeed, technical, as will be our focus here—have a number of benefits. Imagine society, eg, without the agreed standard of a common and well-defined language. Imagine legal affairs without the agreed standard of criminal or civil process. Without standards, life would become somewhat unbearable; as a result of the virtue of standards, however, society can operate in a more effective and beneficial manner. The fundamental benefit of having standards in place concerning specific activities or objects is, therefore, a rather simple one: they ensure a

[1] SM Spivak, and FC Brenner, *Standardization Essentials: Principles and Practice* (New York, Marcel Dekker, 2001) 1. A rather more formal definition of the term standard is provided by the International Standards Organisation ('ISO'), who suggest a standard is 'a document, established by consensus and approved by a recognized body, that provides, for common and repeated use, rules, guidelines or characteristics for activities or their results, aimed at the achievement of the optimum degree of order in a given context', ISO/IEC Guide 2, 'Standards and Related Activities, General Activity' (2004).

degree of surety for the various actors involved as to how things will be done or made. This surety is argued to be a liberating framework, subsequently allowing for an increase in innovation and free competition in a context of the agreed rules of the game.

Standards will, however, emerge from a number of different sources (the source of a standard, it will be argued, is crucial in understanding just how much openness or lack of openness will be associated with it). The basis of a standard agreement might have emerged, over a period of time in society, without a formal consensus on the matter, but becoming generally accepted as a standard (as in a common and repeatable) way of doing a certain thing. It may have been given some type of *imprimatur* as 'standard' by an agreed body with the ability and competency to decide on such matters, such as an industry specific standard setting body.[2] Or it might be a standard as 'law', laid down by one or more governments with an interest in, or responsibility for, the practice in question.[3] However, irrespective of how standards are developed, be they market/society/committee-based (*de facto*) or government/official/regulator-based (*de jure*), they represent an attempt by society to ensure a common point of reference for conformity, similarity, compatibility, or adaptability.[4]

The aspect of a standard that determines its success in providing organization, compatibility, and harmony, is the fact that it is available, and expected, to be freely used. The term 'free' is not necessarily meant here as in 'free beer'.[5] Rather it refers to freedom as in 'minimal restrictions'; note, this does not equal *no* restrictions. Standards only become standards because they are common, widely promulgated, and 'free' from the excessive restrictions that would subvert their 'standard-ness'. Standards, whether they are *de facto* or *de jure* can only fulfil their purpose if control is (relatively) minimal and, more importantly, their exposure vast.

[2] Sometimes, however, bodies with the ability and competency to agree on standards can miss out on the innovative standards advanced through *de facto* evolution. eg, the useful hyper-text transfer protocol ('http') standard that revolutionized internet communications was not recognized by the Internet Engineering Task Force ('IETF') until much later in its development and use, by which stage, of course, the success of http was secured and it was well established as a *de facto* standard.

[3] eg, in the UK, the Office of Communications Regulator ('Ofcom'), a statutory body, has some responsibility for certain technical standards such as relating to radio equipment. Some of the technical standards responsibility has been shifted to NICC (UK Interoperability Standards). Historically NICC was formally constituted as a committee reporting to Ofcom and previously Oftel. In June 2008, NICC reformed as an independent industry body that is owned and managed by organizations involved in interoperability standards development.

[4] See the typological hierarchy of standards proposed by leading US authority Ken Krechmer:

K Krechmer, 'The Fundamental Nature of Standards: Technical Perspective' (2000) 38(6) *IEEE Communications Magazine* 70–3.

[5] The phrase 'free as in free beer' was used in the definition of free software provided by GNU.org, GNU, 'What is free software?' <http://www.gnu.org/philosophy/free-sw.html> accessed 6 April 2013.

10.1.1 Technical standards

One of the main benefits of a standard is that, when adopted for use as a technical standard in what are called 'network industries',[6] (as many modern technological industries are) it will often allow for and encourage increased use of the network as a whole. Technical standards promote compatibility and increase connectivity, allowing for more users to become attached to the network, and for such attachment to be undertaken easily. Such technical standards therefore increase the benefit that can be accrued from the network so that the more standardization is present, the greater the network effects.

For example, having a standard mark-up language for constructing basic web pages (Hyper-Text Mark-up Language ('HTML')) ensured a rapid increase in the creation of such pages, and increased the compatibility of pages with the variety of different browsers. Another notable aspect of HTML as a technical standard, an agreed way of creating web pages, was that it was free to use, both in cost terms and liberty terms (apart from requiring that those who use it adhere to the standards of the language, of course). These features, in turn, also facilitated the emergence of HTML as *the* standard language for the time.

Finally, HTML was also aided in its advancement by the fact that it was supported by a number of technical standards bodies; it had an *imprimatur*, of sorts. The ETF and World Wide Web Consortium ('W3C') (and, subsequently, the ISO/IEC) supported and promulgated HTML as a standard way of creating web pages so that they would be compatible with a variety of browsers and therefore be displayed as intended. The authority of these institutions, combined with the technical quality of the language, the zero cost associated with use, and the minimal restrictions surrounding use, led to the establishment of HTML as both a *de jure* and *de facto* technical standard.

Often, technical standards get no such assistance from authoritative bodies, are not free (either in the sense of cost or liberty), are developed neither in publicly funded institutions nor by volunteers and, confusingly, may not even be the 'best' technology for the task. Consider, eg, the continuing dominance of the Windows operating system and, in particular, the Windows Office suite of software in the 1990s and early 2000s (even, arguably, to this day, although Apple and other software companies have since made some headway into Microsoft's vast market share): this was not a free product, it was the product of a private, for-profit company, and the software was

[6] Crampes writes that: 'In its simplest economic definition, a network is a set of points (or nodes) and interconnecting lines (or edges) organised with the object of transmitting flows of energy (electricity, heat), information (sound, data, pictures) or material (water, freight, passengers, and so on). Each point can be an *initial node* from which the flow is emitted, a *terminal node*, receiving the flow, or a node that plays an *intermediary* role of transmission, storage, amplification, co-ordination, dispatching and so on. Some networks are one-way, like gas, cable TV and water delivery while others are two-way, like passenger transportation or telephone.' C Crampes, 'Network Industries and Network Goods' (1997) *IDEI* 3.

protected by a variety of IP and licensing laws. In contrast with HTML, Windows and Microsoft Word became the standards in their field as a result of a certain amount of technical proficiency (many would argue Apple products and Free Software/Open Source products of the same period were as good, if not better), ease of use, strategic IP deployment and, eventually, customer lock-in, and not because they were handed down from on high, free, or the best in the field.[7]

10.1.2 The role of IP

For such *de facto* proprietary standards, strategic use of the exclusivity offered by IP protection was/is crucial in establishing the product as a standard, especially in the context of network industries where connectivity is key. Simply because IP law allows for exclusivity does not mean that keeping the IP closed is the most strategic use of it. In fact, being open with one's IP can be an important part of establishing dominance in the market. Because of the interconnected nature of network industries, and the benefits of large network externalities, controlling one's IP too strongly may lead to others—those who are more flexible, or open—succeeding.

The computing industry provides a perfect example of this type of strategic failure. In the 1980s and 1990s, Apple arguably pioneered much of the technological innovation of personal computing, producing many radical and successful concepts which are now ubiquitous in computing. However, at the end of 2007, its US market share consisted of approximately 8.1 per cent of the personal computer market, with Microsoft and the generic personal computer accounting for the rest. Although now recovering market share from a low in the early 1990s, the inability of Apple to benefit from technological superiority is in no small fashion the result of its strategic (mis-) management of IP during the 1980s and early 1990s. For example, the important process of mass early acceptance and promulgation of a technology largely bypassed the Apple Macintosh.[8]

Why? Product distribution was hampered by the lack of application software, a deficiency partly compounded by Apple's strict rules on distribution of materials for software developers; in other words, the result of how it controlled its IP. Because Apple was refusing to allow mail-order companies to sell Macintoshes, it also forbade mail-order distribution of *Inside Macintosh*, the guidebook to the Macintosh architecture that was the programmer's bible for the system. Apple also put tight restrictions on the Apple Certified Developer Program, by which software developers were

[7] See, on standards 'wars,' C Shapiro and H R Varian, 'The Art of Standards Wars' (1999) *California Management Review* 41(2) 16–20; and on word processing software specifically, TJ Bergin, 'The Proliferation and Consolidation of Word Processing Software: 1985-1995' (October–December 2006) 24(4) *Annals of the History of Computing IEEE* 48–63.

[8] See, for a good overview of Apple history, O Linzmayer, *Apple Confidential 2.0: The Definitive History of the World's Most Colorful Company* (San Fransisco, No Starch Press, 2004).

able to obtain Macs at a discount and receive informational materials. A few daring employees worked around these restrictions to get development materials into the hands of every software programmer possible, with the sensible idea that each Mac out in the field would help sell additional Macs simply through its presence. They might do so because if companies are encouraged to select their IP, the network effects theory would lead to it becoming a *de facto* standard. Customers would want to stay with the technology that provides them with the greatest reach, and can also become locked into a *de facto* standard. Even if the other technology is better, the fact that its release into the market was delayed because of an overly protective perspective regarding IP could spell its doom. In the computing arena, the case of Apple and Microsoft is a prominent example of the importance of this continual strategic choice, although there are many other examples. Interestingly, Apple appears to have learnt from this early strategic mistake in their utilization of IP; subsequently, it placed some of the technology of its iPod music system into the hands of actual or potential rivals in order to create network effects and attempt to establish a *de facto* proprietary standard[9] and, after a cautious start, it is likewise 'opening up' the iPhone and other devices.

Therefore, while there are indeed two main ways in which technical standards can emerge, *de jure* or *de facto,* the openness or lack of openness of *de jure* or *de facto* standards will in many respects be a reflection of their place of origin, the philosophy of their originator, and the perspective taken by that originator about the role of IP law. As illustrated, ownership of IP does not always equate to a closed technology, or, even, an expensive one to license; conversely, the development of a standard does not always mean that it will be free, either in cost or liberty terms. It depends on the strategy of the player involved, which will be the result of their commercial/organizational 'nature' and their purpose in the marketplace. In addition, however, and complicating matters somewhat, some standards will also be a heady mix of the two. For example, they could emerge from a private company, become a *de facto* standard without which the industry cannot function (an 'essential' technology) and then required by the industry standards authority to 'come into the fold' and become a *de jure* standard capable (and necessary) of being used by everybody.

In such a scenario, the technology in question, having been developed by a private company, will undoubtedly be subject to IP laws; use of the technology as a standard will therefore be subject to a compromise between the conditions laid out by the IP owner and those outcomes of the inevitable negotiation with the standards bodies and its members. It is not necessarily the case that the technology will become a standard without any restrictions as to use, or without recompense to the IP owner,

[9] S London, 'Product to Platform: the iPod's big play' *Financial Times* (11 January 2004); P Lewin (ed), *The Economics of QWERTY: History, Theory and Policy. Essays by S J Liebowitz & S E Margolis* (New York, Palgrave, 2002).

and, many argue, nor should it be. In such cases, the rules of membership of the standard setting organization will act to regulate the incorporation of the essential technology into the 'standard' fold.

However, one might question why an IP owner of what has become an 'essential' technology would agree to allow such a proprietary technology to become an industry standard, promulgated by the standards body. There are a number of benefits. One is strategic: other technologies, developed by other private companies, might become standards in the future. In this way, allowing the use of their technology as a standard is analogous to a social contract amongst industry players: you scratch my back and I'll scratch yours. Another benefit is that even though they may be required to license the technology as a *de jure* standard on less competitive terms than they would have done ordinarily, the fact that their technology is the *de jure* standard gives them a certain degree of leverage, important as a negotiating tool in other situations. Finally, to have your technology known to be an essential aspect of the industry and a standard adds a certain degree of qualitative pedigree to the company.

Intermingling with all of the above, public law might coincide with the private rules of their membership of the standards body to produce a 'perfect storm' of regulatory pressure. Competition law, plus the terms of their membership, might mean that to refuse to license the technology on some kind of fair, reasonable, and/or non-discriminatory terms, or charging an excessive rate of royalty would be either an infringement of competition law, an infringement of their terms of their membership, or both.

The issue of how to encourage private companies to license proprietary technology on fair, reasonable, and/or non-discriminatory terms (or, as is sometimes also requested, especially in the context of open standards, on fair, reasonable, non-discriminatory, and/or *royalty free* terms) is a key problem in the standards debate, and has implications for our exploration of the open standards phenomenon in relation to computing, innovation, and governance. The issue is largely one of a private interest versus a public interest (or interests).

10.2 PUBLIC INTEREST V PRIVATE INTEREST

Standards, in general, are a response to public interest issues; this might be a very limited public interest, in that it might extend, initially, only to the members of a certain industry who need access to a specific technology so that they can function in the industry. In the sense that these needs are exterior to the individual entity that owns the technology, these needs have a 'public' quality, (and, in the context of industries such as telecommunications and energy networks (and, increasingly, internet based services), that public quality can become truly public, affecting statutory public service obligations). Subsequently there may in fact be a benefit to the public at large as a result of this use of a standard within an industry on fair, reasonable, and/or non-discriminatory terms. The public quality of standards should therefore be understood in the same way that competition law is public law (in fact they can be seen as having similar ends, the creation of rules of a game, a framework, within which innovation and competition can thrive).

Any private, for-profit company would of course love to have ownership over a *de facto* technical standard, especially one easily protected from competition by IP law. However, and here we come to the defining feature of standards, the technical standard, like the company, usually does not operate in isolation. Especially in the context of software, telecommunication, and internet industries, the more connection that is possible with other competing products the better it is for the industry as a whole (although perhaps not initially or obviously for particular individual companies). In order that more connection be possible, either *de jure* standards operate for the industry, laid down by industry bodies or standards bodies and developed by private companies, not-for-profit institutions, public authorities, or groups of interested individuals working for a common goal, or privately owned *de facto* standards become *de jure* industry standards.

Here, private companies have a strategic role, in line with competition law and the rules of any standard setting bodies which they might well be members of, to standardize their 'product' to the benefit of the industry while attempting to maximize, as much as possible, the private benefit of their creation. It is important to understand that this does not mean, however, that standards ought to be free, or, indeed, that they are often free. The reason for this, of course, is that those technologies that are often considered essential for the development of a standard are also protected by intellectual property laws. Thus private interests come into conflict with public interest.

Of course, as Bekkers and Liotard have pointed out, in a sense *both* IP rights and standards are ultimately created to serve the public interest. Standards 'can overcome many disadvantages related to too wide a variety of products, services or methods,' while 'a framework of property rights is deemed necessary to ensure that individuals or companies can employ innovative activities.'[10] However, in addition they admit that standards and IP will conflict because of the essentially public character of standards,[11] which is looking for equal access for all, and the private nature of property rights, which provide exclusive ownership to individuals. This conflict between the public good nature of standards, and the private interest personified in an IP right, has become the predominant issue of difficulty surrounding the post-liberalization and digital-era standardization process.

[10] R Bekkers and I Liotard, 'European Standards for Mobile Communications: The tense relationship between Standards and Intellectual Property Rights' [1999] *EIPR* 110.

[11] Bekkers and Liotard call this a quasi-public character because not all parties have equal access to the standard and to the standardization process: (n 10).

Fully liberalized and competitive markets in most sectors of technology now mean that owners of IP may have to engage in one of two problematic scenarios: either protect their rights exclusively, or allow the use of their IP in standards for strategic purposes. They might decide that they do not want to allow their property to be used in the development of standards, or they do want it to be used, but under what others might consider unfair and unreasonable (or anticompetitive) terms. Such behaviour, especially when the IP in question is considered technologically necessary in the development of the standard, is understandably problematic. Standard setting bodies attempt to address this problem in a 'soft' legal fashion applying rules to members.

For example, the European Telecommunications Standards Institute ('ETSI') states in Clause 6 of its IP policy that: 'When an ESSENTIAL IPR relating to a particular STANDARD or TECHNICAL SPECIFICATION is brought to the attention of ETSI, the Director-General of ETSI shall immediately request the owner to give within three months an irrevocable undertaking in writing that it is prepared to grant irrevocable licences on fair, reasonable and non-discriminatory (?FRAND?) terms and conditions.' Such licences must at least allow the following in relation to the IP: the manufacture, including the right to make or have customised components and subsystems to the licensees own design for use in manufacture; the sale, leasing, or otherwise disposal of equipment so manufactured; the reparation, usage, or operation of equipment; and usage methods. The above undertaking may be made subject to the condition that those who seek licences agree to reciprocate.[12] Importantly, while this policy of ETSI puts forward rules relating to certain things the licences must allow, nowhere it is stated that the licensing of the technology should be done for free.

Fair, reasonable, and/or non-discriminatory terms do not, therefore, always equate to free, and here we come to a central difficulty with standards (as least in the context of standardization efforts that are not completely private). Incorporating an essential technology into a standard simply means that the owner of the essential patent must balance their private interests with the more public interests of the industry at large and, indeed, the interests of the public as users and purchasers of associated services and goods.[13] Admittedly, as has been discussed by other commentators, there is a wide continuum of approaches amongst standard setting bodies: as Miller points out, 'SSOs [standard setting organisations] respond to this tension between common access and proprietary control by choosing an approach to participant's patent rights that falls somewhere along the continuum from closed (that is there

[12] ETSI Rules of Procedure, 20 March 2013, <http://www.etsi.org/about/iprs-in-etsi>. <http://www.etsi.org/about/iprs-in-etsi%3E>.

[13] Of course, having to pay a fee can be seen as a considerable barrier to entry, and thus unfair in relation to new market entrants or those competing against major players in an industry. In such cases, competition law can come to bear down on the actions of SSOs or, indeed, of the more private phenomenon of that organization, the patent pool, or consortia.

is no stated patent policy at all) to open (that is the policy requires participants to make any standard-pertinent patent available to all comers on a royalty-free basis).'[14] However, as the same commentator also points out, citing research undertaken by Mark Lemley,[15] 'what has come to be the most common patent policy "occupies a middle ground" requiring those who participate in setting a standard to promise to licence on reasonable and non-discriminatory terms (RAND) the patents they own that prove essential to implementing the standards.'[16]

A key question is therefore: what does RAND, or, indeed, fair, reasonable and non-discriminatory (FRAND) licensing mean in practice? Miller points out that 'the non-discrimination part of the promise is straightforward, requiring that participants licence similarly situated adopters on the same terms.'[17] He goes on to state that 'perhaps most important, an SSO participant who competes downstream with other adopters in the market for the standardized technology must treat its adopter-licencees no less favorably than it treats itself.'[18] It is the concept of what is reasonable (and fair) that is more difficult to establish, especially when there is no obligation to license the technology for inclusion into a standard for free. In the context of a non royalty-free RAND licence, where some payment is expected to be made, Shapiro and Varian have written that 'reasonable should mean the royalties that the patent holder could obtain in open, up-front competition with other technologies, not the royalties that the patent holder can expect once the other participants are effectively locked in to use technology covered by the patent.'[19] Miller points out that in the US the default damages rule in patent law provides an extensive body of case law from which to develop a standard of what a reasonable royalty is in the context of RAND standard setting licences.[20]

It is often suggested, however, that the (F)RAND concept is so nebulous and unclear a concept that it is hard to take seriously: Swanson and Baumol write that 'a RAND commitment is of limited value in the absence of objective benchmarks that make clear the concrete terms or range of terms that are deemed to be reasonable

[14] JS Miller, 'Standard Setting, Patents, and Access Lock-in: RAND Licensing and the Theory of the Firm' (2007) 40 *Ind L Rev* 351, 353–8.

[15] MA Lemley, 'Intellectual Property Rights and Standard-Setting Organizations' (2002) 90 *Cal L Rev* 1889.

[16] Miller (n 14). [17] Miller (n 14). [18] Miller (n 14).

[19] C Shapiro and HR Varian, *Information Rules: A Strategic Guide to the Network Economy* (Boston, Mass., Harvard Business School Press, 1999) 241.

[20] This rule, also known as the 25%, states that 25% of the infringer's profits is the baseline determinant for 'reasonable' royalty damages. As Epstein points out 'The 25% Rule originated as a 5% running royalty negotiated in the 1950s by Robert Goldscheider on behalf of Philco, which, at the time, manufactured televisions and other appliances. The royalty covered a portfolio of exclusive patent rights, trade secrets, trademarks, copyrights, and other intellectual property rights. Mr. Goldscheider compared the 5% running royalty in this arrangement to the pre-tax profit rate of approximately 20% for Philco licensees and calculated that the royalty constituted about 25% of the pre-tax.' See, further, R Epstein, 'The "25% Rule" For Patent Infringement Damages After Uniloc' (2012) *Duke L & Tech Rev* 1, in which Epstein criticizes the 25% as 'essentially arbitrary' in his support of a similar decision by the US Federal Circuit Court in *Uniloc USA, Inc v Microsoft Corp*, 632 F.3d 1292, 1315 (Fed Cir 2011) while accepting that some still maintain the usefulness of the rule.

and non-discriminatory.'[21] Paterson points out that 'while the non-discriminatory element of [RAND] policies is straightforward, the definition of reasonable is not so clear.'[22] One can quite easily add 'and the definition of fair' to this sentence.

It is this difficultly to clearly define (F)RAND that puts intellectual property rights in conflict with the standard setting process, and especially so with the concept of 'openness' within the traditional standard setting process. Balancing intellectual property rights within the standardization process—as also is the case outside it, where owned technology becomes a *de facto* standard, only more so—involves openness only to the extent that it is a strategic perspective in a broader, market based strategy for market dominance.

New trends in the development of software products over the last 30 years have illustrated, however, that the exclusivity offered by intellectual property protection does not have to be an aspect of a software product's life cycle; that software can, in fact, be developed in a variety of more 'open' ways than ever before, leading to innovative, efficient, and effective products. The lessons from Free and Open Source Software (FOSS) have spilled out into the realm of standards and talk of open standards has become in itself standard. While true 'openness' *is* indeed an aspect of open standards we will also see that open standards themselves are also often but a mere strategy in a larger market orientated play, depending on who is pushing and developing the open standard and for what purpose.

10.3 SOFTWARE, FREEDOM, AND OPENNESS

In the field of software, this debate about the standardization of private property has been complicated by the emergence of viable and successful FOSS. Other chapters in this book will provide more detailed explorations of the characteristics of FOSS; discussion here will be focused on the implications of the existence of FOSS for standards and innovation.

As regards innovation, and irrespective of whether one is referring to free or open source software, FOSS illustrates that it is possible and indeed practical to develop software in a way that largely bypasses the 'public interest vs private interest' issue inherent in most IP/standards debates, specifically because there are less private interests at stake in a FOSS product; the very nature of the product and the way it is licensed are directed at satisfying a broader public interest. This is the inherent nature of a FOSS product, and the only debate involved is the degree to which openness is

[21] D Swanson and WJ Baumol, 'Reasonable and Nondiscriminatory (RAND) Royalties, Standards Selection and Control of Market Power' (2005) 73 *Antitrust L J* 1, 8–10.

[22] MR Paterson, 'Inventions, Industry Standards and Intellectual Property' (2002) 17 *Berkeley Tech L J* 1043, 1056–73.

allowed and the fundamental objective of the openness. Is openness mandated in order to make more efficient code and better products, and subject to restrictions based on when it goes beyond this limited mandate? Or is openness considered to be more a tenet of faith, a belief that the code should be available to be modified and should not be controlled by intellectual property rights and the royalty payments that flow from such authority. In the faith section of the FOSS church (the free/libre section) freedom more often than not relates to freedom of expression as a fundamental human right and to royalty free access.[23]

In this way the broader public interest will be different depending on whether one is referring to free software or open source. Free software has very clear goals with regard to the openness of software; as Gupta points out in discussing the objectives of free software movement 'Openness as regards applications was three-tiered: first, access to source code for the purpose of understanding how a program operates and adapting it to one's own needs; secondly, users ought to be enabled to disseminate source code, for facilitating ease of software interoperability for others; thirdly, it was envisaged that whosoever is interested ought to be permitted to modify the code and also distribute modified code free of charge.'[24]

Open source modifies this baseline approach slightly; as Gupta writes, 'royalty free (RF) is certainly not a prerequisite for software to be classified as 'open source'. The Berkeley Software Development (BSD) licence lacks a RF patent clause.'[25] In addition, he points out that 'Apache represents the other (non-RF) branch of the open source movement. This branch is not committed to the value of free code as free speech; instead, they see the open source movement as a better method for developing high quality code. The Apache project did not use the GPL [General Public License], and instead favoured a type of licence most widely associated with BSD Unix. This licence also requires that source code be kept free, but modifications to the source code are not required to be kept free. It allows derivative or modified open source code to be incorporated into commercial products.'[26]

Richard Stallman provides another perspective on the difference between free/libre and open source: 'In the free/libre software movement, we develop software

[23] See further Chapters 1 and 2.

[24] A Gupta, 'Are open standards a prerequisite to open source? A perspective in light of technical and legal developments' (2009) 15 *Computer and Telecommunications Law Review* 3. Gupta misses one important objective, the first of the four freedoms of the FSF as stated on their website:

- The freedom to run the program, for any purpose (freedom 0).
- The freedom to study how the program works, and change it so it does your computing as you wish (freedom 1). Access to the source code is a precondition for this.
- The freedom to redistribute copies so you can help your neighbor (freedom 2).
- The freedom to distribute copies of your modified versions to others (freedom 3). By doing this you can give the whole community a chance to benefit from your changes. Access to the source code is a precondition for this.

[25] Gupta (n 24).

[26] Gupta (n 24). See further chs 1 and 3.

that respects users' freedom, so we and you can escape from software that doesn't. By contrast, the idea of "open source" focuses on how to develop code; it is a different current of thought whose principal value is code quality rather than freedom.'[27]

However, although there are variations within the FOSS movement, dependent on the level of approach, one can state with certainty that FOSS emerged as a definite theoretical and practical alternative to the standard and traditional model of software licensing. Ordinarily, software is licensed in an exclusive fashion with limited rights of use being passed on to the licensee: just enough to enable them to use it adequately and no more, for payment of a fee. Control is the default, and payment is expected in return for an easing of control over the technology. The difficulty with such a licensing model, as Richard Stallman illustrated with his infamous story of the laboratory printer and its associated software at MIT,[28] is that the licensing model is in contradiction to what can be done with software, from a purely technical, non-legal, and non-political perspective. In this way, the traditional licensing model was ignorant of another mode of innovation; it reflected innovation as the product of an established company, developed in-house and in secret and strictly controlled (at the time IBM might have been seen as a perfect example of this type of R&D and innovation process). Stallman had other ideas, reflecting his own approach to how innovation comes about. That is to say: software can be adapted, made better, copied, and distributed at zero cost, once the traditional licensing model, based on exclusivity, is ignored. These were Stallman's central beliefs, still reflected in his criticisms of a number of open source products that view making code better and more efficient as the *main* purpose in being open. Open source thus represents a next, but not necessarily more advanced, step in the evolution of the free software mantra.

Stallman was one of the first to recognize the benefits in treating code as simply code, and, in pursuit of an alternative to the norm, developed a different licensing model, the GNU General Public License ('GPL'), that would allow those who wanted to, and there are many, to release their software for public use under licence terms that opened up what the potential user could do with the code. The catch? Future users of software distributed in this way had to attach the same conditions to any modified codes that they used. At no point could anyone stop the game and say, no more, this is all mine. Importantly, a framework around this was the following: when they talk of free, they meant free as in freedom, not free as in free beer. Not, that is, free as in no cost.

To which point we will return, in further clarifying the distinction between free software and open source. First, one has to consider the important technological

[27] R Stallman, 'Is Android really free software?' (*The Guardian*, 19 September 2011).

[28] As described in some detail in S Williams, *Free as in Freedom: Richard Stallman's Crusade for Free Software* (Sebastapol CA, O'Reilly Press, 2002) ch 1.

benefits such a re-realization of the way in which software can be produced and distributed had on the way in which software was created, the quality of software, and on those users of software who found themselves financially constrained by the fees, and the constant need to update to only a proprietary system because they had become locked in. The benefits were immense: flexibility, adaptability, and reduced cost (even where there were costs).

Importantly, for certain types of software users (and, indeed, developers), this new type of licensing of software was a major boon. For example, for governments and other more public orientated institutions of developing countries, who did not have the large budgets available to governments of more developed countries, but nonetheless required software to administer, the concept of freeing software from the normative and exclusionary method of licensing was a very attractive alternative to the high cost and low flexibility of licensing proprietary systems.[29] More interestingly, for smaller technology companies and start-up companies, open source licensing was an opportunity to circumvent the weight of intellectual property monoliths in the market place and the standard setting arena, an arena where such IP giants often had a large degree of leverage. In 2007, eg, a consortium of 86 hardware, software, and telecommunications companies (the Open Handset Alliance)[30] unveiled Android, an open source, licensed, operating system designed primarily for touch screen devices such as smartphones.

Interestingly, the source code for Android is available under *both* free and open source software licences. Google, the central partner of the Alliance, publishes most of the code under the Apache Software License ('ASL') version 2.0, an open source licence and the rest, or the 'kernel,' under the GNU General Public License version 2. The Open Handset Alliance develops the changes to the kernel, in public, with the source code publicly available at all times. The rest of Android is developed in private by Google, such source code only being released when a new version is launched. While the software is thus open source, device manufacturers who want to use Android must also comply with their Compatibility Definition Document ('CDD') and pass the Compatibility Test Suite ('CTS'); in this way quality is maintained but such measures also act as a way of vetting use of the product and maintaining a degree of centralized control. Richard Stallman and the FSF have been critical of Android because aspects of it are not licensed under the GPL License. He has written how: 'Android is an operating system primarily for mobile phones, which consists of Linux (Torvalds's kernel), some libraries, a Java platform and some applications. Linux aside, the software of Android versions 1 and 2 was mostly developed by

[29] See, eg, RA Ghosh, 'Licence fees and GDP per capita: The case for open source in developing countries' (December 2003) 8 *First Monday*12.

[30] <http://www.openhandsetalliance.com> accessed 6 April 2013.

Google; Google released it under the Apache 2.0 license, which is a lax free software licence without copyleft.'[31]

The Android License does not have the same qualities that a GPL License does. For example, Ryan Paul has written about how the Apache Software License is a permissive licence that is conducive to commercial development and proprietary redistribution and that code that is distributed under the ASL can be integrated into closed-source proprietary products and redistributed under a broad variety of other terms.[32]

Android Open Source thus operates very much like a patent pool or consortia, the benefit of openness being that for hardware manufacturers they get a reputable product with the name backing of a player such as Google, without having to pay the large royalty fees they would have to pay for more traditional proprietary systems. Google, on the other hand, benefits from having control over the emergence of a standard, however open. Here, one sees the openness of the process as having two objectives; one, the production of a technically proficient product that can run on a number of disparate hardware products; and two, the strategic role of Google as lead developer, allowing some elements for free, but maintaining an element of control. In other words Android Open Source is an entirely strategic play focused on the circumvention of other market players. It thus reflects the comment by Shapiro and Varian: 'a corporation will accept and use standards only if it believes it cannot control the market directly and that standards can.'[33]

The case of the ASL and the use of it within Android illustrates perfectly the distinction between open source and free software, and it also serves as a useful case study in illustrating the use of openness as a broader market strategy, something that can be read, in fact, as an exchange of 'royalty rates paid now' for a degree of openness and leveraging that openness for future gains once a standard is established. As Ryan has written, 'such licenses make it possible to use open-source software code without having to turn proprietary enhancements back over to the open source software community.'[34] Android Open Source is part of a very long term strategy.

For their part, Android state that the reason for employing the Apache licence for certain aspects as opposed to the GPL licences for all is that: 'Android is about freedom and choice. The purpose of Android is to promote openness in the mobile world, but we don't believe it's possible to predict or dictate all the uses to which people will want to put our software. So, while we encourage everyone to make devices that are open and modifiable, we don't believe it is our place to force them to do

[31] Stallman (n 27).

[32] P Ryan, 'Why Google chose the Apache Software License over GPLv2 for Android' (6 November 2007) *Ars Technica*; See chs 2 and 3 for further discussion on the issue of the distinctions between open source and free software licences.

[33] Shapiro and Varian (n 19).

[34] Ryan (n 32).

so. Using LGPL libraries would often force them to do so.'[35] Android cites some specific concerns with GPL, particularly that it undermines the static fashion in which Android software is shipped, and that it would restrict the manufacturer freedom in design: in other words, using the GPL limits ultimate control; 'LGPL requires allowance of customer modification and reverse engineering for debugging those modifications. Most device makers do not want to have to be bound by these terms, so to minimize the burden on these companies we minimize usage of LGPL software in user space.' Free software would be too messy in getting hardware companies on side; and, finally, 'Historically, LGPL libraries have been the source of a large number of compliance problems for downstream device makers and application developers. Educating engineers on these issues is difficult and slow-going, unfortunately. It's critical to Android's success that it be as easy as possible for device makers to comply with the licences. Given the difficulties with complying with LGPL in the past, it is most prudent to simply not use LGPL libraries if we can avoid it.'[36] Ultimately Android is a project expected to be sold on the market place, not an experimental domain for software and hardware issues. Openness in Android supports this goal above all others; shipping a product that uses openness only as a means to an end and not the end in itself. Ryan echoes this view by writing 'The counterargument [to GPL] is that distributing Android under a copyleft license could potentially limit the evolution of the mobile software ecosystem by discouraging commercial development on top of the platform. Proprietary mobile software development companies that integrate Android into their technologies would have to dramatically change their business models if they aren't given the ability to keep their enhancements proprietary.'[37]

Google are not, therefore, getting involved in such 'open' standards initiatives out of the goodness of their hearts. There is a clear strategic advantage to being involved in developing and administering such an initiative. Google's involvement in the Open Handset Alliance and in the development of Android is a response to the emergence of a possible player for the title of *de facto* industry standard: Apple and the iPhone. Not being able to control the market in competition with this proprietary technology, Google realized that a play for market share in the mobile smartphone market had to be a standards based model, and perhaps that to get other hardware vendors on board in order to adopt that standard it would have to be 'open' and royalty free. In this sense open standards were as much a strategic play as the use of proprietary technology alone, or the use of a proprietary technology within a more traditional standard setting organization.

[35] Open Source Project, 'Android Open Source Project License' <http://source.android.com/source/licenses.html> accessed 6 April 2013.

[36] Open source project, 'Android Open Source Project License' <http://source.android.com/source/licenses.html> accessed 6 April 2013.

[37] Ryan (n 32).

Governments, however, are also interested in the capabilities of open source over free/libre software.[38] For a government, however cash poor, to use completely free software without the guarantees companies like Microsoft could provide would perhaps be a step too far. Start-ups and technology companies can experiment with free software kernels because they have the know-how to use them effectively. The benefit of paying for a proprietary system, and indeed the benefit with certain open source products as opposed to completely free software, is that you do not pay for simply a product; you pay for a service and when issues arise there is a dedicated support team ready to assist. Open source is the compromise system between free and proprietary; it married the benefits of completely free software (flexibility, adaptability, reduced cost) with the benefits of dealing with an established product and a company who could provide product support. A number of companies emerged that gained an enviable reputation as open source providers but who also charge for their software, or, rather, for the support services associated: eg, Red Hat.

Within this use of open source software by governments, however, has emerged and developed the model of what are being called 'open standards' and the desire for open standards as mandated for government (often the largest customer for software in respective markets); most usually this mandate is limited to the administration of the internal IT systems of the government itself, but see the Chinese policy later in this chapter. Open source licensing and the business model behind it illustrated the benefit to public institutions of using systems that had proven technical capability, but were not proprietary, and therefore not dependent on high royalty payments for profit. The 'open standard' was promoted as a way of combining the benefit of open source licensing with the benefit of standards: of enabling a vast number of software and hardware devices, most usually used in a public or quasi-governmental capacity, to interact efficiently and without the need for payment that was often associated even with the most fair, reasonable, and non-discriminatory of standards licences. In effect, the open standard was a combination of the open source model and the concept of software standards.

10.4 OPEN STANDARDS

The idea of an 'open' technical standard is very much an attractive one, particularly with governments enacting austerity measures in the midst of attending to their

[38] Public Sector spending on ICT in the UK is approximately £16.9 billion (4.6% of public sector expenditure) each year with the top 12 suppliers getting 60% of the IT spend; see John Suffolk, 'HM Government CIO speech, Shifting the paradigm of Government ICT.' See, also, Openforum Europe, 'Open IT Procurement in the UK Public Sector' <http://www.openforumeurope.org/openprocurement/openprocurement/open-procurement-library/Open%20IT%20procurement%20final%20version%2001_11_2010.pdf> accessed 6 April 2013.

duty of administering complex information technology ('IT') systems, but also, as has been illustrated, for certain market players attempting to circumvent events in the market. In the UK, eg, the Cabinet Office (in a consultation on open standards) has written: 'Information Technology across the government estate is expensive and the way that government departments previously purchased IT has resulted in hundreds of small, separate platforms operating across a landscape of disconnected, self-contained departments... Open Standards are crucial for sharing information across government boundaries and to deliver a common platform and systems that more easily interconnect.'[39]

It is in the interests of governments to develop standards concerning open standards, although there will always be controversy in relation to the approaches that governments take. For example, the Indian Government recently enacted a Directive on the application of open standards in e-government.[40] The Directive establishes that such standards shall be used for administration which are totally free of licensing costs.[41] The Indian policy only relates to a very specific sector; the use of software solutions for an interoperable public administration network. Similarly, the UK policy is limited in effect; it relates only to 'standards for software interoperability, data and document formats in government IT,' which, while admittedly a large market, is still confined to public administration.

In China, however, a proposed standardization policy that affected all standardization efforts (and in particular those in the high-tech industries) defined FRAND in relation to the licensing of essential technologies for standards as meaning royalty free, or at least marginal royalties for patents included in standards.[42] Such moves frighten companies that sell proprietary technology products, and/or who allow their incorporation into technical standards for a fee, especially as governments are an important customer base for IT solutions. Admittedly, the extreme proposal put forward by the Chinese Government represents, in part, their communist history, but when one factors in that China is liberalizing quickly and moving to a post-communist economy the move can also be viewed as a potentially rational decision by any government. Open standards, as a concept, is a perfect fit for government,

[39] Cabinet Office, 'Welcome to the Open Standards Consultation' (*HM Government*, February 2012) <http://consultation.cabinetoffice.gov.uk/openstandards> accessed 6 April 2013. As of November 2012 the UK *Open Standards Principles: For software interoperability, data and document formats in government IT* specifications are compulsory across government departments. See <https://www.gov.uk/government/consultations/open-standards-open-opportunities-flexibility-and-efficiency-in-government-i> accessed 6 April 2013.

[40] e-Governance Standards, 'Indian Policy on Open Standards for e-Governance' <http://egovstandards.gov.in/policy/policy-on-open-standards-for-e-governance> accessed 6 April 2013.

[41] See Open Source Initiative, 'Indian Open Standards Policy Finalized' <http://opensource.org/node/551> accessed 6 April 2013.

[42] Standardization Administration of China, 'Regulations on Administration of Formulating and Revising National Standards Involving Patents' (*GTW Associates*, 30 November 2009) <http://www.ipeg.eu/blog/wp-content/uploads/China-SAC-standard-proposal.pdf> accessed 20 March 2013.

as they run complex IT system across platforms and departments in the public interest. Standards are therefore necessary, and one can also see the argument for government mandating that the use of standards at this level should be as cheap as possible (although arguments for openness are, in theory, distinct from arguments relating to cost).

The UK policy argues that 'IT specifications must be based on open standards—standards which can be implemented by all.'[43] However, they also accept that there is no universally accepted definition of what open standards mean in fact. As a result, one of the tasks of the consultation was the proposal of a definition for open standards. The proposal stated that:

> For the purpose of UK Government software interoperability, data and document formats, the definition of open standards is those standards which fulfil the following criteria:
>
> - are maintained through a collaborative and transparent decision-making process that is independent of any individual supplier and that is accessible to all interested parties;
> - are adopted by a specification or standardisation organisation, or a forum or consortium with a feedback and ratification process to ensure quality;
> - are published, thoroughly documented and publicly available at zero or low cost;
> - as a whole have been implemented and shared under different development approaches and on a number of platforms from more than one supplier, demonstrating interoperability and platform/vendor independence;
> - owners of patents essential to implementation have agreed to licence these on a royalty free and non-discriminatory basis for implementing the standard and using or interfacing with other implementations which have adopted that same standard. Alternatively, patents may be covered by a non-discriminatory promise of non-assertion. Licences, terms and conditions must be compatible with implementation of the standard in both proprietary and open source software. These rights should be irrevocable unless there is a breach of licence conditions.[44]

The final definition of open standard as laid out in the Open Standard Principles is:

> Open standards for software interoperability, data and document formats, which exhibit all of the following criteria, are considered consistent with this policy:
>
> **Collaboration**—the standard is maintained through a collaborative decision-making process that is consensus based and independent of any individual supplier. Involvement in the development and maintenance of the standard is accessible to all interested parties.

[43] See n 38. [44] See n 38.

Transparency—the decision-making process is transparent and a publicly accessible review by subject matter experts is part of the process.

Due process—the standard is adopted by a specification or standardisation organisation, or a forum or consortium with a feedback and ratification process to ensure quality.

Fair access—the standard is published, thoroughly documented and publicly available at zero or low cost.

Market support—other than in the context of creating innovative solutions, the standard is mature, supported by the market and demonstrates platform, application and vendor independence.

Rights—rights essential to implementation of the standard, and for interfacing with other implementations which have adopted that same standard, are licensed on a royalty free basis that is compatible with both open source and proprietary licensed solutions. These rights should be irrevocable unless there is a breach of licence conditions.[45]

Many of these features are to be found in standard setting bodies where the membership is composed of private companies; the independent and accessible collaborative and transparent decision making process, the requirement for adoption by a body that can ensure quality, the requirement for publication at zero or low cost, and the requirement for demonstrable interoperability, especially if they will have to operate on a number of platforms.

One of the more controversial aspects of the UK proposals concerning open standards is the stated preference that open standards are licensed on a royalty free basis. This is the key issue on debates concerning standards and their openness, and the debate, in many ways, can be reconfigured as one rather between standards and intellectual property, since it is the potential royalty forthcoming from IP rights concerning software that leads to the difficulty. The requirement that open standards be royalty free is *not*, however, often a feature of how standards are traditionally created, and this illustrates the influence of the open source movement on open standards.

The controversy concerning defining open standards has been mirrored in other European countries. For example, the French Government adopted the European Interoperability Framework ('EIF') on 9 November, 2009. The French Parliament defined 'open standards' in the law no 2004-575 for the Confidence in the Digital Economy (*Loi pour la Confiance dans l'Economie Numérique—LCEN*) as: 'By open standard is understood any communication, interconnection or interchange protocol, and any interoperable data format whose specifications are public and without any restriction in their access or implementation'. Although the definition of open

[45] Open Standards Principles: For software interoperability, data and document formats in government IT, 9 April 2013, <https://www.gov.uk/government/publications/open-standards-principles/open-standards-principles>.

standard is not clear, it seems that under French law the expression 'without any restriction in their access or implementation' could be interpreted as meaning that an open standard should be made available on a royalty free basis only. A report issued by the European Telecom Institute dated 12 December 2005 and entitled 'Open Source Impact on ICT Standardization' assists in understanding the meaning of the French legal definition of open standards. It states that: 'Even though the definition is not crystal clear, some recent French legal developments[46] do refer to "standard ouverts" and there will certainly be more in the future. All of them interpret this definition as being Royalty Free even if the text is not specific about it.' On 10 October 2012, the National Council on Open Source Software sent ten propositions to the Minister in charge of Innovation and Digital Economy relating to issue of open source software. In these propositions, the National Council asked for a general recognition of the principle of royalty free in each legal text in France. Therefore, it seems that France currently precludes open standards requiring fees for use, but this is not clearly established by the law. The definition of what and how open any standard is in fact will always, admittedly, be a reflection of the attitude of the governing nation, or the philosophy of the particular organization involved. For example, the W3C, one of the main standard setting bodies for the internet, has in the past defined openness as follows:

> Using the W3C process as a model, we define the following set of requirements that a provider of technical specification must follow to qualify for the adjective Open Standard.
>
> - **transparency** (due process is public, and all technical discussions, meeting minutes, are archived and referenceable in decision making)
> - **relevance** (new standardization is started upon due analysis of the market needs, including requirements phase, e.g. accessibility, multi-linguism)
> - **openness** (anybody can participate, and everybody does: industry, individual, public, government bodies, academia, on a worldwide scale)
> - **impartiality and consensus** (guaranteed fairness by the process and the neutral hosting of the W3C organization, with equal weight for each participant)
> - **availability** (free access to the standard text, both during development and at final stage, translations, and clear IPR rules for implementation, allowing open source development in the case of Internet/Web technologies)
> - **maintenance** (on going process for testing, errata, revision, permanent access).[47]

A central thread throughout WC3's relationship with the open standard concept is a reluctance to advocate royalty free in isolation from other solutions. WC3

[46] Such as the Law no 2006-961 dated 21 August 2006 on copyright and related rights in the Information Society.
[47] W3C, 'Definition of Open Standards' <http://www.w3.org/2005/09/dd-osd.html> accessed 20 March 2013.

plays an important role in the emergence and administration of technical standards for the internet; XML, http, and CSS are just some of the standards for which they have responsibility. Their membership is comprised of commercial companies, as well as a number of universities and other research organizations. Design principles of the organization are 'web for all' and 'web on everything'.[48] However, the organization is responsible for establishing standards for what is, now more than ever, an environment as much used for commerce as anything else. To imagine that the W3C would advocate royalty free in all standard situations would be naïve.

The Organization for the Advancement of Structured Information Standards ('OASIS') takes a similar approach. The standards policy at OASIS is a complicated mix, reflecting what they see as commercial reality. OASIS states that it 'does not mandate a single, one-size-fits-all IPR mode for standards development' and, instead it permits each Committee to choose for itself, in its charter, one of three IPR modes under which it will operate.[49] They are:

- **Reasonable And Non-Discriminatory (RAND)** defines a basic set of minimal terms a patent holder is obliged to offer (such as granting a licence that is worldwide, non-exclusive, perpetual, reasonable, and non-discriminatory, and so forth) and leaves all other non-specified terms to negotiations between the patent holder and the implementer seeking a licence.
- **Royalty Free (RF) on RAND Terms** operates in the same manner as RAND, however, it does not permit the patent holder to charge fees or royalties for the licence.
- **RF on Limited Terms** specifies the exact Royalty Free licensing terms and conditions that may be included in a patent holder's licence and that must be granted upon request without further negotiations.

OASIS justifies this three-tier approach by arguing that it 'seeks to create the greatest possible incentive for patent holders to participate productively in an open standards process, responsibly disclose their interests, and make available, without prejudice, licenses for any essential claims they may have'.[50] OASIS understands that participating in the standards process is ultimately a commercial strategy for the owner of essential technologies, as well as being essential for the advancement of the field as a whole. To disallow the option of negotiation on terms such as royalties might, in

[48] Web for all being described in further detail as: 'The social value of the Web is that it enables human communication, commerce, and opportunities to share knowledge. One of W3C's primary goals is to make these benefits available to all people, whatever their hardware, software, network infrastructure, native language, culture, geographical location, or physical or mental ability'. See, further, W3C, 'W3C Mission' available at <http://www.w3.org/Consortium/mission#principles> accessed 20 March 2013.

[49] OASIS, 'Intellectual Property Rights (IPR) Policy' <https://www.oasis-open.org/policies-guidelines/ipr> accessed 20 March 2013.

[50] OASIS (n 49).

fact, limit the interaction between the standards organization and a number of useful technologies that could enhance the state of the art for all, even if required to be paid for.

As an example of open standard policy from outside the computing field, the ITU-T (the International Telecommunications Union's Telecommunications Standardisation Sector) also provides a definition of open standards on their website.[51] The either/or approach that emerges is consistent with their role as an industry led body. On their website they state that 'recently some different external sources have attempted to define the term "Open Standard" in a variety of different ways' before going on to state that 'In order to avoid confusion, the ITU-T uses for its purpose the term 'Open Standards' per the following definition:

> 'Open Standards' are standards made available to the general public and are developed (or approved) and maintained via a collaborative and consensus driven process. 'Open Standards' facilitate interoperability and data exchange among different products or services and are intended for widespread adoption.
>
> Other elements of 'Open Standards' include, but are not limited to:
>
> - Collaborative process—voluntary and market driven development (or approval) following a transparent consensus driven process that is reasonably open to all interested parties.
> - Reasonably balanced—ensures that the process is not dominated by any one interest group.
> - Due process—includes consideration of and response to comments by interested parties.
> - Intellectual property rights (IPRs)—IPRs essential to implement the standard to be licensed to all applicants on a worldwide, non-discriminatory basis, either (1) for free and under other reasonable terms and conditions or (2) on reasonable terms and conditions (which may include monetary compensation). Negotiations are left to the parties concerned and are performed outside the SDO.
> - Quality and level of detail—sufficient to permit the development of a variety of competing implementations of interoperable products or services. Standardized interfaces are not hidden, or controlled other than by the SDO promulgating the standard.
> - Publicly available—easily available for implementation and use, at a reasonable price. Publication of the text of a standard by others is permitted only with the prior approval of the SDO.
> - On-going support—maintained and supported over a long period of time.[52]

[51] ITU, 'Definition of "Open Standards"' <http://www.itu.int/en/ITU-T/ipr/Pages/open.aspx> accessed 20 March 2013.

[52] ITU (n 51).

Here, again, we see the development of a pragmatic approach that reflects the history of the organization and, also, the manner in which standards have been developed for the telecommunications industry;[53] thus openness is always defined dependent on source of the definition and its purpose. For example, prior to the trend of market liberalization of telecommunications that swept across developed countries during the 1980s, standards in the telecommunications industry were largely set either by the government as owner of the telecommunications provider, or by the monopoly provider itself, if privately owned. In this respect the standards process was reasonably constrained and restrained. Existing without competition in their field, telecommunication providers only had to ensure conformity and coordination across their own networks; there was little need for consensus building or agreement among companies apart from that needed to ensure international telecommunications was effective (and that was not hindered by the pressure of fully competitive concerns). The only requirements in deciding what a standard would be were issues of technological efficiency, effectiveness, and cost.[54] The additional factor of minimal transnational telecommunication prior to the middle half of the nineteenth century meant that not only were monopolistic telecommunication companies responsible for setting their own standards (without national difficulty), but they also had little to worry about regarding international telecommunication standard-setting.

As a result of such factors, Schmidt and Werle suggest that in the telecommunications sector the pure market-driven process of standardization, the *de facto* method, has been historically of minor importance.[55] In this judgment they are correct. They point out that due to the historical high infrastructural, and military significance of the industry, national governments played a strong role in the development of its evolution, and subsequently its standards. Prior to the liberalization process of recent decades, one central organizational paradigm emerged and dominated—the single network operator, owned or controlled tightly by the state. As Schmidt suggests 'the close affiliation of the network operator to the government resulted in a hierarchical quasi-imposition of technical standards as regulations.'[56]

However, the increasing requirement for transnational telecommunications combined with market liberalization instigated the modern telecommunications standards process, as it is now known. Split up and forced to compete, telecommunications companies realized that the main part of their strategic arsenal was IP that they

[53] See, further, A Cunningham and G Lea, 'Telecommunications, Intellectual Property and Standards' in I Walden (ed), *Telecommunications Law and Regulation*, 3rd edn (Oxford, Oxford University Press, 2009).

[54] Although, for monopolistic companies, even the issue of cost was not really an issue; see, eg, the phenomenon of the 'gold-plating' of technical systems by monopolies.

[55] SK Schmidt and R Werle, *Coordinating Technology: Studies in the International Standardization of Telecommunications* (Cambridge, MA, MIT Press, 1998).

[56] Schmidt and Werle (n 55) 44.

owned, and they could no longer rely on a captive audience of customers. Of course they would require standards and would have to be involved in setting standards, and of course this would be done on (F)RAND terms; but, the ability to compete on the basis of IP ensured that royalty fees would not be left out of the standard setting process. This history goes some way to explaining the definition of open standards put forward by the ITU-T, and, *mutatis mutandis*, for other standard setting bodies that have a perspective on open standards.

As a last example, the Internet Engineering Task Force ('IETF') also has a perspective on what is meant by open standards. In section 7 of its Request For Comments ('RFC') memo 2026, the IETF classifies specifications that have been developed in a manner similar to that of the IETF itself as being 'open standards.' They list the standards produced by ANSI, ISO, IEEE, and ITU-T as examples.

However, the IETF has not adopted a specific definition of 'open standard'; both RFC 2026 and the IETF's mission statement (RFC 3935) talk instead about 'open process,' but RFC 2026 does not define 'open standard' except for the purpose of defining what documents IETF standards can link to.[57]

In August 2012, however, the IETF combined with the W3C, the Institute of Electrical and Electronics Engineers ('IEEE'), the Internet Society, and the Internet Architecture Board ('IAB') to launch Open Stand and to publish principles concerning 'the modern paradigm for standards.'[58] On the Open Stand website it is stated that principle number four is availability and that, 'Standards specifications are made accessible to all for implementation and deployment. Affirming standards organisations have defined procedures to develop specifications that can be implemented under fair terms. Given market diversity, fair terms may vary from royalty-free to fair, reasonable, and non-discriminatory terms (FRAND).'[59] Open stand represents another move forward in establishing open standards as not necessarily royalty free.

Admittedly, money is always an issue in relation to technology, whether it be in response to IP ownership, or payment for the testing of standards.[60] The fact that modern standards are not being developed for nationalized industries means that expecting royalty free from open standards is unrealistic. In the same way that Google's involvement in Android Open Source is as much about market strategy as it is about advancing open standards, it would be too hopeful to expect anything other than a national institution, or an institution that has a philosophy that advocates royalty free, to view open standards as necessarily this way. However, one might ask how

[57] IETF, 'Request for Comments (RTC) 2026 (BCP 9)' <http://www.ietf.org/about/standards-process.html> accessed 20 March 2013.

[58] See, Open Stand, 'Principles' <http://open-stand.org/principles> accessed 20 March 2013.

[59] Open Stand (n 58).

[60] Testing is often done by standard setting organizations in order to ensure whether a system meets a specific standard.

availability is always achieved if a payment has to be made, and whether the question of royalty payments in the context of (F)RAND terms has been adequately explored, given that those who do always advocate (F)RAND in relation to open standards might be slightly missing the point? In cases of extreme unfairness and lack of availability, especially as a as result of excessive licensing fees, it is useful to know that competition law can step in to address such inequities.

10.4.1 Competition law

While the soft law approach of the standard setting body, or, indeed, the consortia, is only as effective as the intention of the parties, a number of traditional hard law remedies are available in cases concerning conflict between IP ownership and standards. As Bekkers and Liotard have pointed out, a most interesting issue surrounding the standards/IP process is to what extent the owner of an essential IPR, perceived as required for a standard, can be forced by law, as opposed to persuaded by a standard setting body, to license it to others.[61] Competition law provides us with the most insight here.

In a European context, the presence of abusive behaviour by the owners of IP rights who also have a dominant position in the relevant market might speak of anticompetitive behaviour.[62] In addition, Article 101 regulates agreements between companies, so patent pooling or cross-licensing activities in standards development might come under scrutiny. The response to such activities might even be compulsory licensing or similar.

Previous European case law regarding similar circumstances provides us with some assistance. In *Volvo v Veng* (Case 238/87 [1988] ECR 6211), it was decided that a refusal to license does not necessarily constitute an abuse. In *Magill* (Case T-70/810 [1991] CMLR 6610), however, famously, television broadcasters were held liable for refusing to license programme information to *Magill* magazine. Here the Court of First Instance (now the General Court) held that the exercise of an IPR constitutes abuse if it is used in a manner falling outside the specific subject matter of the IPR claimed. Two situations were mentioned where claiming exclusivity of an IPR might constitute abuse. First, where a company is 'preventing the production and marketing of a new product, for which there is potential consumer demand.' Secondly, if the right is used in 'order to secure a monopoly in the derivative market.' As Prins and Schiessl point out, 'assuming that the language of the CFI is sufficiently general, the first exception might be relevant in standard setting cases.'[63]

[61] See Bekkers and Liotard (n 10).
[62] Article 101 TFEU.
[63] C Prins and M Schiessl, 'The New Telecommunications Standards Institute Policy: Conflicts between Standardization and Intellectual Property Rights' [1993] 8 *EIPR* 263.

More recently, the European Court of Justice ('ECJ') decided in *IMS Health Gmbh & Co OHG v NDC Health GmbH & Co KG*[64] that the refusal by an undertaking in a dominant position to grant a licence for a copyright *can* constitute an abuse of a dominant position, but only in certain circumstances. This case involved two companies, IMS and NDC, who were both involved in the tracking of pharmaceutical and healthcare product sales. IMS provided pharmaceutical laboratories with sales data, formatted in a particular fashion: a structure of numbered 'bricks' was used, each corresponding to a particular geographical area (in this case Germany). The IMS data model became in some sense a standard, as it was not only sold, but also distributed free of charge to medical institutions in Germany. As a result, these medical institutions became 'locked-in' to the use of the IMS methodology, changing their processes and systems to accommodate it. However, a separate company, Pharma Intra Information ('PII'), began to distribute medical sales data using a similar 'brick' methodology. PII was subsequently purchased by NDC. IMS sought an injunction preventing NDC from using any structure derived from the 'brick' method it used, asserting its copyright in this database structure. The German national court was of the initial opinion that IMS could not refuse to grant a copyright licence to NDC permitting them to use the database structure, since such a refusal would constitute an abuse of a dominant position under EU law. It referred the case to the ECJ looking for particular clarification on the issue of when such a refusal to license could be considered an abuse of dominance. The ECJ first suggested that the national court must assess the issue of indispensability of the product or service, looking at the existence of alternative solutions as evidence either way. In the case of the 'brick' method, the ECJ pointed out that there might have been a high degree of 'lock-in', since the medical institutions that used it modified their systems to do so, but also acted to modify the structure by their use, improving it by their participation. These factors led to high dependency, making the cost, in both time and money, of changing, impractical. The ECJ then asserted that a refusal to license cannot, in itself, constitute an abuse of dominance, since exclusive rights to reproduction are part of the copyright granted. However, the manner in which a right is exercised can, in exceptional circumstances, lead to abusive conduct. Specifically, the ECJ suggested that in order for a refusal, by an undertaking which owns a copyright, to give access to a product or service indispensable to carry on business to be considered an abuse, three criteria must be satisfied. First, the undertaking requesting the licence must intend to offer new products or services not offered by the copyright owner, and for which there is a potential customer demand. Secondly, the refusal cannot be justified by objective consideration. Thirdly, the refusal must be such as to reserve to the copyright owner the relevant market by eliminating all competition.

[64] [2004] 1 ECR 5039; [2004] 4 CMLR 1543.

In the US a number of cases have also been decided on analogous issues. In *Wang v Mitsubishi* 41 USPQ 2d 1263 (Cir Ct App 1997), the Court of Appeal for the Federal Circuit found that a patentee's conduct, including that in a standard-setting group, gave rise to a perpetual, royalty free implied licence to Mitsubishi. In *Stambler v Diebold* 11 USPQ 2d (NY Dist Ct 1988), the plaintiff continued to sit on an American National Standards Institute Committee, even after realizing that a proposed standard might infringe his patent. Stambler subsequently quit the committee without notifying it of the alleged infringement. When Stambler attempted to enforce his patent, the District Court for Eastern District of New York considered that Stambler could not remain silent while an entire industry used the convention. The court ruled that he could not do so on grounds of equitable estoppel and laches, finding that Stambler's course of conduct had reasonably allowed other members to believe that he would not assert any patent covering the standard's subject matter. Finally, the Federal Trade Commission also took action against Dell Corporation for unfair competition under the Federal Trade Commission Act.[65] The action was based on Dell's failure, while at table, to disclose patents as required by an SDO's rules[66] and Dell's later conduct in trying to enforce patent rights against users of a standard adopted by the group. The result in this case was a consent order entered into whereby Dell agreed not to enforce its patent against computer manufacturers incorporating the so called VL bus design in their products.

Competition law, therefore, can be a powerful weapon in combating suggestions that outside the terms of the standard setting organization there is no method to address the unfair practice of dominant undertakings in involved in setting standards.

10.4.2 Institutional pragmatism on openness

The UK is not alone in defining open standards as being royalty free, but it is worth remembering that this is not the only way to interpret open standards as a regulatory body; eg, the definition put forward by the European Commission in the European Interoperability Framework (EIF) v 2 is much less explicit. The European Union developed the European Interoperability Framework in order to address the interoperability of services and systems between public administrations as well as between administrations and the public (citizens and businesses). The most recent version of the EIF, version 2, was adopted by the European Commission on 16 December 2010.[67] It states that: 'All stakeholders have the same possibility of contributing to the development of the specification and public review is part of the decision-making

[65] *Re Dell Corporation* (20 May 110106) doc #C-3685 (unreported).

[66] In these cases, the Video Electronics Standards Association ('VESA').

[67] Annex II, EIF (European Interoperability Framework) of the Communication, 'Towards interoperability for European public services' [2010] COM 744 final.

process; the specification is available for everybody to study; intellectual property rights related to the specification are licensed on FRAND [(Fair) Reasonable and Non-Discriminatory] terms *or* [author's italics] on a royalty-free basis in a way that allows implementation in both proprietary an open source software.'[68] The EIF v 2 thus also presents an either/or approach.

As the UK consultation points out, however, (F)RAND *is* a term notoriously difficult to describe with any degree of accuracy; in addition, being (F)RAND will not necessarily appease the wrath of the open source community, nor will it ensure compliance with an open source licence. Perhaps allowing flexibility in defining open standards—as illustrated with the EIF v 2 definition—defeats the very purpose of the standard being truly open, and allows one to suggests that they are simply promoting standards in the same way that traditional industry led standard setting bodies do. For a regulatory body this is perhaps strange The (F)RAND terms created by standards bodies, indeed the concept of (F)RAND in the context of standard setting amongst industry players, emerge in quite a different context than that of open source software products (although there are some similarities in intention), and, to a certain extent, have to respond to very different problems than those encountered by the supporters and users of truly open standards.

Another point worth making is that appearing to be magnanimous by preferring flexibility rather than absoluteness—(F)RAND or royalty free, as opposed to (F)RAND and royalty free—means the role royalty payments have in making the use of technology possible is ignored. It might be fair to contain within a licence reasonable terms as to the use of the licensed technology, but if access to the technology is limited to only the very wealthy because of a very high licence fee, there is another element of fairness that has been ignored. The question of what an open standard is can, therefore, be rephrased: is royalty free the defining aspect of what separates an open standard from a more traditional standard? Perhaps it might be, with the proviso that even if royalty free there may be a strategic element involved, as with the Android system. On the other hand, without royalty payments, organizations involved will often want (though not always) an alternative revenue stream. Without royalty payments, one argument runs, the company can instead focus on obtaining revenue from service concerning the software, but it is important to note that service revenues will often not exist (as there is no need and therefore no market) or will not be sufficient. In addition, certain companies who may innovate in the field of software may not want to dabble in downstream revenue alternatives at the cost of going royalty free, and may see IP protection and payment resulting as the main justification for their innovation.

Aside from the royalty issue, another important distinction between the open standard and the traditional standard is the differing respect given to the variety of

[68] See n 64.

intellectual property laws that might be involved in becoming standards or becoming open source. Standard setting outside the scope of an open or open source philosophy more usually will accept the exclusionary approach of IP protection as a background to any standardization process, and thus such standardization incorporates the desire for royalties as a default above and beyond any openness or reasonableness required as a standard; indeed, at any point an essential technology might cease to be essential to an industry and could find itself being dropped as a standard. Crucially, this does not mean that the technology itself is still open in the sense that open source software is; it was only the effect of the standardization process that brought it outside the fold of being anything other than IP and subject to royalty payments. IP laws, and their exclusionary effect, in such a case would still apply and are expected to apply in the context of normative standard setting in industry. Why wouldn't they? If there were no IP laws protecting the technology, what would be the point in having a standard setting body for industry bodies in the first place? Conversely, the anti-exclusionary approach is arguably central to open source, and whether open source software becomes a standard or not is a secondary consideration. This would explain the anomaly of Android Open Source; the standard is the primary consideration, I would argue, not the openness. Having openness as the primary consideration involves a different perspective. Consider, eg, the definition of open standard put forward by the Open Source Initiative ('OSI'):

> An 'open standard' must not prohibit conforming implementations in open source software:
>
> To comply with the Open Standards Requirement, an 'open standard' must satisfy the following criteria. If an 'open standard' does not meet these criteria, it will be discriminating against open source developers.
>
> 1. No Intentional Secrets: The standard MUST NOT withhold any detail necessary for interoperable implementation. As flaws are inevitable, the standard MUST define a process for fixing flaws identified during implementation and interoperability testing and to incorporate said changes into a revised version or superseding version of the standard to be released under terms that do not violate the OSR.
> 2. Availability: The standard MUST be freely and publicly available (e.g., from a stable web site) under royalty-free terms at reasonable and non-discriminatory cost.
> 3. Patents: All patents essential to implementation of the standard MUST:
>   - be licensed under royalty-free terms for unrestricted use, or
>   - be covered by a promise of non-assertion when practiced by open source software
> 4. No Agreements: There MUST NOT be any requirement for execution of a license agreement, NDA, grant, click-through, or any other form of paperwork to deploy conforming implementations of the standard.

5. No OSR-Incompatible Dependencies: Implementation of the standard MUST NOT require any other technology that fails to meet the criteria of this Requirement.[69]

As the UK consultation outlines in justifying its definition of open standards: 'Software that is open source must be provided under one of a range of recognised open source licences. Some suggest that the most commonly used of these licences do not allow the development of software that requires royalty payments (Valimaki and Oksanen, 2005). In relation to software, standards must be compatible with free and open source software licensing terms to enable all suppliers to have fair access to competition for government contracts (Ghosh 2005), therefore the potential issue with patents and royalty payments must be considered.'[70]

In the light of this, the principles developed by the Cabinet Office can perhaps be seen as more pragmatic than the either/or approach put forward by the EIF v 2; often what is an available standard might not be suitable for the purposes of being a standard that can be implemented by all; conversely, a standard that can be implemented by all, technically, might not be suitable because of an onerous licensing condition. Sensibly, they are suggesting requiring suitable standards available for implementation by all, thus the preference for royalty free *and* non-discriminatory. To be fair and reasonable, if expected to be an *open* standard, is not enough. It might be in the context of industry standard setting bodies where a proprietary technology has become a *de facto* standard, or, indeed, where a commercial entity is using openness as a Trojan horse for a standard; but for the purposes of a public orientated body such as a government, with, one would hope, a balanced perspective, this is perhaps not the correct approach.

10.5 INNOVATION

Is the desire to have open standards on royalty free terms, as opposed to either (F)RAND terms *or* royalty free, consistent with the broader policy of technological innovation, however? Requiring a royalty to be paid by the users of a technology contained in a standard is not necessarily inconsistent with the overarching requirement

[69] Open Source Initiative, 'Open Standards Requirement for Software' available at <http://opensource.org/osr> accessed 20 March 2013.

[70] See n 39. It is worth pointing out that Valimaki and Oksanen also note the following: '... requiring patents on standards to be always royalty free is not necessarily the optimal solution.... Allowing heterogeneity on the markets may be more important than categorical discrimination against some established business practice such as patent royalties on standard.... Royalty-free terms do explicitly prohibit discrimination against open source software but at the same time they can decrease the possible business models available to those companies, which actually develop new technology on the standards.' See M Välimäki and V Oksanen, 'Patents on Compatibility Standards and Open Source—Do Patent Law Exceptions and Royalty-Free Requirements Make Sense?' (2005) 2:3 *SCRIPTed* 397.

that the technology also be capable of being used within the standard on FRAND terms; not necessarily, but of course there is a distinction between a standard and normal commercial licensing of intellectual property right. That is to say, standards should be, *qua* standards, somehow distinguishable. What makes them different? What is a standard? Perhaps we need to view the definition of a standard in a different light, especially when considering innovation. Indeed, a standard is there to allow different technical instruments to work together, such as interoperability and interconnection, but the idea that the industry linking those systems is run other than in a market orientated fashion is not so often the case. Standards are *technical* standards, in this sense, and do not have any economic goal in the sense of controlling the industrial economy of a sector.

All of this, of course, has to be considered within the broader context of technological innovation more generally. While recognizing that innovation can happen, and often does happen, in spite of attempts to theorize what things might be better or worse in terms of cultivating it, intellectual property rights, standards, openness, and freedom from royalties all offer advantages to the general innovation landscape. IP rights offer the advantage of a return on investment, a spur to innovators and inventors to undertake research and development in order to make the next technological breakthrough. Standards, somewhat conversely, and especially in the context of network industries, can allow for the growth and development of what would otherwise be fractured and underdeveloped industries; standards can open up the advantages of a technology to all the players in an industry, because of their very unrestricted accessibility. Openness encourages experimentation and can indeed lead to better made product; as the saying goes, 'given enough eyeballs, all bugs are shallow'.[71] And, finally, royalty free often means that companies who otherwise might not be capable of getting involved can; or indeed, that large public orientated systems can get off the ground instead of lingering unsatisfied for want of finances to afford royalties. All this openness can be seen as good for innovation. As Chesbrough has argued, modern society is undergoing a paradigm shift from closed innovation towards open innovation and one of the major benefits of this for innovation generally is the 'recovery of false negatives', previously ignored projects that seemed to be worthless turned out to be valuable.[72] Equally, of course, and dependent on circumstances, all of these characteristics of openness can be seen as bad for innovation. Chesbrough himself called the closed innovation system a virtuous circle, only sometimes dangerous for companies if they are exposed to erosion factors from third parties assuming responsibility for post-innovation commercialization.

[71] Commonly known as Linus' Law.

[72] HW Chesbrough, *Open Innovation: The New Imperative for Creating And Profiting from Technology* (Boston, Mass., Harvard Business Review Press, 2005).

It is the intent involved, and the manner in which the principles and instruments are deployed that will encourage or discourage innovation.

10.6 CONCLUSIONS

It would be strange to expect that a for-profit company, having spent years on research to develop a time limited patent for a technology, wouldn't want to recoup some of that money in licensing, even if the technology became essential to the functioning of the sector. The royalty/non-royalty argument in the context of open standards is a red herring, in this sense; one should not look to see whether the standard is open or not, but look to see in which context the standard is expected to be deployed and who is pushing the standard. Openness will depend on the context, not on whether a standard is involved or not. For context here read industry, sector, maturity of the market player, market share, and philosophy. If a commercial entity wants to develop a standard, they will strategize the degree of openness they allow in line with capturing market share, and Android Open Source is a perfect example of this. If a standard setting body is pushing a standard it may well argue that a royalty is only to be expected. Open standards, similarly, will be defined dependent on purpose and origin.

Outside the overtly commercial context of standards development, standard setting organizations vary. If they are comprised of members of industry, they may well have a mix of (F)RAND terms plus a royalty expectation. If they are not, or if they are tied to an industry that supports complete openness, they may well favour royalty free. Government and regulatory bodies such as the European Commission can be seen as a standard setting organizations in this context, pushing their own respective perspectives on openness that reflect their particular mandate and the extent of their responsibility. While open standards have developed on elements of the open source movement, they are very different things serving a radically different purpose.

Openness thus depends very much on the context in which it is being deployed as a concept. If one is referring to openness in the sense of using the lessons from open source software development to establish 'open' standards for a particular industry or sector within an industry, it must be borne in mind that such openness is probably (but not necessarily always) a part of a larger strategy, what Shapiro and Varian meant when they wrote about using standards when competition on the market won't or can't work. In such a scenario the licensing of the open standard may well be royalty free, but the openness of the technology will be a commercial strategy, so the royalty free aspect is moot. It may well simply be a question of pay now or pay later.

If one is referring to openness in the sense of using lessons from the open source software community to advance projects that have a public ethos, one might very well expect it to be open and royalty free. Given the changing understanding of what a public ethos is, one could imagine this changing in the future; if government can privatize sectors such as health, transport, and education, they can and are privatizing IT services. In this sense, the UK policy of open standards as royalty free is better understood as a political proposal framed by budget constraints. Museums, public institutions, and other governments will follow in the footsteps of proposals such as those made by the Cabinet Office about royalty free open standards because the fundamental ethos of such bodies is a public one, but that ethos is also established in the light of available finances. This public v private/finances debate is key in understanding openness in the context of standards because it is the ethos and the financial purpose of the organization that will determine whether openness is seen as an end in itself, as with free/libre software, or whether it is just a means to a more private orientated end.

11

PUBLIC SECTOR AND OPEN SOURCE

Iain G Mitchell QC

11.1 INTRODUCTION

In the competition for market share amongst operating systems and different types of software, there can come a time when one particular model achieves a position that is so dominant it may threaten to create a kind of electronic monoculture. When everyone else has Microsoft Office, it can take a lot of nerve for users to swim against the tide.

In theory, provided that there is full interoperability, that should not be a problem, but anyone who has tried to create a document either in open source or a proprietary program other than MS Word, such as Lotus Word Pro, save it as a .doc file, send it to a recipient, who then tries to open it in MS Office will know that this is at best a hit and miss operation—sometimes it will open perfectly well, sometimes the formatting will be distorted, sometimes it will not open at all, and sometimes Office will generate a scary (and entirely inaccurate) warning that the file may be infected with a virus.[1] A plea to the recipient to install Open Office seems to fall on deaf ears and, on balance, it all seems so much easier for the author of the document just to go out and purchase a licence for MS Office and be done with it.

Further, companies with a dominant position can be tempted to abuse it in order to cement their market dominance by restricting access to operating system code by developers seeking to write programs to interoperate with the system and by bundling software along with the operating system, as in the case of the proceedings taken by the EU Commission against Microsoft.[2]

Though enforcement action, such as that taken against Microsoft by the Commission, can rein in the worst excesses, essentially the way for competing systems to break out of the ghetto of being a minority enthusiasm for geeks is to achieve a significant market share. But the forces which maintain the main player's market dominance can often be those same forces which stop a breakthrough for competitors.

Historically, this is a problem that has confronted open source, though its clear economic advantages over proprietary software have been gaining it an increasing share in the market despite the long-term bias towards proprietary software. What is needed to ensure that it achieves its full potential is both a level playing field and a sufficiently large user base to ensure that the next time the Open Office user suggests that his correspondent download Open Office, that will be a request which is taken seriously.

The EU Commission and national governments have a clear role to play in the creation of a level playing field, but also, and less obviously, through the medium of public procurement have the opportunity to achieve it. Public procurement in general accounts for, on average, about 15 per cent of the GDP of the OECD countries.[3] Figures for the IT market are not readily available, but it is clear that, on any view, the

[1] At the root of the problem is that Microsoft unilaterally declared its own Office Open (OXML) code as a standard, and obtained recognition of it as such from ECMA, though it has not been recognised by the ISO. It is not fully compatible with software written to ISO standards, see K A Zelnio, 'A concise, bulleted list of grievences against.docx' (17 November 2009) <http://www.zelnio.org/2009/11/17/a-concise-bulleted-list-of-grievences-against-docx> accessed 8 April 2013.

[2] See *Microsoft Corp v Commission* case T-201/4, paras 1088–1090 of the judgment dated 17 September 2007.

[3] See OECD, *Size of Public Procurement Market* in *Government at a Glance 2011* (OECD, Paris, 2011) para 40.

public sector is a major player in IT procurement—large enough to have a significant influence on the respective market shares of open source and proprietary software respectively. Further, with the creation of a 'critical mass' of public sector customers, there is the hope that this will serve also to encourage private sector buyers.

The exercise of that extensive buying power might be proactive in its support for open source software, or it might merely set out to be neutral so that there are, at least, no barriers to the procurement of open source, or, indeed, in some cases, the power may even be exercised with a bias towards particular proprietary solutions. Some, but not all governments and public sector bodies may have a specific policy with regard to open source, but, whatever the policy, there are both obligations and limits on what a public authority can do as part of the procurement process: for public procurement sits within a framework of international and European law which binds also the Member States.

At the international level, the World Trade Organisation ('WTO') recognizes the key role which public procurement has to play in stimulating world trade. It states, on its government procurement gateway:

> Open, transparent and non-discriminatory procurement is generally considered to be the best tool to achieve 'value for money' as it optimises competition among suppliers. At the same time, many WTO Members still use their purchasing decisions to achieve domestic policy goals, such as the promotion of specific local industry sectors or social groups.
>
> Government procurement is an important aspect of international trade, given the considerable size of the procurement market (often 10-15 percent of GDP) and the benefits for domestic and foreign stakeholders in terms of increased competition.[4]

Notwithstanding the undoubted importance of government procurement, it was excluded from the General Agreement on Tariffs and Trade ('GATT'), originally negotiated in 1947, and, more recently, was also excluded from the main market access commitments of the General Agreement on Trade in Services ('GATS'). The WTO has been working with member governments to try to plug that gap, starting with the signing in 1979 of the first Agreement on Government Procurement ('GPA'), which has since twice been renegotiated, the most recent version being adopted on 30 March 2012.[5]

There are, however, some drawbacks, chiefly that the Agreement is plurilateral, binding only those states which have joined and not all the members of the WTO, and, second with not all forms of government procurement being covered in all signatory states.[6]

[4] WTO, 'Government procurement' <http://www.wto.org/english/tratop_e/gproc_e/gproc_e.htm> accessed 8 April 2013.

[5] WTO, 'GPA/113 dated 2 April 2012' <http://www.wto.org/english/tratop_e/gproc_e/overview_e.htm> accessed on 8 April 2013.

[6] WTO (n 5).

There are also proceeding negotiations on the possible amendment of Article XIII:1 GATS, from the ambit of which government procurement of services is currently excluded. A Working Party has been looking at this since 1995, but there does not appear to be an end in sight. The sort of difficulties which are being encountered are blandly hinted at on the WTO Procurement Gateway:

> Some Members take the view that negotiations under this mandate can involve market access and non-discrimination as well as transparency and other procedural issues. Other Members do not share this interpretation, considering that Article XIII excludes MFN treatment, market access and national treatment from the scope of the mandated negotiations.[7]

Finally, there is a Working Group on Transparency in Government Procurement set up in 1997 following a decision of the 1996 Singapore Ministerial Conference, but that Working Group has also yet to report.

So far, the only solid achievement is the GPA to which there are currently 42 signatories including the EU and all 27 of its Member States.[8]

Set against this international context, it is intended, first, to consider the European public procurement regime before considering the policy approaches in relation to procurement of open source software adopted by the Commission and Member States, how far those policy positions accord with the legal requirements, and how, in practice, legal obligations are being observed in procurement exercises. Thereafter, the question needs to be asked whether enlightened public procurement alone is enough to level the playing field and enable open source to build its market share.

11.2 THE EUROPEAN PROCUREMENT LAW CONTEXT

Although a full exposition of public procurement law does not fall within the scope of this book, it is useful to have some understanding of the underlying principles in order to understand some of the issues surrounding software procurement.[9]

The European Union acts within the terms of the competences accorded to it by the European Treaties. In particular, Article 3(3) of the Treaty on European Union ('TEU') provides:

[7] WTO (n 5).

[8] The other signatories are Armenia, Canada, Hong Kong, China, Iceland, Israel, Japan, Korea, Liechtenstein, the Netherlands with respect to Aruba, Norway, Singapore, Switzerland, Chinese Taipei, and the United States. A further nine members are in process of acceding.

[9] See generally C Bovis, *EU Public Procurement Law*, 2nd edn (Cheltenham, Edward Elgar, 2012); AS Graells, *Public Procurement and the EU Competition Rules* (Oxford, Hart Publishing, 2010); and P Trepte, *Public Procurement in the EU: A Practitioner's Guide*, 2nd edn (Oxford, Oxford University Press, 2007).

> The Union shall establish an internal market. It shall work for the sustainable development of Europe based on balanced economic growth and price stability, a highly competitive social market economy, aiming at full employment and social progress, and a high level of protection and improvement of the quality of the environment. It shall promote scientific and technological advance...

In terms of Part 3, Title I (Articles 26 and 27) of the Treaty on the Functioning of the European Union ('TFEU'), the Union is given power 'to adopt measures with the aim of establishing or ensuring the functioning of the internal market, in accordance with the relevant provisions of the Treaties.'[10] Title II makes provision in respect of the Free Movement of Goods and Title IV for the Free Movement of Persons, Services, and Capital.

The Union exercises those competences by a number of means, including legislation which includes the making of Regulations, which are immediately effective throughout the EU, and Directives, which impose requirements upon Member States to transpose the provisions of the Directive in question into their respective national laws.

In the area of public procurement, the applicable Directives, at the time of writing, are Directive 2004/18/EC ('The Public Sector Directive');[11] Directive 2004/17/EC ('The Utilities Directive');[12] and Directive 2007/66/EC ('The Remedies Directive'),[13] all collectively referred to as the Procurement Directives. For the purposes of illustration, reference will be made primarily to the Public Sector Directive. The European Commission has adopted a proposal for the replacement of these Directives,[14] which will be considered later in this chapter.

Article 16 of the Utilities Directive and Article 7 of the Public Sector Directive set minimum thresholds below which the Directives do not apply. In the case of the Public Sector Directive, this threshold is normally €6,242,000.[15] However, that does not mean that contracts of a lower value fall outside the European public procurement regime.

[10] Article 26(1).

[11] Directive 2004/18/EC of the European Parliament and of the Council of 31 March 2004 on the coordination of procedures for the award of public works contracts, public supply contracts and public service contracts [20 April 2004] OJ L134/114.

[12] Directive 2004/17/EC of the European Parliament and of the Council of 31 March 2004 coordinating the procurement procedures of entities operating in the water, energy, transport and postal services sectors [30 April 2004] OJ L134/1.

[13] Directive 2007/66/EC of the European Parliament and of the Council of 11 December 2007 amending Council Directives 89/665/EEC and 92/13/EEC with regard to improving the effectiveness of review procedures concerning the award of public contracts [20 December 2007] OJ L335/31.

[14] European Commission, 'Reform proposals' <http://ec.europa.eu/internal_market/publicprocurement/modernising_rules/reform_proposals_en.htm> accessed 8 April 2013.

[15] This is the normal threshold, though there are lower thresholds stipulated for certain specified types of contract.

At the heart of the Single Market are not only the abolition of customs barriers, but also non-tariff barriers, such as differing national standards, and the creation of a level playing field on which businesses from all of the Member States can compete fairly. At the time of the introduction of the original Procurement Directives[16] there was a concern that public authorities could make direct awards of contracts, cutting would-be contractors out of the opportunity to bid. Accordingly amongst the preambles to, eg, the 1992 Public Services Contracts Directive, there was a statement:

> Whereas, to eliminate practices that restrict competition in general and participation in contracts by other Member States' nationals in particular, it is necessary to improve the access of service providers to procedures for the award of contracts;

It is because EU procurement law is rooted in the Treaties that the 2004 Public Sector Directive narrates, in recital 2 of the preamble:

> The award of contracts concluded in the Member States on behalf of the State, regional or local authorities and other bodies governed by public law entities, is subject to the respect of the principles of the Treaty and in particular to the principle of freedom of movement of goods, the principle of freedom of establishment and the principle of freedom to provide services and to the principles deriving therefrom, such as the principle of equal treatment, the principle of non-discrimination, the principle of mutual recognition, the principle of proportionality and the principle of transparency. However, for public contracts above a certain value, it is advisable to draw up provisions of Community coordination of national procedures for the award of such contracts which are based on these principles so as to ensure the effects of them and to guarantee the opening-up of public procurement to competition. These coordinating provisions should therefore be interpreted in accordance with both the aforementioned rules and principles and other rules of the Treaty.

Thus, it will be seen that, in addition to the specific rules in the Public Sector Directive, public sector contracts are also governed by both the principles laid down in the Treaties, and the principles derived from those Treaty principles, namely:

- equal treatment;
- non discrimination;
- mutual recognition;
- proportionality;
- transparency.

This is underscored for contracts falling within the scope of the Public Sector Directive (that is above threshold contracts) by Article 2, which provides:

[16] Directives 92/50/EEC (Public Services Contracts), 93/36/EEC (Public Supply Contracts), and 93/37/EEC (Public Works Contracts).

> Contracting authorities shall treat economic operators equally and non-discriminatorily and shall act in a transparent way . . .

However, as the European Court of Justice has developed the law, starting with *Telaustria Verlags GmbH and Telefonadress GmbH v Telekom Austria AG*,[17] it has applied these principles not only to above-threshold contracts but also to most below-threshold contracts. At paragraph 60 of its judgment, the Court said:

> In that regard, it should be borne in mind that, notwithstanding the fact that, as Community law stands at present, such contracts are excluded from the scope of Directive 93/38, the contracting entities concluding them are, none the less, bound to comply with the fundamental rules of the Treaty, in general, and the principle of non-discrimination on the ground of nationality, in particular.

The Court expanded upon this reasoning in the case of *Bent Mousten Vestergaard v Spøttrup Boligselskab*[18] where it stated at paragraphs 19–21 of its judgment:

> 19. To rule on the questions, it should be noted, to begin with, that the Community directives coordinating public procurement procedures apply only to contracts whose value exceeds a threshold laid down expressly in each directive. However, the mere fact that the Community legislature considered that the strict special procedures laid down in those directives are not appropriate in the case of public contracts of small value does not mean that those contracts are excluded from the scope of Community law.
>
> 20. Although certain contracts are excluded from the scope of the Community directives in the field of public procurement, the contracting authorities which conclude them are nevertheless bound to comply with the fundamental rules of the Treaty (see, to that effect, Case C-324/98 *Telaustria and Telefonadress* [2000] ECR 1-10745, paragraph 60).
>
> 21. Consequently, notwithstanding the fact that a works contract is below the threshold laid down in Directive 93/37 and thus not within the scope of that directive, the lawfulness of a clause in the contract documents for that contract must be assessed by reference to the fundamental rules of the Treaty, which include the free movement of goods in Article 30 of the Treaty.

These cases have subsequently been followed in a number of other cases, including *Parking Brixen GmbH v Gemeinde Brixen & Stadtwerke Brixen AG*[19] and *Medipac-Kazantzidis AE v Venizeleio-Pananeio*.[20] In each of the cases cited here, the contract value fell below the threshold, yet the court, whilst not applying the provisions of the directives, did apply the Treaty and derived principles.

[17] Case C-234/98 [2000] ECR 1-10770.
[18] Case C-59/00 [2001] ECR 1-09505.
[19] Case C-458/03 [2005] ECR 1-08585.
[20] Case C-6/05 [2007] ECR 1-04557.

Given, however, that the Treaties are the ultimate source of the principles, it follows that European procurement principles ought not to apply in those cases where the contract in question does not fall within the scope of the Treaties, which is to say where there is no cross-border interest. The Treaties aim to create a Single Market by ensuring competition across borders. Thus, in the case of *Consorzio Aziende Metano (Coname) v Comune di Cingia de'Botti*[21] the Court stated at paragraph 20:

> With regard to the case in the main proceedings, it is not apparent from the file that, because of special circumstances, such as a very modest economic interest at stake, it could reasonably be maintained that an undertaking located in a Member State other than that of the *Comune di Cingia de'Botti* would have no interest in the concession at issue and that the effects on the fundamental freedoms concerned should therefore be regarded as too uncertain and indirect to warrant the conclusion that they may have been infringed...

The wording here is a little convoluted, but the principle was, perhaps, expressed more clearly by the Advocate General in the conjoined cases of *SECAP SpA* and *Santorso Soc. Cooparl v Comune di Torino*[22] at paragraph 23:

> The setting of a financial threshold above which contracts are subject to public procurement directives is based on a single premise, namely that contracts of small value do not attract operators established outside national borders; such contracts are thus devoid of Community implications. However, that rebuttable presumption is open to evidence to the contrary...

The threads were brought together by the Court in its judgment in those cases where it said, at paragraphs 19–21:

> 19. The strict special procedures prescribed by the Community directives co-ordinating public procurement procedures apply only to contracts whose value exceeds a threshold expressly laid down in each of those directives (order in Case C-59/00 *Vestergaard* (2001) ECR 1-9505, paragraph 19). Accordingly, the rules in those directives do not apply to contracts with a value below the threshold set by those directives (see, to that effect, Case C-412/04 *Commission* v *Italy* (2008) ECR 1-619, paragraph 65).
>
> 20. That does not mean, however, that contracts below the threshold are excluded from the scope of Community law (order in *Vestergaard*, paragraph 19). According to the established case-law of the Court concerning the award of contracts which, on account of their value, are not subject to the procedures laid down by Community rules, the contracting authorities are nonetheless bound to comply with the fundamental rules of the Treaty and the principle of non-discrimination on the ground of nationality in particular (*Telaustria and Telefonadress*, paragraph 60; the order

[21] Case C-231/03 [2005] ECR 1-07287.

[22] Cases C-147/06 and C-148/06 [2008] ECR 1-03565.

> in *Vestergaard*, paragraphs 20 and 21; Case C-264/03 *Commission* v *France* [2005] ECR 1-8831, paragraph 32; and Case C-6/5 *Medipac-Kazantzidis* [2007] ECR 1-4557, paragraph 33).
>
> 21. However, according to the case-law of the Court, the application of the fundamental rules and general principles of the Treaty to procedures for the award of contracts below the threshold for the application of Community directives is based on the premiss that the contracts in question are of certain cross-border interest (see, to that effect, Case C-507/03 *Commission* v *Ireland* [2007] ECR 1-9777, paragraph 29, and *Commission* v *Italy*, paragraphs 66 and 67)

At paragraph 30, the Court added:

> It is in principle for the contracting authority concerned to assess whether there may be cross-border interest in a contract whose estimated value is below the threshold laid down by the Community rules, it being understood that that assessment may be subject to judicial review.

One sees that the approach of the court is to see public sector contracts as falling into two categories, those where there is and those where there is not a cross-border interest. However, it may be more helpful to treat public sector contracts as, in effect, falling into three classes: first, there are those which are of such a negligible value that no cross-border interest is likely to arise; second, there are those contracts (not falling in the first category) in which the contract value falls below threshold, and in which there is a rebuttable presumption that no cross-border interest arises, but if that presumption is rebutted, then the Treaty principles and derived principles are applicable; and third, there are those contracts in which the contract value is above threshold, in which case there arises an irrebuttable presumption that there is a cross-border interest, and accordingly those contracts are subjected to the strict and detailed rules set forth in the Procurement Directives.[23]

Those which are above threshold clearly fall into the first category (cases where there is a cross-border interest); those which are below threshold might fit into either category depending upon the view taken as to whether the presumption that there is not a cross-border interest is overcome by the facts. The responsibility for making the judgment of whether a cross-border interest arises is for the public body concerned, though any such decision is always open to judicial review.[24]

[23] For a more detailed analysis of the jurisprudence of the ECJ in this matter, see the submissions by the present author as Counsel in *Sidey Ltd v Clackmannanshire Council and Pyramid Joinery and Construction Ltd* 2010 SLT 607, paras 22 *et seq*.

[24] *SECAP* (n 22); *R (on the application of Chandler) v Secretary of State for Children, Schools and Families* (2010) CMLR 19; *Sidey Ltd v Clackmannanshire Council* 2010 SLT 607. In the Petition for Judicial Review which followed the case just cited, the court determined on the facts that, in the below threshold contract in question, no cross-border interest had been engaged, even though the Council had voluntarily conducted the revelant tendering exercise in question according to the rules for above-threshold contracts (*Sidley Ltd v Clackamnnanshire Council* 2012 SLT 334).

Assuming that there is a cross-border interest and whether or not the contract value is above threshold, the public authority will be required to conduct the procurement exercise in accordance with the Treaty and derived principles, including the principles of equal treatment, non discrimination, mutual recognition, proportionality, and transparency.

How, then, does this legal structure impact upon questions of software procurement?

11.3 ISSUES IN SOFTWARE PROCUREMENT

11.3.1 Is there procurement at all?

It is important to stress that the EU procurement regime (the Procurement Directives, the Treaty and derived principles) apply to procurement by the public sector, defined in Article 1(9) of the Public Sector Directive thus:

> (9) 'Contracting authorities' means the State, regional or local authorities, bodies governed by public law, associations formed by one or several of such authorities or one or several of such bodies governed by public law.
>
> A 'body governed by public law' means any body:
>
> (a) established for the specific purpose of meeting needs in the general interest, not having an industrial or commercial character;
>
> (b) having legal personality; and
>
> (c) financed, for the most part, by the State, regional or local authorities, or other bodies governed by public law; or subject to management supervision by those bodies; or having an administrative, managerial or supervisory board, more than half of whose members are appointed by the State, regional or local authorities, or by other bodies governed by public law.

The definition of a body governed by public law is of considerable importance, encompassing, as it does, bodies which do not have an industrial or commercial character, placing such bodies within the ambit of the EU procurement regime, whereas a body not having a commercial or industrial purpose would not be regarded as an 'enterprise' and so not fall within the ambit of competition law.[25]

The procurement regime does not apply to the private sector. If a private enterprise in its procurement activities, whether in connection with IT purchases or anything else, is opaque and treats potential suppliers unequally, then, whatever other remedies there

[25] See the conjoined cases of Cases C-159/91*Poucet* and C-160/91 *Pistre* [1993] ECR I-637; Case C-67/96 *Albany* [1999] ECRI-5751; and Case T-319/9 *Nacional de Empresas de Instrumentación Científica, Médica, Técnica y Dental (FENIN) v Commission of the European Communities* [2003] 5 CMLR 1 and, on appeal, Case C-205/03 [2006] 5 CMLR 7.

may be for an aggrieved potential tenderer, there are none under the European procurement regime.

Further, the procurement regime will not apply if there is no procurement at all. For there to be a procurement exercise, at least two separate parties dealing with each other are required. If the public authority is developing its own software, then securing that software for its own use is not a procurement exercise at all. This applies even if the departments involved are organizationally separated.

It should also be noted that certain specific contracts are excluded from the ambit of the Directives. Of most relevance to IT suppliers are likely to be 'public contracts for the principal purpose of permitting the contracting authorities to provide or exploit public telecommunications networks or to provide to the public one or more telecommunications services'[26] and secret contracts or contracts requiring special security measures.[27]

A particular issue with open source software is that if a contracting authority wishes to acquire such software, it might usually do so as part of a larger package, eg, involving also services provided by a supplier who uses open source software or implements an open source solution. However, there may be cases where all that the contracting authority wishes to do is simply to acquire the software either with a view to developing the software itself or simply using it 'as is'. In that situation, it might choose to buy the software, but it might also be able simply to download it for free. If it chooses to download it, then, since it is not buying anything, there is no 'public contract' within the meaning of Article 1(2)(a) of the Public Sector Directive[28] and, hence, no procurement exercise falling within the ambit of EU procurement law.

Paragraph 2.2.4 of the IDABC *Guideline on Public Procurement of Open Source Software*[29] comments on this and, in paragraph 2.3 gives guidance on best practice for downloading. The process which is recommended is that the public authority should first determine its acquisition requirements, and then should download the relevant software itself without fee as part of that already-determined acquisition process, whilst simultaneously issuing an invitation to tender for commercially provided services and support, where required. The *Guideline* stresses that the downloading of the software should be seen as, in effect, an alternative to the step of publishing a tender for the supply of software, and counsels against the unsupervised downloading of software by individuals within the organization.

[26] Article 13. These are subject to their own special regime: see para 23 of the preamble, referring to Council Directive 93/38/EEC of 14 June 1993 coordinating the procurement procedures of entities operating in the water, energy, transport and telecommunications sectors [9 August 1993] OJ L199/84.

[27] Article 14. See also para 22 of the preamble. The reason for this exception is self-evident.

[28] Article 2(1)(a): ' "Public contracts" are contracts for pecuniary interest concluded in writing between one or more economic operators and one or more contracting authorities . . . .

[29] European eGovernment Services, *Guideline on Public Procurement of Open Source Software* (March 2010) <http://joinup.ec.europa.eu/sites/default/files/OSS-procurement-guideline%20-final.pdf> accessed 8 April 2013.

For those interested in the future of open source software, this is something of a double-edged sword. On the one hand, it means that an informed public authority would be able to acquire the open source software that it wants, without having to be concerned about possible challenges from disappointed would-be tenderers who would have hoped for the opportunity to sell proprietary software to the public authority. On the other hand, if a public authority, perhaps not as well informed, embarks on a public procurement exercise, it may end up with a proprietary solution, simply because there is no open source supplier in the race; no one would go to the cost and trouble of submitting a tender with a nil value. Of course, most open source licences are concerned to ensure that software is kept free (as in free speech) and not free (as in free beer) and there may be nothing to stop a free software developer tendering at an economic price from bundling in software support services, even though the public authority might have downloaded the same software for free. How far this is a real dilemma may be open to question, but it may be that most software acquisitions by public authorities will involve some element of added value, even if it is only installing, testing, and maintaining the solution.

11.3.2 Cross-border interest

As discussed earlier, both the TEU and TFEU set out principles that may be relevant in matters of public procurement. Neither these Treaties nor the derived principles apply where there is no cross-border interest. It is for the public authority concerned to make that judgement in the first instance, though subject to the possibility of judicial review. There may be cases where the public authority may decide that there is a cross-border interest, or fails to apply its mind to the question, and then proceeds to run the procurement exercise according to either the Procurement Directives or at least the Treaties and derived principles, but then finds itself as the respondent in a judicial review for having gone through the European procurement procedure. It might be thought unlikely that this would arise in the real world, for who would have an interest to object if the process is conducted openly, fairly, and transparently, which is what the European procurement regime requires? Yet, in rare cases this can happen when the public authority, in conducting the procurement exercise, infringes any of the principles contained in the Treaties (known as 'Treaty principles'), or principles derived therefrom (known as 'derived principles'). In that event, it may seek to defend itself by asserting that there was no cross-border interest in the first place.[30] In reality, the cases where economic operators dealing in software, who bring proceedings before the courts for breaches of the procurement regime

[30] This in fact happened in *Sidey Ltd v Clackmannanshire Council* 2012 SLT 334 though the defence only succeeded up to a point.

by public authorities in respect of a software procurement contract will be met with such a defence will be rare.

Of more practical concern are those cases where the public authority might decide that there is no cross-border interest and so does not put the contract out to tender. It is all very well to say that a disappointed would-be tenderer could bring judicial review proceedings, but how is he to know that he missed the opportunity in the first place?

This is particularly so since, although there is a strict requirement on a public authority, in terms of Article 36 of the Public Sector Directive, to publish a Contract Notice in the Official Journal in the case of an above-threshold contract, in the case of a below-threshold contract, publication of such a notice is merely permitted, but not mandated.[31]

The answer may be eternal vigilance. If the would-be tenderer subsequently comes to find out about a failure to advertise a contract which does engage cross-border interest (whatever the public authority may think), then the courts will not be slow to invoke the principle of transparency to set aside any contract made without sufficient advertising.[32] The obligation is to ensure 'for the benefit of any potential tenderer, a degree of advertising sufficient to enable the . . . market to be opened up to competition and the impartiality of procurement procedures to be reviewed.'[33]

11.3.3 An own goal?

Although a detailed survey of the rules of public procurement, including the rules governing the assessment of the economic operator's suitability and competence, lies outside the scope of this chapter, it is worth mentioning one issue which may have a particular resonance for software developers. It may from time to time happen that a would-be tenderer or his employees have been involved in the preparation of the contracting authority's invitation to tender, contract notice, or specification. At one extreme, it may be a particular developer or supplier who has got, as it were, too close and cosy with the contracting authority. At the other end of the spectrum, a contracting authority may have chosen to download open source software and develop that software itself. Then, some years later, it decides to put out for tender a further development of its IT systems. Assume, however, that its former chief developer has gone off to join a private sector company which might like to tender for the new work, or that the public authority has chosen to float off its former IT department to become a stand-alone section, which is interested in tendering. This situation is one of some legal delicacy, as is illustrated by the case of *Fabricom*.[34]

[31] Article 37. [32] *Telaustria* (n 17); *Parking Brixen* (n 19). [33] *Telaustria* (n 17) para 61.
[34] Cases C-21/03 and C-34/03 *Fabricom SA v Belgium* [2005] ECR I- 1577.

In that case, a company, Fabricom, was prevented from tendering by a Belgian Royal Decree in (inter alia) the following terms:

> No person who has been instructed to carry out research, experiments, studies or development in connection with public works, supplies or services shall be permitted to apply to participate in or to submit a tender for a contract for those works, supplies or services.

The European Court of Justice overturned that decree, but on the ground that it was expressed in absolute terms. The Court did, however, recognize the underlying principle of the prohibition of unequal treatment. It stated:

> 29. Indeed, a person who has participated in certain preparatory works may be at an advantage when formulating his tender on account of the information concerning the public contract in question which he has received when carrying out that work. However, all tenderers must have equality of opportunity when formulating their tenders (see, to that effect, Case C-87/94 *Commission* v *Belgium* [1996] ECR I-2043, paragraph 54).
>
> 30. Furthermore, that person may be in a situation which may give rise to a conflict of interests in the sense that, as the Commission correctly submits, he may, without even intending to do so, where he himself is a tenderer for the public contract in question, influence the conditions of the contract in a manner favourable to himself. Such a situation would be capable of distorting competition between tenderers.
>
> 31. Taking account of the situation in which a person who has carried out certain preparatory work may find himself, therefore, it cannot be maintained that the principle of equal treatment requires that that person be treated in the same way as any other tenderer.

However, the Court, having observed that there may be circumstances in which such involvement might not in fact lead to an unfair advantage, decided that the Royal Decree should be amended to the following effect:

> ...a person who has been instructed to carry out research, experiments, studies or development in connection with public works, supplies or services is not permitted to apply to participate in or to submit a tender for those works, supplies or services and where that person is not given the opportunity to prove that, in the circumstances of the case, the experience which he has acquired was not capable of distorting competition.

In these circumstances, a would-be tenderer should be vigilant for possible earlier involvement by a competitor at an earlier stage, and a contracting authority should be careful lest it end up accidentally running the risk of disqualifying a person whom it might have wished had been free to tender.

11.4 ISSUES WITH THE SPECIFICATION

11.4.1 Introduction

The problems which are most likely to be met with in practice are not so much to do with whether the procurement rules apply at all, or whether a tendering exercise has been sufficiently advertised, but, rather, whether the technical specification has been drawn up in a way which unfairly tilts the playing field, eg, by specifying a particular product (eg 'Microsoft Office') or, indeed, specifying 'Open Source', or producing an apparently open specification which, upon closer examination turns out can be met by only one supplier.

11.4.2 Specified products

The law is quite clear that it is forbidden to specify a particular brand or product, without, at least, adding the words 'or equivalent'. The leading case is *European Commission v The Netherlands*.[35]

Interestingly, the *Netherlands* case involved an IT contract where the contracting authority's general terms and conditions stated that the operating system required was 'UNIX'.[36] The words 'or equivalent' were not added.

The judgment of the Court gives a good flavour of the argument advanced by the Netherlands Government, which seemed to have made a half-hearted attempt to set up UNIX as a kind of industry *de facto* standard:

> 24. The Netherlands Government contends that the UNIX system must, in the field of information technology, be regarded as a technical specification generally recognized by traders and that, accordingly, it is unnecessary to add the words 'or equivalent'.
>
> 25. It should be borne in mind that Article 7(6) of Directive 77/62 prohibits the indication of trade marks unless it is accompanied by the words 'or equivalent' since the subject-matter of the contract cannot otherwise be described by specifications which are sufficiently precise and fully intelligible to all concerned.
>
> 26. The parties agree, however, that the UNIX system is not standardized and that it is the name of a specific make of product.
>
> 27. Hence the fact that the term UNIX was not followed by the words 'or equivalent' may not only deter economic operators using systems similar to UNIX

[35] Case C-359/93 [1995] ECR I-15; see also Case C-59/00 *Bent Mousten Vestergaard v Spøttrup Boligselskab* [2001] ECR 1-09505.

[36] A software system developed by Bell Laboratories of ITT (USA) for connecting several computers of different makes.

from taking part in the tendering procedure, but may also impede the flow of imports in intra-Community trade, contrary to Article 30 of the Treaty, by reserving the contract exclusively to suppliers intending to use the system specifically indicated.

28. Accordingly, the contracting authority should have added the words 'or equivalent' after the term UNIX, as required by Article 7(6) of Directive 77/62.

In short, to specify a particular product is clearly impermissible, even if the product in question has achieved sufficient market dominance that the uninformed begin to think of it as some kind of standard. To revert to the issue raised in the introduction to this chapter, a public authority could not specify Microsoft Office by name, even though it might find that it would be easier and give it a quieter life.

That said, might the same objection not be taken to specifying 'Open Source'?

This is a more complex issue, but it is best postponed until after a consideration of effectively exclusive technical specifications in general.

11.4.3 Effectively exclusive technical specifications

It is all very well to say that one can add the words 'or equivalent', but what if there is no equivalent, and, in any event, how is equivalence to be judged? Further, what if the technical specification is such that only one potential tenderer is in a position to meet it?

The leading case is *Concordia Bus Finland Oy Ab*.[37] That case concerned the awarding by the city of Helsinki of a contract for the operating of buses for its public transport system. The contract notice published in the Official Journal stated that the city would select the most economically advantageous tender, rather than the one with the lowest price.[38] Where the 'most economically advantageous' criterion is used, the contracting authority selects a number of criteria, allocates a specific number of points to each and carries out a scoring exercise on the admissible tenders which have been submitted. In the interests of transparency, the authority is required to publish the criteria and points to be allocated to each.

In *Concordia Bus*, the contract notice specified that additional points would be available for a tenderer who would use buses with nitrogen oxide emissions below 4g/kWh (+2.5points/bus) or below 2g/kWh (+3.5points/bus) and with external noise levels below 77dB (+1point/bus). The lowest price was offered by Concordia, but it was unable to meet those specifications, whereas a rival tenderer, HKL (which belonged to the city) was able to do so, and won the contract. Concordia challenged this award, inter alia, on the ground of unequal treatment, before the national courts

[37] Case C-513/99 [2002] ECR I-7251.

[38] This is permissible under the Directive: Article 53 of the current Directive.

who, on appeal, referred the matter to the European Court of Justice for a preliminary ruling.

The Advocate General, in his comments,[39] proceeded on the basis that, on the criteria in the tender documentation, there was only one tenderer who was capable of succeeding. At paragraphs 94 to 98 he expressed the view that, provided that the criterion in question observed the fundamental principles of community law, and, in particular, the principle of non discrimination, 'there is nothing which prohibits the taking into account of a criterion which serves the general interest, such as an environmental criterion.'[40] In this case, the criterion was applied to all tenderers, so did not offend against the principle of non discrimination.[41]

At the core of his reasoning lies the following observations:

> 148. In order to decide that the criterion in question had given rise to indirect discrimination towards Concordia, it would not be sufficient to find that that company had been treated differently from HKL, in the sense that the latter had been given points which had not been given to Concordia.
>
> 149. It follows from settled case-law that the principle of equality of treatment requires that comparable situations are not treated differently and that different situations are not treated similarly, unless such a difference in treatment can be justified objectively.
>
> ...
>
> 151. Finally, the specification of the criterion which gave rise to a difference in the awarding of points could only be considered to reveal the existence of discriminatory tactics if it were to appear that this criterion could not be justified objectively, having regard to the characteristics of the contract and the needs of the contracting authority.
>
> 152. As was seen above, a contracting authority cannot be prevented from requiring that the service in question be provided using a fleet which possesses the best available technical specifications.
>
> 153. To reach a contrary view would mean requiring the contracting authority to lay down the criteria having regard to the potential tenderers. As each call for tenders contains a whole series of criteria, the contracting authority would then require to establish those which could be provided by only one tenderer and remove them from his draft call for tenders. It could be that one tenderer was unable to meet one criterion, while another tenderer could not meet a different one.
>
> 154. Not only would such an approach result in a form of levelling down of the award criteria in eliminating all those which were truly selective, it would equally strip all content from the right recognised by the Court for the contracting authority to select

[39] [2002] ECR I-6319. [40] Para 98. [41] Para 116.

> the criteria for awarding the contract as it chooses. I would observe on further consideration that laying down criteria having regard to the potential tenderers would in my view result in a denial of the principle of equality of treatment. If a contracting authority were to remove a criterion from the tender notice on the basis that one or more tenderers were unable to meet it, the authority would in so doing disadvantage a tenderer who was able to comply, by neutralising the advantage he could have made use of.
>
> 155. My conclusion on the first point is therefore that the mere fact of including in a tender notice a criterion which can be met by only one tenderer does not contravene the principle of equality.

The Court dealt with these issues in two parts. First, in relation to the specification, it stated:

> 64 It follows from the above considerations that, where the contracting authority decides to award a contract to the tenderer who submits the economically most advantageous tender, in accordance with Article 36(1)(a) of Directive 92/50, it may take criteria relating to the preservation of the environment into consideration, provided that they are linked to the subject-matter of the contract, do not confer an unrestricted freedom of choice on the authority, are expressly mentioned in the contract documents or the tender notice, and comply with all the fundamental principles of Community law, in particular the principle of non-discrimination.

It then applied that principle to the particular facts of the case in paragraph 69, to find the criteria stipulated in the contract in question to be permissible.

It then turned to consider the circumstance that the criteria shut out other tenderers. It came to a similar conclusion to the Advocate General, even though its view of the factual basis differed from that of the Advocate General, who had proceeded upon the basis that there was only one tenderer (HKL) which could satisfy the criteria, whilst the Court appears, rather, to have taken the view that the criteria did offer the possibility of a limited number of tenderers (of which HKL was one):

> 85 It must therefore be held that, in such a factual context, the fact that one of the criteria adopted by the contracting entity to identify the economically most advantageous tender could be satisfied only by a small number of undertakings, one of which was an undertaking belonging to the contracting entity, is not in itself such as to constitute a breach of the principle of equal treatment.
>
> 86 In those circumstances, the answer to the third question must be that the principle of equal treatment does not preclude the taking into consideration of criteria connected with protection of the environment, such as those at issue in the main proceedings, solely because the contracting entity's own transport undertaking is one of the few undertakings able to offer a bus fleet satisfying those criteria.

This reasoning was developed in *EVN AG and Weinstrom GmbH v Austria*[42] which concerned a contract for the supply of electricity which stipulated that a minimum proportion of the electricity should be generated from renewable resources, and, additionally, gave a weighting in the scoring for electricity to be generated from renewable sources above that minimum.

The Court found this to be permissible. It stated, under reference to *Concordia Bus*:

> 34. It follows that the Community legislation on public procurement does not preclude a contracting authority from applying, in the context of the assessment of the most economically advantageous tender for a contract for the supply of electricity, a criterion requiring that the electricity supplied be produced from renewable energy sources, provided that that criterion is linked to the subject-matter of the contract, does not confer an unrestricted freedom of choice on the authority, is expressly mentioned in the contract documents or the contract notice, and complies with all the fundamental principles of Community law, in particular the principle of non-discrimination.

The outcome of this is that, although a contracting authority may set criteria beyond the purely economic, it cannot arbitrarily select those criteria. From the comments of the Court in *EVN* one might single out the requirements that the criteria should not be such as to confer an unrestricted freedom of choice on the contracting authority, and should be linked to the subject matter of the contract, and, from the comments of the Advocate General in *Concordia Bus*, the requirement that the criteria should be objectively justifiable.

Following *Concordia Bus*, the European Commission issued advice that:

> [under] the EU public procurement rules, contracting authorities may refer to a brand name to describe a product only when there are no other possible descriptions that are both sufficiently precise and intelligible to potential tenderers.[43]

If this advice were followed, it would not normally be possible to refer, eg, to 'MS Office or equivalent' or to 'Intel or equivalent' microprocessors in public tender specifications, and it may be difficult to posit (at least in the IT market) a situation where the qualification would come in to play.

This might all seem relatively hopeful in furnishing arguments to mount a challenge against a procurement exercise where open source software providers find themselves shut out by the technical criteria, but there is a danger that the courts will judge reasonableness from the perspective of the contracting authority, rather than on a wider view.

[42] Case C-448/01[2003] ECR I-14558.

[43] European Commission release reference IP/06/443 dated 4 April 2006; this is also a reference to Directive 2004/18/EC, Article 23.

That is what happened in the Scottish case of *Elekta Ltd v Common Services Agency*.[44]

That case concerned a tendering exercise carried out by the National Health Service ('NHS') in Scotland for the replacement of linear accelerators and certain associated equipment for delivering radiotherapy in the treatment of cancer in all of the five cancer units in NHS hospitals in Scotland. A linear accelerator, which is an extremely expensive piece of equipment, is the machine that delivers the radioactivity dose in a controlled and focussed way. In order to operate properly, the linear accelerator needs to be controlled by specialized software.

In five out of the six hospitals concerned, there were already in place systems that had been purchased some years previously from a company, Varian. The software in question (the 'ARIA' radiotherapy management system) was described by Elekta[45] as a 'closed system,' in that Varian kept its code secret and did not publish its communications interface, so that it was not possible for other manufacturers' machines to interoperate with it, whereas Elekta's operating system was 'open' and permitted full interoperability.[46] The NHS did not wish to replace its software system, even though by far the most expensive part of the entire system was the hardware which the NHS sought to replace.[47]

The technical specification required, first, that the new equipment should be compatible with the existing ARIA system, and, second, made certain functional requirements that could not be met without such interoperability. Elekta, and any other potential tenderer, found itself effectively shut out of the tender process: only Varian was in a position to bid.

Elekta raised a legal challenge against the tender process on the basis of the Treaty principles and derived principles, in particular, the requirement of equal treatment.

The judge, Lord Glennie, having considered the *Concordia Bus* and *EVN* cases, expressed the view:[48]

> ... the contracting authority must be entitled to decide what it wants, what is the subject matter of the procurement which it seeks to obtain, the subject matter of the contract, or to put it another way it must be entitled to decide upon the functional requirements it wishes to satisfy. Second, the fact that the criteria included in the tender notice can only be met by one tenderer, or a limited range of tenderers, does not of itself contravene the principle of equality. And third, that the inclusion of these criteria can only be considered discriminatory if they cannot be justified objectively having regard to the characteristics of the contract and the needs of the contracting authority.

[44] 2011 SLT 815. [45] See para 7.

[46] One should be careful about terminology here. Elekta's system was not *Open Source*: it was merely that Elekta published the communication interface and so facilitated interoperability.

[47] The contract value was £21m excluding VAT. [48] At para 14.

At paragraph 17 he continued:

> [17] In the present case the defender wishes to procure the purchase of a range of radiotherapy equipment including, in particular, linear accelerators. These are for incorporation into an existing system or systems, a feature of which, in four of the five hospitals in question, is the use of a Varian RMS system with which the equipment to be purchased has to be compatible. Except in the case of Tayside, the defender does not want or need to purchase a new RMS system. In those circumstances, the adoption of criteria which recognise that the new equipment must be compatible with the existing equipment and, in particular, with the existing RMS system is to my mind self evidently justifiable and objectively so. On that basis, in line with the reasoning in the *Concordia Bus* case and *EVN*, those criteria which, as I say, essentially define what the defender wants to purchase, cannot be regarded as discriminatory, even if the application of those criteria results in there being only one tenderer.

The solicitor advocate appearing for Elekta sought to argue, under reference to the *Netherlands* and *Vestergaard* cases, that effectively what the contracting authority had done was to specify a Varian machine, which was not permissible under EU law. Lord Glennie's response[49] was:

> Those cases say that the contracting authority cannot stipulate for goods of a specific brand or name but must allow for an equivalent to be offered in a tender. It is important to note in the present case that the defender did not specify that they required a Varian linear accelerator. Taking the matter at its strongest for the pursuer, they specified, in effect, that they required a linear accelerator which was compatible with Varian ARIA RMS; and it might be said that they thereby specified for something like 'a Varian linear accelerator or equivalent.' If that is the right construction to be placed on what they did, it seems to me that they have fulfilled their obligation in terms of those cases rather than acting in breach of them.

In paragraph 20, he emphasized that:

> ...it is for the defender as the contracting authority to decide what it wants. It has an existing RMS system in four out of the five cancer units which will remain in place for some years, the precise length of time depending upon a rolling system of replacement which was shown in the documents put before the court. It does not presently wish to replace that system. There are no doubt many factors leading to its decisions in this regard, including the question of cost, disruption and teething problems likely to be encountered if one system is replaced by another which then has to interface it with other equipment which is already in operation. It cannot, in the interests of equal treatment, be compelled to seek tenders for something it does not want. I note, as senior counsel for the defender submitted, that there has been no attack on the present procurement exercise on the grounds that the criteria adopted by the

[49] At para 19.

> defender are not objectively justifiable; and the solicitor advocate for the pursuer, in his oral argument, did not seek to argue that they were not objectively justifiable. I therefore proceed on the basis that they are. That being the case, no purpose would be served by requiring the defender to invite tenders for something other than what they in fact want.

For those practising in the area of IT, this may all sound depressingly familiar, a classic case of vendor lock-in. The reason why the NHS needs its new and extremely expensive equipment to be interoperable with the Varian system is that, because of what one might argue was a poor procurement decision made in the past, it is locked forever into Varian's system, or at least for so long as it continues to operate a rolling replacement system. Indeed, the present procurement exercise compounds the situation as the hospital which was not locked in was to have its RMS system replaced as well as its linear accelerator, with the inevitable effect that it too would be locked in for the future. Further, it shuts out competition, giving Varian a monopoly.

It is interesting that after the decision was published, representatives of NHS Scotland were heard at conferences to say that the decision vindicated their excellent public procurement policy.

It may be arguable that the case was correctly decided on the basis of the arguments that were presented to the court, but it might also be suggested that the case was badly argued.

The key is the requirement for objective justifiability of the criteria and the incomprehensible decision of Elekta's solicitor advocate to decline to argue that the criteria were not objectively justifiable.

In one sense, the judge may have been correct to identify the factors that led the defenders to their decision, but it might be argued that a key element of justifiability is reasonableness. In particular, it might be fair enough, as far as it goes, to say that you do not want the inconvenience of changing the software, but that leaves altogether out of account other factors such as the continuing and future cost of lock-in (or even the recognition that you are locked in), the possible extra cost of the extremely expensive hardware which, for all that you know, may be much more expensive than similar hardware might be if provided by a competitor, (you cannot say, as you have locked competitors out of the process) and, set against that, the relative cost of breaking the vendor lock-in.

Of course, if, in setting the criteria, a contracting authority had considered all of those matters and come to a careful decision to remain locked in, it might be more difficult to argue that the criteria were not objectively justifiable (though perfectly possible to do so: a challenger would have to engage in a careful filleting of the contracting authority's reasoning process). On the other hand, if no thought had been given to such matters, it may be much easier to argue a lack of objective justification for selecting the criteria in question.

In short, *Elekta v Common Services Agency* represents a lost opportunity to advance this area of the law in what, I should suggest, is its natural direction of travel, though, as will be discussed later, there is already some movement in this direction at the policy-setting level.

There is a similar, though much earlier case in Spain.[50] In that case, the terms and conditions specified an educational computer program having certain characteristics, and it was stated that the software had to be MS Windows compatible, without incorporating the compulsory expression 'or equivalent'.[51] Apple raised an administrative appeal against the procurement exercise and, once rejected, a court action, which reached the Supreme Court in 2004. The Supreme Court found this specification not to be contrary to any of the public procurement principles (most relevantly regulated by the Royal Legislative Decree 3/2011[52] and, concerning in particular software procurement, Decree 2572/1973).[53] The principles of non discrimination, publicity, free competition, equal treatment, and legal certainty were analysed and found to be unchallenged by the specification. The Supreme Court found the choice of a particular operating system to be justified in order to meet a need of the administration, which, in the opinion of the Court, was adequately explained within the terms and conditions. Also, the Court stated that the administration must enjoy a higher degree of discretion in these kinds of contracts, allowing more flexibility in public procurement.

One might have some reservations about the reasoning in this case. Particularly, the view that one accords greater flexibility to public administrations in software procurement than in other forms of procurement, which scarcely seems justifiable in procurement law, but, in view of the requirement for objective verification, it may be that we are left with a decision which is difficult to reconcile with the underlying principles of procurement law.

11.4.4 Specifying open source

'Open source software' is not a brand name or an identifiable product, so including in a tender specification a requirement for the use of open source software ought not to cause problems under the *Netherlands* and *Bent Mousten Vestergaard* line of

[50] Sentencia del Tribunal Supremo de 6 de julio de 2004 (Supreme Court decision, 6th July 2004). Available at <http://www.poderjudicial.es/search/doAction?action=contentpdf&reference=2106595> accessed 8 April 2013.

[51] The decision cites the former version of this provision (Article 53.2 of Act 13/1995 on Contracts of the Public Administration, no longer in force), currently stated in Article 117.8 of the Royal Legislative Decree 3/2011 on Public Sector Contracts, as harmonized by the 96/36/EEC Directive. This provision clearly provides that, in the exceptional case where a particular brand, patent or type has to be stated in order to provide a precise description of the object of the procurement procedure, this 'must be accompanied by the expression "or equivalent"'.

[52] Royal Legislative Decree 3/2011 on Public Sector Contracts.

[53] Decree 2572/1973, approving the General Administrative Terms and Conditions for the Procurement of Information Treatment Systems and Equipment, as well as its Maintenance, Renting and Programming.

authority. In particular, such a requirement would not restrict competition to only one supplier, or group of suppliers (eg Microsoft resellers): anyone can seek to tender. Rather, open source software might be regarded as having a non-technical characteristic, which is to say the licensing terms under which it is written, or even a technical characteristic; namely the ability of the source code to be modified, whereas with proprietary software the source code may not have been provided. Viewed in this light, one is firmly in *Concordia Bus* territory, and the issues relate to whether such a requirement can be objectively justified.

Notwithstanding this legal analysis, in practice some doubt appears to surround whether a technical specification may specifically call for 'Open Source Software'. Under the auspices of the European Commission, the IDABC in March 2010 published the *Guideline on Public Procurement of Open Source Software*,[54] paragraph 2.4 of which provides:

> This guideline is about promoting good practices that clearly meet procurement regulations and provide for a competitive and transparent procurement process. So the authors do not recommend issuing a call for tender for the supply and service of installation of a specific open source software. The authors do not even recommend issuing a call for tender for un-named software, with 'open source' as one of the selection criteria. As discussed in the previous section, the authors recommend best practice procurement based on the definition of functional requirements—which may include properties that are equivalent to the characteristics of open source software, or the characteristics of open standards.

However, it is made clear that the *Guideline* is intended as a guide to good practice, and not as legal advice[55] and, in that context, one can understand why this recommendation is made.

In particular, it is made clear in the Public Sector Directive that award criteria must be detailed with 'the necessary transparency to enable all tenderers to be reasonably informed of the criteria'.[56] It might be thought that the phrase 'open source' might be open to being differently understood by different potential tenderers and so lack the necessary transparency. Certainly a reference to functional characteristics might be thought preferable. Equally, if there were a concern over the use of the term, then the necessary transparency could equally be assured by referring to a recognized definition of that term, such as that provided by the OSI.[57]

There has also been some discussion at the level of individual Member States of whether or not specific reference to 'open source' can be made in a Specification.

[54] See n 29. [55] Disclaimer at end of para 1.

[56] Recital 46 of the preamble, and see also Case C-496/99 *Commission v CAS Succhi di Frutta SpA* [2004] ECR 2004 I-03801.

[57] Open Source Initiative, <http://www.opensource.org> accessed 8 April 2013.

There has been little by way of guidance from the courts on this matter, though there are some useful cases in France and Italy.

For example, in Germany, the Directives are transcribed and public procurement regulated inter alia by *VGV Vergabeverordnung* (procurement order)[58] and *VOL/A Vergabe- und Vertragsordnung für Leistungen, Teil A* (procurement order for services). Those rules are required to follow the principle of the Wettbewerbsprinzip by virtue of section 97(1) GWB (Act Against Restraints of Competition). The principle dictates that all applicants shall be treated equally and distinctions made only on the grounds of technical qualifications, efficiency, and reliability.[59]

Section 7 of *VOL/A* requires the specification in the tender documents for the procurement of software to be kept neutral, though section 7(3) does permit specification of open source software where reasonable, based on the type of the offer.

Interpreting these provisions, some writers argue that normally specification of 'open source' would be in breach of the principle,[60] whereas other writers suggest that if the public body is able to explain why it is only open source software which would fulfil their requirements, it would be permissible to specify open source.[61] It has been suggested that such reasons for the specification of open source software may lie in higher security requirements which may indicate a need to alter the source code against 'back door' hacking, or a need for the contracting authority to acquire an open source licence together with the source code to allow it to develop or modify the software to meet its particular requirements.

In France, there is a similar legislative provision. The Directive is implemented by the *Code des Marchés Publics* (Code of Public Procurement Contracts). Article 6, III of the Code provides that:

> Technical specifications shall afford equal access for tenderers and not have the effect of creating unjustified obstacles to the opening up of public procurement to competition;

and Article 6, IV provides that:

> Technical specifications shall not refer to a specific make or source, or a particular process, or to trade marks, patents, types or a specific origin or production with the effect of favouring or eliminating certain undertakings or certain products.
>
> Nevertheless, such a mention or reference is possible whether it is justified by the particular subject-matter of the contract or on an exceptional basis where

[58] The paragraphs particularly applicable to open source are paras 4–7.

[59] Section 97(4).

[60] Heckmann, 'IT-Vergabe, Open-Source-Software und Vergaberecht' (2004),*Computer und Recht* 401, 408 ('IT-Procurement, Open Source Software and Procurement' (2004) *Computer and Law, Law Review* 401, 408).

[61] Rechtliche Aspekte der Nutzung, Verbreitung und Weiterentwicklung von Open-Source-Software, November 2011, Bundesbeauftragte für Informationstechnik, Begleitdokument zum Migrationsleitfaden 4.0, S.30 ('Legal aspects of the usage, distribution and development of Open Source Software' November 2011, 30).

> a sufficiently precise and intelligible description of the subject-matter of the contract is not possible; such reference shall be accompanied by the words 'or equivalent'.

Thus, the Conseil d'État, the highest French administrative court, held that reference to a specific trade mark is possible if it is the only means of describing the requirements of the contracting authority and provided that such reference is accompanied by the words 'or equivalent'.[62]

Apart from this general principle (which is consistent with the jurisprudence of the ECJ) there has been no case in France which deals with a tender for the acquisition of open source software as a species of good, though there is one case which deals with it in the context of the public procurement of services.

The case in question is a decision of the Conseil d'État dated 30 September 2011 regarding the Region of Picardie[63] (req no 350 43 Région Picardie). In that case, the Region of Picardie, as an acquiring authority, launched a procedure for the award of a public contract in order to 'carry out, exploit, maintain and host' an open source solution for the Digital Work Platform 'Lilie' (Espace Numérique de Travail ('ENT')) for use in the colleges of the region. Two companies claimed that the Region failed to guarantee equal access and treatment to all tenderers. They contended that the technical specifications drawn up by the Region, by referring to an open source solution, had the effect of favouring certain undertakings.

Given the nature of the public procurement in question, the aim of which was not to supply software, but to *provide a service related to the software,* the Conseil d'État held that mention of the open source solution in the technical specifications neither favoured nor penalized any potential tenderer. Indeed, the Conseil d'État pointed out that open source software being freely accessible, changeable, and adaptable by each company, to specify it in the technical specifications did not have the result of favouring any one tenderer over another.

It is important to emphasize that this case addresses the issue of public procurement *of services* (to carry out, exploit, maintain, and host the open source solution) and does not deal with the supplying of that open source solution itself (which may be regarded as public procurement of goods). Whether it is lawful for a contracting authority to specify open source in an exercise for the public procurement of goods remains a question which the French courts have yet to address,[64] though it may be pointed out that, as discussed earlier, it would be possible for a contracting authority to obtain open source software as a product without going through a formal procurement exercise at all.

[62] Conseil d'Etat, 11 September 2006, Commune de Saran c Sté Gallaud, req no 257545.

[63] Req no 350 43 Région Picardie.

[64] See *La Semaine Juridique Entreprises et Affaires no 48,* 1er Décembre 2011, 1854.

In Italy, there is an important decision of the Constitutional Court regarding the Region of Piedmont.[65] In that case, Piedmont enacted a Regional law permitting contracting authorities when assessing tenders to give greater weight to those tenders that provide for the use of open source software.

The national law regarding public software procurement[66] requires a contracting authority to choose amongst a number of specified options, one of which is open source software. That choice is required to be made on the basis of a technical and commercial comparison,[67] but no further guidance is given on how to effect that comparison, so the general principles of procurement law apply.

What the Region sought to do was to give a boost to open source software by enacting a regional law which stated that the Region should use software applications of which the source code is available to it, and which it can freely modify to adapt them to its needs;[68] providing that in the procurement of software, the Region should give preferential treatment to free software and software where the source code is accessible.[69] It further provided that if the Region were to choose proprietary software, it is required to justify the reasons for its choice.[70] Similarly a preference for open source was expressed in other provisions regarding data protection[71] and publicly accessible documents.[72]

The national government challenged those provisions in terms of Article 117 of the Italian Constitution, as being in conflict with the rules of competition law laid down by the jurisprudence of the ECJ and the National Code of Public Contracts. The national government argued that the Region had to remain neutral in respect of the different technologies that might compete in a procurement exercise, that naming one particular technology over all others is clearly prohibited, and by extension, giving preferential treatment to certain technologies, including or 'on the basis of' their licensing regime, should also be prohibited.

The court's analysis, however, was that:

> The choice is not an exclusive one, but just preferential and requires a comparative evaluation, as is confirmed by the reference to the possibility to use proprietary formats... under the condition that in such case the Region shall provide reasons for its choice...
>
> Finally, it must be once more remembered that the concepts of free software and software with inspectable code are not notions concerning a given technology, brand

[65] Decision no 122 of 22/03/2010 available at <http://www.cortecostituzionale.it/ accessed 21 January, 2013. See also C Piana, 'Italian Constitutional Court gives way to Free Software friendly laws' (2010) 2 *IFOSS Law Review* 61.

[66] 'Codice dell'Amministrazione Digitale' Dlgs no 82/2005, Article 68.

[67] *Assoli v Ministero del Lavoro* TAR (Regional administrative court) Lazio, Decision no 428 of 23/01/2007, available at <http://www.giustizia-amministrativa.it/DocumentiGA/Roma/Sezione%203B/2006/200603838/Provvedimenti/RM_200700428_SE.DOC> accessed 21 January 2013.

[68] Article 6.1. [69] Article 6.2. [70] Article 6.4. [71] Article 5. [72] Article 4.

> or product, instead they express a legal characteristic. At the end of the day, what discriminates between free and proprietary software is the different legal arrangement of interest (licence) upon which the right of using the program is based; and the choice concerning the adoption of one or the other contractual regime belongs to the will of the user.
>
> It follows that the damage to competition feared by the Avvocato dello Stato with regard to the law in question, is not envisaged.

As Piana argues,[73] the distinction is based upon not only the technical and economic merit of the tenders, but a non technical characteristic, namely the nature of the legal rights offered. He suggests:

> The licensing conditions of a software product are—as the Court said—a non technical characteristic, not unlike the price or the level of support offered. Nothing prevents a proprietary vendor from choosing a more liberal license or to confer more rights if so weighs favourably. If this is prevented by the upstream licensing conditions, the case is identical for Free Software developers, who also are constrained by the requirement of the upstream suppliers and again it is a matter of choice.

11.4.5 Excluding open source

The other side of the same coin is the issue of whether a contracting authority can specifically exclude open source solutions. Logically that may be so, consistently with *Concordia Bus*, provided that there is an objectively justifiable reason for doing so, though the issue that seems to be encountered more frequently is simply a specification which, in functional terms, excludes open source.

Interestingly, the debate in Poland regarding open source in procurement specifications seems to have been conducted in terms of the exclusion of open source software, rather than a positive requirement for open source.

In Poland, the principle of equal treatment is found not only in the Treaties, but is enshrined in national law in Article 32 of the Polish Constitution, which provides:

> Everyone is equal before the law. Everyone has the right to equal treatment by public authorities. No one shall be discriminated against in political, social or economic life for any reason.

According to the Constitutional Court, this means that persons who can be characterized by the same important feature are required to be treated equally without any discriminative or favourable diversification.[74]

[73] Piana (n 65).

[74] Judgment of Constitutional Court of 9 March 1988, file no: U 7/87, OTK 1988, no 1, poz 1, 14.

Public authorities carrying out procurement exercises are bound both by this overriding constitutional requirement, as well also as by the Polish laws on public procurement, in particular, the Law of 29th January 2004 on Public Procurement,[75] which by Article 7 obliges public authorities to prepare and conduct public procurement proceedings in a manner which maintains fair competition and equal treatment of suppliers. All the activities related to the preparation and carrying out of the procurement exercise are required to be conducted impartially and objectively. Article 29(2) contains a general prohibition on framing the tender in such a way as would impede fair competition, and Article 29(3) prohibits describing the object of the tender by indication of trade marks, patents, and origin, unless such description is justified by (1) the character of the order, (2) the public authority is not able to describe sufficiently the object of the tender by means of precise terms, and (3) the description is followed by the phrase 'or equivalent'.

The net result[76] is that all requirements must be justified by the real and objective needs of acquiring authorities. Only such limitation as is justified by real needs does not violate the law.[77] The formulation of stringent requirements without reasons is forbidden and is considered as discrimination.[78]

In commenting upon this, Siewicz (a leading Polish legal writer), comments that its effect is that a public authority may not exclude or refuse to choose software just because it is open source software.[79] Any requirements which lead to the exclusion of open source software are required to be objectively justified. He suggests that a formulation of requirements, which excludes providers of free software would seem not to be objectively justifiable since, as he explains, open source software differs from closed or proprietary software because of the wider range of users' rights; but there is no objective reason why it could not have the same or similar functionality. According to Siewicz, this means that the public authority may not refuse to choose software just because it is open software.[80]

11.4.6 Summary

What then are the conclusions which can be drawn from all of this?

The application of the Treaties and derived principles is, according to the jurisprudence of the European Court of Justice, quite clear: a contracting authority may generally not express a requirement or a preference for a particular named product

[75] Dz, U z 2010, r no 113, poz 759. [76] Consistently with the position in EU law.

[77] Decision of Krajowa Izba Odwoławcza of 5 August 2009 (file no: KIO/UZP 961/09).

[78] Decision of Krajowa Izba Odwoławcza of 13 January 2009 (file no: KIO/UZP 1502/08).

[79] K Siewicz, *Prawne aspekty zamowień publicznych na oprogramowanie* (Fundacja Wolnego i Otwartego Oprogramowania, Poznań, 2010) 15, available at <http://www.fwioo.pl/media/attachments/prawne_aspekty_zamowien_publicznych_na_oprogramowanie.pdf> accessed 8 April 2013.

[80] Siewicz (n 79) 15.

or system. That prevents a specification which names UNIX, Intel, or Microsoft. However, that does not prevent the addition of the magic words 'or equivalent'. But what if there is no real equivalent, so the words 'or equivalent' are, in reality writ in water? This amounts to much the same thing as a specification which, functionally, closes down competition, because it can be met by only one tenderer, or, at any rate, a very limited number of tenderers.

That situation is governed by the principles articulated in *Concordia Bus.* Such a closed or exclusive specification may be permissible, provided that the contracting authority can articulate reasons for drawing up the specification in those terms. But merely having reasons, which seem to the contracting authority to be good ones, is not enough. The absolute requirement, as the Advocate General makes clear in *Concordia Bus,* is that the reasons should be *objectively justifiable.* Note the combination of words: the focus is on justifiability, and, what is more, objective justifiability.

These objectively justifiable reasons may relate to technical characteristics or non-technical characteristics. The *Piedmont* case appears to have been founded upon the proposition that open source software was preferred for its non-technical characteristics, but it is worth bearing in mind the peculiar circumstances in which the argument came to be based in Italian constitutional and administrative law, drawing on competition law, albeit that the context was acknowledged as involving procurement law principles. However, if one looks at the ECJ jurisprudence, ignoring the special Italian context, it is difficult to see why, in theory, a decision to specify open source software or, sauce for the goose being sauce for the gander, to exclude open source software, could not be justified on technical as well as non-technical grounds. Both would be equally permissible, provided that the contracting authority's reasons were objectively justifiable.

Similarly, the distinction drawn in the *Picardie* case between procurement of goods and procurement of services may not be one which is of importance, for a decision to prefer or exclude open source solutions might equally be justified whether the procurement exercise relates to goods or to services, though it might be that the actual reasons may differ depending on whether the procurement exercise was characterized as one for goods or for services. It may be that, in the *Picardie* case, the Conseil d'État was mindful of the provisions of Article 6, IV of the *Code des Marchés Publics* with its references to 'products', and was reluctant to engage with whether open source software was a product, especially as the case could be (and was) decided without having reference to that issue.

In the event, it seems reasonably clear that whatever open source software is, it is not a specific product or brand, such as would bring into play the *Netherlands* and *Bent Mousten Vestergaard* principles. Accordingly, it is difficult to understand why there is academic disagreement in Germany on this point, unless it be concerned with the detail of the manner in which the Directives have been transposed into

German law, though one can perhaps understand why at the EU level the *Guideline on Public Procurement of Open Source Software* expresses its preference for a specification of functional characteristics as a matter of good practice.

What it comes back to is that the seemingly absolute rules suffer exception where the contracting authority's reasons for departing from them are objectively justifiable, and one may be slow to state, categorically, as Siewicz does, that the exclusion of open source can never be justified (any more than one can assert that stipulating for it can always be justified). In any given case, what will matter is the objective justifiability of the reasons.

It is for this reason also that one might part company with the comments of Lord Glennie in *Elekta* if, in saying that a contracting authority 'cannot, in the interests of equal treatment, be compelled to seek tenders for something it does not want', he intended to lay down a rule of general application. This is because not only is the object of the tender something which the contracting authority wants, and not only must it have its reasons for wanting it, but also those reasons must be objectively justifiable. Of course, surprisingly Elekta's solicitor advocate declined to argue that the contracting authority's reasons were not objectively justifiable, and so, in the context of the arguments before him, the judge's comments may have been fair enough.

11.4.7 Arguing objective justifiability

It may be that in any given case, the ingenuity of the litigants will be able to produce plausible reasons why a decision by a contracting authority as to its requirements was or was not objectively justifiable. Such arguments may involve the economics of open source as against proprietary software, or may involve technical issues or non-technical issues such as the licensing regime. However, in the existing legal framework, in the European Commission's 'Proposal for a new Procurement Directive'[81] and elsewhere, there is to be found a wide range of potential arguments that might be used to assist those who would wish to justify a selection (or attack the exclusion) of open-source software.

First, there is the economic argument. The underlying criticism of the reasoning of NHS Scotland in the *Elekta* case is that its decision to remain locked in was based on headline cost, and took no account of the ongoing cost of perpetuating (indeed, extending) lock-in. That this is not objectively justifiable is arguable from first principles, but it is helpful that paragraph 2 of the Explanatory Memorandum attached to the Proposal makes specific reference to the ability to use lifecycle costing (which also extends to take in 'green' issues such as environmental costs of sourcing and

[81] European Commission, 'Reform proposals' <http://ec.europa.eu/internal_market/publicprocurement/modernising_rules/reform_proposals_en.htm> accessed 8 April 2013. See in particular para 2 of the Explanatory Memorandum: 'Strategic use of public procurement in response to new challenges'.

disposing of products). Even more explicitly, the UK Government Paper, 'Open Standards Principles: For software interoperability, data and document formats in government IT specifications'[82] states, at page 14:

> Short-term financial savings based only on cost could risk longer-term lock-in and are not necessarily the most cost-effective in terms of whole-life or when broader cross-government working or re-use is considered.

and at pages 15 and 16:

> As part of examining the total cost of ownership of a government IT solution, the costs of exit for a component should be estimated at the start of implementation. As unlocking costs are identified, these must be associated with the incumbent supplier/system and not be associated with cost of new IT projects.
>
> For existing systems that are not being modified, these should be considered as legacy and should not be extended. Transition to open standards for software interoperability, data and document formats must be considered by government bodies within exit management plans, in accordance with the timescales for the refresh lifecycle of the existing technology.
>
> In preparation for any technical refresh projects, or in exceptional circumstances, where extensions to IT contracts or to legacy solutions have been agreed, government bodies must formulate a pragmatic exit management strategy. These must describe publicly the existing standards used together with the transition to open standards and compulsory open standards. Transition should take place within a specified timescale (agreed as part of the Standards Hub process).

Two important warning notes should be sounded. These comments are made in the context of a policy on open standards and they are intended to bind only the UK Government and not the devolved national governments, local government or other public bodies. That said, whatever the context, the comments clearly embrace procurement policy; and, more importantly, the reasoning is so compelling that its influence should spread more widely than the UK Government, and, indeed, the United Kingdom. If the rationale of these comments is borne in mind, it is extremely difficult to see how anyone could have thought that, on economic grounds alone, the contracting authority's decision in *Elekta* could have been objectively justifiable.

So far as the technical and non-technical policy arguments are concerned, Article 53 of the Directive provides that the criteria shall be:

> ...when the award is made to the tender most economically advantageous from the point of view of the contracting authority, various criteria linked to the subject-matter

[82] HM Government, 'Open Standards Principles' (2012) <https://www.gov.uk/government/uploads/system/uploads/attachment_data/file/78892/Open-Standards-Principles-FINAL.pdf>. See also ch 10.

> of the public contract in question, for example, quality, price, technical merit, aesthetic and functional characteristics, environmental characteristics, running costs, cost-effectiveness, after-sales service and technical assistance, delivery date and delivery period or period of completion ...

Concordia Bus plainly allows a wider policy view to be taken by a contracting authority, but there have been suggestions that the list might be restrictive, or, at least require that any benefits are enjoyed directly by the contracting authority itself. In *Concordia Bus*, it was pointed out that environmental matters were not listed in the applicable definition in the predecessor (which then applied) of the current Directive.[83] In the event, the court, at paragraph 54 explained that the use of the words 'for example', clearly demonstrated that the list was not intended to be exhaustive, and at paragraph 55 it stated that the applicable article:

> cannot be interpreted as meaning that each of the award criteria used by the contracting authority to identify the economically most advantageous tender must necessarily be of a purely economic nature. It cannot be excluded that factors which are not purely economic may influence the value of a tender from the point of view of the contracting authority. That conclusion is also supported by the wording of the provision, which expressly refers to the criterion of the aesthetic characteristics of a tender.

The article in question did not exclude the possibility for the contracting authority to use criteria relating to the environment,[84] but:

> 58. However, that does not mean that any criterion of that nature may be taken into consideration by the contracting authority.
>
> 59. While Article 36(1)(a) of Directive 92/50 leaves it to the contracting authority to choose the criteria on which it proposes to base the award of the contract, that choice may, however, relate only to criteria aimed at identifying the economically most advantageous tender (see, to that effect, concerning public works contracts, *Beentjes*, paragraph 19, *Evans Medical* and *Macfarlane Smith*, paragraph 42, and *SIAC Construction*, paragraph 36). Since a tender necessarily relates to the subject-matter of the contract, it follows that the award criteria which may be applied in accordance with that provision must themselves also be linked to the subject-matter of the contract.

That formulation as expressed by the Court clearly gives a contracting authority plenty of scope to specify open source, since it would be extremely difficult to see how such a specification could not be linked to the subject matter of the contract.

However, matters become even easier under the Commission's Proposal.

[83] The relevant provision, however, was in similar terms to Article 53. [84] Paragraph 57.

It will be recollected that Article 3(3) TEU already stipulates that the Union 'shall promote scientific and technological advance...', and paragraph 2 of the Explanatory Memorandum to the Proposal states:

> 2) Strategic use of public procurement in response to new challenges:
>
> The proposed Directive is based on an enabling approach providing contracting authorities with the instruments needed to contribute to the achievement of the Europe 2020 strategic goals by using their purchasing power to procure goods and services that foster innovation, respect the environment and combat climate change while improving employment, public health and social conditions.

And, later:

> Innovation: Research and innovation play a central role in the Europe 2020 strategy for smart, sustainable and inclusive growth. Public purchasers should be enabled to buy innovative products and services promoting future growth and improving efficiency and quality of public services. The proposal provides for this purpose the innovation partnership, a new special procedure for the development and subsequent purchase of new, innovative products, works and services, provided they can be delivered to agreed performance levels and costs. In addition, the proposal improves and simplifies the competitive dialogue procedure and facilitates cross-border joint procurement which is an important instrument for innovative purchasing.

Also of relevance is paragraph 3:

> 3) Better access to the market for SMEs and Start-ups
>
> Small and medium-sized enterprises (SMEs) have a huge potential for job creation, growth and innovation. Easy access to procurement markets can help them unlock this potential while allowing contracting authorities to broaden their supplier base, with positive effects of higher competition for public contracts...

This is reinforced by the inclusion, amongst the examples in the proposed Article 66(2) of the other criteria which can be considered in assessing the most economically advantageous tender:

> (a) quality, including technical merit, aesthetic and functional characteristics, accessibility, design for all users, environmental characteristics and innovative character.

In short, if the new Directive, when it is promulgated, reflects the terms of the current Proposal, there will be, if anything, even more scope to justify a requirement for open source software, and, consequently, more scope for challenging as not being objectively justified a decision to exclude open source, whether specifically, or by way of an unduly restrictive specification.

11.5 THE ROLE OF PUBLIC POLICY

11.5.1 Introduction

Arguably, the whole of EU law is an expression of public policy, being rooted as it is in treaties which themselves frankly both acknowledge and set public policy goals. However, as the preceding section of this chapter shows, initiatives such as the UK Government's 'Open Standards Principles' and the Commission's 'Proposal for a new Procurement Directive' can drive those policies forward. If open source wins the policy argument and has the backing of governments or local administrations, then that can considerably assist it in operating on a level playing field. Furthermore, as the discussion of the *Piedmont* and *Picardy* cases discloses, such policy backing is unlikely to lead to a successful challenge under EU procurement law.

How, then, does the policy picture stand?

11.5.2 European Union

Although one can detect a general policy trend at the EU level, as explained earlier, there is no unequivocal policy commitment to open source software. The *Guideline* is a document about how to go about procuring open source software, rather than a policy committing anyone to do so.

Similarly, the Commission co-funds through the Interreg IVC programme, the Free Open Source Software Policy for European Public Administration project[85] ('OSEPA') as an EU-wide initiative to promote open source software and the benefits of its application within public administrations.[86] With the Central Union of Municipalities of Greece leading a consortium of 12 partners, OSEPA explores the main qualitative and quantitative benefits resulting from FOSS adoption and use by public authorities.

Since the establishment of OSEPA, various EU or national documents and guidelines providing directions and indicating good practice on how public organizations should purchase software and services have been published. These include OSOR *Guidelines: public procurement and Open Source Software*, public draft version 1.0,[87] the IDABC, *Guideline on Public Procurement of Open Source Software*, referred to earlier and OSEPA's own *Guide on free and open source software procurement*

[85] OSEPA <http://osepa.eu> accessed 8 April 2013.

[86] OSEPA, 'Open-Source Policy Statement' <http://osepa.kr-vysocina.cz/prilohy/policystatement/osepa_policy_statement_en_v3.pdf> accessed 8 April 2013.

[87] European Commission, 'General information about the Joinup platform' (10 October 2008) <http://www.osor.eu/idabc-studies/OSS-procurement-guideline-public-draft-v1%201.pdf> accessed 8 April 2013.

for European Public Administrations.[88] These last-mentioned guidelines address general principles that should be adopted in public procurement of OSS: planning and defining a procurement method, estimating costs and benefits, setting interoperability, and the use of open standards as a priority, avoiding discriminatory practices such as naming trade marks, understanding and assessing licensing schemes, software provision models and suppliers, and establishing fair tendering processes. OSEPA has also published a Policy Recommendation Paper, dated 23 November 2012[89] which sets out a series of 25 recommendations aimed at improving and increasing the use of open source in the public sector.

Against that background, though the Commission has not, as it were, expressly declared for open source, the underlying intent to encourage its use (or, at the very least, to level the playing field) seems clear. Indeed, that aspiration is very clearly expressed in the European Interoperability Framework 2.[90]

So far as material to the present issue, paragraph 5.2.1 of the Communication requires, inter alia:

> Intellectual property rights related to the specification are licensed on FRAND terms or on a royalty-free basis in a way that allows implementation in both proprietary and open source software.

'FRAND' is defined in footnote 19 as 'Fair, reasonable and non-discriminatory'; and this particular provision is justified in footnote 20 thus:

> This fosters competition since providers working under various business models may compete to deliver products, technologies and services based on such specification.

The intent which lies behind the provision referred to in paragraph 5.2.1 could not be more clear: interoperability requires a level playing field between proprietary and open source software.

11.5.3 The Netherlands

At the national level, an early leader in adopting a public policy position was the Netherlands, with the Netherlands Government action plan published in November 2007.[91] The plan recognizes that public procurement must not discriminate between

[88] OSEPA, 'FOSS guidelines' <http://osepa.eu/pdeliverables/TAL18D_3.2.3_GuidelinesFOSS.doc> accessed 8 April 2013.

[89] OSEPA, 'Open Source software usage by European Public Administrations' (23 November 2012) <http://www.osepa.eu/pdeliverables/Policy%20Reccomendation%20Paper.pdf> accessed 8 April 2013.

[90] Published on 16 December 2010, as Annex II to Commission Communication *Towards Interoperability for European Public Services*, COM (2010) 744 final, available at <http://eur-lex.europa.eu/LexUriServ/LexUriServ.do?uri=COM:2010:0744:FIN:EN:PDF> accessed 8 April 2013. See also ch 10.

[91] Ministry of Economic Affairs (Netherlands), 'The Netherlands in Open Connection: An action plan for the use of Open Standards and Open Source Software in the public and semi-public sector' (2007) <http://www.opensource.ch/knowhow/2007_TheNetherlandsInOpenConnection.pdf> accessed 8 April 2013.

individual vendors, but noted that a preference towards a specific business model is generally accepted and widespread in several areas, such as when a preference is expressed for leasing instead of buying capital equipment in a call for tender.

The plan then articulated the Cabinet Office Policy towards open standards as follows:

> The Cabinet intends to encourage the use of open standards within the public and semi-public sector. The key focus here is: use open standards, or come up with a very good reason why this is not possible, and indicate when open standards will indeed be implemented. This is the principle of 'comply or explain, and commit.' Through this the use of open standards will be given a firm foundation.[92]

The report then set out a series of 'Action Lines,' including:

> 6. Central Government Departments will from April 2008 support ODF13 alongside existing file formats for reading, writing and exchange of documents. Subsidiary government bodies and general institutions will follow as soon as possible, at the latest by December 2008.
>
> 7. All ministries will have developed an implementation strategy by January 2009 for tendering and purchase and the use of open source software—by June 2008 more than half of the ministries. This may also relate to communal or interdepartmental implementation strategies.
>
> 8. Subsidiary government bodies and general institutions (education, healthcare, social security) will have developed an implementation strategy by January 2010 for tendering, purchase and the use of open source software.
>
> 9. A good example tends to be followed. Initiative takers should be encouraged.

Action line 11 committed the Cabinet Office to seek to encourage open standards and open source in a European context.

One of the purposes of the policy is to encourage individual public agencies at the regional, national, or local level to acquire open source software, even if there is no existing policy in place regarding open source. Justification for this guideline is provided by the existence of widespread 'poor practices' in public procurement that lead to non-transparent, anticompetitive discrimination in software procurement. This discrimination is stated to be in favour of proprietary software, and typically, in favour of specific proprietary products and their vendors.

The Policy Document was followed up in 2008 with the publication by the Office of Nederland Open in Verbinding of *The acquisition of (open-source) software: A guide for ICT buyers in the public and semi-public sectors*,[93] which provides detailed guidance to public sector bodies on how to go about acquiring open source software.

[92] At 12.

[93] NOiV, 'The acquisition of (open-source) software' (22 April 2008 updated) <http://www.ictu.nl/archief/noiv.nl/the-acquisition-of-open-source-software/index.html> accessed 8 April 2013.

11.5.4 Sweden

The current Swedish Framework Agreement for the procurement of open source,[94] though dating from 2011, is rooted in what was the first framework for the procurement of open source software in Europe. The earlier and similar framework had run from 2007 to 2011 and had been created by the National Procurement Services department ('NPS').

Under EU procurement law, it is possible to have a two-stage tendering process whereby a number of economic operators submit tenders for a Framework Agreement. The successful tenderers then provide a pool of economic operators who are able to compete for individual contracts which are let under the Framework Agreement. Under the current Swedish Framework Agreement, in which central government, the public educational sector, all 20 county councils, and 225 out of the 290 Swedish municipalities participate, five open source suppliers[95] have been contracted to provide software and services.

The framework defines open source software as code available under a licence approved by the Open Source Initiative ('OSI'). Besides promoting free software, the OSI maintains a list of licences that have been checked against the Open Source Definition ('OSD'). This model differs from the recommendations made in the *European Guideline on Public Procurement of Open Source Software*, which regards explicit calls for open source software as bad practice. However, the NPS believes that requiring an open source licence for the software procured by public authorities is not against the Public Procurement Directive, and this has not been challenged.

There exists a parallel framework agreement called *Licensförsörjning 2010* that customers can use to buy any kind of software (including open source). The strength of this parallel agreement is that it provides an entry to the public procurement market for SMEs which would not make it on to the other framework agreement, but the perceived disadvantage of this dual solution is that the public authorities may find themselves unable to compare open source directly with proprietary software in the context of an open competition, given the requirement first to choose under which Framework Agreement to proceed.

11.5.5 Italy

Where Piedmont led, the national government in Italy has followed.

[94] <http://www.ch-open.ch/fileadmin/user_upload/events/itbeschaffungskonferenz2012/08_DanielMelin.pdf> accessed on 16 June 2013.

[95] Arctic Group, Init, Pro4u Open Source, RedBridge, and Redpill Linpro, who together have about 75 subcontractors.

As discussed earlier, the Piedmont Regional Law was found by the Italian Constitutional Court to be consistent with Article 68 of the *Codice dell'Amministrazione Digitale* ('CAD') as it stood at the time of the Court's decision in 2010.

Since then, possibly partly for pragmatic reasons (Italy's latest economic crisis), the Italian Government, as part of its programme to encourage economic development, promulgated a decree on 7 August 2012.[96] Article 22 of the new law modified the public procurement rules set out in Article 68 of the CAD so as to exclude first resort to proprietary software, instead creating a presumption in favour of certain specific software categories (custom-developed software, reused custom software, open source software, or any combination thereof).

Article 68, in its amended terms read (in part) as follows:

> Only when the comparative assessment of technical and economic aspects demonstrates the impossibility of adopting open source solutions or any other software solution already developed (at a lower price) within the public administration system, the acquisition (by license) of proprietary software products is allowed.

That decree required to be approved by the Italian Parliament. There was intensive lobbying from the proprietary software industry for the very clear commitment to open source to be watered down. Separately a decision was made to include also cloud computing solutions. Thus, when the Senate approved the new legislation on 17 December 2012 (the Italian Digital Agenda Reform) the options set out in the revised Article 68 were extended in order to include also cloud computing solutions, and the criteria for comparison were both widened from lowest cost alone and spelled out more fully. There was also some relatively insignificant weakening of the text in respect of the open source preference.

In its final form, Article 68 provides:

> 1) In accordance with the principles of economy and efficiency, return on investment, reuse and technological neutrality, public administrations must procure computer programs or parts thereof as a result of a comparative assessment of technical and economic aspects between the following solutions available on the market:
>
> a) develop a solution internally;
>
> b) reuse a solution developed internally or by another public administration;
>
> c) adopt a free/open source solution;
>
> d) use a cloud computing service;
>
> e) obtain a proprietary license of use;
>
> f) a combination of the above.

[96] *Legge Sviluppo*, Law 134/2012.

1-bis) For this purpose, before procuring, the public administration (in accordance with the procedures set out in the Legislative Decree 12 April 2006, no.163) makes a comparative assessment of the available solutions, based on the following criteria:

a) total cost of the program or solution (such as acquisition price, implementation, maintenance and support);

b) level of use of data formats, open interfaces and open standards which are capable of ensuring the interoperability and technical cooperation between the various information systems within the public administration;

c) the supplier's guarantees on security levels, on compliance with the rules on personal data protection, on service levels, taking into account the type of software obtained.

1-ter) In the event that the comparative assessment of technical and economic aspects, in accordance with these criteria of paragraph 1-bis demonstrates the impossibility of adopting an already available solution, or a free/open source solution, as well as to meet the requirements, the procurement of paid-for proprietary software products is allowed. The assessment referred to in the above subparagraph shall be made according to the procedures and the criteria set out by the Agenzia per l'Italia Digitale, which, when requested by interested parties, also expresses opinions about compliance with them.[97]

Although there are certain infelicities in the drafting of the new Article 68, with a looseness in the setting out of the criteria, and a great deal of responsibility for advice delegated to the Agenzia per l'Italia Digitale, it does represent a considerable government commitment to open source. Indeed, it should be noted that even internally developed software is required to be made available for reuse by other public authorities, free of licensing fees and with the source code also made available. Perhaps the most remarkable feature is that the hurdle that must be overcome before proprietary software can be acquired is that the use of the other forms of software listed in Article 68 is 'impossible'.

That is a high hurdle indeed, and, as might be expected, the new law has continued to meet substantial opposition from the proprietary software industry with intense lobbying by Microsoft and other software companies, along with the *Confindustria Digitale* and the American Chamber of Commerce in favour of restoring Article 68 to its form prior to its first amendment by Law 134/2012.

Whatever the outcome of the political lobbying, it is unlikely, so long as Article 68 remains in its present form, that it could successfully be challenged legally, since, as discussed earlier, it is strongly arguable that to express such preferences as are set out in Article 68 is permissible under EU law. Furthermore, given the decision of the

[97] An updated and verified text of the CAD is available at <http://www.digitpa.gov.it/amministrazione-digitale/CAD-testo-vigente> accessed 8 April 2013.

Constitutional Court in the *Piedmont* case, it is unlikely that a challenge based on competition law principles would succeed. In any event, even if Article 68 were put back to its pre-2012 form, this would certainly not preclude regional laws giving a preference to open source, as in the *Piedmont* case.

Software procurement in Italy has changed fundamentally.

11.5.6 The United Kingdom

The UK Government Paper, *Open Standards Principles: For software interoperability, data and document formats in government IT specifications*[98] is explicit in its encouragement of open source software. It proceeds upon the political commitment expressed by the Conservative and Liberal Democrat parties contained in the *Coalition Agreement for Stability and Reform*[99] dated 20 May 2010 which provides, at page 22:

> We will create a level playing field for open-source software and will enable large ICT projects to be split into smaller components.

On the basis of that commitment, the *Open Standards Principles* have been specifically drawn up so as to encourage full and equal access to the market for open source. However, it should be borne in mind that this is a commitment made by the United Kingdom Government in respect of its own procurement. It does not bind either the devolved administrations in Scotland, Wales, or Northern Ireland, nor does it bind local authorities or the many other public authorities such as the NHS. However, even before the publication of the Coalition's policy statement, some local councils and other public bodies were beginning to adopt open source and it may be that the *Principles* will help encourage this trend.

11.5.7 Spain

In Spain, at the national level there is a Proposal for Recommendations by the Ministry of Public Administration dated 2005, stating the benefits of open source software and recommending its use to bodies of the central administration, but it remains a proposal, and does not have mandatory effect. However there is a legislative framework which encourages the creation of a level playing field, including Law 11/2007 for Citizens' Electronic Access to Public Services, which by Article 39 provides for access to source code to audit automatic procedures; by Article 45 provides for declaration of applications such as 'open source' for reuse; by Article 46 creates

[98] See n 82.

[99] HM Government, 'The Coalition Document' <http://www.cabinetoffice.gov.uk/news/coalition-documents> accessed 8 April 2013.

a reusable applications directory, and in the Annex sets out a definition of an 'Open Source Application.'

There is also Law 56/2007 on Measures to Promote the Information Society and Royal Decree 4/2010, which regulates the national scheme for interoperability, and expresses a clear commitment to interoperability.

At the regional level, in Andalusia, Decree 72/2003 establishes a rule of preference in favour of open source in the education sector in that region. Elsewhere in Spain, though there is no mandatory requirement or formal guidance, there is evidence of public procurement practice favouring open source, eg, in Extremadura and Galicia, as well as at local level, eg, in Zaragoza.

11.5.8 Germany

Germany is also prominent in OSS adoption in the EU. The ICT Strategy of the Federal government, 'Digital Germany 2015'[100] claims that standardization and interoperability in the field of ICT are of strategic importance for the German state. It contains clear commitments to open standards and, in that context, to open source:

> The German federal government focuses on 'Open Standards' in order to ensure unhindered access to ICT markets. Open Standards support interoperability and the functioning of complex technical systems in the best way...the use of Open Source Software in Public Administrations augments interoperability and sustainability of Information Technology Systems and it contributes to the consolidation of IT-competencies in Germany as well as to the enhancement of competition and of security on the software market.

Within the federal pact on employment and stability, a Competence Centre Open Source Software ('CC OSS') has been established with the aim of increasing knowledge of open source software and to transfer this knowledge to public administrations. The Federal Ministry of Economics and Technology funds an open source project, the Open Source Solutions Stack, which aims at building up an integrated and comprehensive open source software stack providing customised software solutions for companies and the public sector.

There have also been significant commitments at the local level to open source software, such as the City of Munich, the City of Freiburg, and the City of Schwäbisch Hall. A further notable example is the project to implement an open source infrastructure in schools, UCS@school, promoted by the senator for education and research of the City of Bremen.[101]

[100] ICT Strategy of the Federal Government, 'Digital Germany 2015,' Ministry of Economics and Technology, November 2010 <http://www.bmwi.de/English/Redaktion/Pdf/ict-strategy-digital-germany-2015,property=pdf,bereich=bmwi,sprache=en,rwb=true.pdf> accessed on 16 June 2013.

[101] Uninvention <http://www.univention.de> accessed 8 April 2013.

11.5.9 The rest of the EU

The situation elsewhere in the EU is patchy. In some Member States, such as Romania and the Czech Republic, there are encouraging noises made at central government, but no formal policy initiatives, and in other Member States, such as Cyprus, some localized initiatives seem to succeed in spite of a resistance at national level to the use of open source software. A useful survey on the comparative experience in several Member States is published by OSEPA.[102]

11.6 THE SITUATION ON THE GROUND

It is one thing to have clear legal rules or national or local policies, but it is another actually to follow them. The situation on the ground is not necessarily encouraging, where even the European Commission itself has made a direct award of an IT contract to an individual preferred supplier, in the case in question, Microsoft.[103] As *Computer Weekly* reports, the European Commission has been buying Microsoft software since 1993 without an open and public competition to assess alternative products. It is pointed out that:

> As a result of striking its sixth successive uncontested deal with Microsoft in May 2011, the Commission has ensured Microsoft will have dominated the desktop computing environment of European institutions for 20 years without allowing a single rival to compete for the business, using legal exceptions meant only for extraordinary circumstances. The so-called 'negotiated procedures', were used to secure purchasing arrangements, the last of which concerned approximately €50m of software licences for 36,000 PCs and their supporting infrastructure across 42 European institutions, including the European Parliament and Court of Justice.

The justification advanced by the Commission in 2003, 2007, and 2011 was that 'any alternative software would be technically incompatible and migration unusually burdensome, so it had no choice but to carry on buying Microsoft'.[104] One might observe that this may or may not be a good reason to draft the specification narrowly so as to effectively exclude software which was not compatible with existing legacy systems, though such a restriction would require to be objectively justified,[105] but it is extraordinarily difficult to see how it could lawfully be used as a reason not to have a tendering process at all. The matter becomes even more difficult to understand when, as *Computer Weekly* reports:

[102] OSEPA, 'FOSS European and National Policies and practices: Analysis and Recommendations' <http://osepa.eu/pdeliverables/Report_of_evidence_of_national_FOSS_policies_v6.pdf> accessed 8 April 2013.

[103] M Ballard, 'European Commission buys Microsoft for 20 years without competition' (*Computer Weekly*, 15 September 2011) <http://www.computerweekly.com/news/2240105617/European-Commission-buys-Microsoft-for-20-years-without-competition> accessed 8 April 2013.

[104] Ballard (n 103). [105] See the discussion of *Concordia Bus* and *Elekta* earlier in this chapter.

> Maroš Šefčovič, the Commission vice president and commissioner for inter-institutional relations and administration, who is leading a major reform of IT at the EC, told MEPs the Commission was committed to 'promoting interoperability' using standards. But he said these standards could include those implemented by commercial software vendors. He denied the Commission was locked into supply from any single vendor.

It may be that part of the explanation might lie in the circumstance that the Directorate General of the Commission responsible for purchasing IT is not the same as the Directorate General for Competition.

There was extensive discussion of this case within the open source community at the time. Attempts were made to encourage a challenge to what might appear to have been an arguably unlawful direct contract, but the problem was that the contract was too small for extremely large potential suppliers who preferred not to disrupt relations with the Commission, and too large for SMEs who could not have demonstrated *locus standi* as economic operators who would have tendered had they had the opportunity to do so.

The situation at Member State level is scarcely more encouraging. For the past three years, OpenForum Europe ('OFE') has published a report[106] on the EU Member States' practice of referring to specific trade marks when procuring computer software packages and information systems. The latest monitoring exercise examined 585 invitations to tender issued by contracting authorities seeking to procure computer software products during the three months from 1 March to 31 May 2012. It found that almost one in five notices included technical specifications with explicit references to trade marks, which shows a worse outcome than the 2011 OFE procurement monitoring report[107] which showed 13 per cent of the monitored public tenders making an explicit reference to a proprietary software trade mark, thus apparently excluding open source or proprietary alternatives.

In Finland, the Free Software Foundation Europe recently examined over 300 procurement notices, and found clear violations of procurement law in 14 (almost five per cent). The group has announced that it plans to take the country's public administrations to court if they continue to break national and EU procurement rules when procuring IT solutions. The group's campaign is supported by several OS IT service providers.[108]

[106] OFE, 'EU Member States practice of referring to specific trademarks when procuring for Computer Software Packages and Information Systems between the months of March to May 2010' <http://www.openforumeurope.org/openprocurement/open-procurement-library/Report_2012_1stSnapshot_FINAL-1.pdf> accessed 8 April 2013.

[107] OpenForum Europe, <www.openforumeurope.org> accessed 8 April 2013.

[108] FSFE, 'FSFE to Advance Fair Public IT Procurements in Finland' (19 June 2012) <http://fsfe.org/news/2012/news-20120619-01.en.html> accessed 8 April 2013.

A similar monitoring exercise was carried out in Poland covering the period from July 2006 to June 2007 by UBIC BC Business Consulting. The results were published in an analytical report published in August 2007.[109]

170 procedures were analysed with respect to the description of the product.[110] In 150 procurement exercises, to the value of about 99 million zloty, the specification named a specific application or manufacturer. In 17 proceedings, to the value of 54.5 million zloty, the specification specified a trade mark, though with an 'or equivalent'. In only three cases, with a value of 1.3 million zloty, did the public authority set out functional requirements and specifications without giving product names.[111] The biggest contracting authority was ZUS (Zakład Ubezpieczeń Społecznych 'Social Security Authority') which sought 27,000 licences for MS Office, Windows updates, and three years' support.[112] The words 'or alternative' were not used. ZUS specified the detailed conditions for the computer programs in such a way that companies other than Microsoft resellers were not able to meet the tender requirements. The report also highlights the procurement process carried out by the Central Anti-corruption Office ('CBA') for 574 computers with software. In all of the individual specifications software with the Microsoft trade mark was specified, and in only two out of five of them was there reference to an equivalent, but there were no detailed performance specifications to give any objective basis upon which a would-be tenderer might be able to judge what might constitute an equivalent.[113]

The Free and Open Software Foundation in Poland suggests that Polish public procurement law does not make proper provisions for economic operators to challenge defective procurement exercises. Frequently, if a challenge or protest is made to the contracting authority carrying out a tendering exercise, the authority often does not know how to deal with such challenges, and sometimes it simply ignores them, thinking that such lack of reaction will have no consequences. The FOSS Foundation, within the framework of its PPP IT project,[114] takes an active role in intervening in the case of improper tender specifications, contacting the contracting authorities in writing and requesting them to bring the terms of their tender specifications into compliance with the law. For some time they have been using the threat of reporting the authority to the Polish Public Tenders Office if the tender is not corrected, and this strategy is said to have proved quite effective.

Anecdotal evidence is equally dispiriting. In Cyprus in 2008, the Cyprus Ministry of Education & Culture ('MOEC') launched, in a pilot stage, a web-based learning

[109] UBIC BC Business Consulting Report available at: <http://ubikbc.pl/files/ao/UBIKBC_200708_Raport_o_przetargach_ICT_w_sektorze_publicznym.pdf>.

[110] UBIC BC Business Consulting Report (n 109) 4.

[111] UBIC BC Business Consulting Report (n 109) 14.

[112] UBIC BC Business Consulting Report (n 109) 17.

[113] UBIC BC Business Consulting Report (n 109) 19.

[114] PPPIT <http://pppit.org.pl> accessed 8 April 2013.

platform, named DIAS.[115] Teachers are called on to utilize the system's capabilities by trying out new teaching methodologies so that all students are motivated to use DIAS virtual tools for constructing their own knowledge. However, the system is entirely based on proprietary software (the DIAS home page even carries Microsoft advertising) and any expansion in use of the system brings with it additional licence fees payable by the Ministry of Education and by individual schools. Not only the software but also the content is copyrighted. An attempt to provide the software and content to the Greek Ministry of Education was stalled because of licence issues. One questions whether the contracting authority in framing the tender specifications gave any thought to the possible advantages of free software.

Similarly, the Cyprus Ministry of Education is offering funded laptops for all students in Cyprus. However, the rules provide that only computers with Vista or Windows 7 operating systems are eligible for funding. Free educational systems are completely ignored. The Ministry is also offering several proprietary educational packages.

There is a particularly egregious example in Slovakia where a law was enacted that mandated electronic means as the only way of fulfilling certain statutory obligations including the submission of tax returns. However the dedicated web solution provided by the Slovak Government operates only with Microsoft Windows. The practical result is that every taxpayer in Slovakia had to acquire licensed software from Microsoft in order to perform their statutory obligations. Several companies have taken exception to this and attempted to file their tax returns on hard copy, but this is not permitted under the regulations. The Slovak tax administration has already imposed 12 fines on EURA Slovakia, s.r.o., which submitted its monthly tax returns in hard copy, and other taxpayers attempting to use hard copy face similar fines.[116]

In April and July 2008, the Portuguese Ministry of Public Works, Transport, and Communications directly awarded public contracts for the supply of notebook computers and the provision of internet services to three telecommunications operators. The notebooks and internet service were for students, teachers, and trainees for use within four educational programmes. More than one million notebooks with internet access were supplied under the first programme. The Portuguese authorities claimed that no public tendering procedure was required for these contracts as they considered that the notebooks formed part of the payment by the telecommunications providers for operating third generation GSM telecommunication services. The Commission issued a reasoned Opinion[117] (the first stage in formal enforcement

[115] DIAS <http://www.dias.ac.cy> accessed 8 April 2013.

[116] EDRI, 'Digital Civil Rights in Europe' (9 May 2012) <http://www.edri.org/edrigram/number10.9/mandatory-eforms-slovakia-only-windows> accessed 8 April 2013.

[117] Europa, 'IP/10/678' (27 January 2011) <http://europa.eu/rapid/press-release_IP-11-83_en.htm?locale=en> accessed 8 April 2013.

proceedings), which caused the Ministry to agree to conduct a proper tendering exercise in connection with the remaining three programmes.

In 2007, following a public procurement procedure, the Greek authorities awarded a contract to a company for the development of the ERMIS national portal, the online Greek Government portal. Soon afterwards, the Greek authorities awarded a supplementary contract worth €1.5 million to the same company for the development of an information system to be used by staff working in the Greek Government's KEP centres (government service centres where citizens can obtain information and official documents such as birth certificates, licences, and identification papers). The Greek authorities used a negotiated procedure to settle the terms with the company for the development of the information system. No prior contract notice was published. The view of the EU Commission was that the development of the ERMIS online portal was different from the development of the internal information system. The contract should not have been awarded on the basis of a supplementary contract following a negotiated procedure, but rather in a formal tender procedure with a Europe-wide publication of a tender notice, as required by the rules of the Public Procurement Directive. No satisfactory response having been obtained from the Greek Government, the Commission commenced infringement proceedings.[118]

In another case involving Greece,[119] the Greek Social Security Foundation ('IKA') in 2009 launched an open public tender for the provision of services for operating an information system. The contract was valued at almost €7.5 million. The call for tenders stipulated that bidders needed to present project references for successfully implemented contracts in Greece which had the same profile as the one for the IKA. According to the jurisprudence of the Court of Justice of the European Union, contracting authorities are not allowed to impose conditions causing direct or indirect discrimination (such as local preference) against potential bidders established or active in other Member States. The call for tenders also stipulated that bidders could not invoke the experience of their potential sub-contractors in order to cover all the selection criteria of the call for tenders. However, the Public Procurement Directive does clearly allow this possibility. The view of the Commission was that as a result of the conditions imposed, other IT service companies which had provided similar services in other Member States were unlawfully excluded from participating in the tendering procedure in question. The Commission commenced enforcement proceedings.

Finally in this depressing narrative, since 2006, the Italian Region of Molise had failed to comply with EU procurement rules by directly awarding IT services contracts to a company whose shares were held both by the Region of Molise and a private

[118] Europa,'IP/10/1441'(28October2010)<http://europa.eu/rapid/press-release_IP-10-1441_en.htm?locale=en> accessed 8 April 2013.

[119] Europa,'IP/11/1263'(27October2011)<http://europa.eu/rapid/press-release_IP-11-1263_en.htm?locale=en> accessed 8 April 2013.

undertaking. The total value of the contracts was estimated at more than €14 million. In all of these cases the contracts were awarded directly, with no tender procedure. Although there is a limited exception,[120] where the company which the contracting authority owns has the same degree of control exercised over it by the authority as does an internal department of the authority, that was not the situation in the *Molise* case. The Commission again commenced enforcement proceedings.[121]

What these examples show is that, whatever the law may provide, and whatever the applicable policy statements may say, contracting authorities persist in failing to follow the legal requirements. Sometimes this consists in the making of an unlawful direct award without conducting a public procurement exercise, such as in the cases of Molise, the Portuguese Notebooks, the Greek KEP centres, and arguably, the EU Commission's own IT procurement. Other cases involve shutting out competition on a geographical basis, as in the Greek Social Security Foundation. Some involve procurement exercises which produce results which seem on any rational basis of securing value for money difficult to justify, as in the Cypriot DIAS system, but by far the most common appears to involve defective specifications which unlawfully specify software and IT solutions by brand name, without providing for equivalents.

Some of this catalogue of errors may be down to mischief, but a less sinister explanation may be widespread ignorance as to what the law requires (an error which one may suggest is inexcusable in a public authority), or in relation to the relative merits, for any given task, of open source and proprietary solutions. In this regard, reference might be made to the 2011 Report of the Spanish Survey on open source software in the State Public Administration,[122] conducted by CENATIC.[123] According to this report, a significant number of public entities have a perception that open source software suffers from lack of support, this being considered as a critically (19.8 per cent) or very (30.8 per cent) important concern in deciding whether to proceed to the procurement of open source software. Other concerns are seen as being the lack of expertise of public workers with open source, issues with the migration from proprietary platforms, and interoperability issues.

Even when public authorities do get it right, there is evidence that the large proprietary vendors are becoming more prepared to fight back. For example, the City of Munich started a project in 2004 to migrate 13,000 of its computers from Windows NT 4 and Microsoft Office 97 to a custom build of Ubuntu and OpenOffice as part

[120] Case C-107/98 *Teckal Srl v Comune di Viano and Azienda Gas-Acqua Consorziale (AGAC) di Reggio Emilia* Case [1999] ICR I-8121.

[121] Europa, 'IP/11/1119' (29 September 2011) <http://europa.eu/rapid/press-release_IP-11-1119_en.htm?locale=en> accessed 8 April 2013.

[122] *Encuesta sobre el Software de Fuentes Abiertas en la Administración General del Estado (ESFA-AGE) 2011*, published by CENATIC on 10 January 2012. Available at <http://www.cenatic.es/publicaciones/onsfa?download=121%3Adossier-encuesta-esfa-age-2011> accessed 8 April 2013.

[123] A public body in charge of OSS policies, integrated within the Spanish Ministry of Industry.

of its 'LiMux' project. A further 2,000 computers will stay on Windows but are being switched to OpenOffice. The migration is due to be completed in the autumn of 2013. This decision was made by the city after it had calculated that to upgrade its Microsoft systems would cost it €34 million, whereas to migrate to open source would cost it only €23 million. In January, 2013, Hewlett Packard, under commission from Microsoft, produced a report, *Studieüber die Open Source Software Strategie der Stadt München,*[124] which purported to show that migrating to Windows XP and MS Office would cost only €17 million (as opposed to the €34 million estimated by the city), and to migrate to open source would cost €60.6 million (as against €23 million). The city has responded claiming various false assumptions underlying Microsoft's figures.[125] The Munich project has been running for a number of years and Microsoft's late intervention has been made in the public forum, but it may well be that challenges to future similar projects will increasingly be made in the judicial arena.

11.7 CONCLUSION

Where then stands the relationship between public procurement and open source software?

The legal regime is relatively clear, though given the level of disconformities with it revealed in both the surveys and anecdotal evidence, one might be forgiven for thinking that the law was more complex than it is. In particular, it is clear that all procurement exercises where there is a cross-border interest, whether above or below threshold, have to conform to the Treaty principles and derived principles, including transparency and equal treatment. Those principles exclude the limiting of technical specifications to named proprietary software, but permit the specification of open source software in general, or a functional definition which permits or even favours open source. The key is that the requirements of the specification (whether favouring or excluding open source) have to pass the test of being objectively justified.

It is questionable how far, in many tendering exercises, objective justification for the choices made was really a consideration, or, at least, the justifications were being looked at too narrowly by the contracting authority, and wider questions of, eg, vendor lock-in were considered.

[124] The conclusions of which are available at Scribd, 'Studie über die Open Source Software Strategie' <http://www.scribd.com/doc/122167337/Studie-OSS-Strategie-der-Stadt-Munchen-v1-0-Zusammenfassung> accessed 8 April 2013.

[125] See, for a news report of the dispute: N Heath, 'No, Microsoft, open source software really is cheaper, insists Munich' (*ZDnet*, 7 February 2013) <http://www.zdnet.com/no-microsoft-open-source-software-really-is-cheaper-insists-munich-7000010918>; and S Narisi, 'Open source costs more than commercial software (says Microsoft)' *Finance Tech News,* 18 February 2013) <http://www.financetechnews.com/open-source-software-costs> both accessed 8 April 2013.

In the final analysis, procurement law is about how contracting authorities go about contracting, but it is neutral as to the content of the outcome of the tender exercise, provided the process meets the requirements of, inter alia, transparency and equal treatment. Those requirements may go some way towards levelling the playing field for open source, but for open source to be given proper consideration by public authorities who may have got comfortable with their existing proprietary solutions, clear and coherent public policy guidance has a hugely important role to play.

Public procurement can be a valuable tool in levelling the playing field, but it would be a mistake to see it as a panacea. Also critical to ensuring proper competition is the requirement for interoperability.[126] Without interoperability, proper competition is prevented: would-be inventors who do not use Microsoft Windows and Microsoft Word are denied the fee reduction offered by WIPO for the filing of their international patent Applications in XML format[127] and cannot use the European Patent Office's online filing software, which works only with Microsoft Windows;[128] Irish householders looking for their local recycling depot and using any browser other that Microsoft Internet Explorer are condemned, like the flying Dutchman, forever to wander the web without ever loading the page which tells them where to go,[129] and the entire tax paying population of Slovakia finds itself forced, under penalty of a large fine, to purchase a Microsoft Windows licence.

The European Patent Office has, apparently, frequently been asked by frustrated inventors why their PatXML software works only with MS Office. That may be inferred from the fact that the Office's response appears in a section of its website entitled 'Frequently Asked Questions.'[130] The justification given by the EPO is as follows:

> Most people now use Word as their preferred word processor. However, if you wish, you can still author your applications in WordPerfect or any other word processor and import them into PatXML, but you will still need MS Word.[131]

[126] See further ch 10.

[127] WIPO offers software called PCT-SAFE together with a PCT-SAFE Editor for filing international patent applications, and the European Patent Office offers software known as PatXML the use of which together entitles one to a discount on the filing fee, but the PCT safe tools can be used only in conjunction with Microsoft Windows and the PatXML tool can be used only in conjunction with MS Word. WIPO, 'PCT e-Services' <http://www.wipo.int/pct-safe/en>; and EPO <http://www.epo.org/applying/online-services/online-filing/auxiliary/patxml/faq.html#faq-155> both accessed 8 April 2013.

[128] See the Installation Manual for Online Filing version 5: EPO, <http://www.epo.org/applying/online-services/online-filing/documentation.html> accessed on 8 April 2013.

[129] <http://dev.govdata.eu/DataBrowser/ieOpenData/BringBanks#param=NOFILTER--DataView--Results> no longer available.

[130] <http://www.epo.org/applying/online-services/online-filing/auxiliary/patxml/faq.html#faq-151> accessed on 23 March 2013.

[131] <http://www.epo.org/applying/online-services/online-filing/auxiliary/patxml/faq.html#faq-151> accessed on 23 March 2013.

And so, neatly, we end up where we began: even the European Patent office, which ought to know better, requires the use of MS Word because that's what everyone else uses. Despite all of the policy papers, mandatory procurement requirements, and fine words, there is still a long way to go before the Open Office users mentioned at the outset of this chapter will be taken seriously when they suggest, in their Frequently Asked Questions, that their correspondent should himself accept the use of Open Office.

At the end of the day, experience teaches that whatever the law or the policy, compliance with it has to be purchased at the price of eternal vigilance.

12

EVERYTHING OPEN

Andrew Katz

12.1 INTRODUCTION

Openness abounds. Open source software,[1] is now joined by open source hardware[2] (and open hardware),[3] open knowledge,[4] open content,[5] open data,[6] open software services,[7] open politics,[8] open democracy,[9] open government,[10] open public services,[11] open standards,[12] open specifications and formats, open innovation,[13] open education,[14] open publishing,[15] and open access.[16] There is a clearly a connection between these *opens*, but trying to determine the common thread is far from straightforward.

An evident feature of *opens* is that they are intended to remove restrictions to use (including modification and reuse) and access. The terminology may be relatively new, but the openness describes an old idea[17]—of sharing and facilitating reuse[18]—which was often the default in the relevant field, until someone had the idea, implemented through law or other mechanisms, to restrict access. Suddenly, there was a need to differentiate between that field in its restricted form, and the same field made available to all. For example, the free software movement was formed as a reaction to businesses placing restrictions on the use of software and access to source code, in contravention of the then default hacker culture of sharing and making the code and its source available.

[1] Open Source Initiative <http://ww.opensource.org> accessed 4 April 2013.

[2] Open Source Hardware Association <http://www.oshwa.org> accessed 4 April 2013.

[3] Open Hardware <http://www.openhardware.org> accessed 4 April 2013.

[4] Open Knowledge Foundation <http://okfn.org> accessed 4 April 2013.

[5] Open Content 'Defining the "Open" in Open Content' <http://www.opencontent.org/definition> accessed 4 April 2013.

[6] Open Definion <http://opendefinition.org> accessed 4 April 2013. [7] Open Definition (n 6).

[8] Sunlight Centre for Open Politics <http://www.sunlight-cops.org.uk> accessed 4 April 2013.

[9] Open Democracy <http://www.opendemocracy.net> accessed 4 April 2013.

[10] Open Government Partnership <http://www.opengovpartnership.org/about> accessed 4 April 2013.

[11] <http://standards.data.gov.uk/challenge/open-public-services> accessed 4 April 2013.

[12] Principles <http://perens.com/OpenStandards/Definition.html> accessed 4 April 2013.

[13] Open Innovation Community <http://www.openinnovation.net> accessed 4 April 2013.

[14] JISC, 'Open education—case studies' <http://www.jisc.ac.uk/whatwedo/topics/opentechnologies/openeducation.aspx>, and open educational resources: UNESCO, 'Open educational resources' <http://www.unesco.org/new/en/communication-and-information/access-to-knowledge/open-educational-resources> both accessed 4 April 2013.

[15] M Arnison, 'Open publishing is the same as free software' <http://www.purplebark.net/maffew/cat/openpub.html> (March 2001) accessed 4 April 2013.

[16] Open Access <http://open-access.net/ch_en/communication/downloads> accessed 4 April 2013.

[17] Charlotte Waelde argues that the first English language scholarly journal, *Philosophical Transactions* (published in 1665) was, in effect, the first open access journal: C Waelde, 'Scholarly Communications and New Technologies' in L Edwards and C Waelde (eds), *Law and the Internet*, 3rd edn (Oxford, Hart Publishing, 2009).

[18] As we see later, there are a number of movements which seek to define the characteristics of their particular *open*. These definitions are frequently based on the Free Software Foundation's *Four Freedoms* or the Open Source Initiative's openness criteria.

There is no 'open cuisine' or 'open gardening' movement, because recipes and gardening have not been significantly affected by any form of intellectual property restriction. This may change if intellectual property rights start to impinge on these areas (eg, plant breeders' rights, and patents in genetically modified plants).

The openness evident in many free software projects goes beyond the ability to access and reuse the code: it also extends into areas like the governance of the projects themselves (although, as we discuss,[19] it is by no means necessary for an open source project to have an open governance model). Thus the word *open* has established additional shades of meaning, and its usage varies from field to field. There are, we suggest, four different but related connotations to the word *open*.

12.2 USE-MAXIMIZATION OR ANTI-CLOSURE?

The most accessible definition of *open* emphasizes freedom of sharing and reuse. Its aim is to maximize the availability of knowledge and data. However, within each of these fields, there is a tension between those who want to maximize sharing and reuse (irrespective of what the recipients might do with the shared material), and those (who tend to use words like *freedom* more) who want to place obstacles in the way of those who would limit sharing and reuse. These goals are not mutually exclusive and are frequently well aligned, but to understand the dynamics within (and sometimes between) each of the *open* fields, it is necessary to appreciate this distinction.

For example, free software advocates promote the GNU General Public License family of software licences. By implementing copyleft, these licences attempt to ensure that a program subject to the GPL can only be distributed by a recipient if the recipient also makes any work based on the program subject to the same licence, which becomes binding on downstream recipients. On the one hand, this fights the perceived evil of 'closure'. On the other, the implementation of copyleft is itself a restriction on sharing and reuse, and there are many examples of software which has not been adopted by a business because it is subject to the GPL, and for the business, copyleft is an unacceptable restriction.

In contrast, the Apache Software Foundation releases its software under a liberal licence which presents very little restriction to recipients. Those recipients are able to take the software, adapt it, and redistribute it to third parties, even under a closed, proprietary licence. The foundation's aim is to maximize utilization and promulgation of the code, even if that means it is capable of becoming closed.

[19] See further ch 2.

The Free Software Foundation ('FSF') is associated with an anti-closure view; the Open Source Initiative ('OSI') with a use-maximization view.[20] The subtle distinction is clear in the world of Free and Open Source Software ('FOSS'), but is less clear in other areas, where the word *open* may be used without distinguishing between the two different (but frequently aligned) concepts. The distinction becomes clearer when looking at the types of licence which are adopted within the various fields.

Use-maximization also requires that the material in question can be used by as many people as possible and for as many purposes as possible, without discrimination, either in relation to characteristics of the individual (or organization) seeking to use the material, or in relation to the intended use to which the material may be put.[21]

A further connotation of use-maximization is that the material must be amenable to development, amendment and modification for any reason, including extending functionality or field of use, and for correcting errors.

12.3 TRANSPARENCY

The word *open* carries a third connotation: that of transparency (and, to a degree, that of the ability to influence and participate on a non-discriminatory basis, and also that the governance structure allows accountability). Transparency is often a characteristic of open development, and especially the open source development model described by Eric S Raymond in 'The Cathedral and the Bazaar', noting 'release early, release often' (let everyone have access to your development process) because 'given enough eyeballs, all bugs are shallow'.[22] Open source software projects are often portrayed as meritocracies, in which any contributor has an equal opportunity to have his or her efforts recognized in each code release, based solely on the merit of their submissions.[23] (This may be the case in some high profile projects, but there are plenty of projects in which the code development, although ultimately released

[20] The FSF will argue that by ever increasing the pool of GPL software, it will become more difficult for non GPL software to be developed (given that very little software is developed from scratch these days, but is an assemblage of different components), and that, accordingly, it will maximize the use of free (GPL) software. The Apache Foundation (and, to an extent, the OSI) will argue that, although proprietary companies may close Apache code, they will realize that it is better business to keep the code open and contribute to the code base, as the benefits in community participation will lead to a better business outcome, and as such, there is a normative effect for code, even under a no copyleft licence like Apache, to become open. Thus in practice there is significant commonality between the two viewpoints.

[21] This requirement, contained in both the FSF's *four freedoms* and the open source definition from the OSI, causes some counterintuitive consequences. eg, both sets of criteria outlaw a licence which only allows non commercial use, and a notorious seemingly liberal software licence (JSON) which exhorts the licensee to use the software for good, not evil, also falls outside both criteria, as discriminating against those who want to be evil.

[22] ES Raymond, 'The Cathedral and the Bazaar' <http://www.catb.org/~esr/writings/cathedral-bazaar/cathedral-bazaar/index.html> (*Thyrsus Enterprises*, 2000) accessed 5 April 2013.

[23] See further ch 2 at p57.

under an open source licence, is effectively undertaken in-house by a development team structured in a way very similar to the development teams at any proprietary software company.) This is part of the meaning of *open* which is invoked in terms like *open politics* or *open government*.

12.4 ANTI-LOCK-IN

Finally, there may be an assumption that a user of something open is not *locked-in*. This means that adoption of the *open*—usually a standard, a specification, or specific software or hardware—does not create barriers to the adoption of another solution, or from moving away from an existing solution. For example, the adoption of an open standard for a document format means that the document can be edited, at least in theory, by a number of different word processors, whereas a proprietary format may only be capable of being read by a specific supplier's product. This is the connotation which is foremost in the definition of *open standard* or *open specification*. A further connotation of this is persistence: for an *open* to avoid lock-in, it must also be persistent: in other words, the user must be able to trust that the means of access used at a particular time will continue to be available for some significant time into the future.

12.5 INTERRELATIONSHIP BETWEEN OPENS

Free software and open source software are, more often than not, the same thing, even though the organizations that are behind them differ in their aims. The development of open source software (or at least the poster-child projects, like the Linux kernel or the Debian Linux distribution) often involves open development methodologies and transparency. Open source software often complies with open standards (and, arguably, any interfaces which it implements are *de facto* an open standard, because it is possible to see the code which implements it, and reuse or reimplement the standard in an open form).[24] Likewise, it is difficult (but not impossible, as we shall see in the context of open software services) for open source to implement a lock-in solution, as access to the code means that a solution can be reimplemented using different means.

However, sometimes there are conflicts between opens. Open standards are useful only to the extent that they remain stable and consistent. If someone unilaterally 'improves' a standard by amending it, so that devices or software built to that standard no longer interoperate (either at all, or unreliably), then it is no longer of

[24] See further ch 10.

any use as a standard. To be of use, open standards need to be developed in such a way that improvements and amendments are co-ordinated, and standards bodies have a role here. Ideally, the process leading to the formation of the standard itself should be transparent and allow for non-discriminatory participation, but, the process and the result are often confused, and to say that it is necessary for both the process and the result to be open (in two quite different meanings of the word) for a standard to be open is unhelpful and an over-simplification (see later in this chapter, and Chapter 10). The outcome of a standards process (whether open or otherwise) should be a standard which is documented on an open content basis (for which detail, see later) and which anyone can implement without payment of royalties or other restriction. This is one definition of an open standard.[25]

Each of the opens we consider in this chapter places slightly different emphasis on each of these characteristics, anti-closure, use-maximization, transparency, and anti-lock-in.

12.6 OPENNESS AND INTELLECTUAL PROPERTY RIGHTS

We have seen that for a field to develop an open movement, there has to be a corresponding closure, or at least a threat of closure. These threats are largely facilitated by intellectual property rights. Thus free software and open source software exist as movements, because the existence of copyright (and patents) makes it possible for the owners of those rights in software to control the use and distribution of that software, even in the absence of a contractual relationship between the rights holder and the infringer of those rights.

Where there are no intellectual property rights (such as the preparation of food to a particular recipe) it is more difficult to close the field: a diner in a restaurant who enjoys a particular aubergine curry is free to try to recreate the recipe at home without the permission of the chef. Further, if someone watches the chef prepare the dish on television, they can make notes of the ingredients, quantities, and process, and the viewer is, again, under no restriction regarding creating a recipe accordingly.[26] It follows that there is no 'open recipe' movement, as there are no closed recipes against which it can rally.[27]

[25] See ch 10.

[26] Although clearly a written recipe would be subject to copyright as a literary work, making the dish is not infringement of that work (it's interesting to speculate whether a recipe could possibly be considered analogous to 'performing' it like a dance). It may also be the case the dish is associated with a trade mark, registered or unregistered, so selling the dish as McDonald's Special Sauce would invoke a different set of intellectual property rights.

[27] There have been a few attempts to release 'open recipes.' However, it's not clear what they are trying to achieve. OpenCola is a recipe for a flavoured sugar syrup intended to be similar to the base for Coca Cola. Coca Cola may

That is not to say that where there are no intellectual property rights there is no possibility of a corresponding *open* movement developing. Lawrence Lessig has famously drawn a distinction between East Coast code (laws) and West Coast code (physical or technological constraints).[28] Thus in the absence of laws, it is possible to construct constraints technologically. A simple example is that manufacturers may deliberately make items which are difficult to fix, with the intention of either ensuring that only that manufacturer (or its licensees) has the ability to repair and maintain those items, or that broken items are discarded and a new replacement is purchased.

To repair such items, the owner would ideally have access to blueprints and circuit diagrams; any device would be easy to open using readily available tools, rather than employing special security fastenings; replacement components of the device would be readily available; and re-assembling the device would be possible without special jigs or adhesives. These are the sorts of freedom that are set out in the *Maker's Bill of Rights.*[29]

A more subtle application of intellectual property rights consists in their importance in facilitating copyleft. The copyleft principle provides that if someone makes use of material available under a copyleft licence, then that person will be required, under certain circumstances,[30] to make their amendments, design documents, and/or source code relating to that material available to downstream recipients under the same licence. Sometimes known as *sharealike*, this principle is designed to ensure that once material is available under an open licence, it, and its derivatives, will remain available under that licence. Clearly, however, for copyleft to be effective, there does need to be an intellectual property right which would be infringed at the appropriate time but for the licensee's compliance with a condition in the licence. If the licensee is able to do that act in question without impinging on any intellectual property right, then there is no requirement to comply with any licence. This is explored in greater depth later.

famously keep its recipe confidential, but anyone purchasing a bottle of Coke is entitled to reverse-engineer it (a mass spectrometer may help) and publish the results without restriction. The Coca Cola Corporation is unable to exercise any intellectual property rights to prevent the purchaser from making a clone drink, in the way that it *would* be able to prevent someone from using its name or its distinctively-shaped bottle. Open Cola adopts the GPL as its licence, but since making a drink from a recipe does not impinge on copyright in the way that compiling a piece of software does, it's hard to see how any obligations can be placed on downstream recipients of the cola. Reproducing the recipe (that is making copies of its text) does impinge on copyright, so it's not so much the cola that is open, than its recipe, in the form of a literary work. 'OpenCola Softdrink' <http://www.colawp.com/colas/400/cola467_recipe.html> accessed 5 April 2013.

[28] L Lessig, *Code Version 2.0* (Version 2.0, Penguin Books, 2006) 72 *et seq* available at <http://codev2.cc/download+remix/Lessig-Codev2.pdf> accessed 5 April 2013.

[29] Mister Jalopy, 'Owner's Manifesto' (*Make*) <http://makezine.com/04/ownyourown> accessed 5 April 2013.

[30] The circumstances will depend on the licence: eg, the GPL is concerned about distribution. The AGPL, additionally, is concerned about access to the software across a network.

12.7 DEFINITIONS OF OPENNESS (AND FREEDOM) IN SOFTWARE

The most venerable criteria for openness, as currently understood, are the *four freedoms* espoused by the FSF.[31] The other *opens* frequently adopt criteria that are modelled on the four freedoms. The FSF's *four freedoms* are:

> The freedom to run the program, for any purpose (freedom 0).
>
> The freedom to study how the program works, and change it so it does your computing as you wish (freedom 1). Access to the source code is a precondition for this.
>
> The freedom to redistribute copies so you can help your neighbor (freedom 2).
>
> The freedom to distribute copies of your modified versions to others (freedom 3). By doing this you can give the whole community a chance to benefit from your changes. Access to the source code is a precondition for this.[32]

These cover use-maximization (and, in a roundabout way, through the words 'access to the source code is a precondition of this' anticipates anti-closure), but the definition does not cover transparency or anti-lock-in. As we have seen, anti-lock-in is an emergent characteristic of free and open source software, and the open source development model, although applicable to a number of projects, is by no means universal (and not automatically emergent).

Accordingly it is dangerous for other *opens* to assume that the four freedoms can be transmuted into other areas, and the same connotations of openness preserved.

For example, the Open Hardware and Design Association has established the following freedoms based on the FSF's four freedoms, with a reasonable degree of success:[33]

Freedom 0: The freedom to use the device for any purpose.
Freedom 1: The freedom to study how the device works and change it to make it to do what you wish. Access to the complete design is precondition to this.
Freedom 2: Redistribute the device and/or design (remanufacture).
Freedom 3: The freedom to improve the device and/or design, and release your improvements (and modified versions in general) to the public, so that the whole community benefits. Access to the complete design is precondition to this.

[31] GNU, 'What is free software?' <http://www.gnu.org/philosophy/free-sw.html> accessed 5 April 2013.
[32] GNU (n 31).
[33] Open Source Hardware and Design Alliance <http://www.ohanda.org> accessed 5 April 2013.

We will see that there are some fundamental problems with this definition—around the definition of 'complete design'—but subject to that, it makes sense. However, how can this definition be meaningfully adopted in a way that makes it clear what 'open government' or 'open politics' are?

12.8 OPEN KNOWLEDGE

The Open Knowledge Foundation ('OKF') is a body that has attempted to establish a universal definition for the *opens*.[34] Its definition of open knowledge is as follows:

> A piece of content or data is open if anyone is free to use, reuse, and redistribute it—subject only, at most, to the requirement to attribute and/or share-alike.

The first half of this definition is use-maximizing. The second is anti-closed. As we have seen before, there is significant commonality between the two. But it fails to convey transparency or anti-lock-in, and even though these are either irrelevant or emergent in relation to some of the opens, it fails to cover the connotation of *open* which is anticipated by open government or open politics.

Aware that the open knowledge definition is not all-encompassing, the OKF presents another, specific definition, the Open Software Service Definition:

> A service is open if its source code is Free/Open Source Software and non-personal data is open as in the Open Knowledge Definition.

This cleverly uses the Open Knowledge Definition to define the scope of the data (excluding personal data) which the service contains and processes, and also (indirectly) to define the scope of the software which must be used (free and open source software falls within the open knowledge definition). However, this definition is not ideal, in that it still allows for a software service which can be locked in, as we discuss later.

One of the activities of the OKF is, like the FSF or the OSI, to consider which licences are approved, such that material released under such a licence can be regarded as compliant with the open knowledge definition.

Open Data Commons[35] is a project of the OKF, which seeks, like the Creative Commons organization discussed later, to facilitate the availability of content, in this case database, as part of a knowledge commons. The tools used are a set of licences, the Public Domain Dedication and License, the Attribution License and the Open Database License.[36] These licences are drafted to take into account the special characteristics of databases, such as the European Union's *sui generis* database right,

[34] Open Knowledge Foundation <http://okfn.org> accessed 5 April 2013.

[35] Open Data Commons <http://opendatacommons.org> accessed 5 April 2013.

[36] Open Data Commons, 'Licenses' <http://opendatacommons.org/licenses> accessed 5 April 2013.

and the practical consequence of a multi-source database potentially containing contributions from many thousands of different sources, and therefore it becoming impractical to provide attribution for them all.[37]

12.8.1 Open data

The Open Data Foundation focuses not just on making data available, but making it useful, by seeking to promote global metadata standards (metadata is data about data), so that information from diverse databases conforming to the standards can be combined in practical and interesting ways. As such, its activities are intended to help people:

Discover the existence of data;
Access the data for research and analysis;
Find detailed information describing the data and its production processes;
Access the data sources and collection instruments from which and with which the data was collected, compiled, and aggregated;
Effectively communicate with the agencies involved in the production, storage, distribution of the data;
Share knowledge with other users.

12.8.2 Open content

Open content is another blanket term, and is broadly equivalent to 'open knowledge'. At least terminologically, the movement is roughly as old as the OSI (the terms *open source* and *open content* were both coined in 1998). Initially intended to refer to content licensed under the Open Content License, the definition extended to any content which meets these criteria:[38]

Reuse: the right to reuse the content in its unaltered/verbatim form (eg, make a backup copy of the content);
Revise: the right to adapt, adjust, modify, or alter the content itself (eg, translate the content into another language);
Remix: the right to combine the original or revised content with other content to create something new (eg, incorporate the content into a mash-up);

[37] Open Data Commons, 'Licenses FAQ' <http://opendatacommons.org/faq/licenses>; and Interview with Jordan Hatcher, (*Poynder blogspot*, 18 October 2010) <http://poynder.blogspot.co.uk/2010/10/interview-with-jordan-hatcher.html> both accessed 5 April 2013. Jordan Hatcher is the principal drafter of the Open Data Commons licences.

[38] Open Content, 'Defining the "Open" in Open Content' <http://www.opencontent.org/definition> accessed 5 April 2013.

Redistribute: the right to share copies of the original content, your revisions, or your remixes with others (eg, give a copy of the content to a friend).

These criteria are very similar to the FSF's four freedoms, so it will come as no surprise that the Open Content License[39] is modelled on the GNU GPL, in that it is a copyleft licence. It does restrict the ability to charge for access (and to that extent is partially non-commercial).[40]

12.9 CREATIVE COMMONS

One of the most prominent organizations in the open content movement has been Creative Commons. The brainchild of Professor Lawrence Lessig, with co-founders Hal Abelson and Eric Eldred, the name *Creative Commons* draws on the metaphor of creative activity being a commons. However, whereas a physical commons (eg fish in the sea, or a piece of common land in a village) can be exhausted by harvesting or over-grazing, a commons of ideas cannot be exhausted, as using an idea does not remove it from the commons (in economic parlance, use of material subject to intellectual property is non-rivalrous).

Creative Commons is intended to cover a wide range of material, such as literary works, photography, video and film materials, and other works such as choreography, with the intention that as many works as possible are available for reuse.

Creative Commons consists of a series of licences, which are currently on their third version. They have been localized for use in a number of jurisdictions worldwide to address differences in copyright and other laws between jurisdictions. A content owner choosing to use a Creative Commons licence has a number of options: BY (attribution), ND (no derivatives), NC (non-commercial), and SA (share alike); these can be combined in various ways. Thus, a licence designated CC-BY-NC would allow the user to take the work and exploit it for non-commercial purposes (NC), provided that the originator is credited (BY). Permission is also granted to amend the work. The ND (no derivatives) tag prevents derivative works from being made. SA (share alike) is a copyleft-like provision that requires any redistribution of the work or a derivative to be subject to the same licence.

Creative Commons licences have gained wide acceptance: eg, the whole of Wikipedia is released under CC-BY-SA. The use of simple tags to establish the applicable licence has the benefit of making material that is available under a specific licence to be easily identified and searched using a search engine such as Google.

[39] OpenContent License <http://opencontent.org/opl.shtml> accessed 5 April 2013.

[40] Non-commercial licenses are incompatible with the four freedoms, because commercial activity is a legitimate field of endeavour and restriction of the right to charge is a restriction on this legitimate endeavour.

Sites such as flickr.com have added functionality to make it easy to identify material which is available under particular licences.[41]

Works such as software or hardware are occasionally released under Creative Commons licences. This is not appropriate, as the licences do not deal effectively with the distinction between source code and object code, and they do not cover patents. (If the material relates solely to design document rather than the hardware instantiation of the design, then a Creative Commons licence may be appropriate.)

On the other hand, where there is material which is more analogous to computer software (such as a multi-track source material for use in a digital-audio workstation such as Reason[42] or Ableton[43]) then a licence like the GPL may be more appropriate.

Material is sometimes released under 'a Creative Commons licence' without any further information: this is unhelpful. Creative Commons is a suite of licences, and without further information it is not possible to determine which licence is intended. In this case, the best assumption is that BY-NC-ND (attribution, non-commercial, no derivatives) is intended.

Despite their *open* credentials, not all Creative Commons licences comply with the various free/open criteria. In particular, the non-commercial (NC) option discriminates against commercial fields of endeavour. (It is also difficult to determine exactly what non-commercial means, at one extreme it could be taken to limit use of material for which direct payment is taken, and at the other, it could be taken to mean use in any context that involves an organization which receives money.) Likewise, an ND (no derivatives) version of the licence prevents amendments being made to the content, and also fails to meet the free/open criterion of use maximization.

Creative Commons have also suggested a mechanism for dedicating works to the public domain[44] called CC0. Because dedication to the public domain is not possible in many jurisdictions, including England, Wales, and Scotland, CC0 includes a 'public license fallback' which grants the widest licence possible should dedication fail.[45]

12.10 OTHER DOCUMENTATION LICENCES

A number of other open licences are available for documentation, the best known of which is probably the GNU Free Documentation License ('FDL').[46] The FDL is a part copyleft licence which contains some complex terminology intended to ensure that

[41] Flickr, 'Creative Commons' <http://www.flickr.com/creativecommons> accessed 5 April 2013.

[42] Propellerhead <http://www.propellerheads.se> accessed 5 April 2013.

[43] Music Production with Live 9 and Push <https://www.ableton.com> accessed 5 April 2013.

[44] Creative Commons, 'Our Public Domain Tools' <http://creativecommons.org/publicdomain> accessed 5 April 2013.

[45] Creative Commons <http://creativecommons.org/publicdomain/zero/1.0/legalcode> accessed 5 April 2013.

[46] GNU Free Documentation License <http://www.gnu.org/copyleft/fdl.html> accessed 5 April 2013.

software documentation in particular remains free, but useful and relevant to the software which it documents.

12.11 OPEN HARDWARE AND OPEN SOURCE HARDWARE

There have been several attempts to apply open principles to physical objects. The step from free and open source software to physical hardware seems at first sight to be fairly straightforward. However, there are issues which make this more complex.

12.12 INTELLECTUAL PROPERTY RIGHTS

Primarily, software is governed by copyright. There are software patents, and other intellectual property rights such as database extraction right do impinge, but intellectual property affects hardware in a more complex and inconsistent way. As we have seen, copyleft relies on there being some form of intellectual property right which impinges each time an item is distributed, in order for that distribution to be licensed under that intellectual property right, and for the licence to be conditional on the grant of another licence to the distributed item on the same terms; thus perpetuating the licence to derivative works as they are distributed. If the act of distribution requires no licence under any intellectual property right (or any of the necessary precursors to distribution, such as copying), then the distribution of the item cannot be controlled.

To take an extreme example: it is obvious that a work in the public domain cannot be subject to any licence, so it is not possible to apply any copyleft restrictions to this. Richard Stallman (founder of the FSF) was aware of this when he criticized the Swedish Pirate Party's recommendations for a very short period of copyright (five years).[47] At the end of five years, under their plans, computer software would enter the public domain and therefore what was previously available under the GPL would be capable of being incorporated into proprietary software without the requirement for the corresponding source being made available. In other words, the core purpose of the GPL—to ensure that free software remained free—would be defeated after five years. This offended Stallman's anti-closure views, and after considering (and rejecting)[48] a special exception for software which would *extend* the Pirate Party's

[47] Richard Stallman, 'How the Swedish Pirate Party Platform Backfires on Free Software' (*GNU*) <http://www.gnu.org/philosophy/pirate-party.html> accessed 5 April 2013.

[48] Not surprisingly, Stallman did note the apparent contradiction in someone so generally anti-intellectual property that he rejects the term *intellectual property* itself, promoting a position of extended copyright.

proposed five-year term of copyright for the specific purpose of allowing the GPL's copyleft mechanism to continue working for longer, he concluded that it would be better for the source code for non-free software to be placed in escrow and automatically released at the end of the five-year term.

Several open hardware licences attempt to create a form of copyleft, but this lack of impingement of copyright on distribution does cause problems, as we see later.

Whereas almost any activity involving software—running it, distributing it, copying it, amending it—will involve an act reserved to the copyright owner (primarily the copying), it is by no means clear that similar acts relating to hardware are similarly controlled.[49] For example, it is not an infringement of copyright under English law to make a 3D copy of a Stormtrooper helmet (from the Star Wars films),[50] despite the fact that the underlying design documents clearly do attract copyright. Simply using a mechanical device does not require a copyright licence,[51] but the same is not true of a device incorporating software, including firmware.

The two most prevalent open hardware licences, the CERN open hardware licence,[52] and the TAPR Open Hardware License[53] both attempt to apply a form of copyleft. The lack of impingement of intellectual property rights on hardware causes issues for both licences, as discussed later.[54]

12.13 THE COSTS OF REVERSE ENGINEERING

The marginal cost of making a binary copy of a piece of software is close to zero. In contrast, because hardware always involves physical material, there will always be some cost involved in instantiating a piece of hardware. For example, even if the hardware can be replicated by 3D printing, the cost of the feedstock needs to be considered. Many hardware designs will be more complex than something which can be replicated using a 3D printer: eg, the front suspension sub-assembly for a car may require some complex milling and machining of the steel components which make it up. Even if the design documentation includes CNC (computer numerical control) files to control the machine tools like the lathe and milling machines, the effort required in setting the machines up, monitoring them, and finishing and assembling

[49] Except in relation to patent, which is dealt with later in this chapter.

[50] *Lucasfilm v Ainsworth* [2011] UKSC 39.

[51] Although it is possible to imagine circumstances in which other intellectual property rights, such as patents or registered designs, may be infringed.

[52] OHWR, 'CERN Open Hardware Licence—Introduction' <http://www.ohwr.org/projects/cernohl/wiki> accessed 5 April 2013.

[53] The TAPR Open Hardware License <http://www.tapr.org/ohl.html> accessed 5 April 2013.

[54] For further analysis of these issues, see Katz, 'Towards a Functional Licence for Open Hardware' (*IFOSS L Rev*, 2012) <http://www.ifosslr.org/ifosslr/article/view/69>; and R Stallman, 'On "Free Hardware"' (*Linux Today*, 22 June 1999) <http://www.linuxtoday.com/infrastructure/1999062200505NWLF> both accessed 5 April 2013.

the mechanical components is significantly greater than the effort required to compile the binary of a piece of software from the source code, or, even more simply, copying an existing binary.

If a piece of software is covered by a copyleft licence, like the GPL, someone wishing to make use of the functionality of that software can either agree to comply with the terms of the GPL, or can decide to replicate the functionality of the software by reverse-engineering it.[55]

Recall that copyright protects the expression of an idea, and not the underlying idea itself. Thus, it is possible to determine the functionality (idea) of a piece of software, and then replicate that software independently (using a different expression), so that the rights in the new piece of software belong to its author, and it may be exploited freely by that author without reference to the rights holders of the original piece of software.[56] Compaq famously employed a reverse-engineering and rewrite technique to replicate the BIOS of the original IBM PC, to enable it to create the first IBM PC clones.

A similar technique can be employed with hardware, such as mechanical and electronic devices.[57]

To take an extreme example, there is a monumental difference in cost between taking a copy of the Linux kernel (almost zero), and replicating its functionality by reverse-engineering and recoding it (estimated by the Linux Foundation at $1.4 billion).[58] It is not surprising that businesses opt to comply with the GPL rather than try to re-create their own compatible kernel.[59]

The economics for hardware are liable to be different. Even if it is possible to create an effective copyleft licence for hardware (an issue discussed later), given that the instantiation of any piece of hardware is liable to require significant effort in any event, the differential in cost between recreating a design which does not impinge on any intellectual property rights, and using an existing open hardware design will be dramatically smaller than the equivalent scenario in software.

The upshot of this is that it is a more difficult proposition to apply a copyleft licence to hardware (even if it can be made to work), than to software.

[55] For completeness, two further options are to ignore the licence, and infringe the copyright (with the legal consequences that that might entail), or to persuade the copyright owners of the software to grant a licence which is more amenable (possibly at a price), something Richard Stallman calls, scathingly, buying exceptions to the GPL.

[56] Ignoring, for the time being, other rights, particularly patent rights, which may cover the original software.

[57] As we have seen, it is by no means clear that the hardware itself is covered by copyright. Accordingly, the process of creating an alternative design containing the same functionality, free of any intellectual property rights, is relatively more straightforward for hardware than for software. Furthermore, it is even simpler when open hardware is concerned, because the design documentation will be available.

[58] A McPherson et al, 'Estimating the Total Development Cost of a Linux Distribution' (*The Linux Foundation*, October 2008) <http://www.linuxfoundation.org/sites/main/files/publications/estimatinglinux.html> accessed 5 April 2013.

[59] Another option is for businesses needing a Unix-like kernel who are not keen on using software covered by the GPL to adopt FreeBSD, which is licensed under the much more liberal BSD licence.

12.14 THE BOUNDARY PROBLEM

If copyleft is to work in open hardware, there must be some clear limit to the degree in which it is intended to affect the rest of the design. For example, if a wheel hub is released under an open hardware licence, does that mean that, if it is included in a front suspension sub-assembly, all of that sub-assembly will become subject to the copyleft licence? What if that sub-assembly is incorporated into a car: does the whole car need to be released under the same licence? These issues exist for free and open source software as well, but the boundaries are well understood (although even here, they continue to generate a great deal of debate). The definitions are somewhat easier in the software world. The Mozilla licence, eg, is intended to apply file level copyleft, where the term 'file' is reasonably well understood; at least it is more understood than a vague term like 'sub-assembly'.

The boundary problem also impinges in the detail. The wheel hub just referred to, if it is to comply with the Open Hardware and Design and Association's four freedoms (the 'OHANDA freedoms': see earlier), will need to be provided with a complete set of documentation. The hub is likely to require a ball bearing assembly. Ball bearings are available in a number of common sizes and specifications, and consist of two concentric hardened steel rings (races) with a number of hardened steel balls in between them. A strict interpretation of the OHANDA freedoms would require that the wheel hub design also contains complete documentation for manufacturing the ball bearing. To take this to a ridiculous extreme, instructions would be required for the manufacture of the entire hub assembly from atoms.[60]

One way of approaching this issue is to distinguish between *open hardware* on the one hand, and *open source hardware* on the other.[61] Open hardware is hardware for which the complete specification is known, in all material and necessary respects (so for an electronic component, it will not only be its electrical characteristics, but also its physical characteristics and environmental operating conditions, eg).[62] Knowing that information, it is possible to source the component, and also, at least in theory, to recreate an equivalent component to those specifications (it may be regarded as equivalent to a software library for which full specifications of the interface are known, but not the underlying code). Open source hardware goes one

[60] An explanation for this oversight may be that many people think of open hardware as being mainly electronic devices. Electronic construction tends to consist of components, such as resistors, capacitors, ICs, transistors and inductors, all being soldered onto a circuit board. The components are all standard items, with well understood specifications, and therefore, it is fairly clear that the level of abstraction required of the design is at component level.

[61] Katz (n 54).

[62] For a component to be described as open hardware, it must be possible to recreate it and use it without infringing any third party rights, such as patents.

stage further, in that it must have complete design documentation for that hardware itself, and all the components are either themselves open hardware or open source hardware.

The CERN Open Hardware Licence takes a slightly different approach by requiring the design documentation for derivatives to be at the same level of abstraction as the original design documentation.

12.15 THE COMPETING COPYLEFTS PROBLEM

It is clear that if a copyleft licence requires derivatives to be released under the same licence, then it becomes impossible to combine two works into a third, being a derivative of both the original works, if each of the original works is subject to a different copyleft licence. This is a well-known problem for free and open source software, with compatibility lacking between even different versions of the GPL.[63]

The practical issue is that the effectiveness of an open project is understood to grow, as a network effect, in proportion to the square of the participants.[64] If two projects of a similar size are unable to interoperate, then each project on its own would be a quarter as effective as the two projects combined.

Attempts have been made to deal with this: some free and open source software licences allow relicensing under similar licences. For example, the EUPL allows relicensing under the GPL. If someone has chosen a licence with relatively strong copyleft, then they are unlikely to be happy with the ability of anyone downstream to choose a licence which has weaker copyleft, or no copyleft at all. Discussions are currently underway between the drafters of the CERN and the TAPR licences about how some form of relicensing may be possible.

12.16 PATENTS

Copyright has been an effective way of controlling the use and exploitation of software (and the implementation of copyleft), in part because, under the Berne Convention, it arises automatically, without the formality of any assertion or registration. Patents, in contrast, may provide a number of opportunities to impinge on the use and exploitation of a piece of hardware, but require extensive formality to obtain and maintain. At first glance, it may seem that if patents give a number of opportunities for a licence to impinge during the lifecycle of a piece of hardware that copyright does not, then

[63] Unless there is an option to take a later version, eg, GPLv2 or later is compatible with GPLv3.

[64] Metcalfe's law.

for a hardware licence to be effective, and, in particular, for it to be able to implement copyleft, it should concentrate on patents rather than copyright.

This assumption has a number of difficulties:

1. It has been noted that a characteristic of the open source development model is that there is low barrier to entry for participants. Each participant in a software project will automatically obtain copyright in the work that he or she submits, and this can form the basis of the licensing applicable to the project, both in relation to third parties, and, also in relation to the relationship between the participants themselves (as in the case of the Linux kernel), or the participant and the project sponsor. In contrast, patent protection is not automatic, so there has to be a more complex mechanism in place to mediate the relationship between the participants, the sponsor (if any), and the end users. This will have to take into account the issues noted here.
2. Even relatively small pieces of software code may attract copyright protection. Only a relatively small number of designs, whether hardware or software, will potentially have the necessary quality of inventiveness and novelty to qualify as a patentable invention.
3. Patents are expensive and take time to apply for. This militates against many open projects, which have minimal funding. It also requires that some mechanism is in place to decide how funding is obtained and is spent, and which inventions are worthy of being applied for.
4. Patentable inventions need to be kept secret at the initial stages. This means that the invention needs to be kept to a small number of people until (dependent upon jurisdiction) it has been filed. This adds complexity (non-disclosure agreements need to be entered into, and the various recipients of the information need to be trustworthy), and, crucially, it is contrary to the open source business model, as it is directly in opposition to both 'given enough eyeballs, all bugs are shallow' and 'release early, release often.'
5. A patent is only effective in the jurisdiction in which it is granted. Worldwide coverage requires multiple patent applications and grants, and this multiplication rapidly becomes very expensive.

That is not to say that is impossible to establish an open development model based on patent protection, but these barriers suggest that it is likely to be more challenging than the equivalent open source software model.

For example, the secrecy problem may be addressed by having an inner circle of developers who have signed mutual non-disclosure agreements, and anyone who comes up with an invention which they feel may be patentable may apply to join the inner circle, and therefore share his or her invention subject to the mutual NDAs.

12.17 OPEN HARDWARE LICENCES

The main open hardware licences are the TAPR Open Hardware License[65] and the CERN Open Hardware Licence.[66]

The TAPR license was developed by attorney and radio amateur John Ackermann. Ackermann acknowledges many of the difficulties of applying copyleft to hardware.[67] The TAPR license is intended to be a copyleft licence, and although it acknowledges copyright in the design documentation, it attempts to cover the impingement issue by acting as a contract, and thus contractually binding anyone who relies on the licence to release modifications to the design under the same licence.[68] The contract is formed by presenting an offer which is capable of acceptance by anyone wishing to make use of the licensed invention, and as such presents itself as a unilateral contract, capable of acceptance by conduct, without communication of that acceptance to the licensor.[69] Ackermann is aware of the potential problems of consideration, especially where the licensor does not have any rights (such as a patent to license). He attempts to deal with this, not by granting a licence which he believes would be failed consideration if there is no underlying IPR to license, but by granting a patent non-assert, which he claims would be effective as it anticipates, eg, that the licensor might acquire a relevant patent in the future.[70]

The CERN Open Hardware Licence takes a different tack. It concentrates on the design documentation, and the user's rights (and the conditions applying to the licence) impinge once the user performs any act that would otherwise impinge on an intellectual property right in the design documentation. From version 1.2 of the licence, it is intended that amendment of the design documentation is conditional

[65] OHWR, 'CERN open hardware licence—Introduction' <http://www.tapr.org/ohl.html> accessed 5 April 2013.

[66] <http://www.ohwr.org/projects/cernohl/wiki> accessed 5 April 2013.

[67] John Ackermann, 'Toward open source hardware' (*University of Dayton Law Review*, 2009) <http://www.tapr.org/Ackermann_Open_Source_Hardware_Article_2009.pdf> accessed 5 April 2013.

[68] A number of mechanisms based on contract have been suggested to make copyleft work. The principle is generally that in order to use design A, the licensee enters into a contract with the licensor, and then whenever the licensor distributes an article made to design A (or a derivative), this must be subject to the same licence, which is itself a contract, binding on the next downstream licensee, and so on. It has been suggested that this can be used to create, contractually, pseudo-intellectual-property-rights that do not otherwise exist at law. However, a contract is only effective as between the parties to it. If someone receives the design, or the documentation, for whatever reason, not subject to the contract, then they will not be a party to the contract, and will not be bound by the pseudo-intellectual-property-right. If the licence is reliant on *real* intellectual property rights, then someone seeking to exploit the design will have to have some form of licence, and will be in breach unless they do so, irrespective of whether there is a contract with the rights holder. There is therefore no necessity for a contractual chain.

[69] *Carlill v Carbolic Smoke Ball Company* [1892] EWCA Civ 1.

[70] J Ackermann (n67); and a telephone conversation between John Ackermann and the author.

on the release of the amendments. However, that obligation is suspended until such time as an instantiation of the design is made available to the public.[71]

At the time of writing (March 2013) John Ackermann has proposed updating the TAPR Open Hardware License. He and the CERN drafting teams are working together to discuss different approaches and to consider possible routes for licence compatibility.

12.17.1 No copyleft hardware licences

Many of the issues surrounding open hardware licensing arise from attempts to apply copyleft. It follows that no copyleft licences may be a more straightforward approach. In particular, a version of the Apache 2.0 software licence has been modified slightly to make it more applicable to hardware. The changes revolve mainly around terminology (eg, expanding the definition of 'source form' to cover more hardware-related forms of documentation), and also the expansion of the types of intellectual property right that are covered (the database right, eg).[72]

A proposal has been made to CERN that a slightly modified version of the CERN OHL should be approved alongside the copyleft version, for those who would prefer to use a more permissive licence, (this is similar to the relationship between the Open Software License and the Academic Free License, which are two open source software licences, copyleft and permissive respectively, which differ in only a few words of drafting).[73]

12.18 OPEN DATA

Open data is a form of open content, and arises in many contexts. Proponents of open government are keen to see governmental statistics (and their underlying datasets) being made freely available, and indeed freedom of information legislation is a useful tool to facilitate this.[74] In academia, projects such as genetic research and nuclear physics have generated vast amounts of data which it has been argued should be

[71] The wording of 1.2 has not been finalized at the time of writing (March 2013) nor has it been made public. However, the principle has been accepted by the core licence drafting team, and should be published in due course on OHWR, 'CERN open hardware licence—Introduction' <http://www.ohwr.org/projects/cernohl/wiki> accessed 5 April 2013.

[72] Solderpad, 'The Solderpad Hardware License' <http://solderpad.org/licenses> accessed 5 April 2013.

[73] The author made this proposal to the core CERN licence development team. If accepted, it will be published at OHWR, 'CERN open hardware licence—Introduction' <http://www.ohwr.org/projects/cernohl/wiki> accessed 5 April 2013.

[74] In the UK, Freedom of Information Act 2000, Freedom of Information (Scotland) Act 2000, and Environmental Information Regulations 2004. The Aarhus Convention (1998) also provides for public access to certain information: UNECE <http://www.unece.org/env/pp/welcome.html> accessed 5 April 2013.

made freely available to facilitate research. There are also specific initiatives, such as Openstreetmap, which are intended to facilitate crowdsourcing geographical data, and open genealogy, covering family history.[75]

In the United States, the Government has launched data.gov,[76] which is a central repository of governmental data. The UK has data.gov.uk.[77] In each of these cases, the emphasis is on transparency (although the licensing structure is intended to facilitate reuse). The licensing regime of projects like Openstreetmap places more stress on use-maximization.

In particular, the United States has historically had neither a *sui generis* database protection right, nor protection for databases as an extension of copyright.[78] Further, in the US, copyright protection is not available to works created by the Government,[79] and such works are assumed to be in the public domain, the theory being that if tax dollars have been expended in creating them, they should be free to use by anyone (including, for that matter, anyone outside the US). The situation in the EU, in particular, is very different. The EU possesses a *sui generis* database protection right,[80] and the EU Directive on the reuse of public sector information (2003/98/EC)[81] has as its rationale that copyright works owned by the Government should be exploited by licensing them to commerce for the highest bidder. So, eg, mapping data which in the US has historically been available universally as it is in the public domain, is considered public sector information in the UK, the use of which is made available under a restricted licence through the Ordnance Survey.[82] Despite these philosophical issues, much information is now made available through the data.gov.uk portal under less restrictive licensing. The data available through data.gov.uk is available not only as dumps of data in various database formats (the simplest being CSV), but access is also available through an API.

The licence under which much of the data on data.gov.uk is released is the Open Government Licence, which is a liberal database licence, requiring only attribution.[83] It does limit its own scope to personal data (and it is unclear whether the definition of *personal data* employed is the fairly restrictive definition contained with the Data Protection Act 1998 which deals solely with data relating to a living individual, or a

[75] Open Genealogy Alliance, 'Manifesto' <http://www.opengenalliance.org> accessed 5 April 2013.

[76] <http://www.data.gov> accessed 5 April 2013.

[77] <http://data.gov.uk> accessed 5 April 2013.

[78] *Feist Publications v Rural Telephone Service* (1991) 499 US 340.

[79] 17 USC para 105.

[80] Directive 96/9/EC of the European Parliament and of the Council of 11 March 1996 on the legal protection of databases [27 March 1996] OJ L77/20.

[81] [31 December 2003] OJ L345/90.

[82] Ordnance Survey, 'Licences and agreements explained' <http://www.ordnancesurvey.co.uk/oswebsite/licensing/index.html> accessed 5 April 2013.

[83] Open Government Licence for public sector information <http://www.nationalarchives.gov.uk/doc/open-government-licence> accessed 5 April 2013.

wider interpretation which covers any data relating to a living individual, irrespective of whether the individual is living or dead).[84]

The US site data.gov does not specify a licence, possibly because of the twin assumptions that (1) data as such is not amenable to intellectual property protection under US law, and (2) that governmental data would, in any event, be in the public domain.

Both availability of the data and ability to reuse under a liberal licensing framework are important to advocates of openness, but as services are built on top of government data portals, the reliability and persistence of the API are also important. In addition, where people wish to compare data between portals from different jurisdictions, it becomes increasingly necessary that those portals adhere to standards, so that to extract equivalent data from different portals, it is not necessary to customize the interface code each time. Thus the additional connotation of anti-lock-in—persistence—is critical in this context. To address these issues, the Open Knowledge Foundation has developed CKAN, an open source data management system[85] which is intended to act as a platform to facilitate data transfer, in part by using standardized data catalogues which facilitate the comparison of data within, and between, datasets.

There are a number of different mechanisms to facilitate interoperability between datasets. One of these is the *semantic web* project, which aims to provide a way of categorising data to create what it calls a *web of data*. In this way, data presented by different entities from different datasets is provided in a predictable way to facilitate programmatic access to web sites and the data behind them. The Semantic Web Project[86] is led by the World Wide Web Consortium ('W3C'). The Open Data Foundation also seeks to facilitate interoperability and combination of data sources.[87]

The Open Data Institute, founded by web inventor, Tim Berners-Lee, and Nigel Shadbolt, also seeks to promote access to government data.[88]

12.19 OPEN SOFTWARE SERVICES

As we saw earlier the Open Knowledge Foundation also proffers a definition of Open Software Services,[89] which is based on the *open* connotations of use-maximization and anti-closed.

[84] Data Protection Act 1998, s 1(1).
[85] CKAN <http://ckan.org> accessed 5 April 2013.
[86] W3C Semantic Web Activity <http://www.w3.org/2001/sw> accessed 5 April 2013.
[87] The Open Data Foundation <http://www.opendatafoundation.org/?lvl1=projects> accessed 5 April 2013.
[88] Open Data Institute <http://www.theodi.org/about> accessed 5 April 2013.
[89] Open Software Service Definition <http://opendefinition.org/software-service> accessed 5 April 2013.

However, a better way to look at openness in software services is that they must also embrace the other connotations of open: they must also minimize lock-in and embrace persistence, and they must be transparent (in that the mechanism which underlies them must be visible).

Lock-in can impinge in two ways: the interface presented by the API must be open, in the standards sense of it being fully documented, and available for use without payment of any royalty.[90] It must also provide appropriate and complete functionality on a non-discriminatory basis. 'Appropriate and complete' means that that functionality must do everything that the user would need it to, including facilitating bulk extraction of data (including metadata and, where necessary, pending transactions) at any time during the lifecycle of the solution. 'Non-discriminatory' means that each user has access to the full API, and that the API performs in the same way for each user (so that there are no hidden API calls for privileged users, and that the performance is not dependent on which user is accessing the API; a vendor, eg, might seek to lock in one customer by only allowing a certain number of API calls per second, preventing bulk transfer of data).

Transparency is related to the documentation of the API, but requires a further step: that the mechanisms underlying the provision of the service are also fully documented, in a form that would enable them to be reproducible (this is similar to one distinction between *open hardware* and *open source hardware* which is discussed later). Of course, providing the source code of all of the software providing the service would fulfil this requirement (at least assuming that there is no non-software element of the service which is also required to provide the service).[91] However, even without access to the underlying source code, if the API and the mechanism for delivery of the service are available, then a competing service can be provided.

It's relatively easy to imagine a service which fulfils the requirements of the Open Software Service Definition, but which still fails to be *open* in any practical sense because the data which it contains are not capable of being extracted. It may be because the software does not contain appropriate functionality to allow the data

[90] This does present a problem: there must be some mechanism to enable to the providers of open software services to charge for their services. One logical way to gauge whether charging is reasonable or not is to look at the model of the GPL, which does not prohibit or limit charging for software (except in the specific case of providing a copy of the source code in response to a request), but relies on economics to lower the cost of the software to the marginal cost of copying it, on the basis that any licensee with a copy of the source code is able to copy and distribute it without any fee to the licensor, so competition between licensees will tend to drive the cost of copies down to the marginal cost of copying it. Likewise, if the software providing the open software service is available on an open source basis, then it would be open to any person with a copy to instantiate their own competing service, which would tend to drive the cost of providing the service down to the marginal cost.

[91] It was rumoured that one provider of mobile speech-to-text services performed a large proportion of its work by using human labour offshore, rather than computers. There is no requirement for the services provided on the back side of an API to be provided by computers.

to be extracted,[92] or even because the dataset is too big. An appropriate definition of an open software service must, therefore, address the issues of transparency and lock-in. The user of a service described as open must be able to transfer to another service with minimal effort:[93] the data must, both theoretically and practically, be portable.

Practical portability means that it must also be possible to extract all of the user's data, including metadata, from the service in a meaningful and sensible way. There are two ways in which access to data can be restricted: by law (or by terms of use restricting certain activity in relation to API, such as number of calls per second) and by code (there is a hard-coded restriction on the number of API calls per second, eg). Both of these must be absent for a software service to be properly regarded as open.

Therefore, a better definition of an open software service will be one which takes into account not only anti-closure and use maximization, but also transparency and, crucially, anti-lock-in.

12.20 OPEN POLITICS AND OPEN GOVERNMENT

Open politics and open government are about transparency and accountability. In addition, open politics and government principles require the information and data used to make decisions to be made freely available to as wide a group as possible, and accordingly, use-maximization becomes relevant.

The UK Government has published a White Paper which defines open public services[94] as an important branch of open government. Open public services are those which display the following characteristics:

[92] Just because the software is released as open source does not mean that the user of the service will have any ability to change the version used in that instance of the service to rectify problems with the API's functionality, although they may be able to create their own instance and modify the code to deal with those issues. However, the new instance is unlikely to be of any use unless the data accessed through the original instance is accessible.

[93] Rufus Pollock, who happens to be on the board of the Open Knowledge Foundation, makes a relevant point about lock-in as it applies to virtual worlds. Virtual worlds are different from the real world, in that it is relatively straightforward to up sticks and move from one virtual world to another. In the real world, moving from one country to another can be enormously disruptive. As complex as it may be to move from World of Warcraft to Second Life, it's an order of magnitude easier than moving countries in the physical world. In the physical world, we need democracy to exercise control over the governance. In the virtual world, a governor who fails to provide an amenable environment for the subjects will find all those subjects leaving to a more conducive domain. Governors will, of course, be aware that failing to provide for the needs of their subjects will cause them to lose subjects. Accordingly, even if they are dictators, they will still have a normative pressure imposed on them to behave well and keep their subjects happy. The same applies so far as software services are concerned: if it is relatively easy to transfer from one software service to another, then the provider of the software service will work that much harder to provide a service which its users are happy with.

[94] <http://data.gov.uk/opendataconsultation/policy-challenge-questions/setting-open-data-standards> accessed April 2013.

Choice and control—Wherever possible [the government] will increase choice.
Decentralisation—Power should be decentralised to the lowest appropriate level.
Diversity—Public services should be open to a range of providers.
Fairness—[the government] will ensure fair access to public services.
Accountability—Public services should be accountable to users and taxpayers.

Where information or data are made available under an open government basis, it is important that they are capable of broad reuse. See 12.8.1 on open data for more information about how this is typically carried out.

12.21 OPEN STANDARDS AND OPEN SPECIFICATIONS

Standards exist to promote interoperability.[95] As such they need to be applied consistently. Any standard which is subject to the ability to adapt, amend, and extend in an uncontrolled or arbitrary fashion rapidly loses this consistency, and becomes untrustworthy, and ultimately valueless. Accordingly, the application of the description *open* to a standard is necessarily subtly different from its application in other contexts. This does mean that an open standard may be subject to restrictions that are not necessarily applicable to other opens, in order to ensure consistency.

There are a number of different definitions of open standard. The first version of the European Interoperability Framework ('EIF')[96] contained the following criteria:[97]

USE OF OPEN STANDARDS

To attain interoperability in the context of pan-European eGovernment services, guidance needs to focus on open standards. The following are the minimal characteristics that a specification and its attendant documents must have in order to be considered an open standard:

— The standard is adopted and will be maintained by a not-for-profit organisation, and its ongoing development occurs on the basis of an open decision-making procedure available to all interested parties (consensus or majority decision etc.).

[95] See further ch 10.

[96] The first version of the EIF was published in 2004 and is a non-binding recommendation, primarily aimed at governmental organisations within the European Union, but also ultimately at businesses (especially when interacting with governments) and citizens. See IDABC, 'EIF—European Interoperability Framework for pan-European eGovernment services' <http://ec.europa.eu/idabc/en/document/2319/5938.html> (last update June 2009) accessed 5 April 2013; and ch 10.

[97] European Commission, 'European interoperatbility framework for pan-European eGovermnet services' (2004) <http://ec.europa.eu/idabc/servlets/Docd552.pdf?id=19529> accessed 5 April 2013.

— The standard has been published and the standard specification document is available either freely or at a nominal charge. It must be permissible to all to copy, distribute and use it for no fee or at a nominal fee.
— The intellectual property—ie patents possibly present—of (parts of) the standard is made irrevocably available on a royalty-free basis.
— There are no constraints on the reuse of the standard.

This requires not only use-maximization of the standard itself (bullets three and four), but of the documentation comprising the standard (bullet two). Additionally, transparency in the standards creation process is dealt with in bullet one, as is anti-lock-in (in that the standard cannot be amended without an appropriate decision-making process open to all interested parties).

One contentious issue which this definition directly addresses is the requirement for an open standard to be usable without payment to any holders of intellectual property holders (in particular, patent holders). Clearly, if a standard becomes adopted, this is likely to significantly increase its use. A patent holder whose patent would necessarily be infringed by implementation of the standard is potentially in a position to demand significant sums for licensing the patent. This sometimes happens when the patent holder is part of the team establishing the standard in the first place (in which case the patent holder can either be open about holding the patents from the outset—as was the case with Sony and Phillips when they established the various CD and CD-ROM formats—or the patent holder can keep the existence of the patents or the applications for them secret).[98] It can also happen when an entity is not involved in the standards setting process, but begins to assert its patents after the standard has been put into effect.

If a standard is an open standard (under the EIF version 1 definition, eg) then a licence to the patents which would be infringed by its implementation must be available on a royalty free basis to anyone. It is an open question what happens if patents are later discovered which impinge on a standard which was previously understood to be open, either because they belong to a party who participated in the standards setting process and who concealed the existence of the patents, or because patents belonging to a third party are subsequently discovered which impinge on implementations of the standard. It can be assumed that, if the patent holder is unwilling to

[98] This is known as a 'patent ambush.' Rambus was alleged to have done this, by participating in setting standards for RAM through the standards setting body JEDEC. After the standards were ratified, Rambus started to demand royalties from entities using the particular technologies covered by its patents. It was alleged that Rambus kept details of the patents secret from the standards body and the other participants, an allegation which Rambus denied. The facts of the case are complex, and impinge on competition law both in the US and the EU. A good summary of the issues from a European perspective can be found in: R Schellingerhout and P Cavicchi, 'Patent ambush in standard-setting: the Commission accepts commitments from Rambus to lower memory chip royalty rates' (2010) <http://ec.europa.eu/competition/publications/cpn/2010_1_11.pdf> accessed 5 April 2013.

make licences to the patents irrevocably available on a royalty free basis to all implementers of the standard, then the standard can no longer be described as 'open'. However, this can have consequences: what happens, eg, if a procurement process is already underway which specifies that the items to be procured must comply with an open standard? What if some items have already been procured in the belief that the standard is open, the standard then becomes closed, and further items need to be procured which, to interoperate with the already-procured initial items, now need to comply with a standard which is no longer open?

A further issue is that, even if licences to the patents are available on a royalty free basis, those patents are likely to impose other terms on the licensee, and those terms may be equally problematic to proponents of openness, and particularly those who would wish to implement the standard in free or open source software, as we explore later.

12.22 FRAND

Patent holders may argue that it is a step too far to demand that they make a licence to their patent available to all implementers of the standard on royalty free terms. They may offer to make the patents available under 'reasonable and non-discriminatory' terms ('RAND') or 'fair, reasonable and non-discriminatory' terms ('FRAND').

RAND and FRAND have been dismissed as being meaningless platitudes by proponents of openness[99] in that the interpretation of what is fair and reasonable is too subjective, and that, if royalties are payable, then the licences will necessarily discriminate against free and open source software. This is explored more thoroughly later.

A further variety of patent licence, FRAND-Z adds a requirement that zero royalties are payable, which does render the licence compatible with EIF1 requirements, but does not address interaction between other aspects of the licence and certain FOSS licences. This is particularly problematic in relation to the GPL, as discussed next.

12.23 INTERACTION BETWEEN FOSS AND OPEN STANDARDS

The GNU GPL family of licences (from GPL version 2 onwards) contains a 'liberty or death' clause which, although it varies slightly from one version of the licence to another, provides that if a licensee cannot license the covered code to a third party so that the third party gets the same rights that the licensee has, then the licensee may no longer distribute the covered code. This is intended to prevent a scenario where a

[99] Simon Phipps, 'RAND: Not So Reasonable?' (*Computer World Blogs*, 17 November 2010) <http://blogs.computerworlduk.com/simon-says/2010/11/rand-not-so-reasonable/index.htm> accessed 5 April 2013.

licensee obtains a personal licence (to a patent, eg) which enables it to use the covered code, but any downstream licensee cannot benefit from that licence, and must approach the patent licensor for another licence (which the licensor may charge for), to allow the software to continue to be used. This was seen as an unwarranted restriction on freedom (and would permit the implementation of a relatively simple mechanism to be employed allowing a patent licensor to subvert software freedom; something that the Free Software Foundation, with its anti-closed stance was unwilling to countenance).

In order to be compliant with the liberty or death clause, any patent licence which impinges on a GPL program must allow the same patent licence to be made available to any downstream recipient of the code. In particular, this means that the patent licence needs to be sub-licensable to any downstream recipient of the GPL code, or that at the very least that a patent licence is available to any downstream recipient of the code. Whilst it is possible that a FRAND licence could be constructed which complies with the GPL requirement, is it unlikely to do so, as such a licence would have to be so wide[100] that it would be equivalent to a patent surrender (in other words, giving up the patent entirely). In practice, FRAND licences are not sub-licensable. Even if the FRAND licences are available to downstream recipients, they are likely to be conditioned on the downstream recipient implementing the standard, and not deviating from it. The GPL, however, requires that a downstream recipient must be free to modify the code, even if the modification means that the code deviates from the standard. (This is an illustration of the conflict between *open* principles: use-maximization, in the guise of allowing modifications conflicts with the anti-lock-in principle that needs standards to be maintained.) The original licensee of the GPL code cannot comply with its obligation to allow downstream recipients to modify the code,[101] the *liberty or death* requirement is not satisfied, and the GPL code cannot therefore be distributed.[102] It has also been argued that the cascade licensing model of GPL itself (that is that each downstream recipient of GPL code receives a number of licences, one from each contributor to the code received) is incompatible with the direct licensing model that is present in almost all FRAND licensing structures.[103]

[100] It is possible to imagine a FRAND-Z licensing structure broad enough to be compatible with the GPL licensing model; it would have both to allow sub-licensing, and also to allow implementations other than those that implement the standard.

[101] This right does not have to extend to the right to allow the downstream recipients to modify the software in such a way that it might infringe a different patent which was not licensed under the original FRAND licence.

[102] A counterargument is that the original recipient of the GPL code (assuming it takes the benefit of the same FRAND licence as are available to downstream recipients) is limited in the same way as any downstream recipient, and that therefore, since the original recipient has no greater rights than are granted to any downstream recipient, there is no loss of freedom, and the liberty or death clause does not impinge.

[103] I G Mitchell QC and S Mason, instructed by A Katz, 'Compatibility Of The Licensing Of Embedded Patents With Open Source Licensing Terms' (*IFOSS L Rev*, September 2011) <http://www.ifosslr.org/ifosslr/article/view/57/99> accessed 5 April 2013.

Thus even FRAND-Z is incompatible with a GPL licensing model, and FRAND, more so.

Other definitions of 'open standard' are covered in Chapter 10.

12.24 OPEN INNOVATION

'Open innovation' is a term coined by Henry Chesbrough in his book *Open Innovation: the new imperative for creating and profiting from technology.*[104] It differs from the other *opens* in that it does not envisage universal access to knowledge and the use of innovative intellectual property licensing structures or governance to facilitate access, but more restrictively, to make organizations more amenable to the inventions and innovations from outside the organization, and to allow organizations to license their IPR to others more freely. This is likely to result in a wider dissemination of invention and innovation, but only under a traditional network of non-disclosure agreements and licences. Accordingly, *open innovation*, except in its most extreme forms, does not embrace the openness considered in this chapter.

12.24.1 Open publishing, open education, and open access

Open publishing and open access mainly concern academic articles and journals, and refer to the ability of a researcher to access the journal or article without payment, and, ideally, to reproduce the relevant text also without any restriction (including payment).[105] There are a number of competing definitions, but possibly the most succinct is that developed by the US Public Library of Science (PLoS):

> Free availability and unrestricted use.

Open access publishing is not incompatible with traditional 'consumer pays' publishing, and open access journals can still provide high quality peer-reviewed material. Since electronic publication and distribution is inexpensive and effective, almost all, if not all, open access journals are available online.[106] Many have print versions available as well. The print versions may be paid for by advertising, sponsorship, or by a charge to the purchaser (the fact that an open access journal is available at a price in print form does not preclude it from being an open access journal, so long as it is possible to obtain a version, usually electronic, without charge). Someone downloading a copy of an open access journal can, of course, also print one or more copies of the journal, or use a print on demand service like Lulu.com to create a physical copy.

[104] Harvard Business School Publishing Corporation, 2003.

[105] See also Waelde (n 17).

[106] eg, the *International Free and Open Source Software Law Review* ('*IFOSS L Rev*'), <http://www.ifosslr.org/ifosslr> accessed 5 April 2013.

In practice, many open access journal articles are published under an appropriate Creative Commons licence, although other licences, like the free documentation licence, are also employed. Open access is divided into *green* and *gold* standards.[107] The chief difference is not in terms of licensing, but that the green standard refers simply to the information being made available, but without a formal mechanism for review. The gold standard adds a requirement for the information to be peer reviewed, and is thus competitive (and seeks to be as authoritative) as academic peer reviewed journals published under the traditional mechanism.[108]

The main *open* addressed in open access publishing is use-maximization.

'Open education' has a connotation that is similar, and refers mainly to courseware being made available on an open access basis (also referred to as open courseware).[109]

However, the meaning may be much broader, and refer to elimination of barriers restricting access to education. A prime example is the Open University ('OU')[110] which opened in the UK in 1971. Open education providers rely heavily on (and contribute to and create) open courseware, but also provide more traditional services provided by open education bodies: tutorials, access to academic staff, examinations, and so forth. The OU requires no academic qualifications for entry (although qualifications are required to move on to more advanced courses, which can be obtained within the OU itself, so that a sufficiently dedicated and able student can enter the OU with no qualifications and leave with a doctorate, or even post-doctoral qualification). The OU does charge fees (although grants may be available to qualifying students).

Other open educations institutions operate on a similar basis. Use-maximization is the goal, although the governance of open education institutions may also involve transparency. Open educational institutions are often keen to ensure that their academic qualifications are regarded as equivalent to those from non-open institutions, and, accordingly, will submit to review by bodies, often governmental, which are established to ensure that standards are maintained. An example in the United Kingdom is the Quality Assurance Agency ('QAA').[111]

[107] UK Open Access Implementation Group <http://open-access.org.uk/information-and-guidance/open-access> accessed 5 April 2013.

[108] eg, The *IFOSS L Rev* (n 106) is published under a Creative Commons licence, generally CC-BY-ND with an exception to allow for translations to be made. It is available online, and in print versions, and raises money through print subscriptions and sponsorship. Because its academic articles are peer-reviewed, they meet the gold standard of open access (it does carry opinion articles which are less rigorously reviewed, and these, despite being licensed on the same basis, meet the green open access standard).

[109] OCC <http://www.ocwconsortium.org> accessed 5 April 2013.

[110] The Open University <http://www.open.ac.uk> accessed 5 April 2013.

[111] <http://www.qaa.ac.uk/Pages/default.aspx> accessed 5 April 2013.

12.25 SUMMARY

An increasing number of fields describe themselves as 'open'. The term most frequently connotes access to, and the ability to reuse data and information, but within those connotations, there is a tension between maximizing the use of content, and preventing it from being reclosed (use-maximization, and anti-closure).

This is not all. Transparency in governance (including access to and influence over the decision-making process) is frequently connoted by the term 'open', as is a rejection of structures which would allow dominance by a specific entity or group of entities: 'lock-in'. An understanding of these four different connotations assists in determining the commonality between the many different *open* fields.

Index